Sir Ronald Wilson

A MATTER OF CONSCIENCE

Sir Ronald Wilson

A MATTER OF CONSCIENCE

Antonio Buti

University of Western Australia Press

First published in 2007 by
University of Western Australia Press
Crawley, Western Australia 6009
www.uwapress.uwa.edu.au

National Library of Australia
Cataloguing-in-Publication entry:
Buti, Antonio.
A matter of conscience: Sir Ronald Wilson.

Bibliography.
Includes index.
ISBN 978 0 9802964 1 9 (pbk.).

1. Wilson, Ronald, Sir, 1922– . 2. Australia. Human Rights and Equal Opportunity Commission—Biography. 3. Murdoch University—Presidents—Biography. 4. Uniting Church in Australia—Presidents—Biography. 5. Judges—Australia— Biography. I. Title.

347.9403534

Cover photograph courtesy News Limited
Cover painting by Mandy Buti
Consultant editor: Bruce Gillespie, Melbourne
Designed by Anna Maley-Fadgyas, Perth
Typeset in 10pt Janson Text by Lasertype, Perth
Printed by McPherson's Printing Group

For my Parents,

Mimma

and

Andrea Buti

CONTENTS

ACKNOWLEDGEMENTS

I have accumulated enormous debts of gratitude to so many people in researching and writing this book.

My first debt of gratitude is to the subject of this biography, Sir Ronald Wilson. This book was not his idea. In fact, initially he was lukewarm about the project. Sir Ronald was an extraordinarily self-effacing man; a book about himself was not his style. But over a number of coffee chats at Murdoch University's cafés he warmed to the idea, and once he had agreed, he provided invaluable assistance: letters of introduction; access to his personal papers; access to interview transcripts held at the Perth's Battye Library previously under embargo (until twenty-five years after his death); and countless interviews.

Sir Ronald never sought to interfere in the writing of this book, but what he wanted most was that the story of the National Inquiry into the Separation of Aboriginal and Torres Strait Islander Children, and its report, *Bringing Them Home*, be brought to the attention of the public. He believed that some commentators and politicians (current and former) had unfairly criticised and misrepresented the contents of the report.

He had always accepted personal criticism as being 'par for the course'. However, although never making an issue of it, he was hurt by some of the criticism directed at him after the release of *Bringing Them Home*. Also, he did not believe that he warranted being labelled a ruthless Crown prosecutor.

Whether Sir Ronald would agree with how I have presented and interpreted the national inquiry and his role as a prosecutor, and for that matter other parts of his life, I will never know, as sadly he died before the task was completed. What I do know is that we would have had some enjoyable coffee chats and debates about the book, as he was the most agreeable person to disagree with.

My deepest thanks also go to Lady Leila Wilson and the children: Bruce, Helen, Geoff, Robyn and Ian. They were all willing to talk openly about many personal matters, which immensely enriched this biography. Lady Wilson also unearthed some valuable correspondence written by Sir Ronald as a young wartime pilot, and she read the entire manuscript. She was scrupulous in checking the accuracy of a number of events, and at no stage did she seek to interfere editorially with the contents of the book. Any errors and omissions that remain are my responsibility.

I express a special thanks to three people—Eric Fisher, Chris Smyth and another (who wishes to remain anonymous)—who kindly gave of their time and talents to read earlier versions of the manuscript. Their kindness and suggestions have been invaluable, and I will remain forever thankful. Equally, I am indebted to the literary and editorial talents of Steve Hawke. His contribution to the final draft of this book cannot be overstated.

I was most fortunate to have research assistance from a number of outstanding individuals. Sam Nunn and Catherine Hall provided valuable early research assistance when it was much needed. I then had the significant assistance of the very talented Linley Batterham. She was a rare find.

Besides interviews with Sir Ronald and his children, I was fortunate that many others agreed to be interviewed. Without their assistance this book would never have happened. I sincerely thank them all: Jeremy Allanson, Professor Geoffrey Bolton, John Bond, Sir Gerard Brennan, Ron Cannon, Fred Chaney, Jeffery Christie, Sir Charles Court, Laurence Claus, Des Cousins, Mick Dodson, Sir Daryl Dawson, Sir William Deane, Robert Ellicott QC, Sir Harry Gibbs, Beryl Grant, Reverend Gregor Henderson, Ahlia Harris, Jonathon Hunyor, Judge Hal Jackson, Justice Michael Kirby, Bart Kakulas, Ian Ladhams, Theo Mckay, Chief Justice David Malcolm, Kenneth Martin QC, Sir Anthony Mason, Ian Medcalf, Judge Michael Murray, Paul Nicholls, Kerry O'Neil, Rob Osborn, Sue Osborn, Peter Panegyres, His Excellency Judge Kevin Parker, Richard Price, Susan Roberts, Reverend David Robinson, Lucy Robinson, Justice Ralph Simmonds, Melanie Sloss SC,

Diana Temby, Jim Thomson, Joan Tonkin, John Toohey QC, Peter Travers, Peter Van Hattem, Justice Christine Wheeler, Meredith Wilkie, Hazel Wilson, Jim Wilson, Leopold Woods and Judge Mary Ann Yeats.

I am thankful to Kaye McLennan, who transcribed many hours of taped interviews with skill and professionalism.

I was fortunate to have access to a number of interview transcripts conducted by others, which are noted in the bibliography. Some of these interviews are held at the Battye Library, the staff of which I thank. I also thank Tony Caravella and his staff at the State Records Office.

A number of media outlets, including the *West Australian*; *Subiaco Post*; the *Age*; News Limited; and ABC TV and Radio (Sydney and Perth) provided film and radio footage, photographs and newspaper articles. This is very much appreciated, as are the efforts of Anne Calverley and Martin Flanagan, who helped me access vital media material.

I thank the Western Australian attorney-general, the Hon. Jim McGinty MLA, for permission to reproduce selected court transcript extracts from the criminal trials and appeals of Eric Cooke, John Button and Darryl Beamish. Similarly, I appreciate the efforts of Geoff Wilson and other staff members of the Supreme Court of Western Australia in retrieving these transcripts from the archives.

Angie Goldie from the Office of the Western Australian Solicitor-General was of invaluable assistance in retrieving archival material and providing details of Sir Ronald's professional achievements. I thank her, as I do the Western Australian solicitor-general, Robert Meadows QC, for providing space in his office for me to peruse the archival material.

I was fortunate to have the assistance of many people at University of Western Australia Press, including Terri-ann White; Janine Drakeford; Maureen de la Harpe; Anastasia Stachewicz; Michael Hermann; Linda Martin; Anna Maley-Fadgyas; Emma Matson; Olivier Breton and the rest of the crew. I could not have asked for a more helpful, understanding, insightful and professional editor than Bruce Gillespie.

Many other people and institutions assisted me in a number of ways: Richard Bartlett; Andrew Bastow; Helen Bedwell; Estelle Blackburn; Margaret Breen; Patti Brook; John Button; Robert Castiglione; Michael Christie; Rebecca Cohen; Christine de Maupeou; Russell Elsegood; William Emilsen; John Farley; Jane Fleming; Arran Gerrard; Anne Greenshields; Stephen Hall; Camilla Harding; Michael Heath; Barbara Hocking; Anne Hunter; Jeremy

Kirk; Owen Leitch; Tim Loh; Kath Mallot; Judge Robert Nicholson; Lee O'Conner; Debra Osborn; Michael Owen; Bob Pearce; Robert Pinkerton; Kay Regan; David Rogers; Linda Spearman; Lyn Walker; Joyce Wilkins; High Court of Australia; Human Rights and Equal Opportunity Commission; National Press Club; and the Uniting Church Library (Perth). I would also like to make special mention of Murdoch University, an institution where I have spent many happy years as an academic and that provided valuable research funding for this project. There may be others who assisted in some way—if so, please accept my sincere apologies for my lapse in memory.

One person to whom I owe a huge debt of gratitude is Bill Johnson. With the support of Bill, I have for a number of years held a JLV/Louis Johnson Memorial Trust Fellowship, which has provided me with significant financial assistance. It is an immense honour to hold this fellowship.

Finally, I am deeply grateful to my family who helped me through this project. To my children, Alkira, Paris and Tennessee, thanks for your patience and love through this long process. To Mandy, my greatest supporter, thanks for allowing me to take over the dining table for so long and for being loving and caring in so many ways. And thank you for the portrait of Sir Ronald.

The journey is finally over.

PREFACE

Sir Ronald Wilson was an accomplished Crown prosecutor, solicitor-general, High Court justice, president of the Uniting Church, president of the Human Rights and Equal Opportunity Commission (HREOC), Royal Commissioner and university chancellor. That list of appointments provides little indication of the nature of the man behind them or of his lifetime struggle to maintain the highest professional standards and at the same time a complete commitment to his religious principles.

In this book, the author relates in a direct and straightforward way the story of a remarkable man whose achievements, the product of dedication rather than ambition, were accompanied by a simplicity in his personal life that was an inspiration to many and an example to us all.

From the humblest of beginnings, Ron Wilson emerged in the Western Australian public service as an outstanding Crown prosecutor. His success in that position has led some to criticise his performance on the basis that it involved the pursuit of advocacy at the expense of a balanced presentation. The author sets out those cases on which controversy centred, and the reader may make his or her own judgement. But it was in his role as advocate that Wilson felt the most satisfaction, and this was to stay with him for the rest of his life.

His advocacy could be seen in the church, where his sermons as a lay preacher have been described as fiery. In a quieter, but no less effective mode, his advocacy as solicitor-general of Western Australia's cause in battles between the states and the Commonwealth made him the doyen of solicitors-general, and undoubtedly led to his being appointed to the bench of the High Court of Australia. As a justice of the High Court, he rightly felt himself required to adopt a balanced and dispassionate approach to the cases coming before him, and his judgements were the product of an accepted judicial method. Perhaps it was the constraints imposed by the judicial method that led to some feelings of dissatisfaction on his part with his life as a judge. But there must have been other reasons. Life in Canberra, removed for long periods from his family, was lonely, and the opportunity for engagement in other activities was limited. Moreover, Ron Wilson was an active rather than a contemplative man, and the curbs that judicial life placed upon his natural enthusiasms may have led him to minimise in his own mind his talents as a judge.

With his retirement from the bench and appointment as president of HREOC, he was once more in a position to exercise his skills as an advocate, and to do so in causes about which he was able to feel passionate. The inquiry by HREOC into the history and effects of the forced separation of Aboriginal and Torres Strait Islander children from their families offered Wilson an opportunity that he seized. The resultant report—*Bringing Them Home*—was criticised by many, particularly in the legal profession, as being the product of inadequate investigation and an unbalanced approach. That was to judge Wilson for failing to adopt the objectivity and restraint expected of a judge. However, it is clear that he no longer regarded himself as a judge but as an advocate, and the report was, given the constraints of time and money, what he considered appropriate to advance a cause of which he personally was utterly convinced. The author sets out the criticisms, and the reader is again able to make his or her own judgement.

The life of Sir Ronald Wilson was very much a public life, and this book is a comprehensive account of that life. It also manages to draw a picture of a close and rewarding family life. Wherever he was, Ron Wilson was a man of captivating charm and immense ability. Any impression his small stature may have given was immediately eclipsed by the strength of his personality. His simplicity, humility and generosity are legendary, all strengthened by a deep religious conviction. He was a distinguished man, but his distinction was of an unusual and memorable kind. It is fitting that there is now an account of his life.

Sir Daryl Dawson
formerly Justice of the High Court of Australia (1982–97)

AUTHOR'S EXPLANATIONS

Although this book has extensive endnotes, I have sought not to clutter the narrative with them. To this end, I have not sourced to endnotes interviews conducted by the author. The reader can assume that quotes and paraphrases not sourced to an endnote have been obtained from interviews with the author (although on occasions the same information was found in the interview transcripts conducted by others). A full list of interviews conducted by the author is listed in the bibliography.

In referencing, I have as much as possible followed the standard style of UWA Press. Therefore I have departed from standard legal referencing style on occasions.

Abbreviations

ALSWA	Aboriginal Legal Service of Western Australia
ACTU	Australian Council of Trade Unions
AIF	Australian Imperial Force
ALP	Australian Labor Party
ASCM	Australian Student Christian Movement
ATC	Australian Treaty Committee
CIB	Central Investigation Bureau
HREOC	Human Rights and Equal Opportunity Commission
IUS	International Union of Students

JCCU	Joint Commission of Church Union
NAC	National Aboriginal Conference
NUAUS	National Union of Australian University Students
NEAF	New Era Aboriginal Fellowship
PFA	Presbyterian Fellowship of Australia
QC	Queen's Counsel
RAAF	Royal Australian Air Force
RAF	Royal Air Force
RCADIC	Royal Commission into Aboriginal Deaths in Custody
RDA	*Racial Discrimination Act*
SC	Senior Counsel
SMF	Special Mobile Forces
UK	United Kingdom
UN	United Nations
US	United States of America
UWA	University of Western Australia

PROLOGUE

On 26 May 1997, the prime minister of Australia, the Honourable John Winston Howard, walked to the podium. This was the moment that a small but significant section of the audience had been waiting for. He was about to address delegates at the opening session of the Australian Reconciliation Conference in the incongruous setting of the Melbourne Crown Casino Convention Centre. As he spoke, in the full glare of the media, a number of conference delegates, black and white, stood and slowly turned their backs on the nation's leader.

Meanwhile, the man whose work was to define the conference remained quietly seated in the audience. He was no fan of Howard, but symbolic gestures of disrespect to Australia's elected leader were not his preferred method of expressing his disapproval. Sir Ronald Wilson had impeccable manners and a respect for the 'office'. He believed in allowing people the right to be heard. He also believed that the only way forward for the reconciliation process was by remaining engaged, even in the face of a dissenting opponent.

Instead, Wilson focused his attention on Patrick Dodson, sitting on stage, the grey-bearded chairman of the Council for Aboriginal Reconciliation. He had great confidence in his friend and colleague, a well-respected Aboriginal leader, whom he had seen in action over the years diffusing potentially volatile situations with his intelligence and measured temperament. But he wondered how Dodson was going to handle this hostile situation.

Since coming to power the previous year, Howard had railed against the tide of reconciliation that had welled up in the Labor years, backed by bipartisan support since 1991. Turning their backs on Mr Howard was a symbolic echo of what the protesters felt Howard and his government had done to Australia's first people.

Upon claiming the Treasury benches in Canberra, Howard had been quick to criticise Aboriginal organisations for their perceived or real failure to improve the lot of their people. But what had really incensed many of those who turned their backs on the prime minister was his government's opposition to the High Court's *Wik* decision, which held that a pastoral lease did not necessarily extinguish native title. Tim Fischer, the deputy prime minister and leader of the rural-based National Party, had publicly attacked the High Court justices, accusing them of inappropriately engaging in judicial activism, and warning that the next appointment to the High Court would be a big-C conservative. Howard had appeared on ABC-TV's *7.30 Report*, brandishing a map of Australia with a significant portion coloured brown, in order to demonstrate the areas of land that potentially could be vulnerable to native title claims. Many viewed this as an attempt by Howard to spread fear among Australians by suggesting to them that their suburban homes were at risk of being claimed by Aboriginal people.

Just nine years earlier, as a justice of the High Court, Wilson had been in the minority in *Mabo (No 1)*, the first of three landmark decisions regarding native title. If one more member of the High Court had sided with him and Justices Anthony Mason and Daryl Dawson, the core issues of Eddie Mabo's case may never have been determined in *Mabo (No 2)*. Mabo's quest for recognition of native title rights would have been consigned to history.

Over the course of his decade on the High Court (1979–89), Wilson, the country boy and World War II fighter pilot, would often find himself in the minority in decisions involving constitutional matters, especially those that sought to expand the constitutional reach of Commonwealth legislative power over the states. Wilson, who had been solicitor-general of Western Australia (1969–79), earlier had forcefully argued in the High Court on behalf of Western Australia and its agencies in constitutional battles against the Commonwealth and Commonwealth legislators. Wilson's attitude was not based on beating the drum for his home state, but based on balance in a federal system. He was essentially cautious; conservative even.

The backs forming the silent wall of protest remained stiff and straight as the prime minister began to speak. Instead of the cheers that might have accompanied his declaration that he was 'personally sorry for those of my fellow Australians who suffered injustices under the practices of past generations towards Indigenous people', his words prompted jeers as the audience realised he was not going to apologise on behalf of the nation. He was not going to allow the nation to recognise those Aborigines who, as children, had been forcibly separated from their families—the so-called 'stolen generations'. Heckling increased as Howard proceeded to attack Aboriginal leaders and stridently defend his ten-point *Wik* native title plan. This heckling incensed the prime minister who, becoming angrier and angrier, took to waving his fist and shouting at his detractors. Wilson remained seated and silent, privately wondering whether Howard's behaviour gave the protesters even greater justification for their actions.

It looked as if the conference on reconciliation was going to turn into an exercise in retribution. But then Dodson intervened, appealing for calm. Eventually order was restored. Wilson afforded himself a private chuckle as his friend once again demonstrated that his peacemaking skills, perhaps honed during his time as a Roman Catholic priest, were as effective as ever.

Over the three days of the conference, delegates heard speeches from a number of prominent Australians, including the governor-general and former High Court justice, Sir William Deane, who received long applause when he made a personal 'profound' apology to the Aboriginal people of Australia for the historical practice of separating Aboriginal children from their families. His apology was accepted, unlike the statement of the prime minister. Deane had been in the majority in both *Mabo (No 1)* and *(No 2)*, and had at the inaugural Lingari Lecture at the Northern Territory University in Darwin in 1996 stated the importance of acknowledging past injustices to Aboriginal people. He was already a conference favourite.

In his speech, Deane made special mention of Wilson, his former High Court colleague. He spoke with affection and respect for Wilson, and observed that his friend and former colleague seemed to be having 'a hard time of it lately'.

Deane was referring to the Howard government's criticism of *Bringing Them Home*, the report of the National Inquiry into the Separation of Aboriginal and Torres Strait Islander Children from Their Families. The criticism had started even before the report was tabled in the Commonwealth parliament on 26 May 1997, the very same day as the opening of the Australian Reconciliation Conference and a day before the thirtieth anniversary of the 1967 referendum that granted power to the Commonwealth parliament to legislate for Aborigines and count them in the national census. The inquiry had been conducted by the Commonwealth Human Rights and Equal Opportunity Commission, of which Wilson was president. Wilson and Mick Dodson—the Aboriginal and Torres Strait Islander social justice commissioner and brother of Patrick—had been the leading hearing commissioners of the inquiry.

Even as the politicians in Canberra debated the report, Wilson rose to address the conference in Melbourne. Wilson was doing again what he loved best, advocating. His years of tough forensic prosecuting for the Crown had earned him a reputation as a dogged, even ruthless, advocate. But his advocacy was heartfelt. He had a profound point to make. In his speech he was advocating not just for Aboriginal Australians and the members of their 'stolen generations', but for all Australians and their future as a reconciled and united people. He spoke passionately about how he had been changed by his exposure

> to the stories of my fellow Australians, Australians for whom I have now unbounded respect because of their courage, their dignity, their suffering, and through it all, their generosity of spirit.

He urged the government and people of Australia to recognise what the report had found:

> I want to say this is no ordinary report...much of it is expressed in the actual words spoken to us by those who suffered personally from the process... words which were spoken from the heart, to the heart, and the report must be read in that spirit. It must be read with an open heart and mind. I make this appeal not only to the citizens of Australia, but particularly to those with the authority and responsibility of government. It must be listened to with open heart and mind, and with a willingness to listen intently so as to understand.

Wilson had already come a long way on his journey to this understanding. As the former moderator of the Presbyterian Church of Western Australia

(1965–66), he had been responsible for overseeing the management committee that ran Sister Kate's Children's Home in Queens Park, Perth, a receiving home for light-coloured children or 'half-castes' whose colour had prompted their separation from their families. He had played some part in the practice of separation. His enquiry, three decades later, into that practice had surely caused him to listen and understand.

But he was compelled to take a further step. In an interview screened on the *7.30 Report* on 1 May 1997, he apologised for his involvement in the practice of separating Aboriginal children from their families:

> Listening leads to understanding, understanding leads to acknowledgement, and I acknowledge that on behalf of the church and on my own behalf the wrongs the church played in the separation of the children and I confessed my deep sorrow for that association…I deeply regret that the church was involved in the implementation of a process that is now seen to be so dreadful, and of course, I mean to say one is sorry sounds pretty light-hearted but it is a matter of deep grief that one acknowledges a responsibility and as I say I hope that I am the better for it and I hope that I will continue to earn the trust of Aboriginal people.

The inquiry had changed him. For those who had known him as a deeply religious man and Uniting Church leader, this change, and his apology on national television, would come as no surprise. But for some of those who had known Wilson only as the tough Crown prosecutor, a man not given to conceding an inch on a point, the apology was astonishing.

1

The Boy from Geraldton

I have never begrudged my childhood, you know. I wouldn't have liked to have been a silver-spooned kid at Uni with the best of everything. I never hankered for it.

The Melbourne-bound Ansett flight had just left Perth domestic airport. Wilson sat in economy class. As president of the Human Rights and Equal Opportunity Commission (HREOC) he could have sat business class. But that was not the way of the man, who lived by the motto: 'Living simply, so others may simply live.'[1] At Melbourne he would catch another flight to Hobart, for the commencement hearings for the National Inquiry into the Separation of Aboriginal and Torres Strait Islander Children from Their Families.

Wilson was excited that the hearings were finally commencing. He had hoped that they would have started sooner after the official launch of the inquiry in Adelaide in August. His knowledge on the past history of removing or separating Aboriginal children from their families was still limited, but he was aware that many Aborigines claimed that their lives had been ruined by the removal policies and that they had lost their childhoods. But he wondered how different were the origins of many of these Aborigines from his. Had he not, for most of his own childhood, been devoid of parental love and care?

The plane was still low enough on this fine early summer day in December 1995 for Wilson to spot a group of cyclists on a narrow country road in the hills east of the airport. The sight reminded him of his youth a lifetime ago, in Geraldton, where the sun shone brightly for most of the year and the Indian Ocean westerlies brought afternoon relief from the summer heat. For a moment in his mind's eye he could see his brother cycling ahead of him.

'Come, Ron, hurry up!' called Jim, slowing down long enough to turn toward his younger brother. The year was 1933; Ron was ten years old and trying to keep up with his brother, who was two years older. They were on their way to the Home of Peace Hospice in Perth, where their father lay incapacitated by a stroke. The two young boys cycled all day and spent their nights along the roadside in abandoned farm sheds. In all, they travelled 480 kilometres to visit a father who had always seemed distant to them. They had undertaken the ride for adventure.

Harold Wilson was a solicitor living in London's East End when he decided to set sail for Australia, driven by the elusive desire that motivates every emigrant—a better life. Arriving in Western Australia in early 1912, he moved to Geraldton, a trading and business hub, where he established himself as a small-town solicitor. Working on the everyday legal problems of members of his community, he never dreamed that one of his sons would grow up to become a justice of the High Court.

Shortly after Harold's arrival in Geraldton he met Jean Isobel Darling. After a brief courtship, they married in late 1912. There was a considerable age difference between them: Harold was forty-four years old and Jean was thirty.

Jean was the daughter of Robert Darling and Mary Anne Ferguson. She was born in South Australia on 29 June 1882. Her grandfather, John Darling, emigrated to Adelaide in 1855 when he was twenty-four, with his wife and two sons, John and Joseph. After their arrival in Australia, another five sons and a daughter were born, including Robert.

From the time John arrived in Adelaide in 1855, with virtually no financial or other assets, but with a will to succeed, the Darling family accumulated considerable wealth through business ventures revolving around agricultural properties, flour mills and grain exports.[2]

John the elder was a religious man and lay preacher, and he became a member of the South Australian parliament in 1870. He served three periods in the Legislative Assembly between 1870 and 1887. Then for nine years (1888–97) he represented North District in the Legislative Council.

On his death in 1905, after leaving gifts to charities and favoured employees, he bequeathed to his wife and eight children an estate worth £67,000. His son John continued to amass wealth, and by 1897 he had become known as the 'Wheat King' of Australia. Like his father, he was a religious man and a generous supporter of the Baptist Church. He also served in the South Australian parliament as a member of the Legislative Assembly (1896–1905), and ended up as leader of the conservative Australian National League opposition. He served on a number of company boards, including the BHP board. The family connection with BHP continued for some ninety years, with at least one and sometimes two Darlings serving on its board.[3]

The second son of John the elder, Joseph, distinguished himself as a cricketer, playing in thirty-four Tests for Australia from 1894 to 1905, and serving as captain for twenty-one of them. In the 1897–98 season, he became the first left-hander to score a century, the first player to score 500 runs in a series and the first player to score three centuries in a series. He moved to Tasmania, entered politics, and became a strong performer in the Tasmanian Legislative Council.

Another son, Robert—Wilson's grandfather—who also became a successful businessman, lost most of his fortune through gambling. He was considered the black sheep of the family. He left South Australia for the West, and settled in Geraldton. He and his large family lived in a grand home on top of Hospital Hill and were regular attendees at the Wesleyan church, being transported to church in a bus drawn by horses. It was from this house that daughter Jean left to marry.

Harold and Jean did not wait long to commence a family, and Robert (Bob) was born in 1913. For the duration of World War I (1914–18), Harold Wilson continued his work as a solicitor in Geraldton. Two more children, Emily in 1915 and Douglas in 1917, were born. After the war two more sons followed: Arthur James, known as Jim, born in 1920, and on 23 August 1922, Ronald Darling Wilson.

By this time, Harold was a well-regarded solicitor in Geraldton, and had even declined an invitation to become a magistrate in the town. Although he was well established as a professional in what was a small town in 1922, with a population of approximately 5000, the Wilsons did not live in luxury. The house on Francis Street was large, with many rooms and a verandah. Toddler Ron had his own room, which was small and minimally furnished with a wooden cot, a chest of drawers and a number of toys on the wooden floorboards.

Keeping the house clean and tidy and looking after five children was Ron's mother's responsibility. She received little help from her husband, who busied himself with his legal practice and paid little attention to the children's nurturing.

When home, Harold spent considerable time reading books from his wonderful home library. It was said that Harold could read in thirteen languages and speak at least seven. His library contained a full set of Chaucer, volumes of Shelley's poems, and Victor Hugo's novels in French.

It was in this library that Harold was most at rest and peace, sitting in a rocking chair immersed in a book, occasionally raising his eyes from the book and focusing a gaze on nothing in particular, contemplating what he had just read. Harold was a quiet man, carefully thinking about what he was to say before speaking.

Ron was a healthy, cheerful and active toddler, entertaining himself by playing with the toys handed down from his older siblings. He loved being with his brothers and sister. When he was a toddler, his constant companion was Jim, the nearest in age to him.

The family became well known. Through his legal practice Harold came into contact with many people from the small Geraldton community. Although not overly friendly, and somewhat pompous at times, he was courteous and pleasant to those with whom he had contact. Jean was more relaxed around people. She was popular, and made friends easily.

Jean attended to young Ron's day-to-day needs, but fate prevented a long-lasting bond being established. On 18 January 1927, Jean died from complications caused by a serious bout of pneumonia. Ron, still only four, didn't fully appreciate the loss of his mother. She soon became a distant figure in Ron's memory, and by the time he was a teenager, Jean was absent from his consciousness.

Very soon after Jean's death, Harold secured the housekeeping services of Ellen Jane Clover (née Wintle), who became a major influence on the young Ron. She emigrated from the west country of England sometime in the mid 1920s. Shortly after her arrival in Western Australia she married a man from Dalwallinu. He died in a car accident soon after.[4]

Mrs Clover quickly went about organising the house and confirming her authority over the children. She ran the household and raised the children while Harold busied himself with his legal practice.

Ron commenced school aged five at the only state primary school in Geraldton. It was a rather miserable-looking place painted in dull brown paint, shabby compared with the local parish Catholic primary school. Jim, only two grades ahead, was his constant companion. Doug was in grade 6 when Ron commenced, and left three years later after completing grade 9. His eldest brother Bob had already left school, and Emily was in Perth attending St Mary's Anglican Girls College. Jean Wilson's two sisters covered the cost of this private education, and Emily commenced at St Mary's not long after her mother died.

Ron and Jim walked to and from school together. Often they were joined by other children, including Joan Wheat, who in later life became Joan Tonkin, wife of state Labor Premier John Tonkin (1971–74). Joan was the same age as Jim.

The two youngest Wilson boys were popular among their peers. They were funny, often telling silly jokes to the rest of the walking group. They were bright children. Some of the other children were envious of Jim and Ron, as they didn't work too hard at school but always finished at or near the top of their respective classes.

When reaching Francis Street on the afternoon walk home from school, Jim and Ron would part company with the other kids and sprint towards their home. As the group watched Jim and Ron dodging each other as they ran down Francis Street, Joan would feel sorry for them, running home to a large house, but without their mother to greet them.

But the Wilson boys were not sad: they were greeted every day by Mrs Clover. She wasn't a naturally gregarious and warm person, but cared for the children and they respected her. They turned to her when they needed something or required reassurance. To them she was their mother; they called her 'Mumsie'.

When the boys arrived home, Mrs Clover would ask them how their day at school went. Invariably the response would be 'okay'. School did not enthuse Jim or Ron.

Enjoying English and social studies was about the limit of Ron's satisfaction with school. He longed to learn the classics, and although not naturally attracted to the sciences, he was disappointed that chemistry and physics were not on the curriculum. He wished the teachers would move beyond the standard rote learning of reading, writing and arithmetic.

Young Ron often spent time looking at and touching the books in his father's library, and occasionally taking one from the bookcase to flick through. Sometimes he would even sit down and read parts of the books, searching for a paragraph or page that interested him and he could understand. But they seemed unfamiliar, out of reach.

Young Ron's view that his education was too narrow was to have an enduring effect. He believed that his education after leaving school at fourteen had been 'wholly utilitarian', unable to develop in him a side 'that was devoted to simply living a civilised life'.[5] Wilson believed his lack of a classical education deprived him of the opportunity to develop his technical and philosophical skills to the same high level as his colleagues on the High Court.[6] This perception was not shared by his colleagues on the High Court; nor can any lack be found in his High Court judgements. But it is a perception that he carried with him for life.

Wilson the student behaved himself, although on one occasion he did land himself in trouble. The male teacher was giving preference to the girl students, calling them by their first names, selecting them to answer the questions and running the teacher's errands. This was Wilson's perception, and he didn't think it fair. He raised his hand, which remained aloft until the teacher acknowledged him. 'Yes, Wilson!' No first name basis for the boys. With a tremor in his voice Wilson said, 'Sir, you are favouring the girls. It is not fair, sir.' The teacher's face turned red. He yelled at Wilson to come up to the front of the classroom, then bellowed out how rude and disrespectful he had been.

The teacher picked up the wooden cane and ordered Wilson to put out his right hand, palm faced up. He gave him six of the best, Wilson flinching as each swing of the cane came down hard on his small tender palm. But there was no chance of him crying; it was not the done thing to cry in front of the class and the teacher. Wilson had given his classmates a glimpse of the advocate he was to become.

Wilson was only in grade 3 at school when he and his siblings again had to cope with a distressing family event. This time it involved their father.

On 24 October 1929 ('Black Thursday'), the New York stock market collapsed. The same day, the federal Scullin Labor government was sworn in, having defeated Stanley Bruce and Earl Page's Nationalists–Country Party coalition government in a general election on 19 October 1929.

Three days after 'Black Thursday', the *Sydney Morning Herald* stated that the 'insensate optimism' of the decade had been replaced by a 'dire pessimism'.[7] It was the worst of times. Internationally, unemployment had been on the rise for several years. When Scullin was elected prime minister, unemployment in Australia had risen from just above 9 per cent in the early months of 1929, to as high as 12.2 per cent in October.[8]

The Great Depression made things financially tight for the Wilson household. With a major downturn in commercial activity, there was less demand for lawyers and, even when a lawyer was needed, there was little money to pay for services rendered. This only compounded the perennial difficulties Harold had with collecting his legal fees. It also made it more difficult for Mrs Clover to run the household. She was receiving less and less money from Harold, and there was no money left over to pay for her services. She continued to work out of a sense of duty and concern for the children.

Whether because of the stress of work and running a small business that was bringing in less and less money, or a genetic predisposition, Harold suffered a massive stroke in 1930. His working life had come to an abrupt end.

Bob sat opposite Ron at the wooden kitchen table. 'Dad has had a bad stroke.' Ron remained silent. He didn't fully comprehend what Bob was saying. But he realised it was bad, as his dad was in hospital.

With Harold incapacitated, Mrs Clover continued to look after the children, the only other option being for the children to be split up and sent off to different homes. She was determined not to allow that to happen, and for this Ron was eternally grateful. To Ron and Jim, Mrs Clover 'was a wonderful lady' and 'a fantastic foster mother'.

The church provided Mrs Clover with a distraction from the responsibilities of managing the Wilson house. She regularly attended the local St John's Presbyterian Church, where she sang in the choir. The Wilson children attended church with her, but only Ron carried a deep religious faith into adulthood. Although baptised an Anglican, Wilson fully embraced the faith of the Presbyterians.

Without Harold's income, the financial position of the Wilson household was even more precarious. Mrs Clover resorted to taking in boarders, farming children from as far away as Meekatharra, Yalgoo and Mount Magnet, who had come to Geraldton to attend school. The boarders slept in beds on the big verandah attached to the Wilson house in Francis Street. During school term the house was a hive of activity.

Even though the income from the boarders and from Bob's job with the Bank of New South Wales provided much-needed cash, financially it remained tight at the Wilson household. Doug and Jim contributed by wrapping newspapers at the *Geraldton Guardian* and doing other odd jobs.

When Doug left home, Ron helped Jim wrap newspapers, and they both worked in a secondhand store on Saturdays. On the way home they visited the local greengrocer's store to collect the waste lettuce and fruit that couldn't be sold. If the food were edible, Mrs Clover fed it to the children; otherwise it went to the chickens. The children looked after the chickens and vegetable garden. Other household chores had to be done, such as washing and 'tramping' the clothes, although, as the youngest, Ron mostly just tagged along with his siblings, watching them doing the chores with Mrs Clover.

Harold resided at the Subiaco Hospice, less than five kilometres from the centre of Perth, until his death in 1935 at the age of sixty-six. Other than the time he cycled down with Jim, Ron only managed to visit once a year, when Bob drove the two boys and Mrs Clover to Perth in his Whippet.

While in Perth they stayed in Maylands, with an English friend of Mrs Clover. During the hospice visits, Bob and Mrs Clover did most of the talking, telling Harold what was happening in Geraldton and what his children were doing. While this was happening Jim and Ron engaged in tomfoolery. Mrs Clover would often tell them to be quiet.[9]

Ron's sister Emily did not share his affection for Mrs Clover. They disagreed strongly on more than one occasion. Emily was encouraged by her two aunts to take control of the household when she returned home during the school holidays. The aunts' view was that Mrs Clover was the housemaid and nothing more. On her returns to Geraldton for school holidays, Emily ordered Mrs Clover around. Towards the end of one summer school holidays, Ron had had enough of his sister's attitude toward Mrs Clover. He told her so, and wrote letters of protest to his aunts.

'She was virtually the only mother I'd known and I wasn't going to have these aunts interfering,' he later said.[10] He believed Mrs Clover deserved better. She had given everything to the children so they could stay together as one family, even at an economic cost, because she received no salary for her efforts after

Harold's income ceased. Wilson viewed his support of Mrs Clover as an early excursion into an advocacy role that he believed was the principal characteristic of his life.[11]

After Harold's stroke, efforts were made to find a partner for the business. At one stage Sydney Good, then a country lawyer, and who would later became Wilson's boss in the Crown Law Department, contemplated joining the partnership. This did not happen, and a Mr Inglis became a partner in the firm.[12] But for reasons unknown, the partnership failed to flourish, and it quickly dissolved, with the Wilson family retaining some of the business chattels.

The family had to decide what to do with these assets, which included numerous law books. They were of no use to the family. So Jim walked around Geraldton visiting lawyers in an endeavour to sell the books. Some of the law books were sold, but not the leatherbound volumes of the English Law Reports. Who made the decision is unclear, but it was decided to dispose of them. The future High Court justice was complicit in burying a set of reports of the English law in a Geraldton backyard.

Even though financially things were difficult, Ron loved his childhood in Geraldton. It was a typical outdoors lifestyle—swimming at the Geraldton Back Beach, fishing under the wharf for yellowtail, bike riding and generally playing with Jim. Wilson dabbled in sport, playing a little soccer and tennis, but was not good at either. He also commenced learning the piano. Talking of his childhood, Wilson stated, 'I have never begrudged my childhood, you know. I wouldn't have liked to have been a silver-spooned kid at Uni with the best of everything. I never hankered for it.'

Silver-spooned or not, the end of childhood was fast approaching. In 1936, with Ron aged fourteen and about to finish school, only he and Jim were still living with Mrs Clover, when the bank foreclosed on the mortgage and repossessed the family home. This was Mrs Clover's opportunity to move to Perth, which she believed would provide Jim with greater employment opportunities than Geraldton. Bob was working away from Geraldton at a country branch of the Bank of New South Wales, and Emily was a nurse and living at the Royal Perth Hospital nurses' quarters.

Wilson remained in Geraldton, and boarded with the local Presbyterian minister. Young Ron was effectively on his own, and he was never really close to any of his siblings again.

After his father's stroke, Ron's eldest brother Bob became a 'father figure' to him. He particularly enjoyed his brother's Christmas Eve treat, when Bob would take Ron downtown, where he would buy him a spider—a soft drink with ice-cream floating on top.[13] Ron thought his brother was kind and clever.

At the outbreak of World War II in 1939, Bob joined the Australian Army Engineers. While serving in Darwin, he was injured by shrapnel during a Japanese bombing raid on 19 February 1942. He never fully recovered his health, and died in 1963 at the relatively young age of fifty of a cerebral haemorrhage, although it is unclear if this was linked to the war injury.

Emily left St Mary's Anglican Girls School around 1930–31 and returned to Geraldton, where she worked for the local food store owners—Frank Greene and Sons. Later she became a nurse and ended up marrying a farmer, Fraser Lukin.

Wilson did not attend Emily's funeral when she died in 1992. At the time he was interstate, attending to work-related matters in his role as HREOC president. When asked in 2004 why he didn't return to Perth for his sister's funeral, Wilson answered, 'Well I suppose today I would have returned. We have a different view on travel today. Back then travel was considered more involved.' This view seems incongruous, given that he was used to travelling across Australia and air travel was easily accessible in 1992.

Around 1934 or 1935, Doug left Geraldton for Perth to work as journalist. Ron and the family had little later contact with him. After a short period in Perth, Doug moved to Sydney and became a member of the Communist Party. His membership brought a visit to his apartment in Woolloomooloo by the police. They searched his apartment, for what is unknown. One police officer took a second look at the framed photograph above Doug's bed. He asked Doug, 'Who is that?' Without hesitating, Doug responded, 'That's my grandfather.' In fact it was Lenin.

During World War II, Doug joined the Royal Air Force (RAF), flying Wellington Bombers and Stirlings. He became the captain of a Stirling. Returning to his base at about 3.30 a.m. on Saturday, 15 July 1944, for reasons unknown he crashed at a village called Shortgrove Park near Saffron Walden in Essex. There was one other Australian in his crew, and there were no survivors.

Jim also enlisted, in the Australian navy, and for part of the war served in Papua New Guinea. Most of his adult working life was spent in the Commonwealth public service, employed in several departments, such as Taxation and Health. Although Jim and Ron spent much of their childhood together, and in later life resided only a few kilometres apart, they rarely spoke to each other, and came together only once a year, to, as Wilson said, 'make sure they remember each other's face.'

The Wilson children had lost both parents when young, which could have acted as a bonding event for support and protection of each other. But this did not occur. Although Bob did act as a father figure to young Ron, and the children helped with the household income and duties, emotionally they were not drawn together. There was a distinct sense of detachment from each other.

Wilson left school at the end of November 1936. It was three months after his fourteenth birthday. He had completed grade nine and his Junior Educational Certificate. At the time grade nine was the highest grade at the school. In 1937 a public high school opened in Geraldton, but Wilson did not return.

Immediately on leaving school, Wilson found work as a casual messenger boy at the local courthouse in Geraldton. He loved working at the courthouse and earning an income. The thought of going back to school didn't enter his mind.

In 1936 it was not possible to join the Western Australian public service as a permanent until age fifteen. On turning fifteen, Wilson became a junior clerk within the Crown Law Department. His association with that department was to be marked by longevity combined with meritorious and spectacular advancement.

Wilson would arrive early each morning at the courthouse, eager to commence his daily tasks of running errands, fetching lunches and serving at the courthouse counter. Because of his lack of height, Wilson had to stand on a box to reach documents that needed to be filed. He presented a picture of a little schoolboy dressed in shorts and long socks. Doubtless none of his customers imagined that this young and small file clerk would eventually be a High Court justice.

When the local magistrate, Keith Dougall, 'a very tall, fine figure of a man', was not at the courthouse, Wilson would often step into the magistrate's office and snoop around, see what work Dougall was up to and sometimes even make phone calls. One lunchtime the magistrate returned earlier than expected. Wilson, on the phone, could hear the magistrate's heavy steps on the wooden boards in the corridor. The steps were moving closer and closer to the office. Wilson froze with fear. Dougall entered his office. Wilson expected to be severely reprimanded, but to his relief and surprise, the magistrate didn't utter a word. Wilson quickly retreated from the office.

Wilson commenced part-time study while working at the Geraldton Local Court. He undertook this study privately, and not as part of an organised night school program. He had no grand plan worked out. He fleetingly thought about future university studies, but such an idea seemed remote. He was planning a career in the state public service, where he expected to become a middle-ranking public servant.[14]

He was a disciplined young man, studying most nights after work. Discipline was to become a hallmark of his professional career and his attitude to personal fitness. He didn't participate in competitive team sports, because he was not very skilled at ball games and lacked the time to devote to such pursuits. But running and walking he enjoyed and could schedule around his other numerous commitments. Throughout his professional career and in 'retirement', Wilson retained a regime of physical exercise, running and walking.

In 1940, Wilson completed his study of four subjects, English, economics, history and geography. But because it had taken him four years, he could not be awarded a Leaving Certificate, the education certificate in Western Australia at the time for students who successfully completed upper high school, grades eleven and twelve. To be awarded the Leaving Certificate a student had to complete at least three of the four subjects in one year.

On 23 August 1939, just before his seventeenth birthday, Wilson left Geraldton and its local courthouse to work at the Crown Law records office, situated in the basement of the Supreme Court building in Perth. The Western Australian Supreme Court was established in 1861, and since 1903 has been located in the same building.[15]

He was reunited with Mrs Clover and Jim. With the help of the children, she had purchased a house at 67 Hampden Road in Hollywood, which at the time was a comfortable, but not affluent, western suburb not far from the University of Western Australia (UWA).

On 3 September 1939, just after Wilson's arrival in Perth, Robert Menzies, the Australian prime minister, went on radio to inform the Australian public that Britain had declared war on Germany and, as a consequence, Australia was also at war.

Australians as a whole accepted that the nation was at war, and 'accepted Menzies advice of "business as usual" and life went on'.[16] The war didn't command Wilson's attention or spur any great patriotic excitement in the young man. That was to change, but at the time of Menzies' declaration the seventeen-year-old clerk was fully engrossed in learning his way around the records office and continuing with his studies. In contrast, his three brothers enlisted in the defence forces not long after Menzies' declaration. Jim left Perth to join the navy. Wilson remained with Mrs Clover at Hampden Road, Hollywood, riding the 6 kilometres to and from work.

The records office came under the jurisdiction of the Crown Law Department. Wilson's boss was William Hardwick, whom Wilson initially viewed as a 'ferocious sort of person' who walked around the office barking orders at his underlings.[17]

Wilson found his work enjoyable and challenging; he made sure he knew where all the files were, who was working on them and where they should be stored. Typically, he strove to be the best he could be at his job. He proudly described himself as 'the best records clerk imaginable'.[18] Wilson's work ethic and pride in his work were to be defining features of his professional career. He took great pride in being able to produce a requested court file in record time.[19]

When time permitted, Wilson went to the storeroom to examine old files and study trial depositions and judges' handwritten notes. He and other clerks sought out the files that contained details of the juiciest sex cases, reading out the facts and the judges' notes—a group of adolescent boys having a laugh.

Not long after coming to Perth, Wilson sat for the state public service exam, called the 'F' exam. State public employees had to pass this exam to have a chance of promotion. The exam involved typing and rudimentary bookkeeping. In preparation, Wilson became a proficient touch typist, and won a public service prize for typing. From then on, Wilson did most of his own typing, surprising the secretarial and typing staff who worked for him with his speed. Typing was considered unusual behaviour for a man of his generation of lawyers and judges, for whom the pen or, eventually, the dictaphone were the only acceptable methods.

Wilson's youth in Perth was not all work. The church was very important to him. Presbyterians placed great emphasis on preaching and singing of personal salvation and expressions of personal faith. There was also a great deal of formality, and an emphasis on dignity and holding God in awe.

He was involved in the youth fellowship of his local Nedlands Presbyterian Church, which had approximately fifty teenagers and young adults. For Wilson, who didn't form friendships easily, the youth fellowship provided an opportunity to make new friends in Perth.

He was a member of the Presbyterian Fellowship of Australia (PFA), which was nationally organised as a commonwealth council, with separate state councils. Two other churches that were to eventually unite with the Presbyterians to form the Uniting Church also had youth fellowships—the Methodist Youth Fellowship (MYF) and the Congregational Youth Fellowship (CYF). Occasionally, these youth fellowships would meet together socially, but mostly they conducted separate activities.

Wilson participated in the full range of PFA social events, such as excursions, picnics and the annual single-sex Easter camps—the girls camping at Cannington, about 12 kilometres south-east of Perth, and boys a further 10 kilometres south at Kelmscott, on the banks of the Canning River. Although the camps were single-sex, the PFA provided Wilson with his main avenue and opportunity to socialise with females. But during the late 1930s and early 1940s, Wilson, a naturally shy young man, was not looking for a girlfriend or spouse.

Life in the PFA was not all about socialising. Wilson was part of one of the 'evangelistic teams' that would go to congregations on weekends to preach. The teams consisted of enthusiastic youngsters keen to preach the gospel to various Presbyterian congregations. Although there was a social side to the 'evangelistic teams', especially when making a country trip, when they often stayed overnight enjoying various social events such as picnics and barbecues, they also worked hard at preaching and leading the prayers for the service.

This 'youth preaching' gave Wilson early training in public speaking, which he effectively used in his professional career and his involvement with the church. Wilson built up a formidable reputation as a great advocate, public speaker and lay preacher. Des Cousins, a retired minister of the Uniting Church, who first met Wilson in the early 1960s through his involvement in the PFA, has said, 'Wilson's reputation as a tough prosecutor was well known in church circles. He also was a passionate and articulate speaker and preacher. He was very good.'

Life was busy for young Wilson, balancing work with his church and PFA commitments and part-time study, which he completed at the end of 1940. If that were not enough, Wilson spent long hours practising the piano in preparation for a music exam in 1941. He failed, and from then on piano playing receded into the background.

The war was two years old. Young men were joining up, and for Wilson a new sense of duty emerged.

2

Duty Calls

It was hard to be a young man and not seriously consider whether one should enlist.[1]

As Wilson was beginning to find his feet as an adult, the nation too was beginning to mature. In 1926, the Balfour Declaration had formally acknowledged, in principle at least, that Australia had equal status with Britain in matters of external affairs. But in 1931, two events led to Australia assuming full control over its domestic affairs. The first was the appointment of Sir Isaac Isaacs, former Commonwealth attorney-general and Chief Justice of the High Court, as the first Australian-born governor-general. The second was the passing in Britain of the *Statute of Westminster* 1931 (Imp), which repealed the *Colonial Laws Validity Act 1865* (UK), and provided that British laws no longer had Imperial paramountcy in the dominions.[2]

But in the 1930s and 1940s, Wilson and many others in the Australian community still believed in the paramountcy of the British Empire and monarchy. He conformed to the prevailing views of Australian society that Australia owed unquestioning allegiance to Mother England.

Such a worldview was avidly encouraged by Robert Menzies, Australia's prime minister. For example, in 1939 he declared that Australia was at war because Britain was at war. Wilson remembers that sombre broadcast on the evening of 3 September 1939:

> Fellow Australians. It is my melancholy duty to inform you that, in consequence of the persistence by Germany in her invasion of Poland, Great Britain has declared war upon her, and that, as a result, Australia is at war...Where Great Britain stands, there stands the people of the entire British world.

Wilson's own sentiments were cemented by working in the Geraldton courthouse and, subsequently, at the Crown Law Department, where there was a prevailing affinity with Britain. The law had an aura of regal power to it—Australian law has its origins in the courts of England.

The young Wilson was a conformist. Rather than 'rock the boat', he focused his energies on the required tasks, always striving to do his best. He was an inquisitive individual when it came to his work, often venturing into the solicitors' offices to check on files and their contents. But that was about as far as his inquiring mind roamed. His attention was on his work and church activities.

Though he had little interest in major political and social issues, many young men around him were joining up, and Wilson felt a duty to 'King and country'. He joined the armed forces, believing it was expected of him. A sense of adventure was also a motivating factor. The prospect of travelling overseas and being engaged in aerial combat excited young Wilson, who was enthralled with the romance of flying. Although he initially joined the Australian Imperial Force (AIF), he had his eye on the air force.

In early November 1941, Wilson left not only the home he was sharing with Mrs Clover but also his work in the basement of the Supreme Court building. His decision to join up was very timely, given the sinking of the HMAS *Sydney* off the Western Australian coast on 19 November 1941. The *Sydney* had been engaged in a gunnery duel with the German raider *Kormoran*, which also sank. The *Sydney* lost all its crew at sea, while those who survived on the German vessel reached mainland Western Australia. World War II was no longer a distant event on the other side of the world.

On 7 December 1941, Japan entered World War II with the assault on Pearl Harbor. The United States immediately entered the war. Before the year was out, with Wilson still in training camp, John Curtin, Australia's new prime minister, had withdrawn two divisions of the AIF from duties in the Middle East to defend Australia against the increasing Japanese danger.

Wilson underwent induction training at the south-west coastal town of Busselton. He was then attached to the Special Mobile Forces (SMF), an infantry battalion-strength force, which was charged with defending the coastline north of Perth from enemy attack—primarily attacks from Japanese submarine or aircraft. Wilson spent little time near the coastline. Instead, the SMF was stationed at the small town of Dandaragan, 50 kilometres inland and about 140 kilometres north of Perth.

At the first available opportunity, Wilson transferred to the Royal Australian Air Force (RAAF), officially enlisting on 6 July 1942. At the same time, the SMF moved to the Port Walter camp near Fremantle, and was disbanded in July 1942.

Wilson wanted to fly. But at the time of his transfer to the RAAF there was no aircrew intake. He was offered the choice of being a guard or transport driver. He selected the latter, but there was a problem: he couldn't drive. Before his transfer, Wilson took weekend leave and returned to Perth, where he called on his local Nedlands parish minister to elicit help in obtaining his driver's licence. On being greeted by the minister, Wilson said, 'Gilbert, I have got to get a licence.' Without hesitation, the minister replied, 'OK. Hop in.' With Wilson in the driver's seat and the Presbyterian minister in the passenger's seat they drove around the block a couple times and then went to the Nedlands police station.

The police officer was not impressed with Wilson's driving skills. They hadn't even travelled 100 metres when the police office hailed Wilson to stop hopping the car. He turned to Wilson and said, 'Why do you need a driver's licence?' Wilson, with his legs trembling replied, 'It is very important. I need a licence as I am being transferred to the air force.' He didn't tell the police officer that he was to be a transport officer. The policeman remained silent. Wilson was desperate. 'I promise that until I have some more practice I won't drive in the city.' The police officer issued the driver's licence and Wilson joined the RAAF as a transport driver.

In one of his first tasks Wilson was at the wheel of a new Chevrolet. Being rather small in stature, at 5 feet 4 inches, he had difficulty seeing over the dashboard. He was given the duty of transporting the commanding officer of the Fremantle embarkation depot. He had only driven 15 metres when the commanding officer told him to stop the car: 'You get out and sit here and I'll drive.'[3] This was not the only time that Wilson's lack of driving skills was to cause consternation and discomfort to others.

Against the better judgement of his superiors he was rostered to drive a RAAF truck on the 'sick parade'. This meant transferring injured and sick RAAF personnel, seated on unstable stools, from Fremantle to Hollywood Hospital and Royal Perth Hospital in the back of the truck. The RAAF truck's Servo brakes were highly attuned to pressure and, unless skilfully operated, could bring the truck to a juddering halt.

The 'sick parade' truck was coming down the hill past the Nedlands Council offices, picking up speed, when Wilson realised that the truck was quickly approaching the Williams Road turnoff for Hollywood Hospital. He applied the brakes suddenly and forcefully. The truck screeched to a halt to take the corner. Simultaneously Wilson heard an enormous clattering in the back as flying stools and bodies crashed against the insides of the truck. After rounding the corner into Williams Road, he parked the truck and climbed out. He turned to his ruffled passengers, and as an innocent and confident nineteen-year-old enthusiastically asked, 'Anyone for Hollywood?' The responses were immediate: they all wanted to be dropped off at Hollywood Hospital, even those destined for Royal Perth Hospital. They had had enough of Wilson the truck driver.

Fortunately, Wilson's driving exploits didn't bar him from taking control of a potentially more lethal machine, an aeroplane. Soon after the 'Hollywood' incident, Wilson was undertaking his aircrew induction training at Clontarf, on the banks of the Canning River, about 8 kilometres south of Perth. After completion of the induction training, he moved to the wheatbelt town of Cunderdin, where he did his initial flying training in Tiger Moths. Then he returned to his hometown of Geraldton and more training, flying Avro Ansons. He flew up and down the Western Australian coast and out over the sea 'loving every minute of it; it was exhilarating'. He received his flying wings in July 1943.

On the night they were awarded their wings, Wilson and the crew hit the town of his birth. While his mates knocked back beers, Wilson sipped lemonade. But at the end of the night, after much singing and boyish fun, Wilson's mates thought it would be a good idea to have him enjoy the sensation of alcohol. With great laughter from all, including Wilson, they grabbed him and pulled him to the ground. While he was flat on his back they poured beer down his throat, giving Wilson his first taste of the amber fluid. That was some experience for the teetotaller. The temperance movement, which was closely associated with the Presbyterian and Methodist churches, had influenced the young Wilson: 'I thought abstinence from alcohol was the right thing to do. It was the way I was brought up.'

Having gained his wings, Wilson was ready to take on the world—and the enemy. In late July 1943, he commenced on an extraordinary journey from Perth to Melbourne, then across the Pacific to Canada, the United States, and finally by sea across the Atlantic to Liverpool—an ocean passage threatened by German U-boats, primed and ready to attack allied ships. The *Aquitania*, with Wilson and another four thousand on board, would have made a first-rate target. Fortunately, under vigilant navy escort, Wilson and the *Aquitania* made it safely to Liverpool.

The usual Merseyside fog welcomed Wilson. He was excited with all the activity and talk on the docks. He could hear a number of accents from different parts of the UK and the Empire and Ireland, but the dominant accent was the Liverpool Scouse dialect. At the time, Liverpool was the second busiest port in Britain after London. It was the home to many of the biggest shipyards of the day and prominent in servicing the Allied war effort.

When Wilson arrived in Liverpool in late August 1943, the Allies were finally gaining the upper hand in the war in Europe. The German advance eastward into Russia had reached its peak, and would decline into defeat and retreat. On the western front, Hamburg had been destroyed by successive Allied bombing raids, and the conquest of Sicily by the Allies was complete. On Wilson's twenty-first birthday, 23 August 1943, the Allies began night bombing raids over Germany, and by 3 September they had landed on mainland Italy.

Wilson arrived in England under the impression that he would be flying Lancaster bombers over Germany, as many of his Australian colleagues who had joined up earlier were already doing. Among the Western Australians who were in England at that time was Francis Burt, who was flying Sunderland Flying Boats. 'Red' Burt, as he was known, was the great-grandson of Sir Archibald Burt,[4] the first chief justice of the Supreme Court of Western Australia, and would become a professional contemporary of Wilson.

Much to his disappointment, Wilson was prevented from joining the Lancaster squadrons. Someone in authority—exactly who Wilson never discovered—decided that Wilson's 'short legs' would prevent him from exerting sufficient control over the Wellington plane. This was a major problem, because the Wellington was the training plane for the Lancaster. On being informed of this decision, Wilson jokingly castigated himself for not taking a superior's advice when joining the air force to put manure into his boots.

After being denied the opportunity to join the Lancaster squadron, Wilson was posted to an RAF squadron as a fighter pilot. He was the only Australian in the squadron, and was initially stationed at the Winkleigh Aerodrome in Devon. The squadron was not combat active. It kept the Plymouth Defence Forces finely tuned and ready for action. Plymouth was a strategically important port and, therefore was subjected to extensive German bombing. Many of the women and children who resided in Plymouth were removed for the war's duration to safer places, such as Northern Ireland.

Wilson flew Hurricanes initially, and then Spitfires. The Hurricane's finest moment had been the August 1940 Battle of Britain, where it was crucial in downing enemy aircraft in the air battle. But the Spitfire became arguably Britain's most celebrated World War II plane. It was first flown on March 1936, and became operational in July 1938. By the outbreak of war in 1939, nine Spitfire squadrons were operating with the RAF, increasing to nineteen by the autumn of 1940.

Wilson's squadron flew their fighters out over the English Channel, dragging a drone behind them; they would then fly back over the Cornwall coastline providing a simulated target for the Plymouth ground forces to practise shooting at the German bombers. It was important to shoot the enemy before they crossed the English coastline, because to bring them down over the mainland could cause considerable damage to property and people.

Wilson loved flying, being in control of a Spitfire that 'fitted him like a glove'.[5] He loved the thrill of flying at 450 miles an hour, coming over the south coast of England at Brighton and in no time reaching London, 'playing hide and seek around cumulus clouds'. It was a great adventure, and a 'marvellous life for a 21 year old'.[6]

He particularly enjoyed flying over the cityscape of England's south coast on a clear day. Usually his view of London was marred by grey mists, but on the days he was greeted by blue skies he felt especially fortunate and happy.

He could see Big Ben and the imposing dome of St Paul's Cathedral. He might even have been able to pinpoint the place of his father's birth, if he knew where it was. East End, London, he'd been told. It didn't matter. The young pilot's remembrance of his father was as fleeting as the receding terrain.

Gliding over the outskirts of London on his way back to the RAF Winkleigh Aerodrome, Wilson took in the full view of his ancestral home. Rows of densely packed houses gave way to expanses of green fields, so much greener than the coastal bushlands of home.

On his arrival back at Winkleigh, he attended to filling in his flying logbook and other regulation paperwork. It was all part of his duties as a pilot of His Majesty's air force. But the young conformist did occasionally slip up.

Once he was taxiing in a Spitfire, but was going too fast, and collided with another parked Spitfire. The consequences were a few thousand pounds damage and a negligence mark in his logbook. Wilson ripped out the evidence from his flying logbook, but didn't destroy the offending page. He just tucked it into the back of the logbook.

On another occasion, Wilson flew a Spitfire longer than was scheduled for the session, returning to base on an empty fuel tank. Fortunately, his commanding officer remained ignorant of Wilson's indiscretion, for otherwise his logbook might have been missing another page.

On his free weekends, Wilson often travelled up to London for a day out with Eva Pepperdine, attending concerts at Albert Hall in London, visiting museums or having picnics in Hyde Park. She was a cousin of Mrs Clover. He also visited the Charlesworth family in Grantham in Lincolnshire. He searched out the family and friends of Mrs Clover, 'virtually the only mother I knew'. By contrast, he displayed no interest in searching out his father's family.

During his time in England he never heard from his family back in Western Australia. Through a friendship scheme organised by the Royal Commonwealth Society—of which he remained a member throughout his life—he met the Kuhns, who would become like a family away from home. Heine Kuhn and his wife Mariele were Jews who had fled Germany after Hitler was elected chancellor in 1933. Both were well educated, and Heine was a Fellow at Balliol College, Oxford University. The Kuhns had two sons; one of their grandsons would marry an Australian in Melbourne in 1993. Wilson visited them frequently, often flying himself without permission from Winkleigh Aerodrome to the Kidlington airfield near Oxford and back.

Wilson also corresponded with Mariele Kuhn. Throughout his life Wilson, the reserved man, felt uncomfortable talking about himself. The letters to Mariele provide some insight into the man and what he was thinking at the time.

Although deeply religious, he gave little thought to the morality of war, seeing it essentially as a national issue. It was simply a matter that Australia was at war and he had a duty to join the services to fight the enemy of Australia, Hitler:

> I just accepted the prevailing view that Hitler was bad. Nazism was a menace that had to be stopped and you just accepted the war as inevitable and joining up was the thing to do.

In a letter to Mariele dated 11 July 1944, he wrote:[7]

> Isn't it ironical (or is it?) that two countries are at war when the men that do the actual fighting and killing have no real desire for war or for anything except the right to live their own lives in an atmosphere of peace, security and goodwill.[7]

Wilson then commented on his noncombatant role. He was philosophical, although disappointed, about being denied active combat. He felt he had an important job, but was embarrassed that he had a relatively 'cushy' time compared to his colleagues engaged in combat. He had no 'battlefield trauma' or nightmare memories, and he could not claim to have suffered the rigours of war, as many others did.

While not necessarily wanting to go out to kill the enemy, he would have preferred to have experienced the danger, excitement and importance of operating in combat missions. Wilson wrote to Mariele:

> I'm beginning to doubt that I shall be given the opportunity to kill anybody in this war (sounds callous, doesn't it?), any Germans anyway and I shall be very thankful not to do. That's one reason why I never wanted to be a bomber pilot because in the course of his duty he brings death and destruction to hundreds of innocent civilians, whereas with a fighter pilot it is just like a duel, you are both on equal terms and the best man wins.

To Wilson, being a fighter pilot was like a game of chess, with one seeking to outwit and outperform one's opponent. But unlike chess, defeat invariably meant death. Wilson displayed a clinical detachment to the consequences of military death; it was just part and parcel of being a serviceman.

Again in another letter to Mariele Kuhn dated 28 July 1944,[8] the issue of death in war is prominent—this time in the context of his brother Doug's death, only two weeks earlier on 15 July 1944. Although both were in England serving as RAF pilots, Ron and Doug had not met up. Wilson did not receive notification until after Doug had been buried at the regional cemetery in Cambridge.

Wilson told Mariele that he had been unable to find out much about his brother's death. He wrote:

> It was rather a morbid visit altogether last Monday as I heard of several of my old cobbers who have crashed recently. The Aussie padres are kept busy going round the country burying airmen. Still that's enough of that!

He then moved on to saying that he was back into the old routine, and that he was happy at Winkleigh base.

Obviously worried that his communication to Mariele of his feelings about the death of his brother may have seemed unemotional and detached, he finished the letter with a PS:

> I've got an idea you think I'm a bit cold-blooded or unmoved about my brother's death—if I'm wrong then please forgive this explanation. In our present vocation Death is such a frequent visitor that we have to keep our emotions under a leash, as if we let them run riot we should soon lose our own nerve.

Wilson did not appear to view the death of his brother as any different from the death of others in time of war—no special and understandable family grieving. But then, they had never had a close relationship, with Doug leaving home when Wilson was still relatively young.

Wilson then expressed how his faith guided his response to death:

> I have always said I believed in the Resurrection of the Dead and that makes death a very paltry thing. In the words of Bishop Brent: 'Life is eternal and Love is immortal, and Death is but a horizon, a horizon being the limit of

one's sight.' I hope you can understand what I mean Mariele—If not, then don't bother about it.

Wilson was very fond of Mariele and the Kuhn family, and he enjoyed his visits to Oxford. Many years later, in the 1960s and 1970s when he was in England appearing in the Privy Council, he would often pay a visit to Oxford to see them. He would disembark from the long flight from Perth to London in the early hours of the morning and head straight to the Heathrow bus terminal to catch a bus directly to Oxford and the Kuhn family.

During the war, Wilson and a good friend in his squadron both fell for the same girl, a young lady called Betty. He fell in love, but the relationship was purely platonic. Wilson the serviceman was inexperienced in the matter of sex, and remained true to his Presbyterian beliefs and sheltered upbringing. He was also a young man reticent about forming relationships that required him to open up to the other person. This was particularly the case when the opposite sex was involved.

It was a shock for the naïve, sheltered Wilson to be in the company of service comrades as they belted out bawdy songs, told smutty jokes in the troop truck and talked about their sexual conquests: 'I used to shudder to my backbone. The crudity and the sex, well, the sexual crudity of it was, oh, it was just too shocking for words.' He gradually acclimatised to his more boisterous and lewd comrades, but he never went as far as having sex. Indeed, Wilson remained a virgin until he married at the age of twenty-eight. But hearing about the conquests of his sexually adventurous service mates made him wonder what he was missing.

His friend was more forward, and more interested in marriage. He married Betty in 1944, with Wilson acting as best man. Sadly, his friend was killed not long after the wedding. The way was now open for Wilson to step in and become the new man in the widow's life. But he still was not keen on marriage. He didn't propose to Betty.

Sometime after the war, Betty immigrated to Denmark, a town on the south coast of Western Australia. In the early 1990s, her son contacted Wilson when he enrolled to do law at UWA.

Religion and the church remained important to Wilson during his war years in England. While based in Devon near the Winkleigh Aerodrome, he attended the local Methodist church, and occasionally took a few services as a lay preacher. While attending a service at the Anglican church in Blackheath, in the south-east of London, Wilson had his most graphic firsthand experience of German bombing raids. The parishioners were in church reciting prayers when they heard V-1 flying bombs overhead. Then the noise cut out. Wilson's thoughts moved from the prayers of intercession to survival. A V-1 bomb landed 50 to 100 metres away, damaging the church, which had been weakened by prior bombing. Showing the resilience and stoicism that was emblematic of Britons during the blitz, they continued with the service, even as part of the ceiling came down and dust filtered through the church.[10]

Wilson was impressed with this stoicism. The British didn't complain about the shortages and rationing and bombing raids, and continued on with normal daily routines. Wilson liked this attitude—just get on, whatever the situation and hurdles in front of you.

After about nine months at Winkleigh Aerodrome, around the end of June 1944, Wilson was briefly transferred to Gatwick. Earlier that month, 6 June 1944, Allied troops landed on the coast of Normandy in France. The D-Day invasion of France resulted in Paris's liberation on 25 August 1944. By the end of September 1944, all of France and most of Belgium had been cleared of German forces, apart from German prisoners.

After Gatwick, Wilson moved to North Weald in Essex, not far from London. There he flew Tempests over the Channel and back in training exercises for coastal forces. Tempests were ideal for this purpose, as they were similar in size, weight and speed to the German bombers. Wilson enjoyed flying the Tempests, as they were easy to control. Although Wilson did not fire a shot in combat, other Tempest squadrons were engaged in intercepting the deadly German V-2s before they could penetrate too far inland and blitz London.

Wilson remained at North Weald until the war ended in Europe with the surrender of the Germans on 7 May 1945. But hostilities continued in the Pacific for another three months, coming to a dramatic end when the United States dropped an atomic bomb on Hiroshima on 6 August 1945 and another on Nagasaki on 9 August 1945.

The young Wilson was not profoundly affected by the atomic bombing of Hiroshima and Nagasaki: 'It was just a piece of news without any particular relevance to me. I never really thought about it.' In fact, there were many people who would have felt the same. There was a feeling of exultation and relief that the six long years of war were now coming to an end. Moreover, because of the excruciating freshness of the knowledge of Japanese atrocities against Australian soldiers, many Australians were not inclined to show sympathy to the Japanese.

After victory in Europe, Wilson made some flights into France and visited Paris. He was tempted to remain in Europe and join the occupation force in Germany for a regulation two-year stint. It would be exciting, and he felt comfortable in the forces. No need to make day-to-day decisions, such as selecting accommodation and a job. But it would have only being delaying the inevitable. He never contemplated a lifetime career in the military, so going to Germany would only have postponed and made more difficult the transition back to civilian life.

In November 1945, Wilson left Southampton for home, but the MV *Athlone Castle* broke down in the Bay of Biscay and returned to England. After repairs were made, the ship set sail again for Australia. While on the voyage he wrote to Mariele Kuhn, posting the letter from Port Said in Egypt on 5 December 1945.[11] Reflecting on his time in England he wrote:

> I'm just beginning to think that we really have said goodbye to England, for a few years at any rate. And even already I feel that my sojourn there is just an episode, a part of my life that is separate, closed complete in itself; and yet coming as it did at the most formative part of my life it cannot have failed to leave its mark indelibly upon me. I feel I want to compare myself as I was 2 and half years ago with what I now am, and I honestly think my life is based on firmer foundations, that the youthful ideas and ideals I had have become crystallised into mature convictions, thanks largely to the friendship I made in England, notably you and my mother's cousin [here he is referring to Mrs Clover's cousin, Eva Pepperdine] in London.

After thanking Mariele for her friendship, he apologised for his failure to learn the 'greatest lesson' that she had tried to teach him, 'namely to give myself fully to my friends to open up completely'. He acknowledged his reserved nature:

> I know I can't live really fully without putting aside all my reserve and yet I still want to cling to it. Maybe I have to really fall in love with someone before I shall be able to gain complete freedom in all my relationships.

In commenting on the journey, Wilson said that the MV *Athlone Castle* was 'bearable' and that he was managing okay. He commented on the long queues, writing that even the English housewife famous for her patience in queuing would be impressed with the ship's 'queues for everything...with about three or four hours per day spent in them'. He noted the fine weather in the Mediterranean—the beautiful blue skies. He added: 'Some of the sunrises and sunsets over the water have been wonderful, I wish I was an artist and could convey their beauty to paper.'

Wilson arrived in Fremantle on Boxing Day 1945. His arrival home confronted him with having to make a career choice.

3

A Lawyer or a Padre?

I was in two minds whether to go into the church when I came back from the war. I made enquiries as to whether there were any plans to institute aerial padres in the North. If the answer had been yes, that might have swayed me. Anyhow I chose law…I'm not conscious of any influence that my father's profession might have had, but going into the Courthouse, of course, brought me in touch with the law and it was a natural progression.[1]

The Australia that greeted Wilson on Boxing Day 1945 was a nation seeking to find its feet after the war. Perth was still a small city, with the total population of the state being around 500,000. Perth remained a conservative place in which the British immigrant still dominated. The mass immigration from southern Europe had not yet commenced.

On his arrival back in Perth, Wilson in his usual energetic manner didn't stand still for long. He was in a hurry to sort out what he was going to do with the next stage of his life. But before doing so, he travelled by car to Point Peron, just south of Fremantle, to catch up with some friends who were attending a PFA camp.

Wilson turned up in his RAF uniform, after having arrived back from service just twenty-four hours earlier at Fremantle. He was not really sure why he went to the camp in uniform. Perhaps it was to impress his friends, whom he hadn't seen for more than two years. Many of the young women at the camp gathered around the young man in uniform. But not Leila

Gibson-Smith, who thought he was a bit of an upstart and showoff arriving in blue serge:

> He came down in his air force uniform and I can't say I was terribly impressed with him at first. I thought he was a little bit above himself, but I think it was all the girls making a fuss of him and I didn't want to be one of them.

But at least she recognised him. Wilson didn't even notice her.

After his day visit to the Point Peron camp, Wilson returned to Mrs Clover at the family home in Hollywood. Just 'Mumsie' and him. She was relieved that he had survived, and delighted in Wilson telling her stories about his meetings with her close friends and relative in England. But Wilson didn't have time to spend lounging around and talking about his time in England and the RAF. He had the important matter of his future to sort out.

Some of Wilson's air force colleagues pursued careers in aviation, becoming commercial pilots. Although toying with such an idea, Wilson was more set on a career as a flying padre, where he could marry his love of flying with his religious convictions and interests. But his enquiries with the Presbyterian Church were not encouraging. The idea was in its infancy in the 1940s. The nascent flying padres didn't become a regular feature of the outback ministry until around the 1970s, first in Queensland, then later in Western Australia.

Having reluctantly abandoned this dream, in February 1946 Wilson decided to take advantage of the Commonwealth Reconstruction Training Scheme for returned servicemen and enrol at university. The scheme paid a living allowance and associated educational fees and costs. This was an offer too good to forgo, thought Wilson, significantly reducing the financial strain normally associated with obtaining a university degree.

At the time, students did not pay tuition fees at the University of Western Australia (UWA). Other universities followed UWA's example only after the Whitlam Labor government abolished university tuition fees soon after coming into office in 1972. But for most families in 1946, the collateral costs of a university education for their children were prohibitive.

Wilson found that his lack of secondary school qualifications—something which he remained sensitive about for all his life—would prevent him directly enrolling in the UWA law school. So Wilson enrolled in the Bachelor of Arts program, selecting to study English, French, economics and industrial relations. His selection of French was interesting, considering he had only studied it to the rudimentary junior school level. But Wilson viewed mastering French as part of his quest to become better educated and cultured. By contrast, industrial relations was selected for study because he believed it was a relatively lightweight subject, allowing him more time to spend learning the other subjects.

Wilson arrived on campus on the first day of term in late February 1946, eager to learn and keen to do well. He attended all his lectures, although many of them were not overly stimulating. In the main, the lecturers were not keen to have their prepared lectures interrupted by student questions or debate, not that Wilson was inclined to do so. He found it relatively easy to master the details and issues of his subjects, apart from French. Initially, he struggled with it, receiving marks as low as 10 per cent for some of his early assessments.

Within the first week or two of first term, Wilson joined the Australian Student Christian Movement (ASCM). It was only natural that Wilson, a deeply religious young man who was very involved with his local Nedlands Presbyterian Church and the PFA, would be attracted to the ASCM on campus.

The philosophy or objectives of the ASCM can be ascertained from the following excerpt from its 1947 pamphlet:

> The Australian Student Christian Movement is a fellowship of students who seek God and the truth by which to live.
>
> The Aim of the Movement is—
>
> - To confront students with Christ and His Gospel,
> - To lead them to commit themselves to Christ and His way of life,
> - To unite them in the fellowship of His Church and in the service of the Kingdom of God.
>
> The Basis of the Movement is its affirmation of the Christian principles:
>
> - That Jesus Christ is the supreme revelation of God and of true manhood.
> - That Christian faith in God requires from men and women the devotion of their whole lives to the service of the Kingdom of God.
>
> On these principles the Movement bases its study, prayer and service and other activities.
>
> Membership of the Movement is open to students, teachers and others who have decided to test with their lives the truth of Christ's way of life.[2]

These philosophies resonated with Wilson's own firmly held beliefs in matters of morality, personal behaviour and interpersonal relations. And he was particularly attracted to belonging to an organisation that had a Christian faith as central to its being, but one that also fostered debate on what such a faith meant.

The ASCM was an interdenominational student fellowship body affiliated with the World's Student Christian Federation. It viewed the inter-denominational nature of its mission as very important:

> a natural source of power for the ecumenical movement, by which the Churches have begun to understand and appreciate each other, and to see their task as an indivisible and co-operative commission.

It busied itself with activities such as addresses, camps, study groups and conferences. It viewed these activities as 'the means by which students are confronted with Jesus Christ, and His Gospel, and are led to commit themselves to Him and His way of life'.

The ASCM was one of a number of religious student groups with a presence on the UWA campus. The Evangelical Union (EU) and the Roman Catholic Newman Society were also present. The Newman Society and the ASCM sometimes held joint activities, such as debating events and social gatherings. But the EU was a different matter. Wilson had little time for their fundamentalist attitude to religion and refusal to engage in debate with others who held a different view of Christianity. Wilson was opposed to the EU's policy of demanding that potential members sign a pledge that bound them to the Christian views espoused by the EU. Wilson did not support a prohibition on religious debate. His view was that people should be able to hold a variety of views on religion and other things, never more so than in a university environment that was supposed to foster debate and diversity of opinions.

Soon after becoming a member of the ASCM, Wilson went on one of their camps, where he found himself leading a study group. Before long they were discussing deep theological issues, including the most crucial issue of all, the existence of God. Wilson viewed it as probably the greatest challenge he had confronted up to that stage of his life, much greater than any challenge he faced in the armed services.

Then and for the remainder of his life, Wilson saw the existence of God as a very personal matter. He had no physical concept or image of God; for him it was spiritual, with God being everywhere. His religious philosophy started from an inclusive concept of God who touched him in a deeply personal sense. In describing his faith, he recited the opening verse from the Presbyterian hymn 'God: His Being, Works and Word':

> Lord of all beings, throned afar,
> Thy glory flames from sun and star;
> Centre and soul of every sphere,
> Yet to each loving heart how near.

Wilson believed that the God who created a magnificent universe could still value equally His creation of even the humblest being. God was often in his thoughts. He did not have a daily commitment to Bible reading and prayer, but he would pray spontaneously 'as and when the occasion arose'. Often when preparing a speech or participating in a community event, he would think about the presence of God. He worked at worship, as it was the way he linked his life with his God.

Wilson did not unduly 'rely' on God to intervene. His God 'is not the one on whom you can foist the responsibility of the way human beings behave'. He saw God as being there to support people, with this support reflected in the sacrifice of His son Jesus, who died on the cross for the sins of the people. Wilson explained it as being the epiphany, which was the centrality of his faith. He viewed Jesus as suffering for humans, but also rejoicing in the joys of humanity. Jesus (and God) identifies with human beings and humanity, but 'that doesn't mean that he will over-rule people'. For Wilson, God's will is that humans He created should have the free will to negotiate the path between good and evil and to reach God's promise of everlasting life. This does not mean that there was not an omnipotent, omniscient God; but Wilson did not believe that God would intervene in the life chosen by people. Although his God is capable of shouldering that responsibility, Wilson did not put that responsibility on Him.

According to Wilson's view of God and faith, life is not predetermined or ordained. This would 'rob humanity of its freedom of will'. Wilson's God maintains relationships through love with human beings, and in that relationship people are stimulated if they are conscious of it; they are stimulated to live in accordance with what they believe to be His truths and His ways and they take, as the epitome of that, the ways of Jesus. For Wilson,

Jesus Christ was central as a companion and a saviour. In other words, there is a saving power, a saving from a fear of death, a saving from a sense of futility in life and meaninglessness when a person asks 'what is life about?' For Wilson, faith in Jesus Christ was one answer.

While at university, Wilson attended the annual national conferences of the ASCM in the eastern states. He engaged in the various conference forums and debates, and was very excited to rub shoulders with the leadership of many of the Protestant churches. He was particularly impressed by his conversations with Anglican Bishop David Garnsey and the Presbyterian Davis McCaughey (who later became governor of Victoria).[3] He found both men to be highly intelligent and wise thinkers with a great sense of justice for their fellow human beings. He considered them to be outstanding individuals.

Even though the ASCM was Wilson's 'spiritual' home, he continued to be involved with his local Nedlands Presbyterian parish and the PFA. The Presbyterian Church prided itself on its democratic government structure: the 'priesthood of all believers', which was played out through the lay members having the opportunity in the government of the church as elders; the equality in rank between the ministers and the ruling elders; and the unity of the church via a series of councils.

Wilson was attracted to the egalitarian government structure of the church and the liberty of opinion on nonessential doctrinal matters of faith. He always had what he saw as a personal relationship and belief in God. The importance given to the laity meant that Wilson was able to have significant input to and impact on the governing of the church over the years before the Presbyterian Church became part of the Uniting Church of Australia in 1977.

After a first year of diligent study, Wilson achieved credit grades in all his four arts subjects. He expected the credits in English, economics and industrial relations, but credit in French was something that surprised and delighted him after his initial difficulties. He even managed to play a significant role in the university production of Molière's *Le Bourgeois Gentilhomme*.

After completing the first year of arts, Wilson transferred to the law school at the end of 1946. By the end of his first year of law in 1947, he stood in the same position as second-year law students. The only difference was that he had spent 1946 exclusively doing arts and 1947 doing law, rather than the usual two arts and two law units per year for the first two years of study.

In 1947, Wilson entered the law school with just fifteen other students. By today's standards this is a very small intake,[4] but the 1947 numbers were greater than the annual intakes before and during the war (teaching was suspended at the university for 1943 and 1944).

It was the enrolment of returning ex-servicemen that increased the number of students in the immediate years after the war. It was an interesting time to be in the law school, as there was a mixture of the older returned servicemen and the younger school leavers. One such school leaver was John Toohey, later a colleague of Wilson's on the High Court from 1987 to 1998. He believes that the younger students were enriched by the presence of the returned servicemen, some of whom were experiencing the rigours of study for the first time, and that they in turn benefited from the students who were fresh from secondary school. These younger students were able to pass on hints about study or tell the older students about study habits that worked for them.

The returned servicemen were considered to be an asset, as they brought a seriousness and urgency to the school. Even though they received a weekly allowance (just over £3 under the Commonwealth Reconstruction Training Scheme), for those who had families to support it was a financial struggle to continue at university. They believed in having a good time, but most were in a hurry to obtain the knowledge and qualifications needed to practise law. Although there was a wealth of social and sporting activities, the law school at that time was a serious place of learning. Many students had to juggle study with family responsibilities.

The times were far from buoyant. People were recovering from the horrors of war and facing a 'cold war' scenario, unsure about what the future held for the human race. There was much concern about atomic war. Also, there was still some food rationing, and housing was difficult to obtain. Although Wilson did not have a melancholy or pessimistic outlook on life, he viewed university as a time for study and doing as well as possible.

Until 1947 there had only been one full-time academic appointment in the law school. In that year, the school appointed a second full-time academic position. The law school still relied heavily on the interest and goodwill of the local profession to teach many of the subjects. Students were required to study four non-law units and sixteen or seventeen law units; all the law units were compulsory.

Professor Frank Beasley, who had founded the law school in 1927, ran a tight organisation. He was an enthusiastic administrator and educationalist, and was always concerned with students' interests. He was a very 'hands on' administrator, so much so that he had a hammer and screwdriver in his desk drawer for repairs around the school. He gave much to the school and to the student body, but expected in return that students would wear appropriate dress to university and apply themselves to their studies. Students were expected to wear an academic gown in the tradition of his alma mater, Oxford University.

Beasley's contribution to the UWA law school was duly recognised with the striking of the Frank Beasley Award in 2003 to commemorate the seventy-fifth anniversary of the law school. There were two inaugural recipients of the award for outstanding service to law, the legal profession and legal education, Wilson and Sir Francis 'Red' Burt.

As he did during his year of arts, Wilson attended all his law lectures. He was most attracted to subjects with a more human dimension that were strongly case based and dealt with real-life situations, such as torts, evidence and criminal law. Of course, criminal law was to play a major part in Wilson's legal career, as was constitutional law, which he found interesting and thought was very important in the Australian legal and political system. Other subjects, such as property and legal method, he found uninspiring.[5]

Wilson and the other law students were left to their own resources when it came to studying. Wilson had few textbooks to refer to. Those in existence were based on the English law and procedure, with little commentary on Australian law. Comprehensive course outlines or summaries of lectures were nonexistent. Wilson attended about 20 hours of lectures per week, spending most of his remaining time in the law library reading cases. Assessment was solely exam based; generally one end-of-year exam, with mid-year exams being infrequent.

But Wilson didn't mind or complain about the lack of assistance or resources. He and the other students just got on with learning. For students who had been to war, complaining about the lack of resources seemed a trifle self-indulgent.

Wilson was liked by his fellow law students although he didn't take part in the school's social activities, of which sporting events occupied a significant portion. He enjoyed debating and public speaking, but stayed away from these activities at law school. And he eschewed student politics.

The UWA law student body at the time was a breeding ground for some of Australian's future politicians, people such as Peter Durack, a future senator and Commonwealth attorney-general; Billy Snedden, a future Federal Liberal opposition leader and speaker of the House of Representatives; and Bob Hawke, who went on to become Australia's longest-serving Labor Party prime minister.

Hawke entered law school in the same year as Wilson, but, like most first-year law students, he did two law and two arts units, and graduated later than Wilson. Just as John Toohey had, Hawke also viewed positively the large presence of returned servicemen on campus and in the law school:

> I admired the way in which these men, many without secondary level qualifications, adapted to the unfamiliar discipline of study after the rigours of war. They were generous in their attitude to us young people who had enjoyed such an easy run compared to them.[6]

Wilson and Hawke were not mates, although they did have contact with each other through their involvement in the ASCM. But even there, they rarely socialised or spoke to each other, though there was no animosity between the two. Hawke, who later became agnostic, shared the speakers' stage at Winthrop Hall with Wilson for an ecumenical, nondenominational church service to celebrate Empire Youth Sunday on 23 May 1953, four years after Wilson had graduated from UWA.

Within two years of joining the UWA branch of the ASCM, Wilson was elected branch president. Being an ASCM officer placed further demands on his time, but he was organised, energetic and enthusiastic. Wilson had to be organised, because he still maintained a full commitment to his Nedlands Presbyterian parish and the PFA. In 1948 he was also the state president of the PFA. That year, the state secretary was the young woman he failed to impress in his military uniform two years earlier at the Point Peron camp, Leila Gibson-Smith.

Leila was born in Perth in 1925. Her parents were from Sydney. All her grandparents were from England. She was the second eldest child in the family, and had a brother Keith, born in 1922, and two younger sisters, Nancy, born in 1928, and Judith, born in 1931.

Leila's father was a cable engineer with Cable and Wireless. Through his job, the family travelled around Australia to such cities as Adelaide, Darwin and Sydney, before resettling permanently in Perth in 1943 when Leila was eighteen years old.

Leila and Wilson shared in common the death of a parent while still a child. Her mother died in 1937 of a cerebral haemorrhage, aged forty-one. Leila, only twelve, took over many household duties, including much of the cooking for the family.

On leaving school at age fifteen, with a New South Wales Intermediate High School Certificate, Leila enrolled in Mrs Hale's Model Business College. Later she worked as a stenographer in Sydney. When the family moved back to Perth, Leila worked for Wesfarmers as a stenographer and secretary. In early 1949 she moved to the Western Australian Department of Industrial Development. Later in the year, Leila suffered the early loss of her father who, aged fifty-seven, died of a coronary occlusion.

Also like Wilson, Leila was baptised an Anglican. She had been an occasional churchgoer, but on returning to Perth in 1943 she met up with some old friends who were regular attendees of Presbyterian services. Within two years she had joined the Nedlands congregation of St Paul's Presbyterian Church. Her conversion to Presbyterianism was to lead to a strong faith commitment that continues still.

Wilson and Leila slowly but surely got to know each other through their joint commitment to the PFA. They were often at the same meetings, and socialised with other PFA members. They found it easy to talk to each other and enjoyed being together. In early 1948, Wilson asked Leila to the grand PFA ball. From then on they started going out as a couple.

Only a couple of months later, on Anzac Day in 1948, Wilson and Leila went for a picnic to Kalamunda in the hills east of the city. The food was laid out on the blanket and Wilson and Leila were seated on the grass. Wilson proposed to Leila, 'Will you marry me?' Although at the time short courtships were relatively common, Wilson had moved quickly on the marriage front. He thought he had reached the stage in life where he was ready for marriage. He needed a partner he could depend on for support for the next phase of his life. Leila was that woman. She was dependable and she was religious.

Leila contemplated the proposal. There was silence for about a minute. Wilson then said, 'I have to be honest with you, Leila, and tell you that my faith will always come first. My second priority is my professional duty and then you, Leila, and the family I hope we will have.'

Leila was speechless with surprise. She thought quickly. Did she love him enough to accept the conditions he was placing on any marriage between them? She decided she did, and accepted his proposal of marriage.

In later life, when reflecting on Wilson's priority choices, she said that if she had been younger (she was twenty-five years of age when he proposed) she would not have had the maturity to evaluate the situation before her. She is uncertain if she could have coped with Wilson's priority statement.

During Wilson's time at university, student politics was dominated by the threat or perceived threat of communism. The 'communist menace' was never far from student discussion. One controversial topic was the International Union of Students (IUS). It was alleged that the IUS was a communist front, and at the very least included officeholders who were sympathetic to the communist cause. *Pelican*, the official UWA Guild student newspaper, had numerous articles and letters to the editor in relation to the merits of affiliation or non-affiliation of the National Union of Australian University Students (NUAUS) with the IUS. The 1948 Guild president, Peter Durack, a law student colleague of Wilson's, supported the NUAUS decision in December 1947 to disaffiliate.

Was the IUS a front for communist sympathisers? The campus debate was at times heated, with many passionate supporters on both sides. There were numerous debates on the issue, in *Pelican*, at Guild meetings and formal and social student gatherings. Wilson never took a public stance on this issue, although he was anticommunist. This was part of church orthodoxy: communism was antithetical to the Christian faith.

At the time the student population was small, fewer than two thousand. But apart from his involvement with the ASCM, one would not have known that Wilson was on campus. Prominent Australian historian and former Murdoch University chancellor, Professor Geoffrey Bolton, who edited *Pelican* during the time of the 'communist debate', had no strong impression of Wilson. He remembers that there were several law students who were prominent on both sides of the IUS communist debate, but Wilson was not one of them.

In class Wilson excelled. He was in the top echelon of an exceptional 1949 graduating class of sixteen students, nine of whom were awarded first class honours. Normally first class honours would not be awarded to more than 10 per cent of a class—but many of this class would go on to outstanding careers in law and other professions. A fellow first class honours graduate,

Bob Jones, became a Western Australian district court judge (1970–73), and was later elevated to the Western Australian Supreme Court (1973–82). Another classmate, Eric Edwards, eventually became dean of the UWA law school and the author of a number of law books.

In most subjects, Wilson vied with Ron Cannon for scholastic honours. Cannon was one of the younger graduates in Wilson's year, being only seventeen when he commenced at the school. Cannon achieved fifteen distinctions in his law subjects, compared with Wilson's twelve. Cannon, who went on to have a colourful and successful legal career in Africa, Hong Kong and Perth, specialising in criminal law, remembers Wilson as a quiet student with impeccable manners. Wilson never put his fellow students down. He was always prepared to listen and give due respect to others, and then go on to indicate how he agreed or disagreed with their viewpoint, but never in a condescending or patronising manner. For Cannon, 'Wilson was a real gentleman.'

In December 1949, Wilson graduated. Normally graduation would take place in the following year in March or April. To allow the returned servicemen to commence work as soon as possible, the university brought the date forward. Also, these returned servicemen were only required to do one year of articles training, rather than the normal period of two years. The Western Australian Law Society considered that, because the servicemen were more mature than graduates who had gone to university from high school, they should be prepared for practice after only one year.

Another exception was created for Wilson. In 1949, the Crown Law Department had no authority to take on articled clerks. Wilson, who had continued to work as a filing clerk in the Crown Law Department during the university holidays, wanted to do articles with that department and, reciprocally the department wanted to retain him. During 1948, Wilson consulted the under-secretary of law to see if he could do articles at the department. In 1949, the *Legal Practitioners Act* 1893 (WA) was amended to allow Wilson to do so.

In late 1949, Wilson made a trip to Ceylon and India, attending a World Student Christian Federation conference in Kandy in Ceylon. Wilson enjoyed the conference immensely, and was particularly stimulated by the interaction with some leaders of Christian churches around the world. One noteworthy speaker was Philippe Mauray, a leader of the French student Christian movement and the French underground resistance during World War II. Mauray discussed the dilemma facing Christians who engaged in war.

At one point in the address, Mauray paused as he surveyed his audience. He then said: 'In so far as we do not use force, we are ineffective. In so far as we do we are diminished.' This raised an important issue: when is it just for a Christian to engage in war? Wilson never felt a dilemma in volunteering for military service in World War II. He viewed it as an adventure and a way of serving one's country. But he also thought it was a just war, fighting the evil of Nazism.

Wilson had little opportunity to meet the locals in Ceylon and India. He spent most of his time with conference delegates. Wilson had no recollection of the poverty found on the streets, the child beggars, the maimed and sick lying in squalor. His university contemporary Bob Hawke attended a World Conference of Christian Youth at Kottayam in the southern Indian State of Travencore-Cochin (later named Kerala) in 1952. In stark contrast to Wilson, Hawke indicated that seeing the poverty of so many people while the conference delegates feasted on a plentiful supply of food 'marked the beginning of the end of my belief in the organised Christian religion.'[7]

Wilson returned to Perth in early 1950, and on 29 April 1950 he and Leila married at St Paul's Presbyterian Church in Nedlands. It was a beautiful April autumn day—sunshine and showers—and a happy day. But for Leila that happiness was mixed with a tinge of sadness, because her parents were not alive. Her father had died only six months earlier, and was not there to give her away. Instead, John Adams, the father of her best friend Beryl Adams, walked down the aisle with her. Beryl's mother, Jeanie, had acted as Leila's 'substitute' mother. Leila confided in her, and went to live with the Adams family for the six months leading up to the wedding.

Wilson and Leila were married before about sixty guests, friends and a small number of family. Leila's younger sister, Judith, acted as bridesmaid, along with Beryl. Jim Wilson acted as best man, and Wilson's friend from the ASCM, Norman Groom, was the other groomsman. The parish minister was away on a trip to the eastern states, so Reverend Harry McAndrew was a late replacement to celebrate the wedding. After a forty-five-minute church service, the wedding party and guests attended a quick reception at Reno's Restaurant in Piccadilly Arcade in the city. Then the newlyweds rushed to the Perth Central Railway Station to catch a train down to the south coast town of Albany for a two-week honeymoon.

Wilson's marriage to Leila created some difficulties with Mrs Clover, who was lukewarm towards Leila and anxious about losing her Ron. Wilson felt an obligation to Mrs Clover, the rock of support for him in his childhood, and with whom he lived for many years as a young adult. Now he was leaving her. Wilson believed that she never got over this disappointment, and never quite forgave him.

On their return from the honeymoon, the newlyweds moved into a friend's flat at the bottom of Mill Street in the city, near to where the Perth Hilton Hotel now stands. Access to the friend's flat eased the financial strain on the newlywed couple. They had delayed their marriage until Wilson had commenced articles with the Crown Law Department and they could rely on a regular, albeit small, income. They were completely dependent on Wilson's income because public service policy decreed that, as a married woman, Leila had to resign her job.

The Wilsons' tight financial situation did not go unnoticed. Roy Neville, crown solicitor (and later Justice Neville of the Western Australian Supreme Court, 1955–70) remarked at the crown law staff party thrown for Wilson before the wedding: 'How can an articled clerk afford to get married?' The newlyweds managed well enough because they didn't seek luxury items or engage in expensive pastimes or extensive socialising. They lived within their means. They even saved enough to purchase an old weatherboard house in Bulimba Road in Claremont only six months after their wedding. By then Wilson was very busy at the Crown Law Department.

4

The Prosecutor

I had difficulty in understanding why I attracted a reputation for being a ruthless prosecutor. I would have said that I concentrated on being a fair prosecutor but from the defence side you get a different perception.

Wilson commenced his one-year articles with the Crown Law Department in March 1950. It was a small outfit, with only six solicitors, headed by solicitor-general Sydney Good, who had nearly bought into Wilson's father's legal practice in the 1930s. Wilson was the sole articled clerk. His work was varied, helping out on both criminal and civil litigation, and drafting wills, contracts and conveyance documents.

In March 1951, Wilson was admitted as a barrister and solicitor of the Western Australian Supreme Court, sixty years after his father's admission as a legal practitioner. Wilson joined a small profession—in the early 1950s, the whole Western Australian legal profession numbered around 200 lawyers.[1]

On his admission, Wilson was made a Crown law solicitor. Within a month, he and Leila celebrated their first wedding anniversary, and within six weeks Wilson was undertaking jury criminal trials solo. This is what he wanted to do—advocate, not sit behind a desk drafting documents.

Wilson's first jury trial was in Bunbury, Western Australia's second city, 200 kilometres south of Perth. Representing the defendant was Ken Hatfield, who had a formidable reputation as a defence lawyer, and would often appear against Wilson over the next fourteen years. Hatfield had a prodigious capacity for work. He once told a solicitor and his client to come to his office the next day at 4.30 for a meeting. The solicitor and client arrived at Hatfield's office at 4.30 p.m. the next day. They were 12 hours late; Hatfield had meant 4.30 a.m., the normal start to his working day.

The Bunbury hearing had its origin in a trial that occurred just before Wilson's admission to the bar. Assistant Crown prosecutor Leo Regan had prosecuted an unlawful wounding case in Bunbury. The defendant's name was Dominic Recchici. There was disagreement in the jury room, and thus the jury had been unable to make a decision. This in itself was highly unusual, because Hatfield was a Bunbury boy and had never lost a trial there. The consensus back in the Crown Law Department was that the Crown had little chance of succeeding in the retrial. This was because a retrial nearly always went against the Crown, and the likelihood of defeating the local Bunbury lawyer on home turf was remote.

The department had given up hope of securing a guilty verdict and could see little risk sending the fresh-faced, enthusiastic Wilson to Bunbury to put the case again for the Crown. He might even learn something that may help him in future trials. One of the senior prosecutors, Gerry Ruse, said to him, 'Wilson, you might as well get some experience and go and do this trial.'

Wilson did the trial and, against the odds and the expectations of his more senior Crown Law colleagues, the accused was convicted. Wilson couldn't believe it. He thought he had done a terrible job, mumbling his way through the proceedings. At times during the prosecution he required assistance from Les Stotter, the chairman of the sessions, as to what he had to do next. Wilson thought the jury took pity on a novice up against the experienced Hatfield.

Hatfield did not like losing to the young Wilson. For the next few months after the trial, whenever they met Hatfield would sarcastically ask Wilson, 'And how is Her Majesty's learned Crown prosecutor this morning?' After Hatfield had overcome the ignominy of losing to an untested newcomer in Bunbury, the two developed a warm professional relationship, with mutual trust and respect. Over the years they would often appear against each other, including in several famous criminal trials in the 1960s: Wilson for the Crown and Hatfield for the accused.

Wilson was busy with his career, but also had other matters to attend to. Leila gave birth to their first child, Bruce, on 15 July 1951 at King Edward Memorial Hospital in Subiaco, fifteen months after he and Leila had tied the knot. Wilson had been thrilled with the prospect of their first child, but as was the norm in those days, Wilson was not involved in the delivery process. The first sighting Wilson had of Bruce was through the window of the hospital nursery. What he saw was an angelic-looking, blond, blue-eyed newborn boy.

Wilson may have warned Leila before the marriage that family would not be his number one priority, but he took to the task of fatherhood with enthusiasm and devotion. He bucked the norm of the time, changing nappies and helping with the feeding. Wilson was to be just as devoted with all his children, but he did spend considerable time away from home, prosecuting on the Western Australian country circuits.

Bruce had not reached his second birthday when Leila became pregnant again. This time around it was to be twins. Both Leila and Wilson were excited that Bruce would have not just one, but two new playmates.

The pregnancy was tiring for Leila. She had an active and inquiring toddler to keep entertained while dealing with the lethargy and nausea of pregnancy. The Wilsons decided to take a short break to Rottnest, a popular island holiday spot for Western Australians, 20 kilometres off the coast of Fremantle. Wilson thought the break would also do him good, as he had been working long hours.

Taking the ferry from Fremantle to Rottnest and back could be rough, the last thing the nauseous Leila needed. So they decided to fly. At the time, the Rottnest Island air service comprised one aeroplane, an Avro Anson, the same type of aircraft in which Wilson trained in Geraldton. The pilot was the legendary Jimmy Woods, whose name is synonymous with the history of Rottnest. He had also served with the RAF in the war. For Wilson and Leila the flight to Rottnest was memorable. Wilson, who sat in the right-hand seat alongside Woods, had to wind up the undercarriage by hand. This required about a hundred turns. By the time Wilson had fully retracted the undercarriage it was time to let it down again for the descent.

The flight back from Rottnest was even more memorable, but not for happy reasons. While on Rottnest, Leila started to miscarry. Wilson contacted their doctor back on the mainland, who said that while they remained at Rottnest there was little he could do. So they caught the first flight back from the island.

One of the back seats of the plane was removed to allow Leila to lie down for the fifteen-minute flight back to the Guildford airport. Leila was then transferred to the Tresillian Hospital in Nedlands, where she miscarried.

Wilson did not endure the same sense of loss and grief as his wife, who was hit hard. At that stage he did not feel the same connectedness to the unborn children as Leila did, and he quickly got back into the groove of normality and work: 'There's always a sense in which miscarriages—provided you're not too old—are very sad but not necessarily the end of the road, and one does learn from it.'[2]

During this period Wilson was constantly in the courtroom prosecuting for the Crown; he wanted as much advocacy as he could get. His appetite and capacity for work were demonstrated in March 1953. With the chief crown prosecutor unavailable, Wilson prosecuted nine successive criminal cases, some involving homicide, in just five weeks.

Wilson's usual practice for all trials was to spend the last week of the preceding month talking to the CIB detectives and settling the briefs. This included typing out his opening address to the jury, in which he would tell a story and not name the witnesses that he was going to call:

> I was convinced then, and I still think it was right, that the jury wants to know what the case is they're going to hear, and...their attention will be better if it's put in as interesting a way as possible and they don't need to know the linkages that go to make up that story. So you tell them a story. Then I'd put that story with the papers and forget it, and go on with the next one.[3]

Then, as each trial commenced, he picked up the brief and addressed the jury, often without having a clear recollection of all the facts and issues of the case. He would invariably be nervous, a slight quiver in the voice. But a few sentences into his address the quiver would be replaced by a firm, controlled voice. And, as if by divine guidance, the facts and issues would return to Wilson, and he would present the Crown's case in a logical forensic manner, with great enthusiasm and attention to detail. He was a tough cross-examiner, not hesitating to pursue witnesses on a question or point if he thought a witness was not telling the truth or had given an incomplete answer.

After the defence counsel completed the re-examination of his last witness, he commenced the summing-up or closing address. Wilson would sit on the edge of the chair, leaning forward with pen in hand ready to scribble brief notes as cues for his own closing address to the jury. He paid attention to every word the defence counsel uttered, and keenly observed the reaction of the jury members—their body language, where they were looking and their facial expressions. All this provided clues that might indicate what they were thinking or what he needed to address in summing up. Wilson was well aware it was the members of the jury he had to convince. They were the final arbiter on the matter of the defendant's innocence or guilt.

In his closing address Wilson would focus on answering the defence's closing address and reiterating the strengths of the Crown's case. As soon as he had completed this summing up and the jury had been sent away to deliberate, he would immediately transfer his thoughts to his next brief and trial. There was no time to contemplate how the jury may be deliberating or whether he could have done better.

The presiding judge for all of the nine trials in March 1953 was Justice Laurence Jackson, a Sydney-trained lawyer who had travelled to Perth after World War II. He was appointed a judge of the Arbitration Court in 1947 and a justice of the Western Australia Supreme Court in 1949, but his main focus was on the Arbitration Court. His first criminal session with the Supreme Court was in 1953. Wilson came to respect Justice Jackson who, in 1969, was to become Chief Justice of the Supreme Court, and whom he credits with humanising the court and making it an easier forum in which to appear.

Wilson felt that during his initial period on the Supreme Court's criminal list, Justice Jackson treated the court like the Arbitration Court. From Wilson's prosecutor's perspective, Jackson sought to elevate the defence case to that of the Crown, so as to have the scales more evenly matched between the parties, as was more common in the Arbitration Court. Because of the higher standard of proof in a criminal court—that is, 'beyond reasonable doubt' as compared to the lesser civil burden of 'on the balance of probabilities'—Jackson's directions to the jury made the chances of conviction less likely. Whatever the merit of this assertion, the fact is that Wilson's rate of conviction success was abysmal for March in 1953. In the nine trials, there were eight acquittals. The other was a conviction for manslaughter.

Although Wilson's success rate was poor, it didn't diminish his growing reputation within the Crown Law Department as an advocate with intelligence and great potential. He was on the rise.

Wilson got on well with his colleagues, and found them helpful. Gerry Ruse was always prepared to offer advice, and they became good friends. He credits another colleague, crown solicitor Ted Dunphy, with offering him the best piece of advice—when advising government departments, give them the answer in a few crisp sentences; they are not interested in how you reached the decision. This advice Wilson followed throughout his career, whether he was providing a legal opinion to the government or writing a High Court judgement. He always kept to the point and used short sentences.

Wilson's growing reputation was rewarded with his elevation in 1954 to assistant crown prosecutor. Criminal law was his main fare, even though his civil case work increased during the 1950s. Most of the cases were in the Supreme Court. Wilson was also required to prosecute on the country circuits, which kept him away from home for periods of up to six weeks.

Just over a year after the miscarriage of the twins, on 4 November 1953 Leila gave birth to Helen at King Edward Memorial Hospital. Wilson and Leila were proud parents and happy, and relieved that this pregnancy had gone the full length without complications. Now Bruce had a playmate.

In 1953 Wilson prosecuted Bunny Morris, who killed a policeman at Northampton, not far from Wilson's hometown of Geraldton. Morris was found guilty and appealed to the High Court. The appeal revolved around Wilson's cross-examination of Morris. He had got Morris to demonstrate in court how the accidental shooting had occurred. It was one of the first times a demonstration technique was the subject of an appeal.

Wilson flew to Brisbane for the High Court appeal, but he was not called on to speak by the court. It was reported sardonically by the Perth *Daily News*, a now-defunct afternoon tabloid, that Wilson had travelled to Brisbane and had won the case without being asked to utter a word. Although the High Court appearance was uneventful, the trip still proved memorable for Wilson. Sir Owen Dixon, for many people the greatest Australian jurist ever, invited Wilson to his chambers. Dixon's love of the common law and distaste for statutory interpretation was on display during their meeting. Wilson recalled:

> I can remember him picking up an Appeal Book, it was coming up that week, a smile came on his face and he said, 'A problem in contract—what a marvellous relief.'[4]

No one could accuse Wilson of not keeping busy. In addition to his Crown Law and family duties, Wilson lectured at the UWA law school, and remained heavily involved in church affairs. He commenced lecturing part time in 1952. Although the 1950s was a time of gradual 'academicisation' of the law school as more full-time legal academics were appointed, heavy reliance was still placed on the goodwill of the legal profession to assist in the delivery of lectures.

Wilson commenced teaching mercantile and commercial law, not because he had any particular interest or knowledge in these areas, but because it was offered to him and he wanted to retain some involvement with the law school. Later, to Wilson's satisfaction, he taught criminal law, evidence and constitutional law. Only when he was appointed solicitor-general in 1969 did he relinquish his lecturing.

Although Wilson had little spare time to prepare for lectures, he was highly regarded by his students. One student, former Chief Justice of the Western Australian Supreme Court David Malcolm (1988–2006), remembered Wilson as a brilliant lecturer who was extremely erudite and intelligent and who, importantly, made note-taking easier. Malcolm, the 1959 Western Australian Rhodes Scholar, later followed the tradition and also lectured at the law school. Around the same time that Wilson was teaching, the law school was fortunate to have a number of high-quality lecturers, such as John Toohey for property, Bob Jones in matrimonial law, Dean Beasley for constitutional law and Dave Allen for equity.

One of Malcolm's former colleagues, current Supreme Court justice Michael Murray (from 1990 on), who joined the Crown Law Department in 1964 as an articled clerk, was also lectured by Wilson. He remembered him as a 'very clear, very concise, effective lecturer' and a forgiving examiner. Murray failed evidence, and had to sit a supplementary exam. Wilson marked his exam paper and passed him. Murray was reminded of this when, shortly after joining the Crown Law Department, he met Wilson, who greeted him with a welcoming smile and generous handshake and said, 'Oh yes. I remember you. I felt I had to pass you because I couldn't bear the thought of inflicting you on to the lecturer the following year.' A backhanded reminder, but Murray was delighted and impressed that Wilson had remembered him.

Wilson and Leila remained committed to the church. They attended weekly Sunday services at Nedlands Presbyterian Church. Not content to restrict their church involvement to attending Sunday service, they were involved in a number of church committees, and Wilson became a commissioner of the Presbyterian Church. This made him a trustee of church property; his expertise was of great assistance in relation to the legalities involved in maintaining the property and the constitutional structures of the church.

From 1951 to 1956, Wilson was the honorary secretary of the Western Australia Council of Churches. In this role he worked with people from other churches, fulfilling his strong commitment to ecumenism. He was involved in organising a number of ecumenical and interdenominational events. The highlight for Wilson was attending the annual meetings of the Australian Council of Churches, which was generally held at Gilbillorah, the New South Wales Anglican Church's retreat centre. Wilson enjoyed meeting people from different denominations, something that had attracted him to the ASCM during his university days. He was in his element at the annual meetings, socialising and discussing ecumenical issues with most of the leaders of the various Australian Protestant churches and some of the Orthodox churches. The Catholic Church was not a member of the Australian Council of Churches.

Wilson loved his work with Crown Law, but a break from the constant grind of prosecuting criminal cases, many with their sordid details, was an appealing prospect. He viewed postgraduate study in the United States as his chance to have a break from prosecuting. In 1955 Wilson tried to find a scholarship to study in the US.

Wilson was short-listed for the Harkness Fellowship, a prestigious fellowship awarded for American study. He was interviewed by the selection committee, which was chaired by Sir Owen Dixon. He failed to convince Dixon that he was a serious enough researcher. Probably a fair enough assessment, Wilson thought.

The 'Harkness experience' whetted Wilson's appetite, and he continued his search for a scholarship. He read an advertisement for the Benjamin Franklin Bicentennial Fellowship in Criminal Law at the University of Pennsylvania law school. The fellowship had been established in 1940. This time he was successful, and became the first non-American resident fellow. The Americans were impressed by his position as assistant Crown prosecutor.

The fellowship was worth around $US4000 a year, just enough for him and the family to live on, but it did not provide for transport costs to and from Philadelphia. Wilson solved this problem by applying successfully for a Fulbright Scholarship. Named after Arkansas Senator J. William Fulbright, the Australian Fulbright program was established in 1949. It provided financial support for people from around the world to study, research and travel in the US, and for Americans to do likewise overseas.

The high regard the Crown Law Department had for the young prosecutor was reflected in its decision to continue to pay Wilson half his normal salary while away. This was very welcome, as the costs of taking the family were considerable. On 21 May 1956, baby number three, Geoff, was born at Tresillian Hospital.

In August 1956, Wilson, Leila, Bruce, Helen and Geoff boarded the *Strathnaver* bound for Philadelphia. The initial leg of their trip was via the Suez Canal, where Egyptian troops were visible on the banks of the canal. This was the time of the Suez Crisis. From the Suez, the family continued their voyage to Tilbury in England where, after a ten-day stopover, they boarded another ship from Southampton to New York.

The Wilsons arrived in New York in early September 1956, with Wilson commencing his Master's of Law (LLM) course on 10 September 1956 at the law school of the University of Pennsylvania. Leila's initial impressions of Americans were not positive. The customs officers were rude, people were unfriendly and taxi drivers unhelpful. Because there were five of them plus luggage, two taxis were required for the journey from the port to the train station. One of the taxi drivers had no idea where he was going. He lost the other taxi carrying Wilson and one of the children. Three hours passed before they were all reunited at the train station.

Leila was shocked by the ignorance of the Americans. She found that many had no or little knowledge of Australia. One day she was standing in the queue at the supermarket, when the woman behind her asked, 'Where do you come from?' When Leila told her Australia, the woman's surprised response was, 'You speak very good English, don't you?'

On another occasion, a woman in a shop said to Leila: 'Australia, that is way down south below Louisiana isn't it?' Leila smiled and responded, 'Yes, a long way down south.'

After the initial difficulties, Leila and Wilson found Americans to be friendly and warm. But their circumstances meant they had difficulty making friends. They were living about 13 kilometres away from the law school, as accommodation closer to the campus, where most of Wilson's class colleagues resided, was taken before they arrived.

Each week day Wilson headed off to campus in the Chevrolet they had purchased. But things were tougher for Leila, who was housebound in the rented part of a house they shared with the owners, an elderly doctor and his wife. She was without friends and support. She had to care for three young children, with one, Geoff being only four months old when they arrived in the US.

On arrival in Philadelphia they sought to enrol Bruce into the district school where they were living. But they were too late; it was full to capacity. Lacking the money needed to enrol him in an out-of-district school, Leila taught him at home via correspondence with the Western Australian Education Department.

Wilson and Leila found the Americans much more security conscious than Australians when it came to personal safety. Back in Perth, people slept with their doors and windows unlocked. Leila would think nothing of leaving Bruce or Helen, when they were babies, sleeping in the pram out on the front verandah. When she did this in Philadelphia for the first and last time, the next-door neighbour came over and said: 'Dear, you can't do that. Somebody might take your baby.' Coming from the relaxed atmosphere of Perth, Leila found this very restricting. But not too many years after the Wilson's return to Perth, events in their home city changed people's sense of freedom and safety.

There was little money available to splurge on buying 'special' things for the children, and the weekly groceries were limited in variety. Reminiscing about his time in the US, Wilson remarked, 'Leila learnt to cook mince 100 different ways.'

By the end of the week, Leila looked forward to spending Saturday afternoons downtown window shopping. There was also the occasional dinner invitation from faculty members, but as back in Perth, the church provided the major avenue for socialising. The Wilsons attended the First Presbyterian Church in German Town, where they were warmly received. While Wilson and Leila attended the weekly Sunday service, the children were well cared for, with a nursery for baby Geoff, a romper room for the crawling Helen and a toddler room for Bruce.

By arriving in the September of a presidential election year, Wilson was able to experience electioneering American style. He was fascinated with the 1956 presidential campaign: incumbent Republican President Dwight 'Ike' Eisenhower versus the Democratic challenger, Adlai Stevenson. It was the razzamatazz of it all, with candidates addressing large crowds accompanied by marching girls and slogans such as 'We're gladly and madly for Adley' and buttons with 'I like Ike', that fascinated Wilson. The election was held on 6 November 1956, and Eisenhower was easily re-elected.

With the Crown Law Department continuing to pay Wilson his half-salary, he acceded to the department's request that he visit and report on state prisons in Philadelphia and New York. He was impressed and surprised by what he observed. The prisoners had fully sanitised cells, and living conditions superior to those given to prisoners in Western Australia. Wilson was also impressed by the use of an internal TV monitoring system to observe cell blocks and corridors without intruding into the cells.

It didn't take long for Wilson to notice that he was surrounded by bright confident students. He lacked the same confidence, still hamstrung by his view that his education has been limited and narrow. He did not trust his intellectual ability against these American law students in competitive exams. He worried that he would be ashamed by his results, so he endeavoured to excuse himself from having to do the exams. He argued to the LLM program chair that he had a good case because of his professional experience and status as assistant Crown prosecutor and part-time university lecturer.

Wilson's advocacy skills, this time used to advance his own cause, succeeded. He still had to attend courses, but was not required to sit exams. He felt a great release of pressure. He now had more time to devote to his dissertation, which dealt with jury selection and service in the United States, particularly in Philadelphia.[5] As a prosecutor, he was keenly interested in the issue of juries.

In his dissertation Wilson wrote that the complexity of modern late 1950s life placed increasing demands on citizens, and thus the civic obligation to jury service 'should be attended with such economy as is consistent with the ends to be served'. He believed the rigid requisition of twelve jurors to serve in every case was an unjustified concession to a tradition of obscure origin. He opined that a smaller jury could do the task of decision-making adequately and efficiently.

He also expressed concern with the system of jury selection in which the chief electoral officer balloted a certain quota of names from the list of voters. Potential jurors could be disqualified from service for a number of reasons, including if they were not born in the United States or were not a naturalised citizen; if they were convicted of a crime or misdemeanour; were an undischarged bankrupt; or could not read or understand English. Also there were people from a range of occupations exempted from jury service.

Wilson wrote that the random selection process and categories of exemption increased the likelihood of having jurors not sufficiently competent to judge complex fact scenarios. He recommended the appointment of a jury commissioner unfettered by 'excessive statutory regulation', who in jury selection would place emphasis on 'the honesty, intelligence and general competence of the juror while preserving a reasonably representative character.'

Wilson's concern for jurors to be competent to understand and able to judge fact did not end with his dissertation. In an address at the UWA law summer school on 13 February 1976, Wilson queried the usefulness and reliability of the jury system in complex cases, such as 'white-collar' crimes. He argued that such cases were often so complex that it was unrealistic to expect lay people to deal competently with the facts and reach a just result. Also, the length of some complex criminal trials was so great as to impose extraordinary demands on the physical and mental capacity of jurors as well as their time. Wilson suggested possible reforms: for example, jurors being able to take notes, special juries, or a special tribunal sitting with judges and lay 'assessors' selected by ballot from a special panel.

In 1995 he publicly repeated his concern about the jury system for white-collar crimes.[6] His views grew more strident. Indeed, Wilson advocated the abolition of the jury system.[7] He believed that 'a judge is trained to analyse facts and to know the principles and apply the two', and that the jury system is 'deliberately inviting the community to exercise their prejudices'. He didn't agree with the argument that the jury system allowed representation from the broad community, which overcame biases and prejudices of judges who are overwhelmingly appointed from a narrow socioeconomic class. He didn't believe that, once a person had been charged with a crime, the community, through the jury system, should retain a role. Rather, a properly trained and competent judge should be able to produce the correct results.

Wilson argued that, from his experience in the majority of criminal cases, the weight of evidence favoured the prosecution, but that the jury was often used by the defence as a device to gain a sympathy verdict of acquittal. He conceded that the jury system allowed 'a measure of mercy into the system', which a strict judicial approach may not readily permit. He didn't necessarily consider this as bad or improper because, he said, there were some cases where an innocent defendant may be found guilty. He admitted that there may have even been cases he had prosecuted in which the defendant was innocent of the crime but found guilty. He always sought to detach himself from deciding questions of innocence or guilt. He believed his task was to take police briefs

> and deal with the defence as you saw fit and very often in simply testing the submissions put up by the defence and discussing them with the jury to assist them to appreciate where the truth may [reside].

Wilson's dissertation provided hints that it was written by a prosecutor seeing through the prism of prosecuting. He stated that the need for a unanimous decision in criminal matters 'does offer to a biased juror the opportunity to convert the entire proceedings into an elaborate and expensive farce'. He recommended that in all cases, except capital charges, majority verdicts should be allowed. He added that majority verdicts requiring a three-quarters or five-sixths majority decision would meet 'the objection that to allow majority verdicts may preclude any real effort at unanimity, and so stifle a proper deliberation by the jury'.

The concluding paragraph of Wilson's dissertation contained a criticism of the Philadelphian legal profession, which he believed would probably resonate with the Australian situation. The greatest obstacle to reforming the jury system was the prejudice of the legal profession. He noted that, when he raised the issue of jury sizes and majority verdicts with a dozen defence counsel in Philadelphia, with a single exception 'the reaction was one of strong opposition to any "tampering" with the jury [process]; indeed, even a discussion of such proposals proved impossible'. He concurred with the argument that many criminal defence counsels favoured an inefficient jury system because this increased the chances of obtaining an acquittal of a 'guilty defendant' or, at the very least, provided opportunities for appeals after convictions.

Wilson expressed, in the final sentence of his dissertation, his distaste for the blind refusal of the defence counsel to consider change:

> Whatever may be the merit of the suggestions which emerge from this study, the blind antipathy to the consideration of any reform cannot be too strongly condemned, for the survival of the jury depends upon the

> extent to which its character and functions are relentlessly and realistically examined and moulded to meet the changing conditions under which justice is administered in a modern society.[8]

His examiners were impressed with his dissertation, and he graduated in June 1957. He was encouraged by a number of faculty members to continue with the dissertation and convert it into a SJD (doctorate in law). Wilson had only ever contemplated the one year in America. He was committed to the Crown Law Department and, consequently, had to return to Perth.

The next ship going to Australia was departing from San Francisco six weeks after graduation. This provided the Wilsons with the opportunity to see a large slice of America on the drive from Philadelphia to San Francisco. They travelled to Chicago, the vast expanse of South Dakota, and Yosemite National Park. Here Wilson had a close encounter of a dangerous type. He decided to park the car to photograph a brown bear near the roadside. He left the car with his box brownie camera. He paused until the bear was near enough for a nice close-up shot. Wilson tracked the progress of the bear through the box brownie camera viewfinder, which made images look farther way than they really were. After taking the shot, Wilson looked up from behind the camera to see a bear closer to him than he would wish. He made a hasty retreat back to the safety of the car. Leila had never seen him move so fast.

After Yosemite, they travelled south-east through Utah, where the highlight was the explosion of a nuclear atomic bomb at the Utah nuclear testing site about 35 kilometres away from where they were driving. Leila recalled seeing a vivid spectacular flash. From Utah they drove to Los Angeles, where they spent five days.

In Los Angeles the children's highlight was the visit to Disneyland. For Wilson, Los Angeles was also the place for excitement of a different type. At a motel where the Wilsons were staying, a hostile parent accused Wilson of slapping her daughter. The woman's daughter was throwing sand at young Geoff. Wilson told the child to stop it, but she continued throwing the sand at Geoff. Wilson decided to take matters into his own hands, literally, and gave the young girl a tap on her hands. Her mother went into a rage and threatened to call the police and have Wilson charged with assaulting a minor. The matter was diffused by the motel staff and the allegations were taken no further.

From Los Angeles the family drove north along the coast towards San Francisco, where for two weeks they rested and went sightseeing before boarding the ship for Fremantle. Just before their departure, though, the family was to endure one more traumatic experience, courtesy of Wilson.

Wilson had decided not to sell the car until immediately before departure. Learning he was running rather late, he put Leila and the three children on the P & O liner, the *Orunsay*, a few hours before departure and headed off to sell the car. Because of time constraints, he didn't have a lot of bargaining power. He sold it for a very low price. He arrived back at the port to see nearly all the gangplanks up. Leila was trying to comfort the distraught children, who were screaming because Daddy wasn't coming back. Wilson just managed to jump on the last gangway before it was closed off.

They enjoyed the leisurely journey across the Pacific. The ship called into Sydney, Melbourne and Adelaide before the Wilsons saw the 'dirty old petrol tanks' along the Fremantle foreshore.

The Wilson family quickly settled into life at their Claremont home. Bruce was enrolled into the last term of grade 1 at the nearby Claremont Demonstration Primary School, so called because the teachers there often performed demonstrations for the student teachers at the nearby Claremont Teachers' College. Leila must have done a good job in America, as Bruce was ahead of his peers, academically if not socially.

Wilson quickly returned to prosecuting. His reputation as a formidable prosecutor was growing within the small Perth legal fraternity. Within two years of his return, and approximately two months from his thirty-seventh birthday, he was appointed chief Crown prosecutor, leading a team of six.

Also in 1959, Leila was to suffer another miscarriage when she was five months pregnant. On visiting the doctor in his rooms she was informed that he would have to perform a dilation and curettage. Wilson and young Bruce, who was about to turn nine, were also in the doctor's room. Bruce asked the doctor: 'Can you tell if it is going to be a boy or girl?'

'Why do you ask, Bruce?' the doctor wanted to know.

Bruce responded, 'Oh, I wanted to know if I was losing a member of my cricket team.'

The doctor and Wilson quickly walked out of the room. They could barely control their laughter. But of course, as with the previous miscarriage, there was also much sadness, more so for Leila than her husband. The passage of time has not removed the sadness for Leila.

Leila was told that she could have no more babies. She informed the doctor that she and her husband would very much like more children. The doctor conceded, saying that they could have one more only. Robyn was born on 5 October 1960 at Devonleigh, a private hospital in Cottesloe.

In 1959 Wilson was appointed counsel assisting the Gambling Royal Commission, whose establishment fulfilled an election promise of the David Brand-led state Liberal–Country Party coalition, which on 21 March 1959 won government back from the Australian Labor Party.

The Royal Commission was a response to concerns about off-course SP (starting price) bookmaking, allegedly the subject of racketeering. Off-course bookmaking was illegal, but tolerated by the police. In this context, it was similar to the longstanding containment policy in relation to brothels and prostitution in the west.

Sir George Ligertwood, a retired judge of the South Australian Supreme Court, was appointed Royal Commissioner. The commission was very revealing for Ligertwood and Wilson, who were both Presbyterian elders. Conforming to the Presbyterian Church's general abhorrence of gambling, they had never entered a racetrack. Therefore, they commenced the Royal Commission completely ignorant of the racing and pacing industry's operations and activities. They quickly learnt about all aspects of the industry, particularly the gambling. Both were given free passes for six months to every racing and pacing meeting in the state.

The Royal Commission recommended the complete banning of off-course bookmaking and the establishment of a state government-approved Totalisator Agency Board (TAB) system. This had the benefit of being a revenue source for the government and for the racing and pacing industries.

The 1950s was the decade of prosecution for Wilson, although he continued doing civil litigation. He also continued to do his own typing and retyping, which was unusual for the times. Most lawyers relied on their secretaries. His typewriter became as much part of the Wilson legend at the Crown Law Department as his ability to reduce complex legal arguments and propositions into succinct synopses or précis.

His little black typewriter would be positioned on a little desk beside his main desk. He would swing round to the small desk and tap away, recording his thoughts and points that would come out of conversations. Wilson had the ability and self-discipline to reduce into point form the issues as they were discussed.

Kevin Parker, former solicitor-general of Western Australia (1978–94) and justice of the Western Australian Supreme Court (1994–2003), who in 2004 commenced a five-year term as a judge on the International Criminal Court for the former Yugoslavia at The Hague in the Netherlands, joined the Crown Law Department in December 1958 to do his articles. He had received offers from private law firms, but the best they could offer was £4 a week. Crown Law offered £14 a week. While money was a determinant in Parker selecting Crown Law, the reputation of the lawyers there, in particular Wilson, was also a motivating factor.

After his admission to practice, Parker began working more closely with Wilson. Parker enjoyed the experience, finding Wilson friendly and patient with others. Wilson was self-effacing in his dealings with his colleagues, but he did expect a lot from them. It was no more than he expected from himself. He worked long hours at high intensity. If a colleague was not prepared to show similar commitment, Wilson 'would tend to seek someone else's assistance'.

Towards more senior staff, Wilson was sterner and more direct, but not offensive, if they 'let the show down'. Parker comments: 'With junior colleagues he would be encouraging so as not to shake their confidence.'

As Parker's career progressed in the Crown Law Department (he became solicitor-general in 1978 after Wilson's High Court appointment), he worked more and more with Wilson on major criminal and constitutional matters. He observed a man always thinking ahead on legal issues and how cases should be approached, and writing tasks to be done on anything he could find, including the backs of envelopes. After writing his list of things to be tackled he would say to Parker, 'Well, which of these do you want to look at?' Parker would work on part of the list and Wilson on the rest. Often they worked on each other's tasks, with Wilson being there at the beginning of the preparation, fostering ideas and planning the strategy.

Parker also observed a lawyer not afraid to change his mind, often arriving back at work the next morning with a position different from that which he and the other lawyers had agreed to when they left the office the night before. There was little complaint, as it would have been Wilson working at night at home on the redirection.

Parker's observations are echoed by other Crown Law Department lawyers. Peter Panegyres, who commenced articles at Crown Law in 1962 and became the crown solicitor (1985–2003), found Wilson friendly and encouraging. Over time Panegyres observed Wilson's 'hard work ethic'; early into the office and among the last to leave. He found Wilson to be very modest and 'polite and deferential'. He would bring the juniors into discussions of legal issues and, to the extent that he 'would debate them with you', accepted their views. As Ron Cannon recognised at law school, Wilson would not disparage others' points of view or put them down without debate.

Justice Michael Murray, who considered Wilson a very good university lecturer, also thought he was a great teacher at the Crown Law Department. After a few years in the department, Murray got to do more and more work for and with Wilson. He found him encouraging and non-authoritarian. Murray found Wilson amenable to being questioned as to why he tackled a particular issue or argument in a certain way. Wilson would take the time to explain in detail his rationale behind a tactic or argument, and willingly debated different points of view.

Wilson's relationships with his colleagues, whether in the air force, university, church, the ASCM, the Crown Law Department or other organisations that he was later to be involved with, were marked by civility and respect. Although the young cheeky Wilson was there on display in his years as a records clerk and fighter pilot, in the main he conformed to the dominant models of conduct for the various organisations and also with his own personal moral view on how others should be treated. But Wilson also had a strong Protestant work ethic, so he demanded high standards for himself and from others. His Protestant sensibilities also disinclined him to be boastful about his successes.

Although those who worked with Wilson were generally very complimentary about him as a 'boss' and a colleague, such compliments were not as forthcoming in relation to Wilson the prosecutor. Judge Hal Jackson of the Western Australian District Court (1986–   ), who never saw Wilson in action, has commented that he had a 'fearsome reputation' as a prosecutor.

David Malcolm, who did watch Wilson in court and had a high opinion of him as an advocate, confirms Jackson's comment on Wilson's reputation as a tough prosecutor: 'He had a reputation as being a really tough opponent in criminal cases. There were some people who said that he was almost too zealous in prosecuting in that way.' Malcolm's own view is that Wilson was tough, but scrupulously correct and ethical.

Former High Court colleague, John Toohey, although unable to recall ever appearing against Wilson in a criminal matter, was well aware of his reputation as a strong prosecutor. Interestingly, Toohey contrasted Wilson's prosecution reputation with his personal humanitarian side. He mentioned that for a number of years Wilson and Leila helped overseas students, particularly from Sri Lanka, with their lodgings and other support. Toohey comments: 'He certainly did have the reputation for being a very strong prosecutor, but he had this aspect of his life which was very much caught up with helping people.'

Long-time Perth barrister Paul Nicholls believed that Wilson was too intense as a prosecutor. Nicholls believes that, to convince a jury, prosecutors have to approach their duties in a more relaxed fashion than Wilson did. Nicholls remarks that Wilson would rarely concede a point to the defence counsel and that, although he was a man who 'had a certain streak of compassion in him', it was missing when Wilson stepped into his prosecuting role.

Perhaps Wilson's greatest critic is Leopold (Leo) Woods, a well-known Perth criminal defence lawyer admitted as a lawyer in 1937. For five decades until he retired in the 1980s he practised in the criminal law. Woods came from a working-class Perth family, and attended three Perth schools before going to New Norcia's St Ildephonsus College to complete his secondary education.

Woods was in the top echelon of Western Australian criminal defence lawyers. Indeed, Wilson considered him a formidable opponent, equal to the redoubtable Ken Hatfield QC as a defence counsel.

Woods was not only a talented defence lawyer, he was also a colourful legal character. When addressing the jury, he was prone to removing his false teeth, hoping to grab the attention and perhaps the jury's sympathy. He was also known to confront, in a friendly manner, people on Perth's streets to discuss with them the latest trial in which he was acting as defence counsel. His objective was simple: to gauge how they viewed his client, hoping to gain some insight into how a jury, drawn from the local Perth community, was thinking.

Woods never had a high regard for Crown Law Department lawyers. He thought Gerry Ruse and Leo Regan were competent enough, and he got on well with them, but they typified 'a tired Crown Law Department'.[9] He said that Wilson reinvigorated the department:

> He was fresh from the war scene, real fresh. He got into there and he was like a livewire. He was into everything, prosecuting, rushing around and doing

> everyone else's work, you know, he was a real dynamo. I had no trouble beating him nine times straight at one stretch.[10]

Woods considered Wilson to be hardworking, with talent and intelligence. Even so, he doubted Wilson's effectiveness as a prosecutor. Woods had several major criticisms of Wilson. Probably the least critical on the personal level was that Wilson was too naïve and ignorant of 'real life' and the public, as a result of working in the Crown Law Department since he was fourteen and spending most of his spare time with church friends. Woods believed Wilson's puritanical, Presbyterian lifestyle made it hard for him to associate and connect with average Australian males who enjoyed a few drinks and gambled at the races, and that this lack of knowledge about how the average Australian male lived and enjoyed himself was, on occasions, a handicap for him in court.

Wilson readily admits that he didn't patronise pubs or racecourses, but disputes that he could not 'connect' with your average Aussie bloke.

To illustrate his point, Woods recalled a fatal hit-and-run case he defended against Wilson. Woods said that he should never have been able to get the accused acquitted. His client had accidentally swerved and fatally hit a pedestrian and, without stopping, left the scene of the accident and drove home. Soon after arriving home he was arrested and recorded a 0.2 per cent blood alcohol reading. When cross-examining the accused about how much he had been drinking, Wilson raised the issue of the size of the drinks. After the accused answered that he was drinking schooners, Wilson, whose knowledge of the different glass sizes in pubs was nonexistent, said: 'Well, what is that? What's that size? How many ounces is that?' This played into Woods's defence strategy. When summing up to the jury he said:

> Well, when I sit down, as the procedure normally is, after I make my final address, you'll hear from Mr Wilson and he'll talk about the alcohol the accused had and his level of alcohol…I can only anticipate what he might say but I can guarantee he'll say something about this and so and so, but all I want you to remember, Mr Foreman and members of the jury, is that when he starts to tell you his view of these things and that you should adopt that view, don't forget that he doesn't know the difference between a schooner and a glass of beer, so just be careful about taking notice of anything he says about that.[11]

Woods reckoned this appealed to the jury, who consequently viewed Woods more as one of them than was Wilson. Given the secrecy of the jury room and deliberations, we'll never know the full story, but Woods was successful in obtaining an acquittal. His argument was based on convincing the jury that the victim had stepped out from behind the bus, and the driver, even though he swerved, had no chance of avoiding him regardless of whether or not the accused was drunk.

Woods disliked most what he believed was Wilson's antagonistic style of prosecuting and a desperate desire to win. Woods recalled Wilson's voice continually rising if he perceived he was losing a case:

> If he started to lose and was starting to become aware that he was losing ground...his bloody voice used to be raised up hundreds of decibels with the effort of making up ground. A striver, something seemed to be motivating him more than just ordinary winning.

While many prosecutors were prepared to concede cases or disputed facts or issues before a trial, Woods said Wilson would not. For Woods, defence lawyers had to watch Wilson 'like a hawk; you got no concessions, he wouldn't give you an inch'. Woods attributes this to Wilson's absolute determination always to win the case:

> He was a striver after convictions—he had his sight clearly on what he was doing and knew bloody well what he was doing and you would get nothing off him pre-trial or during the trial—no concessions. I've had cases where a good prosecutor has agreed to what the defence has said—and a good bloke will do that—he will be fair, he won't disagree with you, but he'll leave it to the jury and say it could be this or it could be that, it is up to you—you're the judges. But Wilson would try to get on to that thirteenth seat of the jury...That's the best way I could express it. He wished to hell he was on the jury and could go away with them.[12]

Woods said Wilson saw opposing counsel not as colleagues in law, but as enemies to be defeated. Even so, he did not believe Wilson acted unethically. But the point was clear: Wilson was too 'gung ho' as a prosecutor. This made Wilson dangerous, because it increased the risk of convicting an accused who should probably have been acquitted.

Woods, like many defence lawyers of the time, held the view that Crown prosecutors should present the facts and evidence in a neutral manner and leave it to the jury to decide the verdict. This was the modus operandi of prosecutors, Woods remarked, until Wilson came along and 'upset the apple cart'.

Woods indicated that Wilson's 'win at any cost' attitude attracted opposition and dislike of the man: 'Some of the blokes hated him, but I'm not a hater. Others would never forgive him. Others hated him until the day he dies. He incites opposition.' These are strong words from a colourful ninety-year-old-plus criminal defence lawyer who confronted Wilson in a number of cases. Did the defence lawyers of the time hate him? As most of are dead now, we will never know, but there is no doubt that he did attract criticism, and some defence lawyers referred to him as the 'Avenging Angel'.

Another prominent Perth lawyer, Bart Kakulas, agrees with Woods that Wilson changed the style of prosecuting. Kakulas, a Greek immigrant who relinquished a very successful motor vehicle insurance law practice to become a Queen's Counsel, had in his early legal career appeared in several criminal cases against Wilson, sometimes as a junior to the prominent defence lawyer, Ken Hatfield.

Kakulas acknowledges that Wilson was very effective and talented, but also says he was much harder and more aggressive than other Crown prosecutors at that time. This offended some Perth lawyers: 'Many of the Crown prosecutors had the view that they have to be seen to be prosecuting rather than persecuting. So you find them almost being dull, but not Wilson.'

The general view of the legal profession was that the Crown should merely present the evidence. With Wilson, Kakulas says, it was very different. Defence lawyers did not go to him trying to reach a deal. In Kakulas's dealings with Wilson, he found him very reluctant to concede points unless it was absolutely necessary:

> If it was clear that he couldn't go down that track; he was a realist, but he wouldn't just concede because it was a weak point; he'd concede because it was a hopeless point.

Wilson agreed that he would not concede much. For example, he would never initiate plea bargaining; it had to come from the defence counsel. And he never conceded a case. In summing up to the jury, the closest he would go to conceding would be: 'Well, it's a matter for you to determine where you think the truth lies.'[13] His view was clear: if it was a proper case, there was no need for such concessions; if it was a case that should not be prosecuted, the judge would have intervened to ask the jury if they wished the case to proceed. It was not a prosecutor's role to concede.

Wilson acknowledged that: 'I attracted a reputation as a ruthless prosecutor.' He found it difficult to understand why, although he does agree he was forceful: 'I would have said that I concentrated on being a fair prosecutor, but from the defence side you get a different perception.' He was a fluent speaker who sought to address the jury in a persuasive manner, and 'if there was a strong defence counsel, then you had to put up a strong defence of the crown case'. Wilson has no qualms or regrets about his style of prosecution and his role as a Crown prosecutor. He did not believe he had a 'win at all costs' attitude.

Whether it was 'win at all costs' or just 'forceful', what motivated Wilson to prosecute in such a manner? Did he see prosecution as a competitive game? Or was it because of a religious zeal to prosecute? Or was it motivated by Wilson's view of his duty as a prosecutor?

Wilson admitted to having an upbeat aggressive style, and to enjoying the contest of courtroom advocacy. It was the challenge of persuading judges and juries and the thrill of the contest. It is interesting that Wilson viewed advocacy in court as a contest. Others consider the reference to a contest by a Crown prosecutor as worrisome. People's freedom and even life was often at issue, so considering court proceedings as a contest—some sort of sport—may devalue the issues. But Wilson has said that, although he enjoyed the contest of the prosecution, this is not what motivated him.

Retired Police Commissioner Owen Leitch, who had much to do with Wilson in the 1950s and 1960s when he was a CIB detective sergeant, was very impressed with Wilson's talents and with his commitment to the job. For him, Wilson believed in the cause: 'The cause being to prosecute those that have been accused of a crime and if they had committed a crime they should be convicted.' Leitch adds: 'However, Wilson realised the issue of guilt and innocence was up to the jury. His job was to prosecute the case, which he did well and with commitment.'

Kevin Parker, who worked closely with Wilson at the Crown Law Department, has an interesting view about Wilson's motivation or guiding principle as a prosecutor:

> In his early days as a prosecutor he drew on his religious faith a lot to give him the confidence that to prosecute people was right. He had to reconcile that in his mind and his conscience and then to prosecute them hard and I know that he was helped through the conviction that it was right as long as you were honest and fair, that it was right to prosecute and, in appropriate cases, to prosecute hard. He was known as a fairly determined prosecutor. He didn't let go of your tail if he was after it. Dealing with a criminal bar, who were often fairly relaxed in those days, he came with a sort of higher intensity of dedication and preparation. It worried some of them. Not others.

Wilson would not agree that his religious faith influenced his prosecution style. Whenever Wilson had been asked about how his religious faith influenced his legal career, he constantly replied that it had no influence, or at least no conscious influence. A point in case is the death penalty.

In later life, Wilson expressly opposed the death penalty. He said: 'Finality is one of the important arguments against it. It is too final and I don't think any human being has the right to take the life of another.' But back in the 1950s and early 1960s he prosecuted cases where a conviction resulted in the imposition of the death penalty.

Wilson had just completed his articles year when he assisted Crown prosecutor Gerry Ruse in prosecuting a Czechoslovak immigrant, Karol Tapci, for murder. He had been charged with wilful murder, but after evidence was presented that he was drunk when he fought with and killed another man, the jury convicted him of the lesser crime of murder. Tapci was the first person to be executed in Western Australia since 1932, and the only person to be executed for the lesser crime of murder since 1913.

His execution was opposed by many, including a large number of Christians. Over 6000 people petitioned the state government for a reprieve for Tapci, but to no avail: he was executed on 24 June 1952. The fact that he was sentenced to death for the lesser crime of murder contributed to the public protest.[14] Subsequently, issues of the death penalty gained added significance and prominence after the conservative Brand government was elected, because it demonstrated a great readiness to allow the law to take its course in relation to those sentenced to death.[15]

Western Australia became known as the capital punishment state in the early 1960s, with four executions between 1960 and 1964. At the time the trend in the Western world was to abolish the death penalty. It had been already abolished in Queensland (1922) and New South Wales (1955), and from 1959, when Brand was elected, there had been no executions in any other state, apart from one in South Australia in 1964.[16] Wilson prosecuted the last person to be hanged in Western Australia in 1964, Eric Cooke.

> A 1962 Gallup poll found that 61 per cent of Western Australians favoured capital punishment but there was still much protest against the practice from academics, lawyers, religious people and the Western Australian Anti-Hanging Committee. Many letters of protest were published in the *West Australian* and the *Daily News* in relation to the executions in WA. Many of the letters of protest were based on the argument that capital punishment was contrary to Christian principles.[17]

The churches were at the forefront of the public campaign against capital punishment, with people such as the Congregational minister of Perth, the Reverend John Bryant, and Wesley Methodist Church's Reverend Ralph Sutton being prominent. They were supported by leaders from other congregations, such as the Church of Christ, the Baptists, the Anglicans and Wilson's Presbyterians, as well as the Jewish faith.[18]

The most enthusiastic and persistent politician in the anti-capital punishment debate was the Labor member for Balcatta, Herb Graham. He repeatedly sought to introduce measures to abolish the death penalty, including a private members' bill, the Death Penalty Abolition Bill, in 1960 and 1964. When he introduced the Bill in 1960, a number of academics, lawyers and church people signed a petition to the members of the Legislative Assembly advocating abolition. But capital punishment was not removed from the Western Australian statute books until 1984; it was the last state to do so.

As a prosecutor, Wilson would have been placed in an untenable position if he had publicly identified with the church opposition to the death penalty. In cases he was prosecuting, the death penalty was a real possibility following guilty verdicts. So what was Wilson's personal view at the time about the death penalty? In an interview with this author in 2004, he said he had no vivid memory of having any view on the death penalty in the 1950s and early 1960s when he prosecuted in several death penalty cases.

It is surprising that an intelligent, deeply religious man, who was intricately involved in the death penalty cases, did not have or cannot recall having a particularly strong view. Maybe it was a way of coping with the issue at the time. He was a religious man, very much involved in the Presbyterian Church, which was part of a broad church movement opposing death penalty; at the same time he played a significant role in sending people to death. Maybe he needed to detach himself from the religious and moral issues in order to do his job properly, while maintaining his strong commitment to his church.

But Wilson said that, even if he were opposed to the death penalty while a prosecutor, this would not have affected his role for the Crown:

> I didn't allow any personal views affect my professional role and duty. That would have also been the case with the death penalty. But I can't recall my personal views on the subject at the time.

Leo Woods, his harshest critic, has remarked that Wilson made a distinction between his personal and professional views and life 'that led [him] to avoid any tremendous conflict in [his] own mind about [capital punishment]'.[19]

Wilson's position on separating his personal and professional views or duties and his ability to implement this distinction in practice was a constant hallmark of his professional life. Clearly, this allowed him to avoid a sense of tension or conflict. As a trained lawyer, he had to concern himself with the law as it existed, not as he or others might think the law ought to be. Such normative considerations, in a parliamentary democracy, were for politicians to determine. A Crown prosecutor should be concerned with professional, not personal, duties and views.

For Wilson, his guiding or motivating principle as a prosecutor was his duty to prosecute the case to the best of his ability. It mattered not whether the death penalty were a possible outcome of a conviction. In Wilson's eyes, it was his duty of office and not some competitive urge or religious zeal that motivated and guided him as a Crown prosecutor, and that duty was to present the evidence and let the jury decide on questions of innocence and guilt.

In a 5 August 1997 interview with Lynne Haultain on ABC Radio National's *The Law Report*, he was asked: 'Sir Ronald, talking about your church life and your legal life—is there, or has there been, any moral tension there that you've have to deal with?' His response:

> Not that I can recall. I had principles that governed my conduct, for example, as a prosecutor that my job was not to strive too hard for a conviction, but

> rather to ensure that the evidence was presented fairly and completely to the jury and that I would assist them with an analysis of the evidence. If you think this, then that would tend to a conclusion along that way. And this evidence might be persuasive. So that was okay. I wasn't a brutal prosecutor or someone who sought a conviction at any price.

He viewed his role as establishing the elements of the alleged offence beyond reasonable doubt, and that was the end of his job and responsibility. After that, it was for the jury to decide if he had done so, and for the judge to determine the sentence. Wilson said that, 'I deliberately divorced any sense of personal judgement of guilt or innocence of any accused person, it being the province of the jury, not me.'

In practical terms, the demands of prosecuting in the 1950s meant he had no time to concern himself with what the jury might decide. Often the members of the jury would file out of the courtroom before lunch to consider their deliberation, and Wilson would have another trial commencing that afternoon. As soon as he had addressed the jury for the final time, Wilson would turn to the opening address for the next criminal trial: 'It was as disjunctive as that.'

Wilson saw his role as a prosecutor very clearly: accepting CIB briefs that were given to him. He said he had no responsibility or involvement in those briefs, but once he received them he did his job. However, Wilson did have discretion as to what information and evidence he used from the police. The police were the foot soldiers, gathering the evidence to be considered by the prosecutor.

In the 1950s and 1960s it was not unheard of for the police to engage in some intimidation and roughing up of suspects. For example, after one particular incident where some youths were brought in for questioning, police commissioner James O'Brien advised one officer 'to "try and remember to keep his hands in his pockets" in the future'.[20] As if to underline the police view at the time that sometimes it was necessary to engage in 'robust policing', O'Brien drafted a lengthy statement for public consumption, in which he said in part:

> Whilst I agree entirely with the necessity of fair play and justice in dealing with suspected persons or offenders, I sometimes feel that the pendulum has swung a little too far in restricting the police in their investigations which, after all, are made in the interests of society generally.[21]

One may have expected a prosecutor, especially one as experienced as Wilson, to be mindful of the possibility of 'improperly' obtained evidence by the police. This raises the question of whether there was a 'right level' of energy and intensity to be displayed by prosecutors in light of potential problems with police evidence, particularly in a era where the forensic evidence was not as sophisticated as today, which made witness statements even more important.

Wilson had a very good relationship with the CIB and the detectives he regularly dealt with, some of whom, such as John Porter and Leitch, rose to the position of police commissioner. Before Wilson left for the US in 1956, the CIB gave him a mock passport as a going-away present. During the early 1960s, when there had been a series of unresolved murders around the vicinity of the Wilsons' home in Nedlands, where they had moved from Claremont, the CIB would ensure that a patrol car intermittently went past the family home. The detectives would shine their torches and walk around the house to ensure all was in place and there were no prowlers on the premises. Leila felt more secure, knowing that the detectives 'were keeping an eye on things for us', especially when Wilson was away at night, a fairly regular occurrence as his career progressed.

When Wilson was home, some of the detectives would drop in for supper or a cup of tea if near by. It was an interesting gathering—the university graduate and deeply religious man enjoying a meal or a cup of tea with the blokey detectives who spoke in broad Australian accents about 'footy' and horseracing. But Wilson welcomed them and enjoyed their company and was interested in their various investigations and their lives and families.

He had a great respect for, and trust in, most of the detectives he worked with. There were cases that he prosecuted where the defence was successful in challenging the voluntary nature of witness statements and confessions. Despite such examples, he trusted that the facts and evidence constituting the CIB brief were true and had been gathered in accordance with the law.

Later in life, when talking of his relationship with the police, he said that, apart from one detective he refused to name, he believed that the detectives he dealt with were men of high integrity who would conform to the rules and conduct regulations of their organisation; just as he did with the rules of the Crown Law Department. Thus he did not turn his mind to the possibility that some police may not have been upholding the standards of their office. But in more recent times, he acknowledged that given the numerous examples of improper police behaviour, such as police verballing of witnesses, which have been publicised since his tenure as prosecutor, there was a chance that this may also have occurred while he was a prosecutor. But he was not aware of any such inappropriate behaviour when he was prosecuting.

Leitch remarks that the police enjoyed dealing with Wilson:

> He was a talented prosecutor so you knew he would do a good job with the brief you gave him. Also, unlike some of the other prosecutors, he rarely questioned the brief or whether to prosecute. He just got on with his job of using the brief to prepare his arguments for the trial.

It may be argued that Wilson was naïve in his near-absolute belief in the integrity of police evidence. It may also be argued that he was too forceful as a prosecutor. But what is widely acknowledged is that Wilson changed prosecuting in Western Australia. As Kakulas says: 'Wilson was a brilliant prosecutor. He brought a new degree of professionalism and energy to prosecuting. Defence lawyers were not used to coming up against such aggressive and intelligent prosecutors.'

Some did not like it, and thought Wilson should have been working for the defence. Kakulas thought it could be dangerous having someone as good as Wilson prosecuting, because innocent people may wrongly be found guilty:

> It was better to have a guilty person acquitted than have an innocent person convicted. It was not acceptable to discover the truth years after an innocent person had already been in prison for a crime in which they should not have been found guilty.

Likewise, Leitch believed that Wilson's prosecuting abilities were such that he 'achieved' guilty convictions that less talented advocates would not have done. Leitch adds that Wilson's professionalism and energy also rubbed off on some other prosecutors and improved their performances, men such as Alan Dodd and Michael Murray.

Wilson's belief in the integrity of the prosecution process and the police force was reinforced by a paper he presented many years after his prosecuting days. On 23 April 1983, while on the High Court, Wilson delivered a paper titled 'Truth and Justice' at the national symposium on 'Lying', organised by the Australian Academy of Forensic Sciences and the World Psychiatric

Association at the University of New South Wales. In the paper, he said that even though the offender may be clever, 'there is comfort in the fact that, however clever an offender may be, the law enforcement officers have the advantage that they are working on the side of truth.'[22]

Wilson the prosecutor was on the same side; he had right on his side. The statement reaffirmed Wilson's strong belief in the integrity of the police and the criminal investigation process, which arguably could be viewed as naïve in light of a number of recent successful petitions in overturning criminal convictions in Western Australia.[23] Some of these successful petitions, dealing with criminal trials that occurred in the early 1960s, placed intense scrutiny on the propriety of the police and Wilson's reputation and modus operandi as a prosecutor.

5

The Prosecutor's Trilogy

The town is in a frenzy down there. This is what it means to be a city, they say, locking their doors and stifling behind their windows. On the streets at night no one moves. No one goes out. There's a murderer out there and no one knows what he wants, where he is, who he is, and why he kills. This is Perth, Western Australia, whose ambitions know no limit and the streets are empty.[1]

Seeing the 'dirty old petrol tanks' on Fremantle's foreshore on their return to Perth from the United States in August 1957 gave Wilson and Leila a comforting feeling. They were back home, a place they loved and where they felt safe to live. Unlike in Philadelphia, ignition keys were left in cars parked overnight in the driveway. People left their house doors unlocked and windows open at night and slept on the front or back porch.

Within a few years this would all change: Perth would lose its innocence, to be replaced by fear, a fear of someone unknown who could strike terror into the hearts of people in the suburbs. Soon, apprehension was to overwhelm the sense of comfort and safety Leila felt when she returned to Perth. And she was not alone.

As Perth entered the 1960s Wilson was a man in the prime of his life, and at the peak of his powers. Over the next five years he would become a central figure in three sensational murder trials. The murders, the trials and their seemingly endless repercussions would change Perth forever. And they would come to both define Wilson's career as a prosecutor, and raise questions that he was still being asked to address four decades later.

On 29 January 1959, Pnena Berkman was startled awake by a burglar in her house. The next day her naked body was found lying in a pool of blood. She had been repeatedly stabbed with a diver's knife.

By the end of the year, with the police no closer to solving the Berkman killing, another young woman was murdered. She was also sleeping naked, in her apartment in Brookwood Flats on Stirling Highway in Cottesloe. The date was 19 December 1959. The woman was twenty-two-year-old Jillian Brewer, heiress to the MacRobertson chocolate fortune.

> The killer had begun with a hatchet. He hacked into her face, breasts, thighs, stomach and pelvis. He severed her windpipe and fractured her skull and pubic bone. He struck so hard he split the hatchet's wooden handle. Then he snatched up a pair of scissors and stabbed her in the breasts, abdomen, liver and buttocks.[2]

The Berkman and Brewer murders bore similarities that were noticed by the mortuary staff where the bodies were held for post-mortem examination.

The Berkman case remained a mystery, but a breakthrough on the Brewer murder came in April 1961. Darryl Beamish was a nineteen-year-old deaf mute, who had been charged with aggravated assault on four young girls, each of whom was four or five years of age. Over a period of five months, Beamish had taken each child to a secluded spot in Kings Park, partly undressed them, and masturbated while handling the girl's vagina. Beamish pleaded guilty to all charges, and was sentenced to seven months' imprisonment.

Beamish, who became a deaf mute as a result of contracting cerebral meningitis as a baby, was well known to the police. Previously, he had been charged with vandalism, and with stealing from a car, shops, offices and homes in the Perth area. Beamish was only slightly below 'normal' intelligence. He was capable of holding a driver's licence and a job as a metal worker. Although he learnt finger spelling, sign language and writing, his vocabulary was limited (approximately that of a six-year-old), and he had major communication problems. All of these attributes marginalised Beamish in the Perth community.

In *Offcuts from a Legal Literary Life*, Nicholas Hasluck (a Western Australian Supreme Court justice since 2000) reminisced:

> It is January 1953 or thereabouts and I am swimming at Claremont baths, a boy of eleven. On the afternoon in question two policemen come to the baths and within minutes of their arrival, everyone knows they are present but not exactly what they want. They sit down in a far corner of the baths and seem to be interviewing a boy about my age.
>
> I know that boy sitting between them in his wet bathers, shivering. He is skinny and has a hawk-like face. He is the leader of a gang, and at the Windsor Picture Theatre on Saturday afternoons when the lights go down, he and his mates sometimes clamber over several rows of seats to reach the girls. He acts strangely and he often rushes at the girls without any preliminaries, and the girls don't like it and they complain. Something like that has probably happened at Claremont baths on that afternoon I am speaking of. But the policemen won't get anything out of the boy. He is deaf and dumb. His name is Darryl Beamish.[3]

Shortly after being remanded in custody for the Kings Park sexual assault charges, Beamish was questioned by Detective Sergeant Owen Leitch in relation to the Brewer murder. The interrogations were spread over two days and various locations—Brewer's flat, in a police car, and CIB headquarters. Also in attendance were Detective Jack Deering and Mrs Florence Myatt, a public relations officer and interpreter for the Western Australian Adult Deaf and Dumb Society, who interpreted for Beamish.

On the first day, 7 April, after first denying he knew anything about the Brewer murder, Beamish confessed. He repeated his confession the next day in written responses to questions put to him in writing by Leitch.

Also, on 8 April, while in the Perth Police Station exercise yard, Beamish was allegedly observed by another prisoner writing on the bitumen with a piece of plaster. He wrote four separate lines: 'Cottesloe'; 'where drunk'; 'I killed lady'; and '7 months'.

On 10 April, Leitch queried Beamish, via written questions, about these lines. As to whether he wrote the lines, Beamish nodded with his head and wrote 'yes'. But he also wrote: 'not me killed lady Cottesloe.' When questioned by Leitch on the inconsistency of this answer with his lines on the police station courtyard bitumen, Beamish wrote, 'father said, say nothing.'[4]

Two months later, on 12 June 1961, Leitch attended Fremantle Prison to interview Beamish again, with Detective Sergeant Balcombe, Reverend Christopher Chetwynd, Myatt and Dr Thompson, a former Inspector-General of the Mental Health Services as well as the visiting psychiatrist to the Fremantle Prison. Even though Myatt was present, Chetwynd acted as interpreter.

At that interview, Beamish was taken through his answers given at the 8 April interview, the written statement of confession. Beamish nodded his acceptance to each paragraph of that written statement. At Beamish's trial Chetwynd, during his examination in chief, confirmed that this was correct, but he did indicate that there were some difficulties in interpreting for Beamish. Chetwynd also stated that Beamish answered the questions 'quite readily and without displaying...any great emotion—until...the end of the interview [when] he put his head down in his hands and appeared to have a little weep to himself'.[5]

On 16 June 1961, Leitch returned to Fremantle Prison to charge Beamish with Jillian Brewer's wilful murder.

Beamish's trial for the wilful murder commenced in the Western Australian Supreme Court on 7 August 1961, before a jury and Chief Justice Sir Albert Wolff, who was appointed a Supreme Court judge in 1938. Wolff, like Wilson, was born in Geraldton. Before his elevation to the Bench he had been a Crown prosecutor with a reputation as 'thorough and relentless',[6] and Crown solicitor and parliamentary draftsman. There was a brief period in which both Wilson and Wolff would have been at the Crown Law Department together, but Wilson never recalled his presence there.

The prosecution of Beamish was led by the chief Crown prosecutor, Wilson. The defence was led by a relatively junior counsel, Athol Gibson.

During the six days of the trial the jury heard the evidence against Beamish, consisting solely of his four statements and how closely they matched the facts known to the police. Beamish's 'confessions' or 'statements' to the police were central to the prosecuting case. There was no other evidence linking him to the crime scene, although in February 1961 Beamish had gone to the Brookwood Flats to see a Susanne Delaney even though he knew she no longer lived there. Wilson believed that it was Beamish's confessions that were so telling. From Wilson's perspective they read like a confession from someone with Beamish's very limited vocabulary, and much of it was in Beamish's handwriting.

Beamish gave evidence at the trial through a sign language interpreter. When examined in chief by his defence counsel, Beamish denied the confessions. He said that, in relation to the 7 April 1961 interview, Leitch shook him and had his fist in Beamish's face. Also, he gave evidence that Myatt suggested the answers he should give in relation to Leitch's written questions. At trial, Myatt denied this was the case, although she said that, because of Beamish's limited English vocabulary, she modified or amended the questions that Leitch had asked her to convey to Beamish. She also denied that Leitch had thrust his clenched fist towards Beamish's face.

Beamish admitted that he had written the police station courtyard lines, but said they were written in response to questions asked him by a boy in prison, and that he wrote 'I kill lady, not me', rather than the more damaging 'I kill lady'. In relation to the words 'Cottesloe, drunk', he said that he wrote 'Cottesloe' and the boy wrote 'drunk'. Beamish said he wrote '7 months' in response to being asked what sentence of imprisonment he had received. In fact, he had received seven months for the assaults on girls in Kings Park.

Beamish held firm under Wilson's cross-examination. The renowned prosecutor was unable to trip him up on the matter of the confessions, with his answers remaining consistent with what he had said to his own counsel in his evidence in chief.

Beamish's defence at trial was that his statements to the police were untrue; the answers were suggested to him; and that they were made in an atmosphere in which Beamish felt threatened by Leitch. The Crown's position was that the statements were true, given freely and voluntarily. But Wilson did acknowledge at trial that the police questioning was relentless, and he argued that this was necessary with a person like Beamish. That is, because of Beamish's disability, it was necessary for the police to 'keep at' Beamish to obtain answers to their questions. It is interesting to note that in later life Wilson became a strong and passionate advocate for people with disabilities.

Wilson was singly focused on the prosecution. But the issues of the veracity and voluntariness of Beamish's confessions were relevant to the prosecution, because prosecutors, like defence lawyers, had an obligation to assist the court in the administration of justice. Untrue or involuntarily confessions should not be admissible if the objective is a fair criminal trial.

To counter the defence claim that Leitch had been untruthful in his trial evidence, Wilson decided to attack the character of Beamish. Surprisingly, Beamish's counsel, Athol Gibson, did not object to Wilson cross-examining Beamish about his prior offences, including aggravated assaults on young girls, and also Beamish's alleged behaviour as a child in relation to property damage and cruelty to animals:

WILSON:	Darryl, do you like hurting people?
BEAMISH:	No.
WILSON:	Or animals?
BEAMISH:	No.
WILSON:	When you were young, did you use to play a game with the neighbours' fowls?
BEAMISH:	Yes.
WILSON:	What was the game?
BEAMISH:	Open and feed them with wheat.
WILSON:	Did you used to chase the fowls, catch them, break their legs, and then wring their necks?
BEAMISH:	No.[7]

Wilson returned to this line of questioning when he cross-examined Beamish's father:

WILSON:	Do you remember some incidents concerning a neighbour or fowls, or fowls of somebody who lived near by?
MR BEAMISH:	Only when he was a baby—practically a baby—aged about five years of age; do you wish me to tell?
WILSON:	Please tell the incidents that my learned friend referred to.
MR BEAMISH:	Well, he went to a house and opened the fowl-house door and allowed a dog that had followed him in to the fowl-house, whereupon the dog had a lot of fun with the fowls. Fowls flew over the fence and went everywhere.
WILSON:	Mm?
MR BEAMISH:	And the other occasion was—he went down the road in a—about—down at the corner of Loch Street—it was about 200 or 300 yards away from my home, and he was playing with a hose in the front garden and he squirted water into the lounge. Although there was no direct complaint made to me I found out about it; I went down and saw the lady concerned, and she told me not to worry about it, that he had done no damage and everything was quite OK—just a babyish, practical thing.
WILSON:	How old was he when that happened?
MR BEAMISH:	About six years of age—five—about five. I should say.[8]

These passages were quoted by Professor Peter Brett, Professor of Jurisprudence at Melbourne University Law School, in his 1966 pamphlet that argued that the *Beamish* case was a miscarriage of justice. He criticised Chief Justice Wolff for allowing this—which Brett characterised as 'an utterly tasteless piece of cross-examination'—to pass without critical judicial comment.[9]

Pursuant to evidence law, because Beamish alleged he had been intimidated by the police, he opened himself up to cross-examination by Wilson in relation to his character. Past adverse or criminal activity cannot be used to argue a propensity to commit the crime for which the defendant is being tried, but it is admissible in questioning the truthfulness of the defendant's evidence given on oath. That is, as a matter of law, prosecutors can use the witness's past activity to attack his or her credibility as a truthful witness.

As the Beamish statements were central to the prosecution case, it was vital for the Crown to have the jury believe they were voluntarily and freely given by Beamish. Wilson himself always thought the statements were voluntarily and freely given by Beamish. But did this acceptance conflict with Wilson's 1961 trial statement that Beamish's confessions required the police to 'keep at' Beamish? And a further question remains: was it 'utterly tasteless' for Wilson to cross-examine Beamish and his father in relation to a tendency to injure animals? It is unclear what evidence there was of such behaviour by Beamish. Surely it could have prejudiced a jury that heard the chicken coop incident.

A modern answer to this question emerged forty-four years later, in 2005, in Beamish's eventual and successful appeal. The Western Australian Court of Criminal Appeal (CCA), which is part of the Supreme Court, stated that this aspect of Wilson's cross-examination of Beamish was 'extraordinary, and highly prejudicial', not only in relation to the allegations of cruelty to animals but also in relation to theft, property damage and sexual assaults against young girls. The court also noted that Wilson's attack on Beamish's character continued in his final address to the jury. The court stated:

> The justification which was offered for this extraordinary, and highly prejudicial, cross-examination was that Beamish had told the Court that Leitch had not been truthful in his evidence. This attack on Leitch's character was said to justify, under the then provisions of the [WA Criminal] *Code*, a similar (but very much more damaging) attack on Beamish's character. We should add that the attack on Beamish's character continued during the course of the

> prosecutor's address to the jury. The jury, being aware, as a result of the cross-examination, of the aggravated sexual assaults which had been committed by Beamish on the little girls, were told by the prosecutor that Beamish was 'sexually perverted' and that 'the killer...[of Brewer] must surely have been sexually perverted'. He went on to urge upon the jury a form of propensity reasoning, which would be most unlikely to be permitted in more modern times...[10]

The court quoted the following portion of Wilson's summing up to the jury:

> I say the killing itself indicates it's the work of a sexual pervert; it's a sadistic killing, such as you would—could only square up with the kind of person who is sexually perverted, and you might also say, the kind of person who is overborne with a sense of inadequacy—overwhelmed with the sense of his own disabilities. The feeling that he's got sexual urges with no knowledge of how to satisfy them.[11]

Perhaps today's standards would not permit Wilson's summing up. Even by 1961 conventions, it was playing hard. Remember, the death penalty was in the Western Australian *Criminal Code* 1913. Surely, a prosecutor would want to ensure that, if a person was going to hang if convicted, the jury was not influenced by prior prejudicial, and irrelevant, behaviour of the accused. In 1961 there was a greater likelihood of the death penalty being imposed for murder: 'the State Government elected in 1959 showed a greater readiness to let the law take its course with murderers sentenced to death.'[12]

At the end of the trial Beamish was found guilty by the jury of the 1959 murder of Jillian Brewer. Chief Justice Wolff had no option but to sentence Beamish to death, despite the jury making a strong recommendation to mercy. Because of the state government's policy towards people with disabilities, Beamish's death sentence was commuted by the governor to life imprisonment with hard labour.

Shortly after the trial, Beamish appealed against his conviction. The appeal commenced before the CCA on 19 September 1961.[13] It concerned whether the chief justice should have used his discretion to exclude Beamish's statements to the police made on 7 and 8 April 1961 because they were not shown to be voluntary.

Francis 'Red' Burt QC acted as senior counsel for the defence, and Wilson represented the Crown. Burt argued that the confessions were obtained by the police when Beamish was already in custody over the Kings Park incidents, and by use of threat or promise so as to interfere with Beamish's freedom of choice. Burt also argued that Chief Justice Wolff had misdirected the jury about the burden and standard of proof, and he criticised the judge's summing up to the jury. Both arguments failed, and the appeal was dismissed. The matter was over, it seemed.

On 1 November 1961, Wilson was appointed Crown counsel. This was a new position, especially created for Wilson within the Crown Law Department. It carried a wage of £3718 per annum. His appointment did not end his criminal work. Wilson was to represent the Crown in all major civil and criminal matters and appeal hearings. For Wilson, who loved advocacy more than anything else, this was a job 'made in heaven'.

The early 1960s were exciting times for Wilson. His reputation was rising as a Crown prosecutor in criminal cases and a Crown advocate in a variety of civil cases. These were exciting times for the state, too. Perth hosted the Empire Games in 1962, which put Perth on the map for a couple of weeks and made the people of Perth feel proud of their city.

Then came the 'extraordinary summer' of 1962–63. To be more precise, it was the night of Australia Day, 26 January 1963. It was to be a night of terror in the suburbs of Perth. Five people were shot that one night. Two of the five—John Sturkey and George Walmsley—died; and another—Brian Weir—was brain damaged and died three years later.

The utter surprise was captured in Tim Winton's famous novel *Cloudstreet*:

> It's right in our bloody backyard, said the Sarge, Cottesloe, he shoots and wounds two in a car. Then he goes to a flat, puts a hole in a bloke's forehead. An hour later he shoots a bloke on his doorstep in Nedlands when he answers the door. Then he kills a kid sleeping on a back verandah in the next street. The CIB are shitting themselves...[14]

For days following, the people of Perth clutched at straws.

> In their awe and fear of the mysterious killer, people could speak of little else. The mystified police appeared helpless and confused. Indignant

> letters-to-the-editor writers demanded they ask the FBI and Scotland Yard to step in. Locksmiths and gun shops did a thriving trade. Dogs' homes sold out of watchdogs...[15]

The Wilsons had the CIB as their watchdogs. Squad cars would frequently call around to check in on them. Two of the murders had taken place in their neighbourhood. Wilson had no fear for his personal safety, but was happy to have the police visit to ensure that Leila and the children were safe. This was particularly so when he was away from home.

On the night of 9 February 1963, two weeks after the awful shooting and murder spree in Cottesloe and Nedlands, Rosemary Anderson, a seventeen-year-old girl, was deliberately run down on Stubbs Terrace in Shenton Park. Later that night, at Royal Perth Hospital she died.

Her boyfriend, nineteen-year-old John Button, was arrested the same night. In a statement to the police he said that after an argument over a missing piece of fish Anderson had left his parents' Subiaco home to walk to Mount Claremont, 5 kilometres away. Later he told the police that the argument ensued after he had touched her breast during a game of strip poker played by Button, his younger brother Jimmy and Anderson while his parents were out.

When Anderson left the house, Button followed in his Simca, repeatedly asking her to get in the car. She refused. He stopped his car as Anderson approached the railway subway on Nicholson Road. After a few minutes Button started up his vehicle, drove under the subway and turned left into Stubbs Terrace. Then the story gets messy.

Button gave two statements to police that night—one before he had been told she'd died of injuries and one after. In the first, he said he drove up and saw Anderson lying on the side of the road. In his second statement, he said that when he saw her walking on Stubbs Terrace he decided to scare her by driving his car as close as possible to her, but instead he hit Anderson with the left-hand side of the front of his Simca.

The first statement was made by Button at 2.15 a.m. on 10 February 1963. The second statement was made around 3.40 a.m. that morning.

In both statements Button said he picked up Anderson and laid her in his car. This was witnessed by others who drove past the scene. One witness followed Button as he drove Rosemary to Dr Joseph Quinlivan's surgery nearby. By then it was about 11.00 p.m. Button was wearing just trousers.

This was because he had removed his shirt during the strip poker game at his parents' home. After examining Anderson, Dr Quinlivan telephoned for an ambulance and then telephoned the police.

On 2 April 1963, Button was charged with the wilful murder of Anderson. The trial commenced in the Western Australian Supreme Court on 29 April 1963 before Justice Oscar Negus and a jury. Again Wilson appeared for the Crown, with Alan Dodd. Ken Hatfield QC and Bart Kakulas represented Button. Hatfield was the defence lawyer whom Wilson had appeared against in 1953 in his first criminal trial before a jury.

So, the Button trial involved a confrontation between two of the finest exponents of criminal advocacy in Western Australia. Wilson had the utmost respect for Hatfield, considering him a first-rate lawyer and advocate. At his death in January 1969, Hatfield was described by the *Daily News* as the most well-known lawyer in Perth.[16] The *West Australian* described Hatfield as:

> A gifted, persuasive pleader who won the esteem of judges and the hearts of juries; he was [a] daunting cross-examiner; he was a champion of seemingly lost causes; he was a one-man band.[17]

Wilson did not fear Hatfield. He feared none of the lawyers who stood at the defence side of the bar.

At the commencement of the trial, Hatfield sought to have Button's second statement to the police ruled inadmissible on the grounds that it occurred after persistent questioning of Button by the detectives, and that it was not a voluntary statement. Justice Negus, who had been appointed to the Supreme Court bench only in 1962 from private practice,[18] ruled that Wilson could not refer to the second statement in his opening address to the jury but, of course, this did not necessarily prevent Wilson from subsequently referring to it during the trial.

Whether the second statement could subsequently be put to the jury was the subject of lengthy *voir dire* (where counsel argue before a judge alone as to whether some issue or evidence can be put to the jury) before Justice Negus in the absence of the jury. During the *voir dire*, Wilson cross-examined Button.

The cross-examination was set against the context of Button denying the truthfulness of the second statement. Button said that after he was told that Anderson was dead he didn't want to answer any more questions, but he knew that the police would not believe him until he admitted that it was his car that hit her. Therefore, he felt 'forced' to give the second statement. In cross-examination, Wilson pressed Button on the truthfulness of the second statement. This led to Hatfield protesting over Wilson's style of cross-examination:

HATFIELD:	May it please Your Honour, I think the witness should be questioned without being shouted at. I don't think there's any point for him to be shouted at and be oppressed in the witness box and I ask, your Honour, that you protect the witness from this sort of conduct.
NEGUS J:	I'm quite satisfied with the conduct so far, Mr Hatfield. I propose to allow the cross-examination to continue. I'm listening to it.
HATFIELD:	Your Honour, all I'm saying is that the method in which it's put to him—he can be asked a question without being shouted at.
WILSON:	One moment we talk too softly and the next we talk too loudly. Will you answer the question?
BUTTON:	Could you give me the question again, sir?
WILSON:	You have told us that you have told this lie about getting fresh with Rosemary during the evening and the fact that she got wild about it because you thought it was the only thing that would satisfy the police?
BUTTON:	That was the suggestion that Detective Deering gave me and was the only reason that they'd believe for an argument which did develop that night.
WILSON:	And you thought all this out when Wylie wanted to know what happened after the game of strip poker finished?
BUTTON:	No, it had already been given to me by Detective Deering.
WILSON:	When? A couple of hours before?
BUTTON:	No—well, before but I couldn't say how long before.
WILSON:	Just tell us how long before?
BUTTON:	I couldn't really say, sir.
HATFIELD:	He can't really say again.
WILSON:	Will you stop interrupting?
HATFIELD:	No, not until…
NEGUS J:	Don't let there be any argument at the bench, please.

HATFIELD: May it please Your Honour. I think if a witness says, 'I can't remember, I can't tell', he can't be pressed to make something which he knows to be untrue. The witness says, 'I can't really tell you how long it was.'

NEGUS J: You are saying that counsel who is cross-examining is not allowed to press the witness.

HATFIELD: Once the witness says, 'I can't say', he couldn't be allowed to press him to make up some story to satisfy this particular counsel.

NEGUS J: No, I think he's entitled to question his statement that he can't remember, Mr Hatfield, and I again rule...[19]

Justice Negus had no trouble with Wilson's line and style of questioning. Doubtless, Wilson was pursuing a vigorous cross-examination, and it is not difficult to see why he would want to test Button's denial of the truthfulness of the second statement. After all, it was the prosecutor's trump card—the accused had confessed to running Anderson over. If the truthfulness of that statement were destroyed, the prosecutor's case would be destroyed.

Towards the end of Wilson's cross-examination, he got the answer he wanted. Button admitted that the second statement was given of his own free will but under the pressure of the circumstances that night; that he had been questioned continually and that he had been emotionally upset over the death of Anderson. Justice Negus ruled that the second statement was admissible and thus could be put before the jury.

Wilson's cross-examination of Button's father, Charles, given in the *voir dire* proceedings, also raised the ire of Hatfield. As a youngster, John Button had been taken to the Havelock Children's Clinic in West Perth. Wilson put to Charles that the reason for this was that there had been a complaint that John was lying a lot. Even after Charles denied that this was the reason, Wilson persisted in asking him that question. Each time Charles denied that there were concerns that John was lying.[20]

This line of questioning by Wilson led Hatfield to demand that Wilson produce the material on which he had based his cross-examination of Charles Button. Wilson responded by saying that Hatfield's request had no basis in propriety because he had put the questions to the witness, who denied the matter put, and that was the end of the issue. Hatfield did not agree. He considered that the airing of these allegations may have some influence on the judge, and it may later go before the jury. Hatfield then stated that he would not believe that Wilson would dare cross-examine without a factual basis for the cross-examination. To do so 'would be most improper and it would be reprehensible in the highest degree.'[21]

Justice Negus did not see the need to take this issue further. But an important question remains. If Wilson had based his questions of lying by Button on some medical or other evidence, didn't Hatfield, as Button's counsel, have the right to see it? Alternatively, if there were no evidence, wasn't it inappropriate to put a question to Charles that had no any evidentiary foundation?

Wilson's cross-examination of Button in the presence of the jury was as robust and detailed as had occurred in the *voir dire*. Wilson's final address to the jury displayed all his skills in bringing together the Crown's case. He pointed out that the police stood up to the rigorous cross-examination by Hatfield, which attested to their truth and propriety and, therefore, countered Button's claim that his second statement (the guilty statement) was tarnished by improper police questioning.

The fact that Button had confessed that his car had hit Anderson was also significant to the Crown's case. This, together with the damage to the front left-hand side of Button's Simca, and the blood smears near the Simca's front-left headlight and mudguard, made the Crown's case very strong. Button didn't help his cause by giving vague answers to Wilson's questions. This probably raised the jury's suspicion, as did Button's initial story that the argument between him and Anderson occurred over a piece of fish.

Wilson also stressed to the jury the issue of coincidence:

> What a tremendous coincidence that she [Anderson] should be struck... when the accused was sitting in his car just 300 to 400 yards away. What a tremendous coincidence...what a coincidence that they [Anderson and Button] should have had an argument. What a coincidence he doesn't seek help from cars that stop in the vicinity, that he doesn't volunteer anything to Dr Quinlivan about how it happens; that his car should have blood spots; that there should be dents on the bonnet consistent with the girl's body having at some stage come up on the bonnet.[22]

In response to the defence's claim about the small dents on the car being inconsistent with hitting a girl of ten stone, Wilson submitted to the jury that:

> …it is quite impossible, I suggest to you, to be able to look at a car and look at certain damage on a car and say 'that couldn't have killed a pedestrian'.[23]

The prosecution's case and evidence convinced the jury. On Saturday, 4 May 1963, the foreman of the jury, after first saying, 'Not guilty Your Honour', quickly corrected himself to return a verdict of guilty of manslaughter.[24] Button was guilty of a crime, but not wilful murder as Wilson had submitted. The matter was then adjourned to Monday, 6 May 1963, for sentencing, and to allow Hatfield to call testimony in favour of Button.

Before the court adjourned, Wilson informed Justice Negus that he would see that Hatfield had access to the police report. But on returning to court on the Monday, Hatfield objected that he had not, as yet, received that report. Wilson responded by indicating that he had a copy for Hatfield and that he had 'followed the time-honoured practice of having it available to counsel at counsel's request.'[25] Hatfield took exception to this, and reminded Wilson not only that he had been practising in the court longer than Wilson but also that it was the time-honoured practice that as soon as the jury retired the Crown prosecutor would usually say, 'Here is a copy of the police report.' Hatfield added that he should not have to be 'like a penitent or an incumbent and ask' for the report.[26]

When it came to the sentencing, Justice Negus informed Button that he could give him imprisonment for life with hard labour. But after considering the testimony on Button's behalf, the fact that he had picked Anderson up from the road and the strong emotional strain, Justice Negus sentenced Button to ten years with hard labour.

In both the Button and Beamish trials, the defence raised concerns about the 'confessions'. Both of the accused alleged that the confessions were the result of police pressure, and in the case of Beamish, was actually got by prompting or suggesting answers from the police. But the thought of the police not acting in an appropriate and ethical manner was foreign to Wilson. He had a very good working relationship with the CIB, and there was mutual respect and trust. Professor Geoffrey Bolton has said that Wilson was seen as a man of considerable integrity himself, who like many in the judiciary and the Crown Law Department of the time held, probably more so than today, 'a great faith in the integrity of the Police Force'.

Less than a week after Anderson had been run down and killed, Perth was to experience another murder of a young woman in her home. The victim was twenty-four-year-old social worker with the Native Welfare Department, Constance Lucy Madrill. On the night of 15 February 1963, she was strangled in the bedroom of her West Perth flat, then dragged outside and placed under the rotary clothes hoist, where she was defiled with an empty whisky bottle that was left under her right arm.

Beamish and Button might have been under lock and key, but the Berkman killing of 1959, the rampage of Australia Day 1963 and this new outrage remained unsolved, and the hysteria gripping Perth continued unabated. Unexplained break-ins and burglaries continued in the western suburbs. Then, on 10 August, university student Shirley McLeod was shot dead as she sat on the couch while babysitting at a house in upmarket Dalkeith.

A week after this, an elderly Mount Pleasant couple, William and Leila Keehner, stumbled across a .22 rifle hidden in the bushes near their home. In hope and desperation, the police began a stakeout. For a fortnight they waited, until the night of 31 August 1963.

> When Bill Hawker grabbed him in the dark as he reached for the rifle, Hawker wondered what sort of weirdo he'd caught. This creature was burbling strange nasal sounds, and when he went to handcuff him the hands felt slick and smooth, almost slimy. [He] was wearing the kid gloves, of course, and in the policeman's anxious mood the skin of the gloves felt creepy, other-worldly. But Hawker held on. He handcuffed him to the fence. He had him.[27]

Eric Edgar Cooke was born on 25 February 1931 in Victoria Park, just south of Perth over the Swan River. He was the eldest child of Vivian and Veronica Cooke, loved by his mother and despised by his father. The source of his father's loathing was Eric's deformity, a hare lip and cleft palate. He underwent a number of operations, which reduced some facial signs of deformity and slightly improved his speech, although he still mumbled. His father would yell at his mother: 'If you think I'm going to keep that misfit all my life you've got another think coming! Banging his head on the wall. Talk properly, Uglymouth.'[28]

Vivian Cooke was an alcoholic who failed to provide for his family, instead spending his money on the booze. Consequently, Veronica had to work. She also lived with violence, because Vivian beat her and Eric and two younger sisters. Eric was the principal target for most of the beatings, being hit with a belt and punched in the face.

Eric was intelligent and did well at school, but missed a lot through illness, and teasing by other children made it an unhappy place for him. They made fun of his comical mumble and facial appearance. He was expelled from Subiaco State School when six years old, and was in trouble at the four other state schools he attended. His father forced him to leave school at age fourteen and start work.

It was not long before he started on a life of crime, committing petty theft for money and food, then moving on to more serious home burglaries as he roamed the streets, away from home and his abusive father. In 1949, a week after his eighteenth birthday, he was arrested and held in custody after trying to burgle a house in Nash Street, Perth.

The same year he was sentenced to three years' imprisonment for stealing, breaking and entry, and arson. Based on a report obtained by the Inspector-General of Mental Health, who had examined Cooke in Fremantle Prison, the sentence was reduced. After three months in Fremantle Prison, he was released on probation by the Indeterminate Sentences Board.

The inspector-general opined that Cooke was not certifiably insane. He was a young man of normal intelligence, emotionally underdeveloped, who was finding it difficult to adjust from adolescence to being an adult. The inspector-general said that the maladjustment was the result of many factors, including deformity at birth, his psychological trauma—particularly as a result of his father's hatred and abuse—and physical illnesses. As a result, Cooke was displaying the onset of a psychoneurotic state and delinquent behaviour.

As part of his parole conditions Cooke voluntarily admitted himself soon after his release to a local psychiatric centre, the Heathcote Reception Hospital, for a month's assessment. The superintendent of Claremont Mental Hospital, psychiatrist Frank Prendergast, examined Cooke at Heathcote. He thought that Cooke was an embroiderer of stories and a liar.

Not long after leaving Heathcote, Cooke was employed at the confectionery factory where his mother worked. He also came under the pastoral care of Reverend George Jenkins, who had volunteered to help rehabilitate Cooke. This brought Cooke into the fold of the South Perth Methodist Church. He found the parish members friendly and supportive. He became a Methodist and attended Bible studies. In addition, Cooke joined the Methodist Church in the affluent Nedlands parish.

While working as a truck driver at the Metropolitan Markets in West Perth he met his future wife, Sarah Levin, who had emigrated with her mother and two sisters from Liverpool in 1942. The Catholic Levin married the Methodist Cooke in the Cannington Methodist Church on 14 November 1953. Within seven months their firstborn arrived, a son they named Michael. Another son followed a year later, one of a total of seven children.

Even though Cooke enjoyed being a father, he found it difficult to accept and meet his parental responsibilities. He was violent to his wife. He again roamed the streets at night-time and continued burgling houses, mostly in the affluent western suburbs. He came unstuck after pinching a car, and was convicted and sentenced to two years with hard labour. To mark the centenary of Fremantle Prison, Cooke was granted a sixty days special remission, so that he was released on 6 January 1957.

Cooke had a chronic, longstanding resentment against society: against those more fortunate than him, against those who made fun of him, those who scorned him. He later confessed to thirty burglaries and more than 250 occasions on which he unlawfully entered houses. But his malign attitude meant he was never going to be satisfied with committing house burglaries. He was primed to progress to serious and violent crimes that would irrevocably change Perth.

After being captured at the Mount Pleasant stakeout, Cooke was taken to CIB headquarters. Initially he admitted only to burglaries he had committed that night. By the next day the police scientific team had concluded that the cartridge case found in Cooke's Holden sedan had come from the gun that had killed Shirley McLeod. Cooke confessed to killing her, and he was charged with wilful murder.

That was only the beginning. By Tuesday, 3 September 1963, he confessed to the Australia Day weekend murders and shootings, and to the murders of Berkman in 1959 and Madrill in February 1963.

There was great public rejoicing and celebration at Cooke's capture, at the removal of this spectre that had hung over the city for years. Of course the police were delighted, and hugely relieved. Yet there were complications.

Cooke kept talking. In addition to these major unsolved crimes, he claimed that between 1958 and 1963 he was responsible for six hit-and-run attacks against young women using stolen motor cars, eight attacks against women asleep in their beds, and to other shootings.

He did not admit to two crimes that clearly fitted his modus operandi—the 1958 murder of Barbara May Williams, and the 1961 hit-and-run of Alice Kathleen Bennett.

On 10 September, he claimed responsibility for two other murders—those of Jillian Brewer and Rosemary Anderson—for which Darryl Beamish and John Button had already been convicted.

In early 1960 Cooke had actually been questioned about Jillian Brewer while being interviewed by police in Fremantle prison after being arrested for loitering.[29] He had denied any involvement or knowledge of the murder.

Exactly how the police responded in the first instance to Cooke claiming the Brewer and Anderson murders is not clear. But after further questioning, Cooke retracted these two admissions.

Cooke was charged with four wilful murders, an attempted murder and an unlawful wounding. Clearly, defending Cooke in a criminal trial would be a very difficult task. The brief was given to Ken Hatfield, who had previously defended Button.

Thirty-three year old Desmond Heenan was appointed Hatfield's junior. Heenan was part of a prominent Perth legal family. He was later to become a founding judge (1970–82) and chairman and chief judge of the Western Australian District Court (1982–95), and a Supreme Court justice (1995–2000).

Heenan made six visits to interview Cooke in Fremantle Prison. Sometimes he was accompanied by Hatfield. Heenan was impressed with Cooke's phenomenal memory. He was able to provide detailed descriptions of the interior of many of the houses he had entered as well as the cars he had stolen. On one of these visits from Heenan, Cooke admitted again to killing Brewer and Anderson.

At the request of the police, in October 1963, Reverend Prestage Sullivan visited Cooke without anyone else present. Sullivan had known Cooke for twelve years, and had officiated at Cooke's Cannington Methodist Church wedding. At this meeting, Cooke again confessed to killing Brewer and Anderson. Cooke told Sullivan that he had retracted the confessions about killing Brewer and Anderson because the murders were of such a horrific nature that he was ashamed of them.

On 5 November 1963, Hatfield wrote to Wilson, who would be prosecuting at Cooke's trial. Hatfield sought confirmation that Cooke had confessed to the killings of Brewer and Anderson and requested copies of every written confession on these matters. Wilson rejected the request, saying that it was contrary to public policy to discuss or disclose details of police investigations of matters that had not yet been the subject of preliminary proceedings for committal for trial and, therefore, remained within the CIB's responsibility.

In desperation, Hatfield wrote to the attorney-general seeking copies of the Cooke confessions. At a conference between Cooke's defence team and the prosecution team it was agreed that Hatfield could have copies of them. But Wilson clearly indicated that they were only to be seen by defence counsel, Cooke, and any medical advisers. Also, they were only to be used in connection with the Cooke trial and were not to be copied.

Western Australia's trial of the century began on Monday 25 November 1963. But the trial of the Nedlands monster was to be forced off the front page by the breaking news of an equally monstrous event occurring in the United States, the dramatic picture and story of Jack Ruby shooting Lee Harvey Oswald.

The second day's report of the trial was moved from the front page, to make way for the emotional photograph of three-year-old John Kennedy Jr saluting his father's casket. It wasn't till the final day of the trial that it received the extensive newspaper coverage it deserved, with a front-page report and photograph of Cooke. In addition, two and half pages inside the newspaper covered the trial.[30]

When it came to court, Cooke was standing trial only for the wilful murder of Sturkey.

As in the Button trial, it was Wilson against Hatfield QC. But now Wilson was also a Queen's counsel, having been appointed on 24 July 1963. He was forty years old, one of the youngest barristers in Australia to be appointed a QC and the first from the Western Australian Crown Law Department. Heenan was junior to Hatfield, and Wilson's junior was Kevin Parker.

The judge was Justice John Virtue, who had been appointed to the Western Australian Supreme Court in 1951. He was a man of emotional warmth, but this was not to be mistaken for softness. In 1964, the year following the Cooke trial, he imposed a sentence of whipping, the last Western Australian judge to do so.[31]

> Only in real life, I thought, could a judge in the State's most notorious murder trial be named Mr Justice Virtue. You couldn't get away with that name in a movie or a novel. It was too much.
>
> But in the real world there was Virtue on the bench. And there was Evil in the dock, the man who had brought fear and chaos to Perth, trying earnestly now to oblige his lawyer, Ken Hatfield QC, by politely stressing how insane he'd been.[32]

At 10.15 a.m. on Monday, 25 November, Wilson rose to address the jury. He was nervous, as he always was at the beginning of a trial. But he was even more nervous at Cooke's trial because of its public interest. His voice cracked as he spoke the first few lines of his opening address, telling the jury what the charge was against Cooke. After the first tentative sentences he was able to calm his nerves, and his voice became firm and clear as he sought to convince the jury of the strength of the prosecution's case.

The Crown listed twenty-one witnesses, but only called fourteen of them. Few of them were cross-examined by the defence. The Crown's case was finished by the end of the trial's first day. This was not surprising, because Cooke had already confessed to Sturkey's murder. The only real issue for Wilson to confront would be the defence plea of insanity.

A critical weakness of the insanity plea was the available psychiatric assessment. The only psychiatrist to thoroughly examine Cooke was Dr Area Samuel Ellis, the state's most senior mental health practitioner. He found Cooke fit to plead to the wilful murder charge. Hatfield had requested that Dr James, a psychiatrist employed at Heathcote, examine Cooke. But for reasons unknown Wilson withdrew his original approval to the request.

Even so, the defence called Dr James as a witness. He discussed schizophrenia in general. But, of course, he was not in a position to give a psychiatric assessment of Cooke based on an actual examination. Therefore, the probative value of Dr James's testimony was questionable.

To rebut the defence of insanity Wilson made an application, granted by Justice Virtue, to examine Dr Ellis. To the prosecution's satisfaction, Dr Ellis opined that, based on his examination of Cooke, the accused was not suffering from schizophrenia.

Inevitably, Hatfield cross-examined Dr Ellis. At the end of this cross-examination, Hatfield put to the psychiatrist that the constant headaches and blackouts that Cooke suffered could indicate brain damage. Dr Ellis replied: 'It could.'

Wilson re-examined Dr Ellis.

WILSON:	Just taking up that last point—if there was brain damage, is there a type of examination (I think it is called an 'encephalogram') to reveal brain damage?
DR ELLIS:	Yes.
WILSON:	Has the accused been subjected to any encephalograms?
DR ELLIS:	Yes, at least twice.
WILSON:	And did either of those tests reveal any brain damage?
DR ELLIS:	No.[33]

Wilson had gone directly to the issue that may have given the Cooke defence some hope; for Cooke's defence the result was devastating.

In his closing addresses Hatfield—no doubt conscious of the loathing of the jury members for Cooke—reminded them that their role was to consider the evidence presented in court. They had to divorce their minds from any feelings they would have had when they first heard of these crimes. He also asked the jury not to consider him and his junior as 'termites or people who are here to obstruct the course of justice'. He reminded the jury that the defence team were in court because they had been assigned the case, and that it was their duty to fulfil their tasks as defence counsel to 'the end and with the courage and honesty that befits a barrister'.[34]

Hatfield wasted little time getting to the core element of Cooke's defence—the insanity plea:

> We say without apology, without any mock humility, that at the time—in January 1963 when the accused fired the shot that resulted in the death of Sturkey—he was undoubtedly suffering from a mental disease known as 'schizophrenia' which deprived him of the capacity to control his actions, and deprived him of the capacity to know that what he was doing was wrong. That is the defence.[35]

Wilson, like Hatfield, commenced his summing up to the jury by reminding them of their duty, and the duty of the defence counsel and the judge. He reiterated to the jury that Cooke could not be trusted to tell the truth. He had admitted to telling a 'pack of lies' to a doctor in 1949. He informed the jury that Cooke had 'a capacity to spin yarns' and was an attention seeker. He reminded them of Cooke's statements: 'I wanted to hurt somebody' and 'I am just a cold-blooded killer'.

Wilson told the jury that Cooke had 'a longstanding resentment against society' and 'a kind of moral irresponsibility that has nothing to do with any mental disease'. He added that most crimes were committed by people who 'are not 100% normal in their thinking and thought processes and so on', and even though they may be maladjusted and defective in character, that could not excuse them from the responsibility for their crimes. He said that the law did relieve certain people of criminal responsibility if a mental disease deprives them of the capacity to understand or control their actions. But the law did not relieve people of criminal responsibility merely because of a character defect, which he alleged Cooke had:

> the moment you talk to relieving a person who suffers from a character defect, who suffers from some kind of moral irresponsibility—then where do you draw the line? For every person who is charged with a crime, and shown to have committed a crime may be said to have suffered from 'moral irresponsibility'. In order that he should have done what he did.[36]

The jury deliberated for just over an hour to convict Cooke of Sturkey's wilful murder. Justice Virtue told them they had made the correct decision. The judge produced a black cap—the signal for the death penalty—and placed it on his bewigged head. He proceeded to sentence Cooke to death by hanging.

Wilson didn't have any elation about the guilty verdict. He had prosecuted to the best of his ability, the jury had decided on the guilt of the accused, and Justice Virtue had imposed the death penalty. The Perth community, which had lived in fear, was happy with the guilty verdict. No doubt, many were happy with the death penalty too.

6

The Prosecutor's Trilogy Concludes

I have no sense of failure in having prosecuted John Button and Darryl Beamish and Eric Cooke because I was doing my job.

After Cooke's conviction, lawyers for both Beamish and Button visited him on death row with the intention of testing his admissions to their clients' crimes. This was a dramatic situation—here we had lawyers visiting a mass murderer in the same prison in which their clients were incarcerated for crimes that Cooke said he had committed.

On 2 December 1963, in front of Button's solicitor at trial, Bart Kakulas, Cooke wrote out a confession to the murder of Anderson. Ivan Thorpe, the prison's deputy superintendent, was on hand to witness the making of the statement by Cooke. As a result, on 4 December 1963, Button's legal team made an application for an extension of time in which to appeal. The prescribed time in which to appeal or to apply for leave to appeal had expired in May 1963. But they based their application on the ground that there had been a miscarriage of justice; namely that Cooke, by his own confession, was the person responsible for the crime for which Button was now in prison. A hearing date was set for 27 February 1964, but was adjourned until 17 March

1964. Eventually, the appeal was heard on 7 April 1964. Button's appeal meant that the execution of Cooke would be delayed.

Beamish's solicitor, Howard Smith, had also been active. During Smith's visit to see Cooke at Fremantle Prison on 4 December 1963, Cooke confessed that he had killed Brewer. He provided a detailed statement about the night in question.

Smith wrote down the oral confession made to him by Cooke. The statement was once again made in the presence of Ivan Thorpe. Cooke signed each page of the written statement, and swore an affidavit attesting to the truthfulness of his statement to Smith. Reverend Sullivan also swore an affidavit to the effect that Cooke's statement to Smith was consistent with the oral statement Cooke had made to him in October, before his trial. A third affidavit was obtained from a private investigator, Maxwell Blight, who had gathered independent corroboration of some matters referred to by Cooke in his written statement to Smith.

On behalf of Beamish, Smith petitioned Western Australia's governor for mercy, and requested that the matter should be referred by the minister of justice to the Supreme Court. This was duly done pursuant to section 21 of the Western Australian *Criminal Code* 1913 on 4 February 1964. The petition was listed for hearing in the Supreme Court on 27 February 1964, where some preliminary considerations on procedure were discussed and the hearing was adjourned to 17 March 1964. The defence was not seeking the quashing of Beamish's conviction, but that he should have a new trial.

Appearing for Beamish on the morning of 17 March 1964 were Smith and Francis Burt QC, the same silk who had represented Beamish in the first appeal. The Crown was represented by Wilson and Dodd. Again, this was a monumental match of two of the finest advocates. Subsequently, these two men from vastly different backgrounds would appear in a number of cases on opposite sides. Indeed, Chief Justice Sir Garfield Barwick, at a High Court dinner, stated that 'the best legal argument [the High Court] got in Australia was when they had Burt on one side and Ronald Wilson on the other'.[1]

On the Supreme Court bench to hear this second appeal were Chief Justice Wolff, Senior Puisne Judge Jackson and Justice Virtue. This was a situation where the chief justice had presided at Beamish's trial and the other judges had sat in judgement on the first Beamish appeal. Understandably, Professor Peter Brett of Melbourne University was very critical of the constitution of the Supreme Court for this second appeal. As Brett pointed out, the bench was being asked to decide on whether a miscarriage of justice might have occurred in their own court:

> It needs no expert knowledge of psychology to realize that any man, however scrupulous, might well be swayed unconsciously by a desire to believe that he had not been a party to such a tragic error.[2]

Brett also referred to the well-known principle that justice must not only be done but must manifestly be seen to be done. This should, for example, prohibit a judge sitting in judgement on an appeal against his own decision. Also, Justice Virtue had been the judge in Cooke's trial, and would have already formed an opinion of Cooke's propensity for telling the truth.

In a strong critique of Brett's pamphlet, Professor Douglas Payne, of the UWA law school, noted that Brett himself had been less than disinterested. He had failed to reveal in his pamphlet that he had assisted in writing an opinion on the *Beamish* case, and commented on Beamish's notice of appeal to the Privy Council.[3] Payne had concluded that there was no problem with the composition of the Supreme Court for the second appeal. He considered that, because the appeal related to new evidence, it did 'not impeach the propriety of the conviction on the evidence available at the trial'.[4]

But the defence were also seeking to cast doubts on the voluntariness of Beamish's statements to the police and, as Chief Justice Wolff said in his judgement of this second appeal, the strength of the case against Beamish was an important question for consideration,[5] as was the veracity of Cooke's confessions. Thus, as we had justices here who had in previous hearings formed opinions on the case against Beamish and the veracity of Cooke as a witness of truth, Brett's view that Chief Justice Wolff and Justices Jackson and Virtue should not have sat on the second appeal has much merit. But these were not matters that Wilson had control over.

For the first two and half days of the second appeal hearing, Burt and Wilson presented arguments in relation to aspects of law and facts, and then several Crown witnesses who had filed affidavits were called to give evidence and be cross-examined. Burt submitted that the Court should have no regard to any evidence adduced by the Crown at this hearing because, he argued, that would in effect be usurping the function of a hypothetical jury that might be called on to decide on the case in the event of a retrial.

On the third day, Wilson raised the issue in Cooke's statement about a peculiar aspect of the murder. Apparently, after Cooke had hacked her, Brewer spoke. Wilson said that Dr Pearson, who conducted the post-mortem examination, had testified at the trial that the hatchet blows would have caused immediate unconsciousness. Wilson submitted that:

> The thought of [Brewer] being able to make herself intelligible in speech would perhaps—well, in the crown's submission, it's a distinct inconsistency with the proven facts at the Beamish trial and might well rank…as being ornamentation or a certain tendency to exaggerate in the description of something.[6]

On the fourth day of the second appeal, 20 March 1964, Cooke appeared in court to be cross-examined by Wilson. The second appeal relied heavily on Cooke's confessions. It was Cooke's confessions to the Brewer murder that were all-important—it was the prosecution case that these confessions were untrue. Here we had an exquisite moment in Western Australian criminal justice history—a case of the 'ruthless' prosecutor saying no and the convicted serial killer saying yes.

This was the pivotal moment, because Cooke's credibility as a witness was crucial to the outcome of Beamish's second appeal. Wilson was fully aware of this, and his line of attack on Cooke's confessions included testing how much of them came from the media. Wilson also asked Cooke why he had introduced further detail as time went on in the investigation of his confessions. Cooke replied, 'I was playing it shrewd, so that I'd be in—where I am at this moment.' Then Wilson said to Cooke, 'No prospect of staying alive longer by playing it shrewd here today?' Cooke conceded, 'No sir. I know that as soon as my evidence has gone I'll get the axe.'[7]

Then, in response to questioning from Justice Jackson and Chief Justice Wolff, Cooke again admitted to playing it shrewd, and that even on oath he would leave things out. But he added: 'I never told an untruth.'[8]

Cooke had mentioned earlier that he omitted certain details from his statement to Smith, which was attached to the affidavit before the Court, because Cooke wanted to buy some time.

WILSON: You say that your sudden compulsion to murder a woman was a little thing?

COOKE: It wasn't a little thing by any means but.

WILSON: Why did you leave it out of your statement?...

COOKE: At the time I made this statement, I was under the sentence of death, as you well know, sir. I had in my mind that if I left out little things in this statement, I would be used as I am at this moment and that would keep me alive that much longer.

WILSON: I see. If you didn't make a complete statement, investigations would have to be made and they would be protracted and it would keep you alive a little...?

COOKE: Alive that much longer.

WILSON: That much longer?

COOKE: Yes.

WILSON: Would I be wrong if I suggested that's why you confessed to this murder in the first place?

COOKE: No, sir. You would be wrong.

WILSON: I would be wrong?

COOKE: Yes, sir.

WILSON: You're not just saying this to try and keep alive a little bit longer?

COOKE: No, never, because, sir, when I was arrested I told the authorities about this.

WILSON: We may refer to that later, but your explanation then for not including some of the detail, including the statement you have told us this morning—that you made up your mind to murder this girl whilst in the bus. You didn't include that because you thought, 'If I put everything here now, it might be cleaned up too quickly and the other way I might stay alive a little longer'?

COOKE: A little longer, yes.

WILSON: That's a fair statement of your reason?

COOKE: Yes.[9]

During this cross-examination, Wilson returned to Cooke's statement that Brewer made intelligible speech after he had attacked her with the hatchet. After taking Cooke through his statement of the attack with the hatchet, Wilson sought to have Cooke confirm the time that Brewer spoke. He laboured the point when Cooke responded that he was now not sure about the precise time that Brewer spoke, whether before or after being hit in the throat with the hatchet.[10]

Wilson asked Cooke a number of questions about his statements to the police, and to Beamish's and Cooke's lawyers, that sometimes he got so engrossed in reading books that he projected himself as the characters in the books. Wilson queried why Cooke would have made such comments if he was sure he had killed Brewer and Anderson. As part of his response Cooke said that because of his insanity plea he was seeking to build himself a case of being a person of low mental standard, 'and that is one of the reasons I have said it, about, "I read these books", and things like that'.[11]

Wilson's cross-examination of Cooke went from 11.00 a.m. until 3.30 p.m. Cooke proved at times a tenacious and even stubborn witness, able to provide many of the details of the known facts of Brewer's murder. But there were also inconsistencies between the known facts of the murder and Cooke's recollection that he made earlier in statements and in court. This was also true of Beamish.

Cooke's stature as a witness of truth and credibility was severely dented by his admissions that he had deliberately omitted certain facts from his previous statements to police and lawyers to 'buy some time', and that he had made certain statements to improve his insanity plea. There were also the admissions in cross-examination that Cooke had read the reports of the *Beamish* trial, and that he had been following closely the activities of the police investigations. He also agreed that when Detective Sergeant Leitch picked him up in 1960 for loitering he was shown the hatchet used on Brewer. And, that when he had informed his lawyer, Desmond Heenan, about killing Brewer and Anderson, he was 'still a bit hazy about them'.[12]

Cooke admitted that, even though he knew the statement he made to police on 12 September 1963 was not completely true, he signed it because '[the] easiest way out of anything is to sign anything'.[13] Cooke admitted that on occasions he played loose with the truth. He confirmed a number of untruths he had told over the years, including when he was examined by Dr Prendergast at Heathcote in 1949. Cooke didn't like the man, and he told an untruthful story to him 'for the simple reason I wanted to get out of [Heathcote]'.[14] Cooke said that he was prepared to mess people about if it helped him.

Following Wilson's cross-examination, Burt very briefly re-examined Cooke and addressed the bench for just over thirty minutes. Wilson did not feel the need to address the bench at the conclusion of the hearing. The Beamish appeal was adjourned at 4.16 p.m. on 20 March 1964, and the court reserved its decision.

Originally the *Button* appeal was scheduled to follow the *Beamish* hearing immediately. Because of the latter's duration, Button's appeal was rescheduled for 7 April 1964. Again, Wilson represented the Crown and Hatfield represented Button, the appellant. The Supreme Court comprised the same three justices who had just heard the Beamish matter. Although none of them had sat on the original *Button* trial, it was still problematic that they were sitting on his appeal. As Justice Virtue admitted, he had already formed an unfavourable view of Cooke as a witness of truth before Beamish's second appeal. The other two justices would, of course, have formed a view on Cooke too, after the second *Beamish* appeal, less than three weeks earlier.

Cooke was called to the witness box on the second day of the appeal. Again, Wilson engaged in a vigorous cross-examination by taking Cooke through his previous confession and retraction statements. Cooke again admitted that he didn't tell the complete truth in his statements or reveal the total picture, in an attempt to 'play it shrewd' and prolong the time to his execution.[15]

Cooke's practice was to tell fibs and not the whole story to the police and to Button's lawyer, Bart Kakulas.[16] The continual admissions by Cooke in cross-examination that he hadn't been telling the total truth did not impress the bench.

Wilson asked Cooke why he signed a retraction statement if he didn't believe it. Why did he put his name to a statement in which the last paragraph says: 'I give this statement of my own free will and it's true'? Cooke responded, 'Mr Wilson, excuse the smile, but every police statement you make is dictated in that way to you, no matter if they've given you a thousand thumpings under the ear, and it's still the same, "I have made this statement of my own free will".'[17]

Wilson vigorously cross-examined Cooke in relation to inconsistency between his various statements and his admission that he didn't tell the whole truth. In one exchange between Wilson and Cooke over his confession of the Anderson killing, Cooke seemed rattled, as he admitted to lying to the police.[18]

After Wilson had completed his cross-examination, Hatfield very briefly re-examined Cooke. Then the owner of the car that Cooke had stolen on the night of Anderson's killing was questioned by both Hatfield and Wilson. Remarkably, like Button's Simca, this car had also been damaged in a way that might have been consistent with hitting a pedestrian. That brought the day's proceedings to an end. The court reconvened for the next day, 9 April 1964, to hear Hatfield's summing up. Wilson, as with Beamish's second appeal, declined the opportunity to do likewise. The matter was reserved for judgement.

On 22 May 1964, the court delivered the unanimous decisions dismissing both appeals.[19] Chief Justice Wolff wrote the major judgements.

In the *Beamish* judgement, Chief Justice Wolff concluded that the Crown's case was of great probative strength. The criticism that had been levelled at it 'is no different from what one may expect to find in any case where as here the bulk of the evidence carries conviction'.[20] He was not troubled by any inconsistencies between Beamish's various confessions and the known facts of the case. Chief Justice Wolff then turned his attention to Cooke. He described Cooke as a 'monster', and said that having seen and heard him trying to explain away the various discrepancies in his statements 'he emerges not unexpectedly as a low, cunning liar who, when cornered, will say anything to try and escape from a denouement'.[21] He added that Cooke was still attempting to cling to life and develop his compulsive insanity theory.

In reaching his view on the lack of credibility of Cooke's statements, the chief justice made particular mention of Cooke's assertion that Brewer spoke after he had attacked her with the hatchet:

> One of the most incredible statements concerning the killing of Brewer as described by Cooke is the detail which he gives of going out of the flat to dispose of the hatchet—suspending operations during the killing. At this time Brewer had received severe wounds on the scalp which must have rendered her unconscious. After a lapse of time Cooke says he returned and set about stabbing her with the scissors. Describing the girl he says with lying detail: 'Every breath she took made a rattling noise in her throat and she awoke and said "who is it"—in a very slow manner.'
>
> It is clear from his description of when he got the scissors that he must have chopped her through the windpipe with the hatchet before he got the scissors.[22]

Wolff stated that the unanimous view of the court was that Cooke's 'evidence given on affidavit and under cross-examination is perjured.'[23] He concluded that Cooke's account of his claim to have killed Brewer 'is so circumstantially inaccurate and so obviously fabricated' in light of all of his statements, and the evidence in the Beamish trial, 'that no Court could conscientiously disturb the verdict against Beamish and order a new trial'.[24]

As in the Beamish second appeal, in the Button appeal the court held that the Crown's case was very strong, and that Cooke's confession to the killing of Anderson lacked credibility and was fabricated. Wolff said that, although the appellant placed great store in the small amount of damage to Button's car, he would venture that the three justices sitting on the appeal would have seen cases where the damage done to the car that collided with a person was small but the injuries sustained were great. He also said that the damage to Button's car, as seen on the night of 9 February and early morning of 10 February 1963, was 'materially significant in pointing to the conclusion that it was the car that hit the girl'.[25] The chief justice then discussed the confession made by Button and the totality of the evidence against him, opining that 'the evidence for the Crown presented a very strong case against Button'.[26]

Wolff then turned to consider the sworn testimony of Cooke. He said that the court's conclusion in *Beamish (No 2)* (the second appeal) about Cooke also applied in this case; that is, Cooke was a dreadful character who had no regard for moral values, had a tendency to show off and gild the lily, and that his word in and out of court was utterly worthless. He concluded his comments on Cooke by writing:

> It would not be necessary to go beyond the various statements made by Cooke to determine that his whole claim to have killed Anderson is a fabrication. Cooke has been caught in the web of his own lies.[27]

At the end of his judgement, Wolff said that the evidence presented by Button's legal team about other similar offences (hit-and-rundowns of women on five separate occasions) was not compelling. He said these offences 'must be regarded as an open question so far as this Court is concerned', and they could not help Button, against whom the evidence is very strong.[28]

Justice Virtue agreed with the decision of the chief justice, but provided no written reasons. Justice Jackson also agreed, but in his written reason for his decision he limited the Crown's case to the probative value of Button's second written statement, where he confessed that his car hit Anderson. He added that, as with Beamish's second appeal, Button's appeal depended on the court's view of the credibility of Cooke's confession.

Jackson concluded that in light of the known facts, Cooke's confession lacked credibility, and 'is devoid of cogency or plausibility and no reasonable jury could believe it'.[29] He added that, even though the police may have believed Cooke's confession in relation to five other hit-and-run incidents, this did not strengthen Cooke's credibility as a witness, because he was disposed to telling lies when it suited him and to making up fanciful stories. Jackson felt that, in any case, the personal credibility or lack of it was not important, as the story Cooke 'tells is itself beyond belief by reasonable men'.[30]

So at the end of the 1964 appeals, Beamish and Button remained in jail, guilty of the killings of Brewer and Anderson respectively, and Cooke remained on death row.

Both Beamish and Button applied to the High Court for special leave to appeal the court's decisions. The special leave applications were heard in the Perth sitting of the High Court on 11 September 1964. Wilson again appeared for the Crown, as did Burt for Beamish and Hatfield for Button. The *Beamish* hearing was first, followed by Button. The decision was the same in both. The High Court bench of Chief Justice Barwick and Justices Kitto, Menzies and Windeyer dismissed the applications.

On 14 October 1964, a month after the special leave applications to the High Court had failed, the conservative state government announced that it had decided that the Cooke execution would go ahead at 8.00 a.m. on Monday 26 October 1964. Cooke was duly informed.

The Labor opposition were opposed to the death penalty. A few hours after the government's announcement of the date for the Cooke execution, the Labor member for Balcatta, Herb Graham, reintroduced a private member's bill to abolish hanging in Western Australia.[31] It was defeated.

Even after the announcement of the scheduled date for the execution, Cooke still insisted that he had murdered Brewer. Subsequently the Labor opposition asked the premier a parliamentary question in relation to the *Beamish* case. In response, the premier revealed that an officer of the Crown Law Department had sought and received advice from three medical specialists on Cooke's claim that Brewer had spoken a few words before dying, in order to test the veracity of Cooke's statement on this point.

The advice received was that, although speech was highly improbable, it was not impossible. This advice was given to the police but was not put to the court, because the opinions expressed were equivocal and did not persuasively support or refute Cooke's statement.[32] It should be remembered that, in answering questions from Wilson during the cross-examination in the second *Beamish* appeal, Cooke qualified his earlier statements to the police by saying that he was not sure whether Brewer spoke before being struck on the head or after.

In 1966, Professor Peter Brett wrote a stinging critique of the *Beamish* case, in which he said that it was unbelievable that advice sought in relation to testing Cooke's veracity was not put to the court. Brett wrote that it was known to the Crown Law Department but:

> It cannot have been known to the Crown Prosecutor [Wilson], for if it had he would never have made to the court the argument that he did. But the fact remains that he quite unwittingly led the court into an error on a matter which two of its members regarded as of great importance. And the error remained uncorrected when the High Court of Australia dismissed Beamish's application in September, for special leave to appeal—doubtless because the Crown Prosecutor had still not been informed of the advice which had been communicated to the Crown Law Department and the police.[33]

In fact, Wilson was aware of the medical opinion prior to the 1964 appeal hearing in the Supreme Court. He later acknowledged this in correspondence he sent to the attorney-general of Western Australia, in October 1966, in response to the Brett article. Wilson stated that he had no hesitation in putting aside the medical opinion, which stated that speech was possible but highly improbable, because:

> In doing so I believed that I was giving Beamish the benefit of the very slender chance that Cooke's statement that Miss Brewer spoke was medically possible. If the evidence had been tendered, [it would have adversely affected the] credibility of Cooke's 'confession', because the opinion plainly was that given a ruptured windpipe speech was highly improbable.[34]

One would have thought that the proper course for Wilson to have followed was to release this information to the defence, and allow them to decide whether the medical opinion lent any support to Cooke's statement. In a highly critical review of Brett's article, and supportive of the Court's decision in Beamish's second appeal, Douglas Payne (of UWA) even conceded as much.[35]

While on death row, Cooke received regular visits from the honorary Fremantle prison chaplain, the Reverend George Jenkins. But at the time Cooke's execution date was announced, Jenkins was otherwise engaged at a church conference. He was unable to visit Cooke until 23 October 1963, three days before execution day. When Jenkins visited Cooke then, Cooke said that it was just that he be hanged, and that he was concerned that Beamish and Button were still in jail for crimes he had committed. Without any prompting from Jenkins, Cooke took the Bible that Jenkins was holding and said: 'I swear before God I did these two.' The 'two' obviously referred to Brewer and Anderson.

Reverend Jenkins visited Cooke again two days later, and then again the next day, only fifteen minutes before Cooke's execution. On this last visit, Reverend Ralph Thomas accompanied Jenkins to see Cooke. Cooke again took the Bible in his hand and said, 'I swear before Almighty God that I did these two [Anderson and Brewer].'[36] Ten minutes later Cooke was dead. He was the forty-fourth and last person to be hanged at the Fremantle Prison gallows since they were built in 1888.

There is no doubt that many residents of Perth were happy that Cooke's life was coming to an end. But for Wilson there was no rejoicing. Indeed, on the morning of 26 October 1964, Wilson gave little thought to the execution. As far as he was concerned he had prosecuted Cooke according to his legal duty as a Crown prosecutor. It was the judiciary that had decided that Cooke should hang, and it was the state that followed through with the execution. It was not until later in life that Wilson was to become a strong opponent of the death penalty.

When Cooke was executed, Beamish and Button were nearby in the prison yard.

The Beamish legal team decided not to stop at the High Court. They petitioned the Privy Council. Wilson and Burt both travelled to London to appear before the Privy Council. Burt travelled economy class. Wilson was impressed, and joined him in the back half of the plane. So impressed was Wilson by Burt's humility and modesty that it launched Wilson into following a rigid and simple lifestyle. As Wilson put it: 'Living simply so others may simply live.' Part of this was travelling economy class even when his station in life afforded him the luxury of first or business class.

This did not always go down well with his judicial brothers. In fact, when Wilson had been elevated to the High Court, a Federal Court judge wrote to the chief justice of the High Court complaining about Wilson travelling economy class, as it was not fitting of a federal judge. No doubt the judge in question was concerned that Wilson's travelling did not lead to a move to downgrade judges from first class to business to 'cattle class'.

The Privy Council brought no joy for Beamish. On 12 April 1965, Beamish's petition to the Privy Council for special leave to appeal against the decision of the Court of Criminal Appeal (CCA) in *Beamish (No 2)* was dismissed.

In 1969 the *West Australian* published an article that said that the Western Australian Chapter of the International Commission of Jurists would be asking the state government to reconsider the conviction of Beamish.[37] Whether the request to the government was ever made is unclear, but if it was, nothing came of it.

It seemed that the cases of Beamish and Button had run their course, and that whatever opinions might exist in the legal fraternity and the wider community, as far as the law was concerned, they were both guilty men.

On 20 December 1967 Button was released on parole, and in 1968 he was married to Helen Featherstone. Her father was Sergeant Ralph Featherstone, who believed in the innocence of his son-in-law. Beamish was released on parole in June 1976.

A chance meeting in 1992 between Jimmy Button—younger brother of John—and Perth journalist Estelle Blackburn was to prove momentous for John Button. After that meeting, Blackburn commenced her long and detailed investigation that led to the publication in 1998 of her highly significant book, *Broken Lives*.[38] In the book, Blackburn recorded the various murders, shootings, home attacks and hit-and-runs of Cooke. She also discussed the Brewer murder and, in even more detail, Anderson's killing. Blackburn's thesis was that Cooke was guilty of Anderson's death. Although not focusing on the murder of Brewer, Blackburn leaves the reader in no doubt that she believes that Cooke was again the culprit.

Broken Lives was published on 30 October 1998. On the day before, the ABC screened an *Australian Story* documentary on Button. It was the first of two episodes. The second episode, telecast the week after, brought together Button, Sally Cooke and her well-known son, union official Tony, and Rosemary Anderson's parents. Sally Cooke believes that her husband was the murderer, but Rosemary's parents still believed that Button was rightly convicted of the killing of their daughter. It was a memorable and weird piece of television.

The producer of the Button *Australian Story*, Wendy Page, sought out the views of Wilson. In a written response dated 13 September 1998, Wilson wrote to her:

> 1. It is now 35 years since the trial. I have only the most general recall of the trial, or of the subsequent appeals based on Cooke's confession to the crime.
>
> 2. It was my practice as a Crown Prosecutor to receive the brief in the form of the depositions recorded in the course of the preliminary hearing and to marshal that evidence for presentation to the jury in the course of the trial. I would omit evidence contained in the brief that I thought was unnecessary, but the same brief was usually available to the defence and it was open to defence Counsel to ask me to call any witnesses I failed to call or to call such witnesses themselves.
>
> 3. I saw my task as being to present the evidence contained in the brief to the jury in as clear and fair a manner as possible. I had no reason to think that, on the evidence available, John Button did not have a fair trial. He was represented by an experienced Counsel who was probably the best criminal lawyer in Perth. I have no doubt that if any complaint could have been made of the trial, then the verdict would have been appealed to the Court of Criminal Appeal.
>
> 4. There was no appeal from the verdict until fresh evidence came to light in the form of Eric Cooke's confession. Successive appeals to the Supreme Court and the High Court of Australia were unsuccessful.
>
> 5. It has never been my responsibility to make a decision on John Button's guilt or innocence and I have not done so.
>
> 6. If further relevant evidence has now been uncovered, as I understand to be the case, then I would support further examination of the totality of the evidence by an appropriate authority with a view to determining whether the verdict is safe and should stand. If that question is determined in John Button's favour, then obviously the record should be put right.

> 7. John is a Christian. As a fellow-Christian, I accept him readily as a brother in Christ. The question of his guilt or innocence is immaterial to this relationship.[39]

This public airing in 1998 was not the first time Wilson had had cause to look back on the Button case.

Button had turned to God when he was on remand for the wilful murder of Anderson, and from then his faith in God grew. In 1995, he was ordained as a ruling elder of the Westminster Presbyterian Church.

While attending the annual general meeting of the Bible Society of Western Australia in 1989, Button came face to face with his prosecutor, Ronald Wilson, who was the guest speaker at the meeting.[40] At the time of the trial which put him in prison, he disliked Wilson immensely. He perceived Wilson to be very aggressive in his cross-examination of him. He viewed Wilson as a 'nasty little man'. But time had mellowed that view. By the time he meet Wilson at the 1989 Bible Society meeting, he no longer disliked Wilson. He saw Wilson as a 'fellow Christian, a good man'.

At the end of the meeting, Button went up to Wilson and introduced himself before saying, 'First, you were wrong—I didn't do it.' Second, he thanked Wilson for helping him on the course to God. He believed being incarcerated was part of God's plan to draw him closer to God and eventually turn over his life to him. Wilson smiled back, not knowing what to say. Button's view on Wilson had changed over time.

A few days later, Wilson received a letter from Button in which Button once again thanked Wilson for helping him on his spiritual walk with God. He signed off: 'Your brother in Christ.'[41]

Wilson paid a visit to Button just before Christmas 1989. Wilson was a member of Legacy, the organisation that assists returned servicemen's families. As part of his Legacy duties, Wilson would visit their homes. Although Button was not one of them, he included him in his Christmas round of Legacy home visits because he thought it was the decent thing to do—go and visit the man who had written him a thank-you letter. Button welcomed Wilson into his home. They talked about life in general and the word and work of God. The Anderson case and Button's conviction were not discussed.

Wilson met up with Button again in April 1990. The occasion was the graduation of Button's son Gregory from Murdoch University. Wilson, as chancellor of the university, was in attendance. The meeting between the two was ever so brief, but the encounter led to Button writing again to Wilson on 19 April 1990.

Button once again wrote how God had helped him to turn his life around. His felt that his chance meeting with Wilson at the Bible Society meeting and the discussion they had at his home were a sign from God, placing one of the last pieces of the jigsaw in place. It was a signal for him to tell his story to the world, to tell the world how God had turned his life around. But to tell the whole story would have implications for others, including Wilson as a fellow Christian. He concluded the letter by stressing that he was concerned with Wilson's feeling on the matter and sought his advice. Again he signed off: 'Your brother in Christ'.[42]

Wilson telephoned Button a week later. He gave his blessing for Button to tell his story to the world if he felt the need to do so.

In 1991, Button sent Fremantle Arts Centre Press the manuscript of his life story. The reply was not encouraging. His story never appeared as an autobiography, but it was to be told by Blackburn, and it led to a remarkable series of events in the late 1990s.

Meanwhile Brett Christian, the editor of the metropolitan newspaper the *Subiaco Post*, was seeking to tell the story of the conviction of Darryl Beamish. He had provided Blackburn with support and assistance during her investigation and writing of *Broken Lives*. Christian published a number of articles on Beamish in his newspaper. The 10 June 2000 edition of the *Subiaco Post* contained two such articles. One talked about his mother's hope that her son's name would be cleared,[43] and another about how new evidence gathered for a pending appeal in the matter of Button provided new hope for Beamish.[44] The article contained a quotation from Beamish's counsel Sir Francis Burt in the second appeal (1964 appeal to the CCA) and appeals to the High Court and Privy Council: 'The two cases, although entirely different on their facts, should stand or fall together.'

This publicity flushed out Beamish's nemesis, the now retired former Detective Sergeant Owen Leitch, who was police commissioner between 1975 and 1981. Leitch was quoted in the *Sunday Times* on 3 September 2000, saying that Cooke only confessed to the Brewer murder after he was sure of his fate for the murders that he had done. Kerry Welham, the author of the article, wrote:

> Mr Leitch described Cooke as an 'unscrupulous liar' and said personal contact was vital in coming to the correct conclusion in the murder...He said he

> was addressing today's police to enlighten those subjected to the 'hype' over the appeal.[45]

Christian responded to the Welham article in the following week's *Sunday Times*, writing in part:

> Mr Leitch is wrong to say there is no new evidence. Estelle Blackburn's book, *Broken Lives*, details a lot of evidence that was available at the time of the original appeals, though not known to Darryl's defence and not presented to his Appeal judges.[46]

The hype that Leitch referred to was generated by the 1998 publication of *Broken Lives* and screening of the *Australian Story* Button episodes. New evidence and old, undisclosed evidence had been amassed by Blackburn and Christian. Blackburn's inquiries had uncovered previously undisclosed evidence from a former police officer in relation to the likelihood of Button's Simca striking a pedestrian. Christian had been interested in the case through Blackburn, and had paid for an American car-crash expert, whose evidence cast doubt on the 1960s forensic work.

In light of Blackburn's revelations, then state attorney-general, the Hon. Peter Foss QC MLC, referred the John Button case for reopening in May 2000.

The reference was lodged pursuant to Section 140 (1) (a) of the *Sentencing Act* 1995 (WA), whereby a petition for the exercise of the Royal Prerogative of Mercy in relation to an offender convicted on indictment or the subsequent sentence may be referred by the attorney-general to the Court of Criminal Appeal. The referral can request a hearing of the whole case as an appeal against the conviction and/or sentence, or it may seek an opinion on any specific matter relevant to determining the petition. In responding to Button's petition, Foss requested that the case be heard as an appeal.

The appeal proper commenced before the CCA on 28 May 2001, after earlier sittings for determination of the admissibility of affidavit evidence in support of the appeal, and of evidence of confessions by a deceased third party [Cooke] to the Anderson killing. Tom Percy QC, well-known and colourful Perth barrister, led the charge for Button, and Shane Stone from the Department of Public Prosecutions (DPP) appeared for the Crown. They appeared before Chief Justice David Malcolm and Justices Henry Wallwork and Neville Owen.

It was a momentous point in Western Australia's criminal justice history. They were being asked to undo and throw out the decisions of many judges.

Chief Justice Malcolm, the outstanding law student, Rhodes Scholar and commercial and equity barrister, was the first chief justice for over 100 years to be appointed directly from the independent bar rather than from the bench of the Supreme Court. Malcolm as a judge was considered a reformist and liberal and a person generous with his time, attending many community events and supporting many community causes.

Malcolm has very fond memories of the man who had prosecuted the case that he was now reviewing. Although never appearing against him in court, Malcolm did witness Wilson the prosecutor, the Crown counsel and the solicitor-general in action. Malcolm feels privileged to have seen Wilson the advocate in action: an outstanding barrister who used his meticulous planning, penetrating analysis and persuasive charm to good effect.

Justice Wallwork, the son of a chief magistrate, became a justice of the Supreme Court on 31 October 1989. He did his articles at the Crown Law Department in 1957–58, at the time Wilson was building his reputation as a prosecutor. He also served on the senate of Murdoch University from 1984 to 1990, a period in which Wilson was the chancellor. He had earned a reputation for compassion towards the less privileged who came before the courts.

The third justice to sit on the Button appeal was Justice Neville Owen. He had built up a formidable private practice reputation in corporations law. He became a justice of the Supreme Court in 1991, and also was involved in the establishment of the law schools at Murdoch University and University of Notre Dame in Fremantle.

The appeal proper opened to the clicking of cameras and frenzied activity of television crews. As the *West Australian* reported it: 'Lights, camera, action.'[47] Chief Justice Malcolm had agreed to media requests to allow cameras in to court for the first time, given the public interest in the case. The reporters, photographers and television camera crew were there to catch Button and his supporters arrive at the Supreme Court and follow them into the courtroom. When the doors opened at the front side of the courtroom to allow the three justices to enter, there was silence. The chief justice's associate called, 'Button versus the Queen.' There was one last flurry of clicking cameras and then the appeal was on.

A crucial witness for Button at the appeal was William Haight, of San Diego in the US, an expert in traffic accident reconstruction. In 1999 he was asked by Christian to review documents and materials from the 1960s hearings, including photographs of Button's car and Cooke's car and the collision scene. Haight was asked to assess the Crown's case in relation to the collision investigation technology at the time and what has since been developed. As part of his investigation, Haight reconstructed the scene and carried out crash tests to simulate the collision that killed Anderson.

Haight concluded that it was highly unlikely that Button's Simca motor vehicle was involved in the running down of Anderson. This finding was crucial to the appellant's case, because the opposite was crucial to the Crown's case at trial. When opening the Crown's case at trial, Wilson told the jury that the indentations on the bonnet of Button's Simca had nothing to do with his accident three or four weeks before the Anderson death, and that the damage:

> was caused when the car driven by the accused [Button] struck Rosemary and she was flung heavily onto the bonnet of the car with her tummy, her abdominal region, thereby causing these serious abdominal injuries that I have described and which, by the way, were not attended with any external injury indicating that it was a very severe blow in this region on a smooth, flat or comparatively flat object with no projections to break the skin or lacerate the body.[48]

But Haight's evidence, which was compiled using the superior technology available now as compared to the early 1960s, was that there was no physical evidence that the Simca driven by Button had at any time struck a pedestrian.

Another crucial witness at the appeal was Trevor Condren. At the time of the Anderson killing he was a first class constable in the Western Australian Police Force, and a fatal accident vehicle examiner attached to the Traffic Branch in Perth. On 12 February 1963, at the request of the CIB, he inspected Button's Simca and prepared a report. When examining the car he was informed by CIB officers present that the car had been involved in an accident with a pedestrian and the driver had been charged and had confessed. He was also told that the Simca had been involved in a minor accident with a Ford Prefect a few weeks earlier. At the appeal, he said that he had commented to the officers present that he did not think the vehicle had struck a pedestrian. But he did not express this at the trial or in his report, because his role was to report on the vehicle in terms of its mechanical condition and damage.

This evidence from both Haight and Condren that the Simca did not strike a pedestrian was significant. So was Haight's conclusion that the front-end damage suggested in the body shop documents for the Holden that Cooke claimed to have used for the crime, and the tests done by Haight, were consistent with a pedestrian being struck. This went to supporting Button's case that his car did not strike Anderson, and that Cooke's confession to the running down of Anderson was true.

There were a number of other witnesses and evidence presented at the appeal for the appellant. The most compelling of these related to Cooke's propensity to run down women walking on the side of the road. Percy for the appellant called several of the hit-and-run victims of crimes to which Cooke had confessed to give evidence. He also presented the evidence of Cooke's confession to the Anderson killing.

On 25 February 2002, the appeal judgement was read out by Chief Justice Malcolm before a packed courtroom of Button supporters and family members and the media. Once again the photographers and film crews were there to catch this piece of courtroom drama. In concluding his judgement, Chief Justice Malcolm said:

> I have concluded that the evidence of Mr Haight supported by the evidence of Mr Condren is sufficient to raise a reasonable doubt whether the appellant's Simca motor vehicle was involved in running down Ms Anderson on 9 February 1963. The evidence of Mr Haight also tends to substantially corroborate the evidence of Mr Cooke, whether the latter was mistaken about the side of the vehicle which hit Ms Anderson or whether he swerved off the road in the manner he described and constituted the alternative scenario described by Mr Haight. The evidence of Cooke's propensity to seek out women walking on the side of the road and run them down is compelling. In my opinion, it overwhelms whatever doubts may have been held concerning its credibility by the remarkable coincidence between his recollection of the events described in his

> confessions and the recollection of the victims. The fact that Mr Cooke maintained his guilt in relation to the death of Ms Anderson in the 'gallows' confession on 26 October 1964 shortly before he was hanged takes on some additional significance against the background of the other matters to which I have referred.[49]

The chief justice allowed the appeal, and quashed Button's conviction for manslaughter. His brothers, Justices Wallwork and Owen, agreed that if all the evidence that had been presented to them had been available for the jury's consideration, there was a significant possibility that a jury acting reasonably would have acquitted Button. They considered the verdict unsafe and unsatisfactory on the ground that there had been a miscarriage of justice. There was also to be no retrial.

Of course Button, his legal team, family and supporters were delighted. Outside the courtroom Button said: 'Unbelievable, to think that after 40 years we finally got there today…I don't suppose I could believe it, that it actually happened. It was such a wonderful feeling.'[50]

That night Button and his family celebrated with about 100 friends at a Subiaco hotel. Wilson watched the news reports of the appeal and then retired to bed. He wished Button well, though he had some concerns with Button's quest for a large compensation package from the government.

Wilson said one needed to form a distinction between 'not proven', 'unsafe' and 'innocent', and that Button's case fits into one of the first two. The government as a matter of public policy would need to be careful with creating a precedent over the matter. Not that Wilson was against Button receiving some form of compensation for spending five years in prison for a conviction that a court has subsequently quashed. In the end, Button received $400,000 from the government. Wilson believed $50,000 would be the upper limit in a case like Button's, where there was no evidence of judicial, prosecuting or police misconduct.

The Button success refocused attention onto the *Beamish* case. It didn't take long before the case was also referred to the CCA by the attorney-general on a petition by Beamish. Some preliminary matters were heard on 24 October 2003, and the appeal proper, which got under way on 11 October 2004, lasted four days. Again Tom Percy QC appeared for the appellant and Shane Stone for the state of Western Australia.

PHOTOGRAPHS

1 A two- or three-year-old Wilson, Geraldton, 1925 or 1926.
Photograph courtesy of Lady Wilson.

2 Wilson and his siblings in Geraldton, circa 1930. From left to right: Bob, Jim, Ron, Doug and Emily.
Photograph courtesy of Lady Wilson.

3 Family photograph (minus Doug) in Geraldton, circa 1934. From left to right: (back row) Bob, Emily's friend, Emily and Jim; (front row) family dog, Mrs Clover and Ron.
Photograph courtesy of Lady Wilson.

4 The Wilson Boys (minus Doug) in Geraldton, circa 1934. From left to right: Jim, Bob and Ron.
Photograph courtesy of Lady Wilson.

5 The Wilson siblings (minus Doug) at the Hollywood home (Perth), circa 1939. From left to right: Bob, Emily and Jim with Ron kneeling.
Photograph courtesy of Lady Wilson.

6 Wilson just after joining the Australian Imperial Forces, 1941.
Photograph courtesy of Lady Wilson.

7 Wilson in RAAF (Royal Australian Air Force) uniform just after gaining his wings, and before leaving for England, 1943.
Photograph courtesy of Lady Wilson.

8 Wilson with friends at PFA (Presbyterian Fellowship of Australia) Camp at Point Peron, a day after his arrival from England on Boxing Day 1945.
Photograph courtesy of Lady Wilson.

9 Wilson, second row, far right, at the PFA boys' camp in Kelmscott, circa 1946.
Photograph courtesy of Lady Wilson.

10 Wilson in Northam as part of the Evangelistic Bible team, circa 1946.
Photograph courtesy of Lady Wilson.

11 Wilson inside the girls' quarters at the PFA campsite in Cannington, Easter 1948.
Photograph courtesy of Lady Wilson.

12 Leila and Wilson at the Law School Ball, which doubled as their engagement party, 6 May 1949.
Photograph courtesy of Lady Wilson.

13 Wedding portrait, 29 April 1950.
Photograph courtesy of Lady Wilson.

14 Wilson with toddler Bruce, Claremont, 1953.
Photograph courtesy of Lady Wilson.

15 Wilson with Geoff in arms, Bruce and Helen, Philadelphia, 1957.
Photograph courtesy of Lady Wilson.

16 Darryl Beamish, circa 1959.
Photograph courtesy of Western Australia Police Service and Estelle Blackburn.

17 John Button during his courting days with Rosemary Anderson, circa 1962.
Photograph courtesy of Western Australia Police Service and Estelle Blackburn.

18 Eric Cooke, location and time unknown.
Photograph courtesy of Western Australia Police Service and Estelle Blackburn.

19 Daryl Beamish leading his legal team and family out of Supreme Court after his successful appeal against his murder conviction, 1 April 2005.
Photograph courtesy of Subiaco Post.

20 John Button in a media scrum outside the Supreme Court of Western Australia after his successful appeal against his manslaughter conviction, 25 February 2002.
Photograph courtesy of Subiaco Post.

21 Beamish and Button embrace outside the Supreme Court after Beamish's successful appeal, 1 April 2005.
Photograph courtesy of Subiaco Post.

22 Wilson with delegates at the Third Assembly of the World Council of Churches in front of the Taj Mahal, November–December 1961.
Photograph courtesy of Lady Wilson.

23 Wilson being congratulated by the outgoing moderator of the Western Australia Presbyterian Synod, Bill Maley, on Wilson's instalment into that position, 4 May 1965.
Photograph courtesy of Lady Wilson.

24 Wilson's instalment as the inaugural moderator of the Western Australian Uniting Church synod, Perth Entertainment Centre, 26 June 1977.
Photograph courtesy of Lady Wilson.

25 Outgoing Murdoch University chancellor Justice John Wickham congratulating Wilson as his successor, Bush Court, Murdoch University, 1980.
Photograph courtesy of Lady Wilson.

26 Wilson on the day his High Court appointment was announced, 21 May 1979.
Photography courtesy of the West Australian.

27 Wilson and Leila in Brisbane for the swearing in of Wilson as a High Court justice, 29 May 1979.
Photograph courtesy of Lady Wilson.

28 Wilson's investiture as a Knight of the Realm (KBE) by Governor-General Sir Zelman Cowen at Yarralumla, 31 July 1979.
Photograph courtesy of Lady Wilson.

29 Wilson in his High Court chambers, Canberra, 1979.
Photograph courtesy of the High Court of Australia.

30 Queen Elizabeth II at the official opening of the High Court building in Canberra, 26 May 1980 with, from left to right: Wilson, Murphy, Gibbs, Barwick, Stephen, Mason and Aickin.
Photograph courtesy of the High Court of Australia.

31 Justice Wilson the labourer, part of the volunteer Uniting Church building team building an Aboriginal Community Centre in Wiluna, 1985.
Photograph courtesy of Lady Wilson.

32 Justice Wilson on a hot roof, Wiluna, 1985.
Photograph courtesy of Lady Wilson.

33 Ceremonial seating of the Mason High Court, circa 1987. Left to right: Toohey, Deane, Wilson, Mason, Brennan, Dawson and Gaudron.
Photograph courtesy of the High Court of Australia.

34 The Mason Court in 1987. Left to right: Mason, Wilson, Brennan, Dawson, Gaudron, Toohey and Deane.
Photograph courtesy of the High Court of Australia.

35 Wilson as President of the Uniting Church of Australia being presented with a ceremonial spear at Barrkira, Northern Territory, 20 July 1989.
Photograph courtesy of Lady Wilson.

36 Installation of an Aboriginal Uniting Church minister at Yirrkala, Northern Territory, July 1989.
Photograph courtesy of Lady Wilson.

37 WA Inc Royal Commissioners walking down St Georges Terrace towards the National Mutual Centre, the home for the Royal Commission, on the first day of hearings, 12 March 1991. Left to right: Wilson, Kennedy and Brinsden.
Photography courtesy of the West Australian.

38 Papa Wilson with the Christie boys at Harvey Weir, 1994. Left to right: (back row) Michael and Peter; (front row) Daniel and Caleb.
Photograph courtesy of Lady Wilson.

39 Family portrait, July 1997. Left to right: (back row) Robyn Christie (nee Wilson), Geoff Wilson, Allyson Ladhams, Ian Ladhams, Helen Ladhams (nee Wilson) (seated), Lynette Ladhams, Bruce Wilson, Ronald Wilson (seated), Kerrie O'Neil, Nur Khamidah ('Ida'), Leila Wilson (seated) holding Jalada Wilson, Ian Wilson; (front row): Alice O'Neil Wilson, Daniel Christie, Jeffery Christie (behind), Rosie (Christie family dog), Caleb Christie, Michael Christie, Peter Christie, Emily O'Neil Wilson.
Photograph courtesy of Lady Wilson.

40 A courtesy visit to the High Court while president of the Human Rights and Equal Opportunity Commission in 1997. Left to right: Kirby, Gummow and Wilson.
Photograph courtesy of Lady Wilson.

41 Wilson during a media conference at the Australian Reconciliation Conference in Melbourne on the same day that *Bringing Them Home* was tabled in federal parliament, 26 May 1997.
Photograph courtesy of Human Rights and Equal Opportunity Commission.

42 Wilson signing his last decision as president of the Human Rights and Equal Opportunity Commission, July 1997.
Photograph courtesy of Human Rights and Equal Opportunity Commission.

43 Wilson in the back streets in the Gaza Strip, October 1998.
Photograph courtesy of Lady Wilson.

44 Wilson in a Palestinian Girls' School in the Gaza Strip, October 1998.
Photograph courtesy of Lady Wilson.

45 Wilson with Sandra Hill at Stolen Generations' Forum at Lawrence Wilson Art Gallery, University of Western Australia, National Sorry Day, 26 May 1999.
Photograph courtesy of Lady Wilson.

46 Wilson flanked by Mick Dodson (on Wilson's right) and Geoff Clark (Aboriginal and Torres Strait Islander Commission chair) at the launch of ANTaR's (Australians for Native Title and Reconciliation) campaign for a treaty, Sydney, 27 May 2000.
Photograph courtesy of Lady Wilson.

47 Wilson presenting certificates at an award ceremony for achievement in the area of disabilities, Perth, circa 2000.
Photograph courtesy of Lady Wilson.

48 Wilson teaching English to refugees, Perth, circa 2000.
Photograph courtesy of Lady Wilson.

49 Newspaper reporting of Wilson's death, July 2005.
Photograph courtesy of the West Australian.

50 John Button at Wilson's funeral service, Karrakatta cemetery, 22 July 2005.
Photograph courtesy of the West Australian.

51 Lady Wilson and grandson Jalada, Karrakatta chapel funeral service, 22 July 2005.
Photograph courtesy of the West Australian.

1

2

3

4

5

6

7

8

9

10

11

12

13

14

15

16

17

18

19

20

21

22

23

24

25

26

27

28

29

31

32

33

34

35

36

37

38

39

40

41

42

43

44

45

46

47

48

Human rights fighter dies

Ronald Wilson was an outspoken and tireless supporter of the Stolen Generation, reports **Gareth Parker**

WA's first High Court judge, Sir Ronald Wilson, has died at 82.

Sir Ronald, born in Geraldton on August 23, 1922, was a hard-hitting prosecutor, eminent jurist and outspoken human rights campaigner.

Sir Ronald sprang to national prominence in 1997 after the release of Bringing Them Home, a report into the so-called Stolen Generation he co-authored with Aboriginal leader Mick Dodson.

The report, produced while Sir Ronald was president of the Human Rights and Equal Opportunities Commission, explosively labelled government policies that saw Aboriginal children removed from their parents as "genocide".

The report called for an apology from governments, police and other bodies and paved the way for National Sorry Day and recommended stolen children be compensated. His recommendations, many of which were never adopted by the Federal Government, remain controversial today.

Mr Dodson yesterday said working with Sir Ronald had been a privilege and a pleasure. He was very energetic and a great intellect.

"Some of the establishment attacks on him after the report came out were gutless and unnecessary, but he was a tough old bugger and did not let it get to him," he said.

Ronald Darling Wilson left school at 14 and started work as a messenger boy at the Geraldton courthouse.

He faced hardship when both of his parents died while he was still young.

After serving as a fighter pilot in the Royal Australian Air Force in Britain during World War II, he returned to Australia and graduated with a bachelor of law degree from UWA.

Sir Ronald became a barrister and solicitor in 1951 and was appointed a Queen's Counsel in 1963 — the youngest ever in WA — and between 1969 and 1979 he served as WA's solicitor-general.

Renowned as an uncompromising prosecutor, Sir Ronald oversaw the prosecution of John Button and Darryl Beamish for murders that serial killer Eric Edgar Cooke confessed to.

Both men spent many years in jail for crimes they did not commit.

Murdoch law senior lecturer Tony Buti, who is writing a biography of Sir Ronald, said he never regretted the prosecutions.

"He always did what he believed was fair in law," Mr Buti said yesterday.

In 1979 Sir Ronald was appointed to the High Court by Malcolm Fraser's coalition government.

The appointment was criticised by then Labor deputy leader Lionel Bowen, who thought he was too conservative. Ironically, it was Mr Bowen as attorney-general who appointed Sir Ronald president of HREOC in 1990.

'I think he was controversial because he was willing to stand up for what he believed in.'
PREMIER GEOFF GALLOP

Sir Ronald was chancellor of Murdoch University between 1980 and 1985 and with judge Peter Brinsden and Justice Geoffrey Kennedy, oversaw the WA Inc. royal commission.

In his later years, Sir Ronald devoted his time to many human rights groups and causes, including asylum seekers and the disabled.

Premier Geoff Gallop said Sir Ronald was a man of great personal modesty, enormous intellectual capacity and moral courage.

"He's made a very significant contribution, not only to WA, but also to the nation," Dr Gallop said.

"I think he was controversial because he was willing to stand up for what he believed in."

Attorney-General Philip Ruddock said Sir Ronald served Australia with distinction.

His distinguished career could not be overstated, particularly his tireless work for indigenous Australians.

He died in his Applecross home on Friday after a 12-month illness. He is survived by his widow, Lady Leila, and five children.

Gift: Sir Ronald Wilson is presented with art work by Inawinytji Williamson, left, and Katie Curley of the Kaltjiti community in South Australia in 1999.

Legal life: Sir Ronald Wilson chairs a committee hearing of the Stolen Generation inquiry, left, and when he was appointed as a judge of the High Court in 1979.

figure 49

Wilson remained quiet on the latest developments, taking on the position as an interested onlooker. However, as this latest *Beamish* appeal was about to commence Wilson still believed he had prosecuted the case properly, and that the evidence, particularly Beamish's written confession, went to his guilt. He said:

> Beamish was charged with the murder of Jillian Brewer. She was a model and a very attractive woman, about twenty-one, and Darryl was a roamer, he would go out at night and just roam the streets, deaf mute, all sorts of problems arising from that and he was attracted by a window with the blinds, the blind up and Jillian Brewer lying on the bed naked and it aroused him and he chopped her up. I always saw it as a rebellion against a situation which had everything going for it, a beautiful young lady and so on compared with his disability and he just wanted to destroy it and I never doubted his guilt...[but] who knows, he may get up and have his conviction quashed...[however] I still remember Owen Leitch, who later became Commissioner of Police, was the detective, he was very careful and in this case he had Darryl write out his own confession and it is typical, the sort of writing you would expect from a deaf mute, can still see it, 'I fuck lady' and so on surrounding things and I thought that was fairly persuasive, his guilt, because both the choice of words and the manner in which it was his own handwriting was one of the more telling confessions you could have against the accused.

The constitution of the CCA bench was different from that which decided the Button appeal. Chief Justice Malcolm had disqualified himself from sitting on the appeal because he had enjoyed a number of conversations with his predecessor, Sir Francis Burt, over the matter. The CCA bench consisted of Justices Christopher Steytler, Christine Wheeler and Carmel McClure.

South African-born Justice Steytler was appointed to the Supreme Court in 1994. Justice Wheeler has the distinction of being the first woman appointed to the Western Australian Supreme Court, and also one of its youngest members at the time of her appointment in 1996, having been born in 1954. During her final years of study for her law degree at UWA she had worked as a professional assistant to Wilson the solicitor-general. Justice McClure had only been appointed to the Supreme Court three years before hearing the Beamish appeal.

The three justices completed hearing the *Beamish* appeal on 14 October 2004. They handed down their judgement on April Fools' Day, 2005. But the result was not a joke for Darryl Beamish. The court held that there had been a substantial miscarriage of justice, and set aside his conviction of the murder of Jillian Brewer in 1958. As Beamish had served his sentence of imprisonment, no retrial was ordered.

The key to the decision of Justices Steytler, Wheeler and McClure was the 'gallows confession' of Cooke. Only fifteen minutes before his hanging, and also three days earlier, Cooke had confessed to Reverend Jenkins that he had killed both Brewer and Anderson. The court said there was no good reason for Cooke to lie when making the gallows confession.

The court commented that the justices who heard the 1964 appeal did have the advantage of seeing and hearing Cooke give evidence when they formed their poor view of his general credibility. But the court added that the 1964 court's view was based, in some part at least, on the conclusion that Cooke was seeking to prolong his life by creating confusion and winning support for his theory that he suffered from compulsive insanity. Justices Steytler, Wheeler and McClure said this could not possibly be the case with the gallows confession, which was made after the 1964 appeal, because Cooke 'had appreciated that his execution was inevitable and had acknowledged to Jenkins what he saw as the justice of the decision to hang him'.[51]

The court stated that the gallows confessions, along with other evidence, supported Cooke's confession to the murder of Brewer. This other evidence related to Cooke's details about the time of the crime and contents in Brewer's flat that went to supporting the view that Cooke had committed the murder. There was evidence that Cooke had stolen a car from Brookwood Flats on the night of the murder, and there was corroboration from a bus driver that Cooke had caught a bus on Stirling Highway near the flats on the same night.

Of more crucial significance was Cooke's observation in relation to the two milkmen who serviced the flats on the night of the murder, 'more especially given that one of them had, on that night only, changed the ordinary time of his delivery between 4 and 5.00 a.m. to between 2.00 and 2.15 a.m'.[52]

The court also said that the fact that Cooke was a serial murderer and brutal criminal meant that the Brewer murder was 'nothing out of the ordinary for him.'[53] The court said similar fact evidence in relation to Cooke's other crimes on young women, which on two occasions included a sexual element, may have had some bearing on the minds of a reasonable jury.[54]

The court did acknowledge:

> the very strong case against Beamish, given...[his] detailed confessions to the same crime, made in the presence of a number of people, including persons who were independent of the police (although there was no other evidence linking him directly with crimes).[55]

Then the court went on to say that there were a number of unsatisfactory aspects of these confessions. These were in relation to Beamish's communication level, possible prompting by the police to give certain answers, and the destruction of a piece of paper by Leitch, in which he had recorded questions given by him and answers received from Beamish where he denied killing 'the lady'.

The court also referred to some inconsistencies between Beamish's confession and the known facts of the circumstances of the murder and his predisposition to admit to crimes that he had not committed. Even allowing for all these weakness or concerns at the end of their judgment, their honours wrote: 'We reiterate that the case against Beamish was very strong.'[56] The court went on to conclude:

> We also accept that many of the difficulties in Cooke's evidence which were pointed to by the 1964 Court are present (bearing in mind, however, that the Court did not have available to it the gallows confession and, as we have pointed out, was influenced by some considerations which have since been shown to have been mistaken). However, it seems to us that when regard is had to the fresh evidence of the Reverend Jenkins, supported by the other matters to which we have referred, it cannot be said (even allowing for the poor view of Cooke's credibility formed by the 1964 Court) that Cooke's gallows confession is so incredible that a reasonable jury could not accept it as true. Rather, it seems to us that Cooke's confession is capable of giving rise to a reasonable doubt in the mind of the jury and that, when that confession is considered in combination with all of the other evidence... there is a significant possibility that a jury, acting reasonably, would have acquitted Beamish.[57]

Although over the years the *Beamish* case had not received as much publicity as the *Button* case, the media coverage, in Western Australia at least, was extensive after the Supreme Court handed down its decision. Outside the court, the media shot photographs of Beamish, his family, supporters and legal team. Beamish gave a victory shake with his hand while his sister spoke on his behalf. Obviously he was happy with the verdict, but unlike Button, he would not be seeking compensation from the state government. Button was in court to see and hear the verdict, and outside the court he joined arms with Beamish and raised them to express their joint victories. An interested bystander at the court was Tony Cooke, son of Eric Cooke, who expressed his happiness for Beamish for the nightly TV news coverage. The journalists Christian and Blackburn were there to savour the result of their years of campaigning.

Former Detective Sergeant Owen Leitch denied on the evening TV news that he had done anything wrong in the investigation. The president of the Western Australian Police Union said that Leitch was 'deeply disappointed' with the decision.[58] Even five months after the successful appeal, Leitch strongly maintained that the evidence against Beamish was very strong. He said that:

> Beamish may have been a deaf mute but he was able to obtain a driver's licence and communicate, even if he did it by finger speaking. Also he had that woman Myatt helping him, she was his supporter.

In relation to Cooke, Leitch commented:

> He was an unscrupulous liar. It took him three attempts to get his story right in relation to how Jillian Brewer was killed. And even then he said he had stabbed her in both buttocks but it was only one.

Leitch denies that he intimidated or pressured Beamish. He also says that Wilson at all times acted with propriety and professionalism: 'As usual Wilson acted ethically. He received the brief from us and prosecuted the case with his usual professionalism and talent.' But Leitch also acknowledged the toughness of Wilson the prosecutor. In a *Sydney Morning Herald* feature article on the *Beamish* case, Leitch's admiration for Wilson's performance in the 1964 appeal was reported as follows:

> 'Ronnie Wilson is very adept,' says Leitch, recalling that historic hearing. 'He's a little fellow with bright eyes, look like butter wouldn't melt in his mouth, but

> they used to reckon he would twist the knife. In his perfect English, and with his face, he got the better of Red Burt.[59]

Wilson was asked by the media to comment on the decision. He declined to give extensive commentary on the decision, but in response to the court's finding that Beamish had been subjected to an 'extraordinary, and highly prejudicial, cross-examination' by Wilson and that his summing up 'would be most unlikely to be permitted in more modern times',[60] Wilson said:

> But as the judgement emphasises, there was no objection to the use I was making of it [Beamish's prior criminal and deviant behaviour]...It was an extraordinary killing, with the use of the hatchet, and I wouldn't deny that I had that in mind when I drew the jury's attention to [Beamish's] perversions.[61]

Wilson had throughout the years before and after the successful Button and Beamish appeals maintained a consistent position on his role in both cases and, for that matter, Cooke:

> I have no sense of failure in having prosecuted John Button and Daryl Beamish and Eric Cooke because I was just doing my job. I didn't create the brief that was given to me. I took it and did my job in relation to it.

Even Wilson's strongest critic as a prosecutor, Leo Woods, offers no criticism of Wilson over the Button case. Woods says the fact Button had confessed to the killing of Anderson provided the Crown with a very strong case, and at the time of the Button trial there was no criticism around, and that the ensuing attention and criticism of the conviction is 'simply a media beat up'.

Bart Kakulas, junior counsel for Button at the trial and the first appeal, who always was convinced of the innocence of Button, believes that if Wilson had not been the prosecutor, there would have been less chance of a conviction, although he acknowledged the Crown had a strong case against Button. Kakulas's belief is even stronger in relation to the 1964 appeal, where Wilson was able to discredit Cooke as a witness of truth. Not that Kakulas believed that Wilson acted in an unethical manner. He was just sharp and unwilling to concede points fully, if at all.

In relation to the 1964 appeal, Kakulas said that he and Hatfield kept saying to Wilson that the appeal should have been conceded:

> We were saying 'Look, you have got your man now. Why do you want to keep this other man Button in gaol?' But that wasn't the way Wilson worked. His stand was that Button had confessed and we got our conviction and that was his approach to the matter.'

Tom Percy QC, who led the successful appeals in *Button* and *Beamish*, says that no question can be raised in regards to Wilson's role in the trial prosecution and earlier appeal in *Button*. He remarks that every prosecutor is entitled to proceed on the basis that a confession is true and voluntary, and Button 'had a motive and had opportunity and with limited material available to him, it looked very much like Button was responsible.'[62]

But in relation to the *Beamish* case, Percy is more qualified, stating that Wilson's conduct at the trial was fine, but 'there were certain things which, on current standards of disclosure, should have been disclosed'.[63]

The issue of disclosure has been one of the more consistent criticisms of Wilson in relation to the *Beamish* case, especially in relation to the second appeal in 1964. Percy mentions the nondisclosure by the Crown to the defence of medical reports in relation to Brewer's ability to speak after being attacked but before death, a statement from one of the milkmen saying he had delivered milk to Brewer's flat earlier than normal, and a statement from a person who corroborated Cooke's statement that he had observed people at an engagement party in the Brookwood Flats. These documents would have given the defence ammunition to argue the credibility of Cooke's confession.

Although Percy was critical of the Crown, he makes it clear that, even though the prosecution had many things in their possession that they didn't disclose to the defence or the court, it cannot be assumed that Wilson was responsible for this, or even that he knew about much of this evidence. He comments that, when he has acted as a prosecutor rather than as a defence lawyer, there have been times when he has not had what he considers relevant documents released to him because the police thought it was not relevant. Also, the Chief Prosecutor may not receive evidence that has been disclosed to the prosecution because a junior officer in the Crown Law Department has not considered it relevant.[64]

But whoever was to blame for the nondisclosure of certain documents, Percy believed that the conduct of the Beamish prosecution would not meet today's standards, where there is a greater onus on the Crown engaging in full and comprehensive discovery of evidence in their possession. But he can understand how it happened, because the prosecutors had a confession of the murder by Beamish. Percy adds that probably the major reason the Crown conducted the case the way it did was because Wilson never contemplated that Beamish wasn't guilty, and he also believed that Cooke was a villain and liar.[65]

Leitch says that he and Wilson thought that what Beamish meant by 'I fuck lady' did not refer to sexual intercourse—no semen was found inside Brewer's vagina or on her body. What Leitch and Wilson think Beamish was referring to was handling Brewer's vagina like he had done with the young girls in Kings Park.

The CCA in 2004 never found that the Crown or Wilson had failed in their professional duties in relation to disclosure of evidence and documents. But, in any case, the CCA said that, in considering whether the duty to disclose had been breached or if there had been a miscarriage of justice, it was unnecessary to find fault on the part of the prosecutor.[66] Also, the fact that there has been a broadening of the prosecution's duties to disclose over the last twenty years made it difficult to consider through today's eyes what should have happened if decided through yesterday's eyes.[67]

It is worth noting that, on the specific issue that had outraged Professor Brett in 1966—the nondisclosure of the advice that had been sought on Cooke's claim that Brewer had spoken just before dying—the CCA found Wilson's action was 'entirely proper', particularly as Wilson did not intend and, in fact, did not base his argument at the trial on a view that speech was impossible. But in fact, in *Beamish (No 2)*, the second appeal hearing (1964), Wilson had raised the issue of Brewer speaking and cross-examined Cooke on it. Further, Chief Justice Wolff had referred to it in his judgement as a factor in his negative determination of the credibility of Cooke's confession to the murder.

Wilson believed that throughout his career he conformed to the highest contemporary professional and ethical standards. But he acknowledged, as the CCA did, that today the standards are higher. For example, a prosecutor today is legally obliged to disclose all information that may be relevant to the case. Previously, that had not been the law.

Even so, Wilson said he regarded it as improper to withhold evidence: 'If I didn't want it, then I ought to give it to the defence and that was my practice. That was the standard practice.' But when Wilson was prosecuting, the Crown had a right of discretion not to disclose all of the evidence to the defence, and it used that right to deny evidence. Consequently much less was disclosed then than now.

Rarely does a court review a case in such a public and controversial way, and scrutinise a man's professional work in such detail, as happened to Wilson in relation to Button and Beamish. His work as Crown prosecutor has been picked over to a rare degree. Wilson's role in *Button* and *Beamish* has been scrutinised by academics such as Professor Brett, the media, counsel such as Tom Percy and the court, forty years after the event. This is unprecedented in Western Australian criminal justice history. And throughout the hype and attention, Wilson, apart from some brief media comments, remained silent in public.

But back in 1983, way before the media, legal and political hype of the late 1990s and early part of the twenty-first century, Wilson made a clear public declaration of his views in relations to Cooke's confessions of the killings of Brewer and Anderson. In his paper 'Truth and Justice', which he delivered on 23 April 1983 at a national symposium on 'Lying' in Sydney,[68] he noted that, while Cooke's confession to the murder of Brewer was 'superficially plausible', it 'was inaccurate in certain crucial respects', and that much of the details of the murder that Cooke described could have been learnt from the newspaper accounts of the crime.[69]

In relation to the fatal running down of Anderson, Wilson said that Cooke's confession 'revealed superficial conformity to the facts of the case as they had been revealed at the trial [of Button]', but as Chief Justice Wolff observed: 'the mathematical odds against not only one but two such serious miscarriages of justice arising out of the actions of one person beggared the imagination.'[70]

Wilson concluded his recital of the Cooke confessions to the murders of Brewer and Anderson with the following sentence: 'Apparently he [Cooke] went to his death with the lies still on his lips, perhaps hoping to secure a last-minute reprieve or perhaps indulging in one final gesture of defiance.'[71]

Unlike his expressed views in the 1983 paper, Wilson declined to offer his views to the media when they did ask him to express an opinion on the successful Button and Beamish appeals in the early part of this century. He refused to offer an opinion publicly on the merits of the successful appeals, except to say that he remained satisfied with the way he prosecuted the cases. But in private, even after the successful appeals, he still believed that the circumstantial evidence pointed to the guilt of Button.

In relation to Beamish, he believed his written statements were very strong evidence of guilt, but maybe a good defence lawyer would have made more of Beamish's literacy difficulties.[72]

In any case, Wilson believed that, as the prosecutor of the cases, it was not his role to decide on the guilt of Button or Beamish or, for that matter, Cooke or anyone else; his job was to prosecute in an honest and ethical manner, which he maintained he did.

7

Crown Advocate, Church Moderator and Family Man

You have to remember when you walk through the door of that courtroom, you are the Crown.[1]

The *Beamish*, *Button* and *Cooke* cases of the early 1960s were the public high points of Wilson's prosecuting career. But in fact, although he continued to take on selected high profile criminal trials and appeals such as these, over the course of the 1960s the majority of his work, and the focus of his career, shifted primarily into the field of civil advocacy.

It was also a decade in which Wilson's church commitments became even greater. Simultaneously, the children's various school and extracurricular activities increased, which of course placed greater demands on Wilson and Leila. Wilson's work commitments meant that Leila had to assume the bulk of parenting duties, for which Wilson always remained indebted to her. His prenuptial warning that Leila and family would have to defer to his faith and professional duties came into full effect.

As the 1950s ended, Wilson's civil court load was increasing, with appearances on civil matters in the Western Australian Supreme Court and High Court. His first noncriminal appearance in the High Court was in 1959, in the *Professional Engineers* case, in which the parties were arguing over the application of the Commonwealth's arbitration powers in a dispute involving state public servants.[2] Wilson had little opportunity to address the court, as John Kerr QC, acting for the Professional Engineers' Association, dominated the court's time. He was amazed at Kerr's ability to spend more than two days arguing over one case—the *Teachers* case.[3] Wilson lapped up the chance to listen to some of the leading counsel of the time, including Kerr and Keith Aickin, who was later to become a High Court justice (1976–82).

Wilson's civil work also involved him travelling to Melbourne each year to represent the Western Australian government's view in the annual *Basic Wage* case. The *Basic Wage* case was a feature of the centralised Conciliation and Arbitration system established in 1904. The Conciliation and Arbitration Commission was the arbiter of the system, setting the minimum wage that an unskilled person could be paid. Until the 1953 *Basic Wage* case abolished the practice, the system had been for this minimum to be indexed for inflation, so that cost of living adjustments were automatically made to the wage. Larger adjustments came via the *Basic Wage* cases, and other secondary large adjustments occurred via the *Margin Wage* cases. The *Margin Wage* cases dealt with the money to be paid for a skill that was to be added to the basic (unskilled) wage to make up a single paypacket.

At the *Basic Wage* cases, counsel or advocates appeared for the Commonwealth and each state. The Australian Council of Trade Unions (ACTU) attended, representing the workers, and employer representatives were also present. In acting for the state, his home state, Wilson would invariably be arguing against an increase in the basic wage. Although not an economist, he was quickly able to grasp the brief prepared for him, which inevitably would involve a large quantity of statistics and economics.

Wilson was not one of the main players in these cases. He was relatively junior at the time compared with some of the other counsel, and he was representing one of the smaller states, which was not yet a powerhouse in the national economy. Nor was he an industrial specialist, a member of the 'industrial relations club', as it was sometimes derided. It is doubtful that any of the other counsel at the commission doubled as prosecutors in controversial murder trials between the annual hearings. Nevertheless, Wilson enjoyed his appearances before the commission; he was just happy to be an advocate.

It was at these *Basic Wage* cases that Wilson was to spar with two of his university contemporaries—with one representing employer groups and the other the ACTU. Bill Snedden, who had moved to Melbourne to practise, built up a good reputation as an industrial barrister, representing the employers' interests. This no doubt assisted him with launching into a career in federal politics, where he rose to the position of opposition leader. The top prize of the prime ministership was to elude him when he was deposed by his parliamentary colleagues and replaced with Malcolm Fraser. Wilson viewed Snedden's efforts in the *Basic Wage* cases as 'workmanlike'.[4]

The other former university colleague, who acted for the ACTU, was Bob Hawke. Hawke had assisted in an honorary capacity with the preparation of the ACTU's presentation for the 1957 and 1958 *Basic Wage* cases, while still on a PhD scholarship at the Australian National University. Although he did not appear in the 1957 and 1958 cases, he nonetheless made an impression on the commissioners. President of the commission, Dick (later Sir Richard) Kirby recalls:

> He was very fresh-faced and we thought he was only twenty-two or three. On occasions he was unable to sit still and we could see he was nearly going mad with frustration, wanting to jump up and have a say. We used to watch him with some curiosity and amusement, and wonder who this young cove was...[5]

By the 1959 *Basic Wage* case, Hawke was employed by the ACTU as its research officer and advocate. Thus he was ready and willing to step into the fray and let the commissioners know that he didn't think much of their 1953 *Basic Wage* case decision. Unlike a barrister, mindful of respecting the bench when criticising their previous decision, Hawke did not concern himself with protocol and niceties. He attacked the legal and economic assumptions of the 1953 *Basic Wage* case, which had abolished automatic indexing or adjustment of the basic wage. The bench did not restore full automatic indexation. However, they did provide for a massive increase of 15 per cent in the basic wage, which brought the minimum wage above the level it would have been if automatic indexing had not been abolished in 1953. In his memoirs, Hawke writes:

> As an advocate I favoured none of the niceties and euphemisms beloved by lawyers when gently suggesting an alternative interpretation, or even the possibility of error, to the Bench. I was enraged by the enormous injustice done to Australian workers by the 1953 decision, and as the representative

> of those workers, I did not feel it within me in those early days to go beyond the necessary formalities of respect…[6]

Wilson described Hawke's advocacy as 'truculent, abusive, intimidatory and effective'.[7] Wilson thought Hawke was 'positively rude' to the Bench as he went about criticising their former judgements:

> He used to abuse the Commissioners and they would take it out of his hand, like lambs. He would tell them their last decision was appalling, disgraceful. I would marvel at this, you know, and of course the reality was that he'd done a law degree but he had never been admitted. He was entitled as an advocate to appear before the Arbitration Court. He couldn't have appeared before any other court. But he would get away with murder because there was no professional etiquette that bound him. But he was very effective…[8]

Wilson's appearances before the Arbitration and Conciliation Commission and his increasing civil workload motivated him to seek a change to his title of chief Crown prosecutor. He thought it was silly for him to appear in civil matters and before the Arbitration and Conciliation Commission in the annual *Basic Wage* case as the chief Crown prosecutor. Moreover, some of the commissioners and advocates wondered why a chief Crown prosecutor was appearing in wage cases.

Wilson's push for a change in title was successful. The logic of a change was obvious, but the timing also assisted. Gerry Ruse, who was the Crown solicitor and principal counsel for the Crown in civil matters, suffered a heart attack in 1959, which curtailed his court workload. The solicitor-general of the time, Sydney Good, did not appear in court; his time was taken up with administering the department and advising various government departments. The time was appropriate for someone to take charge of the civil caseload. On 1 November 1961, Wilson was appointed the chief Crown counsel. This gave him carriage of major civil and criminal matters as well as appeals hearings. His title was unique in Australia, and the appointment was for Wilson 'a job from heaven'.

Wilson loved the fact that his new appointment allowed him to spend much time in the courts, and he was quite happy to remain with the Crown

Law Department, where he had worked since 1937. Private practice held no appeal; nor did the independent Perth bar, then in its infancy, pioneered by Francis Burt and John Wickham.[9]

However, Wilson acknowledged that many in the profession in the 1950s believed that being an employed solicitor was inferior to private practice. In a 1993 interview with Robert Meadows (who became Western Australian solicitor-general after 1995) and historian Geraldine Byrne, Wilson retold the story of how in the late 1950s a Supreme Court justice counselled him to leave the Crown Law Department and move into private practice:

> His reason for counselling me in that way, he had the best intentions, it was that he felt that if I stayed in the Crown and was ever appointed to the Bench from the Crown that I would be exposed to the possibility of a challenge to my authority to sit. He mentioned that I might face...[a] writ of *quo warranto* if I took the judicial office without having been in private practice on my own behalf. I appreciated the advice but as I said I wasn't ambitious and I enjoyed what I was doing and I stayed where I was.[10]

A writ *quo warranto* is an ancient prerogative writ that means 'by what warrant do you to perform this role?' The justice was concerned that employment with the Crown Law Department, especially as a solicitor, may not be regarded as legal practice, and at the time, a person needed experience as a legal practitioner before becoming a judge.[11]

This advice brought home to Wilson the misconception some in the legal fraternity had about working for the Crown Law Department. However, over time, he sensed that the perception of the Crown Law Department as inferior dissipated. As testimony to this, he pointed to the election of Michael Murray to the position of president of the Law Society while an employed solicitor with the Crown Law Department. Now, graduating law students eagerly seek articled clerkships offered by the state solicitor's office.

His job at Crown Law certainly did not handicap Wilson, no matter what some in the profession thought of the department. Within two years of being appointed Crown counsel, he was appointed Queen's counsel (QC), on 24 July 1963. At forty years of age, he was the youngest QC in Australia at that time. The appointment of QCs is the prerogative of the state government. The usual procedure is for the state attorney-general to seek out the views of the legal profession before making recommendations to the cabinet for approval.

Justice William Windeyer sent Wilson a note congratulating him on his appointment. He was the only High Court justice to do so. Nevertheless, even in these early days of his appearances, Wilson was earning respect from the members of the High Court. Justice Douglas Menzies of Melbourne suggested to him that he should leave Perth and join the Melbourne Bar. Menzies felt that Wilson's skills and abilities would be more fully utilised and challenged in Melbourne.

Wilson had no intention of leaving his home state or his position at the Crown Law Department—he enjoyed living in Perth, and he was satisfied professionally by the quality of work at the Crown. Indeed, he believed that the same quality and range of briefs would not be available to him in private practice.

The early 1960s were heady days for Wilson. His star was rising as a Crown prosecutor in criminal cases and as a Crown counsel in a variety of civil cases. To add to the excitement, a few weeks after his appointment as Crown counsel, Wilson was in New Delhi attending the Third Assembly of the World Council of Churches. He was one of the four Australian delegates appointed to represent the Presbyterian Church of Australia. Wilson revelled in ecumenical meetings and interfaith exchanges, and it is not surprising that he viewed his attendance at the assembly as another significant landmark on his Christian journey.

He was still a commissioner of the Presbyterian Church of Western Australia, an elder of his Nedlands Parish, convener of Christian Unity, and in demand as a lay preacher. So, with his increasing family commitments, Wilson led a very full life. Moreover, although his Crown Law work was increasingly taking him into civil jurisdictions, Wilson still prosecuted more serious criminal cases, such as the Eric Cooke trial.

In 1963, Wilson's eldest child Bruce entered high school at Scotch College, the exclusive boys' private school. The Wilsons had not planned to send any of the children to private schools. They thought Bruce would attend Hollywood High, and the other children would follow. Bruce asked if he could sit the scholarship entrance test for Scotch, as some of his friends were going there.

Wilson and Leila hoped that he would not win a scholarship, as their preference was a state education, which they had had. Although Wilson had been dissatisfied with his school education, he, like Leila, thought a state school would provide a more 'normal' atmosphere than the more privileged Scotch College. However, if Bruce were going to go to a private school, they could think of no better one than Scotch College, a Presbyterian institution. He sat the test, and won a scholarship that paid for half of his tuition fees.

Bruce was a bright student, and did well, achieving six out of a possible seven distinctions in the matriculation, or entrance exam, for university. He also had a great time on the sports field, playing cricket, hockey, tennis and athletics for the college, and captained various teams. However, Bruce did not enjoy all aspects of his time at Scotch. He thought the teachers were authoritarian, and many of the students snobbish. Like his father, Bruce particularly disliked snobby behaviour.

Because Bruce went to Scotch College, the other Wilson boys were to follow in his footsteps, but without the same success. Geoff had transferred to Scotch in grade 7, as his parents felt that too much pressure was being placed on him at Claremont Demonstration Primary School to perform as well as his older brother. But the move to Scotch brought no joy. He felt the same pressure there, which was only made worse when his Latin teacher corrected a mistake he had made, and said, 'Your brother would not have made the same mistake.' On hearing of this, Leila communicated with the teacher that 'Geoff was not Bruce, he was Geoff and should not be compared to his older brother'.

To make matters worse for Geoff, he lost six months of schooling in year 9 and three months in year 11, each time because of a broken leg.[12] This had a significant negative effect on his academic performance. This affected his confidence, and he did not pursue tertiary studies, at least not initially. At eighteen years of age he left home, and also got a job in his father's former department, Crown Law, doing clerical work. About six months later, he transferred to the Summary Relief Court, the precursor to the Family Court, which his father later helped establish in Western Australia. Not long after arriving at the Summary Relief Court, he bumped into special magistrate Hillary Ryan, who often visited the Wilson household with his wife to play bridge with Wilson and Leila. Ryan said to Geoff, 'Good to have another Wilson in the department. I hope you end up as successful as your father.' Geoff's response was to seek a transfer to Mental Health Services, where he worked for eight years in a clerical role. Ryan's words vividly brought back the expectation at primary school, and particularly at Scotch, that he would follow in the footsteps of his brilliant brother Bruce. The thought that there was now an expectation that he would rise to the performance of his esteemed father was just too much. He felt very pressured and despondent.

Helen and Robyn also attended an exclusive private school—Presbyterian Ladies College (PLC). Both girls won scholarships to the college, which paid for half of their tuition fees. Compared with the experience of their brothers, their time at an exclusive Presbyterian educational institution was more enjoyable.

Helen enjoyed schoolwork; she says she was an 'average' student in most subjects but did very well in maths. She did well enough at school to gain entry into Claremont Teachers College. Since entry grade 1 in primary school, Helen had wanted to be a primary school teacher: 'I love my first grade teacher so I wanted to be a teacher. But if I couldn't do that I may have gone to UWA to study law.' As far as sport at PLC was concerned, she had no great talent for it, but competed in an array of activities, enjoying netball the most.

Robyn, like her elder sister, participated in a number of sporting activities, but without any great distinction. She particularly enjoyed playing netball. She worked hard at school and excelled, attaining a tertiary entrance admission score that was high enough for her to gain admission into medicine at UWA. But as long as she could remember she wanted to be a nurse:

> I just wanted to be a nurse. I was interested in being involved with people and in a caring profession and I thought nursing was for me. So I applied to do nursing at the Fremantle Hospital Nursing School and I enjoyed it there.

Although Leila and Wilson had not originally made any firm commitments on the children attending a private school, they were happy with the choice of Scotch and PLC, both private Presbyterian schools, which reflected Wilson and Leila's strong commitment to their faith. Wilson's commitment to the church was recognised by his fellow Presbyterians when in 1965 the Western Australian assembly, consisting of parish elders, lay persons, and ministers representing all congregations in the State, elected Wilson as the moderator, that is, the presiding officer of the Presbyterian Church in Western Australia. He was the first lay person to hold this position, which entailed being the administrative head of the church and overseeing the policy direction of the church and its various committees and organisations.

The Western Australian assembly had to persuade Wilson to take the job. Des Cousins, who at the time was the minister of the Presbyterian church in Manning, a southern suburb about 7 kilometres from the city, had known Wilson since the mid 1950s, through his involvement with ASCM. In all that time, Cousins had never known him to push himself forward for positions in the church. But, when it became clear that he could help the church, Wilson did not hesitate to accept. He saw it as part of his commitment to his faith, and as his public service duty.

Cousins believes the election of Wilson as moderator was a turning point for the Presbyterian Church in Western Australia. Wilson was very capable, and commanded wide support among church members. His election gave impetus to the move to elect more moderators from lay persons within the congregation.

As moderator, he was constantly invited to various parishes to deliver the Sunday sermon. Many in the church were well aware of Wilson's reputation as a fiery prosecutor. His sermons were delivered with much gusto, and some would say with the same intensity that he displayed in court as an advocate. Some viewed Wilson as a 'fiery preacher', although Wilson categorically denied such a description, which he considered negative and associated with 'TV specialists and others who rant…'[13] Cousins believes it is a more accurate picture to describe Wilson as a 'highly committed' preacher rather than a fiery one:

> Highly committed to what he was saying, sort of intense sometimes, as you would expect with a very good command of the language and a capacity to sort of speak in ways that were compelling and so on. He was a good preacher.

Many of his sermons reflected his belief in humility and service to God. He believed that man often was too selfish and concerned for material wealth, lacking in humility. This was the theme of a sermon, delivered at his local parish church as part of the Technical Training Year, which demonstrated his skills as an orator and an informative preacher:

> Some people have been saying that God is dead, but despite all the promise of a richer life the possibility that confronts us now is that man is dead, transformed into a thing, a producer, a consumer, unthinking, unfeeling, a blind worshipper of other things.[14]

He said that it was not wrong to have material prosperity, that it should not be feared, but it should also not be worshipped, and it should be 'used to make the whole world a place where men can live fully human lives'. He saw the relationship with God as central to human development and humility:

> There is no human way of dissolving the selfishness and possessiveness and pride which mars our sense of community and frustrates wholesome relationships of person to person save the experience of the love of God, bringing with it forgiveness, release from guilt and an incentive to serve.

This concept of service was central to both Wilson's religious life and his work. He believed that it was important for Christians to serve God through their work in the world, and that this be a sign to others of Christian works. At his induction ceremony as moderator on 4 May 1965, Wilson warned of the 'threat of irrelevance' for the Church. He said that the irrelevance threat was the result of the over-institutionalisation and organisation of the church. He believed that:

> It is no disloyalty to the forefathers of the church to recognise that what was suited to their day and age is not suited to the modern scientific, technological world with its changing social pattern.[15]

He added that he suspected that some of his professional colleagues in law had until his appointment as moderator viewed his church work as a spare-time occupation. But for Wilson this was not the case—for him he was a Christian twenty-four hours a day, and during his daily work he always worked from a position of Christian principle.

Wilson appreciated that, in his role with the Crown Law Department, he had the full support of then premier, David Brand, to take on the role of moderator. And he was delighted to play host to Brand at the luncheon on the first day of the 1965 Assembly of Churches in Western Australia. Brand's successors, John Tonkin and Charles Court, similarly supported Wilson's involvement with the church, and did not object to him sometimes attending to church matters during normal business hours.

Although Wilson believed in the importance of serving God and being obedient to God's rules, and although he never put aside his Christian principles, he always maintained that his religious faith did not influence his decisions as a lawyer or judge. This may have been the case, so far as not consciously allowing his religious views to influence his legal arguments or his judgements, but subconsciously his belief system would have shaped his interpretation of the law.

There are many who believed that Wilson's religious faith did influence his method of court advocacy. As previously mentioned, his close Crown colleague, Kevin Parker opined that Wilson's belief system was shaped by his religious faith—it guided his judgement on what was right and wrong, and it instilled in him a public duty commitment to represent the Crown's case as best he could. He believed that his work for the Crown was the 'right' thing. Justice in its wider sense dictated that he prosecute a case to the best of his ability and in an ethical and fair manner.

However, some of those critical of Wilson as a prosecutor would query his commitment to fairness or Wilson's view on fairness. Justice and fairness, Wilson thought, were best served by complying with professional ethical standards, and for the lawyers on both sides arguing their client's case or position to the best of their abilities. Wilson, unlike some of his critics, did not believe that a prosecutor should not prosecute a case hard.

Fred Chaney, former Fraser government Aboriginal Affairs minister and deputy president of the Native Title Tribunal (2000–07), believes that Wilson had a focused view of right and wrong that bred a single-purpose and forceful prosecuting and advocacy style. Chaney recalls as a young lawyer sitting in court observing Wilson in action. Chaney had briefed Howard Smith QC in obtaining an ex parte injunction against the Western Australian government to prevent the government issuing mineral leases in a specified area in the Pilbara region of the north-west of the state. The government was unhappy with the issuing of the injunction, and a few days later Wilson appeared in the Supreme Court on behalf of the government in relation to the interim injunction. Chaney remembers the experience:

> This was my first, and indeed only experience of being in court with Ron and he was, I would have to say, fearsome. Ah, I mean my vivid recollection of this man as a very diminutive person…he had all his arguments written out in a child's exercise book, cardboard covered school exercise book of the sort that was common in those days, lined paper but…it was the most powerful bit of advocacy and quite frankly I think I describe it as… intellectual bare knuckle fighting and I actually felt we were sort of quite

> bloodied at the end of it and our injunction disappeared but it was a masterful, I would have to say, he was all over us...and we were done over comprehensively.

As moderator, Wilson was responsible for overseeing the management committee of Sister Kate's Home for Children. Sister Kate's was established in 1933 as the Children's Cottage Home by Sister Kate Clutterbuck, an Anglican nun, who had been working at the Parkerville Children's Home in the hills north-east of Perth. Sister Kate's was situated at Queens Park, then on the outskirts of Perth, a twenty-minute train ride south-east from the city. Sister Kate ran the home until her death in 1946. It was then placed under the management of an administrative board until the Presbyterians took control in 1956.[16]

Sister Kate's was one of many government and church homes and missions that were utilised to house and raise Aboriginal children, who would become known as the 'stolen generations'. These were Aboriginal children who had been separated from their families as part of a state-mandated legislative and administrative assimilation scheme. Sister Kate's was government funded, and intended to deal only with so-called 'quadroons' (those with less than 25 per cent Aboriginal 'blood').

Sister Kate's consisted of seven small cottages situated among picturesque farming land, where dairy cows grazed. 'The grounds at Sister Kate's were a child's paradise—expansive and containing many and varied adventures.'[17] There was also a church at the home, where all the children attended Presbyterian services. Situated across the road from Sister Kate's was the local state primary school, where most of the 'homies' attended, and where they were often subjected to racial taunts.[18] Some 'homies', particularly those who were seen to require extra discipline, went to the local Catholic primary school.

The passage of time and the emergence of the accounts of the children who lived there would bring Sister Kate's a degree of notoriety. But at the time the cottage model, based on 'the style that Sister Kate had developed at Parkerville, using theories and attitudes that were progressive for their time',[19] was seen by the administrators and outsiders as an attempt to re-create as much as possible a family lifestyle for the residents, rather than a traditional dormitory-style orphanage.

The cottage system did provide some degree of 'homely' environment, with the children housed in group cottages with a cottage mother. But not all these cottage mothers were necessarily very nurturing and committed to the children. This was a particular problem with the cottage system, which allowed each cottage mother to have significant autonomy in how she treated the children and in establishing the 'cottage rules'. While some cottage mothers were caring, allegations would later emerge of cruelty by cottage mothers[20] and of sexual abuse by family members of the cottage mothers and by some members of the public who came to take the children out for weekends away from Sister Kate's.[21]

There were no facilities to house parents, even for short-term visits. The children were discouraged from maintaining contact with their families, and in many instances lied to about the reasons for being placed at the home, with some being falsely told they were orphans. Ex-resident Sue Gordon (since 1988 a magistrate in the Perth Children's Court) does not have fond memories of the place: 'There was never any love at Sister Kate's. There was love amongst the kids because that was all you had. You didn't have any adult person you could attach yourself to.'[22]

At the time Wilson became moderator, these issues had not become public knowledge. The home was well regarded, with its profile boosted by the outstanding success of former residents Graham 'Polly' Farmer and Ted 'Square' Kilmurray on the football field for East Perth, and in Farmer's case, Geelong in the Victorian Football League.

Wilson sometimes went with his family on Sunday drives to the home, where his children played with the children at Sister Kate's. But as moderator, he was not expected to concern himself with the 'nitty gritty' management and affairs of the home, and, given his extremely busy life, it seems in retrospect that its affairs did not occupy much of his time or attention.

Wilson's involvement with Sister Kate's was his first real contact with the world of Aboriginal people. Three decades later, it would become a matter of controversy, and would indeed give him cause for deep reflection, and some personal pain. But at the time there was no hint of this.

Wilson was not blind to issues of race. As Des Cousins remarks, he was philosophically conservative and cautious, and tended to stick with the established practices until there was some reason to change. However, he spoke out against racial discrimination at church meetings on his return form the US in 1957. This was born out of his contacts with the elders of the predominantly black church in Philadelphia, the nearest church to where he was living. It was not a conscious decision to seek out a black congregation or knowledge of race relations in the US.

From 1963, Wilson was instrumental in the establishment of a program to house students from overseas countries such as Ceylon who had come to Perth to study. Wilson coordinated activities of a number of community organisations involved in the welfare of overseas students studying in Western Australia. He assisted in finding accommodation, English language courses and friendship networks. He and Leila played host to many of these overseas students.

Until 1963 many of the children at Sister Kate's were placed there under the provisions of the infamous *Aborigines Act* 1905 (WA), which gave the Chief Protector or Commissioner of Native Affairs the power to remove Aboriginal children without a court order.[23] By the time Wilson had oversight of the Sister Kate's management committee, the *Native Welfare Act* 1963 (WA) had replaced the 1905 *Aborigines Act*,[24] but in spite of this change, and an increasing focus on education, Aboriginal children were still being separated from their families at a far greater rate than for non-Aboriginal children, with many of those separated still heading to missions and institutions such as Sister Kate's.

As a senior officer in the Crown Law Department in 1963, Wilson might be expected to have been aware of the parliamentary debates and legislative changes, and hence to some degree be familiar with the history of the separation of Aboriginal children from their families. Moreover, during this period many citizens, including some affiliated with the church, expressed their concerns about the separation policy in the newspaper and at public meetings.

But it would seem that Wilson never made the connections. He always maintained that until he became involved in the 1990s' National Inquiry into the Separation of Aboriginal and Torres Strait Islander Children, he was unaware of a state-run Aboriginal child separation scheme and Sister Kate's involvement in that. He thought Sister Kate's catered for Aboriginal children who needed a home, and he thought Sister Kate's had the best interest of the children at heart; he was unaware of the wider assimilation policy in operation.

When the issue did become controversial in 1997, Wilson was asked why 'if those voices [those of protest over the removal policy] were present when you were involved in the church in the 1960s…you didn't hear them? Or was it simply that it didn't make an impact?' Wilson replied:

> I don't recall hearing them. Nothing that I recall focused my attention on what was happening at Sister Kate's. As I say I wasn't involved in the day-to-day administration of it. The only involvement was through my leadership.[25]

Even when he did become directly involved in Aboriginal issues and causes in the early 1970s through the New Era Aboriginal Fellowship (NEAF), he had said that he didn't recall the organisation 'having any nexus to the history of the separation of [Aboriginal] children'.

This ignorance provides another reason to view Wilson as a man lacking in curiosity about the world outside the 'box' of his profession, or unless it had an impact upon his immediate task at hand. There was a sense of detachment from significant issues of public policy, unless he was professionally involved in some way.

Wilson maintained a busy court schedule as Crown counsel throughout the 1960s, including the year (1965) in which he was moderator of the Presbyterian Church in Western Australia. He was forceful in ensuring that the Crown Law Department retained the best work for itself and did not brief it out to silks, be they from Perth or the eastern states. As early as 1956 Wilson had agitated against briefing work out. In that year, the Crown Law Department briefed Sir Garfield Barwick KC, then the leading silk of the Sydney bar, to appear for the state at the Privy Council. Wilson was scheduled to act as his junior, but he came down with mumps and was unable to go. Wilson was greatly disappointed that he could not appear as Barwick's junior.

Although Wilson was not critical of Barwick's performance for the state of Western Australia, he was determined that the Crown Law Department would do its own advocacy in the High Court and the Privy Council. He was partly motivated by a view that the department was competent to handle its own constitutional and complex cases, and also because he wanted to do as much advocacy as possible himself. Wilson admits that he was forceful in demanding the 'best' and most interesting briefs for himself.

The highlight of his appearances before the judicial committee of the Privy Council was the 1967 *Freightlines* Case.[26] Freightlines had challenged the *Road Maintenance (Contribution) Act* 1958–1965 (NSW), which imposed a road charge on owners of prescribed commercial vehicles on the grounds that it violated section 92 of the Constitution, 'which enacts that trade, commerce, and intercourse among the States, whether by means of internal carriage or ocean navigation, shall be absolutely free'.[27] Because of its constitutional significance, the Commonwealth and the states of Victoria, South Australia, Queensland and Western Australia intervened. These states intervened because their parliaments had enacted similar legislation to the New South Wales statute, and the Commonwealth was interested because it was also bound by section 92 of the Constitution, and therefore was concerned to maintain an interpretation of the trade and commerce power (section 51(i) of the Constitution) that would allow the Commonwealth parliament to enact similar legislation. Lords Reid, Hodson, Pearce, Wilberforce and Pearson affirmed the High Court's decision that the New South Wales statute did not contravene section 92.[28]

Counsel appearing for the various parties were a Who's Who of Australian advocates. The list included two of Wilson's future High Court brothers: William (Bill) Deane QC for Freightlines Construction and Holding Limited, and Anthony (Tony) Mason QC for the Commonwealth of Australia. The counsel representing the states and the Commonwealth spent much time together coordinating their strategies and arguments. Although the lawyers got on well together, Wilson thought the eastern states' counsel were seeking to run the case, and not taking sufficient account of the views from South Australia and Western Australia. Wilson's contribution to the argument before the Privy Council was most significant. He was last to speak for the respondents, and is generally credited as having won the case for the respondents. Later, when they were both sitting on the High Court, Deane remarked to Wilson that he was 'to blame for his [client's] loss'.[29]

In Wilson's words, the respondent's and intervener's counsel had 'hammered the law to death'. Wilson

> decided to take a jury approach—I addressed the Privy Councillors as if they were a jury and didn't bother with the law, just dwelt on the facts and persuasion. I talked about the Nullarbor Plain and the camel trains, and tried to give their Lordships an idea of the distances and the cost of upkeep of the roads and the necessity to charge fees, and so on, that shouldn't be viewed as a constraint on interstate trade and therefore offend the freedom of interstate travel...[30]

The Privy Council's judgement, delivered by Lord Pearce, recognised the need to obtain revenue for the maintenance of highways in order for interstate trade to take place, and held that this did not infringe the Constitution's freedom of interstate trade and commerce guarantee.

Wilson spent three weeks in London preparing and arguing the case. He thoroughly enjoyed his visits to London, usually staying at the Royal Commonwealth Society premises in Northumberland Avenue, five minutes' walk from the Privy Council at Number 9 Downing Street, next door to the British prime minister's residence. At the time, appearing before the Privy Council 'was the epitome of one's achievement in the profession'.[31] Wilson was greatly impressed with the Privy Council's lack of pretension. It was nothing like a courtroom, being a large room with a substantial table, their Lords sitting on one side and counsel on the other side.

Wilson's visits to the Privy Council provided a chance to work and socialise with the cream of Australian barristers. One social event that Wilson vividly remembered involved Hal Wooten, who later became a Federal Court judge and the Royal Commissioner into Aboriginal Deaths in Custody. Wooten was challenged by other barristers in London for the *Freightlines* case, including Mason, to call the waiter and have the wine sent back. Wilson laughed with undeniable joy as he recalled Wooten's imperious signalling of the waiter: 'Waiter, take it away. This wine is sour.' The waiter dutifully complied with Wooten's request and came back a few minutes later with a bottle of wine. He had the last laugh as he returned with the same bottle. By the time they had realised, the waiter had disappeared and no one was willing to recall him again.

After his three-week stay in London, Wilson headed for his alma mater, the University of Pennsylvania Law School. He dropped in to do some research on an article he was preparing with Peter Durack, then a Liberal member of the Legislative Assembly of the Western Australian parliament.

It was an unusual pairing, the public servant and the politician. But the paper was not part of Wilson's official duties; rather, a personal contribution to an important legal debate on which he and Durack held similar views. The article, 'Do We Need a New Constitution for the Commonwealth?', which the authors were preparing for the 1967 Australian Law Council Convention in Melbourne, was subsequently published in the *Australian Law Journal*.[32] Since his law school days at UWA, Wilson had been interested in constitutional law, an interest that was magnified with his increased constitutional work as Crown counsel.

The article was a measured exploration of federalism and the Constitution. The authors, both Western Australians, who because of Perth's geographical distance from Canberra were highly sensitive to the issue of Commonwealth–state relationships and the reach of Commonwealth legislative power, concluded that although there was no need for a new Australian Constitution, there was need for some changes. The authors were advocates of federalism:

> ...there is more to be said positively in favour of federalism...It is a method of guaranteeing a decentralization of authority whilst at the same time providing the conditions of a central government in necessary respects. When one is considering the government of a continent the size of Australia this is a consideration of paramount importance. It is not simply a case of seven governments to govern eleven million people: it is a case of seven Parliaments providing the opportunity for greater political participation, for the airing of local sentiment, for the securing of greater correspondence between public policies and that sentiment, and for the speedy remedy of local abuses...[33]

Across a wide range of specific issues the Wilson–Durack paper essentially argued a states' rights position, even to the extent of arguing for a guarantee to the states by the Commonwealth of a fixed percentage of Commonwealth revenue. They warned that, if this were not forthcoming, the consequences would be lack of state funds to serve the needs of its citizens adequately.[34]

Wilson and Durack also made several suggestions in relation to judicial power, including, *inter alia*, enhancement of 'the stature and significance of the State Supreme Courts', and allowing the Commonwealth parliament to create specialised federal courts.[35] Towards the end of the article, the authors argued for no change to 'the present arrangement in Australia whereby fundamental freedoms derive their authority from custom and extra-Constitutional conventions'.[36] They wrote:

> A statement made in another context by a former Chief Justice of the High Court, Sir John Latham, adequately expresses our view in this regard: 'The remedy for alleged abuse of power or for the use of power to promote what are thought to be improper objects is to be found in the political arena and not in the Courts.'[37]

This is of some interest because in later life, during his term as president of the HREOC, Wilson became a supporter of a 'Bill of Rights'. He came to believe that the best way of protecting individual human rights was through a judicially enforced Bill of Rights, rather than leaving this to politicians and pressures of the political process.

Wilson's role as a Crown prosecutor seems to have been influential in his comments about how a Bill of Rights may negatively impact on law enforcement—the classic debate between the state's law enforcement powers and individuals' civil liberties.

The article was confirmation, if any was needed, that Wilson was a strong legal advocate for states' rights in a federal system. He was concerned with the independence and functioning of states, and their survival. Professionally, he was dedicated to this cause.

When representing the Crown in civil and constitutional cases, Wilson's attitude was the same: he was there to do the best for his client—the state Crown. By the time Michael Murray joined the Crown Law Department in 1964 as an articled clerk, Wilson was doing more civil than criminal work, his criminal work primarily restricted to the higher profile cases and appeals to the CCA of the Supreme Court of Western Australia or the High Court. Murray observed a lawyer in action who was a tenacious and forceful advocate in civil as well as criminal cases. He described Wilson

> as a courageous barrister. The judge who could talk him down and make him give away a point which he believed was...pretty good. He was tenacious and was one of those who clearly took the view that if you got the reaction from the Bench that at first your point was not accepted, then your responsibility was to see if putting the point another way, you might get it accepted, particularly if you were of the view that it was not only arguable, but clearly right.

Murray added that Wilson played it 'hard and gave no quarter and, at the same time, was very fair and played no tricks'. He remarked that Wilson

> was always a firm exponent of the proposition that you were practising in an adversarial system which worked best, and still works best, if the practitioners on both sides had done their homework and bring to the process of presentation in the court room a good level of skills, and so he always had a clear view that it wasn't for you to expose, as a prosecutor or crown counsel, things favourable to the defence, leave that to the defence

> counsel, that was their job. Your job was to ensure that all that could be said fairly for the case of prosecution or the Crown was said.

Wilson was the champion of the Crown's cause. This is reflected in his advice to Murray, the novice lawyer: 'You have to remember when you walk through the door of that courtroom, you are the Crown.' Wilson imparted to Murray that he should never forget that he had an obligation to represent the Crown to the best of his ability. In his advice, Wilson also said to Murray that you should not forget that you portrayed the Crown's case

> in everything you said and did, when you went to the Bar Table, when you went across and had a friendly word to defence counsel while the jury were watching you, all these things were part of the game of advocacy which we played.

Part of the advocacy game was meticulous preparation. Wilson had a clear perception that the fundamental truth of good advocacy depended essentially on good preparation. Every angle had to be covered; Wilson expected nothing less of himself and those who worked for him. Murray recalls Wilson being a hard taskmaster, but one who was always polite and respectful of his juniors. He was always prepared to listen to their point of view and include them in discussions with senior counsel. But he also expected them to provide high-quality legal work. He did not expect, as Murray says, for them to collect information that was going to teach him something he didn't know, but rather 'you were to put work together so as to save him the legwork of doing it for himself'. If he was not happy with the work provided and there was time available, he would request further and better particulars of what one ought to do. If there was insufficient time, Wilson would make it obvious that he was disappointed by the steel in his eyes. But he would never lose his temper.

Although Wilson prepared meticulously and was an excellent advocate, he was still nervous before a trial or appeal, despite his experience. Murray recalls an incident when he was carrying the case 'bag' and briskly walking with Wilson to the Supreme Court for the commencement of a trial. They were near the court, in the Supreme Court Gardens, when Wilson dropped some papers he was holding. As he bent down to collect the papers, Murray noticed Wilson's hands shaking. Murray said to Wilson: 'Well forgive me for saying it but you seem to be nervous. I don't know why you would be because you will wipe the floor with these other characters.' Wilson with papers back in his possession, smiled as he replied: 'I always like to feel on edge. I always think if I come down to court really relaxed, it is probably because I have forgotten something terribly important.'

Peter Panegyres, who joined the Crown Law Department in 1962, also accompanied Wilson to court on a number of occasions. He also observed nervousness and tensions:

> For all his unusual knowledge and ability, intellectual prowess, all of the things that you so admire in Ron it was very surprising that whatever the occasion that he would be going to present something orally, to the court or to a group of people, there would be a tension, you could see a tension build up in him which in no way affected what he was doing or saying but he became tense, physically. You could see him being tense but then the presentation that he would make would always be at the highest key as a consequence and would have an unusual impact. Most people would stumble and mumble and scratch and get themselves in order and lose their audience very quickly as a consequence, but Ron would come on full bore from the start.

To aid his preparation, Wilson would often rehearse his court arguments while on his early morning jogs. By the time Wilson turned forty-two years of age, in the mid 1960s, he had became a regular jogger. When appearing before the High Court in Sydney, Wilson would run around the oval near where he was staying at the Travelodge in Rushcutters Bay:

> I used to do seven laps every morning of the oval, quite a big oval, it would have taken me the best part of 20 minutes and I would devote each lap to a different member of the High Court and I would rehearse my argument as I jogged…Roger Jennings was Tasmanian Solicitor-General and he used to stay at the same place but he would stand on the balcony and watch me.

Wilson enjoyed the exercise and found that it provided him with the stamina and fitness to cope better with his workload, which was about to increase substantially.

On 5 December 1968, the state government appointed Wilson to the position of commissioner of the Supreme Court. This was in response to a warning from Chief Justice Wolff that the Supreme Court had a backlog of cases waiting to be heard. As a commissioner, Wilson had the powers of a Supreme Court judge except concerning divorce matters. He retained his position as Crown counsel, but received a judge's salary of $13,600 per annum—$1930 more than he earned as Crown counsel.

The appointment placed him in the curious position of at times sitting in effect as a fellow judge of the Supreme Court justices, whilst at others appearing before them as counsel. However it would be short lived, and contribute little to the court's backlog.

In early 1969, Wilson and Francis Burt were the subject of a cabinet minute advocating their appointments as justices of the Supreme Court of WA. They were seen as the pinnacle of the Western Australian legal profession—the state's two best advocates. Burt accepted the nomination, and he went on to serve as Chief Justice of the Supreme Court. He is widely regarded in the Western Australian legal profession as one of, if not the best Chief Justice of the state's highest court.

This could have been a turning point in Wilson's professional life. If he had followed the same path as his contemporary and frequent courtroom adversary Burt, what would history record of Wilson as a Supreme Court justice? Would it have been as glowing as Burt; would he have also been a Chief Justice, maybe in place of Burt?

However, Wilson made a most unusual choice. At the time it is likely that few lawyers would have declined the opportunity of an appointment to the Supreme Court, especially among the salaried ranks of the Crown Law Department. But in Wilson's eyes there was a more appealing alternative. The position of solicitor-general of Western Australia had become vacant with the appointment of Sydney Good as the inaugural chairman of the Motor Vehicle Tribunal, which was charged with relieving the Supreme Court of a number of motor vehicle accident cases.

Good was not an advocate like Wilson. He had been responsible for administering a department that had increased from four to forty staff during his twenty-three-year tenure, for providing advice to government departments, and settling legal documents for the government in relation to the development of the booming north-west of Western Australia.

The government was proposing a restructuring to make the position of solicitor-general a statutory office, as was already the case at the federal level and in the state of Victoria, and in contemplation in New South Wales and

South Australia. The new solicitor-general would retain the status as the state's second law officer after the attorney-general, but would be relieved of administrative duties, which would pass to the Crown solicitor, allowing him to concentrate on advocacy work and law reform.

Wilson said to the state government: 'Look, if you'd rather have me as Solicitor-General then I don't mind surrendering the appointment as a Supreme Court Judge.'[38] This appealed to the government, and to Wilson because of his love of advocacy. Wilson remarked:

> It always presents as a challenge in communication skills. The capacity to persuade and the techniques that you learn to employ to further that end and there was always the fun of the contest. Well not necessarily the fun of a contest, but the thrill of a contest that appealed to me.

On 24 April 1969, the member for Nedlands and the minister for industrial development, the Honourable Charles Court, representing the attorney-general, who sat in the Upper House, moved for the second reading of the Solicitor-General Bill 1969 (WA), and proposed:

> that Mr. R. D. Wilson Q.C., will be appointed Solicitor-General under the provisions of the new Act. He is known to members and well regarded by the judiciary of all courts before which he has appeared. His appointment as Solicitor-General will enhance his status before the courts and ensure the State is represented in the best manner.[39]

Court argued that the state would be better served if its cases in the superior courts were argued by someone with the title of solicitor-general. Being independent of the public service, a solicitor-general would enhance the standing of submissions to the 'Privy Council, the High Court, and the Supreme Court'.[40] Court also believed strongly that it was necessary to have the best representation in constitutional matters 'if states' rights are to be protected'.[41]

When debate on the Bill resumed, Ronald Bertram, the Labor member for Mount Hawthorn, made a point of saying in his opening: 'I am pleased to say I support this Bill. It is quite different from what has become almost customary in a number of cases.'[42] This led to a jocular interjection by Ross Hutchinson, the member for Cottesloe: 'There must be something wrong with it.'[43] Bertram went on to say that the Solicitor-General represents the state and thus it was important to get the best person for the job, whether they came from the Crown Law Department or outside it. In giving his support to the appointment, he said that Wilson's position as commissioner of the Supreme Court attested to his standing in the profession and 'it also indicates his readiness for promotion to the bench'.[44] He added:

> ...it is good to see that Mr Wilson has been appointed to this office, as I am aware of the tremendous skill and energy he possesses. I understand he has come up from the lower rungs of the Crown Law Department; that he served in the last war; that after he returned he studied; and that from then on he has gone from strength to strength. It is wonderful to see the success he has achieved. I am sure that I speak for every member on this side of the House when I extend to him congratulations on his appointment.[45]

On 21 May 1969, Wilson was appointed as the inaugural solicitor-general under the *Solicitor-General Act* 1969 (WA) rather than the *Public Service Act* 1904 (WA). For Wilson, the position was perfect. He would continue the advocacy role he had as Crown counsel, but now he would have even greater freedom to determine what briefs he would accept.

Meanwhile the busy Wilson household, with its four children ranging in age from eighteen-year-old Bruce to eight-year-old Robyn, was to become busier.

Wilson's job, as Crown counsel and now solicitor-general, frequently took him away from home, sometimes only for a day or two, but it could be a week or more if he were appearing in the High Court in Sydney, or months, if he were appearing in the Privy Council in London. Wilson was away frequently enough for the family doctor to remark when Leila visited him with a sick child: 'Where is he this time?'

Leila took on the bulk of the parental responsibilities. She served in the school canteen, went to most of the children's sporting events, and was home for them when they arrived back from school. However, when home Wilson did significantly contribute to domestic and family duties. He would sometimes wash the dinner dishes or supervise the children washing them, and on weekends did the washing and attended the children sporting activities. Sometimes he made the children's school lunches. Robyn recalled that if her dad made the lunches they were always Vegemite based—Vegemite and celery,

Vegemite and lettuce or Vegemite and cheese. She much preferred her mum making the school sandwiches—there was a greater chance of variety.[46]

When in Perth, he nearly always arrived home for the family dinner at just after 6 p.m. Wilson saw this as a benefit of working in the public service. Unlike many of his colleagues in private practice, he could regularly get away from the office before 6 p.m. After dinner, Wilson would often retire to his study to continue working, or attend a church or professional meeting. But if he were home in the evening working, he remained approachable to the children and would read bedtime stories to them.

Leila acknowledges that Wilson was a devoted father and a supporting husband. It was just that his duties and roles within the church and as a legal officer took precedence over wife and family. The children saw Wilson as a devoted father, but they acknowledge that it was Mum who was always there when they needed her. However, the children all agreed that when their dad was home he was there for the family. He did not engage in personal recreational pursuits like golf, tennis or sailing—favoured pastimes of many lawyers.

When home on the weekend, Wilson would drive the girls to netball games and the boys to hockey matches. That would usually be on Saturday mornings. On Saturday afternoons, the family would often go on picnics to Kalamunda and Mundaring in the Perth hills. On Sunday, the whole family would attend church and come home to the traditional Sunday roast. But more often than not, the Sunday roast would be shared with people from the church, sometimes up to twelve extra mouths.

After the visitors had left, Wilson would often drive the children to the North Mole down at the end of Fremantle Port harbour. If Leila also went along for the drive, the children would most likely be treated to an ice cream at the Leighton Beach Kiosk. There was less chance of this if Leila were absent. Wilson and the whole family loved the ocean. During summer, most Saturday mornings would see them go to Cottesloe Beach early, before the midsummer Perth sun made conditions uncomfortable.

The beach was also an attraction for the one or two weeks' annual holiday. Often they would travel to the south-west port town of Bunbury. When the children were young, the Wilsons would stay at the Hathaway Lodge, as it catered for small children. On another occasion they stayed at a cottage at Walpole, which faces the more treacherous Southern Ocean. They had a few holidays where they had a government car pulling a caravan to some destination away from Perth. Wilson did most of the driving, but Leila shared the duties. Once when returning from a holiday in the south-west, the Wilson car was pulled over by a police officer for speeding. Leila was driving, one of the children was in the front passenger seat and Wilson was in the back with the other children. The police officer poked his head inside the open front driver's window and said, 'I will let you off this time as I can see you have a carload of children in the back.' Wilson's diminutive stature had been advantageous on that occasion.

As the children moved into the teenage years, family holidays with all the children become more infrequent. Some years there would only be a couple of the children. In other years, it would only be Wilson and Leila. Wilson loved holidaying down at the Stirling Ranges and hiking the Porongurups. He loved the closeness to nature and the magnificence of the expansive vista and the roaring wind from the Southern Ocean. He appreciated 'the beauty of God's nature'.

Wilson and Leila also went on cruises to places such as Singapore and Malaysia. Wilson encouraged Leila to go on other holidays when he was busy with work and couldn't spare time off. On some of these occasions she went on cruises with her daughter Robyn or a relative.

Wilson was very helpful to Leila with domestic chores, but he was not much of a handyman. Although not a keen gardener, he did dabble at it, and took some pride in the grooming of the roses at the Nedlands family home. One Saturday when digging out the weeds in the garden, Wilson discovered a number of rotten milk cartons. He had no explanation for this, nor did Leila.

Sometime after Wilson's discovery of the milk cartons, Leila received a knock on the door from the local milkman, who had done a stakeout because so many people were complaining that their milk was going missing. He had followed the family dog, a kelpie labrador named Sally, back to the Wilson home, and watched her go round the back and bury the milk cartons. The milkman could see the funny side of it, but Leila had to hand over a cheque to pay for the milk delivered to the neighbours but not consumed by them.[47]

Family life with four active children brought many joys for the very busy Wilson. And, only three months after being appointed solicitor-general, Wilson's large and lively family was to expand yet again. Leila and he adopted a three-week-old baby. Ian was born on 25 June 1969. He was being held at the Ngala Mothercraft Centre, which was managed by Beryl Grant, a good friend of the Wilsons. Grant was later to become moderator of the

Uniting Church of Western Australia. Leila was to spend twenty-four years on the management board of Ngala. Although the name Ngala suggested an Aboriginal connection, the centre catered for mothers and babies of any racial or ethnic background. Ian was not of Aboriginal heritage, even though an employee of the Western Australian Equal Opportunity Commission in the 1990s, who had never met Ian, assumed, for no apparent reason, that the Wilsons had an adopted Aboriginal child.

The initial catalyst for the adoption of Ian was Robyn. She had a hankering for a younger sibling. She recalls: 'I guess I just wanted a doll that was alive and Mum had always had a hankering herself.'

Ngala had around 400 children available for adoption. Leila believed that this was the consequences of the promiscuous 1960s. Grant would say to her friends: 'If all my friends would take one of my babies I would have no problems.' Because of the overabundance of available children, Ngala increased the maximum age for parents wanting to adopt, thus making the Wilsons eligible. Their friend's plea confirmed Leila and Wilson's decision to seek adoption.

In order to be eligible for adoptions, the prospective parents had to be separately interviewed by an officer from the Child Welfare Department. During her interview, which went for nearly two hours, the officer asked Leila how many homes she had lived in. Because her father had travelled to many parts of Australia with his work, she had lived in around twenty-five houses, including the four (one in Philadelphia) since being married. The officer replied: 'Why did you live in so many houses?'

Leila nearly lost her temper and was tempted to say: 'Because we didn't pay the rent.' But she didn't, and explained the travel situation with her father. At the end of the interview the officer said: 'You nearly lost your temper, didn't you?'

'Yes I did,' Leila responded. The officer then asked why. Leila said that she was married to the solicitor-general and had four normal children and thus could not see the need to answer such questions. The officer remarked: 'It told me one thing. You really want this child.' The officer added: 'You'd be surprised at the number of people who, at that stage of an interview will get up and walk out. The fact that you remained tells me a lot.'

That night at home, Leila said to Wilson, who was to be interviewed the following day, 'Don't you dare blow it.' He was interviewed for only half an hour. Ian was adopted on 26 July 1969.

8

The Solicitor-General

I was thrilled to become the Solicitor-General. I thought it was a great job to be the principal advocate for the Crown and to also be influential in advising the government on developments in legal matters.[1]

Wilson's rise through the ranks of the Western Australian Crown Law Department from being a messenger boy at the Geraldton courthouse in the 1930s was complete. He now occupied the most senior nonjudicial position in the state.

His appointment as solicitor-general came at a time when Western Australia was undergoing rapid population and economic growth fuelled by the Pilbara iron ore boom, and on the eve of a decade of great change for the state and the nation.

His first major task, though, was not as an advocate, but in the field of court reforms. The state's growth had placed an increasing burden on the two-tier judicial system of Western Australia—the Supreme Court and Local Court (which also included a Court of Petty Sessions). The Supreme Court, with only six judges, could not handle the volume of work before it. With the need to give priority to criminal cases—'liberty over property'—the civil list backlog was increasing, with little prospect of it being reduced. It was this situation that had driven Chief Justice Wolff to write to the government about the backlog of cases, and which had prompted the appointment of Wilson in December 1968 to the position of commissioner of the Supreme Court.

A year earlier, Perth barrister William Pidgeon (later a judge of the District Court and Supreme Court) placed the idea of a County Court before the Law Society. This led to a working party on the issue, and after discussions, the Law Society's council endorsed the idea of an intermediate court between the Supreme Court and Local Court. After comments from council member Francis Burt, it was considered that it may be problematic to exclude the Perth metropolitan region from the intermediate court's jurisdiction, and thus the court should have jurisdiction over the whole state.[2]

The government was receptive to the idea and, in July 1969, not long after his promotion to the solicitor-general's position, Wilson advised the Law Society that the government would introduce legislation in parliament setting up a District Court.[3] Wilson closely consulted with the profession on the structure of the court, as there were varying views on the need for it and its proposed form.

The District Court, which today has its own backlog problems, was originally to have three judges, and hear civil matters involving amounts greater than $200 and less than $6000, and criminal cases in which the maximum penalty was no more than fourteen years imprisonment. The court could remit cases to the Supreme Court and vice versa. By mid March 1970, the first four judges of the District Court had been appointed. Wilson's predecessor as solicitor-general, Sydney Good, became chair of the District Court, in addition to chairing the Third Party Claims Tribunal. The other judges appointed were Des Heenan (deputy chairman), William Pidgeon and Robert Jones (a law school colleague of Wilson).

The early 1970s were a time of change in Australia. The Labor Party under Gough Whitlam, campaigning with the slogan of 'It's Time', won the federal election on 2 December 1972, bringing an end to twenty-three years of unbroken conservative parliamentary and executive power in Canberra.

One of Whitlam's first acts as prime minister was to bring the Australian troops home from Vietnam. The late 1960s and early 1970s had seen unparalleled marches in the streets as part of the anti-Vietnam War moratorium. One of the protesters in Perth was Bruce Wilson. But in deference to his father's public service profile, whenever Bruce participated in a public protest he attempted to walk in the second row or further back, so as to reduce the chances of clashing with the police and embarrassing his father. However, on one occasion he was almost arrested for civil disobedience. His parents were not impressed, but their admonishment to him was mild.

Bruce engaged in the anti-war marches while a student at UWA, which he had entered in 1968. He didn't really know what he wanted to study. At his father's suggestion he enrolled to do law, which at the time involved doing two law units and two arts units in the first year. Law was not to Bruce's liking. The following year, he transferred to do an arts degree, taking politics, anthropology, psychology and economics.

It was during his time at university that Bruce developed a keen interest in social and political activism, forming a close friendship with a Jesuit priest, John Hart, who was one of the anti-war moratorium leaders in Western Australia. On one of his summer breaks, John took Bruce and a few other students to India, where they worked with Mother Teresa and slept on the floor of one of her Calcutta orphanages. This experience heightened Bruce's interest in social justice, and he moved further to the left on the political spectrum.

During most of his period at university Bruce resided at St Columba College, a Presbyterian residential college for UWA students. But on most Sundays, he would return home for the weekly family roast, accompanied by anything up to ten university friends. His parents warmly welcomed Bruce's friends. His father revelled in the chance to engage in discussion with the university students on a wide range of subjects. As in court, he enjoyed the repartee of the discussion. He tried to stay away from giving personal opinions, but Bruce thought he was conservative and a conservative voter. In later life, when asked about his political voting patterns, Wilson said he had always been a Labor voter, although he had admiration for Sir Robert Menzies, who had for twenty-three years been Australia's prime minister. He admired Menzies' oratorical eloquence and political strength.

During the Vietnam War, Wilson was not opposed to Australia's involvement. He had no firm position on it. He didn't give it too much thought. Rather, he accepted the fact Australia was involved and left it at that. Again, Wilson displayed a lack of interest or engagement in major public policy issues.

Whitlam's government, though it lasted just short of three years, was a reformist government. As prime minister, Whitlam attempted to instigate a legislative program that would be constitutionally valid and adhere to what he called the 'doctrine of positive equality'.[4] By this, Whitlam meant greater equality of services provided by government, with the national government playing a vital role in this. Whitlam and his ministers' reform agenda implemented changes in many areas. Two areas that were to touch on Wilson's interests and professional responsibilities were Aboriginal affairs and family law.

During the 1960s, Wilson attended many church meetings where various committees and subcommittees discussed issues relating to Aborigines. Wilson often found these meetings frustrating—there seemed to be a lot of talk but little action. More disturbingly: where were the Aborigines? They talked about Aborigines, but there were none at the church meetings. Wilson felt the meetings lacked direction, and there was no engagement with the people they were purportedly seeking to help.

This was to change when Wilson attended a presentation by H. C. 'Nugget' Coombs, a Western Australian and governor of the Reserve Bank. Coombs was also an advocate for Aborigines and their rights. Wilson joined other interested people as Coombs delivered a speech on Aboriginal affairs at the 1969 Summer School at UWA. Coombs talked passionately about the need for a new era in Aboriginal affairs, a need to engage Aborigines and the need to increase the government and community awareness of the problems facing Aborigines and their communities. The talk inspired Wilson and others at the presentation. This led to the establishment of the New Era Aboriginal Fellowship (NEAF). Wilson did not become an officebearer of the organisation, but he attended many of the meetings and was particularly delighted to mix and discuss issues with Aboriginal people. This provided a welcome change from the church meetings of the 1950s and 1960s.

NEAF provided a forum for the development of Aboriginal leadership, as Wilson described it in a 1972 letter to Fred Chaney, seeking a donation:

> We of the New Era Aboriginal Fellowship are a non-political non-sectarian group of Australians—Aborigines and others—who are trying to help Aborigines to help themselves. We believe that Government efforts in this field, however great, can never be a complete substitute for the personal concern and involvement in practical tasks of voluntary groups such as NEAF.[5]

NEAF was involved in many and varied activities. It assisted Aboriginal couples find accommodation, purchased a mobile health clinic to visit Aborigines in the rural areas, provided city hostel accommodation for rural

Aboriginal girls, and sought to increase Aboriginal participation in sporting activities. NEAF also referred Aborigines in need of legal assistance to willing lawyers.

Initially the NEAF office was staffed predominantly by non-Aborigines. Within a few years, in accordance with NEAF policy, the organisation's headquarters in Wellington Street, East Perth was predominantly staffed by Aborigines.

Lack of free time was one reason why Wilson did not seek to become an officebearer with NEAF. Another reason was his uncertainty whether any such position could at some stage involve a conflict of interest with his role as solicitor-general, especially because Aboriginal issues were often played out in the political arena. As the number one legal adviser for the state, Wilson might be required to give advice to the government that was at odds with NEAF policies, although Wilson recalls no such occasion during his ten years as solicitor-general.

Wilson was particularly interested in the NEAF proposal to establish an Aboriginal Legal Service. Wilson encouraged and supported a group of young lawyers, including Robert French (who became a Federal Court judge in 1986 and was president of the NTTT from 1994 to 1998) and Fred Chaney, as they discussed and later established the Aboriginal Legal Service of Western Australia (ALSWA). Chaney comments that Wilson's presence at meetings and his advice were invaluable to the young lawyers and idealists seeking to establish the legal service.

The ALSWA, which grew out of the Justice subcommittee of NEAF, commenced as a modest operation in 1973. It was heavily dependent on pro bono advice and representation from the WA legal profession. Slowly solicitors were employed in the Perth office along with Aboriginal field officers. It was difficult to service the vast geography of the state. However, the Legal Service achieved a real coup when John Toohey QC left his very successful practice at the Bar to work for the service at their Port Hedland office.

Toohey, who later became a High Court colleague of Wilson's, had a rapid rise in the legal profession in Western Australia. He was only thirty-one when he made his first appearance in the High Court as leading counsel. He became a QC at aged thirty-nine, a year younger than Wilson did. He, like Wilson, had a strong sense of public duty. This is what led him to leave his lucrative bar practice to establish the ALSWA office in Port Hedland in 1974. From then on he represented many Aboriginal plaintiffs and defendants, appeared as senior counsel in a Royal Commission dealing with police relations with Aborigines, and in 1977 was appointed the first Aboriginal land commissioner for the Northern Territory (with concurrent appointments to the Federal Court and Supreme Court of Northern Territory judiciaries). Then in 1987, he was appointed to the High Court.[6]

Whitlam had come to office intent on implementing change to the political and social policy framework of Australia. One of his more reformist ministers was the controversial New South Wales Senator, Lionel Murphy, the Commonwealth attorney-general and minister for customs and excise. During Murphy's time as attorney-general he secured the passage of a number of pieces of legislation such as the *Law Reform Commission Act* 1973 (Cwlth) and the *Trade Practices Act* 1974 (Cwlth). He also introduced the Family Law Bill, which sought to radically change the way family law was administered in Australia.

The Family Law Bill sought to remove the *Matrimonial Causes Act* 1959 (Cwlth) as the statute dealing with divorce and introduce a 'no-fault' divorce system. This reflected the progressive political agenda of the Whitlam government, and was more in line with contemporary attitudes of society. Many, including the supporters of the new Bill, felt that the 'fault in marriage' principle often discriminated against wives. For example, in a 1956 case, the High Court heard that a man hit his wife several times across the face while driving. He told her she deserved to die, but wasn't worth hanging for. The High Court held that the husband's actions did not amount to cruelty, and were not grounds for divorce.[7] Under Murphy's proposals, evidence of guilt by at least one party to the marriage was to be replaced by the irretrievable breakdown of the marriage, which could be evidenced by twelve months' separation of the parties to the marriage. The Bill also recognised the noneconomic contribution made by wives to marriages and, therefore, made it easier for the wife to obtain a share of the sale of the family home. The Bill proposed a specialist Family Court to deal with divorce issues.

The Bill became the *Family Law Act* 1975 (Cwlth), receiving assent on the 12 June 1975. This was after Murphy had been sworn in as a justice of the High Court on 14 February 1975. The legislation sought to establish one Family Court of Australia, but it did provide the opportunity for each state to establish its own family court exercising Commonwealth and state jurisdictions.

Wilson seized the opportunity. Displaying his parochial pride and mindful of encroachment of Commonwealth power into the state's judiciary system, he championed the establishment of a Western Australian Family Court. Wilson recalled:

> I think my incentive at the time was pride in Western Australia and the conviction that it was as good or better than any other State and it could run a State court better than being dependent on the Commonwealth.

Wilson had a receptive ear in the Western Australian attorney-general, Ian Medcalf QC, and the equally proud Western Australian, premier Sir Charles Court. Court, like Wilson, was a strong supporter of states' rights, and resisted Commonwealth attempts to enter areas that traditionally had been the province of the states. Court also was wary of giving increased power to Canberra, which he thought rarely gave Western Australia the respect it deserved.

There was also a jurisdictional reason to support Wilson and the state government's position. Under the Constitution, the Commonwealth parliament could deal with matters of marriage (section 51(xxi)) and divorce and matrimonial causes (section 51 (xxii)), which included parental rights and the custody and guardianship of children of a marriage. But the Commonwealth parliament had no express constitutional powers to deal with such matters for de facto couples and their offspring. Thus the Family Court of Australia could not deal with such matters, unless they were referred to it by state legislatures. All other state parliaments referred such power to the Commonwealth parliament. Consequently, the Family Court of Western Australia is the only state court exercising state jurisdiction under the *Family Court Act* 1977 (WA) and federal jurisdiction under the *Family Law Act* 1975 (Cwlth).

Wilson's strong legal advocacy was paramount in underpinning the political process of establishing the Western Australian Family Court. The opposition Labor Party queried the need for Western Australia to go it alone, but Wilson thought it showed the maturity of the legal system and judiciary in his home state. The inaugural chair of the Western Australian Family Court, Justice Alan Barblett, acknowledged Wilson's role at a special sitting to mark the opening of the court on 1 June 1976. He said:

> A special thanks must be paid to you, Mr Solicitor. What now seems a long time ago, when the Government first decided on a State Family Court, there were no officers of the court, there were no judges; there was only the

> Solicitor-General and if anyone could be designated the father of this court it is you.[8]

Wilson considered this one of his greatest achievements as solicitor-general, and pointed to subsequent jurisdictional problems between the Family Court of Australia and courts in other states, which did not arise in Western Australia, as vindication of his strong advocacy for a separate state Family Court.

During this period, the Whitlam government's extensive program of legislative reforms led to many constitutional challenges from the states. This gave Wilson more opportunities to enhance his growing reputation among the High Court justices as an advocate on constitutional matters. Moreover, when more than one state challenged the Commonwealth government in the High Court, Wilson was the person to whom other solicitors-general turned to lead the argument or to develop strategies.

Sir Daryl Dawson, who before joining Wilson on the High Court had been solicitor-general of Victoria from 1974 to 1982, has said: 'When I became Solicitor-General of Victoria in 1974, Ron was at the height of his powers.' It was a time when Wilson was happiest in a professional sense. He loved advocacy and constitutional law, and he loved appearing before the High Court.

Wilson also passionately believed in what he was arguing. Sir William Deane, who during part of the mid 1970s was on a retainer to appear for New South Wales in many of their constitutional cases before the High Court, commented:

> 'Ron the person' and 'Ron the advocate' were normally identical and I think to a large extent that was Ron in constitutional matters as distinct from other matters. [He] really strongly believed in the State case in just about all of those disputes involving the limits of Commonwealth and State powers whereas there were at least a few of those appearing for the States in that series of litigation arising out of the activities of the Whitlam government who weren't nearly as much convinced about the limits of power from the State point of view as they had been as advocates.

Presumably Deane was referring to himself here, as many of his High Court opinions favoured the expansion of Commonwealth legislative power.[9]

Wilson did believe in the state cause. He was mindful of the encroachment of the Commonwealth on the powers of the states. His geographic location only strengthened this belief. Western Australia was a long way away from Canberra and the eastern seaboard. Western Australians often felt forgotten by the rest of Australia, and Wilson, like the state government, was keen to preserve the rights of the states and to ensure they were fairly treated by the Federal government. As Deane remarked: 'Wilson was completely committed to the cause.'

The isolation of Western Australia from the 'main' game should not be underestimated. Dawson believes that Wilson's mantle as unofficial leader of the state solicitors-general was all the more remarkable because he came from Western Australia, a state that many in the legal profession on the east coast treated with little respect. But Wilson's advocacy abilities and passion for the 'states' rights cause' made it difficult for him not to be noticed.

He was also charming and likeable. Although naturally a shy and reserved man, Wilson did not find it necessary to search out company in a social gathering; company usually found him. On first meeting Wilson at a conference, Daryl Dawson's wife, Lady Lou Dawson, thought he was 'extraordinary'. Later when talking to her husband she said: 'Here was this man, this man with charm. He had verve for living, a capacity to take in everything that was around him with an electric personality.'

Nevertheless, behind this charm lay a steely determination, a trademark of his days as a prosecutor in the 1950s and early 1960s and now as the solicitor-general before the High Court. His belief in the states being strong in the federation was not just a professional belief that he was obliged to argue and from which he could then walk away. Wilson believed that the constitutionally established federal system was the correct form of government of a country the size of Australia. Even when confronted with aggressive questioning by someone like Chief Justice Barwick, he was not going to be deterred from that commitment or argument.

Barwick, the judge, was well known for seeking to 'persuade' his brethren and the advocates before him that his view of the law was the correct one; he was a brilliant advocate who carried that mindset on to the bench. Wilson believed that Barwick often used his exchanges with counsel as an opportunity to convince his brethren of the virtue of his position. But Wilson never took a backwards step when being questioned aggressively by Barwick or any other judge. He was often advised by others, such as his fellow state solicitors-general, that he would be better served if he backed off from arguing with the bench. But that was not Wilson's way. If he believed in what he was arguing, which he invariably did in constitutional cases for the state of Western Australia, he would continue to press his point. Also, because of his quick mind and erudition, he was ready to abandon his prepared oral argument and answer the questions put to him by the bench, even if it meant engaging with the bench without notes. Such exchanges could last hours, but Wilson thrived on the competition and argument.

Wilson acknowledged that the High Court, with seven esteemed jurists sitting high above, behind a heavy wood panelled bench, could be intimidating; though not enough to deter him from pressing his arguments to their limits. He did find Justice Frank Kitto, who retired from the bench shortly after Wilson's elevation to the position of solicitor-general, sometimes difficult to argue with.

Kitto was very acerbic, and as Wilson remarked, 'could strike fear in many counsels' breasts'. Even Wilson was affected in his early years of appearing in the High Court. However, as time went on he lost that fear, although he still found Kitto tough to deal with. One of Wilson's most treasured memories came after Kitto's retirement, when he unburdened himself to Wilson. Kitto told Wilson that being on the High Court was very difficult. Deciding cases was an arduous task, as law was complex, especially so when seeking to apply it to some complicated fact scenarios. And being on the High Court, with its status in the legal system, weighed heavy on Kitto's shoulders: the need to make sure he got it right.

Kitto unburdening himself in this way was reflective of his respect for Wilson. Kitto considered Wilson a very fine advocate, this view even finding its way into the Commonwealth Law Reports. Soon after becoming solicitor-general (in 1969) Wilson was off to the High Court to argue the state's position in *Western Australia v Hamersley Iron*.[10] Wilson did not persuade the court to grant a section 74 certificate (under the Constitution) to have the matter of the state's capacity to impose excise duties referred to the Privy Council. However, Justice Kitto spoke in glowing terms of Wilson's submission:

> The Solicitor-General of Western Australia, whose argument was as distinguished by its candid recognition of difficulties as by the strength and clarity of its presentation, sought to show that the case is so exceptional that these considerations should not conclude the matter.[11]

Wilson's forceful style and preparedness to argue, rather than placate the High Court bench, did not turn off the justices or make them dislike him. The opposite was the case, as Kitto was not the only justice who liked Wilson. Deane and Dawson, who appeared in a number of cases with Wilson before the High Court, have both remarked that, although Wilson was forceful and would not let a point go if he believed in it, his charm was appealing to the justices. The fact that he was prepared to abandon his planned submission and, without notes, go on a tangential 'foray' with one or more justices, drew respect and admiration from members of the bench. This was reflected in some of the remarks they made to Wilson, such as: 'When are you coming to join us, Ron?' Sir Harry Gibbs, who later became his colleague, said that Wilson, the High Court advocate, 'was universally liked and respected' by those that he appeared before.

Wilson had his most consistent 'battles' with Chief Justice Barwick. One of the more memorable moments for Wilson was in the *MacRobertson Miller Airline* Case,[12] which concerned the constitutional power of the state parliament to impose a tax on airline tickets. The airline was successful in having the High Court reverse the Western Australian Supreme Court's decision to allow such a duty to be imposed. On his final day arguing the case before the High Court, Wilson went 'toe to toe' with Barwick and some of the other justices from 10.30 a.m. till 4.00 p.m. Wilson could see he wasn't making much headway. At the end of the day he said to the bench: 'Well, Your Honours, there's not much more that I can say. I don't think I'm going to persuade Your Honour, the Chief Justice, on the matters we've discussed.' Barwick replied: 'No, you're certainly not.'[13]

It was inevitable that Wilson and Barwick would have lengthy and forceful exchanges. Barwick, a New South Welshman and former Commonwealth attorney-general, was a centralist. Wilson, a Western Australian, was the federalist, concerned about further diminution of power from the states to the Commonwealth. Despite their gladiatorial exchanges, the two had something in common. Often during the lunch adjournment of a High Court hearing Wilson would go for a walk. On one such occasion, in the early 1970s in a case being heard in Melbourne, Wilson was waiting at an intersection for the lights to change. Suddenly, he heard a familiar voice at his side: 'Come on Wilson, let's go for a walk.' It was Chief Justice Barwick. After that there would be many days when Wilson the advocate and Barwick the judge would walk together during the lunch adjournment. Not that this mellowed Barwick in his aggressive approach to questioning Wilson from the bench. Barwick loved the argument, as did Wilson.

Wilson had his disappointments in arguing before the High Court. Most of the litigation that resulted from the Whitlam agenda was not decided in favour of the states. Indeed, only one piece of legislation during the Whitlam years—the *Petroleum and Mineral Authority Act* 1973 (Cwlth)—was held to be invalid, and that was on the basis of procedural irregularities. But that was just an inevitable part of the litigation process. It did not make Wilson morose or depressed. He strongly believed in and was committed to the state's arguments. A decision going against the state did not take a personal toll on him. There was always another case to argue.

In July 1976 Wilson made what would be his last appearance in the Privy Council, in the matter of *Oteri v The Queen*.[14] The plaintiffs were the brothers, Santo and Gaetano Oteri, naturalised Australians who resided in Fremantle. Santo and his wife owned a boat, the *Providence*, licensed under the *Marine Act* 1948 (WA). They were charged in the District Court of Western Australia with two offences of having stolen crayfish pots and tackle while fishing 'on the high seas approximately 22 miles from the coast of Australia within the jurisdiction of the Admiralty of England'.

The *Oteri* charge was framed in this way because Western Australia's jurisdiction did not extend beyond the low-water mark—an issue that Wilson was trying to address in other forums. But legal convention held that local courts were responsible for administering justice on behalf of the Admiralty if its jurisdiction applied.

The District Court, acting pursuant to section 49 of the *District Court Act* 1969 (WA), reserved for the consideration of the Full Court of the Supreme Court the issue of whether the alleged offence was an offence under Western Australian law, triable in Western Australia, and if so, whether the District Court could deal with the matter, either under its ordinary jurisdiction or Admiralty jurisdiction. After the Supreme Court held that the Oteris could be charged and convicted under Western Australian law and within the Admiralty jurisdiction of the District Court, the Oteri brothers appealed the matter to the judicial committee of the Privy Council.

So in the Western Australian winter of 1976 and in the middle of the English summer, Wilson and his junior, Kevin Parker, travelled to London to appear in the Privy Council—one of the benefits of working for the Crown that Wilson always savoured. Appearing for the Oteri family were F. Robinson QC and K. Allan from the Western Australian bar.

Although the close proximity of their lordships just across the table from Wilson was intimidating, he always enjoyed speaking to the lords, putting his case to these elderly wise men of law. As usual, Wilson went to what he saw as the seminal points to his argument. He conceded that the criminal law of Western Australia did not extend beyond the territorial boundaries of the state, and thus was inapplicable in this case, as the alleged offence occurred twenty-two miles from the coast. Wilson argued that the criminal law of England applied, and that the Oteris were properly charged under the *Theft Act* 1968 (Imp).

Wilson knew that their lordships may have some trouble with understanding how English law would apply to an alleged offence just off the Australian coast. He was right. They raised that concern with him. At that moment Wilson knew that his answer to this query would be the determining factor in which way their lordships went. No vacillating—it was not Wilson's way. His *modus operandi* was to present his argument in line with how he thought a judge would write a decision. He believed that if this were done, it stood a better chance of resonating with the judge and thus persuading the court to his point of view.

Wilson's method worked to perfection in *Oteri*. In a succinct, decisive manner he laid out how the English law applied. He won their lordships over. When Lord Diplock delivered their lordships' judgement on 4 October 1976, Wilson's arguments formed the framework of the judgement—as he had hoped it would.

Lord Diplock stated that at first sight it would seem strange that Australian citizens could find themselves the subject of English criminal law even though they were fishing only a 'few miles' off the coast of Australia in a Western Australian licensed vessel. But, in reflecting the logic and appeal of Wilson's argument in relation to this issue, he wrote:

> In the submission of the Solicitor-General [Wilson], however, the explanation of this apparent oddity is simple. It depends upon four propositions: (1) The *Providence* was a British ship; (2) the criminal law of England extends to all British ships; (3) offences which are committed on British ships are within the criminal jurisdiction of the Admiralty; (4) in Western Australia the district court of Western Australia exercises the criminal jurisdiction of the Admiralty.

> In the opinion of their Lordships, which accords with that expressed by the Full Court [of the Supreme Court of Western Australia], each of these propositions is correct.[15]

The first proposition, as expounded by Wilson, was the most critical. If that was not established, the state of Western Australia's case would have come to an end. Wilson argued that the *Providence* was a British ship, because the *Merchant Shipping Act* 1894 (Imp.), which at the time was still in force in Western Australia, declared that a ship was British if the owners were 'British Subjects', which, subject to the *British Nationality Act* 1948 (UK), included Australian citizens by naturalisation, as were Santo Oteri and his wife, the owners of the *Providence*. From establishing this, the rest of Wilson's propositions followed.

After stating it agreed with Wilson's four propositions, the court's judgement went on for two pages, expounding these four propositions as argued by Wilson. It was as if Wilson had written the judgement for their Lordships.

The *Oteri* case was not the first time Wilson had immersed himself in matters of offshore jurisdiction. Back in 1963, in a very similar case, the Crown had charged a local fisherman, Vince Lombardo, with illegal crayfishing. Wilson's sparring partner in a number of prominent Western Australian cases, Francis 'Red' Burt QC, acted for Lombardo, and he argued that the state had no jurisdiction below the low-water mark, and thus could not charge and convict Lombardo.[16] The court held that the conclusive finding on the issue was a constitutional matter, which had to be referred to the High Court.

When the *Lombardo* case went to the High Court, the other states were interested. Barwick, a known centralist, had just been appointed chief justice, and the other solicitors-general were fearful that he might persuade his High Court colleagues that, below the low-water mark, sovereignty belonged to the Commonwealth. This was weighing heavily on their minds, and they convinced Wilson to have the case withdrawn from the High Court list.

The Whitlam government sought to end the uncertainty when it passed the *Seas and Submerged Lands Act* 1973 (Cwlth), asserting the Commonwealth's sovereign control over the seabed off the coast of Australia from the low-water mark to the outer limits of the continental shelf. The New South Wales government challenged the legislation in the High Court, and was joined by Western Australia. The states had no problems with Commonwealth sovereignty beyond the three-mile limit from the low-water mark, but the states claimed that state parliaments had jurisdiction within the three-mile limit.

Twelve years on, Wilson got the chance to argue before the High Court the case that he had been dissuaded from pursuing in 1963. But he was unsuccessful; the *Seas and Submerged Lands* case[17] was another victory for the Whitlam government in its series of constitutional battles with the states.

Wilson later said of his 1963 backdown:

> I think it was the biggest mistake of my professional career because if I'd taken the argument then and argued it I would have had a majority of the court, which when we did it in 1975 [in the *Seas and Submerged Lands* case] we lost on a 5–2 majority.[18]

The tenacious states' rights advocate did not let the 1975 *Seas and Submerged Lands* decision remain the final position on this matter. At the end of that year the political landscape changed with the defeat of the Whitlam government, and as solicitor-general, Wilson now had a role in policy as well as advocacy. Taking his initiative from 1950s political settlements in the US between its federal and state governments, Wilson proposed a similar scheme for the Australian states to seek a negotiated agreement with the Commonwealth. His plan was to persuade the Commonwealth to 'return' jurisdiction of the seas and submerged land within the three-mile limit to the states.

Ian Medcalf, Western Australia's Attorney-General, liked the idea, as did the attorneys-general in the other states. Wilson had the issue placed on the agenda of the standing committee of state and Commonwealth attorneys-general. This also involved their legal advisers, including the solicitors-general, and thus the standing committee of solicitors-general.

As the initiator, and the most experienced solicitor-general, Wilson led the negotiations for the states. His Commonwealth counterpart was the equally experienced Maurice Byers QC. Wilson had great professional and personal respect for Byers. They frequently opposed each other in High Court constitutional cases.

Wilson's research officer, Mary Ann Yeats (Western Australian District Court judge since 1993), was present in Adelaide in March 1978 when all the attorneys-general and their solicitors-general gathered there. She was left in no doubt about Wilson's influential role in having the states and

Commonwealth agree that the states should have jurisdiction out to the three-mile territorial seas.

Yeats enjoyed watching how he took his ideas, met opposition, gathered strength and made things happen, knowing when to push a point and when not to. She recalls:

> He was the one who made the agreement happen. He was excellent and understanding, with the Solicitors-General, some brilliant minds at work, such as Maurice Byers QC, Daryl Dawson QC from Victoria and Brian Cox QC from South Australia. It took a lot of work and Sir Ronald was so influential in putting the whole thing together.

Wilson rightly believed that he was primarily responsible for the agreement happening, but as always in such matters, the negotiations were detailed and protracted, and by the time they were formally concluded in 1979, Wilson had left his position as the Western Australian solicitor-general.

In September 1976, not long after his return from arguing the *Oteri* case successfully before the Privy Council, Wilson's secretary informed him that Robert Ellicott QC, the Commonwealth attorney-general, was on the phone. A cousin of Barwick's and a former Commonwealth solicitor-general, Ellicott became attorney-general in the first term of the Fraser government in 1975. He had first met Wilson while attending a church service at Wilson's local Nedlands Presbyterian church in the mid 1950s while visiting a friend in Perth.

They met again in unusual circumstances in 1966. Ellicott, his wife and two of his children were holidaying. They were on a passenger liner heading across the rough ocean seas off the Great Australian Bight coastline on the way to Singapore, when Ellicott's wife Colleen fell sick. Colleen was still feeling sick when the ship berthed at Fremantle. They were not sure if she was up to spending more days on board as the ship made its way to Singapore. Ellicott telephoned Wilson to seek recommendations on accommodation in Perth. Without hesitation, Wilson and Leila invited the Ellicotts to their home to stay as long as they wanted. Ellicott still remembers with fondness the generosity that the Wilsons offered him and his family in their time of need.

Wilson's and Ellicott's paths crossed many times, especially after Ellicott became Commonwealth solicitor-general in 1969. Sometimes that would be at law conventions, meetings of the Commonwealth and state solicitors-general and in the High Court—often on opposite sides of a constitutional argument. Ellicott viewed a 'very careful and effective advocate' in action. Like many of his state colleagues, Ellicott considered Wilson the leading state solicitor-general in constitutional matters before the High Court during the 1970s.

On 12 September, the longest serving justice of the High Court, eighty-six-year-old Justice Edward McTiernan, had retired from the High Court, having been appointed on 20 December 1930. McTiernan's insistence on remaining on the bench, despite his increased fragility and apparent feebleness, was at least one of the motivating factors for the bipartisan support for the successful 1977 constitutional amendment imposing a statutory retirement age of seventy years for federal court judges.

Ellicott had Wilson in mind as a replacement for McTiernan. Before the *High Court of Australia Act* 1979 (Cwlth), the Commonwealth government was not required to engage in consultation with the state attorneys-general on possible appointees to the High Court bench, and Ellicott did not consult the Western Australian government in relation to his intention of offering the vacant High Court position to Wilson.

Wilson took the call from Ellicott. After the usual friendly greetings, Ellicott said: 'I am coming to Perth next week.' Wilson was delighted with this. He enjoyed meeting up with Ellicott, particularly on his home turf. Wilson asked: 'Oh, what are you coming to Perth for?'

Ellicott replied: 'To invite you to join the High Court.' He added that he needed a decision within twenty-four hours, although he gave no reason for the short response period. The phone conversation ended. Wilson had a major career decision to contemplate.

He had never coveted a High Court appointment. He was very happy in his current position, a position that gave him high-quality legal work and, more importantly, the chance to engage in advocacy. That was the professional consideration. There was also a personal consideration. He was concerned with how his long absences in the east sitting on the High Court would affect seven-year-old Ian.

Wilson went to see his attorney-general, Ian Medcalf, and told him about the offer. Medcalf was delighted. At last a Western Australian on the High Court; it was what Sir Charles Court and he had long wanted. Medcalf thought Wilson was highly suited for the position because of his intellect and constitutional law experience.

Medcalf had a very good professional relationship with Wilson. He always received high-quality advice from his solicitor-general, and on a few occasions Wilson even initiated advice when Medcalf had not sought it. But this never annoyed the attorney-general—he found the advice most helpful from the legally astute Wilson.

Medcalf also liked Wilson as a person; he was not pompous or boastful. Although Wilson did have a quick wit and sense of humour that many found charming, the attorney-general found him to be a serious person and very private. He didn't talk to Medcalf about his private life, and gave no indication of his political persuasion, although the attorney-general was confident that Wilson believed in the federal structure and the rights of the states in that system.

Although Medcalf was delighted, he did not urge Wilson to accept the offer. He just listened as the normally very private Wilson unburdened his personal concerns about what this would mean to his family: 'Minister, this is all too sudden. I can't decide by tomorrow.'

He told Medcalf about his concern over Ian, and that he was also worried that Leila would have the extra burden of being both mother and father to Ian while he was away for High Court sittings.

Wilson telephoned Ellicott the next day to decline the invitation. He expressed his concerns about the effect on his family, particularly on young Ian. This time he had placed the family ahead of his job. But he had no great desire to leave his solicitor-general's office to join the High Court. Also, privately, he was annoyed that Ellicott demanded an answer so quickly. Following Wilson's rejection of the invitation, the Fraser government appointed Melbourne QC Keith Aickin to replace McTiernan on the High Court bench.

Both Ellicott and Medcalf view Wilson's rejection of the initial offer to join the High Court in 1976 as indicating Wilson's lack of ambition. Ellicott says:

> He had family concerns. I think it was his son, not a question of any problem with his son, it was a question to be closer to him, he was young and perhaps this was an indication of Ron's personality. Not many people would decline an appointment to the High Court on these grounds. They would think they could cope with the situation and that their son would adjust to it and would be none the worst because of it. But that wasn't Ron's attitude and that is an illustration of what he was really like...always trying to do the right thing.

Wilson had now turned down the two most prestigious appointments open to a Western Australian lawyer, the Supreme Court of his home state, and the High Court of his country.

Wilson's commitment to the Presbyterian Church remained as strong as ever. He remained a commissioner of the church, and was often called on for his legal expertise. He sat on many church committees, and he was the convener of the Home Mission. He also was involved with the Presbyterian-managed St Columba College, a residential college for students attending UWA. He was a founding member of the college, and on the board of management.

It was through his involvement with St Columba College that he formed a lifelong friendship with Reverend Dave Robinson, who was to 'minister' at the weddings of Bruce, Helen and Geoff. Robinson, who had a theological degree from the Presbyterian-established Princeton University, came to Perth from Melbourne to preside over St Columba College. At the time of leaving Melbourne he was the Secretary of the Victoria Council of Churches.

Robinson found Wilson very easy to get along with, someone who was open to ideas. He also remembers Wilson's many visits and mingling with the students at the college. He observed a man at total ease with young people and who was stimulated by their energy and ideas.

Robinson also found a man, in Wilson, who was notoriously frugal in relation to personal expenditure. His wardrobe remained static and limited over time, and the thought of spending money on 'luxuries', such as a new car, was contrary to his philosophy of 'living simply so others can simply live'. He was conscious of not engaging in wasteful expenditure or materialism. This went as far as using the same teabag for a number of cups of tea, even when offering a 'cuppa' to guests to the family home.

Wilson was generous to those asking for help or needing help. Over the years he provided significant financial assistance to his children, particularly Ian, who for many years lived without permanent employment. He also helped many others when they were in need, such as his friend and former Uniting Church moderator, Beryl Grant, to whom he, along with others, provided financial assistance so that she could travel to the United Kingdom. And he provided small sums to many people who wrote to him over the years seeking assistance for this project or that cause. As Robinson remarks:

> He is simultaneously the meanest and most generous person I have ever met. If I went to Ron tomorrow and said, 'I need $30,000 for a good cause,' he would write out a cheque. He wouldn't even probably ask me what it was for. But if his wife said, 'Well, look we do need a new fridge,' he would think twice about purchasing one.

Although Robinson always got on well with Wilson, he remembers one particularly tense meeting when they were on opposite sides of the debate over whether the college should have a quota of first-year students. The college had been established with the main purpose of providing accommodation and pastoral care for first-year university students. Robinson was not in favour of a fixed first-year quota, as he valued the presence of students who had been at the university for some time, and thus thought the college should have discretion in selecting the student mix from year to year. At a meeting to discuss the issue, Wilson and Robinson vigorously argued their respective positions. Robinson won the debate. At the end of it, Wilson approached Robinson and said: 'You know you push a pretty hard line actually.'

'Well Ron you push a pretty hard line too,' Robinson replied.

The Wilsons and Robinsons enjoyed many good times together. On one occasion, in 1977, they met up in Switzerland, where Robinson is a frequent visitor as his wife is Swiss. The Robinsons saw firsthand Wilson's zest and energy for life, as he would rise at 4 a.m. and go running around the hills. Wilson had never needed much sleep, which no doubt gave him extra time to work on his various commitments. While in Switzerland, Wilson also attended the World Council of Churches Central Committee meeting.

Robinson enjoys recounting an incident in Switzerland when the police stopped the car Wilson was driving. Leila was in the front passenger seat and the Robinsons were cramped up in the back of the smallest car possible—barely big enough to accommodate Wilson and Leila, let alone other passengers. Wilson was speeding when hailed down by the roadside police. They asked for his papers. Wilson said to them: 'No need to carry papers.' The police informed him that in Switzerland he needed to carry his papers, to which Wilson pleaded ignorance. The police didn't take the matter further. This is somewhat ironical, as Wilson well knew as a prosecutor and a judge that ignorance of the law was no excuse or defence to a criminal offence.

The issue that was exercising a significant amount of Wilson's time and energy as the 1970s progressed was the issue of the union of the Presbyterians,

Methodists and Congregationalists. As a firm ecumenical believer, Wilson was a strong supporter of the concept of bringing the three denominations together in a new Uniting Church. Not everyone was enamoured with the idea. It is probably fair to say that it was in Wilson's own denomination that the issue of becoming part of the Uniting Church faced the most obstacles.

The national Joint Commission of Church Union (JCCU), with representatives from the three denominations, produced its Basic Union document in 1963, although discussion on the union had commenced just after the beginning of the twentieth century. The document, the proposed blueprint for the new church, allowed all three denominations to feel that part of their particular traditions would be carried into the new church.[19] Wilson, a passionate supporter of union, did what he could to make it a reality.

In the early 1970s, all three churches held a ballot, independently voting on whether to continue with the union process. The Presbyterian Church took its first vote for union in 1970. Then there were subsequent votes in 1971 and 1972 to approve progressing with union. One of the implications for the union vote, which was approved at the national level, was that each Presbyterian parish was to decide if it would go with union or not. It was also decided that the church property would be divided up between those who went into union and those who opted out. To decide on the division of property and church assets, three-member negotiation teams for the pro- and non-union sides were established in each state.

In Western Australia, the pro-union negotiation team consisted of Wilson, Des Cousins and Michael Owen. Cousins, who had ministered in Western Australian Presbyterian churches and had a Master of Religious Education from Princeton Theological Seminary, was at the time the general secretary of the Western Australian Presbyterian Church (1972–77). He was also moderator of the Western Australian Church in 1975, and in 1976 was a member of the Interim Board of Ministry, which was established by the JCCU and also the State Joint Planning Committee. Owen also was a moderator of the Presbyterian Church in Western Australia (and later the Uniting Church of Western Australia in 1984). He had been principal of the Presbyterian Theological Hall and the Uniting Theological Hall in Perth. Later he taught theology at Murdoch University, and became an honorary fellow of the University.

Cousins, reflecting on that period of negotiations, acknowledged the role that Wilson played. Wilson's legal expertise was invaluable in dealing with the complicated legalities associated with the division of church property between those parishes going with union and those that were not. He also had a significant role in creating the structure of the new Uniting Church. The establishment of the Uniting Church required an Act of Parliament. Wilson, in his role as solicitor-general, was in an ideal position to assist in the drafting of the legislation: *Uniting Church in Australia Act* 1976 (WA).[20]

Wilson had more to offer than just his legal expertise—his persuasion skills. This was to prove particularly useful in bringing one 'non-union' congregation over to the union side. In a 1994 interview for the Battye Library Oral History Collection, Wilson revealed some details of the negotiations that led to this result. The members of this particular congregation, which he did not name, had voted against union even though they wanted to be part of the union, because they had erroneously believed that their minister was going to stay out of union. In the 1994 interview Wilson said:

> Had he [the minister] made his intentions clear there would have been no question—it would have voted for union, and they were desperate to come into the Uniting Church. So I bargained with the negotiator for the non-union side. It so happened that we were both stranded in Sydney by an airline hostesses' strike and we had to travel home by train. By the time we reached Perth they'd agreed to let the parish enter the Uniting Church provided we gave them $50,000 for it. So that was the deal. It's very unusual, probably improper, but pragmatic. We got the congregation, we've still got it, [laughs] and they've got the $50,000.

It could be argued that such a deal was an improper inducement. Without further details it is difficult to make conclusive pronouncements. Owens and Cousins, Wilson's colleagues on the Presbyterian pro-union negotiation team, both deny any knowledge of such a deal, and both consider that it would have been most improper to offer a financial inducement for a vote for union. On hearing of the revelations, Owens and Cousins have suggested that Wilson may have been referring to the issue of the proper division of property between the continuing Presbyterians and the uniting side, but they insist no payment was involved, particularly as an inducement to vote for the union. The truth and details of the $50,000 deal remain a mystery. Cousins has said in response to the $50,000 deal revelations:

> Ron was always keen to keep things out of court. Being a lawyer he very well knew how costly and protracted disputes could become once they entered the courts. Thus he was always attempting to negotiate settlements and compromises and often made deals and agreements without others knowing. Who is to know whether he did interest someone from his wide circle of connections to come good with the $50,000? We just don't know.[21]

By the time union came around, there remained five Continuing Presbyterian parishes out of thirty-nine in Western Australia, which amounted to around 10 per cent of Presbyterians in the state.[22] To the immense delight of Wilson, most had voted for union, as was the case also with the Methodists and Congregationalists. But the final vote by the Presbyterians in 1976 to join the union was somewhat comical. There had been a mixup in the counting of the votes, which necessitated a recount. To the delight of the pro-union camp, the vote was in favour of union.

With a new identity—the Uniting Church—there was a need to select a moderator of the church in each state. It was the Joint Planning Committee, of which Cousins was a member, who was charged with putting forward a name or names for consideration as the first moderator of the Western Australian Uniting Church. According to Cousins, 'Ron Wilson's name shone out as that person. By that time he had quite a public profile.' He was seen as someone who would garner broad support across all three denominations.

And so it was that Wilson became the inaugural moderator of the Uniting Church of Western Australia. A service to commemorate the inauguration of the synod (the governing body of the church) and induction of Wilson as the moderator was held at the Perth Entertainment Centre on 26 June 1977. It has been described as a 'solemn and joyous occasion'.[23] Wilson remembered it with great emotion and joy.

Between 7000 and 8000 people filled the Entertainment Centre. They came from all over the state, many on buses. Premier Sir Charles Court was in attendance, which pleased Wilson. He viewed this as a public display of support by the premier of his senior legal adviser's involvement with the church. Wilson always appreciated the support from the premier of the day of his extraprofessional activities. It gave him the confidence to rearrange his work commitments if he needed to attend to church matters.

The inauguration ceremony also saw on stage leaders of many of the other churches in the state. It was a tremendous occasion for Wilson, a deeply religious man who had a longheld commitment to ecumenism and the need for different religions to come together—to share their similarities rather than separate on their differences. Of that day at the Entertainment Centre on 26 June 1977, Wilson recalled some 26 years later: 'I can still remember just standing on the stage at the Entertainment Centre looking at this vast crowd and capturing the excitement of the moment.'

Four days earlier, Wilson had attended the inauguration ceremony of the Uniting Church of Australia at the Sydney Town Hall. This was also a ceremony that Wilson remembered with great fondness. But it was the ceremony at the Perth Entertainment Centre, where he was among his people, that gave Wilson particular joy.

The first synod of the Uniting Church of Western Australia convened over 7–10 October 1977. At the synod, Wilson was re-elected for another two years. In many respects Wilson's role as moderator of the Uniting Church was no different from the position he held in the Presbyterian Church in the mid 1960s. The difference was that in this fledging institution he had to keep abreast of a vast number of activities and attend to a multitude of details. He had many meetings to attend, and there was the endless list of invitations to deliver sermons at weekend services. Wilson had always been in demand as a lay preacher; now, as moderator, his attraction was even greater. With enthusiasm he accepted as many of the invitations as possible.

Wilson never allowed his church and other community commitments to interfere with or compromise his professional duty to the state. What his heavy schedule of commitments did was make him work even harder. It did often draw him away from the family home. But by then the only child still home was Ian. When home, Wilson still attended to domestic chores and family matters. He did not spend time on individual pursuits like golf, tennis or social drinking, which he generally confined to official and informal law-related social gatherings. However, he did play bridge with his colleagues. During his time as solicitor-general there was a thriving lunch bridge club of between ten and fifteen lawyers. Wilson joined in when he could.

In May 1978, Wilson received a phone call from the premier asking him to attend his office. When Wilson arrived, Court greeted him with a friendly smile and the obligatory handshake. He came straight to the point. 'Look, Ron, I want to award you the CMG.' The CMG was an Imperial Honour—the Companion of the Order of St Michael and St George. Wilson showed little enthusiasm. The premier pressed on. 'See this as a stepping stone to a knighthood that you will get when appointed to the High Court.' Court had no knowledge of the High Court offer to Wilson in 1976. Nor had the premier received any assurances that the next High Court vacancy would go to Wilson. He was ever the optimist.

Court saw the awarding of a CMG for community service to Wilson as an appropriate honour for a man who had committed his professional career to serving the interests of the state of Western Australia. He also viewed the bestowing of such an honour as an opportunity to further the profile of Wilson and his chances of a High Court appointment.

Court reached the end of his 'talk' to Wilson. Wilson still remained unenthusiastic about the award. However, he was appreciative of Court's compliments. He accepted the offer, and received the honour on 3 June 1978. In later life Wilson viewed the Imperial-sounding award with some embarrassment.

Less than a year after the awarding of the CMG, Wilson received a phone call from his co-author for the 1967 constitutional article, 'Do We Need a New Constitution for the Commonwealth?'.[24] Senator Peter Durack QC had moved from state to federal politics, and was the Commonwealth Attorney-General in the Fraser government's second term. Durack asked Wilson whether he would accept an appointment to the High Court. A position had become vacant because of the retirement of Justice Kenneth Jacobs, who had been appointed by the Whitlam government in 1974 when Jacobs was president of the New South Wales Court of Appeal. Now, ill-health was forcing him to retire prematurely from the High Court bench. He left on 6 April 1979.

Wilson still held no particular desire to be on the High Court. He was enjoying his 'job made in heaven', and had never held an ambition of being a judge, let alone a High Court justice. He felt pressured. He was well aware that his attorney-general and the premier were very keen for a Western Australian to be appointed to the High Court. He knew the premier would be very disappointed if he declined this opportunity. If the premier found out that he had also declined in 1976, the disappointment would have been even greater. Considering the wishes of the state government and Wilson's belief that an older Ian (eleven years old) would now be better able to cope with his father's constant absence from the home, he was inclined to accept the offer. He would be the first justice of the High Court from a state other then New

South Wales, Victoria or Queensland, and the first appointment from a state where most of the lawyers practised as both barristers and solicitors, not just as one or the other.

He said 'yes' to Durack.

Wilson's appointment, which was announced on the 21 May 1979, was also a first in another respect. His was the first appointment under the formal consultative arrangements that had been discussed between the Commonwealth attorney-general and his state counterparts. At the fourth plenary session of the Australian Constitutional Convention at Perth in July 1978, Durack personally committed himself to consultation with state attorneys-general in the event of a vacancy on the High Court. He reaffirmed that commitment at the ceremonial sitting of the High Court on 6 October 1978, the seventy-fifth anniversary of the first sitting of the High Court.[25] This involved Durack writing to his state counterparts. The responses convinced Durack that Wilson was highly suitable for the appointment to the High Court.

From the ranks of the federal Labor opposition there was public criticism. The deputy leader of the opposition, Lionel Bowen, attacked the appointment, saying that Durack had complied meekly with the demands of the premier, Sir Charles Court. In a newspaper article titled 'Labor Says Wilson Is a "Court Man",' Bowen said Wilson held conservative views, particularly on constitutional questions, that made him very appealing to Court. Bowen remarked:

> While not in any way detracting from the legal eminence of Mr Wilson, the simple fact is that his appointment was made by the Court Government rather than the Fraser Government.

Bowen said that the Labor Party rejected the notion of direct state involvement in appointments to the High Court. He also said that Court had 'been almost fanatical about the need for State participation in the appointment of High Court judges'.[26]

Court denied that his government played a role in the appointment. He said the appointment was the Commonwealth's solely but, as agreed and promised, it was done after consulting the states. Court's press release of 21 May 1978 left no doubt as to how important he viewed the appointment of a Western Australian to the High Court to be. His statement commenced as follows:

> This is an event of historic importance, both to Western Australia and the nation as a whole. All previous appointments to the High Court in its 79-year history have been made from Victoria, New South Wales and Queensland. This has been contrary to the spirit of the Federation, and has left the High Court without a precious asset—the perspective of the less populous but equally important members of the States of the Federation.[27]

The *Australian Law Journal* agreed with the sentiments of Western Australia's premier, saying that many of the crucial constitutional pronouncements of the High Court lacked a 'perspective of the non-Eastern States', and it was difficult to be a true national court of a federation of states if the bench 'is representative exclusively of less than half of such Federation, geographically speaking, and not representative at all of the citizens of the States constituting the balance of the Federation'.[28]

Court defended the appointment, referring, without naming him, to the appointment of Lionel Murphy to the High Court in 1975. At the time Murphy was the attorney-general in the Whitlam government. Court stated that he was appointed 'complete with prior public commitments as to his attitude towards certain constitutional matters'. He then added, 'Happily, Mr Wilson goes to the High Court as an eminent lawyer untarnished by any prior political commitment.'[29]

This was true, but Court was very confident that Wilson would uphold what the premier considered the states' rights in the federal system. Court was also impressed with Wilson's abilities, experience and integrity. Further, Court has made no secret that, while not pushing the case of Wilson to the Commonwealth, whenever he had the opportunity he did press the need for a justice from Western Australia to be appointed.

The Crown Law Department was as pleased as the state government with Wilson's appointment. Some saw it as further repudiation of the previously held perception of Crown Law lawyers as inferior. Peter Panegyres and Kevin Parker both remember how they and others were overjoyed with one of their own being appointed to the High Court, not only because of what it meant for the department, but also for the man so admired by those who worked with him.

The delight over the appointment was not restricted to the government and the Crown Law Department: many of the legal profession in Western Australia saw it as recognition of the quality of the profession in the West.

Judge Hal Jackson (of the Western Australian District Court since 1986) remarked that, while Wilson had those who disliked him as a prosecutor, his High Court elevation was generally well received and seen as being good for the whole Western Australian profession.

His family was proud of him, but Wilson was still the husband or the father they had always known. The High Court appointment was a great achievement. His second daughter Robyn shared these sentiments, but was also concerned with what people would expect of her, the daughter of a High Court justice. In the early stages of a nursing career, she worried that people would expect that her views on politics, religion or morality would be the same as her father's. She was concerned that her ability to create her own self-identity would be clouded by people's preconceived ideas of how she should behave and think. For the first few years of Wilson's tenure on the High Court, Robyn would struggle with these issues, though she kept her fears to herself.

9

The High Court

My time on the High Court was the most unsatisfying time for me professionally. It took me away from my love of advocacy and it was very hard work on the High Court at an age [fifty-six years] when I would have liked to be slowing down or doing something else.

There was crispness in the Brisbane morning air as Wilson entered the Supreme Court of Queensland on 29 May 1979. On its annual circuit visit to Brisbane, the High Court was holding a special session to swear in a new justice—the first ever from Western Australia.

Led by fellow Western Australian and the Commonwealth attorney-general, Senator Peter Durack QC,[1] many tributes and fine words were offered from the bar table. Wilson soaked it up with joy, but also with a tinge of discomfort—he was a modest man who did not overly enjoy being the object of such public displays of praise. His discomfort was softened by his appreciation of the significance of the moment for the Western Australian legal profession, but he felt no inner glow of personal achievement. For Wilson, being made Western Australian solicitor-general ten years earlier was a great achievement; the High Court appointment was no greater attainment.

When it was time for the diminutive new justice to respond, Wilson acknowledged the preciousness of the moment. In humbly accepting the compliments bestowed on him he noted:

> ...what a pity there was not some way for the members of the High Court—now my brothers—to have heard all this about 5 years ago, and then I could have continued to practise and it might just have had some effect.[2]

He paid tribute to those who had offered him personal and professional support. Highest on his list was Leila, with Wilson acknowledging the unwavering support she had provided to him and the family: 'She has borne with me for 30 years and maintained a happy and stable home life, without which I cannot believe that I could have done what I have done.'[3]

One observer of the occasion was Father Frank Brennan, the Jesuit priest, lawyer and human rights activist, whose father, Gerard Brennan, would join Wilson on the High Court in 1981. Many years later, while delivering the Sir Ronald Wilson Lecture in Perth, Brennan recalled that at the end of Wilson's remarks he turned to a friend and said, 'I think they have just put a saint on the High Court.'[4] One may wonder how often a Catholic priest has imparted canonisation credentials on a Protestant judge.

The High Court is a political forum in a manner unlike any other court in Australia. A significant part of its work revolves around interpretation of the Constitution, and in particular, the constantly evolving battleground between the state and Commonwealth governments as they test each other's legislation and powers. Often the court is called on to decide matters that involve high political stakes.

This is one of the reasons that appointments to the court are politically significant, and closely scrutinised. Two of Wilson's new colleagues had direct experience of political life. Chief Justice Garfield Barwick was a former attorney-general in the Menzies Liberal government,[5] and Justice Lionel Murphy had held the same post in the Whitlam Labor government.[6]

Just four years earlier, the court had become directly embroiled in politics when Barwick provided advice to the governor-general, John Kerr, during the 1975 constitutional crisis that led to the dismissal of the Whitlam government. Critics had disputed both the validity of his advice and the propriety of him becoming involved in this manner.

Wilson may have been a political cleanskin, but there is no doubt that he was perceived as a states' righter. He did have a philosophical belief in the legislative division of powers between the Commonwealth and the states, and in the need to protect against the Commonwealth's legislative encroachment into what he viewed as state issues.

More significant, though, was Wilson's philosophical approach to the law. Wilson was a legal positivist. Legal positivism is a philosophy or legal theory that holds that legal validity does not necessarily have a connection with morality or justice. Under this philosophy, the content of law is what is acknowledged or recognised as authoritative by society's 'officials' and institutions, such as parliament and the courts. The content of law is not dependent on its merits or morality.[7] It is more colloquially known as 'black letter law', an approach that demands a literal reading of the relevant legislation and a keen adherence to precedent.

The High Court is the final appellate court in Australia, subject only to limited Privy Council appeals up to 1986. The *Australia Acts* 1986[8] abolished appeals from the state courts to the Privy Council; appeals from the High Court in federal and constitutional matters had been abolished in 1968 and all remaining appeals from the High Court in 1975.[9] Thus the High Court has a pivotal role in shaping the common law of Australia and dealing with legislation across the legal spectrum.

High Court justices are rarely called on to decide matters of fact. These will normally have been determined in lower courts. The nitty gritty of their work lies in interpreting the meaning and intent of legislation, and the application of legal precedents, as they pertain to the cases before them. In Wilson's view, the Australian Constitution, the most authoritative legal and political document in the Australian federation, clearly set out the division of legislative power between the Commonwealth parliament and the state parliaments.

Wilson's adherence to legal positivism meant that he believed it was against his judicial oath to interfere in the polity balance between the Commonwealth and the states, as set out in the Constitution, no matter what the issue at stake. It was a belief that would lead him to deliver judgements that did not necessarily coincide with his personal values.

Wilson's new brothers on the High Court bench, along with Barwick and Murphy, were Justices Harry Gibbs, Ninian Stephen, Anthony Mason and Keith Aickin. They knew him well from his numerous arguments before them on behalf of the state of Western Australia. They respected and liked him, even Barwick, with whom he had many robust exchanges while counsel for Western Australia. In fact, Wilson's appointment to replace Sir Kenneth Jacobs, Murphy's closest colleague on the High Court bench, had an impact on Murphy's contemplation of resigning from the court. Murphy liked the mild-tempered man from humble beginnings, who was not another product of the Melbourne or Sydney bars.[10]

Wilson's frequent advocacy before the High Court had reduced its mystique or aura for him. Even so, he felt intellectually inferior to his fellow judges. It was a view that burdened him throughout his High Court tenure. This burden was noticed by some of his colleagues. Sir Daryl Dawson, the Victorian solicitor-general, who joined Wilson on the High Court in 1982, comments that Wilson felt he did not have the 'intellectual sophistication' of his colleagues. Dawson believes that Wilson's inferiority complex was not justified.

The roots of Wilson's self-doubt lay in his narrow formal education and his lack of study of the classics and philosophy. He believed this prevented him from developing a sophisticated and renaissance intellect. This personal view is reflected in his comments about the writing style of his colleagues. For example, he opined that Sir Gerard Brennan treated each judgement as a work of art and an academic treatise. Reflecting his unpretentious demeanour, Wilson remarked that 'to write like Brennan takes far more intellect than I possess'.

Sir Anthony Mason, who was appointed to the High Court in 1972, to some degree concurs with Wilson's own assessment of his intellect, in the sense that he didn't regard Wilson as having a profound philosophical mind. However, he is quick to add that Wilson had 'an extremely nimble, quick mind', which was best manifested during his time as counsel before the High Court, when he was often required to respond to questioning from the bench.

Sir William Deane, appointed to the High Court in 1982, believes that Wilson was too hard on himself. He also argues that Wilson's view of having had an inferior education made him particularly sensitive to personal banter. On his appointment to the High Court, Deane already knew three of the justices very well—Wilson, Mason and Brennan. But he was more cautious in engaging in friendly ridicule with Wilson than with those other justices. However, others, such as Mason and Dawson, believed that Wilson never took himself too seriously, and that he was happy engaging in friendly banter, even at his own expense.

Often Wilson used self-mocking wit when he was the centre of tributes, a situation he found somewhat uncomfortable. Melanie Sloss, who was his High Court associate from April 1984 to June 1985, thought Wilson was good at telling jokes about himself. She found him witty, although not someone who would come into the office and just tell you a joke. But 'he had that sort of disposition where, if something did occur and it was humorous, he would make the most of it'.

Adding to his self-doubt because of his perceived unsophisticated education, Wilson also felt he was an outsider, the country boy from 'the West' in an institution filled with judges from 'the East'. Of course, as Western Australia's Crown counsel and solicitor-general, he had previously had contact with the legal fraternity in the eastern states. Even though he had good relationships with the other state solicitors-general, and at the time of his High Court appointment was considered the unofficial leader of that group, he still felt apart from them. He felt even more distant from barristers from the independent bars of Sydney and Melbourne, who dominated the appearances in the High Court. They seemed to give little attention to the West, unless being paid by a Western Australian client. Nor did he like the way many of the eastern states' QCs treated their juniors. Wilson never accepted impolite or discourteous behaviour from anyone. He struggled with this sense of apartness but, unlike his educational inferiority complex, this did subside somewhat as he grew into the role of being a High Court justice. It never left him completely.

Wilson also felt that the High Court justices from Sydney, in particular, were more inclined to be centralists and more sympathetic to any push by the Commonwealth government and parliament to extend their powers over the states. He surmised that the reason for this was a general symmetry of the interests of Sydney and Canberra; that is, New South Wales being the most populous state, with the most politicians in the Commonwealth parliament, meant that it had the largest single state voting bloc. While there may be some truth in this, the party system in parliament tends to blur the state groupings, even in the so-called states' house, the Senate. Wilson thought that, regardless of numerical superiority, New South Wales politicians just seemed, for whatever reason, to be attuned to and relaxed about Commonwealth power.

Dawson shared Wilson's view that the High Court was too influenced by the interests of New South Wales and, in particular, Sydney. He too saw himself as an outsider, and like Wilson, noncentralist in judicial and political philosophy. He also considered Chief Justice Harry Gibbs, from Queensland, to be another noncentralist. On the other hand, he thought that Justice Gerard Brennan, though also from Queensland, had lived in New South Wales for many years, and was therefore much more inclined to the centralist point of view.

Although Wilson went to the High Court with reservations, one area where this was not so was criminal law. As a former state prosecutor, Wilson had an insight into criminal trials that most of his brethren on the High Court lacked. The only justice with comparable experience was Gibbs, whose record in deciding criminal law cases while he was on the Queensland Supreme Court and High Court was impressive.[11] These two stood alone with their expertise in criminal law until the arrival on the High Court of Dawson in 1982. Dawson, who had significant experience in prosecuting criminal cases, has remarked that Wilson's vast experience as a prosecutor in criminal trials and appeals gave him the confidence and knowledge to take the lead on the High Court in criminal cases. Mason says that 'apart from constitutional law in terms of expressing his particular perspective, criminal law would have been [Wilson's] principal field of significant contribution to the High Court jurisprudence'.

One of the earliest criminal appeals Wilson had to deal with on the High Court was the *MacPherson* case.[12] Donald MacPherson had been arrested on 13 May 1978 in relation to a murder near Berowra in New South Wales. He was taken to the police station, where swab samples and photographs were taken, and his clothing was removed for examination. He was then questioned by police. On the same day he was charged with the murder. There was strong evidence linking him to the crime.

MacPherson was unrepresented at his trial. In questions he put in cross-examination of witnesses, and in his statement from the dock, he admitted that he had been present when the victim was shot, that he owned the pistol that shot the victim, and that he had disposed of the victim's body in bush. However, MacPherson maintained that the murder had been committed by someone else, whom he named.

MacPherson was convicted of murder, and his appeal to the New South Wales Court of Criminal Appeal was dismissed. He then appealed to the High Court, which heard the matter in May 1981. The appeal centred on the veracity of a confession for murder. The police gave evidence at the trial that MacPherson had confessed to the murder. At trial, the unrepresented accused, in cross-examination of the police officers who questioned him, alleged that the police made threats to him, that he was not warned by the police that anything he said could be used in evidence against him, and denied making a confession to the murder. The trial judge failed to inform the accused of his right to ask the judge to conduct a *voir dire* to determine whether the confession was voluntary.

Wilson joined Chief Justice Gibbs in allowing the appeal, quashing the conviction and ordering a new trial. In their joint judgement, they reiterated that for a confession to be admissible it must be freely given, and not the result of

> fear of prejudice or hope of advantage exercised or held out by a person in authority, or as the result of duress, intimidation, persistent importunity or sustained or undue insistence or pressure...[13]

In other words, the confession must be freely and voluntarily given, absent of any pressure that corrupts the free will of the accused in making the admission. But even if the confession is voluntarily given, Wilson and Gibbs held that the trial judge should retain the discretion to reject it if the voluntary confession was gathered in circumstances that would make it unfair to use it against the accused. In *MacPherson*, they held that the trial judge had a duty to inform the accused about his rights in relation to the conduct of the trial:

> ...once a real question arises as to the voluntariness of a confession tendered in evidence, the judge has a duty to satisfy himself of the voluntariness of the confession, and usually must hold a *voir dire* for that purpose, even if the accused does not object to the evidence or seek a *voir dire*.[14]

Their joint judgement reiterated the importance of judges informing unrepresented accused of their rights and giving them sufficient information to ensure a fair trial. This was not to be the last time the former Crown prosecutor, who had been accused of being too zealous in prosecuting, was to decide cases and write judgements that sought to protect the accused from improper conduct on the part of the police in obtaining a confession.[15] Even in *Barton v R*,[16] where Wilson, in the minority, held that on some occasions trials commenced by *ex officio* indictments (without a committal hearing) were not an abuse of process, Wilson said that a trial would be fair if the trial judge made special provisions for the accused at trial. He was concerned to ensure a fair trial for the accused, particularly unrepresented defendants.

Some may see his judicial approach to criminal trials, where he sought to protect the rights of the accused, as inconsistent with his approach as a prosecutor. Wilson saw no such contradiction. He always maintained that while he was a forceful prosecutor, he never sought convictions unjustly. Some of his critics and adversaries, such as Leopold Woods, a prominent Western Australian defence criminal lawyer, disagreed. Not that Woods suggested that Wilson acted unethically. But Woods was highly critical of what he perceived as Wilson's too-zealous approach to prosecuting. Wilson, as a justice of the High Court, had a different role from that as prosecutor, and whatever the role, he performed it with determination, dedication and conviction.

Melanie Sloss, one of his High Court associates, remembers that Wilson felt it was very important for the court to hold a firm and clear view on prosecutorial conduct and discretion. Dawson comments that Wilson, who had vast experience prosecuting criminal cases before juries, was cognisant of the reality that juries made mistakes and, therefore, it was imperative that their decision was based on properly obtained information, and that they were given clear instructions on the law. Wilson, who had written a master's thesis on juries at University of Pennsylvania, had concerns with the ability of juries to make the correct decisions in complex cases. It was crucial that juries should be aware that, if they had any reasonable doubt as to the guilt of an accused, they should acquit. He was also keen to reiterate that it was for the jury to decide on the evidence before them as to the guilt or innocence of the accused. For example, in the self-defence case of *Zecevic v DPP (Victoria)*,[17] he joined with Justices Dawson and John Toohey (his colleague from the West) in holding that:

> The issue of self-defence was squarely raised. Clearly there was evidence upon which a jury could conclude that the appellant believed it was necessary to do what he did in order to defend himself. There was also evidence of the grounds for that belief. Whether those grounds were reasonable was a matter for the jury…However, if the jury believed the appellant, it is not inconceivable that it might have adopted a view of the facts which would have favoured him in his defence of self-defence. The issue should be left to the jury.[18]

These justices reformulated the test for self-defence by holding that the question to be asked is:

> whether the accused believed upon reasonable grounds that it was necessary in self-defence to do what he did. If he had that belief and there were reasonable grounds for it, or if the jury is left in reasonable doubt about the matter, then he is entitled to an acquittal. Stated in this form, the question is one of general application and is not limited to cases of homicide.[19]

Wilson had gone to the High Court with two pleas from the Western Australian legal profession ringing in his ears. One was to write succinct judgements. The other was for more joint judgements. Practising lawyers wanted to know what the law was. They did not want seven versions of it. They just didn't have the time to ponder over judicial musings in long judgements.

The general view is that Wilson's judgements were 'well crafted',[20] and displayed 'unusually careful attention to the argument of counsel'.[21] Unsurprisingly, this reflected the importance Wilson attached to counsel's arguments. He had come to the High Court after many years of arguing before it. Indeed, he gave greater importance to his role as counsel than being a High Court justice. It is unlikely that his brethren would have held the same view.

His brethren, such as Mason and Dawson, have acknowledged the respect Wilson afforded counsel. One of the more attractive aspects of the job for Wilson was the opportunity to listen to some of Australia's elite barristers presenting their cases before him. However, he was surprised that more counsel in their oral submissions (and any written submissions) did not attempt to present their arguments in a manner that the judge may adopt. This was what Wilson as an advocate had done. He would anticipate a judgement, and present his submissions and arguments in a form that made it easier for the judge 'to just pick it up'. Wilson acknowledged that such an approach may not have worked with some judges, as 'there might be a basic antipathy to a judge being told what to write'. Nonetheless, he was still surprised that more counsel did not take his approach to advocacy.

This is not to say that Wilson wasn't impressed with the calibre of many of those who appeared before him on the High Court. Although some counsel surprised him with their illogically structured arguments, he did enjoy having the chance to listen to strong arguments from some of Australia's elite barristers. None was more memorable than Tom Hughes QC. Hughes became a QC in 1962, then went into federal politics, where he served as attorney-general in John Gorton's government (1969–71), before returning to 'star' status at the Sydney Bar. Wilson described Hughes as a 'colourful advocate', but he added:

> I was never completely happy with the thought that if I was in trouble I would brief Tom. There was a cavalier approach about him that suggested he might have been flying by the seat of his pants and relying on his fluent speech and his imagery and his wit, you got the impression it was very much on the spur of the moment stuff. It was effective though and that's the test.[22]

He viewed Murray Gleeson QC, the current Chief Justice of the High Court, as the most effective, after Hughes, of barristers to have appeared before him. He found Gleeson able to respond quickly and effectively to questions from the bench. He also had great admiration for David Jackson QC from Sydney, S. E. K. Hume QC from Melbourne, and Geoff Davies QC and Tony Fitzgerald QC, both from Brisbane. He particularly enjoyed hearing argument from John Doyle QC, the then solicitor-general of South Australia, who later became the chief justice of the South Australian Supreme Court.

Before entering the courtroom for the commencement of a case, Wilson would read the court papers prepared by both parties and any written submissions available (these not becoming a common feature until after his retirement from the High Court).[23] Wilson found scanning written submissions and other papers useful before a hearing to orientate himself on the important issues at stake: 'I would scan them. Some judges…would not touch them, others might go [into a hearing] with their minds made up…The written submissions…did crystallise the issues for you.'

Sometimes Wilson formed a latent preference for one or the other side, but not to an extent that it couldn't change during the hearing. This was not always so with some of his colleagues. Barwick would often open a hearing already with a fixed view on the outcome. He was not backward in arguing with counsel in regard to his point of view.

As a judge, Wilson was demonstrably opposite to Barwick. For example, Wilson did not seek to carry his love and passion for advocacy on to the

High Court bench. He intervened rarely while sitting on the bench. Even though advocate Wilson loved robust exchanges with the bench, as a judge he showed great respect and courtesy to advocates appearing before him, allowing for the most part the barristers to present their arguments uninterrupted. Wilson did question from the bench, but not consistently during the advocate's oral presentation; when he did ask questions, it was in a pleasant, nonconfrontational manner. Wilson's brethren found him a pleasure to have on the bench, as continual intervention from a colleague could sometimes test the patience of some other justices.

Wilson got on well with the other justices; but he also thought that socialising between them should be limited. He favoured justices maintaining some distance from each other in order to avoid interest groups and power blocs forming on the bench, which he viewed as incongruous with the justice's oath to faithfully obey the law. On the other hand, he felt there was room for greater collegiality in their general day-to-day work. Sympathetic to the pleas from the Western Australian legal profession, Wilson was very keen on joint judgements being reached with his colleagues.

Even though Wilson was keen, and was involved in a number of joint judgements (164 in total), he still felt a lack of judicial collegiality. Wilson thought there could have been greater discussion among the justices in relation to the cases they heard. While not advocating US Supreme Court-style conferences, where a formal vote is taken on the result and the Chief Justice, when in the majority, allocates the writing of the majority decision to one justice, Wilson believed there was room for post-hearing conferences, where the justices could discuss ideas, that may assist in more joint judgements.

During Wilson's time on the High Court, very few conferences were held. The justices occasionally discussed the cases or their thinking on particular legal matters with each other. Wilson often visited a colleague in his chambers to discuss an aspect of a case, or sometimes he engaged in a quick discussion over a cup of tea or when in the lift. He or another justice might say to one another: 'Well, what do you think?' or 'Why don't you write the first judgment?' But it was never a formal arrangement, and Wilson and the other justices would usually write their judgements without too much discussion and subsequently circulate their draft judgements. In Wilson's experience, 'nine out of ten times you wouldn't get any response from the others'. He also said:

> If a justice had not written a draft judgement yet, they may decide to agree with one of their brethren and rather than write their own judgement they would write that they concur with one of the others. They may leave it at that or write a brief explanation as to why they concur with their brother justice.

Sir Owen Dixon, a former chief justice of the High Court, said that it was desirable to get one's judgement circulated first if you wanted to have a greater influence. Wilson did not like to leave a judgement lingering. Most often he was one of the first to circulate a judgement. As Brennan has commented, 'Wilson circulated his judgements with commendable rapidity.' Consequently, Wilson commanded concurrence from his brethren in a number of cases.

Wilson had no desire to seek glory on the High Court. He was more interested in making the right decision and in seeking to uphold the pleas of the legal profession for more joint judgements. He was more than happy to have other justices add their names to his written decisions. Wilson commented that, in relation to joint judgements, he had most difficulty with Deane, whom he felt was most keen to write his own.[24]

Deane recalls Wilson coming to him with a draft judgement that was in agreement with Deane's viewpoint. He offered Deane the opportunity to have his name added to the judgement. Deane declined the offer. He thought it was not fair for him to add his name as a joint author of a judgement that Wilson had laboured over. Wilson did not see it that way. He had no difficulty with his colleagues gaining equal credit or recognition of a judgement that Wilson had spent considerable time crafting.

Deane may have been influenced by the fact that the chief justice or more senior justice would have his name printed first on a joint judgement. Wilson was senior to Deane, having been appointed earlier to the High Court.

At the time of his appointment, the High Court had buildings in Melbourne and Sydney, although until 1980 the court continued to sit at Darlinghurst Court House, rather than the adjacent Commonwealth–State Law Courts Building, which was opened in 1976. When the High Court went on circuit it relied on each state Supreme Court to provide courtrooms and chambers for the justices. In Wilson's home city, he was afforded the privilege of permanent chambers at the Western Australian Supreme Court Building in the Supreme Court Gardens on the corner of Barrack Street and Riverside Drive in Perth.

The quality and suitability of the courtrooms and chambers provided to the High Court justices when on circuit varied from state to state. Chief justice Barwick, a strong centralist in many respects, had long wanted to abolish this circuit and the High Court's state registries, and have a permanent building in Canberra, an arrangement that had been contemplated as far back as 1903 with the *Judiciary Act* 1903 (Cwlth).[25] The building of the current High Court complex in Canberra, on the shore of Lake Burley Griffin just down from Parliament House (now the old Parliament House) had commenced by the time Wilson became a justice. The new High Court building was opened on 26 May 1980 by Queen Elizabeth II during a grand ceremony before dignitaries and judges from all parts of Australia and overseas.

Wilson agreed with the idea of a permanent High Court building in Canberra, the seat of Commonwealth government. He was strenuously opposed to removing the circuit hearings and state registries. As a Western Australian law student, and then practitioner, he was fully aware of the opportunity the circuit hearings gave Western Australians to view and hear High Court proceedings and arguments. Also, he believed that the circuit gave the justices from New South Wales and Victoria an opportunity to gain some experience of the reality of the other states, however fleeting.

In proposing the abolition of the circuits, Barwick also wanted the justices to live in Canberra. At one stage it was proposed that all the justices live in an enclave near the Commonwealth Club in Canberra. Barwick was fond of the US model, where there were no hearings other than in the Supreme Court building in Washington DC, and where the justices made their residence for most of the year in or near the national capital. Wilson and other justices did not agree. This created tension on the bench. It even reached the stage of Wilson and the other justices (minus Barwick) meeting and appointing Ninian Stephen to brief Malcolm Fraser, the prime minister, about their opposition to the chief justice's proposals. The prime minister was told of the importance for each individual justice remaining connected with the environment that had prepared and equipped him or her for a position on the High Court.

Not long after, Barwick received an edict from the Commonwealth government that the justices could remain principally resident in their home states. The circuit would remain, as would the state registries in all capitals other than Melbourne and Sydney. Barwick, who was made aware of Stephen's briefing with the prime minister, was not happy with this result. Fortunately, it did not cause any longstanding rift between the chief justice and the other justices.

Wilson was impressed with Barwick's behaviour toward his colleagues. He treated them courteously and with respect. Wilson has pointed to the Barwick–Murphy relationship to exemplify this. Lionel Murphy was sworn in as a justice of the High Court in Sydney on 14 February 1975. It is a matter of public record that Barwick was strongly opposed to Murphy's appointment. In Barwick's biography, *A Radical Tory*, he states that Gough Whitlam, the prime minister, telephoned him to inform him that Murphy had accepted the offer of an appointment to the High Court to replace the recently deceased Justice Douglas Menzies. Barwick replied: 'But he is neither competent nor suitable for the position.'[26] Barwick admits to being 'considerably upset by the news' of the appointment.

This opposition to the appointment did not demonstrably affect a professional and courteous relationship between Barwick and Murphy. There was no outward sign or display of antipathy between these two strongminded men. This impressed Wilson:

> There was a maturity that enabled difference of opinion not to disturb the surface geniality. We would meet in the common room, just adjacent to the court before going into court, and it would often be a time for story telling and laughter and so on and even though, for example, Barwick hated Lionel Murphy's guts…it was controlled.

Not long after Wilson's swearing in as a justice of the High Court, his eldest son Bruce was married in Melbourne to Kerrie O'Neil. Kerrie grew up in country Victoria, and moved to Melbourne in the early 1970s, attending Melbourne University to do a Bachelor of Arts in politics and history. This was the second marriage in the family. In 1976, Helen had married Ian Ladhams, a high school teacher.

Seven months after his swearing in as a High Court justice, Wilson was the focus of another ceremony. That was his installation as Chancellor of Murdoch University, a relatively new university, established in 1975, 15 kilometres south of the city centre. Wilson replaced the first chancellor of the university, Western Australian Supreme Court Justice John Wickham, who had retired on 6 February 1980 after serving six years.

Although, as a High Court Justice, Wilson had heavy demands on his time, including time on aeroplanes, he was enthusiastic when invited to become Murdoch University's second chancellor. He had a keen interest in higher education, and was attracted to being involved with the fledgling university. It was an extension of his commitment to public service, because he viewed a university as having an important role in the community. He made this clear when delivering the address at his Ceremony of Installation at Murdoch University on 15 February 1980. Wilson's speech was delivered with wit, reminiscent of the humour in his High Court response ceremony in Brisbane:

> I am proceeding at this moment on the assumption that no one will challenge my right to say what I like. That may not always be the case and I shall, therefore, proceed to make the most of this opportunity.
>
> Firstly, Your Excellency [the Governor of Western Australia, Air Chief Marshal Sir Wallace Kyle, Visitor of the University], thank you for installing me. I am sure that whatever mistakes I may make in the future no one will have the temerity to blame it on a faulty installation.[27]

After acknowledging the efforts of the inaugural chancellor, Wilson commented that the health of the university depended on its relationship with the wider community. He went on to express his keen interest in tertiary education, and 'a deep conviction as to the importance of universities to society'. He valued the opportunity of being able to work closely with Murdoch University; wearing his parochialism on his sleeve, he said that he was particularly glad that he would be working closely with a Western Australian university:

> for as one who has been born and bred in this state, and now committed to the national scene in my daily occupation, I am sure that any fitness I may have to discharge the responsibilities of that office, will be enhanced by the continuing nurture of my roots in this state.[28]

Just over three months later Wilson was present at another ceremony, the official opening of the new High Court building in Canberra by Queen Elizabeth II on 26 May 1980. It was an occasion of much pomp and ceremony, with judges from around Australia and the world in attendance, many fitted out in their gowns and wigs. By then Wilson was a Knight of the Realm (KBE), an honour with which he had been invested shortly after appointment to the High Court in 1979 (31 July 1979). The knighthood, which since 1940 in effect was 'automatically' awarded to incoming justices of the High Court, was not something that Wilson craved or felt comfortable about. He was often telling people, 'Just call me Ron.' He normally answered the phone with the words, 'Wilson here.' Wilson could have rejected the knighthood, as Murphy had,[29] but he thought it may have been petty to do so.

In February 1981, Barwick, aged seventy-seven and with failing eyesight, retired after sixteen years as chief justice. History has not been overly favourable to Barwick the judge. Barwick, the pre-eminent advocate, remained in many respects an advocate on the bench, and thus was a strong interventionist. He would often interject to question counsel, and frequently would offer his reactions to barristers' arguments. While it may have been thought by some that Barwick used his interventions during the hearings as an opportunity to influence the bench's thinking, he was very firm against proselytising of individual justices' views. From Barwick's perspective, there was to be no attempt to persuade other justices to agree with a particular point of view. Justices were to reach their decisions independently.

In his autobiography, *A Radical Tory*, Barwick defended his judicial approach, saying that he would not tolerate counsel straying from the relevant issues or being repetitive, as court time, which was public time, was precious.[30] Wilson, like others,[31] thought Barwick's interventionist approach reduced the chief justice's effectiveness as a judge. But the two had a mutual respect for each other, and got on well, even if Wilson did not support Barwick's judicial style.

On 12 February 1981, Queenslander Harry Gibbs was sworn in as the chief justice to replace Barwick. The appointment was generally well received by the legal profession, and commentators viewed Gibbs as a high calibre lawyer untarnished by controversy. He was viewed as the right person to heal any lingering rifts on the bench. Wilson did not see that there were any such rifts. Any tensions over the Barwick push for the justices to reside in Canberra had dissipated before Barwick's retirement.

Wilson found the task of being a High Court justice very demanding. While there were moments he enjoyed—and he took up the task with great dedication—it was not a role that gave him as much satisfaction as when he worked for the Crown Law Department:

> My time on the High Court was the most unsatisfying time for me professionally. It took me away from my love of advocacy and it was very hard work on the High Court at an age [fifty-six years] when I would have liked to be slowing down or doing something else.

He once remarked to Melanie Sloss: 'I sit there in court on this side of the bench but, understand one thing, the fun is on the other side.' Reminiscing about his time as an advocate he told her, 'I would be arguing constitutional cases before Barwick and getting a very tough time but there is nothing like the fun you get out of it.' He advised Sloss, who was contemplating going to the bar, 'Go for it. It is hard work but that is where the fun is.' She followed Wilson's advice and has built an impressive reputation at the Melbourne Bar, especially in corporations law, and is now a Senior Counsel (SC).

One part of the judicial job Wilson did enjoy was the companionship and working relationships he formed with his associates. After the conclusion of a hearing, Wilson would return to his chambers to discuss the case with his associate, who would seek to identify any research avenues that might provide assistance.

Sometimes the associate would provide references, write a synopsis on information gathered and even write a detailed exposé of the relevant issues. But Wilson would write the judgement. Occasionally, associates did write drafts of decisions or parts of a decision. On one occasion, Ken Martin, one of his associates, wrote the judgement delivered by Wilson. After Wilson had discussed with Martin his thinking on the case, Martin went away to write a draft judgement. Wilson read it and said, 'I don't know that I want to fiddle with this. Why don't we publish it?' It was duly published in the Commonwealth Law Reports. Wilson and Martin never disclosed which case it was.

Martin, now a prominent QC at the Independent Bar in Perth, was Wilson's second High Court associate. The first was Jeremy Allanson, who Wilson had seconded from the Crown Law Department. However, Allanson only remained with Wilson for a few months. He recalls the courteous nature of Wilson, and his energy. Allanson had trouble keeping up with him during their walks from their hotel to the courthouse in Melbourne or Sydney.

Wilson was genuinely interested in his associates, who all came from Western Australia.[32] For him, they were there not only to offer him assistance but also to learn more about the law and develop their legal skills. Wilson was keen to assist them in any way he could. Even years after leaving the High Court, he was still prepared to offer assistance.

Wilson enjoyed having young people around him—they were full of energy and promise. He delighted in the successes many of them subsequently achieved. He always enjoyed any chance to meet with them in later years. Often on her trips to Perth from Melbourne for Christmas, Melanie Sloss would phone Wilson. He would always invite her over to his house.

It would be no exaggeration to say that Wilson's associates, or at least most of them, adored him and have always held him in high regard, even in later years, when Wilson was subjected to public and personal criticism from the fallout of *Bringing Them Home*, the 1997 report of the National Inquiry into the Separation of Aboriginal and Torres Strait Islander Children from Their Families.

Martin recalls that, when back in Perth from High Court hearings in Canberra, he and Wilson would often drive together to Cottesloe Beach on a Sunday morning for a swim and jog. Exercise was not their only enjoyment. They would also discuss the cases that were currently before the court. Martin always felt comfortable giving his opinions on various legal issues. Wilson, as he had always done throughout his professional career, listened with respect to the views of his colleagues, especially the younger ones, whom he thought needed to be encouraged to think for themselves and to have their views exposed and discussed.

Wilson's popularity extended to other staff of the High Court. While most of his brethren wrote their drafts in long hand, Wilson typed his draft judgements on a small portable typewriter. He would then give his typed draft to his personal assistant to transcribe and format onto official High Court paper. From 1980 to 1984, Wilson's personal assistant was Western Australian Lee O'Connor. She was replaced by Sandra Riley, who worked for Wilson for the remainder of his time on the High Court. Both women enjoyed working for Wilson. O'Connor has written that she found Wilson to be a 'genuine, considerate, kind, friendly and happy person'.

Referring to her time with Wilson at the High Court, O'Connor commented:

> Sir Ronald was…very hospitable and had an 'open door' to whoever wished to speak to him. To me, there was a friendly atmosphere within the Court amongst the people who worked there, from Justices through to all the

> various positions that people held. This atmosphere, in part, can be attributed to Sir Ronald's down to earth way of getting along with people.[33]

It was Wilson to whom many at the High Court turned to if they needed some advice. Dawson recalls one incident when one of the office workers at the High Court had some personal problems. It was Wilson in whom the office worker confided.

Just three years into his tenure, Wilson was to sit on a case with particular significance to Aboriginal people. It was not to be the last major constitutional case he would adjudicate, nor the last with critical importance to advocates of Aboriginal rights.

John Koowarta, a member of the Winychanam Aboriginal group, had convinced the Aboriginal Land Fund Commission to purchase a lease of Crown land in Northern Queensland for the group. However, under the *Land Act* 1962 (Qld), the Queensland Minister for Lands had to give consent to the transfer of the lease. He refused to do so, because the Queensland government was unfavourably disposed to large tracts of land being acquired by Aborigines.

Koowarta challenged this refusal, on the basis that the Queensland Act was racially discriminatory under the *Racial Discrimination Act* 1975 (Cwlth) (RDA). In response, the Queensland government argued that the RDA was unconstitutional. The Commonwealth government, which was joined in the action, argued that the RDA was a valid exercise of the Commonwealth parliament's legislative power under two clauses of the Constitution: section 51 (xxvi)—the race power—and section 51 (xxix)—the external affairs power—as the Commonwealth was a signatory to the United Nations (UN) 1966 *Convention for the Elimination of All Forms of Racial Discrimination*.[34]

Arguments focused on section 9 of the RDA, which states:

> It is unlawful for a person to deny any act involving a distinction, exclusion, restriction or preference based on race, colour, descent or national or ethnic origin which has the purpose or effect of nullifying or impairing the recognition, enjoyment or exercise, on an equal footing, of any human right or fundamental freedom in the political, economic, social, cultural or any other field of public life;

and section 12, which *inter alia* made it unlawful 'to refuse or fail to dispose of any estate or interest in land, or any residential or business accommodation, to a second person [on racial and other grounds]'.

When the case came to judgement, Wilson was in a majority with Gibbs, Stephen, Mason, Aickin and Brennan, with Murphy dissenting, in holding that sections 9 and 12 of the RDA were not valid laws under the race power—section 51 (xxvi)—because they applied to all persons equally and were not a special law for the people of any one race.[35]

That was not the end of the matter. Wilson, along with Gibbs and Aickin, held that the same sections of the RDA were not valid laws with respect to external affairs within section 51 (xxix) of the Constitution. However the other four justices, Stephen, Mason, Murphy and Brennan, upheld their constitutional validity.[36] By the barest of margins, on only one of the two grounds, the RDA survived. This was to be crucial in the future, when the *Mabo* case came before the court.

The majority of justices considered that, provided there was no breach of a constitutional prohibition, the external affairs powers of the Constitution extended to the legislative implementation of a *bona fide* international treaty obligation, regardless of its subject matter. However, Stephen added that the subject matter—racial discrimination—must be a matter of international concern.

The minority of Gibbs, Aickin and Wilson rejected the argument that race discrimination is anything more than a domestic matter. The minority's overriding concern was the maintenance of the Australian federal system, as clearly stated in the leading minority judgement of Gibbs:

> The distribution of powers made by the Constitution could in time be completely obliterated; there would be no field of power which the Commonwealth [Parliament] could not invade, and the federal balance achieved by the Constitution could be entirely destroyed.[37]

Wilson agreed with the chief justice's reasons, but added some words of his own. Consistent with his longheld opposition to racial discrimination, he commenced his opinion by saying that such discrimination is 'repugnant to the ideas of any human society'.[38] Later he wrote: 'I acknowledge too that of all Australia's international obligations there must be few, if any, of greater humanitarian importance than the obligation to strive for racial equality.'[39] Despite these sentiments, Wilson did not believe the RDA had the necessary external aspect to bring it within the scope of the external affairs power.

In his opinion, the external affairs power did not 'extend to enable the Parliament to implement every obligation which Australia assumes in its international relations'.[40] He added:

> It follows that Australia's obligation to eliminate racial discrimination within Australia will only assume the character of an external affair...if the manner of its implementation necessarily exhibits an international character.[41]

Wilson argued that a narrow view of the external affairs power does not prevent a nation from meeting its international obligations—he pointed to Canada to support his argument.[42] However, as commented by Dennis Rose, Wilson cited only one writer to support his argument, which Rose sees as 'excessively optimistic'.[43]

Wilson's concern to maintain the federal balance ran through his judgement as a guiding force. He suggested that Australia's international obligations should not 'blind us' to the Commonwealth's argument in relation to the external affairs power, as the proliferation of international agreements could give the Commonwealth unlimited power.[44] Wilson observed that the earth may in modern times resemble a global village, with the consequences of a plethora of international agreements in relation to the personal, economic, social and cultural aspects of human beings, which would place no limit to the range of matters that may assume an international character. If the external affairs power of the Constitution were given a wide scope to include any matter in which there is an international agreement, this 'would transfer to the Commonwealth virtually unlimited power in almost every conceivable aspect of life in Australia'.[45]

Wilson's view of the development of the global village pushed him to a different view eighteen years later. In an interview in 2000, he commented that he believed that, with globalisation and the global village, it was silly to have so many legislatures in Australia.[46] His one time 'boss', Sir Charles Court, would been horrified to hear him advocate the abolition of states in favour of a unitary system with a number of smaller counties with diminished powers.

This view was influenced by his concern with states in the federation acting contrary to international human rights conventions.[47] This shows a heightened priority being given to human rights, which may not be surprising, considering that for seven years in the 1990s Wilson was president of HREOC.

Even if Wilson did hold this view back in 1982—which seems unlikely—there was no guarantee that he would have decided differently in *Koowarta*. His view had always been that he had to come to a decision based on his reading of the Constitution and the law, not his personal preference, and Wilson's view of legal positivism meant he interpreted the Constitution as framing a federal system in which the state and Commonwealth parliaments had certain legislative powers that did not favour a dramatic transfer of power to the Commonwealth parliament.

Although his involvement with NEAF in the 1970s attests to Wilson's interest in bettering the lot of Aborigines and his abhorrence of racism, he did not believe that this should be used to justify Commonwealth legislative encroachment into areas traditionally the purview of the states. Concern for international human rights principles did not persuade him to deviate from his view on the constitutional federal balance, which included the need to preserve states' powers.

As a justice, he believed that his obligation was to uphold the Constitution as he saw it, not as he would want it. It was up to politicians to seek changes if they wished (through a national referendum to amend the Constitution). It was not the role of the judiciary to do so. Wilson saw it from the prism of the importance of maintaining the states' position in the federal structure, and was very sensitive to resisting opportunities that would change his view of the federal balance between the Commonwealth and states. The majority in *Koowarta* viewed things differently, which provided a legal result that was advantageous for the Aboriginal plaintiff and to plaintiffs in future High Court litigation in relation to Aboriginal rights. However, John Koowarta was prevented from purchasing the lease in question because, prior to the purchase, Premier Bjelke-Petersen declared the land in question a national park, thus preventing private ownership. Koowarta died in 1991.

Wilson's judgement in *Koowarta* reflected his belief in cooperation through consultation, and perhaps at one level, his unease at the real-life consequences of his legal positivism. He had always believed that it is possible more often than not to work through disagreements with people. In *Koowarta*, he said, 'The Commonwealth must seek the cooperation of the State legislatures to ensure that Australia's international obligations under the Convention are fulfilled.'[48] Examples of such cooperation included the offshore constitutional agreement and the *Australia Acts* 1986, and cooperation between state and Commonwealth governments of different political persuasions. However, having said that, it could be argued that it was naïve of Wilson, or at least optimistic for him to have hoped that Queensland premier Bjelke-Petersen's antagonism towards Canberra (the Commonwealth government of both political persuasions) and Aboriginal land rights could have led to cooperation.

The year after *Koowarta*, the High Court was thrust into the highly charged national politics of environmental protection and state–federal relationships. The Bob Hawke-led federal Labor government, elected on 5 March 1983, was committed to halting the damming of the Gordon River in Tasmania, downstream from its junction with the Franklin River. During the campaign for the election, Bob Hawke, then opposition leader, had promised to block the damming of the Gordon River by the Tasmanian Hydro-Electric Commission.[49] As soon as Hawke had won the election, the federal Labor government was pitted against the Tasmanian Liberal government.

Before the Commonwealth parliament had sat for the first time after the federal election, the Hawke government issued regulations (*World Heritage (Western Tasmania Wilderness) Regulations* 1983 (Cwlth)) under section 69 of the *National Parks and Wildlife Conservation Act* 1975 (Cwlth), enacted while Whitlam was prime minister. Pursuant to the United Nations Educational, Scientific and Cultural Organization (UNESCO) *Convention for the Protection of the World Cultural and Natural Heritage*, the regulations prevented the construction of the dam. In May 1983, the new government passed the *World Heritage Properties Conservation Act* 1983 (Cwlth). This Act reinforced the ability of the Commonwealth government to prevent the damming of the Gordon River, with the dam site falling within national parklands that had in December 1982 been entered on the World Heritage List of UNESCO.

The Commonwealth government then instigated action in the High Court for an order to restrain further work on the dam. The Tasmanian government sought a declaration that the Regulations and Act were constitutionally invalid. The High Court bench to hear the *Tasmanian Dam* case (also known as the *Franklin Dam* case)[50] had two new members from that which had sat the year before in *Koowarta*. Stephen had retired to become the governor-general of Australia, and Aickin had been killed in a car accident. They were replaced by Deane and Dawson respectively.

Wilson remembered the time as being a politically charged period. The justices were under pressure to hear the case quickly and write their reasons for decisions. It was one of the few times during Wilson's ten years on the High Court that the justices, like the United States Supreme Court, held a formal conference to discuss the issues involved.

Again the court divided four to three, with Wilson joining the minority, with Gibbs and Dawson, in holding that the *World Heritage Properties Conservation Act* 1983 (Cwlth) was not a constitutionally valid exercise of the external affairs power (Section 51 (xxix)).[51] The majority, Mason, Murphy, Brennan and Deane, adopted the broadest view of the external affairs power. They held that, as long as the domestic legislation was in conformity with an international treaty (*Convention for the Protection of the World Cultural and Natural Heritage*) obligation, the law would be a valid exercise of the external affairs power.[52] The entry into the international treaty was enough to bring the Commonwealth legislation under the external affairs power, there being no need for the additional requirement, as espoused by Stephen in *Koowarta*, of the legislation dealing with a matter of 'international concern'. However, the majority did say that, in the absence of an international agreement, Commonwealth legislation would only be valid under the external affairs power if it dealt with a matter of international concern.[53]

In his dissent, Wilson expressed a reluctance to revisit his view of the external affairs power as expressed in *Koowarta*. He said that an unbridled interpretation of the scope of legislative power conferred on the Commonwealth parliament pursuant to the external affairs powers was inconsistent with a proper regard to its place in the Constitution when viewed as a whole. He expressed his concerns with an expansive reading of the power:

> I acknowledge, as I must...that I should therefore reconsider the matter in order to accommodate that decision [*Koowarta*]. I do not find this an easy task. I remained convinced, with all respect to those who think differently, that an expansive reading of section 51 (xxix) so as to bring the implementation of any treaty within Commonwealth legislative power poses a serious threat to the basic federal polity of the Constitution. Such an interpretation, if adopted, would result in the Commonwealth Parliament acquiring power over practically the whole range of domestic concerns within Australia.[54]

Wilson, with the other dissenters, was anxious to preserve the 'federal balance' between the Commonwealth and states. Wilson agreed with the views of early constitutional commentators John Quirk and Sir Robert Garran, who warned that the vaguely expressed 'external affairs' power could not be construed too widely, and that the power 'contains a distinct and independent grant of power. It is not intended and it cannot be used to enlarge, or qualify, other distinct and independent grants'.[55]

Wilson's concern about an expansive reading of the external affairs powers found resonance with the views of Dr Colin Howard, a constitutional law expert. Speaking in a debate held by the Samuel Griffith Society in 1995, Howard argued: 'The perversion of the external affairs power has a fair claim to be the most blatant and cynical departure from the original constitutional intention that we have seen.'[56] Another critic of the expansive interpretation of the external affairs power was Peter Durack, Wilson's co-author of the 1967 *Australian Law Journal* article, and federal attorney-general at the time of Wilson's 1979 appointment to the High Court. Durack argued, in conformity with Gibbs's suggestion in *Koowarta*, that an amendment to the Constitution should be made restricting the external affairs power to matters that deal with substantial relations with other countries or people external to Australia, and laws dealing with the movement of people in and out of the country.[57]

Wilson's and the dissenters' adherence to the 'federal balance' stands in stark contrast to the majority's almost suspicious view of the federal balance. For them, the federal system was relevant as far as imposing restrictions on the Commonwealth in relation to the prevention of discrimination against a state or preventing a state from functioning as an independent unit in the federation. That was as far as the majority would go. Murphy viewed the federal balance notion as 'a balance between fallacies'. Mason was dismissive of 'ritual invocations of the "federal balance"'. To which Wilson in his judgement countered:

> Of what significance is the continued formal existence of the States if a great many of their traditional functions are liable to become the responsibility of the Commonwealth? This is not an application of the reserved powers doctrine as it operated before the Engineers' Case. It is a question of the survival of the indissoluble federal Commonwealth as the Constitution conceived it to be.[58]

Wilson always claimed that his judgements were not guided by his heart or the political consequences of his decision but by his mind, his intellectual reasoning of the law. In *Tasmanian Dams* he stated:

> It cannot be emphasized too strongly that, although the subject-matter of the actions before the Court provides the occasion for much political controversy, the role of the Court is wholly divorced from that controversy. The questions which have been referred to it are strictly legal questions involving important issues of constitutional interpretation. The Court is neither equipped, empowered, nor permitted to enter upon the merits of that controversy. In other words, it is not for the Court to decide whether or not Tasmania should proceed with the construction of the dam.[59]

However, in an interview in 1993, Wilson mentioned that he was a pragmatist, and believed 'a Judge of an ultimate Court of Appeal has to keep one foot on the ground and appreciate the consequences that will attend a particular result', although the decision can't be dictated by one's heart and must be guided by one's understanding of the law and precedent.[60] He then admitted that there may be some inconsistency between the practical judge with an eye on the consequences of a decision and coming to a conclusion based on intellectual reasoning of the law and precedent. To this he commented that very seldom does a case fit with precedent, and that 'you could honestly perceive the law leading in alternative directions'.[61]

His reading of the Constitution led him to decide the constitutional cases before him in a way that also supported his personal belief that the federal balance was important for the preservation of the states, which he championed. He believed in the devolution of power, and was concerned with allowing the Commonwealth government unfettered or expanded power over the states, as some states may be badly served. In particular, he had his own state in mind.

Wilson's daughter-in-law Kerrie and son Bruce wished that Wilson's intellectual reasoning would have allowed him the choice of an alternative decision in *Tasmanian Dam*. Kerrie and Bruce were supporters of stopping the dam. They did not agree with Wilson's reasoning in the case, and thought environmental protection of the world heritage-listed site was more important than concerns about 'states' rights' and, apparently, the wishes of many Tasmanians.

Kerrie and Bruce, who considered themselves on the left of the political spectrum, perceived that during the 1980s Wilson was a conservative and a conservative judge. They had many discussions and arguments with Wilson in relation to politics and the law.

These arguments and discussions took place in a spirit of friendly intellectual banter. Kerrie found that Wilson liked to play the devil's advocate so as to stimulate a discussion. He very much enjoyed the debate, and was prepared to listen to the views of his son and daughter-in-law. He also could be determined to hold to his position, as he would when Kerrie criticised prime minister Menzies. While Wilson claimed that he had always voted Labor, much to the surprise of his children, who thought that until the 1990s their father was a Liberal voter, he had great respect for Menzies. He thought Menzies was a good prime minister for the times.

As Bruce and Kerrie were residing in Melbourne, Wilson and Leila sometimes joined them for holidays in the eastern states, or Wilson would visit them in Melbourne when he was in Canberra during the sitting fortnight. Bruce and Kerrie also visited Wilson in Canberra, and were not impressed with his life there. Although he lived in a good standard townhouse, it lacked warmth, and Wilson looked a lonely man. He had little food in the fridge, and he always seemed in need of a good feed. They described Wilson's existence as 'monklike'.

Wilson's life in Canberra was regimented, and for most of the week a lonely affair. The existence of a High Court justice in Canberra was not one of glitz and glamour. For example, Dawson remarked:

> Canberra in the middle of winter at night is not exactly...a glamorous life...You get back to your little flat, freezing cold. You stand there watching the television while eating your solitary sandwich night after night. It is not glamorous I can tell you.

The church provided Wilson with a great outlet in Canberra. He worshipped at St Ninian's Uniting Church. While in Canberra for weekends he would attend the Sunday service, and he socialised with a number of parishioners. Not for the first time in his life, the church was his spiritual focus and the hub of his social life.

If life in Canberra was not easy, he had the added demands of travelling 3500 kilometres from his home in Perth. His usual routine was to catch the midnight flight from Perth to Melbourne (the 'red eye special'), arriving in Melbourne in the early hours of the morning and transferring to a Canberra-bound plane. On arrival in Canberra he would head straight to the High Court building and his chambers, where he would work for the day attending to correspondence, settling judgements and preparing for the week's sittings. By late afternoon tiredness would be creeping in. He would seek to finish working at approximately 5.00 p.m., go for a run, then return to his townhouse in the nearby district of Kingston for a shower, a meal and to bed. Early Tuesday morning, he would jog before going to court and the commencement of the week's hearings. He would stay in Canberra for the weekend and another week of hearings, then take the return flight to Perth on the Friday night of the second week. Usually he would be back in Perth for two weeks working on his judgements, then back to Canberra for another two weeks of sittings, from Tuesday to Friday.

When Wilson became a High Court justice he travelled first class (in the late 1970s and early 1980s there was no business class). This was not his choice; it was protocol. However, this did not sit well with the man whose philosophy of life was 'live life simply so others may simply live'. Within a year of his appointment to the High Court, Wilson had insisted that he fly economy class.

His colleagues on the High Court queried Wilson's insistence on travelling economy class. They thought it was just placing an unnecessary burden on his exacting travel demands. Brennan comments:

> His insistence on travelling economy class and that insistence on modesty in personal indulgence, in my view, was perhaps, unwise on his part and I think he would have been far better served by taking up whatever he could up the pointy end of the plane and trying to get a bit of sleep, but it is an indication of his enormous sense of duty and modesty that he undertook his tasks this way.

Deane recalls on one occasion sitting in business class as Wilson acknowledged him while he continued towards the back of the plane. This made Deane feel decidedly uncomfortable; that is, until he turned behind to see Wilson's diminutive body sandwiched between two rather large women. Deane appreciated his roomy business class seat.

Wilson's philosophy of leading a modest life and striving for simplicity was also borne out by his choice of cars while a justice of the High Court.

He was entitled to a Commonwealth car, with a driver in both Canberra and Perth. Apart from official engagements, when he used the more luxurious Commonwealth fleet car with driver, Wilson travelled in less salubrious vehicles. In Perth he had a red Holden Gemini with the Commonwealth of Australia Z number plates. In Canberra, he saved the taxpayer money and purchased a secondhand car—a Toyota Corolla, a yellow one. His associates often had use of it.

On another occasion, Wilson's insistence on modesty in relation to car usage worked to his advantage when a citizen protested about perceived misuse of a government car. The incident involved his youngest son, Ian. By that time, Ian was the only child still at home. Bruce and Helen had married in the 1970s. Robyn married in 1982. She had been delighted that Jeffery Christie, a fellow nurse and her future husband, had no idea that she was a justice's daughter when he asked her out on a date. He didn't even know what the High Court was. She felt a great sense of freedom and relief of pressure when, in the mid 1980s, she and her husband moved to live in the south-west town of Harvey. For at least three months, no one had an idea of her connection to her famous father. She found this most liberating. Geoff married four years after Robyn in 1986. However, eighteen months later he and his wife Sandra separated, but it took another eight years before they divorced.

On hitting the teenage years, Ian liked to hang out with his mates and go surfing on the weekends. This gave him an excuse for missing Sunday service at the local Uniting Church. Ian had already signalled his lack of interest in church much earlier, when he had walked out of confirmation lessons. Although unhappy and embarrassed by Ian's action, Leila and Ron did not argue with him, and did not attempt to force him to return.

Ian, like his brother before him, disliked Scotch College. Ian the rebellious teenager found the authoritarian nature of Scotch suffocating. He longed to join his surfing mates who attended the nearby public school, Hollywood High. At various times through his five years at Scotch he spoke to his parents about leaving Scotch for Hollywood High, but they would not contemplate it. They saw no reason why Ian should not complete his education at the same school as his older brothers. In their view, he just had to accept it and make the most of it. Ian found some solace in sport, and was a very accomplished cricket player, but he did not seek to play in the college's First XI cricket team, as it would have interfered with his weekend surfing. Ian was an ardent surfer, who never forgave the college for not allowing him to do surfing as a sporting option.

Wilson believed his constant absence from home placed a strain on his relationship with Ian during the period of his High Court tenure. Ian didn't like his father being away so much when he was young, but he always found his father supportive, and very much appreciated that, when home from Canberra, Wilson spent as much time with him as possible. Ian remembers with fondness his father waiting in the Toyota Corolla at the beach for hours on a Saturday reading the newspaper while he sat on a surfboard offshore seeking the best waves. The sight of the car with Commonwealth Government number plate with a surfboard out the back led to a complaint being made to the Commonwealth Department of Administrative Services. The complainer thought this was an example of wasting taxpayers' money. The Department responded by informing the protestor that the driver of the Toyota Corolla was entitled to a larger and more expensive car and a chauffeur to carry the surfboard. That brought the protest to an end.

Making time to spend with Ian and Leila and the other children who had left home was a juggling act of major proportions. As well as meeting the demands of a High Court justice's position and increased travel time, Wilson still maintained a heavy involvement in matters of the church. In 1985, he spent three weeks up in the north-east of Western Australia, in the small town of Wiluna, volunteering as a builder's labourer, while the Uniting Church constructed a community centre for the town's large Aboriginal population. The sight of the diminutive High Court justice on a hot tin roof may have seemed extraordinary to many, but not to Wilson. For him, it was all part of his Christian and civic duty.

Justice Wilson of the High Court also had the extra demands of his chancellorship, whereby he had to chair senate meetings, and attend graduation ceremonies and many other functions. His dedication to Murdoch University impressed his High Court colleagues. Brennan mentioned that, even though Wilson had a very arduous schedule, it was made much more demanding by his chancellorship duties. He never complained or slowed down the pace.

10

Mabo and More

Well I'd rather not be judged by my record on the High Court. I was a conscientious judge of moderate ability in that context. I believe that is for others to express an opinion about...but I was very conscious of my oath, to do justice according to law, and...I really suppressed my personal inclination and it is a lasting cause of sorrow that there were some Aboriginal cases that came before us when I was in the minority. I was so thankful that I was and that the majority decision represented my heart, but...my commitment to my oath [meant] I just couldn't reason myself with rigorous intellectual reasoning to the decision that my colleagues were able to come to. These were four–three...decisions, so obviously it was an issue that permitted sincere differences of opinion but I would not, if I couldn't legally, and intellectually, be comfortable with a decision I wouldn't give it.[1]

As if the pace were not fast enough already for the justice from the West, it was to increase. In June 1985, the Uniting Church's National Assembly, meeting in Sydney, elected Wilson to be the next president of the church, taking over from the Reverend Ian Tanner in 1988.

Reverend Ian Tanner called Wilson to the microphone to respond to his election. Reminiscent of his time as a fourteen-year-old messenger boy at the Geraldton Local Court, where he needed a stool so he could reach over the service bench, Wilson carried a fruitbox to stand on for his speech. He said:

> The only decision I had to make was to assess whether I would have the time to give if I were elected...I decided I would so agree to have my name put forward because I have a lifelong conviction that the community of faith is a vehicle of the Holy Spirit, and I was not prepared to pre-empt anything God was planning. No one has been praying harder than I have that the Holy Spirit would guide this assembly.[2]

There had been speculation leading up to the assembly that, if Wilson were elected as the next president, he would retire from the High Court; and indeed, he had thought about doing this. However, on his appointment to the presidency he made it clear that he did not intend standing down, and that the church position would have no effect on his judicial duties. He said he would give top priority to his High Court duties, and indicated that he expected to serve on the High Court until close to his compulsory retirement age of seventy, in 1992.

In his acceptance speech, Wilson confessed to a limited grasp of the Bible: 'I confess the fitfulness of my faith, my limited grasp of biblical truth, the shallowness of my perception of theological issues, and my preoccupation with worldly affairs.'[3] He added that he was proud to belong to the Uniting Church, thrilled with the gifts of the Holy Spirit, and joyous and confident about the future 'not because we know what it will bring, but because we know WHO it will bring [original emphasis]'.[4]

In reporting on his election, the Uniting Church's national paper referred to a TV interview Wilson had given during the first few days of the National Assembly. The interviewer asked whether his Christian faith or ethics ever conflicted with his vocation. He replied: 'Oh no. Both the law and the gospel stand to rescue man, and then preserve his freedom. And I am always thrilled when the law can be administered with mercy.'[5]

However, time and time again when Wilson was asked about whether his Christian faith influenced him as a justice of the High Court, he answered no. He believed that his integrity as a judge depended on him reaching a decision based on the law and precedent, even if that went against his personal views, which were significantly influenced by his Christian beliefs.

During Wilson's tenure on the High Court there were few cases that specifically involved questions related to religion. One that did was the *Scientology* case,[6] which required the justices to decide if the Church of Scientology were a religion. If so, it would be exempt from paying Victorian payroll tax. The adherents of the Church of Scientology accept and follow the writings of Lafayette Ronald Hubbard. Hubbard claimed that he drew inspiration from the Indian Veda, Buddhism and the *Tao-Te Ching* of Lao Tzu. Scientology has no clear concept of a Supreme Being or a Creator. It was not until 1965 that Hubbard's writings referred to Scientology as a religion, and some have argued that the effort to identify Scientology as a religion was a sham.[7] However, the constitution of the Church of Scientology refers to the religion of Scientology, and article 2, section 1 states that the doctrine of the church is:

> To encourage religious faith and propagate the doctrines that Man's best evidence of God is the God he finds within himself, and that the Author of this Universe intended life to thrive within it, and that the Church is formed to espouse such evidence of the Supreme Being and Spirit as may be knowable to Man and that it is the hope of Man that the teachings of the Church will bring a greater tranquillity to the State and thus the better order and survival to Man upon this Planet.
>
> Scientologists believe that an individual's liberation...is to be attained through the working out of a process of enlightenment which is essentially a practical technology requiring virtually no 'belief', but rather personal application of 'scientific' principles inherent in nature.[8]

Even though Wilson's personal religious view was that the Church of Scientology was not a religion, he came to a different conclusion in relation to the legal characterisation of religion. In a rare joint judgement, he and Deane (who also had a personal religious view opposed to the religious beliefs of the Scientologists) held that, although no single characteristic constituted a formularised legal criterion of whether a system of ideas and practices was a religion, criteria that went towards establishing a religion included a belief in a supernatural being, the ideas and code of conduct were accepted and practised by adherents, adherents were an identifiable group, and the adherents viewed the ideas and practices as a religion. On those criteria they held the Church of Scientology to be a religion.[9] They joined Justices Mason (the acting chief justice), Murphy and Brennan in unanimously ruling that the Church of Scientology was a religious institution.

In later life, Wilson referred to the *Scientology* case when denying that his personal views on religion or his religious faith influenced his decisions on the

High Court. At least at a conscious level he could not recall his religious faith influencing his opinions as a justice. He repeatedly said that he detached any personal religious view or faith from his legal reasoning process.[10] However, on an *ad hoc* basis during the lunch recess, Wilson would sometimes go to the chambers of Brennan, a practising Catholic, and they would share some prayers before enjoying a bite of lunch together.

As a High Court justice, Wilson received many invitations to speak at conferences and symposiums, which, time permitting, he was happy to accept. An address he gave in November 1984 at the Fifth International Congress of the Australian Academy of Forensic Sciences at the University of New South Wales on 'Experimenting with Life' sheds light from a different angle on his thoughts on the interplay of law and religion. He commenced his paper by saying that the twentieth century had produced a paradox, by which war, torture, oppression and violence had violated the sanctity of life, while on the other hand, 'no other century has seen such a determined testimony to the inherent freedom and dignity of every human being'.[11] Drawing on Australian and international case law, and international human rights, he canvassed the law in relation to the right to know, the right to privacy, the right to life and the right to recognition as a person.

His paper offered little in the way of forceful argument on law reform in the area. He acknowledged the varying views and arguments in relation to these so-called rights without nailing his colours to the mast. However, in a conciliatory tone to the debate, he acknowledged the need to balance individual autonomy and choice with the need to harmonise 'individual rights in the peace and well-being of the community of which those individuals are members and to which they owe responsibility'.[12]

He also offered some concluding comments on the 'sanctity of life' *vis-à-vis* 'quality of life' debate. He saw the fundamental issue being shaped by a Judaeo-Christian attitude that life is good and should be preserved, but that 'life is a relative good, and the duty to preserve it a limited one'.[13] Such a qualified view on the sanctity of life could be deemed surprising from such a committed Christian, even though the Protestant churches are not theologically adamant on the right-to-life question as is the Catholic Church.

In later life, Wilson found it difficult to make a definitive statement on the issue of abortion. He said he did not want to diminish the wonder of conception and the reproduction process, which 'obviously is part of God's plan'. He thought it was 'very sad when the unborn is simply treated as a thing that can be disposed of at will', but one needed to also consider the health and mental state and consequences for the mother. Such consideration may justify an abortion, but this should only occur after adequate counselling. He thought that there was merit in the father sharing in the decision to undertake an abortion procedure, but he was not sure how this should work.

Following close on the highly charged 1983 *Tasmanian Dam* case, the High Court again received intense media and public attention during what became known as the 'Murphy Affair'. A phone call from Justice Lionel Murphy to New South Wales chief stipendiary magistrate Clarrie Briese, where he allegedly made reference to his alleged 'mate', Sydney solicitor Morgan Ryan, resulted in the first criminal investigation of an incumbent High Court justice.

As described by Professor Tony Blackshield, the Murphy Affair refers to the series of investigations and criminal trials relating to alleged improprieties by Murphy that began with the publication of the '*Age* tapes' on 2 February 1984, and ended with Murphy's death on 21 October 1986.[14] In describing the tapes, Professor Blackshield wrote:

> 'Age tapes' was itself a misnomer. The reference was to a large body of material, allegedly transcribed from tapes of telephone conversations illegally recorded by the New South Wales police, and allegedly containing evidence of widespread corruption in New South Wales. Tangentially, the material included excerpts from Murphy's telephone conversations with Sydney solicitor Morgan Ryan, obtained through a tap on Ryan's telephone.[15]

The publication of the alleged contents of telephone conversations between Murphy and Ryan over a number of matters, including the possibility of commencing a malicious prosecution against a former federal politician,[16] had commenced as early as November 1983 in the now-defunct *National Times*, although at that stage Murphy was not mentioned by name.[17]

Murphy's biographer, academic Jenny Hocking, has written very critically of the method of publication of the alleged conversations by the *National Times* and the *Age*. She accused the *National Times* of moving 'away from even the intelligence material itself and into supposition in order to fill the gaps where required', and 'displayed none of the spirit of disinterest appropriate to journalism…'[18] She was equally critical of the *Age*:

> [T]he *Age*'s report has since been described as 'a case study in carelessness'. The paper's coverage avoided any distinction between tape, transcripts and summaries, compressed several conversations over different years into one, and established a tone of sinister intrigue, double-dealing, sexual profligacy and dissolute corruption.[19]

Under parliamentary privilege (in the New South Wales Parliament on 21 February 1984 and in the Queensland parliament on 6 March 1984), Murphy was named as the judge in question. This of course received widespread publicity, and placed pressure on the Hawke Labor government. The acting attorney-general, Senator Gareth Evans, who had worked for the then Senator Murphy in 1974, felt particularly uncomfortable. He was faced with a situation where there was political pressure building for the Commonwealth government to investigate the serious allegations being made against a High Court justice, whom Evans knew personally and admired.

Initially, the Hawke government considered a full Commission of Inquiry, but later settled for a Select Senate Committee to inquire into the authenticity of the tapes and whether Murphy's conduct amounted to 'misbehaviour', which could lead to his removal from office under section 72 of the Constitution.[20] Murphy refused to appear before the committee, but he did furnish a written statement. The committee was unable to make a unanimous finding on the authenticity of the material before it. However, the committee heard evidence from New South Wales Chief Stipendiary Magistrate Clarrie Briese that Murphy had made approaches to him seeking favourable treatment for Ryan, with Briese claiming that, in a telephone conversation, Murphy said, 'And what about my little mate?' Briese took this as a reference to Ryan. The alleged 'little mate' phrase was blazoned across the nation's newspapers and became part of Australian folklore.[21]

Morgan Ryan, a friend of Murphy's, was a Sydney solicitor who had been charged in 1981 with falsifying documents and conspiracy in relation to the application from a Korean national for permanent residency. In January 1982, he was committed to stand trial on both charges, but subsequently the charges of forgery were dropped. In July 1983, Ryan was convicted on the conspiracy charges, but a year later the conviction was overturned by the NSW Court of Appeal, and a new trial ordered.

The Briese allegations became the focus of a second Select Senate Committee, established on 6 September 1984, with Murphy again refusing to appear. The second inquiry also heard new allegations from New South Wales District Court Judge Paul Flannery, who had presided over the 1983 Ryan trial, which lent possible corroborative support for the Briese allegations. On 9 July 1983, Flannery had attended a dinner at Murphy's Darling Point home. Flannery did not allege that the Ryan trial was discussed, but that during a general discussion on charges of conspiracy, Murphy referred to his decision in *R v Hoar* (1981).[22] Two days later, the case was cited in Ryan's counsel's opening address in Ryan's trial.[23] This second Senate inquiry, which consisted of four senators and two retired judges, found that on the balance of probabilities, Murphy had attempted to influence the course of justice. Vigorously proclaiming his innocence, Murphy stood down from the bench, but refused to resign from the High Court. On 21 November 1984, Ian Temby QC, the federal director of public prosecutions, recommended that Justice Murphy be prosecuted on charges of perverting the course of justice.

The High Court now faced a possible protracted period sitting with only six justices, while one of its own faced the ignominy of being the defendant in a criminal trial. To make matters worse, Murphy had to contend with the daily media scrum of TV cameras, photographers and journalists waiting for him at the entrance to the courthouse in Sydney.

Wilson remembered this time with much sorrow. He liked Murphy, and wished that he and his family did not have to endure the obvious stress and pain they were feeling. Wilson was not alone in his feelings for Murphy. Wilson had remarked of the period leading up to the first trial:

> We all felt sad for Lionel, Ingrid and the two boys. It was awful for them. A High Court judge standing trial—as you can imagine it was sensational news in the media. But for poor Lionel and his family it would have been just torture.

On 5 July 1985, a jury cleared Murphy of the charges arising from the Flannery allegations, but convicted him of those relating to the Briese allegations. Justice Cantor of the Supreme Court of New South Wales reserved sentencing. Controversy ensued, as some jury members came forward to say they had believed that the trial judge's directions to them meant they had to convict over the Briese allegations even though they believed Murphy had done no wrong.

Murphy appealed the conviction to the New South Wales Court of Criminal Appeal. He also made a jurisdictional challenge in relation to the allegations and Commonwealth power in investing state courts with federal jurisdiction. This matter was heard in the High Court after its removal from the New South Wales Supreme Court. Murphy also referred twenty-one questions of law to the High Court. The High Court refused to answer these questions, saying they should be dealt with by the New South Wales Court of Criminal Appeal in conjunction with the appeal against the conviction. However, it did hear the jurisdictional challenge, which it dismissed.[24] In relation to this hearing, Wilson remembers it as a time of 'great tension.' But he added: 'We went about our task faithfully to our oath. But as you can imagine it was difficult as we were dealing with one of our colleagues.' Ian Callinan QC, a Brisbane barrister who later became a High Court justice, representing the Crown in the High Court proceedings, recalled the tension in the High Court: 'I'll never forget that day…There we were, we had no personal arguments—everyone was just so strained. It was an impossible situation.'[25]

As can be imagined, the guilty conviction of 5 July 1985 and the subsequent eighteen months' imprisonment (with Murphy being released on bail pending his appeals) created a great stir in the media, and placed further scrutiny and pressure on the High Court and the Hawke government. Murphy, his High Court colleagues, and the prime minister and his ministers had to endure headlines such as 'Murphy: 18 Months But Will Not Resign' and 'Words That Made ALP Hearts Sink'.[26]

On 28 November 1985, the New South Wales Court of Criminal Appeal (sitting with a specially constituted bench of five judges) quashed the conviction on the 'Briese allegations' and ordered a new trial.[27] On 28 April 1986, the jury at a second trial acquitted Murphy on these charges. No doubt Murphy hoped that was the end of the matter. On hearing of the acquittal, Wilson also thought that the tension of the last two years could now be put behind everyone, and he and his colleagues could welcome back Murphy. He was happy for Murphy and his family, and also glad that the High Court would now have its full complement of seven justices to hear cases. It had been difficult working with one justice short.

Two days later, Justice Donald Stewart's Royal Commission into the authenticity of the *Age* tapes (which was established in March 1985) released its second report, which raised yet more allegations against Murphy. Also, the *National Times* published allegations that Murphy had spoken to a Commonwealth police officer, before the formation of the Australian Federal Police, offering to assist in his promotion in the new force in exchange for new information.[28] There was now a possibility that Murphy would face new criminal charges. Murphy cancelled his plans to resume sitting on the High Court, but he refused to resign.

This heightened the tension and concern on the bench. Chief Justice Gibbs was particularly worried that the protracted Murphy Affair, which had placed an increasing workload on the other justices, was to continue. Of more concern for Gibbs was the effect on the reputation of the High Court. After the release of the second Stewart report, the chief justice wrote to Murphy, urging him to resign.[29]

The chief justice was not alone in his concern about the damage sustained to the public confidence in the court. The prime minister, Mr Hawke, refused to endorse Murphy's return to the bench, and strong views were being expressed by prominent barristers and academics on the issue. Professor Colin Howard of Melbourne University argued that Murphy's position on the High Court was untenable, while Maurice Byers QC and David Brown, senior lecturer in law at the University of New South Wales, believed Murphy should not resign. A number of prominent Australians, including artist Lloyd Rees, paid for the insertion of a half-page advertisement in the *Sydney Morning Herald* supporting Murphy, and arguing that no further inquiry should take place.[30]

The continual publicity did nothing to ease the concern Gibbs had about the possible damage done to the image and reputation of the High Court. He was joined in his concerns by the other justices who were worried with the 'public disquiet'. According to Wilson, they were angry that Justice Murphy didn't seem to appreciate the harm being done to the court.[31]

Wilson was also angry, but never expressed that to Justice Murphy. While having great sympathy for Murphy's plight, he thought that, as the matter became more and more protracted, it would be best for the integrity and image of the High Court that Murphy should resign. Wilson's fondness for Murphy never diminished over the whole period of the affair. He often disagreed with Murphy's decisions, believing that his judgements were frequently written from a political conviction, rather than legal precedent. With laughter, Wilson recalled how Murphy would often say: 'I have a lot of regard for the doctrine of precedent, I think of it about once a year.' Wilson had great respect for his abilities. He had no intention of shunning his colleague, although there were few chances for social intercourse over this period. Whenever they did meet, they engaged in friendly discussion on a range of matters, but none touching on the issue causing the tension on the court.

Leila also liked Murphy, and had great sympathy for Lionel's wife, Ingrid, and their two sons, Cameron and Blake. During Leila's visits to Canberra over the period of the Murphy affair, she had the occasional social contact with Ingrid. The pain being endured by Ingrid was noticeable. Leila and Ingrid talked about anything but the Murphy affair. Leila felt that Ingrid enjoyed the distraction.

The tension and the concerns of the justices prompted a meeting on 6 May 1986, of all the justices, including Murphy, to discuss the issue. This resulted in media speculation that the next day the justices were going to meet again to sit in judgement on their beleaguered colleague. Gibbs released a statement refuting any such suggestion. The press statement read, in part:

> Yesterday there was a meeting of the Justices of this Court, including Mr Justice Murphy. In some way a misunderstanding of the intentions of the Justices has arisen. The Justices do not intend to conduct any inquiry or to make any finding as to the conduct of Mr Justice Murphy in order to resolve any controversy as to his Honour's judicial status, rights or duties. They did not agree to do so yesterday.[32]

The Hawke government was becoming increasingly concerned over the Murphy Affair. It was not sure which way to respond, with the left wing of the Labor party showing strong support for Murphy, but with the attorney-general, Mr Lionel Bowen, and others in cabinet worrying that Murphy's refusal to resign may have led some of the High Court justices into making public pronouncements on the desirability of their besieged colleague resigning. Wilson never contemplated such an action himself, but it did appear that some of the other justices were thinking about it.

The Hawke cabinet responded by establishing a Special Parliamentary Commission, consisting of three former justices—Sir George Lush, Sir Richard Blackburn and Mr Andrew Wells—to inquire into and decide whether Murphy should be removed from the High Court under section 72 of the Constitution. Hearings commenced in June 1986 in Sydney.

On 31 July 1986, Murphy brought the situation to a head when he announced that he had incurable cancer, and that he would return to sitting on the court for as long as possible. Gibbs, as chief justice, wrote to Murphy urging him not to sit again. The next day Murphy wrote back, stating he had no intention of following the course suggested by the chief justice.

Murphy did return to the High Court for one week of sitting. He died on 21 October 1986. Wilson was sad that a man, who in many respects had a different judicial philosophy from him but he greatly admired, had such a troubled last few years of life. He also felt very sorry for Ingrid Murphy and the two sons, Cameron and Blake.

At the memorial sitting of the High Court following the death of Murphy, Murphy's brother approached Wilson. He said his brother had appreciated their relationship. This took Wilson by surprise, as he believed that he had not been particularly friendly to him.[33] As Wilson commented: '…at least he didn't have to be on his guard [with me] as I think he did otherwise.' In particular, Wilson was referring to the strong stand Chief Justice Gibbs took on the issue of whether Murphy should resign.

Gibbs retired from the High Court on 5 February 1987. The next day Mason was sworn in as chief justice. At the same ceremony, Mary Gaudron and John Toohey were sworn in as justices of the High Court to fill the vacancies created by Gibbs's retirement and Murphy's death.

Gaudron was only forty-three years of age when appointed to the High Court. She came to the High Court from the position of solicitor-general of New South Wales. She was the first female in that position, as she was for the High Court. Wilson found Gaudron a delightful companion, even though he felt that judicially they were generally of different minds.

Toohey became the second justice of the High Court from Western Australia. Wilson had admired Toohey's decision in the early 1970s to give up a lucrative practice at the Perth bar to take up a position as the Aboriginal Legal Service solicitor in Port Hedland. He considered Toohey 'an asset on the court'; he grew strongly into the position after Wilson had left the High Court.

Wilson was happy to see a female and another Western Australian appointed to the High Court. He was also satisfied that they were appointed on their abilities to do the job. Wilson was strongly opposed to the selection of High Court justices on any criteria other than merit. He had never championed the appointment of judges on affirmative action grounds, to improve either the bench's gender or ethnic diversity.

But Wilson was critical of the lack of judicial appointments to the High Court from west of Victoria's border. When Michael Kirby, the president of the New South Wales Court of Appeal, was appointed to the High Court bench in 1996, Wilson criticised the fact that the bench contained four justices from the most populous state in Australia. He was not critical of Kirby's appointment *per se*, having great respect for his judicial qualities. He wanted to make the point that, in a federation of states, it was absurd that four of the seven justices came from New South Wales, when there were many able and competent candidates from other states. In 103 years there have only been two from outside New South Wales, Victoria and Queensland—Wilson and Toohey.

The fifth national Assembly of the Uniting Church opened at Festival Hall in Melbourne on the 22 May 1988. Wilson was installed as its fourth president.

Earlier that year, on Australia Day, 26 January 1988, Wilson had been awarded an Order of Australia (AO).[34] He saw it as a great honour, but felt no great sense of personal achievement. That was not the Wilson way. He knew that he was looked up to by many in the church because he was a justice of the High Court, but he did not seek or want reverence shown towards him. As reported by the church newspaper in 1985: 'Ron Wilson is a humble man whose commitment to the doctrine of the priesthood of all believers makes him edgy when fellow Christians treat him as a VIP.'[35] When lining up to register at the 1985 assembly, Wilson found his name tag written as 'Justice Ronald Wilson'. Wilson asked for a change of tag to 'Ron Wilson'.

In similar vein, Reverend Dr Dean Drayton (who was to become president of the Uniting Church of Australia in 2003) recalled seeing Wilson lining up towards the back of the lunch queue. He stood out, dressed in a loud Hawaiian shirt and shorts. Drayton shouted out, 'Who is that man?' Someone replied, 'He is the next president of the Uniting Church.'

Drayton also recalled a story told to him by former president, James Haire. Lining up for lunch when he had become president at the 1988 National Assembly, Wilson was in conversation with a visiting American dignitary, who asked him, 'Why are you as President lining up in a queue to get lunch?' Without a second thought Wilson replied: 'To get a feed.' As Drayton remarked, Wilson was 'quintessentially Australian', and 'had no airs about himself…One had to remind oneself that this man was a knight of the realm, a High Court Judge and the President of the Uniting Church'.[36]

In light of Wilson's new role as president of the Uniting Church, he informed Murdoch University that it would be difficult for him to serve another term as chancellor after his third three-year term expired in 6 February 1988. The Murdoch University senate asked Wilson to stay. At the time, there was discussion about whether Murdoch would amalgamate with UWA, its more illustrious counterpart across the river. The senate felt it would be advantageous to have the benefit of Wilson's leadership during this period of uncertainty. Again putting his public duty ahead of his personal wishes, Wilson agreed to remain as chancellor for a further twelve months.

Wilson had strong feelings about this issue of amalgamation. At the end of 1987, the Commonwealth government released its Green Paper on higher education. John Dawkins, the federal minister for education and member for Fremantle, was seeking major reform of the higher education sector, which included restructuring and possible amalgamation of institutions to establish larger universities. Amalgamation talks between Murdoch University and UWA ensued.

Wilson had considerable faith in the academic standards and achievements of Murdoch, and was deeply concerned about the possibility of the university losing its distinctive and independent character. However, as an incentive the Commonwealth government was prepared to provide extra essential funding to Murdoch if the amalgamation occurred. Wilson felt that political and financial reality would rule, and that the two universities would amalgamate.

On 17 October 1988, the Murdoch University's senate passed a resolution that agreed to amalgamation, and the UWA senate gave in-principle agreement.[37] It was hoped to implement full amalgamation by 1 January 1990, with the new university to be named The University of Western Australia.

The amalgamation agreement caused much disquiet and concern among a significant number of academics at both institutions. In announcing the Murdoch University senate's decision, Wilson said: 'Our decision has been made to preserve the distinctive and distinguished contribution Murdoch University has already made to higher education.'[38] Wilson said the decision to amalgamate was made with 'deep reluctance'. However, it was considered the only way to safeguard the preservation of the university in light of the Commonwealth government's policy of preferring institutions with larger student populations than could be found at either Murdoch University or UWA. He also believed that a larger institution would provide opportunities for growth and expansion.

Murdoch University and UWA were established under state legislation; therefore, any amalgamation required the approval of state parliament.

Because of pressure from its rural constituents, the National Party blocked amalgamation in the Legislative Council, where the conservative coalition had a majority over the Labor government.

1988 had been a busy and momentous year for Wilson, but his life was about to placed under unexpected new pressures of workload and responsibility. On 8 December 1988, the High Court handed down its decision in *Mabo (No 1)*.[39] Wilson and the other justices had heard argument from counsel in March of that year. The case had commenced its legal journey on 30 May 1982, with the filing of a statement of claim by the plaintiffs in the Brisbane High Court Registry, but the story of the *Mabo* litigation commenced the year before that.

On 28 August 1981, a conference on 'Land Rights and the Future of Australian Race Relations' was held at James Cook University in the northern Queensland town of Townsville. Those attending were committed to the advancement of Aboriginal rights. They were also intent on garnering public support for fundamental change in the relationship of Aboriginal people with the nation. The most significant outcome of the conference was the decision to fight the 'struggle' through the courts.[40]

Some of the nation's most active and significant players in the Aboriginal rights movement attended the conference. They included Aboriginal academic Marcia Langton, Les Collins from the North Queensland Land Council, Bob Collins, the leader of the Northern Territory Labor Opposition, historian Henry Reynolds, Garth Nettheim from the law faculty at the University of New South Wales, and practising lawyers Greg McIntyre and Barbara Hocking. In completing a master's degree at Monash University, Hocking was the first Australian to write a substantial treatise on recognising native title in Australia.[41]

Also attending was the distinguished public servant Herbert Cole 'Nugget' Coombs, who had inspired the formation of the NEAF, of which Wilson had been a member of in the 1970s. In 1978, Coombs had established the Australian Treaty Committee (ATC), which was composed of non-Aboriginal people, including the poet Judith Wright, who was also at the 1981 Townsville Conference. The ATC was committed to a treaty between Aboriginal people and the Australian government. It aimed to secure recognition of Aboriginal rights, identity and culture and greater control by Aborigines over their own affairs. The ATC promoted the treaty idea in the mass media and through public meetings. It also had the support of the National Aboriginal Conference (NAC), which the Commonwealth government had established. However, by 1983, as the influence of the ATC and the NAC waned, the treaty idea lost impetus without achieving any tangible results.

The most significant person at the conference was Eddie Mabo, activist, educationalist and university gardener. Mabo had been to two other Townsville conferences. The first was in 1967, the year of the passing of the referendum to amend the Australian Constitution to give legislative power to the Commonwealth parliament to make laws for Aboriginal people and also to include Aboriginal people in the national census. The 1967 conference drew its inspiration from the civil rights movement in the United States. It focused on the need to end discrimination against the Indigenous peoples of Australia so that they might enjoy the same legal and political rights as non-Indigenous Australians. The second conference, in October 1976, a year after the dismissal of Gough Whitlam as prime minister by the governor-general, Sir John Kerr, focused on protecting Torres Strait Islanders' interests in the management of the resources of the Torres Strait.[42]

Eddie Mabo was born on Mer Island in the Torres Strait. At the time of the 1976 conference, he would still have harboured a keen sense of disappointment at the governor-general's shock dismissal of Whitlam one year earlier.

Elected in 1972, the Whitlam government was committed to radical change in the field of Aboriginal affairs. The momentous, premature dismissal of his government meant that Whitlam was not able to achieve all he had committed to at a February 1972 meeting with Aboriginal leaders at the Aboriginal Tent Embassy. Disenchanted Indigenous leaders had built the 'embassy' at the entrance of the old Parliament House in Canberra. It was a symbolic public display of the sense of disenfranchisement felt by many Indigenous Australians. Nevertheless, under Whitlam's leadership, Parliament passed the *Racial Discrimination Act* 1975 (Cwlth) (RDA). The Act gave legislative force to Australia's international law obligation under the UN *Convention for the Elimination of All Forms of Racial Discrimination*.

The Whitlam government also established a commission of inquiry into Aboriginal land rights, chaired by Justice A. Woodward. As a consequence of this inquiry, the Labor government introduced a Bill into the Commonwealth parliament for land rights in the Northern Territory.

However, the *Aboriginal Land Rights (Northern Territory) Act* 1976 (Cwlth) was not passed until 1976, by which time the Fraser Liberal–National Coalition government was in power.

Eddie Mabo wanted more than a legislative scheme by which parliament defined and created land rights. He wanted to challenge the whole basis of Australian law that made Aboriginal rights subservient to the wishes of Commonwealth, state and territory parliaments. He especially wanted to challenge the common law *terra nullius* doctrine, which conceived that when Europeans acquired sovereignty over Australia, the land had been inhabited by (Aboriginal) people without a system of land ownership—thus equating settlement of Australia with settlement of an uninhabited territory. As Canadian academic Professor Peter Russell writes, it was Eddie Mabo who provided 'the personal energy…to articulate the vision that would convince enough of those in attendance [at the 1981 Townsville Conference] that a law case challenging the *terra nullius* doctrine was the essential next step.'[43] This was to be the *Mabo* case.[44]

On 30 May 1982, a statement of claim on behalf of Mabo and four other Murray Islanders was filed in the Brisbane registry of the High Court. The ultimate aim of the plaintiffs was ambitious: 'to secure from the country's highest court recognition of an Indigenous legal order that preceded and survived the assertion of British sovereignty'. The plaintiffs wanted to overturn the doctrine of *terra nullius* and have the court recognise native title.

The filing of the statement of claim set in motion more than four years of legal manoeuvres and exchanges between Mabo's legal team and lawyers for the state of Queensland. It was not until 1988 that *Mabo (No 1)* was heard by the full bench of the High Court. The claim had already been the subject of a 1986 hearing before Chief Justice Gibbs, who made orders remitting the trial of the action in the Supreme Court of Queensland but under federal jurisdiction.[45]

Melbourne barrister Ron Castan QC, a founder of the Victorian Aboriginal Legal Service and the Koori Heritage Trust, was retained as leading counsel for Mabo and the other plaintiffs.[46] He had also been counsel for the Aboriginal plaintiff in the 1982 *Koowarta* case.

The plaintiffs in *Mabo (No 1)* sought a declaration that they had individual or family ownership over specified plots of land and fishing places in the Murray Islands. The plaintiffs named both the Queensland and Commonwealth governments as defendants, but it was the Queensland government that the plaintiffs viewed as the main opponents. The Bjelke-Petersen-led Queensland government had long opposed Aboriginal land rights. The plaintiffs sought declarations of the existence of their land rights and injunctive relief against Queensland legislation, which sought to deny them ownership of land based on native title recognition. The plaintiffs claimed that the state's legislative power over the Murray Islands was subject to the land rights of the Murray or Meriam people, based upon local custom and traditional title. In respect to the Commonwealth government, the plaintiffs only sought a declaration recognising the plaintiffs' ownership of the land in question.

On 2 April 1985, the Queensland parliament enacted the *Queensland Coast Islands Declaratory Act* 1985 (Qld). This Act purported to extinguish—without compensation—any traditional rights to land that might exist in the Torres Strait. The plaintiffs now needed to challenge the 1985 Queensland Act. Otherwise, even if the High Court were to hold that Queensland's legislative power over the Murray Islands was encumbered by the native title rights of the Islanders, the 1985 Act provided the Queensland government with the power to eliminate any native title rights that existed. Thus the litigation tactics now moved to challenging the constitutional validity of the *Queensland Coast Islands Declaratory Act* 1985 (Qld).

In the 1988 hearing, the High Court had to decide on the constitutional validity of the 1985 Queensland Act in terms of whether it was inconsistent with the RDA. Under section 109 of the Australian Constitution, a state statute is invalid to the extent of any inconsistency with a constitutionally valid Commonwealth Act.

Mabo (No 1) was another significant legal and political case that was decided four to three. As in *Koowarta* and *Tasmanian Dam*, Wilson was again in the minority. This time he was joined by Mason and Dawson. The majority comprised Brennan, Gaudron, Toohey and Deane.

The majority held that the 1985 Queensland Act contravened the Commonwealth RDA. The 1985 Act was inconsistent with section 10 of the RDA, which provides that no Commonwealth, state or territory legislation can deny a person of a particular race, colour or national or ethnic origin 'a right that is enjoyed by persons of another race, colour or national or ethnic origin'. The majority found that the Queensland Act was depriving the Murray Islanders of their legal 'rights'. They held that the Queensland Act 'abrogated the immunity of the Meriam people from the arbitrary deprivation of their legal rights in and over the Murray Islands'.[47] As Professor Russell comments, the key to the majority's decision was the broad view they had of rights protected by the RDA. He adds: 'If the "rights" that cannot be denied in a discriminatory fashion are construed very narrowly, then discrimination against Indigenous rights claimants would be difficult, if not impossible to find.'[48] The majority justices took guidance from the concept of universal human rights and human dignity and equality.[49] If the Meriam people had their property rights arbitrarily extinguished, they would have been deprived of these human rights.

The minority had a more restricted interpretation of 'rights' under section 10 of the RDA. They interpreted the right as a right to 'formal equality'. As the right related to holding property according to traditional Aboriginal law that pre-dated British annexation, and thus could not be enjoyed by non-Aboriginal people, the Murray Islanders were not being denied a right enjoyed by others. Formal equality would only be breached if the Murray Islanders were being denied a right enjoyed by other Australians. Wilson wrote:

> ...if there are no other persons of another race who are shown to enjoy rights of the same kind as those which the plaintiffs [Mabo and others] have been deprived, then it will be impossible to find a foothold for s10(1) of the Commonwealth Act [RDA].[50]

Although the Murray Islanders could enjoy the same property rights as other Australians and, therefore, had 'equality before the law', Wilson did acknowledge that 'a deep sense of injustice may remain'. He said:

> This is because formal equality before the law does not always achieve effective and genuine equality. The latter will only be achieved by reason of the former and when the factual circumstances in which the different groups are placed are comparable. The extension of formal equality in law to a disadvantaged group may have the effect of entrenching inequality in fact.[51]

Wilson was of the belief that genuine or substantive equality could only be brought about by special measure or affirmative action, which would be upheld under section 8 of the RDA; from his interpretation of the Queensland legislation, he believed he was left with no option but to emphasise special or affirmative action as the way to bring about substantive equality. However, he did not believe that section 10 of the RDA 'was directed to the question of special measure', and thus was not relevant to the case before him.

Wilson was alone in deciding that the 1985 Queensland Act, in extinguishing native title, was not inconsistent with section 10 of the RDA and thus unconstitutional pursuant to section 109 of the RDA. The other justices in dissent, Mason and Dawson, in fact did not disagree with the majority in that the 1985 Queensland Act, by extinguishing native title, violated section 10 of the RDA. It is just that they declined to determine the matter because the nature and extent of native title had not been decided.[52]

Although Wilson recognised that formal equality may not remove disadvantage, this did not persuade him to decide for the plaintiffs. His recognition that formal equality does not necessarily equate to substantive equality was again expressed ten years after *Mabo (No 1)*. In an address to the National Press Club in Canberra on 25 March 1998, he said that some people believed that equality for all is achieved by treating all Australians equally. Wilson remarked that he did not agree with such a position: one 'does not achieve equality by treating equally people whose circumstances at that moment are not equal, are anything but equal'.[53] This never persuaded him to the opinion that his decision in *Mabo (No 1)*, as a matter of law, was wrongly decided. However, in later life he did express that he wished he could have reached a different decision.

The legal foundations and the merits of the High Court's decisions in *Mabo (No 1)*, and *Mabo (No 2)* after Wilson had left the bench, continue to be vigorously debated. Whatever one's opinion, the series of decisions in *Koowarta* and *Mabo* provide ample opportunity for reflecting on the ironies of judicial responsibility and judicial appointments.

Even at the time, Wilson would have identified more closely with Aboriginal causes and interests than any of the other justices except Toohey. He would become indelibly identified in this way within a decade. His written judgements make it clear that he was keenly aware of the consequences of his decisions, even to the point of acknowledging in *Mabo (No 1)* that inequality could be further entrenched if his view prevailed. Yet Wilson the legal positivist could come to no other decision.

On the other hand, how different things might have been if Gibbs had remained on the bench for one more year. Both the new appointees Gaudron and Toohey were in the majority in *Mabo (No 1)*. There is little doubt that Murphy would have been in this camp. Given that Gibbs had been with

Wilson in both judgements on the *Koowarta* case, it seems likely the same would have been the case with *Mabo (No 1)*. The four to three judgement would have been reversed.

Wilson had a particularly close attachment to his fellow dissenters in *Mabo (No 1)*. He had said that he was very fond of Dawson on a personal level, and judicially and philosophically he 'often thought on the same lines as Daryl Dawson'.[54] Wilson also commented that, on his retirement from the High Court, he felt sorry for Dawson 'because he was on his own'. Similarly, Dawson has commented that he and Wilson were of a similar mind when it came to constitutional cases. He added that:

> it was not surprising because we [Dawson and Wilson] were people who did believe in Federation and I think, not only believed in it as a matter of argument because we were required to believe in that as Solicitors-General. I think philosophically we believed in Federation as the proper form of government for a country of this size, even at that stage. Others did not.

Wilson also believed that on constitutional matters he was very close in viewpoint to Mason. However, this does not accord with their written opinions, with *Koowarta* and *Tasmanian Dam* being classic examples of them coming down on different sides (although they were both in the minority in *Mabo (No 1)*). Mason and Wilson did collaborate on a number of civil cases, one notable example being the equity case of *Walton Stores v Maher*,[55] the judgement being delivered a month before the hearing of *Mabo (No 1)*.[56]

The *Walton Stores* case was significant because the High Court held that, even if there was no binding contract in existence, certain legal (equitable) obligations may nonetheless be created, which will stop a party from denying that it is bound by an agreement. Chief Justice Mason and Wilson held that voluntary promises may be legally enforceable if to do otherwise would allow a departure from the agreement that would be unconscionable. What was crucial in *Walton Stores* was that the company's behaviour induced the respondents to act, and suffer detriment, on the assumption that a contract would be signed.[57]

Wilson recalled that, five years after the *Walton Stores* decision, he had to defend his decision to a keen law student at a dinner at St Columba College at UWA. He was sitting at a table with a group of students. The keen law student, not knowing who she was sitting next to, commenced to give a critical commentary of the judgement in *Walton Stores*. Wilson listened in silence. When she had finished, he flashed his trademark cheeky smile and introduced himself: 'I'm Ron—Ron Wilson.' After the student had recovered from her embarrassment, she and Wilson had a lively and enjoyable debate about the case, with Wilson defending his decision.

By the time of the *Mabo (No 1)* decision in December 1988, Wilson had decided that he would retire early from the High Court in February 1989, rather than remain on the bench until the statutory retirement age of seventy. He was only sixty-six. Originally he had thought that he would retire from the High Court when he assumed the position of president of the Uniting Church of Australia. However, because some people had queried whether he could do both jobs simultaneously, he decided that he would remain on the bench to show that he could hold down the two positions. This displayed a streak of stubbornness. However, not long after making his decision to stay on, he decided that he would retire in six months' time. He thought this was a long enough period for him to make his point.

When Sir Charles Court heard of the retirement plan, he sought to change Wilson's mind. Court had been very impressed with Wilson's performance, especially on constitutional matters, where he had consistently decided against expanding the power of the Commonwealth parliament to legislate in areas that had traditionally been the province of the states. Recalling his efforts to change Wilson's mind, Court said:

> I was alarmed because I knew we wouldn't get another replacement so I probably did the wrong thing but I sought an opportunity, a discreet opportunity, to have a talk to him about the position...

Court found a man who had made up his mind, and who wanted to devote his energies more to the Uniting Church presidency. Court respected and understood Wilson's position, but he and Western Australia's attorney-general, Ian Medcalf, were disappointed Wilson was to leave the High Court early.

In January 1989, Wilson bade farewell to the staff at the High Court and his friends at St Ninian's Church and headed west towards home. In a style more suited to a student than a retiring High Court justice, he packed his meagre belongings in his yellow 1976 Toyota Corolla sedan and drove away from Canberra. He slept the night in his car in the New South Wales country town of Wagga Wagga, then on to Port Augusta in South Australia, where he boarded the Indian Pacific train for the final stretch across the Nullarbor and home to Perth.

On 1 February 1989, the Western Australian Supreme Court held a farewell ceremony for Wilson. Chief Justice David Malcolm spoke in glowing terms of Wilson, saying he 'had been a consummate judge' who combined 'learning, scholarship and wisdom'.[58] In his response, Wilson criticised the media for labelling him a conservative states'-righter judge. Wilson said, 'I do not care much for labels, and I doubt whether labels gain accuracy through repetition.' He then went on to address the comments that had been made in relation to his judgements in constitutional law:

> In the field of constitutional law, I cannot distinguish between the interests of the states and those of the Commonwealth. Unless and until the Constitution is changed, I believe the interests of the entire Commonwealth and those of the states are served best by a court that faithfully and fearlessly seeks to interpret both the letter and the spirit of the document.[59]

Once again, Wilson was reinforcing what he saw as his obligation to obey his oath to be faithful to the law. He repeated this to journalist Liam Bartlett in a radio interview on the local Perth ABC 720 *Morning Program* on 30 May 2000, where he said that he did not allow his personal views to impinge on 'my oath, to do justice according to law'. Likewise, three years earlier on the ABC Radio National program *The Law Report* he said:

> On the Court…I was sworn to do justice according to law, and I took that oath very seriously. There were some decisions in my ten years on the court of which I'm not proud. I'm not ashamed, because they are the best that I could do in pursuance of my oath. But they're not the sort of decisions that I would have liked to have made. In other words, my heart and my mind went in different directions.[60]

Wilson would not name the cases, but said they divided four–three, and thus one with integrity could have gone either way. He added:

> …I strove to interpret certain sections of the Acts that were in question and I interpreted them in a way that led me to be a dissenter. And I'm very

grateful that I was in the minority, because I would have...preferred the majority view, but couldn't bring myself to accept it.

The cases Wilson was referring to were *Koowarta* and *Mabo (No 1)*. He has said that he was glad to be in the minority, particular in relation to *Mabo (No 1)*. The plaintiffs' success in this case laid the foundation for *Mabo (No 2)*,[61] decided in 1992, after Wilson had left the bench, in which the High Court finally held that Australian common law recognised the pre-existing land rights of Aboriginal people. But in lectures he gave to law students at Murdoch University in 1998 and 2000, Wilson defended his decisions in *Koowarta* and *Mabo (No 1)* as being correct in law.[62]

To the same students he made an additional point: his decision-making process involved writing the judgement that would logically lead him to his decision. He said that some of his colleagues on the High Court would decide what result they desired, and write an opinion to support that outcome. He did not name the colleagues he had in mind, but no doubt they included Deane. In a 1993 interview, he said: 'Bill's got a fine mind but he lets his heart rule his head, I think, on some issues.'[63]

Although Wilson said that he approached his judgements without any preconceived notions of a final decision in mind, he had admitted to thinking about the consequences of any decision. Also, it seems clear that his duty to uphold his oath to the law and the Constitution was guided by a determination to preserve what he saw as the federal polity balance. For example, in the case of *Philip Morris Inc v Adam Brown P. Brown Male Fashions P/L*,[64] he was burdened by the consideration that an interpretation supportive of federal balance arguments was probably not supportive of the best interest of the litigants, but that 'any other decision will not only offend the true intent and operation of the Constitution as established by its proper construction but diminish its effectiveness in maintaining a viable federation'.[65]

The federal balance and his concern to ensure that the Commonwealth parliament did not have an unfettered supremacy in its relationship with the states were crucial to his judicial approach in constitutional cases:

I was inclined to defend the States' position in order to preserve federation as I took the view that there was 'safety in numbers'. I felt anxiety lest the Commonwealth dominate the States and consume them. It was my position that Federalism was good for the country. I won't admit to being biased in

> the sense of a pre-determined goal but rather I worked on the principles of the law itself and arrived at my conclusions through reasoning rather than arriving at a pre-determined judgment. But my decisions were however, influenced by a concern for the Federal State balance.

Wilson considered himself a judge of moderate ability. However, he believed that he faithfully upheld his oath to decide a case on the basis of intellectual reasoning and not emotions. He did not believe that the law should have a greater moral dimension; and he believed that justice was to be done according to the law, not personal judicial preferences. The judge was not to be an advocate for a particular side or a particular issue. Some may argue that, while not 'advocating' for the states from the bench, Wilson's personal and judicial views were sympathetic to the federal balance—more sympathetic to the rights of the states than human rights.

Paradoxically, Wilson's retirement from the High Court was to provide an opportunity for him to place human rights at the centre of his professional duty, and allow him to once again to do what he loved doing most—advocate.

11

The President

A nagging anxiety remains with me. It is that our witness to social justice leaves us too comfortable. Does it cost us enough? Does it lack the struggle, the suffering and the self-sacrifice without which no discipleship is complete?[1]

It was late autumn. The chill in the air could be felt by all those entering Festival Hall in Melbourne on the evening of 22 May 1988. Excitement and anticipation gripped the attendees. It was always the same with the installation of a new president of the National Assembly of the Uniting Church in Australia. Tonight's installation was the fifth in the church's eleven-year history.

For many of those attending, there was that little bit more excitement than usual. Church members felt proud that a member of the judiciary at the highest level in the nation was now their president.

Wilson realised and appreciated that his public profile and High Court status did bring added kudos to the church. However, as he prepared for his installation as president, his mind was focused on the job ahead for the next three years, and how God had brought him to this position. He did not believe he was particularly ambitious, either in his professional career or the church's domain. He just accepted what had come his way 'as fitting in with God's purposes'.

The installation was a grand and moving experience for the humble man who grew up in a small mid-west coastal town. Twenty children led the diminutive Wilson to the dais at the front of Festival Hall. Had it not been for his robes, he would have been indistinguishable from his young escorts.

Wilson was the first lay member of the church to be elected to the position, and during his presidential address he took the opportunity to remind the audience that the church needed to do more for the laity. He said:

> As ordinary men and women scattered in the life of the world engaged in the daily round of labour and family life and community enterprise, you and I will glorify God in the world as we seek in humility and love to represent Him wherever we go…It seems to me that the church has yet to learn to provide you and me consistently with the relevant support that we need in order to be faithful witnesses to the presence of God in the places where we live and work.[2]

Wilson, who believed that God was not interventionist—allowing us to make our own way in life—nonetheless believed that his life fitted with God's purposes and that God provided signposts to give us direction. Wilson said that Christians had a responsibility to ensure that these signposts could be read by the secular world. They had to be written in ordinary language that had resonance with the ordinary human being.

Wilson reinforced his championing of the church's laity, when, in an interview soon after his presidential installation, he commented:

> When I went to the third World Council of Churches Assembly, at New Delhi in 1961, that Assembly coined a delightful phrase to characterise the obedient, well-meaning lay Christians who were so enthusiastic in their service of the church that they never had any time to do anything outside it. The message of the Assembly was: the church doesn't really want 'pasteurised' people. By that was meant the lay people whose merit and worth to the church was judged in terms of how closely they resembled the pastor, the minister. In other words their church life consumed them… If you press me to identify particular emphases that are of concern to me, I would put in the forefront the ministry of lay people in furthering the mission of the church.[3]

Wilson was not a slave to hierarchical structures, and he believed in the legitimacy of people power. In the church this meant the laity. They needed to be included in the decision-making process. This reflected Wilson's Presbyterian background, with its emphasis on the rights and obligations of the lay members of the church.

Gregor Henderson (president of the church for the period of 2006–09), was the general secretary of the National Assembly of the Uniting Church during Wilson's presidential tenure. He believes Wilson's championing of the laity was one of the enduring legacies of his presidency. It brought him even closer to the 'flock'. This, coupled with his esteemed judicial status, made him a highly respected president, who was invited to more municipal and church events than any previous holder of the office.

Very early in his tenure, Wilson had to make a presidential ruling. Under the constitution of the church, any member could make an appeal to the president if he or she were not happy with a decision of the parish or the state assembly. Some ministers in Western Australia and other states were requiring fulfilment of certain preconditions before agreeing to baptise someone, and were refusing to baptise infants. That is, they were restricting baptism to adults and believers. Wilson made a presidential ruling that the ministers were not contravening the rules of the church, and that it was not improper for them to have such discretion.

This upset many in the church in Western Australia who disagreed with such baptismal preconditions. Some Western Australian church members petitioned for a meeting of the standing committee of the national assembly, who ruled that Wilson had made an error, and overturned his ruling. He is the only president who has had a presidential ruling overturned in this way.[4] Discussion papers emanated from this issue, with the matter not being conclusively resolved until the 1994 national assembly, after Wilson's presidential term had ended. It was resolved that, because of the Basis of Union and other documents related to the formation of the Uniting Church, ministers were duty-bound to administer infant baptism.

Had he consulted the general secretary beforehand, Wilson may have avoided the controversy. However, Henderson's appointment only became official after Wilson had made his ruling. From that time on, the two men worked very closely together. Wilson always sent proposed statements and correspondence to Henderson for his view, and often his approval, before sending them out under the president's authority. Henderson saw this as reflective of Wilson's humility and 'down-to-earth' style of doing things. Wilson did not consider that he was 'higher and mightier' than the office of the general secretary. This was consistent with Wilson's work practice. He would often, but not always, include those around him in making decisions.

Wilson didn't behave like the church bureaucrats, who were often reluctant to commit themselves to or advocate a strong position on a matter of concern to a church member. If Wilson thought an injustice was being perpetrated, he would act spontaneously, with passion and anger at an injustice. But he did so with the thoroughness one would expect of Wilson the lawyer. He would investigate the substance of the complaint, consulting relevant people within the church when necessary. If he still felt someone in the church was perpetrating an injustice, he was likely to draft a very strong letter of protest, his passion steaming from its pages. Henderson comments:

> I remember once or twice getting a letter faxed over to me and Ron would ask, 'Do you think it is okay or have I gone over the top?' I would look at the letter and you could see Ron's anger coming off the page. I'd say 'Ooh, Ron. No, no. Settle down a little bit. There may be another couple of political issues in here you haven't thought about.'[5]

On one occasion Wilson telephoned Henderson in Sydney and said, 'I am sending over a letter, a draft in fax.' He giggled, then added, 'It might be a bit strong. Could you have a look at it and then tell me what you think?' Henderson rushed off to the fax machine. He didn't want anyone else in the office reading a presidential letter that he feared would contain strong language.

Henderson was right. Wilson was responding to a letter of complaint from a parishioner, on Tasmania's west coast, who was not happy with what she saw as the church's view on traditional sexual morality. Wilson's response showed that he was not happy with her, saying that it was unjust and unchristian not to reach out to all people and be tolerant of differences. Henderson thought the point could be made a bit more diplomatically. He telephoned Wilson back and suggested, 'Perhaps you could moderate the language a little. I don't think it is going to be very helpful in terms of helping this Church member think seriously about the issue.' As was usually the case, Wilson accepted Henderson's counsel and amended the letter.

Keen to meet with as many parishes and lay members as possible, Wilson travelled extensively within Western Australia and across the country, as well as overseas. In May 1989, he travelled to San Antonio in Texas to attend the World Council of Churches Mission and Evangelism World Conference. He wanted to observe how the council's staff handled the media. Wilson had been appointed to chair the media committee for the council's seventh assembly, to be held in Canberra in February 1991.

Three months later, in August 1989, he and Henderson travelled to South Korea. The primary purpose of this visit was to attend the World Alliance of Reformed Churches General Council meeting in Seoul. Wilson and Henderson went a week earlier, to celebrate the centenary of the first Presbyterian mission in Korea from Australia, which had occurred in 1888.[6]

While in Seoul, Wilson became the recipient of an honorary doctorate in Education bestowed by Keimyung University. Reminiscing on the award, Wilson said:

> I was the beneficiary of the very attractive set of robes and I can sport myself as a Doctor of Education. I think education was chosen because they didn't award Doctorates in law, although they did teach law. Perhaps my role as Chancellor of Murdoch University was the sufficient nexus to education to justify the award, but it was a great honour I think. It gives me a great deal of pleasure now to wear the Korean robes at school speech nights and educational functions and it always typifies the role that the Australian church played in the region.[7]

After his investiture, Wilson and Henderson travelled to Pusan, where they were met by the local Presbyterian Church leaders. Being members of a highly hierarchical society, the Koreans had booked Henderson, the general secretary, into a single deluxe room and Wilson, the president, into a penthouse suite at the Hyatt Regency hotel.

Wilson was appalled at the thought of living in a luxury suite and quickly informed his Korean host, 'We just want an ordinary twin room for the two of us.' The Korean host could not understand. Henderson turned to Wilson and said: 'I am happy with my room.' Wilson, mindful of the cultural sensitivities, was polite but would not give up. He said to Henderson: 'No. No. No. It has got to be a twin, just an ordinary twin room. Just an ordinary room.'

'Come on, Ron. When in Rome do as the Romans do,' Henderson replied. But Wilson would not hear of it. The Koreans were perplexed. It took ten minutes to convince them that this was really what the president wanted.

After they had settled into their twin shared room, their Korean Presbyterian host took them to a fancy restaurant, for a high-quality ten-course French meal.[8]

The next night they were taken back to the same restaurant, this time courtesy of their Korean Methodist host. Early in the day Henderson had informed the Methodist general secretary that it was Wilson's birthday—23 August 1989.

During the meal, a huge birthday cake was wheeled in on a trolley. The cake had dry ice around it, giving it a feel of smoke coming from the cake. Henderson wondered whether a scantily clad woman was going to jump out of its centre. Wilson was blushing with embarrassment, but had a wide grin from ear to ear. He was overcome and overjoyed.

After the main meeting, Wilson and Henderson remained in Seoul for a few days to hold meetings with some Korean church people. Some New Zealand Presbyterians also remained. The New Zealand and Australian contingent decided to share rooms, but by the last night there were only four members remaining: the two Australians and John Murray, the New Zealand Presbyterian moderator, and his compatriot, a woman called Anne.

Wilson displayed his frugality—and perhaps a certain naïvety. 'Oh it is silly to have three rooms. How about we draw straws about who is going to share with you, Anne?' Murray and Henderson looked at each other and simultaneously said, 'Oh my God.'

Wilson didn't know what the fuss was about. He responded: 'I'm sharing a room with you, Anne. You trust me Anne, wouldn't you?' Anne looked at him in astonishment and said, 'Of course I trust you.' This was just as well, because the rooms did not have two beds but one queen size bed.

Towards the end of the day, the four of them were in Henderson's and Murray's room, sharing a cup of coffee. Wilson finished his coffee, stood and announced, 'All right I'm going off to bed now. Give me half an hour and I'll be sound asleep.' Half an hour later, Anne went to the room and Wilson was sound asleep on one side of the bed: plenty of room left for her to sleep in.

Wilson felt privileged to travel overseas as a representative of the Uniting Church, and he was particularly keen to continue his lifelong interest in ecumenism. He was the first national president to ask the general secretary of the church to commence the process towards a national relationship with Muslim, Jewish and other religious leaders.

In Wilson's 1991 presidential report to the sixth assembly, he warned that the Uniting Church had to be careful not to 'be content to become just another denomination'. He was particularly concerned with the lack of ecumenical enthusiasm at the local parish or congregational level:

> At the level of the local congregation there is much more that could be done to project God's will for the unity of His people. Many of our congregations are seemingly unaware of the imperative of the Gospel to break down the walls that separate us from our fellow-Christians. We must realise that the credibility of the churches' witness is seriously impaired by our failure to demonstrate locally in worship, witness and service the reconciling power of the Gospel. I hope the impact of the Canberra Assembly [World Council of Churches Assembly held in Canberra in February 1991] will have opened many doors into the fortress of local denominationalism. Ultimately, it is the oikoumene (the whole inhabited world) that supplies the only valid perspective to everything the local congregation does.[9]

The original draft of the report was even blunter, containing the sentence: 'Too many of our congregations go their own sweet way without regard to the imperative of the Gospel to break down the walls that separate us from our fellow-Christians.'[10]

Wilson spent a considerable time during his presidency reaching out to people from other denominations, as well as various congregations and sections of the Uniting Church. He travelled widely around Australia, to city and rural congregations and to state synod meetings, because he wanted to, and because he received a constant stream of invitations from local congregations. They were delighted and proud to have the president of the national assembly with them, who happened to be a High Court justice up to 1989.

Wilson took a particular interest in reaching out to Aboriginal members of the church. In July 1989, he visited a number of Aboriginal communities in Arnhem Land, including Galiwinku, Yirrkala, Gangan, Barrkira and Maningrida. East Arnhem had been the site of several former Methodist missions. At Maningrida, Wilson participated in the ordination and induction of Aboriginal minister, Dudley Coopey. For Wilson, the trip was a highlight of his term as president. Bringing back memories of his wish to be a flying padre, he flew to these communities with Jim Downing, a Congregational and then Uniting Church minister, who had worked extensively in Aboriginal communities in the Northern Territory. He immediately connected with the local Aborigines, and they adored him. He sat with them on the red desert dirt, sharing food and playing football with the community children. His humility was appealing to a cross section of people he met. Henderson remarks, 'The thing about Ron is when he comes into a new group he is just himself. He has got a terrific sense of humour.'

Wilson strongly supported the establishment in 1985 of the Uniting Aboriginal and Islander Christian Congress. It provided the Aboriginal members of the Uniting Church with a degree of autonomy. The congress, based in Townsville, makes it own decisions in relation to

> training for ministry and the form of ministry and they've been able to pursue their own distinctive insights into the faith with a very great emphasis on the holistic nature of the faith.[11]

He believed it was important to foster an Aboriginal ministry and to give the Aboriginal members of the church as much power and autonomy as possible within the structure and constitution of the whole church.

Wilson was also very supportive of the 'covenanting process', whereby congregations and members of the church were invited to get to know Aboriginal people in their community and to enter into solemn covenants—agreements with them to be supportive and work with them and to advocate for Aboriginal rights. The Uniting Church has long been at the forefront of church support for Aboriginal rights, such as land rights and the improvement in the socioeconomic conditions of Aborigines.

During Wilson's tenure the covenanting process was very active. He viewed it as part of the reconciliation process between the Aboriginal and non-Aboriginal sections of the church. However, this reconciliation process required the church to acknowledge past wrongs or mistakes done by the three denominations that made up the church—the Methodists, Presbyterians and Congregationalists. Wilson believed it was a mistake for the churches in the past to believe that Aboriginal people should shed their culture and assimilate totally into the Christian faith. As a result of talking to Aboriginal church people, he believed that the Christian faith could in contemporary times enrich and illuminate Aboriginal culture, and conversely, Aboriginal culture had 'much to offer the Westernised conceptions of the faith'.[12]

Wilson viewed the reconciliation process as one of the greatest challenges facing the church. His 1991 president's report to the national assembly stated:

> The whole church must demonstrate its love for and solidarity with our Aboriginal sisters and brothers through constant prayer and every possible form of visible support. In this regard, I am sure that the covenanting process, notwithstanding its difficulties, holds great promise for the future of the Uniting Church and also for the nation as it embarks on this decade of reconciliation.[13]

Reaching out to the church's Aboriginal members and the general Aboriginal community, Wilson made what he called a 'pilgrimage to Mapoon' in northern Queensland in August 1990. He was accompanied by John Brown, Shayne Blackman and Don Kube. Brown was the Uniting Church director of missions, an office that, before 1985, also included responsibility for Aboriginal missions in Australia. Blackman was a Uniting Church minister, and president of the Uniting Aboriginal and Islander Christian Congress. Kube was a Uniting Church frontier services patrol minister for the Cape York region.

From 1891 until 1963, Mapoon, on the western coast of Cape York Peninsula, had been a Presbyterian mission. In that year, the Queensland Government declared that conditions at the mission were unacceptable, and decreed that it should be closed down. The community believed that this was a pretence, and that the real reason for the proposed closure was linked to Comalco's plan at the time to develop bauxite deposits in the area. After some debate, the Presbyterians accepted the government's decision, and abandoned the mission in June of that year, leaving the community to its fate.

This history was brought to the attention of the Uniting Church assembly in 1988. Wilson and the others sat in the church at South Weipa listening to Aboriginal people recalling memories of the night of 15 November 1963.[14]

It was the middle of the night. It was very dark; there were no street lights to illuminate the black sky. The police arrived, woke up the sleeping community and gave them only a few minutes to gather their belongings. Most were led away from the settlement, with some women and their children being left behind.

The next day the police returned. With the women and children looking on, the police went through the settlement rummaging through everything in the homes, the store and the church, which had not been in use since the Presbyterians had left five months earlier.

The community was dispersed. Members were forced to resettle in New Mapoon, Cairns and Weipa.

Wilson travelled to Mapoon to express the church's 'deepest regret and sorrow' for not supporting the community in their struggle in 1963, and to offer their humble apology. Some of the community members still were bitter towards the church for not supporting them in their time of need. The general sentiment of the community was acceptance and forgiveness, with many agreeing with the women who said: 'We are Christians. Let's stop worrying about the past and face the future with faith and hope.' One of the community leaders said:

> We accept your apology. We forgive everything and want to face the future for the sake of our children. Please help us to go back. The land, the air, the trees are part of us.

These words remained with Wilson forever. In his report of the 'pilgrimage', he commented on the emotion of the visit and how privileged he felt:

> We spent an afternoon visiting the site of the old settlement. Jack Callope, a fine Aboriginal man 76 years old acted as our guide. He displayed an incredible grasp of the history of the community culminating in the tragic events of 1963. We drove through wonderful forest land for two hours before reaching the vast inland sea and Mapoon country. The events of the past pressed upon us as we moved quietly through the site as Jack pointed to the stumps that were all that remained of the buildings that had once been home. Only one thing remained intact. That was the cemetery. We stopped and silently moved among the graves, still displaying brightly coloured artificial flowers. I was deeply moved by some of the headstones: 'Hold thou thy cross before my closing eyes' was one; there were several which read simply 'Safe in the arms of Jesus'. It was an enormous privilege to be confronted with this mute but poignant testimony to the faith of those who had belonged to this community since the early days of the last century.

Wilson concluded his report by saying that he promised the Aborigines help to rebuild Mapoon if they desired:

> We left them with deep respect for their love for their own land and for their courage and determination to return and for the faith in a loving Father that leads them on. May God bless them!

The church did assist in the rebuilding of Mapoon, which is now a thriving Aboriginal community. It was the focus of an article in the *Weekend Australian* in mid 2006 during the increased media and political attention on the state of Aboriginal communities and allegations of child sexual abuse and neglect in these communities. The newspaper article reported positively on Mapoon, as a shining light in a devastating picture of decay, despair and neglect in many other Aboriginal communities.[15]

Not many months later, Wilson was again at the centre of an apology to Aborigines. It was the first Sunday of the seventh assembly of the World Council of Churches in Canberra in February 1991, with Wilson chairing the daily press conference. The man with the disarming smile and nimble mind handled the daily conferences with ease and aplomb. However, it was to be more difficult at the liturgy on the first Sunday of the assembly.

The evening before, after a day of activities at the Canberra Convention Centre, worshippers formed a procession from the centre to the worship tent on the grounds of the Australian National University for an all-night vigil of prayer and fasting for peace with justice. The procession was being led by children. That was the plan of the organisers, but a group of Aborigines were under the impression they would be leading. When one of the organisers, Reverend Dorothy McMahon, of the Pitt Street Uniting Church in Sydney, saw this, she intervened. She walked up to the Aboriginal group and in a firm authoritarian voice told them that the children were expecting to be leading and asked them to come behind the children.

As McMahon would recount at the liturgy the next morning:

> I used a voice that I didn't recognise in myself—a voice which Aboriginal people and, I guess, black people and indigenous people around the world have come to associate with white people who tell them what to do and who push them aside.[16]

The Aboriginal people did not argue, and moved aside. Tears formed in their eyes. This horrified McMahon. After the procession reached the worship tent, she spent time with the Aboriginal group and apologised. They accepted her apology.

She recounted this event at the commencement of the liturgy at the worship tent the next day, the first Sunday of the assembly conference. Standing beside McMahon on stage, holding her trembling body, was Wilson with microphone in hand. He was first to speak. He told the packed tent of worshippers and international media that the Uniting Church of Australia had been granted a few minutes as part of the liturgy 'to explain a sad incident' the evening before. He then introduced McMahon, who recounted the incident and her subsequent apology, and the forgiveness from the Aboriginal group.

McMahon, in a trembling voice and with tears, said:

> Their grace was as great as the grace of God. It was a very special thing they offered to me. But part of their healing lies in my making this confession.[17]

She believed the confession was appropriate, as the liturgy involved a reconciliation of Communion. She stated that she stood with Aboriginal people, but her actions the evening before meant that she and others had to do more to stop the humiliation of Aborigines that had been occurring for 200 years. She prayed 'that in this Communion we can start again'. She thanked the audience for their attention.

Still holding on to McMahon, Wilson in a soft but controlled voice told the congregation that, as president of the Uniting Church in Australia, he stood side by side with McMahon

> because her confession is our confession. I know that our church, and many others, share her sorrow over the public humiliation inflicted by the failure to accord to our Aboriginal sisters and brothers the love and respect they deserve.[18]

After acknowledging McMahon's work for justice and equal opportunity for all he concluded: 'On behalf of the Uniting Church, I tender our Aboriginal sisters and brothers our humble apology.'[19]

Wilson's commitment to Aboriginal reconciliation was consistent with his desire for the church to engage with its laity and with the wider world. He was strongly committed to the Uniting Church's Commission for Mission, which focused on justice and compassion in the world. He was committed to fighting against discrimination and reaching out to people of all ethnic groups and also to women. He favoured an inclusive church. For Wilson, this was part of his deep faith—a belief that we are all children of God and that Jesus reached out to all. With this commitment and belief, he was a champion of a multicultural church and a supporter of the ordination of women ministers.

Wilson was also a strong believer in the national church. The issue of the Uniting Church being a national church became a focus of debate at the 1991 national assembly. It came up in the context of a move by the New South Wales synod to have the national assembly meet every four years rather than three years. It was argued by the New South Wales delegation that this would provide significant budgetary savings. Wilson did not like what he was hearing.

He delivered a brief but impassioned response to the New South Wales move:

> It might be [okay] for New South Wales but smaller synods of the church, like Western Australia, need a national church. If we went every four years instead of three, it would cost us in Western Australia.

Wilson pleaded with delegates that a national church, looking at national issues such as Aboriginal reconciliation, was fundamental to the principles and belief of the church. Wilson's advocacy skills were once again displayed to all who listened to his speech. The New South Wales motion was lost overwhelmingly.

Wilson wanted a national church, but he also wanted greater dialogue with individual congregations. As during his tenure as solicitor-general for Western Australia and then justice of the High Court, Wilson was mindful to guard against views of smaller congregations in smaller states being swamped by the views of the larger synods of New South Wales and Victoria. However, unlike on the High Court, he did not believe that the church constitution provided for strong state synods.

His own faith and concern for others meant he wanted to make sure the views of the various congregations should be heard. He wanted the laity, the 'little people' of the church, to be taken seriously. Sometimes at national assembly standing committee meetings he would say, 'I am just an ordinary lay member from the Applecross Church in Western Australia.'[20] He was sensitive to lay members' concerns and to have congregations supporting the agenda of the national church.

In his presidential report to the 1991 national assembly, Wilson reiterated his support for a national church. It provided a powerful lobby group and voice in the social justice debate for all Australians. He also said that the most effective way the church fought for social justice was through personal witness of the church members in their daily lives and work. He wrote:

> Much of it goes unseen and unsung. Its value lies in the extent to which such service enhances the quality of life for others and testifies to the eternal verities of integrity, goodness and compassion without which no country can become great.

Wilson was not sure that church members were doing enough:

> Gratifying though all this may be, a nagging anxiety remains with me. It is that our witness to social justice leaves us too comfortable. Does it cost us enough? Does it lack the struggle, the suffering and the self-sacrifice without which no discipleship is complete?

The president of the Uniting Church of Australia is appointed for three years. Wilson's tenure came to an end at the 1991 national assembly. It had been a presidency of significance and distinction. He was the first lay person to be appointed as president. This gave lay members a reaffirmation of their importance in the church's fabric. But Wilson's presidency did much more. It reached out to the lay members. He constantly advocated during his tenure for the church to involve the lay members more in the processes and dealings of the church. This, he believed, was important in relations with all sections of the church, including women,[21] Aborigines and various ethnic groups in the church.

Henderson believed that, along with being a lay person and a former High Court justice, Wilson's humility was a strength that endeared him to church members. They were proud that a lay person had been elected president, especially one with a strong public presence and status—something for which Wilson cared little. He also had a great sense of humour. Henderson comments:

> I remember at Standing Committee meetings you'd never know quite what Ron would come out with. There's a mischievous part of Ron's personality. Sometimes you'd think 'Oh Ron!' He didn't act with airs and graces as President, whereas most of the Presidents develop a bit of a persona in this national position—for good or ill—and there is a sort of dignity that goes with the office. Ron wouldn't have cared two hoots about the dignity of the office. His mischievous humour and desire to be in fellowship with everybody made him a joy to work with, but also at times one thought 'Careful, Ron'. He didn't worry about those things. Because of the integrity of him as a Christian leader, there was a stronger affection for him throughout the church than for most Presidents. Because of his down-to-earth way of dealing with people out their in congregations, there was a tremendous amount of love for Ron.[22]

Wilson's penchant for fun and going along with the flow was on display when he visited the northern synod meeting at Kormilda College, an Anglican–Uniting Church college, just outside Darwin. On the final night of the synod, moderator Ron Brant, a huge man, dressed up in a leopard skin like Mandrake's Lothar. Brant announced to the attendees in the meeting room that a gold Logie was to be awarded to the best performer at the synod meeting. Brant went backstage and came back out carrying on one shoulder Indonesian minister Ini Biri, who stood at only five foot two inches, announcing 'here is the Gold Logie'. Brant called out the name of Ron Wilson as the winner of the Logie. Wilson walked up to the stage, chuckling away and shook hands with Biri. Holding Biri on one shoulder, Brant hoisted Wilson on to the other shoulder and proceeded to parade around the room. Wilson thought it was hilarious.

In reflecting on this event Henderson commented:

> You can't imagine many Presidents that happening to and accepting and enjoying that. Ron just loved that, he thought that was hugely funny. A few more 'proper' members of the Synod were momentarily aghast until they realised that Ron was quite happy in it. Ron didn't know that was going

> to happen, but he accepted that. That was just part of his friendship and generosity of spirit.[23]

Wilson was a very generous man, contributing to a number of charities and church causes. On becoming a justice of the High Court, Wilson anonymously donated $100,000 to the Australian National Council of Churches to establish the Ecumenical Youth Leadership Development Fund to support younger church leaders to gain overseas experience, including, in some cases, studying at the Bossey Theological College in Switzerland. He rarely sought reimbursement from the church for travel expenses, which were considerable, as he travelled extensively within Australia and, to a lesser degree, overseas.

There was another person who was also generous. This was Wilson's wife, Leila. As had been the situation throughout their marriage, Wilson was frequently away from home. Now Leila did not have the company of her children to ease her loneliness. She also became Wilson's unpaid secretary, a fact that Wilson acknowledged in his 1991 report:

> I confess my love and gratitude to Leila. It has not been an easy three years for her and she has spent much time at home alone. She has been a first-class unpaid executive secretary, taking many hundreds of phone calls, dealing with many hundreds of inquiries and sorting through piles and piles of mail. I could not have managed without her.[24]

The end of Wilson's term as president of the Uniting Church, officially a part-time job, did not mean that Wilson could now enjoy blissful retirement. He was actively involved in many community causes, such as Legacy—an organisation devoted to the care of widows and children of deceased ex-servicemen. He was also a member of the Civil Rehabilitation Council of Western Australia, a body that cared for the families of prisoners in custody, and counselled released prisoners and rehabilitated them back into the community. He had other substantial commitments, including teaching English to recently arrived refugees. Leila remarks that he wasn't a very good teacher, as he was too soft on the students. The students loved his company and humour, and Wilson loved their kind spirits and hopes of a better and safer life in Australia.

Wilson was still chancellor of Murdoch University. Although he had originally planned to stay on only until February 1989, he agreed to a further three-year appointment, to end in February 1992. He was excited with the prospect of a law program, and eventually a Law School at Murdoch; the university was in the midst of a Law Library fundraising campaign.

Murdoch law school had been mooted in the early 1980s, but it was not received enthusiastically by some members of the university senate and the legal profession in Western Australia. The University of Western Australia, then home to the only law school in the state, was not opposed to the idea. During discussions on the possible amalgamation of the two universities, UWA's position was to support a substantial legal education presence at Murdoch to complement the UWA program. When the Western Australian parliament voted against amalgamation, UWA continued to support the law school proposal. Wilson championed the idea, because he saw it as further developing Murdoch's importance in the education community, offering alternative and beneficial competition to UWA. He had frequent conversations on the topic with members of the legal profession. Towards the end of the 1980s, they gradually warmed to the idea. This shift in the attitude of the profession gave Murdoch's administration and senate the confidence to implement the law program. It opened its doors to students in 1990.

Remembering his own student experience, when World War II returned services personnel were offered educational opportunities, Wilson wanted the law program to attract mature-age students. In its first ten years, Murdoch University law school did have a significant number of mature-age students—men and women who did not come straight to the program from high school. Wilson also wanted the law school to have strong links to the legal profession. The school set about attracting legal practitioners as tutors, and established an advisory committee comprising judges and practitioners.

Wilson's status in the legal community was pivotal to the success of Murdoch's law library fundraising campaign, which he headed. Launching the appeal to a full house in the University's Lecture Theatre 1, he implored the assembled representatives of Perth's legal community to give generously to the appeal. He followed this up with private meetings with barristers and law firms. Always one to lead by example, Wilson donated $10,000 to the campaign.

His generosity did not stop there. He donated $100,000 towards the building of the first student residential accommodation, and money to establish a perpetual Chancellor's Award. He also established a trust fund to finance an award in the law school, now known as the Ronald Wilson Prize in Law. Reflecting Wilson's priority given to service and civic duty, this prize is awarded to a graduating law student who best combines academic excellence with leadership qualities and service to the university and wider community.

These considerable donations were consistent with his willingness to financially assist people and causes. Wilson was frugal when it came to personal expenditure, but generous to friends and charities. Beryl Grant, a pensioner who became the first female moderator of the synod of the Western Australian Uniting Church (1985–87), has been a beneficiary of Wilson's generosity. One evening, she was enjoying a meal with Wilson and Leila, who were preparing to travel east for a church function. Grant said, 'Oh I would love to be there.' A few days later a cheque arrived in the mail from Wilson to cover Grant's airfare to the interstate function. Grant was also the recipient on other occasions of Wilson's generosity.

Wilson believed that surplus money was not needed. All he needed were sufficient funds to sustain a reasonably comfortable life for him and his family. Much of the surplus was to be distributed to worthy causes and to people who needed the money more than he did. Over the years Wilson received numerous requests from strangers asking for funding for travel to conferences, research, community activities and other matters. When possible, he would write out a cheque to assist, but it was not possible to help all those seeking funding. After providing financial support to various members of his family and substantial contributions to the church and Murdoch University, his financial reserves were considerably reduced.

While Leila was very supportive of Wilson's generous and charitable bent, she sometimes would have liked that new fridge, or car or dress. Although the children were not showered with gifts, whenever they needed assistance while establishing themselves in the 'outside world', their parents were there to help. Ian was to be a major beneficiary of his parents' generosity.

Russell Elsegood, Murdoch University's then head of public relations, engaged Frank Perron, professional fundraising consultant, to coordinate the law library appeal. Early in the campaign, Wilson chaired a meeting at which Perron, a very experienced fundraiser, was to present his report on a feasibility study he had undertaken. Many of Perth's most eminent legal people would be there, including Sir Francis Burt, Western Australia's governor, leading QCs (including Daryl Williams, later the Commonwealth attorney-general in the Howard government), and other barristers and solicitors. Perron explained that, lacking any community 'heartstring'-pulling power, the best the university could expect to raise was $700,000.

In their minds, Elsegood and Perron thought even that target was aiming too high. To their amazement and perhaps consternation, Wilson, far from being overwhelmed by the magnitude of the task, said: 'That's not worth the candle and I don't believe it. We must have a million.'[25] When Wilson opened the law library collection in 1991, he was able to announce that the appeal had raised $1.89 million, at that time the most successful law library fundraising campaign in Australia. In addition to his donations of $10,000, Wilson personally raised $500,000. His status, commitment and charm were a strong combination, so people had difficulty saying no to him. His persuasive skills were also utilised by the university in a fundraising campaign for a worship centre.

The law library collection was enhanced by the considerable private collection of the late Robert Holmes à Court, a Rhodesian-born Australian entrepreneur, who had the nickname 'the Great Acquirer' for his raids on major companies in England and Australia. He died suddenly in 1990, leaving his wife Janet in control of the vast business interests of the family's private company Heytesbury Holdings Ltd. Wilson had a good relationship with Robert and Janet Holmes à Court. Janet asked Wilson to conduct the liturgy at Robert's funeral.

When the law program admitted its first students in 1990, Ralph Simmonds, the foundation professor, attempted to appoint Wilson as a visiting professor, but because of Wilson's other commitments it never occurred. However, Wilson readily agreed to give numerous lectures at the invitation of faculty members, and attended many events for the law program.

Wilson had been part of the selection committee that chose Simmonds in early 1989. It was the beginning of a good professional and personal relationship between the two. Wilson encouraged Simmonds to see him as a 'wise counsel', and someone who was supportive of the law program and school. Initially the program was held in the School of Economics and Commerce.[26] In 1994, the law program had its own law school, with Simmonds continuing as foundation dean.[27]

Wilson was an energetic and dedicated chancellor. He was strongly committed to the development and smooth running of Murdoch University.

He was particularly important to the vice-chancellorship of Peter Boyce (1985–96). Boyce, a very fine historian, had little or no management experience when he assumed the position of vice-chancellor. He often relied on Wilson's advice and support.

Wilson chaired the university's senate meetings. He was courteous and fair, but remained in firm control, not allowing the debate to get out of control. This was how Wilson ran all meetings he chaired at the university. Renowned Australian historian Geoffrey Bolton, foundation professor of history at Murdoch University, senator (1973–76 and 1999–2002) and chancellor of Murdoch University (2002–06), remembers Wilson chairing meetings with firmness if the situation warranted it: 'He didn't allow the business to get out of hand.' Bolton felt that senate decisions never went against Wilson's wishes. If he did not believe in something being proposed he would not hesitate to say: 'Well, you can't do that.'

Wilson was equally meticulous about his role at graduation ceremonies. He insisted on signing each certificate personally rather than using an impersonal, but less onerous, automatic signature. This sometimes created great stress for university staff members, as often Wilson had not been given the total batch of certificates to sign. Sometimes this was discovered only a few hours before the graduation ceremony. This usually resulted in a stressed Elsegood making a dash to Wilson's Applecross home on his way to the ceremony at the Perth Concert Hall. He would be greeted at the door by Leila, with a resigned 'here we go again' smile as she summoned a relaxed Wilson to make some expectant graduand's certificate complete.

As he had been all his working life, as chancellor Wilson was friendly and generous in acknowledging all those with whom he worked. Meeting him for the first time, staff would call him 'Sir Ronald' and he would invariably say: 'Just call me Ron.' At the end of each graduation ceremony, he would remind the audience of graduates and their families that their special night only happened because of the dedicated work of a small, loyal band of Murdoch employees working behind the scenes.

Reflecting on this, Susan Osborn, who worked in community relations, says:

> He would thank them by name and he never ceased to amaze me that he would do that at the end of such an important occasion, but he realised all the hard work that was put in behind the scenes to make things happen and

> he always acknowledged you. It didn't matter what level you were, you were a hard worker and he wanted to make sure that you were acknowledged. It was very, very special.[28]

And, when it was all over, Wilson would join his staff at a nearby bar to celebrate and relax.

While on the High Court, Wilson always arranged his schedule to ensure he was at the graduation ceremony. He considered it imperative that the university chancellor should be at the most special night for the graduates and their families. Whenever possible, before and after the graduation ceremonies he would mingle with the graduands and their families.

From 1990 onwards, the university also held an annual graduation ceremony in Singapore that Wilson always attended. This ceremony accommodated the families of the many Singaporeans graduating from Murdoch, and enhanced the profile of the university in the region.

Already a church president and a university chancellor, at the age of sixty-seven the supposedly retired Wilson decided to take on yet another position, potentially more challenging and time consuming than either of the other tasks. On 7 February 1990, he accepted the post of president of HREOC. Some of his legal and church acquaintances questioned why he was taking on this additional responsibility as president of an institution established in 1986 by the *Human Rights and Equal Opportunity Commission Act* 1986 (Cwlth).

Under its constituting legislation, HREOC has a range of functions relating to the promotion of the observance of human rights, including hearing and determining on complaints of discrimination,[29] community education on human rights, conducting inquiries and publishing reports on human rights issues, intervening in legal proceedings involving human rights issues, and advising the Commonwealth government on matters of legislation in relation to human rights matters. Thus the role of president of HREOC was a busy one, but Wilson approached the task before him with enthusiasm: 'It never occurred to me I'd have an opportunity to enrich my retirement in this way. I'm delighted.'[30]

When Wilson was named a justice of the High Court in 1979, the appointment was attacked by Lionel Bowen, the deputy leader of the federal Labor opposition. He claimed that Wilson had been selected because he held the same conservative views of the constitution as then Western Australian premier, Sir Charles Court. Now, as attorney-general in the Hawke Labor government, Bowen was full of praise for Wilson as he announced that he would replace Justice Marcus Einfeld as president of HREOC:

> He will bring a depth of compassion to this job that will serve as a demonstration both at home and abroad to the ongoing commitment in this country to the protection of the human rights we all need to survive as civilised human beings.[31]

Einfeld resigned early from his term as president, and returned to his Federal Court judgeship. He had earned some respect from the human rights community for his direct criticism of the Commonwealth government's record on human rights and emotional advocacy for improving the living conditions in Aboriginal communities. However, he was criticised for remarks he made in relation to a sexual harassment case before the Federal Court, and from HREOC members, for writing to some Soviet Union 'human rights' organisations suggesting they come to Australia to study the human rights record in Australia. He became estranged from his staff, and there was a public disagreement between Einfeld and his colleague, Brian Burdekin, the human rights commissioner. It was this disagreement that many within and outside HREOC saw as 'life threatening' for the organisation, particularly in light of the stated objective of the Liberal–National Party Coalition opposition of wanting to abolish it.[32] Some had argued that Wilson's appointment to replace Einfeld was motivated in part as a measure to help save HREOC from extinction if a change of government occurred at the next federal election, due in three years.[33]

Wilson was more cautious than Einfeld, who did not hesitate to use blunt language in criticising the Commonwealth government. His measured approach was demonstrated early in his tenure, when a journalist asked for his views on the Hawke government's refusal to sign the First Optional Protocol to the 1966 UN *International Covenant of Civil and Political Rights*, while claiming to be a world leader in human rights. The protocol provided individuals with the opportunity to take their complaints of violation of their civil and political rights to the UN Human Rights Committee.[34]

Wilson responded circumspectly:

> There have been persistent calls for successive governments to sign it, and there has been considerable international interest in our treatment

> of Aborigines…if we did sign it, individuals could complain to the United Nations, but we could still 'thumb our nose' at their decision.[35]

He did say the government was being hypocritical, but added that he had great distrust in using international fora, as it 'indicates that domestic law has failed'.[36] He believed it was best to resolve things through domestic economic and social reforms.

This view was consistent with his judicial dissents on the external affairs powers. Indeed, it was his reputation as a strong states' righter that some thought made Wilson an unusual choice as president of HREOC. When questioned on this, Wilson defended his role on the court, believing the High Court had got it wrong in relation to an expansive view of the Commonwealth constitutional power. But he also showed an awareness of the irony of his appointment to HREOC:

> Tasmanian Dams was incorrect, but because of law of precedent I followed it in Richardson [High Court case]. I see the constitution more in terms of checks and balances and to me the Court's mistakes go right back to the 1930s. I don't believe I'll be more free now to express my opinions on State Rights, but that's why it's so incongruous…here I am president of a Commonwealth body which deals with the very issues and powers I was opposed to being given to the Commonwealth! Some people say I'm unprincipled, but that's not the case at all. I just looked at the offer and saw how I could make a contribution. The past is the past…I want to look to the future.[37]

In the ensuing years as HREOC president, Wilson was to become more forceful in expressing his views. He felt unshackled from the restrictions of judicial office, but also he saw it as his responsibility as president to speak out on human rights. The past, in the form of the historical treatment of Aborigines, was to have a profound effect on Wilson, and his role in this history was to receive attention and criticism.

His term as president of the Uniting Church had been marked by a strong commitment to reconciliation and justice for Aborigines. The Aboriginal social justice issue and rights of Aborigines were high in his priorities when becoming HREOC president, as was the issue of racism in general. But he was careful not to be seen to neglect other issues and sections of HREOC. He was concerned to ensure all forms of discrimination were addressed, whether on the grounds of sex, age, disability or race.

Wilson came to his presidential role with close personal exposure to discrimination and hardship in his family. His youngest son, Ian, aged twenty-one in 1990, was living the life of a squatter in Sydney, having moved there in late 1989. He was into punk music and had dreadlocks. He participated in social and environmental activism. Ian was frequently stopped by the New South Wales police and asked 'Where do you live and where are you going?' Although Ian had chosen the squatter lifestyle and activism, Wilson believed this did not justify the police behaviour towards his son.

Before he moved to Sydney, Ian had participated in a protest at the old Swan Brewery site on the shore of the Swan River on Mounts Bay Road just west of the city. Several protests were occurring at the site in the late 1980s in support of Aboriginal claims that it was a sacred site. The Western Australian government wanted to allow the disused brewery to be developed into a restaurant and residential complex. At one of these protests Ian was charged by the police with trespassing and resisting arrest. His father assisted in obtaining a lawyer to represent him in the Court of Petty Sessions in the Perth Central Law Courts.

Wilson was supportive of his son's protest. After visiting the brewery site, he released a press statement as president of the Uniting Church, saying that the church believed that there was an important principle at stake, and that the government had to be mindful of its obligations under the *Aboriginal Heritage Act* 1972 (WA), and respectful of the rights of Aborigines.

At the court hearing, Ian was not seeing eye to eye with his solicitor. His counsel wanted to appease the magistrate and say that Ian was sorry for breaking the law. Ian was firmly of the belief that morally he was right, and if he had broken the law, the law was immoral. This analysis of the law ran counter to a positivist's jurisprudence that his father followed while on the High Court. When the magistrate asked Ian if he had anything to say, he said: 'I would like to sort this out quickly because I want to leave the state.' Ian was convicted and received a small fine.

After a couple years in Sydney, Ian tired of living the life of a squatter, and in early 1992 headed home. However, he did not ring his parents to collect him at the airport. Instead, he telephoned his biological father to meet him. This act was surprising, because he had never developed a significant relationship with his biological father. Wilson and Leila were hurt, but as was their way, they said nothing to Ian.

The Wilsons had always been open with Ian about his adoption in 1969. In 1987, Ian's biological mother wrote to him. He did not want to meet her. He thought of Ron and Leila as his parents. With Ian's approval, Leila went alone to meet his biological mother, who had been a teenager when Ian was born. She now lived in the south-west of Western Australia. The similarities in appearance and mannerisms with Ian amazed Leila. If she closed her eyes, she could be listening to Ian. Having broken the ice, Leila encouraged Ian to meet his biological mum. He did, and developed a reasonable relationship with her. However, she would not give Ian any information about his biological father. Nevertheless, Ian tracked him down and met him. This never developed into anything meaningful, although he did meet his biological mother on a number of occasions. The contacts with his biological mother were infrequent and punctuated by long periods of no contact. Ian liked her, but Leila and Wilson were the parents he loved.

Wilson's eldest daughter gave him a personal insight into disabilities. Helen had quickly established an excellent reputation as a teacher, and had served for one term as a primary school principal. At age thirty-three she was diagnosed with multiple sclerosis. This was four years before Wilson's HREOC appointment. By 1990 she was in a wheelchair, working as a part-time teacher's aide at her two daughters' primary school near Pinjarra, in country Western Australia.

Wilson could see the deterioration in the physical capacity of his daughter, who was also going blind, and how this restricted her options in life. He was very proud of how Helen had accepted her condition but remained motivated to continue leading a productive life. She realised that her condition would eventually prevent her from working as a teacher's aide. She undertook a course on income taxation preparation with the intention of being able to work from home. For a couple of years she prepared her father's annual taxation returns, but her health deteriorated to the extent that she had to abandon her plans to establish a business from home. She now requires constant care from her husband to move around and do the most basic tasks.

Wilson's interest in disability discrimination was not only motivated by his daughter's condition. His religious convictions in human dignity and belief that we are all children in the eyes of God meant that society must take care of all its members. He had a great capacity to display and give consideration and kindness to people of all creeds and situations, including people with disabilities.

An example of this was during a 1994 hearing he chaired in Adelaide, undertaken pursuant to the *Disability Discrimination Act* 1992 (Cwlth). The Act allowed complaints to be made to HREOC about discrimination on the basis of disability. A complaint had been received from three people in South Australia in relation to their state government's intention to sign a contract for the purchase of 100 new buses that were not wheelchair accessible. The Act gave the president of HREOC the power to make an interim determination. Wilson decided that before he made such a determination he would go to Adelaide to hold a hearing.

The hearing was of particular significance to all parties: the complainants, the state government and the bus company. The company, which intervened in the hearings, engaged a major law firm to represent it.

At lunchtime on the first day of the hearing, Wilson and Susan Roberts, the senior HREOC legal officer with responsibility for the *Disability Discrimination Act*, came out of the hearing room into the corridor to a crowded scene of people with disabilities milling around. Roberts was very hungry. She was sure that Wilson was also hungry, as they hadn't eaten since 5 a.m.

Roberts and Wilson made their way to the lift. Before reaching it, Wilson stopped and said to Roberts, 'Well what about these people, I wonder? What are they going to do for lunch?' Roberts didn't know what to say.

Wilson approached the person with the severest-looking physical disabilities, a woman in her sixties. He asked her if she was all right and if he could give her something. She thanked him and said it would be nice to have a cup of tea. This was the signal for Wilson and Roberts to spend the hour's lunch recess making cups of tea for those in the corridor. Wilson and Roberts managed to skip out just before the end of lunch recess to grab a sandwich and rush back to the hearing room.

12

Royal Commission, Reconciliation and Rights

I could once again do what I loved doing the most — that is, advocating, and now I could do it for the disadvantaged.

On 12 February 1990, only five days after Wilson's appointment as HREOC president, Dr Carmen Lawrence became the first female state premier in Australia, after unseating Peter Dowding in an internal Labor Party coup. As the year progressed, Lawrence was coming under increased pressure to establish a royal commission into the commercial activities of successive Western Australian Labor governments in the 1980s—led by Brian Burke (1983–87) and Dowding (1987–90).

Much of the pressure on the state government to establish a royal commission was coming from the lobby group People for Fair and Open Government. The convener of the group was Perth lawyer, Bevan Lawrence, the premier's brother. This group, and others in the state, were mainly concerned with the commercial activities of the state governments during the Burke–Dowding period, which became known as WA Incorporated, more commonly abbreviated to WA Inc.

Lawrence initially resisted calls for a royal commission. An inquiry had been established a year before into the role of government agencies in investments by Rothwells Merchant Bank, headed by the 'colourful' businessman, Laurie Connell. The inquiry was chaired by Malcolm McCusker QC and a task force of lawyers, police officers and Corporate Affairs Department investigators. The Bevan Lawrence group and others were not satisfied with this inquiry, as it was involved only with allegations of corruption and illegality surrounding the collapse of the Rothwells Investment Bank and attempts to keep it operating. The McCusker inquiry was not examining the propriety of government ministers in relation to a number of commercial activities, which is what the Bevan Lawrence group and others were demanding.

The pressure was relentless on the premier, Carmen Lawrence. She finally succumbed, and on 19 November 1990, with the ALP government's voter support at an all-time low of 22 per cent, Lawrence announced that a royal commission into WA Inc would be established, and set out its terms of reference. The royal commission, named The Royal Commission into Commercial Activities of Government and Other Matters, was to investigate a number of matters relating to Rothwells, and a scheduled list of other government business activities and matters relating to the Stirling City Council. Most of the matters dealt with activities during the Burke and Dowding administrations, but some involved the previous Liberal–National Coalition governments of Sir Charles Court and Ray O'Connor.

The terms of reference were generally welcomed by the media and community groups, including Bevan Lawrence's group. So was the state government's move to introduce legislation, the *Royal Commissions Amendment Act* 1990 (WA), to waive executive privilege for former and current public servants and ministers and for documents, as well as to amend the *Royal Commission Act* 1968 (WA) to compel witnesses to answer questions and deliver documents even though they might incriminate themselves.

The state government approached Wilson to be a royal commissioner. Wilson did not want to do it. He had his part-time HREOC position, his church presidency and his Murdoch commitments, which were far more than one would expect from a person 'in retirement'. Wilson would not contemplate being a sole royal commissioner. When the government decided to appoint three royal commissioners, he was prepared to consider it. He still wasn't enthusiastic about the prospect of spending considerable time on a highly politically charged royal commission, but he viewed it as a public service to his home state that he could no longer refuse to undertake.

On 5 December 1990, Carmen Lawrence appointed Wilson, retired Supreme Court justice the Hon. Peter Brinsden QC, and then current Supreme Court justice, the Hon. Mr Justice Geoffrey Kennedy as three equal royal commissioners. For the purpose of the *Royal Commission Act 1968* (WA), Kennedy was appointed the chairman. All three royal commissioners shared a Presbyterian upbringing, and Kennedy was a former chair of Sister Kate's Children's Home. Both Kennedy (a Rhodes Scholar) and Brinsden had gone to Scotch College, as had Wilson's three sons.

David Malcolm, the chief justice of the Supreme Court of Western Australia, was reluctant to release Kennedy because of the court's workload. Indeed, it was this workload that had been a major factor in Brinsden's decision to retire from the court, before turning seventy. At the age of sixty-seven, he had served fourteen years on the court. Malcolm agreed to release Kennedy on the basis of a commitment by the state government to appoint a new Supreme Court justice.

The government's announcement of the three royal commissioners was well received. Even the *West Australian*, which had been advocating the need to appoint royal commissioners from outside the state,[1] applauded the distinction and abilities of Wilson, Kennedy and Brinsden. Although Wilson had a friendship with Robert Holmes à Court, whose business connection with the State Government Insurance Commission was part of the terms of reference, it was not argued that this would disqualify Wilson from sitting on the royal commission. Bevan Lawrence said that Wilson had the ability to examine evidence dispassionately.[2] Similarly, Lawrence said that the fact that Kennedy had heard and decided a claim by Rothwells' shareholders against Laurie Connell in the Supreme Court did not disqualify him from sitting on the commission.[3]

The announcement of the royal commissioners' appointment received national media attention. Watching Carmen Lawrence's announcement on SBS TV News in Brisbane was Laurie Claus, a young law graduate from the University of Queensland and associate to the chief justice of the Queensland Supreme Court. When Wilson's name was mentioned, Claus became more attentive.

Claus had great respect for Wilson. He had met him when Wilson attended Claus's church in Brisbane a few years before. As a law student, he had read Wilson's High Court judgements with admiration. He agreed with the general thrust of Wilson's judicial interpretation of the Constitution. For several years, Claus wrote to Wilson at the High Court to see if there was a possibility that he could be his associate. Each time Wilson replied, thanking Claus but indicating that there was no opening.

After the SBS news report, Claus immediately wrote to Wilson to ascertain if he needed any assistance. Three weeks later, much to Claus's delight, Wilson telephoned to inform him that they were appointing associates, and could he come to Perth very soon. Claus gladly said yes, and arrived in Perth just after New Year's Day 1991.

The royal commission was formally set up on 8 January 1991. However, a war, rather than the royal commission, was foremost in Wilson's mind in the first month of that year. In August 1990, Iraq's President Saddam Hussein had invaded Kuwait. The United States, under President George Bush (senior), led the international condemnation of the invasion. Bush gave the Iraqi dictator an ultimatum of withdrawing from Kuwait by late January 1991 or confronting military action by the US and its allies. The Australian government immediately supported the position of President Bush. The prime minister, Mr Hawke, reconvened the federal parliament in early January 1991 to debate and vote on sending Australian navy ships to the Persian Gulf to assist the US and its allies in forcing Iraqi troops back into Iraq.

The Uniting Church was against the war, believing that a diplomatic solution had to be found. Wilson supported the church's position, and participated in a twenty-four-hour vigil at St Mary's Cathedral in Perth, praying that a peaceful solution could be found to the dispute. He also joined a list of eminent people who signed a letter of protest to Hawke, requesting that Australia not commit to war. Wilson believed things could have been done differently.

In an ABC TV interview with reporter Alan Hird, screened on 17 January 1991, Wilson said that there had been insufficient diplomacy, and no attempt to negotiate an acceptable solution for Iraq. Instead, the US had given Iraq an ultimatum. He agreed that the Iraqi president had provided the opportunity for the West to engage in war, but he believed there was an insufficient allied effort to find a peaceful solution. He argued that the main reason for going to war was not Kuwaiti sovereignty but rather, national pride and self-interest. There was a determination to prevent Iraq becoming a strong political and military force in Middle East politics, as well as the allies' concern over access to oil.

However, Wilson was not overly critical of Australia's decision to send two navy ships to the Persian Gulf as part of its commitment to the war. Once it had been decided that the US-led coalition would use military force to push Iraq out of Kuwait, Wilson believed that, given Australia's position in the world and its alliance with the US, it had little choice but to commit to the war. However, Wilson failed to develop this argument. There was no treaty in force that compelled Australia to go to war in the Persian Gulf regions. Presumably, Wilson thought that the health of the US–Australian alliance meant it was very difficult for Australia not to support the US, and presumably in a Christian's mind war could be justified.

Meanwhile, the royal commission was building up a large and impressive team of 100 lawyers, investigators, media officers and administrative help. Besides the three royal commissioners, QCs Tony Templeman from Perth, and Brian Martin, who was brought over from Adelaide, were the other public faces of the commission team, presenting the evidence, making submissions, questioning witnesses and giving advice to the commissioners.

The commission commenced hearings on 12 March 1991. A depiction on the TV news that evening, and on the front page of the *West Australian* the next day, showed Wilson, Kennedy and Brinsden walking down St Georges Terrace towards the National Mutual Centre, the home for the royal commission. The artificiality of it all made Wilson and the other commissioners feel uncomfortable, but they agreed to the media's request because of the public interest in the royal commission. Wilson had his characteristic mischievous smile as he walked with his two colleagues, facing the array of cameras.

The media packed the hearing room on the opening day. The commissioners had decided that it was best to allow the media, their cameras and recording equipment into the hearings, the first time this had been done in a royal commission. However, the commissioners would not allow the cameras to operate when the witnesses were giving evidence. They considered this would merely exacerbate a stressful situation for witnesses.

The commissioners thought it was important to allow the hearings to be open, so that the public would be informed about the proceedings. Wilson was mindful that some reputations would be sullied by open hearings and media coverage, but on balance the public interest in being informed was more important. Others, such as Brian Singleton QC and Rene Le Miere,[4] who acted for some of the witnesses before the commission, believed that the widespread publicity, sometimes based on hearsay evidence, unfairly tarnished the reputation of a number of people. Singleton described the royal commission as a Star Chamber.[5]

Wilson was impressed with the professional and efficient manner in which the royal commission team operated. He was most impressed with the superb administrative skills of Gordon Pearce, who had been seconded from his position as chief executive, Department of the Premier (a sub-department of the Ministry of the Premier and Cabinet) to be the chief executive of the WA Inc Royal Commission.

Wilson was also impressed with the forensic and cross-examining skills of Templeman and Martin. For Wilson, the highlight of the hearings was Brian Martin's cross-examination of former premier Brian Burke, who had come back from Dublin, where he was Australian ambassador to Ireland and the Holy See. Wilson thought that Burke entered the hearing room supremely confident. Shortly after, with Martin's firm questioning, Wilson noticed the confidence recede from Burke's face. Claus, Wilson's associate, observed a man resigned to ignominy. In contrast, Claus thought that Laurie Connell presented a bulldog fight to Martin, with an appearance of optimism.

Under the terms of reference, the commissioners were required to report their findings by 8 January 1992; twelve months after the Western Australian governor had signed their commissions. However, the formal hearings of the commission were not concluded until 30 June 1992. They sat for over 278 days, heard from 681 witnesses and took 44,000 pages of evidence. An extension on the reporting deadline was sought and granted. The commissioners were satisfied with the hearings, but faced the next phase of their work with some trepidation.

At the conclusion of the hearings Kennedy said:

> We agreed to endeavour to deliver our report on the specific terms of reference by September 30, and our report on recommended changes to the law of the state and of administrative and decision-making procedures by October 31.[6]

He said the commissioners were determined to adhere to this timetable, but they were under no delusion about the enormous task that confronted them. He concluded his remarks by complimenting the media:

> Our aim was to make this a public inquiry. We believe we have succeeded in this aim, with the splendid cooperation of the media. The public of this state has been exceptionally well served by their news organisations.[7]

The *West Australian* reported that early the following year (1993) Kennedy would return to the Supreme Court bench, and that Brinsden and Wilson 'will resume their very active lives in retirement'. Very active lives indeed, particularly for Wilson.

The first report of the royal commission was tabled in the Western Australian parliament on 20 October 1992.[8] The six volumes made findings of impropriety, conflicts of interest, inappropriate use of money and abuse of office and public confidence. It produced adverse comments against a number of former premiers, their ministers and advisers. The commissioners wrote that Brian Burke 'acted improperly, his conduct being discreditable and amounting to a substantial breach of the standard of rectitude to be expected of a person holding the office of Premier'.[9] On former deputy premier David Parker, the report said that 'by any normal measure of the conduct of a minister of the Crown, his behaviour was grossly incompetent, if not absurd'.[10] In relation to former premier Peter Dowding, the royal commissioners wrote that he was evasive and unconvincing.[11] Of former Liberal premier Ray O'Connor, the commission held that he had retained Bond Corporation 'bribe money', instead of paying off Stirling City councillors, and falsely confessed to paying Liberal parliamentary colleague and former councillor George Cash.

Burke, Parker, Dowding and O'Connor were no longer in the parliament by this time. Among still-sitting members, the first report had an immediate impact. Within hours of its tabling, environment minister Bob Pearce notified the premier, Carmen Lawrence, that he was resigning from the Legislative Assembly. He could be seen speaking to the premier in the assembly; she was close to tears as one of her most senior and high-profile ministers told her of his decision. However, Pearce maintained his innocence against the report's finding that he had misused confidential financial records. Cabinet secretary Bill Thomas resigned his cabinet position over his handling of cabinet records relating to the Burswood Casino. Several senior public servants were stood down pending further assessment of their conduct by an independent panel.

Subsequent to the royal commission, Burke and Parker faced criminal charges. Burke resigned his ambassadorship, and was jailed for two years in June 1994 for 'false pretences' for illegally claiming $17,179 in travel expenses from taxpayers between 1986 and 1988. He served seven months before release on parole. In March 1997 he was again jailed for three years on multiple counts of stealing a total of $122,585 in campaign donations. In his defence, Burke, a keen philatelist, said he had used money donated to the ALP's leader's account to buy stamps as an investment for the ALP, but had not notified anyone of this. He served six months before the convictions were quashed on appeal, on the grounds that the money was Burke's to use as State leader 'as he saw fit'.

In 1994, David Parker also was charged with stealing $38,000 from his election campaign funds between 1986 and 1989, although this offence did not specifically relate to WA Inc business. He was sentenced to one year's imprisonment, which he served out, but the High Court later acquitted him of these charges. In 1996 Parker was charged and convicted of committing perjury before the WA Inc Royal Commission. He was sentenced to eighteen months' imprisonment, of which he served four months, being released on parole from the minimum security Wooroloo Prison Farm.

Three weeks after the tabling of the first report, Part II was tabled in the Western Australian parliament.[12] This report dealt with the commission's responsibility 'to report whether changes in the law of the State or in administrative or decision making procedures are necessary or desirable in the public interest'. The commission stated that its findings revealed

> serious weaknesses and deficiencies in our system of government. Together, they disclose fundamental weaknesses in the present capacity of our institutions of government, including the Parliament, to exact that degree of openness, accountability and integrity necessary to ensure that the executive fulfils its basic responsibility to serve the public interest.[13]

The report made recommendations designed to improve accountability and build public trust in the government and democratic institutions. It recommended that the Legislative Council, the state parliament's upper house, be removed from the daily political battles and become a powerful house of review. Some other important recommendations included the abolition of parliamentary privilege and introducing freedom-of-information legislation, political donation disclosure and whistleblower legislation. The commission also recommended that a commission on government be established to examine issues of honest and open government.

The Lawrence Labor government lost the next state election, held in February 1993. The incoming Liberal and National Party Coalition government was led by the son of Wilson's former boss, Sir Charles Court. Richard Court became premier largely because of the Western Australian electors' negative view of the state Labor Party stemming from the WA Inc period. However, even though the Court government did establish a commission on government, it was given narrower terms of references than that recommended by the royal commission. Deputy premier and National Party leader Hendy Cowan sought to devalue the worth of the second report by alleging that the commissioners 'only had one day in which to consider' that report before agreeing to it.[14]

Wilson refused to respond to Cowan's comment. He thought it was an unspoken rule that royal commissioners should not respond to public comment on the commission's report. However, Brinsden labelled Cowan's comment as ridiculous.[15] Wilson privately applauded Brinsden because Cowan's comment was ridiculous, as the commissioners had been involved in discussions over the shape and content of the both reports. Wilson felt sorry for the exposure it brought Brinsden.

Wilson consistently refused to engage in public discussion on the reports, although, in a 1994 interview for the Battye Library oral history series, Wilson remarked on his disappointment with what he saw as the non-implementation of most of the second report's recommendations. Although freedom-of-information legislation was enacted and the commission on government established, many of the recommendations were never legislatively or administratively carried out. Wilson said that Lawrence should have called the royal commission six months earlier, and not given it so many terms of reference. He believed that, as the sale of the Midland Brickworks had been 'exhaustively examined by a committee of the Parliament', he and his fellow commissioners should not have had to spend precious time on this issue. He added:

> … there simply wasn't time for the [Lawrence] government to implement it [the royal commission's recommendations]. I believe they would have implemented it pretty well across the board had they remained in office. But the [1993 state] election was looming and a change of office, of course, meant that a new government was in a position to take a different stand in relation to the matters that were canvassed.[16]

Wilson added that Richard Court government's protraction in establishing the commission on government, and the limits they placed on the scope of the commission's jurisdiction, reinforced his conviction that the Court government would not significantly implement the royal commission's recommendations. He concluded:

> But I say no more about that. I think in the light of history it was just a pity that those two factors—the amount of work that was given to it, some of which was not worth the time of the commission, and the fact that it wasn't appointed a little earlier so there was time for it to be implemented—has cost the State dearly.[17]

Although for much of 1991 Wilson was working as a royal commissioner, his mind was never far way from his roles as president of both the Uniting Church and HREOC. As to the former, his term came to an end at the July 1991 Brisbane national assembly conference. In his HREOC role, Wilson made several public addresses in 1991.

He would address specific areas of HREOC's responsibilities in these speeches, but what tended to come through most strongly was his emphasis on the human and social aspects of the issues, rather than the legalities. Addressing the Western Australian Press Club in July, with an audience more concerned about the WA Inc Royal Commission than human rights, he argued that complacency was an enemy of the continual need to eliminate discrimination, particularly in relation to Australia's treatment of Aborigines. He remarked:

> One way of combating complacency is to cease dealing in abstractions, in the currency of noble sentiments and fine words detached from the immediacy and tensions of real life, and to remember that behind every human rights problem there are people hurting, people longing for a sense of dignity and self respect, of having a sense of worth in themselves.[18]

On 20 September 1991, Wilson delivered the Mitchell Oration at the South Australian Equal Opportunity Commission in Adelaide, in honour of Roma Mitchell QC, the governor of South Australia, who was a pioneer for women in the law, and the first chair of the Commonwealth Human Rights Commission from 1981 to 1986.

Wilson commenced the oration, titled 'Human Dignity for All: A Pie in the Sky?', by expressing his personal admiration of Mitchell. In his address he said he believed Australia had to do more to ensure human rights for all. He praised the work being done by his fellow HREOC commissioners, such as human rights commissioner Brian Burdekin's advocacy of the rights of homeless children, the disabled, prisoners and many other sections of society; race discrimination commissioner Irene Moss's promotion of harmonious race relations; sex discrimination commissioner Quentin Bryce's work on challenging stereotypes that tended to disadvantage women; and privacy commissioner Kevin O'Connor's pioneering work on ensuring Commonwealth governmental departments observed the privacy of individual citizens. He said that the answer to the question in his oration title was a resounding 'No', and concluded with a rhetorical flourish:

> If you have ever stood on a seashore and watched an incoming tide, you will have noticed how the leading ripple reached a certain point before the rhythm of the sea causes it to recede for a moment before moving forward again. But the next forward movement will take it further up the beach, beyond the previous limit. The growing world consensus of faith in the inherent dignity of every human being is like that incoming tide. It will not be denied. Every day in every continent there are some who learn to read, who gain access to better nutrition and health care, who find justice and peace of mind, a new sense of self-worth. Every day, for those people, human dignity ceases to be pie in the sky.
>
> Laws and institutions can only do so much. Ultimately, as I have said, it is people who by their relationships with each other can pluck that pie down from the sky and make the hope it symbolizes a reality in the life of the other. This means that every one of us here in Australia can contribute to making 'A Fair Go for All' the reality it ought to be.[19]

This conclusion reinforced Wilson's optimistic faith in his fellow human beings. It also reiterated his belief that the best way to overcome injustice is through dialogue between people.

In the Mitchell Oration, and in a speech to the Australian Academy of Forensic Sciences in October,[20] he examined previous High Court cases in which he had been directly involved, from the perspective of human rights.

At the academy he referred to the 1979 case of *McInnis v the Queen*,[21] at which he had argued for the state of Western Australia against McInnis, who took the question of the right to legal representation to the High Court. The court held that the common law did not guarantee a right to counsel at public expense, and in the circumstances of the particular case, there had been no miscarriage of justice. In his 1991 speech, Wilson referred to Article 14 (3) of the United Nations *Covenant on Civil and Political Rights*, which requires a defendant to be afforded a publicly funded counsel 'where the interests of justice so require'. He then discussed whether the *McInnis* case would be decided differently now (1991). He stated that, since the granting of a right to counsel would have public expenditure implications, it may be more appropriate for a legislature to change the law, not the judiciary.

In the academy speech, Wilson referred to the case of *Kioa v West*,[22] where the High Court, with Wilson sitting, held that the immigration decision-maker had properly taken into consideration the benefit of a child (an Australian-born citizen) being cared for by her parents when issuing the parents' deportation orders. At the time, the UN *Convention on the Rights of the Child* 1989 expressed that a child had the right to be with its parents. In his address Wilson asked 'whether the subsequent [1990 Australian] ratification of the *Convention on the Rights of the Child* could be construed as conferring such an [overriding] entitlement may be a matter for argument'. He responded: 'For myself, I doubt it.'[23]

When it came to matters of law, clearly Wilson had not abandoned his belief in positivism and staying true to his judicial record of not using international law to 'introduce' new domestic rights or change the balance between Commonwealth and state powers. However, the longer Wilson spent in the role of HREOC president, the more he championed the need for Australia to comply with its international human rights obligations. However, he saw this as the obligation of legislators and governments, through legislation and policy. He never advocated that the courts should incorporate international law into domestic law.

Wilson may have been a judicial and legal conservative, and in some senses, also a moral conservative, yet he found himself presiding over an organisation at the cutting edge of legal and social policy. It seemed that he was aware of this irony, and at times was almost working his way through the issues in his mind and in his speeches.

In his speech to the forensic scientists, Wilson surmised that human rights law may be making a great impact on Australia's traditional institutions. He rhetorically asked:

> The emphasis in human rights law on the resolution of disputes is upon education, conciliation and mediation. Might not its increasing impact presage a change in the traditional understanding of the role of law and the nature and extent of remedies available through legal process; in other words, a change from a strict reliance on legalism towards a more human and flexible medium?[24]

In the same paper is a comment Wilson makes on the rate of social change. He states:

> In all the circumstances, I see Australia undergoing enormous change in social and legal norms, attributable in part to the development internationally in recent decades of agreed principles that promise in time to affect the life of every person on this planet. For many people, the rate of change in Australia is too slow. For myself, however, except with respect to conditions affecting the Aboriginal people, I am content to welcome change at a pace that allows the community to digest that change and avoid social upheaval. We are dealing with issues of fundamental importance in their bearing on human dignity and the human spirit and so long as we continue to move towards the light of a new day for the powerless and the marginalised, then there is cause to be thankful.[25]

The issue of justice for Aborigines and improving their living conditions was a principal concern of Wilson's. He was not satisfied to accept gradual improvement in this area. Otherwise, he displayed a conservatism or gradualism to change. He displayed sensitivity to social cohesion, not an obsessive or fanatical determination to progress human rights.

When Wilson addressed the Academy of Forensic Sciences in October of 1991 he had opened by saying that he had hoped to have a 'better' quality paper, 'but I am finding that in retirement I no longer have the time to do the extracurricular things that I used to do when I was fully employed.'[26] His 'retirement' was about to become busier.

In May 1991, the Council for Aboriginal Reconciliation Bill had been introduced in the federal parliament to bipartisan support. On 30 May, Robert Tickner, the Minister for Aboriginal Affairs and Minister Assisting the Prime Minister for Aboriginal Reconciliation, arose from his green leather chair in the House of Representatives and strode to the dispatch box to move: 'That the Bill be now moved a second time.' He mentioned how the need for a process of reconciliation had been recognised by all major political parties, Aboriginal groups and also many other groups, including Australian churches and the National Farmers Federation. He stated that the Bill would provide the machinery for the reconciliation process, whereby a Council for Aboriginal Reconciliation would be established. He added that the object of the Council for Aboriginal Reconciliation

> is to promote a process of reconciliation between Aborigines and Torres Strait Islanders and the wider Australian community based on an appreciation by the Australian community as a whole of Aboriginal and Torres Strait Islander cultures and achievements and the unique position of Aborigines and Torres Strait Islanders as the indigenous peoples of Australia, and by means that include the fostering of an ongoing national commitment to cooperate to address Aboriginal and Torres Strait Islander disadvantage.[27]

This speech from a federal minister made Wilson happy. It agreed with what he had been pushing during his presidency of the Uniting Church. Wilson was also happy with the bipartisan support for the reconciliation bill. Dr Michael Wooldridge, the shadow minister for Aboriginal Affairs, spoke at the end of Tickner's speech. He said:

> I rise with pleasure to announce the Opposition's support for the Council for Aboriginal Reconciliation Bill 1991. This is significant because it is the first time in eight years that there has been bipartisan support for a major piece of Aboriginal affairs legislation.[28]

Towards the end of his speech, Wooldridge made a comment in relation to the word 'sorry', a word that at the time he could not have predicted would take on particular importance six years later, and in which Wilson would be intricately involved. Wooldridge said:

> One of the most moving speeches that I heard in my time as shadow Minister for Aboriginal affairs was at a dinner that the Minister arranged and kindly invited me to attend when Bishop Malcolm—an Anglican bishop in northern Australia, an Aboriginal man—got up at the end of the dinner and gave a very moving speech about his hopes and aspirations for the future. They were quite simple. They were not hopes and aspirations that looked to the past at all; they were hopes and aspirations for the future. He said: 'All that Aboriginal people want is for someone to say, "Sorry". We cannot undo the past. We have to look to the future. The first essential step in that is just simply saying 'Sorry'.[29]

On 2 September 1991, the governor-general (former federal Labor opposition leader, Bill Hayden) assented to the Act to establish the Council for Aboriginal Reconciliation. The council was elected soon after, in December 1991, and given a ten-year life span to coincide with the centenary of federation in 1 January 2001.

The Commonwealth government appointed Patrick Dodson as the chairperson and Wilson as his deputy. Wilson served in this position for three years, until 1994. The council consisted of eleven Aborigines, two Torres Strait islanders and eleven non-Aboriginal members from media, mining, farming, business and ethnic groups. Among the non-Aboriginal members were television personality Ray Martin and the National Farmers Federation executive director Rick Farley.[30]

The council's first meeting was on 21 February 1992 in Canberra. The prime minister, Paul Keating, addressed the meeting, as did Tickner. In his usual style, the prime minister was direct and willing in offering advice, telling the council that it must do more than just talk; it needed to come up with ideas and plans for improving the lot of Aborigines. He said, 'It debilitates our nation, it debilitates our culture, our reputation and our self-esteem. It undermines our ambitions to be a good society.'[31]

Although there was ignorance and prejudice in Australian society, he urged the council to be positive, and that most Australians would recognise that the European settlers had taken over the Australian continent from the Aborigines, and this had resulted in many Aborigines being demoralised and left destitute. It was thus important that the council should advance tangible proposals and not just rhetoric:

> On these sorts of bodies you can spend your time debating fine principles and finer points. You can talk about ideal outcomes from now until the end of the century. You can spend a decade in debate and deliberation…I suggest you aim at doing something [to] make concrete improvements in health and education for instance.[32]

As if taking note of the prime minister's words of 'advice', the council decided that it would delay considering the issue of a treaty between Aboriginal and non-Aboriginal Australia. After the first meeting, council chairman Patrick Dodson said that the council would need to decide whether a document like a treaty would enhance the reconciliation process, but acknowledged that the process was fraught with danger. Wilson told the press: 'We are not going to be bogged down on a treaty, certainly in the short term.' He added: 'It will come further down the track than in the first range of priorities. By the time we come to it we hope we will be changed.'[33] But personally, Wilson was against calling any document a 'treaty', as he thought it would raise difficult issues in relation to sovereignty.

He favoured calling any document a 'compact'. This was more in accordance with his personal philosophy of seeking an understanding between Aboriginal Australians and non-Aboriginal Australians. He wanted both sections to understand and appreciate the other—not unlike his support of the ecumenical movement, where all religions come together. His support for the coming together of all Australians, which was his guiding principle in the reconciliation process, was often reflected in his dress sense for much of the 1990s. Wilson would often be seen at public meetings and on television wearing his black jumper marked with Aboriginal paintings and blazoned in white on the front 'Walking Together'.

Wilson was impressed with prime minister Keating and what he was saying. He spoke with strength and commitment. The prime minister and the Aboriginal affairs minister wanted the council to succeed. And Wilson agreed—the council had to be more than a talkfest; it had to deliver with programs and proposals that the Commonwealth government and parliament could accept and take forward. In many respects, it was Wilson's perception of Keating's commitment to Aboriginal justice that governed his generally favourable assessment of Keating.

Just over three months after the first meeting of the reconciliation council, the High Court, on 3 June 1992, released its decision in the landmark case of

Mabo (No 2).[34] The High Court held that there was an established system of Aboriginal legal property ownership that pre-existed and survived European settlement; therefore *Mabo (No 2)* overturned the doctrine of *terra nullius* and recognised a common law native title to land. The plaintiff was Eddie Mabo, who had died on 21 January 1992. This was the same Eddie Mabo, whom Wilson, along with Chief Justice Mason and Justice Dawson, had held against in *Mabo (No 1)* in 1988.

While recognising native title, the High Court did say that Crown grants of land extinguished native title. However, any such extinguishment post 1975 may be in violation of the RDA. Thus the RDA stood as a possible legal barrier to state and territorial governments and parliaments validating mining and other land grants on land subject to native title claims.

A day after *Mabo (No 2)*, Mr Keating in the House of Representatives stated:

> With the *Mabo* decision the Australian law has taken a major step away from this injustice and has finally entered the mainstream of world opinion. As a nation we are now far better prepared psychologically to proceed with the process of reconciliation. With this decision one more barrier—historically perhaps the greatest barrier—has been effectively removed and the foundations of discrimination and prejudice have been kicked away. At least that is what all members of this House hope and want to see pursued in the next decade.[35]

Keating, along with Tickner and Wooldridge, was anxious that the debate on *Mabo* not develop into a partisan issue. That hope was not to be fulfilled. On one side was Keating, a divisive figure who attracted great admiration but also great loathing. With the Australian economy, historically and contemporarily, being highly dependent on mining and farming, the possible effects of the *Mabo (No 2)* decision on these industries created much debate and comment.

Leading the charge against the *Mabo (No 2)* decision, and advocating for the repeal or amendment of the RDA, was Hugh Morgan, the chief executive officer of Newman Mining Corporation. The National Farmers Federation was more moderate in its response, mainly because of the leadership of Rick Farley, its executive director. Farley was a member of the Council for Aboriginal Reconciliation, but, concerned with the uncertainty with some land tenures, such as pastoral leases, Farley demanded that the Commonwealth parliament enact legislation to remove the uncertainty. Aboriginal groups responded positively to *Mabo (No 2)*, and also demanded a Commonwealth government legislative response that would preserve the common law recognition of native title.[36]

The Keating cabinet agreed that a legislative response was necessary. On 27 October 1992, Keating announced that his government would engage in a consultation process with state and territory governments, Aboriginal groups and the mining and pastoral industries as a prelude to introducing legislation into the Commonwealth parliament. However, legislation would not be possible before the 13 March 1993 federal election, which saw Labor surprisingly win against the Liberal–National Party Coalition. Led by John Hewson, the coalition was proposing radical reform, including the electorally unpopular Goods and Services Tax.

Soon after that election, Keating announced that *Mabo* was at the top of the government's legislative program. He wanted native title legislation to be in place by Christmas 1993. As Canadian political scientist Peter Russell stated: 'From mid-March until three days before Christmas, when the Commonwealth Parliament passed the *Native Title Act*, the debate over the response to Mabo dominated Australian politics.'[37]

Wilson was concerned about the heat of the parliamentary and public debate, and he wanted the Council for Aboriginal Reconciliation to stay out of the debate. He advised his fellow council members on those lines: '[M]y conviction was if [the Council] got involved [it] would polarise the debate… we are a cross-party organisation.'[38] It was this concern to retain political cross-party support that made the council a non-player in the *Mabo* debate, although individual council members were, in their private or professional capacities, engaged in the debate. For example, Rick Farley and Senator Cheryl Kernot, the then leader of the Democrats, were involved in the negotiation and passing of the native title legislation.

Even though Wilson was strongly against the council as an organisation being involved in the *Mabo* debate, he was not silent on the matter. He spoke at a 1993 Perth public rally in support of the *Mabo (No 2)* decision. Wearing his 'Walking Together' jumper, Wilson addressed the 1000-strong crowd at the Esplanade (which grew to 4000 people by the end of the march), just across the road from the Supreme Court building, where he had worked as a records clerk and appeared in many high-profile criminal and civil cases. With a microphone in one hand, he softly said that all fairminded Australians would join together in wanting justice and peace for all. He did not criticise the

Western Australian government, which had been outspoken in condemning the *Mabo (No 2)* decision, saying it was unworkable in Western Australia, whose economy depended substantially on mining, farming and grazing.

The Western Australian government's public protest was led by the premier, Richard Court. Among all politicians in Australia, Court was the most vocal critic of *Mabo (No 2)*. He said that the Keating government's proposed legislative response to *Mabo* would result in a form of apartheid where land, with certain rights, was being granted to a group of people.[39] Court said that Western Australia would be affected by the decision more than any other state, claiming that up to 80 per cent of the state was under threat of native title claims.

He wanted a national referendum proposing an overturn of the *Mabo (No 2)* decision. Court's proposal for a referendum received little support from his federal Liberal colleagues, and Tickner responded by asking HREOC race discrimination commissioner Irene Moss to see if Court's call for a referendum breached the RDA. Wilson immediately threw cold water on that, saying, 'To call for a referendum is not, *per se*, unlawful under the Act. However this may change if Court developed his proposal further.'[40]

Bill Hassell, the president of the Western Australian Liberal Party, strongly supported Court's outspoken protest against *Mabo (No 2)*. He was a former state minister and parliamentary Liberal opposition leader, and the Hassell family were large property owners in Western Australia. Hassell aggressively attacked the decision, saying that it was 'illegitimate', and threatened the security of the suburban backyard. He also referred to the decision as 'racist'.

Wilson appeared on the ABC TV current affairs flagship program *7.30 Report* on 31 March 1993, at which time *7.30 Report* was still being produced locally in each state. Being interviewed by the program's host, Alan Carpenter (who subsequently, in 2006, became premier of Western Australia), Wilson applauded the *Mabo (No 2)* decision. He did not believe that the High Court, of which six justices were his former High Court brethren, had overstepped their judicial duty. He said they had a clear duty to enunciate the common law of Australia, which underlies legislation. Carpenter asked Wilson whether the court was making law rather than just interpreting law, and was this wrong. Wilson said this depends on whether the court had neglected its duty of strict legal and intellectual reasoning that underlies the common law.

His view was that the majority in *Mabo (No 2)* had engaged in strict legal reasoning that conformed to the principles of common law. The decision did not violate his legal positivist's philosophy, as it did not overrule existing legislative law. It did change the law of property, in the sense of overturning *terra nullius*, but this did not violate the philosophy of legal positivism. Positive law allows the law to be changed to meet social demands and needs. However, the change in law must be arrived at by reasoning and justification; it cannot be arbitrary.

Wilson held the view that, when he was sitting on the High Court, some of his colleagues had made decisions that were more guided by their 'personal preferred outcome' rather than logical and rigorous legal reasoning. He believed that writing a judgement to justify one's preferred outcome was judicially inappropriate, and that his own decisions were always reached after careful legal analysis, and that he did not seek to write a judgement that would 'fit' his 'personal preferred position'.

For Wilson, the majority justices in *Mabo (No 2)*, in applying rigorous intellectual thinking to the case before them, had 'made a finding of fact that Australia was not unoccupied' when in 1788 the British settled the continent. Wilson argued that the justices then applied long-formed principles of justice in the common law. He added that the fact that Aborigines have a connection to land meant it makes sense they would have ownership of land. He concluded that the *Mabo (No 2)* decision was based on rights and justice that are naturally established, and there was no legislation contrary to this.

In the *7.30 Report* interview, Wilson reiterated that the High Court said that any grant of freehold will extinguish native title. Although he did acknowledge that the decision did create some uncertainties, such as whether pastoral leases could coexist with, rather than extinguish native title, the decision presented many positives. He said that the decision should not be feared. The High Court had said no to sovereignty claims by Aboriginal people. Wilson had always considered this sovereignty issue as settled law that could not be overturned without creating major social and political upheaval.

When Carpenter asked what the positives were of the decision, Wilson said it overturned the *terra nullius* myth, which was 'a sore on the nation—festering on the body politic—as Australia was built on a fundamental injustice.' The decision gave Australia a chance of a fresh start, and provided a catalyst for the reconciliation process.

Wilson must have been relieved that he was no longer a member of the High Court. Clearly he passionately believed in the justice of its decision in *Mabo (No 2)*, and welcomed the opportunities it created. In the Carpenter interview at the time, he mounted a sound legal defence of the decision. However, speaking to Murdoch law students in 2000, Wilson did acknowledge that, considering his record on the High Court and closeness to Justice Dawson's legal philosophy and reasoning, he may have joined Dawson in dissent in *Mabo (No 2)* in not recognising the concept of native title at common law.

From 5 to 7 November 1993, the Council for Aboriginal Reconciliation met in Perth. It held a meeting with Richard Court in relation to his government's proposed legislation, the *Land (Titles and Traditional Usage) Act* 1993 (WA), which extinguished native title in return for the immediate substitution of granting a statutory right to Aborigines of the 'traditional use' of their land. Wilson was the first to greet the premier and introduce him to his fellow council members.

In the meeting, brandishing maps of the state showing areas under consideration in his proposed legislation and also possible native title claims, Court sought to explain the rationale and details of his proposed legislation. The meeting was held in a spirit of civility. While the council believed that the Court legislation was 'a long way from equity and justice', it did believe that the legislation's idea of 'traditional usage of land' was something that Keating should examine for inclusion in the proposed Commonwealth legislation.[41]

Speaking after that council meeting, Wilson expressed reservations with the Western Australian government's decision to extinguish native title and subordinate Aborigines' traditional uses of land to existing land law. He was also concerned at the proposed bureaucratic process, and the powers of the Western Australian minister of resources. He said: 'The Aboriginal people are at the mercy of that process and it clearly is just not good enough.'[42] Wilson, the optimist and conciliator, did offer some praise to the Court government. He viewed the legislation as a breakthrough, in that the Court government was at least now recognising Aboriginal usage of the land. He hoped this would provide a basis for renewed talks between the state and Commonwealth governments to produce a workable solution. Wilson said:

> When you've got a piece of legislation on the table you've got the chance for reasonable people...to negotiate and I think there's enormous public interest in securing a national solution to the High Court decision.[43]

While not supporting the Western Australian legislation, he hoped it would help 'to build a spirit of goodwill to overcome the teething problems of working through the [*Mabo (No 2)*] decision'.[44]

Unlike some of his council colleagues and lawyers representing Aboriginal organisations, Wilson was not sure that the Western Australian legislation would be unconstitutional or violate the RDA.[45] This was to be tested by a group of Kimberley Aborigines in the High Court. When the challenge was announced on 4 December 1993, Peter Yu, the chief executive officer of the Kimberley Land Council, appeared with Wilson on the ABC TV *7.30 Report*.

Again the interviewer was Alan Carpenter. He commenced by asking Yu what was the basis of his challenge. Yu responded that the legal opinion he received was that the state government's legislation violated the RDA because it made Aboriginal interests in land subservient to all other interests in land, and gave the minister of resources the power to extinguish native title. Carpenter then turned to Wilson, asking him for his opinion on the merits of the challenge. Wilson, in his cautious manner and with a wry smile, would only say that there was a chance the challenge would succeed. He said the issue was whether the state law was inconsistent with the RDA; whether the rights of a particular race were dealt with on an equal footing as the rights of another race.

Based on Wilson's reasoning in *Mabo (No 1)*, there would be a good chance that the Western Australian legislation would be held not to violate the RDA. The fact situation in *Mabo (No 1)* was similar to the situation being discussed on the *7.30 Report*. In *Mabo (No 1)*, the Queensland legislation arbitrarily took away property rights of the Meriam people. Wilson had held that this was not in violation of the RDA because

> if there are no other persons of another race who are shown to enjoy rights of the same kind as those of which the plaintiffs [Mabo and others] have been deprived, then it will be impossible to find a foothold for s10 (1) of the Commonwealth Act [RDA].[46]

Native title could only be enjoyed by Aboriginal people and, thus, if Wilson were to be consistent with his reasoning in *Mabo (No 1)*, he would most likely find the Western Australian legislation valid.

Wilson must have believed the ruling of the majority in *Mabo (No 1)*, from which he had dissented, would prevail again. In an earlier interview on ABC Radio he said that a state government wanting to eliminate the effect of *Mabo (No 2)* would be hindered by antidiscrimination law. He added: 'It is unthinkable that the High Court, having been familiar with the *Mabo* case (*Nos 1* and 2) for a decade, would say, "in the light of the reaction of the community we were wrong and we will overrule it".'[47]

On the *7.30 Report* on 4 December 1993, Wilson also said he wanted the Commonwealth parliament to pass the proposed Commonwealth native title legislation. This would strengthen the argument that the Western Australian legislation was unconstitutional under section 109 of the Australian Constitution.[48] Less than two years later, the High Court invoked its decision in *Mabo (No 1)* to hold that the Western Australian legislation was inoperative, as it was inconsistent with the RDA. The court also rejected, in a 7–0 decision (with Dawson the dissenter in *Mabo (No 2)* agreeing with his colleagues), the Western Australian government's constitutional challenge to the *Native Title Act* 1993 (Cwlth).[49]

Wilson also wanted Commonwealth legislation because of his concern that Australia should comply with its international law obligations, such as that required under the *Convention on the Rights of the Child* and the UN *Convention on the Elimination of All Forms of Racial Discrimination*. Wilson said he was speaking as HREOC president, and that he was jealous of Australia's reputation as a nation that respected human rights, although, as a High Court justice, his concern for human rights did not, as his judgement in *Koowarta* exemplified, persuade him that the Commonwealth's external affairs powers prevailed in matters of racial discrimination. Arguably, as a justice of the High Court he was more concerned to interpret the Commonwealth Constitution to maintain the 'appropriate' balance between Commonwealth and state legislative powers. As HREOC president, he was much more conscious of Australia's international law obligations.

On the same day as the *7.30 Report* interview, Wilson also appeared before the public hearing of the Senate Standing Committee on Constitutional and Legal Affairs in Perth. There he reiterated the international human rights obligations. He said that the Western Australian legislation failed to give native title holders a right of due process, and

> it seems to me that that piece of legislation does put Australia, and not just WA, in breach of serious international obligations. There is no protective mechanism...to stand in the way of an unreviewable decision of the Minister which deprives the Aboriginal person of the traditional usage rights. That, in my submission, is a clear breach [of international human rights obligations].[50]

On 16 November 1993, the prime minister, Mr Keating, introduced the Native Title Bill 1993 (Cwlth) into the House of Representatives. The Bill set up a regulatory tribunal system for Aboriginal groups to seek native title recognition, but the legislation also 'validated' grants of land on native title land that had occurred before the Bill would become law.

The introduction of the Bill had been preceded by exhaustive negotiations with state and territorial governments, various industry groups and Aboriginal groups, including the 'A' and 'B' teams. The so-called 'A' team, whose 'membership' was dominated by representatives from Northern Australia, such as Pat Dodson and Noel Pearson, had greater access to Keating. The 'B' team, considered 'tougher and more radical',[51] and consisting of people such as Geoff Clarke (a future ATSIC chair, who later was to face charges of sexual assault) and Tasmanian Michael Mansell, spoke intensively with the Democrats and Greens in the Senate. At times the negotiations with various groups stalled, but the legislation was introduced.

Wilson was supportive of the Commonwealth government's proposed legislation. He understood that some Aboriginal groups and others, such as the Western Australian Greens, favoured legislation that provided greater protection of native title. However, Wilson believed it was best to have the Keating government's proposed legislation enacted rather than engaging in further protracted negotiations. He was concerned that such protracted discussion would be divisive, and not conducive to the reconciliation process between Aboriginal and non-Aboriginal Australia. He believed the Keating legislation provided statutory recognition of the *Mabo (No 2)* decision and an administrative system to allow Aboriginal groups to claim native title.

The *Native Title Act* 1993 (Cwlth) passed the House of Representatives, where the Labor Party had a majority, on 25 November 1993.

The Senate was a different story, because the government needed to rely on the support of the Democrats and the Western Australian Greens for passage of the legislation. After 111 hours of debate, the longest in the history of the Senate, the legislation passed that chamber on 22 December 1993. It was the early hours of Wednesday morning in Canberra. The packed Senate gallery broke into applause.

When Wilson turned on the radio later that morning and heard that the legislation had been passed, he was heartened. He thought this was a major catalyst for the reconciliation process, and provided some certainty for all Australians. The *Native Title Act* 1993 (Cwlth) became law on 1 January 1994. As 1993 drew to an end, Wilson was more confident than he had been at the beginning of the year that the Aboriginal reconciliation process would move forward.

By 1994 Wilson had reached the Biblical milestone of three score years plus ten. He had left the royal commission and the presidency of the Uniting Church behind, but his pace did not slow.

The position as president of HREOC was nominally part time, but it had become Wilson's main focus, and his commitment would have put many a full-timer to shame. Wilson was universally liked and admired by those who worked at HREOC. After the turbulent and tense tenure of his predecessor, Justice Marcus Einfeld, Wilson was welcomed by the HREOC staff and his fellow commissioners. Many at HREOC respected Einfeld's passion and intelligence, but he was seen by many as abrupt, confrontational and egotistical. This could not be said of Wilson.

Susan Roberts, who joined HREOC as a senior legal officer in 1994, recalls her first meeting with Wilson. She noticed this elderly and incredibly small man talking to someone in an office with the door open. The other person noticed Roberts outside the open door and beckoned her in. It was only then she realised it was the president of HREOC. He gestured for a handshake. Roberts immediately felt the firmness of his grip, somewhat surprising for such a small man. Roberts noticed his 'incredibly warm smile and twinkling eyes'. Roberts said to Wilson, 'Hello, Sir Ronald.' With a wry smile Wilson replied, 'Just call me Ron.'

Wilson was charismatic. Roberts comments that he 'engendered love and respect from the staff and he could light up a room with his presence'. She credits Wilson with bringing the HREOC staff together and developing a close sense of camaraderie, especially when the organisation faced severe budgetary cuts under the Howard government. Wilson made people feel positive about the work they were doing, and what they could achieve with reduced resources.

Diana Temby, who joined HREOC as its executive director in September 1995, said that Wilson was 'extraordinarily courteous to staff', but had a wicked sense of humour and a steely determination. She said he was 'absolutely impossible to resist and it was impossible to deal with him on a day to day basis and not love him'.

Wilson was warm and encouraging to all at HREOC. He was particularly keen to encourage the younger lawyers to present their ideas to him, and to develop and defend their arguments. The young lawyers felt it was such a thrill to work closely with a former High Court justice. Jonathon Hunyor, a young lawyer from HREOC's legal section, remarks: 'One of the pleasures of being at HREOC was that even as a junior member of the legal section, you would work quite closely with someone of such high calibre.'

Those who worked with him worked hard. Because Wilson was so encouraging, no one resented it. And no one worked harder than Wilson. When he left HREOC he was presented with a T-shirt, which had a picture of Wilson on the front with the words: 'If you see this man'. On the back was printed: 'Quick give him some work'.

Soon after taking on the appointment, Wilson 'adopted' the legal section of the commission, doing an enormous amount of the hearings that came before HREOC. Roberts and Hunyor observed Wilson in hearings with great admiration. He was comfortable with all who came before him. If dealing with lawyers, he would allow them to act in a formal legalistic way in representing their clients. But if he were dealing with an unrepresented complainant or respondent, he would seek to assist him or her and was patient with the person. Wilson had the ability to make everyone who appeared before him feel relaxed and respected. He was freed from the constrictions of the evidentiary and hearing formalities and rules of court, and appreciated this flexibility.

In dealing with one complainant, a Perth woman, who had made a sexual discrimination and harassment complaint against her employer, Wilson's concern for the wellbeing of the parties before him was demonstrably on display. The complainant's lawyer had managed to negotiate with the employer respondent a $40,000 settlement offer. The complainant would not agree to the settlement. She wanted to take her complaint to a formal HREOC hearing, but there was no guarantee that the complainant would succeed.

After Wilson had spoken to the lawyers for the complainant and the respondent, and with their agreement, he drove himself to the complainant's home to discuss the case with her. Wilson was concerned with the potential emotional toll on the complainant if she proceeded with the formal hearing, and he was not confident that she would win the case. He explained the pitfalls of taking the matter further to a full hearing, and also the possibility that she may not win, or that she would not be awarded an amount as large as the settlement offer. The complainant's lawyer was impressed with Wilson's concern with the welfare of his client. It was all to no avail. The complainant refused to accept the settlement offer. She sacked her lawyer, and in the end the matter did not proceed to a formal hearing; the complainant also lost the chance of a settlement offer of $40,000.

Wilson saw his position at HREOC as liberating. As a spokesman for the commission, he could again be an advocate. As he said: 'I could once again do what I loved doing the most—that is, advocating, and now I could do it for the disadvantaged.'

Wilson never missed an opportunity to speak out in public meetings and in the media on the need to respect human rights and protect many of the more vulnerable or disadvantaged members of society, such as Aborigines and people with disabilities.

In a 1996 address to a conference at Murdoch University on 'Sexual Orientation and the Law', Wilson outlined his philosophy on human rights.[52] He saw human rights as being inherent, something that human beings, by virtue of their being and destiny, already possessed; they were not given by governments. To him:

> it's a question of the inherent dignity belonging to every human being, simply and solely by virtue of his or her humanity. It's a question of equality of opportunity. It is a question of freedom, justice and peace for the whole world community. It is a question of international law and the obligations that Australia has assumed by its adoption and ratification of these instruments.[53]

He said it was unacceptable for Australia to sign international human rights instruments and then only partially enforce them. Wilson saw his obligation as being to advocate for human rights, particularly for the marginalised and disadvantaged sections of the community.

Wilson spent considerable time holding hearings into complaints that were unable to be settled satisfactorily by conciliation. He held hearings in matters under the RDA,[54] the *Sexual Discrimination Act* 1984 (Cwlth)[55] and the *Disability Discrimination Act* 1992 (Cwlth).[56] As Hunyor remarked:

> Sir Ronald had a real sense of basic human dignity and I think he saw as an important part of justice to be able to do a decision that respected human beings and human dignity and I think if he could make a decision consistent

> with the law but that was also going to respect a person's dignity, then that is the decision he would make.

Hunyor added that Wilson seemed to enjoy the freedom from the strict formality and legalism of the High Court, but that 'he was not a radical activist'. He still tried to do 'justice to a case in a way that was consistent with both the law and with those sorts of values that he had about humanity and justice'.

However, Wilson's decisions under the RDA did attract some academic criticism. The decisions that drew most criticism dealt with racism in sport. Because of the prominence of sport in Australian culture and society and the history of Aboriginal sporting stars, racism in sport had long been an issue. It received additional attention in the early 1990s because of the racial abuse suffered by Michael Long and Nicky Winmar, two Aboriginal Australian Football League (AFL) players. Long, in particular, demanded that the AFL address the racism issue more seriously. The result was the establishment of a Racial Discrimination and Vilification Code, which HREOC played a consulting role in formulating.

Two cases that Wilson had heard before the code's formulation, for which he has received criticism, were not in the high-profile AFL competition. Both cases involved incidents that occurred in his home state of Western Australia.

During the 1989 grand final of the Western Australian Southern Districts Football League Australian Rules football competition, Steven Mead, an Aborigine, struck an opponent, Darren James. James suffered a serious injury. As a result Mead was suspended for a season. In early 1990, the league's tribunal reopened the case. Mead provided a statutory declaration claiming that James had called him 'a black cunt', after which he lost control and hit James. The tribunal did not see this as a mitigating circumstance. In fact, because of new evidence on the severity of James's injury, Mead's suspension was increased from eighteen to twenty-five games. The tribunal held that Mead had 'offered little support for a reduction of penalty'. Mead appealed to the Equal Opportunity Commission of Western Australia, and the matter eventually came before Wilson.[57]

Wilson found that Mead was treated unfairly in the second hearing, and he wondered whether the tribunal had fully appreciated 'the import of the complainant's statutory declarations'. But Wilson did not believe there was evidence of racial discrimination against Mead, and accepted

> unhesitatingly that the members of the Tribunal are honourable persons who at all material times have acted bona fide and in the best interests as they saw them of the game of football.[58]

Hannah McGlade, Noongar (local south-west WA kin group) lawyer and academic, asked why Wilson was so confident that the tribunal had not acted with a bias against Mead based on racism? She added that Wilson seemed to not believe that Australia is a racist country, and he seemed to have no understanding and experience of racism. To support this claim, she pointed to Wilson's judgement in *Mabo (No 1)*.[59]

Lawrence McNamara, another legal academic, was also critical of Wilson's decision. He argued that, contrary to Wilson's finding that nothing was said by the tribunal to suggest racism:

> nothing had to be said. It was understood by all members of the Tribunal and of the football community in the Southern District Football League—the interpretative community—this is how things are.[60]

McNamara also wondered why, if Wilson believed that racism was not a part of the Mead case, or that there is no systemic racism in the sport, did he comment that it was good that an Aborigine had been appointed to the tribunal and the Southern Aboriginal Corporation had been invited to send an observer to hearings in which a Noongar is involved.

McNamara's answer to his own question was clear: Wilson 'knows' there is discrimination in football but:

> when racial abuse is immersed in the context of football, he cannot see it as discrimination, because he accepts a certain meaning of what football is. And that meaning is layered with racism.[61]

The other sport case involved the code of rugby union.[62] The complainant, Tomasi Tamanivalu, tackled an opponent in an illegal manner. He was then called a 'dirty black bastard' by an opposing player. He was sent from the ground for the illegal tackle. In the process of leaving the field, someone from the opposing bench said: 'You got what you deserved, you black bastard.' Tamanivalu confronted the player he believed made the statement and hit and kicked him.

Tamanivalu made a complaint to HREOC, arguing that the Western Australian Rugby Union failed to protect him from racial taunts by other players. Wilson agreed that Tamanivalu had been subjected to racial abuse, but there was no breach under the RDA. He held that the Act could only have been contravened if there had been 'a particular problem with racist abuse' and the union did nothing about it. But Wilson held that in this case there was no breach. Although evidence was submitted that there had been a history of racial abuse in games, Wilson determined that 'racist abuse had never been considered to be a major problem by the WARU or its affiliated clubs'. He readily accepted the union's judgement as to whether racism was a problem. Further, even though Wilson acknowledged that the rugby judiciary did not properly understand the nature of racial abuse as provocation, nonetheless the severity of the penalty against Tamanivalu (initially two years, which was reduced to six months with eighteen months' suspended sentence) was not influenced by racism, but was imposed for the good of the game. From this, Wilson appeared to be saying that a player just had to accept the racial abuse.

In concluding his critique of Wilson's decisions in *Mead* and *Tamanivalu*, McNamara wrote:

> The result for the complainants, it has been suggested, is that they were denied justice by our legal system because they were black. They went to Human Rights Commission as black cunts. They left with grand words from Sir Ronald Wilson about 'justice' and 'fundamental freedoms'. But they still left as black cunts.[63]

McNamara's statement is colourful and polemical, but also has merit.

It appears that president Wilson, the expressive advocate of human rights, who was flexible with hearing evidence in the hearings and was sympathetic to allowing the complaints to be heard, retreated to a kind of 'legal shell' when making his determinations as a hearing commissioner. Maybe he was concerned with the consequences to HREOC of his determinations.

It is possible to look at Wilson's decisions in *Mead* and *Tamanivalu* as reflective of his sensitivity of not embroiling the HREOC in political controversy. One can imagine the controversy and criticism that would have been targeted at HREOC if Wilson had held that racism and racial abuse may justify physical retaliation on the sporting field. The critics would have labelled HREOC as social engineers who had no idea of reality on the football field.

With the position that sport holds in Australian society, the debate would have been emotional and protracted.

There are other instances that lend support to the view that Wilson was very sensitive to the reputation of HREOC. In 1995, the Western Australian Police Tactical Response Group stormed a suburban home of an Aboriginal family. This was after an off-duty police officer, one street away, heard what he thought was a gunshot but what was actually a car backfiring. Immediately the Aboriginal family was targeted by the police, with no other homes being considered. However, the off-duty police officer was not in a position to pinpoint the source of the 'gunshot' noise. The ALSWA asked HREOC to investigate the matter, but Wilson refused to do so, saying that there was insufficient evidence to create a *prima facie* case of racial discrimination. One must wonder what further evidence was required to at least instigate an inquiry into the matter.[64]

Although Wilson had great commitment and passion in fighting sexual discrimination and disability discrimination, it would be accurate to say that, from the commencement of his time as HREOC president, racism and the conditions of Aborigines were at the top of his priorities. He had long been passionate in opposing racial discrimination and seeking to redress the plight of Aborigines. He knew as a champion of the reconciliation movement that non-Aboriginal Australia had to confront the longstanding injustices and marginalisation of the Aborigines in Australia. In 1995, Wilson was to be given an opportunity and a challenge on this front that was to have a significant impact on him.

Wilson's long tenure as the chancellor of Murdoch University came to an end early in 1995. Most of the senate and others at the university thought he had wanted to bring his chancellorship to an end. In fact he had wanted to do another term, until a senate member in a private conversation with Wilson suggested that it was probably time for a change of chancellor. It was this suggestion that swayed Wilson's decision not to seek or agree to another term.

His longheld dream of a law school at the university had been finally realised, but the latter stages of his chancellorship were soured to a degree by an academic controversy.

Professor Fred Jevons had been appointed as Director of the Institute of Science and Technology Policy at Murdoch in 1988, but resigned two years later after disputes over his managerial style. Subsequently Jevons criticised, sometimes publicly, the work and staff of the institute. Vice-chancellor Professor Peter Boyce wrote to Jevons expressing concern.[65]

Jevons wrote to Wilson as chancellor in 1992, asking him to use his good offices 'to help achieve a resolution of the dispute in which, to my great regret, I am involved'. Wilson responded, telling Jevons that the dispute had caused him 'anxiety', and pleaded with Jevons that the past be forgotten. He added:

> I accept that you are genuine in desiring a resolution of these difficulties. Two relevant implications of such a desire are that there must be willingness on both sides to compromise and to forgive and forget. By that I mean a willingness to make a fresh start.[66]

This was classic Wilson—seeking to bring parties together and move forward in a positive manner rather than looking into the past.

In later correspondence, Wilson mentioned a possible settlement including an offer of retirement, monetary payout, a written apology and the status of honorary fellow in the School of Social Sciences for two years and an office on campus. But, being a skilled lawyer and concerned to protect the interests of the university, Wilson added: 'Naturally this offer must be conditional on the litigation being discontinued, together with a disclaimer against the University and its staff.'[67]

It was only later that he found out that the settlement between Jevons and the university, which included Jevons being appointed as an honorary fellow for two years, did not contain the disclaimer clause as he had previously suggested. He was most unhappy with this, and wrote to the pro-chancellor, Justice Michael Murray, saying: 'Unfortunately I was not consulted on the form of the settlement and there is no suitable disclaimer clause.'[68]

Jevons continued to engage in public complaints about his treatment and the long-running dispute, and included Wilson in his attacks, calling for his resignation. In one letter he wrote in reference to Wilson:

> I was misled at first by his formidable reputation for integrity. If he had behaved with the integrity I had been led to expect my tasks would have been easy, since the facts are quite clear-cut. When I managed to see him in March I succeeded in getting out of him what he had told the Senate in secret sessions in February. It wasn't easy, because he is so reluctant to

> recognise that he might not be infallible, but I did get it out of him and I showed him evidence that it was directly contrary to the facts. He was clearly taken aback. Ever since he has been fighting like a cornered rat to avoid having to concede that he was wrong.[69]

Eventually the university senate, after considering various documentations on the issue, withdrew Jevons's fellowship, but Jevons did not stop his protest. He complained to the state ombudsman, and eventually to the university visitor, the governor of Western Australia, His Excellency Major-General Philip Michael Jeffery.

It was not until after Wilson had retired as chancellor that the final chapter was written, with a report from Justice Muirhead, who had been appointed by the governor as his assessor, endorsing the withdrawal of the fellowship. Muirhead also wrote that:

> The Chancellor at all times sought to preserve peace, and to counsel the Applicant to withdraw the litigation against colleagues. I find the Chancellor, despite his many responsibilities, did all within his power to preserve not only the University's reputation but the Applicant's reputation.[70]

It seems likely that the Jevons affair was a factor in the quiet suggestion from a university senate member that it was time for a change.

Wilson's long and faithful service to Murdoch University was recognised with the awarding of an honorary degree of Doctor of the University. The award was conferred at the degree ceremony at the Perth Concert Hall on 22 March 1995.

At the ceremony, Wilson delivered the occasional address. Dressed in Murdoch University academic regalia, Wilson commenced his address by thanking the senate for conferring the honorary degree, and then outlining many of the developments at Murdoch that had 'undergirded' his pride in the university. He then moved on to the theme of his address—vision. Reflecting his focus on human rights as HREOC president, he gave a brief overview of the development of human rights law since World War II. He went on to say that, while Australia's record in social justice was better than that of many other nations, it was not good enough: 'From my perspective as President of the Human Rights Commission, I have to say, and to say with conviction, that it is not good enough.' He pointed out the status and living conditions of Aborigines, the gap between poor and rich, issues of sex and disability discrimination and the hostile action by the Commonwealth government against the arrival of boats of refugees.

In the gathering were those graduating from the law school. To them Wilson added:

> Let me add a word directly to those of you who see your future in the practice of the law. Lest you think that the thoughts I have expressed are a bit remote, let me remind you of a remark of one of the most famous lawyers who ever lived. Cicero, the great Roman philosopher, statesman, lawyer, who lived in the first century before Christ, is reported to have remarked: 'We have a natural propensity to love our fellow men, and that, after all, is the foundation of all law.' This remark has intrigued me for years, but, after 60 years in the law I believe the remark to be true.[71]

He congratulated his fellow graduates, and hoped that they would use their life skills acquired at Murdoch for 'the service of your fellow human beings'. He concluded by quoting a US judge:

> You have no goods to sell, no land to till. Your only asset is yourself. If your service does not contain the quality of integrity, it is worthless. If it does, it is priceless. The value is either nothing or it is infinite.
>
> So do not try to set a price on yourselves. Rather be reckless and spendthrift, pouring out your talent to all to whom it can be of service.
>
> Throw it away, waste it, and in the spending it will be increased. Like love, talent is useful only in its expenditure, and it is never exhausted.
>
> A person must eat, so set what price you must on your service. But never confuse the performance, which is great, with the compensation, be it money, power or fame, which is trivial.[72]

Wilson looked up from his speech to observe the graduates one more time. He then said: 'May God bless you all.'

13

Bringing Them Home

I had never been exposed to such pain before.

On 11 May 1995, the Commonwealth attorney-general, Michael Lavarch, signed off on an inquiry to be conducted by HREOC. This was not to be any ordinary inquiry. It was an inquiry for which Aboriginal groups had long been advocating.

As the 1980s ended, there was increased interest among Aboriginal people for a national inquiry into the past governmental (state, territorial and Commonwealth)[1] practice of systematic removal of Aboriginal children from their families. Many of the calls were from Aboriginal leaders who had, as children, been removed from their families. In 1990, the Secretariat of the National Aboriginal and Islander Child Care (SNAICC) group resolved at its national conference to demand an inquiry into the removal issue.[2]

On 4 August 1991, National Aboriginal and Islander Children's Day, SNAICC, in conjunction with high-profile Aboriginal entertainers Archie Roach and Ruby Hunter, publicly launched a demand for an inquiry. Other

Aboriginal organisations, such as the ALSWA and Link-Up (New South Wales), added their support.

On 10 December 1992, in the inner Sydney suburb of Redfern, the prime minister, Mr Paul Keating, uttered words that were to reverberate throughout Australia: 'We took the children from their mothers.'[3] The venue and the occasion were significant. Redfern had been transformed into a residential area for Aboriginal people during Gough Whitlam's prime ministership, from 1972 to 1975. The occasion was the launch of the United Nations' International Year of the World's Indigenous People (1993).

Keating's speech made frequent references to past injustices against Australian Aborigines, including the 'dispossession of their lands'. The prime minister said that White Australia had failed to make the most basic human response and enter into the hearts and minds of the Aboriginal people. As Keating's speech proceeded, voices of approval from the Aboriginal audience could be heard. Keating concluded by stressing the need to provide justice to the Aboriginal people, who had suffered under the dominant political and economic non-Aboriginal systems:

> We simply cannot sweep injustice aside. Even if our own conscience allowed us to, I am sure, that in due course, the world and the people of our region would not.[4]

Two years later in 1994, Joy Williams, an Aboriginal woman from New South Wales who had been removed from her mother as a child, commenced legal action in the New South Wales Supreme Court, claiming that the New South Wales government had breached its duty of care and fiduciary duty to her as a child.[5] Also in 1994, The Going Home Conference was held in Darwin, bringing together Aboriginal people, mainly from the Northern Territory, who had been removed from their families. The conference was emotional, with many in attendance retelling the pain of their separation from their families. Also attending was the Commonwealth Aboriginal affairs minister, Robert Tickner. Deeply moved, he returned to Canberra and pushed the idea of a national inquiry to his ALP parliamentary colleagues.

Many at the conference were also keen to instigate litigation against the Commonwealth, because the Northern Territory removal scheme had been governed by Commonwealth government legislation. The conference delegates heard from Ron Merkel QC about possible litigation actions.[6]

Not long after Merkel's address, the Northern Australian Aboriginal Legal Service established a unit within the organisation to prepare actions against the government. In early 1995, over 700 writs were filed in the High Court registry in Darwin.

The grounds for the actions included denial of familial contact and, in some cases, physical and sexual abuse. The prospect of Aborigines utilising the court system seeking compensation, as well as the continual pressure from Aboriginal groups for an inquiry, focused the Commonwealth government's attention on these issues. The result was Lavarch's announcement on 11 May 1995.

Before Lavarch's announcement, discussions had been held between the Commonwealth government and HREOC over the government's desire for HREOC to conduct the inquiry. Wilson agreed, believing HREOC had a public duty to do so, and that it would be important for the reconciliation process. Wilson had stepped down from the Council for Aboriginal Reconciliation the previous year, but he was still absolutely committed to its cause.

However, he had no well-informed perspective or appreciation of the magnitude of the process involved with such an inquiry. At that stage Wilson was rather ignorant of the history of Aboriginal child removals from family, despite a report in a 2001 *Bulletin* article that, not long after he was appointed as co-head of the inquiry, 'Wilson described forced removals as "virtual genocide".'[7] When asked about it in 2001, Wilson could not recall having used the word 'genocide' just after the announcement of the inquiry. If he had, it would not have been as a consequence of any intense study. In 1995, his knowledge of the issue was superficial at best.

Some other HREOC commissioners were uncertain about what the inquiry could achieve, because the proposed terms of reference did not include the issue of compensation. They were also concerned about additional demands on their already overworked staff. Indeed, human rights commissioner Chris Sidoti wrote:

> The Commission did not initiate the inquiry and indeed the Terms of Reference caused a good deal of trepidation on all fronts—about what could be accomplished, about the level of commitment from politicians and community to do something about the issues, and not least how HREOC could possibly hope to do justice to the subject.[8]

Also, some commissioners were acutely aware that many in the Aboriginal community would be disappointed that the proposed inquiry did not have the status of a royal commission. Even so, the commissioners realised the importance of such an inquiry and the demands for it within the Aboriginal community. It was a step forward, and better than nothing.

Attorney-general Lavarch announced that the Commonwealth government was committed to human rights, social justice, access and equity. Pursuant to powers in the *Human Rights and Equal Opportunity Commission Act* 1986 (Cwlth), he was principally asking HREOC to inquire into, and report on the history and effects of the forced separation of Aboriginal and Torres Strait Islander children from their families. There were two additional terms of reference.

One was to examine the adequacy of the current laws, practices and policies in relation to the delivery of services to those who had been separated, including, but not limited to, measures for family reunification and access to individual and family records. The final term of reference involved an examination of current laws, practices and policies on the placement and care of Aboriginal and Torres Strait Islander children, and possible changes consistent with the principle of self-determination.

Also, Lavarch announced that HREOC was to consult widely with Aboriginal and non-Aboriginal communities. All this was to be done on a budget of only $1.3 million, and HREOC was to report no later than December 1996.

Generally, the announcement of the inquiry was well received by those who had been agitating for it. However, there was some disappointment. For example, Robert Riley, the chief executive officer of the ALSWA and prominent Aboriginal activist, who as a child had been separated from his family, had hoped for a royal commission. Like other Aboriginal leaders and organisations, he was also disappointed that the terms of reference did not include an examination of possible compensation. Further, he was unhappy that Wilson would be the sole chair of the inquiry. He had great respect and fondness for Wilson. However, he was echoing the sentiments of many in the Aboriginal community, and others, when he said to some ALSWA staff: 'Sir Ronald is a fine man but an Aboriginal must also head the inquiry.' A few went further, believing that Wilson, a non-Aboriginal, should not head the inquiry. Most notable was Perth Children's Court magistrate Sue Gordon, who as a child in the 1950s was separated from her parents and placed in Sister Kate's Children's Home,[9] with which Wilson had past connections.

Riley and other Aboriginal leaders telephoned Lavarch's and Tickner's offices registering these concerns. Wilson's only public response was that he was looking forward to being involved in the inquiry.

The protests had an immediate effect. The Commonwealth government appointed Mick Dodson, the Aboriginal and Torres Strait Islander social justice commissioner at HREOC, to co-chair the inquiry with Wilson. The other HREOC commissioners were also to be involved in the hearings and discussion on the inquiry report. It was also announced that the inquiry would appoint a number of Aboriginal women commissioners, who would be invited to sit with Wilson and Dodson in different regions of Australia. But within HREOC at least, this inquiry was perceived as being under Wilson's control. Although at this stage Wilson's knowledge of the history and effects of the past policies and practices of Aboriginal child removals was rudimentary, he was, as HREOC executive director Diana Temby remarked, 'the most enthused about the inquiry, more than anyone else at the Commission'.

Lavarch also stated that the inquiry's terms of references would be amended to include the issue of compensation. At the official inquiry launch in Adelaide on 2 August 1995, with Wilson in attendance, it was announced that the three terms of reference issued on 2 May were revoked, and reissued in the same form with the additional term of reference: 'Examine the principles relevant to determining the justification for compensation for persons or communities affected by such separation.' This did not grant the inquiry power to recommend reparations, only to establish principles on which compensation could be justified. Many of those participating in the inquiry ignored this formal restriction on recommending compensation. Wilson, however, was not, at first, as anxious as some of his fellow HREOC commissioners to consider compensation.

In late August 1995, Wilson attended a meeting at the ALSWA office in East Perth, to discuss the inquiry with Catherine Crawford, the principal legal officer (since 2006 a Perth magistrate), and some lawyers from the public interest section of the ALSWA, including this author. Wilson talked about the honour he felt in chairing the inquiry, and how it had already created much interest within HREOC and the Aboriginal community. He informed the meeting that a secretariat had been established to coordinate the inquiry, and its members were developing protocols and procedures for the inquiry's hearings. The secretariat's principal officer was Jim Brooks, who came from HREOC's Cairns office, where he was the regional director.

Wilson did not mention that HREOC was confronting several difficulties. The $1.3 million budget was demonstrably insufficient to run the inquiry properly, and there were insufficient funds to have a full-time counsel assisting. However, Wilson reduced the need for such a counsel by ensuring that the inquiry was nonadversarial. This would later expose Wilson and the inquiry to criticism that they did not sufficiently test the 'truthfulness' of the evidence and stories told to them.

Also, with a limited budget, HREOC's capacity to establish an extensive secretariat was severely restricted. Employees from other sections were coopted to assist the inquiry, putting further strain on the whole organisation. The inquiry, which had sixteen months to report to the Commonwealth government, appeared to be some time away from commencing hearings. Wilson was not overly concerned. He had great faith that HREOC had the people to 'do a good job'. In public, Wilson consistently expressed this faith. He reaffirmed it at the ALSWA meeting.

At the end of the meeting Wilson enjoyed a cup of tea with those in attendance. In a conversation with an ALSWA solicitor, he expressed concern with the compensation issue: 'I can't see how we are going to be able to recommend compensation. It will just open up a Pandora's box. Who knows where claims for compensation will end?' This was a significant statement. The inquiry had not even started, and already the co-chair was expressing an opinion that was in stark contrast to the views of many of the Aborigines who had agitated for the inquiry over a number of years. One can imagine the controversy that would have been created if Wilson had expressed his view to the media. It would likely have led to some Aboriginal groups and representatives demanding that he stand down from chairing the inquiry.

In developing the inquiry's procedures and practices, the commissioners and Jim Brooks decided that it was essential to establish an Indigenous Advisory Council, with representatives selected from around Australia. Members included Brian Butler and Carol Kendall, who had long advocated an inquiry into the removal issues, and Barbara Cummings, a feisty Northern Territory Aboriginal woman who was keen on court action against the Commonwealth government. Nigel d'Souza, the executor director of SNAICC, although not Aboriginal, was also included.[10] This advisory council met on an ad hoc basis with the inquiry secretariat, Wilson and Dodson (and sometimes other HREOC commissioners), to discuss how to plan for the hearings, and subsequently, the structure and substance of the inquiry report. Most of the meetings were by video conferencing. In addition to the meetings with the council as a group, meetings with individual council members also occurred before the hearings, taking place in the individual council members' respective locations and states.

The meetings were held in a spirit of consultation and consensus. However, in one of the earlier meetings, Wilson did not enamour himself with some advisory council members. He expressed the view that the hearings, which would mainly consist of personal stories and oral submissions from organisations and governments, should be completed in approximately four months. As a High Court justice, he had heard very complicated legal arguments being completed by barristers in a day or less. Although the hearings into the WA Inc Royal Commission had taken sixteen months (but only 278 days of actual hearings), they were extremely complicated. Surely, Wilson thought, the inquiry into the removal policies and practices could not be complex and the number wanting to make oral submissions would not be excessive. Some advisory council members told Wilson that the hearings would take much longer than four months, especially as the inquiry was dealing with matters of great emotional importance for Aboriginal people. They would want and need adequate time to tell their stories. Wilson acknowledged that this inquiry would be delving into sensitive issues. He didn't fully appreciate how protracted the hearings would become.

As the months of 1995 progressed, Wilson's time and thoughts were increasingly devoted to the inquiry. He still retained his duties as HREOC president, including hearing complaints against alleged contraventions of various Commonwealth discrimination statutes that came under HREOC's purview. Even so, the inquiry quickly became the main priority.

Understandably, the inquiry generated great excitement in the Aboriginal community. Some of the 500 Aborigines who had told their stories to the ALSWA for its report *Telling Our Story* were keen to appear before the inquiry.[11]

Rob Riley officially launched *Telling Our Story* in July 1995 at Manguri, the site of the former Sister Kate's Children's Home in Queens Park. In the 1980s, Riley was chair of the National Aboriginal Conference, the forerunner of ATSIC. He had also been adviser to Gerry Hand, Aboriginal affairs minister in the Hawke government. As the chief executive officer of the ALSWA, he had built a high public profile, frequently being sought out by the media for comment.

Holding back tears, Riley launched *Telling Our Story* and told of the punishment he received at Sister Kate's for daring to ask about his parents. He was told his parents were dead. This was a lie. In fact, he was reunited with his mother when he was ten, in 1964. Two years later, he left Sister Kate's to live with his mother, stepfather and siblings.

Within a few days of the launch Rob Riley was engaged in a high-speed police car chase. This signalled the commencement of the decline in his professional status and mental wellbeing, which sadly ended with his suicide on 1 May 1996 at a motel in the Perth southern suburb of Bentley. Consequently, he never told his story to the inquiry, although it featured prominently in *Telling Our Story*.[12]

Because of the interest in the inquiry, Wilson received numerous invitations to attend meetings with Aboriginal organisations, as well as community and church groups, to discuss the inquiry. Whenever possible, he accepted. He was the main speaker at the State Aboriginal Health Conference at the Hyatt Hotel in Perth on 21 November 1995, although he was not the initial choice. Mick Dodson was in Geneva, participating in an Indigenous Working Group of the UN Commission on Human Rights, which was drafting the proposed *Declaration on the Rights of Indigenous People*. Wilson was his replacement.

The title of Wilson's address was 'The National Inquiry into the Removal of Aboriginal Children: Healing the Nation'. He stated:

> While our inquiry has yet to take submissions or consider evidence, I think there can be no doubt in anyone's mind that past policies of removal have a continuing profound effect on the lives of Indigenous people, families and communities across the country.[13]

At times during his delivery, Wilson, the fierce prosecutor and passionate preacher, raised his voice to emphasise a point. He predicted that the inquiry would provide an opportunity for Aboriginal people to tell their stories and for non-Aboriginal Australia to listen. Indeed, he hoped that the inquiry process would 'bring the voices of Aboriginal people into clear earshot of non-Indigenous Australia'. He added that those involved in the inquiry 'hope to build a bridge so that non-Indigenous Australians can learn about, and begin to understand the impact of what has occurred'. In the few months after the announcement of the inquiry, Wilson's ignorance of the history of Aboriginal childhood removal policies and practices had been somewhat remedied. He now was broadly aware that there had been an official systematic policy of separation, and that many of those removed had suffered. But he remained ignorant of the magnitude of the issue and the depth of trauma and ongoing effects. He had little idea of what awaited him at the inquiry's hearings.

The hearings commenced in Tasmania, a state with a dismal history of race relations. Tasmania, unlike other jurisdictions, had not enacted Aboriginal-specific child welfare legislation. From the 1930s, Aboriginal children were removed from their families under general child welfare legislation. They were removed to mainland Tasmania from Cape Barren Island in the Bass Strait, to which they had been transferred in the second half of the nineteenth century. Most had come from nearby Flinders Island, having been moved from the main island in the 1830s, in response to the continual conflicts between the Aborigines and European settlers.

The first hearings were in Hobart on 4 December 1995. Over the next seven days hearings were held on Flinders Island, Cape Barren Island, and in Launceston and Burnie. More hearings occurred in Hobart in August 1996. Wilson and Dodson heard submissions from Tasmanian government officials and from Aborigines who, as children, had been separated from their families.

Wilson empathised with the Aboriginal stories he heard in Tasmania. However, there was still a sense of detachment, emotionally at least, between him and the storytellers, not unlike when he was a High Court justice. He had a job to do: listen to the stories and gather information for the inquiry report. Even so, he could not avoid noticing the pain and trauma in the voices of the storytellers, who had grown up without their parents. Wilson too had effectively grown up without parents. He had thought: how were the Aboriginal people before him so different from him?

Wilson's mother died when he was four, too early for him to have received any lasting impressions of her. At least as far as Wilson could remember, his father, even before he became incapacitated when Wilson was eight, never gave Wilson a hug or sign of affection. Wilson had said of his father: 'He was never a dad. I don't remember him ever playing with me.'

He didn't begrudge these circumstances. He felt no great sense of loss: 'Occasionally I feel a bit guilty in that my parents actually mean nothing to me.' Sometimes he wondered what it would have been like to have grown up with parents playing a major part in his life, but he never dwelt on it or felt miserable about it. He had no affinity with people who treasured the memory of their parents and derived much from them.

Mick Dodson thought that Wilson had an almost dismissive attitude to some Aborigines who came before him at the early hearings. Before the hearings commenced, Dodson viewed Wilson as a conservative judge who had put the interest of the states ahead of the people's human rights. He also thought Wilson's 'position was as an apologist for the past policies, laws and practice'. Dodson said:

> You have to remember that Ron was a lay preacher who was involved with Sister Kate's and I think when the inquiry started he genuinely believed that, you know, the country and governments and others had done the right thing to save Aboriginal kids.

As the hearings proceeded, Dodson noticed a major shift: 'You just had to observe it. He didn't say anything, but the change in him was noticeable, he looked very emotional. You could almost photograph it, such was the shift.' Two or three months into the hearings, Wilson was transformed, overtaken by the sheer emotion of the stories being retold.

He realised that his childhood had indeed been different. He had grown up without the constant presence and love of his parents, but he had 'Mumsie', who cared for him, and he was not denied his culture or subjected to abuse. He now felt great sympathy towards the Aborigines telling their stories, 'for what they went through, their sense of family and their loss of being taken away from their families'. This feeling became stronger as the hearings proceeded to mainland Australia. It had taken the hearings themselves to change Wilson. From the day he was appointed co-chair of the inquiry, he had been advocating the need for the story to be told. However, it was the repeated stories of pain and trauma that changed Wilson from detached support to a passionate and heartfelt advocacy. Wilson had moved a long way.

He became a passionate advocate for having the removal story told to all Australians and for putting in place measures that would address the past's harms and help build a more united Australia. Dodson remarked, 'Once you convince Ron Wilson you can have no one more passionate as an advocate... As an advocate he gives it 120 per cent.'

Dodson's respect for Wilson increased as the inquiry proceeded. They became good friends, developing a good professional relationship and enjoying each other's company in social settings. Wilson discovered that Mick Dodson shared many of the same characteristics he admired in Mick's older brother Patrick. Wilson had got to know Patrick during his time on the Council for Aboriginal Reconciliation. He found both Patrick and Mick to be intelligent, considerate of others, and passionate about a better deal for Aborigines. Similarly, Mick Dodson admired Wilson's stamina and good spirits. He appreciated Wilson's sense of humour and enjoyed spending time with him.

After the first few months of hearings, Wilson realised that his initial estimation of only needing four months of hearings was not achievable. He sought, and was granted, an extension of the timetable and reporting deadline for the inquiry.

The hearing phase of the inquiry concluded where it had started—in Hobart on 22 December 1996. Wilson and Dodson, with some assistance from other HREOC commissioners and a number of regional female hearing commissioners,[14] had travelled throughout Australia listening to Aboriginal people tell their stories. They had taken evidence and submissions from academics, police officers and state, territorial and Commonwealth government representatives, churches and nongovernment organisations. They held hearings in every state and territory capital city, and thirty-two country centres. They had heard from 535 individual Aboriginal people, and in total from 770 people and organisations. The inquiry also received approximately 1,000 stories in writing, and numerous other written submissions. In some instances, the written submissions, particularly from state governments, were voluminous.

The hearings had a great emotional impact on Wilson. After the inquiry, at numerous speaking events, he described how for him

> it was a life-changing experience to listen privately to story after story of pain and loss, told to me in a spirit of trust and simplicity, notwithstanding that I represented the race that had done so much to cause the pain. I have never been exposed to such pain before. The stories so obviously came from the heart that I could not but open my own heart in sympathy and understanding in order to hear them.[15]

When asked to recall some of these stories in an interview with the author in 2003, Wilson was visibly emotional. His voice trembled more than normal, the shaking hand was shakier and the eyes were moist. He mentioned the statement of one woman who came before the inquiry and said, 'The only time I was hugged was when I was raped.' Wilson's response to this was, 'You can hardly call that love.'[16] Another woman had said to him, 'I'm a rotten mother, I've never cuddled my children because I was never cuddled as a baby.' He also recalled the story of 'Evie', who was separated from her mother when only six hours old. Evie's mother had also been separated from her own mother. Wilson said:

> The story of Evie is published in the inquiry report. Evie talked about the sexual and physical abuse at the hands of the priests at Garden Point, Tennant Creek in the Northern Territory. It was terrible. Some of the kids were belted with a stock-whip. Can you imagine the damage done to these children? Evie had her own three children taken away from her when she was in hospital for three months. I think she had septicaemia. She was tricked into signing adoption papers for two of her children. She lost her two boys. They do not consider her as their mother. She was reunited with her daughter eleven years after the separation but it was no good. The daughter blamed the mother for what had happened. Can you just imagine how the mother would feel? I will always remember her saying how every day of her life she feels hurt.[17]

Oral submissions made by governments, churches and nongovernment organisations were conducted as public hearings, although the audience was usually small, consisting of a few Aborigines and their supporters and representatives of the institutions making the submissions. However, most individual Aboriginal stories were told in camera. This was done because it was determined that the storytellers' privacy should be guaranteed, as in many cases they were describing very personal matters, including incidents of sexual abuse.

Often these stories were filled with so much distress, pain and sorrow that Wilson and other commissioners did not ask questions. Seated behind a school table or desk, they only listened. The storyteller sat in front or to the side of the individual commissioner (usually Wilson or Dodson) or the commissioners (usually Wilson, Dodson and a regional female hearing commissioner). The tape recorder was on, but sometimes nothing came from the storyteller. Occasionally it took thirty seconds, a minute, two minutes or even more before the storyteller spoke. Her or his facial muscles twitched and tears rolled down the cheeks. These moments, and the ensuing stories of pain, loss and sorrow, moved Wilson the most.

In some cases the telling of the story was a therapeutic exercise. After telling their stories, some would say, 'I feel better now.'[18]

While some stories were positive, the overwhelming majority were filled with the pain and anguish of family separations and, in some cases, physical and sexual abuse. Wilson had never been exposed to this pain that he was hearing and seeing. At times he found it difficult to cope, and could only bear it 'by opening [his] heart and telling the storyteller that this is a heart to heart communication.' As Wilson would say at a 1999 Gold Coast conference:

> The stories we heard—all 535 of them—were not just coming out of the mouths of the storytellers. The patent display of courage in uttering the words, coupled with the pain associated with their utterance convinced us that we were involved in an exercise of the heart. It was as if the words were being literally wrenched out of the heart, in many cases in words that had never before passed through the lips of the speaker. I found that it was impossible for me to just sit there calmly listening to the words, as I may have been able to do as a judge hearing a case in court. I had to identify with the speaker—in other words, I found myself listening with my heart as well as my mind. I had never been exposed to such pain before.
>
> The reason why this inquiry was so special was because at its centre there was so often a meeting of the hearts—the heart of the speaker and the heart of the listener becoming as one. From that meeting of hearts was born in those of us conducting the inquiry the sense of a precious trust being imparted to us to awaken the nation to this part of its history. I am still conscious of that sense of trust today.[19]

Wilson heard stories of mothers painting their children black, because it was the light-skinned children, the so-called 'half-castes', who were mostly likely to be separated from their parents. Government officials considered that such children were more 'savable' and easier to assimilate into the European community. He recalled the story of a policeman riding into a country town and asking a child if he or she would like a ride on his horse. Once the child was convinced it would be fun, the policeman placed the child on the horse and rode away, without the mother's consent or knowledge. In a hearing in the Kimberley, he was told of how the Aboriginal protector put six crying children in a car and drove off, while being chased by a grieving mother, who collapsed to the ground when she could go no further as the car receded into the distance.

Wilson no longer harboured doubts about recommending compensation. The misery and suffering changed his mind.

Also, the sheer number of Aborigines affected by these removal practices convinced Wilson that a comprehensive system of reparations was required. The magnitude and depth of the effects were large. As Cedric Wyatt, then head of the Western Australian Department of Aboriginal Affairs, admitted at the inquiry: 'All Aborigines in Western Australia have to some extent been affected by the policies and practices of removal.'[20] What he meant was clear: either someone was removed, or had her or his child removed, or her or his sibling or other relative removed from family, community and Aboriginal culture.

During the hearings in Perth, from 13 to 17 May 1997 at the sparsely furnished Aboriginal Advancement Council building in Northbridge, Wilson heard submissions from many people he knew well. For example, he heard from Kath Mallot, the executive director of the Western Australian Deaths in Custody Watch Committee, which was established in response to the Royal Commission on Aboriginal Deaths in Custody. Among other things, the Watch Committee sought to influence government policy in Aboriginal affairs, particularly in relation to reducing Aboriginal incarceration rates. Wilson was a founding member of the Watch Committee, and helped draft its mission statement. Even though he had many demands on his time, he was very involved in assisting the Watch Committee. Mallot remarked:

> [Wilson] was a workaholic. He would often send through faxes to the office suggesting a course of action for a particular issue and he would pave the way for us to make contact with crucial people. He was always there to act as a sounding board and his advice was much valued.

He also heard from Bill Johnson—the brother of Kath Mallot. Johnson, a successful Perth businessman, who had arrived in the Northern Territory with his wife Pauline from Liverpool in 1972, appeared before the inquiry in a private capacity (with Kath Mallot), and his submission was in camera, with Wilson sitting as the sole commissioner.

In the three years prior to the inquiry, Wilson had met Johnson on a few occasions and formed a great respect for him, considering him 'a passionate advocate for justice and a remarkably generous individual'. Johnson appeared before Wilson to tell a very personal story, about his adopted Aboriginal son, Louis St John Johnson, who was murdered in a race-hate crime that took place on North Beach Road in the Perth northern suburbs in the early hours of 4 January 1992, his nineteenth birthday. Two of the five youths involved in the crime were sent to prison.[21]

A very emotional Johnson told Wilson that he and his wife were very upset that they had been party to taking Louis (his birth name being Warren Braedon) away from his mother without her consent. At the time of Louis' adoption they had been told by the Northern Territory Child Welfare authorities that Louis had been abandoned by his mother on three occasions. Indeed, they were under the impression that she had consented to the adoption.

Johnson's oral submission deeply moved Wilson. He and Mallot retold the story of how Johnson and his wife were misled on the facts surrounding the adoption process. Johnson choked up with emotion. He could not conclude his submission, and Kath could not take over. Wilson comforted both of them, and then read the final part of their submission into the record.

During the Perth hearings, the inquiry listened to Cedric Jacobs, an Aborigine from the Swan Valley region who had been removed from his family as a child. Jacobs was a member of the ALSWA oral submission team, which was led by this author. He was an ordained minister in the Uniting Church. In his oral submission, Jacobs talked about separation from his family and his difficulties with the Uniting Church. Wilson became uncomfortable. He shifted in his chair and the muscles in his face tightened as Jacobs criticised the Uniting Church that Wilson loved and to which he devoted so much time.

Jacobs had been a candidate for election to the federal parliament as a member of a small socially and politically conservative party. He had fallen out with the United Aboriginal and Islander Christian Congress and been relieved of his ministerial duties. Wilson had always been keen for Aboriginal people within the Uniting Church to have their own voice, and had strongly supported the Congress. Jacobs's criticism of the congress and church was very uncomfortable for Wilson. But he was there to listen to Aboriginal voices, even if, as in this case, it related to a matter not germane to the inquiry's terms of references.

Wilson was sensitive to the churches' involvement in the removal or separation policies and practices. Stephen Hall, who in his capacity as executive officer of the Anglican Social Responsibilities Commission (WA) had written a paper called *No Better Than Anyone Else*,[22] which discussed the role of the churches, missionary societies and religious orders in the removal and institutionalisation of Aboriginal children, addressed the inquiry on that subject.

Hall appeared before Wilson and regional commissioner Sandra Cummings at the Aboriginal Advancement Council building. Hall's general thesis was clear: the churches played a willing role in child removal. Without their involvement, governments could not have instigated, as widely as they did, their policy of removing Aboriginal children from their families. He was not arguing that the churches were instrumental in the actual removal of the children (although this may have happened in some instances, and there had been a long history of church interest in 'civilising and Christianising' Aboriginal children), but that they provided accommodation for the removed children.

At this juncture, Hall and Wilson disagreed on the history of Sister Kate's Children's Home. Hall correctly informed Wilson that Sister Kate's was originally under the control of the Anglican Church, as Sister Kate Clutterbuck was an Anglican nun. Wilson did not agree, believing that Sister Kate's had always been under the control of the Presbyterian Church and, subsequently, the Uniting Church. Hall disagreed, saying that the Presbyterians did not take control until 1956. Wilson responded by informing Hall that he should know, as he was responsible for overseeing Sister Kate's management committee during the mid 1960s when he was moderator of the Presbyterian Church of WA.

Hall did not take the issue further. It was not why he was before the inquiry. He was there to talk in a general way about the churches' role in the removal policies and practices. But Wilson didn't want to hear from Hall on the churches' link to the policies and practices of Aboriginal childhood removal. During Hall's submission, Wilson repeatedly sought to move Hall away from the churches' responsibility. Wilson knew of Hall's experience and knowledge of youth and juvenile welfare. He started asking Hall questions in these areas. Hall sought to return the discussion back to his submission, but was only partially successful.

The issue of the churches' involvement in the removal process presented a challenge to Wilson. While he opened his heart to the stories told to him by those removed from their families, he was faced with allegations of abuse at institutions and missions run by churches, even his own Presbyterian Church. Wilson later said:

> I was a leader of the Presbyterian Church in Western Australia at the time we ran Sister Kate's home, where removed children grew up…I was proud of the home, with its system of cottage families. Imagine my pain when I discovered, during this inquiry, that children were sexually abused in those cottages.[23]

One such example was the story of Josie:

> Apart from the visits she received from her parents, the most vivid recollection Josie has of SKCH [Sister Kate's Children's Home] is the sexual abuse she was subjected to. She remembers two sons of a cottage parent sexually abusing her. The boys would lock her in their room to 'play games'. They would tell her to shut her eyes and open her mouth and they would give her a lolly. Instead they would take it in turns to place their penis in her mouth. They used to tell her not to tell anyone but Josie did tell some of her friends. The sexual abuse was a regular occurrence.[24]

By early 1996, some inside HREOC and the inquiry secretariat wondered who would coordinate the writing of the inquiry report. The small secretariat was busy coordinating the hearings, and organising appearances for the many hundreds of people wanting to tell their stories, as well as for government and nongovernment organisations. The inquiry process was becoming so large and complex that it was in danger of getting out of control.

HREOC executive director Diana Temby was concerned that the inquiry was becoming too great a task for the inquiry secretariat. She told Wilson:

> We have got no one to take the lead in the research and report writing. The secretariat is working flat out, [HREOC] public relations and community sections are doing a great job keeping the public informed but what are we going to do with research? Do we know anyone who could do this?

Wilson had someone in mind: 'Meredith Wilkie can do it.'

'Who is she?' Temby inquired.

Wilkie, a law lecturer at Murdoch University, had been recommended to Wilson by Chris Sidoti, HREOC's human rights commissioner. Sidoti had been impressed with Wilkie's work on previous HREOC inquiry reports dealing with the problems and needs of Aborigines living on the NSW–Queensland border[25] and homeless children.[26]

Temby thought Wilkie sounded perfect for the inquiry, and urged that she immediately come on board. Wilson phoned Wilkie and, after a further discussion with Temby, she agreed to be seconded to HREOC from Murdoch University for the duration of the inquiry.

Under Wilkie's guidance, consultants were hired to write research papers and draft chapters, and the report's shape and format were developed. Among the consultants were Chris Cunneen from the University of Sydney, and Terry Libesman from the University of Technology Sydney, who drafted papers for the report's juvenile justice section. Sarah Pritchard from the University of New South Wales dealt with the report's international law dimension, and assisted Wilkie in editing parts of the report.

Occasionally, tempers frayed between the consultants and Wilkie. All of them, including Wilkie, had strong personalities, with passionate views on how the report should be shaped and what it should include. They were prepared to argue their positions forcefully. Wilson was also keen for the report to reflect accurately the stories told at the hearings, and to contain practicable and workable recommendations.

Wilson insisted on being kept informed of the report writing. All the commissioners had an opportunity to contribute to the report, but Wilson was keenest and most involved. As Dodson remembers:

> Periodically you would receive chapters of the draft report. You would read them and email your responses and suggestions to the writing team. We would also have regular meetings with Meredith and sometimes others, like Sarah Pritchard, would be there to explain technical terms. Ron was very active. If you look at the Track Changes on the drafts, Ron had a lot of suggested changes.

The inquiry hearings were physically and mentally exhausting. Sometimes during a private moment in the later days of the hearings, Wilson permitted himself a small chuckle as he recalled his initial estimation that the hearings could be done in around four months. But there were very few moments in

1996 when Wilson had time for self-reflection. The inquiry was consuming most of his time, but he still had hearing commitments as HREOC president, and numerous speaking engagements.[27]

Although it did not come under the auspices of his inquiry, Wilson was also looking into the case of an incarcerated young Aboriginal man who had come to the attention of the Western Australian Deaths in Custody Watch Committee through the regular prison visits from the committee's volunteers. The young man was serving a lengthy prison term for murder. He had spent a childhood away from his family in foster care. He had been abused in foster care, and believed the Western Australia child welfare authorities had been negligent in not preventing this happening or removing him from the situation. Wilson visited the Perth office of the ALSWA to examine the young man's child welfare file. He then visited the young man at Canning Vale Prison, accompanied by this author.

Wilson entered the small interview room that had been allocated for the visit. The young man sat on the other side of a small wooden table. On seeing Wilson, he smiled, stood up, walked around the table and tightly hugged Wilson. Wilson reciprocated with a young man he had never previously seen or met. A former prosecutor and High Court justice, in a small interviewing cell of a prison, hugging a convicted murderer he had never seen before. It was a rare and remarkable event.

The young man thanked Wilson for coming to see him. Wilson asked how things were going in prison. They talked about the young man's life and childhood. As Wilson had been doing for most of the past twelve months, he mostly listened. The young man also asked about the inquiry. They talked for an hour. The meeting then ended. Wilson and the young man hugged each other farewell. Wilson's last comment to the young man was, 'I wish you well. Stay strong.'

'Thanks,' the young man replied. Moisture welled up in his eyes. 'Thanks for showing an interest.' Wilson nodded and smiled. He opened the door. He then turned around to face the young man again and said, 'I am happy we met. Good luck.' The young man faintly waved with his right hand. 'Good luck with the inquiry.' Wilson walked out and the door closed behind him.

Wilson urged the ALSWA to consider seriously what they could do for the young man. The ALSWA did file a statement of claim in the Western Australian Supreme Court on his behalf against the relevant child welfare department; however, because of staff departures from the ALSWA, resource implications and anticipated evidentiary and legal difficulties, the matter never proceeded beyond that point.

As the end of 1996 approached, many in the Aboriginal community were anxious for the inquiry to complete its report. It had been due in December 1996, but as the hearings had not commenced until December 1995, and because of the numbers making oral and written submissions, the December 1996 date was never going to be met. However, Wilson was determined that the report would be completed before the Australian Reconciliation Conference in Melbourne, a major event planned by the Council for Aboriginal Reconciliation for May 1997.

The media were also becoming more interested in the report. On 30 December 1996, Wilson appeared on ABC Radio's *World Today* program. He was asked by reporter Ginny Stein how he hoped the report would be received when released. Wilson replied:

> I cannot, personally speaking, conceive of reconciliation if the nation does not respond warmly to our report and by 'responding warmly' I mean to be shocked, to be ashamed...[however]...it is quite wrong to try and impose a guilt complex on current generations, we are not talking about guilt. The only people who have talked about guilt are those who oppose the reconciliation process. It is their way of seeking to discredit the efforts to establish a proper and warm relationship between the original Australians and the later comers.

It was not until the inquiry that Wilson had become more appreciative of the removal policies. In fact, as he had previously said, he did not have knowledge of the removal policies in his own state, even though he had been a senior Western Australian Crown Law Department lawyer and president of a church that ran a home for Aboriginal children. Throughout most of Wilson's life, his views on many issues were formed by his personal experiences, not via reading or researching. While a lawyer, he was focused on the current case, almost oblivious to other voices and views. Stein could not have put it more correctly: 'Obviously your views are formed on the experiences that you have had.' Wilson replied that, although he experienced some deprivation in childhood, he had 'been enormously privileged in life'. He referred to the title of Albert Facey's biography, saying he 'had a fortunate life'.

Wilson then made a statement that reflected his particular satisfaction with his professional post-High Court life. It also reflected what some viewed as a transformation from a forceful prosecutor, Crown advocate and a judge who placed a higher priority on federalism and states' rights than human rights or Aboriginal rights to a passionate human rights advocate:

> The richest experience of my life has been the last seven years. To have been able to have a retirement in which I have continued to be an advocate—I loved advocacy. That is why I became a lawyer. That is why I enjoyed my legal life. But now, in retirement, to have spent seven years as an advocate for the disadvantaged is the most privileged experience that I can imagine.

The interview then returned to the issue of history and guilt. Earlier that year, John Howard's Liberal Party had defeated Keating's Labor government. As the new prime minister, Howard made a number of speeches attacking what he saw as political correctness, including what he described as 'the black armband view' of Australian history. Wilson told Stein that he disagreed with Howard's criticism of teaching schoolchildren about the past treatment of Aborigines. Wilson said it was necessary for children to obtain knowledge of the past if reconciliation was to take place. He was himself ashamed at how Aborigines had been treated by earlier generations.

Stein asked Wilson did his sense of being ashamed equate to guilt. Wilson thought it could, but he did not use the term 'guilt' as imputing direct responsibility for historical injustices. What he thought was necessary was an acceptance of past injustices to Aboriginal people and accepting a responsibility for redeeming the injustices. He said:

> I like the word 'redeeming'. I am a Christian. Redemption means a lot. It is a great word to describe what we have to do for our past. We have to get to know it in order that we can redeem it. I think that is the opportunity that the 21st century is offering to all Australians.

Within HREOC, as the report was being shaped, a significant debate was developing around the question of whether the Aboriginal removal policies and practices constituted genocide under the 1948 UN *Convention on the Prevention and Punishment of Genocide*. Under that definition, genocide is committed when governments or some other identity forcibly transfer children from a racial, ethnic or national group to another group with the intention of destroying that group.[28] Under the definition, actual killing is not necessary; there need only be partial, but substantial, destruction or intended destruction of the group, and there could be mixed motives, even some well-intentioned motives, behind the policy and practice being labelled as genocide.

Pritchard and Wilkie, working independently, both concluded that genocide was relevant to the findings and conclusions of the inquiry. They argued that the removal of Aboriginal children from their families and culture to a European environment (although often the children were surrounded by other Aboriginal children in missions or receiving homes) to be raised as 'White' constituted genocide under the Genocide Convention.

Reference was made to various official statements, for example, from Auber Octavius Neville, the Western Australian Chief Protector of Aborigines between 1915 and 1940. Neville believed that the full-blood Aboriginal population would be extinct within 100 years. The 'half-caste' population, which he considered to be 'quick breeders', should be segregated from Aboriginal influences and brought up within the dominant European culture. At the 1937 Commonwealth, States and Territories Conference on Aboriginal Affairs, Neville said, 'I see no objection to the ultimate absorption into our own race of the whole of the existing Aboriginal race…'[29] The conference passed a resolution:

> DESTINY OF THE RACE.—That this Conference believes that the destiny of the natives of aboriginal origin, but not of the full-blood, lies in their ultimate absorption by the [European] people of the Commonwealth, and it therefore recommends that all efforts be directed to that end.[30]

Neville was a strong supporter of separating the 'half-caste' child from Aboriginal influence. In 1944 he wrote:

> Every coloured child then, must be placed at a residential school at a settlement, and I use the word settlement advisedly, because institutions selected for this purpose must necessarily become what we now describe as Government Native Settlements. The child must be free from all parental control and oversight—it must enter at the earliest possible age—it must

> be considered to all intents and purposes an orphan. Many, of course, are orphans, and there should be no difficulty in these cases. There will be few exceptions other than amongst those of parents who are already assimilated into the community. The children of full-bloods are not of course referred to as coloureds.[31]

This desire to have removed Aboriginal children inculcated into 'White ways' is clearly demonstrated in correspondence from the Western Australian Commissioner of Native Affairs to a Western Australian government official stationed in the state's north-west dated 21 July 1944:

> I regret it is not possible to agree to Mr Cadoux's request. James is a near-white boy. He is being reared as a white child at Sister Kate's Home, and in due course he will be placed out in employment, and will live as a white person. It would be detrimental to his future welfare to permit him to return to his mother who lives in association with natives. If this were agreed to it would undo all the good work in rearing James to white standards.
>
> Children placed with Sister Kate are never released to their parents. This would be a direct contradiction of the principle of their segregation from native persons, as they are placed with Sister Kate for this very reason. By Section 8 [of the *Aborigines Act* 1905 (WA)] I am James' legal guardian up to 21 years [Section 7 of the *Aborigines Act Amendment Act* 1936 (WA) increased the age from sixteen (under the 1905 Act) to twenty-one], notwithstanding that his mother is alive...[32]

Neville's Northern Territory counterpart, Dr Cecil Cook, held similar views.[33] Both wanted to remove Aboriginal cultural influences from mixed Aboriginal children and breed out the mixed descent Aboriginal population under their control. This view of 'breeding out' or 'dying pillow' or 'dying race' concept, as epitomised in the 1937 conference resolution, was based on an idea that a discrete 'race' can somehow 'die out'.[34] This idea had many points of origin, but perhaps the most important is that of eugenics.

Based on the idea of a relationship between racial strength and human heredity, eugenics was seen by its founder, Frances Galton, cousin to Charles Darwin, as practical Darwinism.[35] Galton first defined the idea of eugenics in 1884, but the movement was at its strongest in the first four decades of the twentieth century.[36] The point of difference between eugenics and other racial theories is that eugenicists believed that the 'weaker' races should be bred out of existence.[37]

The eugenics thinking was clearly at the forefront of the mind of Western Australian medical practitioner Dr Cecil Bryant when he made a submission to the 1934 Western Australian Royal Commission on the conditions and treatment of Aborigines. Bryant, who believed that 'half-caste' should not mate with 'half-caste' as 'it would perpetuate the black and coloured elements', submitted:

> The mating of half-castes with half-castes means nothing more than the perpetuation of the black and coloured element against which we all of us are so set against. If we want to do the fair and just thing by these half-castes and their progeny, and if we have desire to save our own children from the terrible problems presented in the United States today, and growing worse with the minutes as they tick by we will do all in our power to prevent the mating of a half-caste and a half-caste, and especially with a black. We will on the other hand do all in our power to displace the black strain by an infiltration of white blood. I am not advocating the marriage of white with half-caste. I am dumb on that aspect. What I am advocating is the mating of half-caste with a coloured person who has more white blood in him or her, with one who, as a quadroon or an octoroon, is higher up on the white scale.[38]

Wilson, acknowledging the shock attached to the genocide label, was receptive to it. In fact, he was more than receptive. The inquiry hearings had been a life-changing experience. He had heard story after story of sorrow and pain that had convinced him a major injustice had been done that needed to be understood by all Australians and measures taken to rectify the historical injustices. He, along with the other HREOC commissioners, believed that they had been trusted with the stories, and had to honour that trust. This meant ensuring that the report presented the story and the case for justice, no matter how uncomfortable it would be for White Australia. Wilson was prepared to proceed with and argue the case that the past removal policies and practices constituted genocide.

Dodson, however, was not so sure that it was wise to label the removal policies as genocide.

At the November 1996 Sydney meeting of all HREOC commissioners, inquiry hearing commissioners and the Indigenous Advisory Council to discuss the final draft report, Dodson was sceptical of the genocide finding and was not prepared to agree to it. But Wilson passionately argued with Dodson that the removal practices and policies constituted genocide as proscribed in the Genocide Convention.

Dodson worried about the political ramifications of such a finding. His concerns were prophetic. However, after listening to Wilson's arguments he was persuaded to agree to the genocide finding, as were the other commissioners. It was decided that the term genocide was correct and appropriate and, as Wilson said, 'it gave greater force and persuasion to the claims for reparations.'

The report argued that the removal policy constituted genocide because the removal policy's intention was to destroy the Aboriginal race by assimilating the next generation of Aborigines into mainstream European society and culture. The crux of the argument was obvious: removal policies intended to assimilate Aboriginal children into White society, so that they would lose their 'Aboriginality'.

While finding that the removal policies as a whole did constitute genocide, as defined in the UN convention, the inquiry and the report made no findings of genocide against any specific individual, organisation or government. The only recommendation made on the subject was a symbolic one, that: 'the Commonwealth legislate to implement the Genocide Convention to full domestic effect.'[39]

Bringing Them Home, the title adopted for the report, was the brainchild of Meredith Wilkie, greatly admired by Wilson for her intelligence, work ethic and commitment.

In giving evidence at the inquiry hearings in Sydney, Aboriginal poet James Miller said, 'We need to bring them home.' Immediately Wilkie thought this had to be the title to the inquiry report. Wilkie designed a mockup cover page: the *Bringing Them Home* title with a photograph of a woman playing with her child (which she had found in a book of photographs by Heide Smith, *Story Time*, at the NSW Art Gallery shop). She showed the mockup cover to Wilson and Mick Dodson. They were impressed.

Wilson and his colleagues wanted their report to tell a story. *Bringing Them Home* was laden with stories and quotes from Aborigines about removal as children from their families; their loss of culture; the abuse they suffered in receiving homes and missions; and their ongoing pain and suffering.

They were wrenching accounts of grief and sorrow. These stories aroused compassion in those sympathetic to inquiry and brought allegations of bias from those who were opposed to the inquiry. It was these stories that had changed Wilson.

Bringing Them Home contained much more than these stories from Aborigines removed as children. It included excerpts from official government documents and quotes from government authorities that provided evidence of the systematic policy and practice of forced removal.

Bringing Them Home found that the policy of forcible removal adversely affected Aborigines in all states and territories. The 'neglected children' legislation[40] and the 'protection statutes'[41] of the mid nineteenth century provided some power and impetus for the removal of Aboriginal children from their families. The first statute that gave legislative power to a state or its officials to remove Aboriginal children came with the enactment of the *Aboriginal Protection and Restriction of the Sale of Opium Act* 1897 (Qld). The Queensland legislation was to provide the blueprint for legislation in many other jurisdictions in Australia, including the *Aborigines Act* 1905 (WA). In many respects, the pattern of Aboriginal-specific legislation was similar across all states and territories,[42] except Tasmania, which removed Aboriginal children under general child welfare legislation.[43] Queensland, Western Australia, South Australia and Northern Territory were most alike,[44] compared with Victoria, New South Wales and the ACT.[45] The power and scope of the legislation in Victoria and New South Wales, particularly in relation to state guardianship powers, were not as pervasive as the other four jurisdictions—in some cases the state or its instrumentalities or officials had custody, care and control and the whole gamut of legal guardianship. In Queensland, Western Australia, South Australia and Northern Territory, for varying periods, the chief protector or commissioner of natives legally was the guardian of all Aboriginal children, whether the Aboriginal child had living parents or was deemed neglected.[46]

Bringing Them Home found that the forcible removal resulted in deprivation of liberty by detaining children and confining them in institutions; the abolition of parental rights by removal, and making Aboriginal children wards of the chief protector or Aborigines Protection Board; abuses of power; and breach of guardianship obligations by protectors, protection boards and other 'carers'. *Bringing Them Home* chronicled several enduring effects: behavioural problems; grief and trauma; and depression and mental illness. There were also claims of 'intergenerational' effects; namely, that those removed were deprived of appropriate parenting models resulting in family dysfunction, and second-generational substance abuse and other horrific consequences.

> There's things in my life that I haven't dealt with and I've passed them on to my children. Gone to pieces. Anxiety attacks. I've passed this on to my kids. I know for a fact if you go and knock at their door they run and hide.
>
> I look at my son today who had to be taken away because he was going to commit suicide because he can't handle it; he just can't take any more of the anxiety attacks that he and Karen have. I have passed that on to my kids because I haven't dealt with it. How do you deal with it? How do you sit down and go through all those years of abuse? Somehow I'm passing down negativity to my kids.[47]

Bringing Them Home argued that the removal policy was not only racially discriminatory but also that many Aborigines were denied common law rights enjoyed by other Australians. Most controversial is the genocide claim. It concluded that Aboriginal removal schemes amounted to 'gross violations of human rights', and recommended a series of reparations that conformed to the van Boven principles of reparations.[48]

The report made fifty-four recommendations. They covered all the components of reparations: acknowledgement of truth and an apology; guarantees of nonrepetition of violations; rehabilitation; compensation; and restitution. A controversial recommendation stated that part of the reason a 'National Compensation Fund' should be established was the procedural, evidential and cost difficulties involved in litigation. It was this compensation recommendation, plus the demand for an apology, that was the focus of the ensuing debate on reparations.

In its submission to the inquiry, the Commonwealth government raised as a concern the difficulty in estimating the monetary value of losses, on the grounds that '[t]here is no comparable area of awards of compensation and no basis for arguing a quantum of damages from first principles.'[49] Sarah Pritchard has written: 'The provision of monetary compensation is largely a symbolic act because the loss, grief and trauma experienced by victims of gross human rights violations can never be adequately compensated.'[50] However, she added that for the 'victim' it provides affirmation of the wrong done to her or him.

The recommendation that lay at the heart of *Bringing Them Home*, though, and the one which would define the debate to follow, was recommendation number five:

> That all Australian parliaments:
>
> 1. officially acknowledge the responsibility of their predecessors for the laws, policies and practices of forcible removal; [and]
>
> 2. negotiate with the Aboriginal and Torres Strait Islander Commission a form of words for official apologies to Indigenous individuals, families and communities and extend those apologies with wide and culturally appropriate publicity...[51]

Wilson thought that the reconciliation process between Aboriginal and non-Aboriginal Australia would be significantly enhanced if the Commonwealth parliament and/or government made an apology to the 'stolen generations' for the pain and suffering resulting from the separation schemes.

An apology can be seen as displaying respect to those that have been wronged. Some argue that it has a justice element to it: that is, one must apologise for a past wrong in order to do justice for the victim.[52] An apology is often seen as a first step in reconciling past wrongs with the intention of providing for a new, more harmonious future between the wrongdoers or their successors and the wronged or their successors. An apology may be looked on as an important element in the restoration of dignity for those wronged, and as part of the healing process for these individuals and even for the nation. The *Sydney Morning Herald* would editorialise:

> An apology is a powerful symbol. It represents a break with past policies that had tragic consequences for the indigenous and non-indigenous alike that the lessons of the past have been learnt, and it lays the foundation for both groups to build a future truly in common.[53]

Wilson believed that *Bringing Them Home* was like no other report he had been involved in. He was determined that it should not gather dust on the shelf, as had happened to many reports to government. For Wilson, it had the capacity to aid the reconciliation process by informing non-Aboriginal

Australians of 'what we did to Indigenous Australians', and thus the need to address this. Reconciliation, Wilson said, required a grassroots movement, in partnership with political leadership, to convince Aboriginal Australians that non-Aboriginal Australians cared about them. Wilson argued that a positive response to the report by the political leadership of the country and the public was needed. But this could only happen, Wilson believed, as written in the report, if 'the whole community listens with an open heart and mind to the stories of what has happened in the past...'[54]

The 689-page report was presented to the Commonwealth attorney-general, Daryl Williams QC, on 5 April 1997, seven weeks before the start of the Melbourne Australian Reconciliation Conference.

14

In the Eye of the Storm

I came to this inquiry a couple years ago as a man over the hill at 73 with about 50 years or more behind me as a hardboiled lawyer mixing it with all sorts of antagonists and people in the courts here and in England and yet this inquiry changed me. The reason it changed me is that it penetrated the heart, it got away from my mind which I have had done for the rest of my life in all the briefs I have had.[1]

Wilson openly confessed that the hearings of the *Bringing Them Home* inquiry had changed him. The furore that followed the handing down of the report would forever change his place in Australian history.

He could not have anticipated the full extent of the furore, but neither could it be said that he entered naïvely or innocently into the fray. He had made a commitment to the cause of the 'stolen generations'; he became an advocate as never before, in heart as well as mind.

It was Wilson's deliberate choice, months in advance, to ensure that the report would be out before the Melbourne Australian Reconciliation Conference. That conference came at a very particular moment in Australian history, and Wilson and his report would become a potent part of a volatile political brew.

The Howard government had been in power just over a year, and the political environment could hardly have been more different than in 1992, when his predecessor made the Redfern speech, in which he acknowledged the nation's responsibility for dispossessing the Aboriginal people, and 'stealing' the children.

Howard had made a series of speeches attacking various aspects of what the conservatives saw as political correctness, including 'black armband history'. Pauline Hanson had come into Parliament at the 1996 election, winning as an independent, but quickly forming the One Nation Party, which bemoaned Asian immigration, and attacked alleged special privileges being bestowed on Aboriginal people. The support she garnered astounded nearly everyone. Race, and especially Aboriginal issues, had become an absolutely central part of Australian politics for the first time.

As if to add fuel to the fire, the *Wik* case, decided on 23 December 1996 by the High Court, found that native title could coexist on pastoral leases.[2] Amid uproar in the outback, the government vowed to protect leaseholders, and began developing a legislative response to the *Wik* decision, with Howard's deputy, National Party leader Tim Fischer, calling for 'bucketloads of extinguishment' of native title. The 'Ten Point Plan' announced late in April 1997 caused outrage amongst Aboriginal groups and their supporters, as it watered down native title rights.

This was the state of play when Wilson delivered *Bringing Them Home* to the attorney-general, Mr Williams. It was a report the government did not want, about an inquiry it did not call, at a time that could hardly have been less welcome.

As the inquiry had been referred to HREOC by the Commonwealth attorney-general, the public release of the report was a matter for the Commonwealth government. Williams refused to say when he would make it public, and as speculation mounted, a subterranean campaign commenced to discredit both *Bringing Them Home* and its principal author. Although twenty-eight commissioners signed the report, Wilson, the former High Court justice, was the focus of the media and critics of the report.

Government sources challenged Wilson's impartiality, and noted his involvement with the administration of Sister Kate's Children's Home. Wilson had not concealed this fact. In an interview on ABC TV's *7.30 Report* on 1 May 1997, he expressed sincere regret for the Presbyterian Church's role in the Aboriginal removal process and his association with it. He noted that there were dissenting voices of protest during the operation of the removal policies, but that he 'did not hear these voices'. He said that during the period he was moderator of the Presbyterian Church of Western Australia (1964–65) he heard nothing that would have focused his attention on what was happening at Sister Kate's. He offered, presumably as a defence of his ignorance, that he was not involved in the day-to-day management of Sister Kate's. It may be understandable that he did not hear of allegations of abuse taking place at Sister Kate's if in fact, which is unclear, such allegations were being made at the time. But it is more difficult to understand how Wilson didn't know of the fact that Sister Kate's was housing Aboriginal children removed from their parents under a systematic state government policy, of which, he says, he was also unaware.

His expression of sincere regret did not satisfy Perth Children's Court magistrate and former 'homie' of Sister Kate's, Sue Gordon, who appeared on the same *7.30 Report*. She said Wilson's regret statement was thirty years too late, and she believed that Wilson should have recused himself from the inquiry, which should have been conducted by Aborigines who had been removed.

In marked contrast, Australian Rules football legend Graham (Polly) Farmer, who appeared on the same *7.30 Report*, and had been at Sister Kate's as a child, said that Wilson was a good man, and he had no problem with him being involved with the inquiry. In fact, Wilson was the inaugural President of the Polly Farmer Foundation, which sought to assist Aboriginal children make the most of their sporting and academic skills. The establishment of this foundation was the precondition to Farmer agreeing to Steve Hawke writing a biography about him.[3] The son of former prime minister Bob Hawke, Steve Hawke has been for many years involved in Aboriginal affairs in the north-west of Western Australia.

Things really began to heat up a week before the Melbourne Reconciliation Conference. On 20 May, the *Sydney Morning Herald* ran a front page story referring to unnamed government sources condemning the report, even though it had not been tabled in the Commonwealth parliament,[4] and in the same issue journalist Margo Kingston wrote about the attempt to discredit Wilson in an article headlined 'Report That Won't Stay under the Carpet':[5]

> Sir Humphrey Appleby gave politician Jim Hacker this advice in *Yes, Minister* on how to suppress an inconvenient official report. 'Discredit the man who produced the report. This must be done OFF THE RECORD.'

Kingston said that the Commonwealth government was withholding the parliamentary tabling of the report, which meant that Wilson had to remain silent, while the Commonwealth government poured 'scorn on it through a "background briefing".' But Kingston commented that the government had a problem in seeking to discredit Wilson because:

> [He] is a former Liberal-appointed High Court judge, widely respected and a man near retirement. Sir Humphrey's lines of attack—that the inquirer harboured a grudge against the government, was a publicity seeker or was trying to get a knighthood—were not available.

Kingston unambiguously attacked the government's actions in seeking to discredit Wilson. It heralds, she wrote:

> a new low in public discourse. 'Government sources' said Sir Ronald lacked credibility because he was the moderator of the Presbyterian Church in Western Australia at a time when the Church was involved in running institutions for stolen children. (Unlike the Government, Sir Ronald has recently publicly apologised for his role in this.).

Kingston added:

> Thus, we have the incredible allegation that a man [Wilson] who was involved in the tragedy who has repented after hearing evidence on its disastrous consequences cannot be trusted to produce a credible report. As Sir Humphrey says: 'You can't put a nation's interest at risk just because of some silly sentimentality about justice.'

That same night Wilson returned to the *7.30 Report* to express concern with the Commonwealth government's attempt to use his link to Sister Kate's to discredit *Bringing Them Home*. He said that he was not personally concerned with the attacks on him, but it was a 'matter of deep concern' if the attacks damaged the reception of the inquiry report by the Australian people and governments. He remained optimistic that the Commonwealth government would give the recommendations proper consideration. But in a determined voice he said that, irrespective of the Commonwealth government's response and comment, he and HREOC would not be 'put off or deterred' in seeking to have the report accepted and acted on. They would visit every state and territory capital and seek consultation with their governments on ways of implementing the report's recommendations.

The next morning, 21 May, in the *Sydney Morning Herald*, Tony Wright wrote that: '"senior government sources" have started the quiet process of disowning it [the report], even to the extent of trying to undermine the credibility of the commission's head, Sir Ron Wilson.' He warned that Wilson, with his tough childhood and distinguished legal career, was 'not the type easily undermined', and that Wilson was 'speaking for decency in recommending acknowledgement of past wrongs, rehabilitation for victims, and monetary compensation.'[6]

Perhaps in answer to these criticisms, the government did come out in the open on the day of Wright's piece, though it did so by selectively revealing aspects of the report to the media. A government press statement on 21 May 1997 attacked the report's genocide finding, and dismissed any suggestion of awarding compensation. It also accused HREOC of seeking to have the report released before being tabled in the Commonwealth parliament. The attorney-general, Mr Williams, reiterated that compensation would not be paid: 'The Government can see no equitable or practical way of now paying special compensation to those persons [Aborigines that had been removed as children], if compensation were considered to be warranted.'[7]

Kingston reentered the fray, commenting on 22 May: 'Yesterday's response by the attorney-general, Daryl Williams QC, to the stolen children inquiry contained perhaps, the most extraordinary claim ever made by an Australian chief law officer.' She added that:

> [Williams'] claim that the Human Rights Commission was mounting a campaign 'to promote a presumption of Government antipathy' is mere Newspeak. It was the Government which attacked the report and its inquirer, Sir Ronald Wilson, before it had even tabled the report (it still hasn't). His statement merely puts on the record the fact that the response is indeed, antipathetic.
>
> The Government is now in the open, landing publicly the punches it first delivered on Monday in a background briefing in the *Herald*. Sir Ronald, the sort of jurist Daryl Williams could only dream of being, will not break his legal obligations to refrain from comment on the report's findings until the report is tabled.[8]

One result of this acrimonious buildup was that many of the key findings and recommendations in *Bringing Them Home*—in general terms at least—were public knowledge before its release. As well as the genocide finding and the compensation recommendations, it was widely known that the report would call on governments to apologise for the child removal practices.

Bringing Them Home was tabled in the House of Representatives on 26 May 1997. This was the opening day of the Australian Reconciliation Conference at the Melbourne Crown Casino Convention Centre. The prime minister, John Howard, attended the opening session, which included Kim Beazley, the leader of ALP opposition, Cheryl Kernot, the leader of the Democrats, Jeff Kennett, the premier of Victoria, and the 'father' of Aboriginal Reconciliation, Pat Dodson, chair of the Council for Aboriginal Reconciliation.

Before the politicians could speak, and after the official welcome by the Kulin elders, Sydney activist Shirley Lomas, the founder of the Disability Services Aboriginal Corporation, appeared unexpectedly on the speaker's stage. She was well known to many of those attending the conference, including Wilson. She had appeared before the inquiry, complaining about the state of Aboriginal affairs in Australia. Before 2000 delegates, she berated the politicians and Aboriginal leaders who she alleged had abused their positions. She told the story of her mother's removal from her family and the tragic plight of her fifteen-year-old severely intellectually disabled son. Wilson felt immense sympathy for her, and hoped that if the recommendations contained in *Bringing Them Home* were implemented they would help people like Shirley.

After Lomas's twenty-minute tirade, with the dignitaries on stage looking on helplessly and with many in the audience cheering, she was led off stage by the Kulin elders. Her appearance heightened the tension in the convention centre auditorium. Much of that tension was directed towards John Howard.

It was at this moment that the stage lights shone on the prime minister as he stood behind the lectern. Patrick Dodson, his white beard prominent in the dim lighting behind the prime minister, surveyed Howard and the audience from his seat. There was an eerie silence in the auditorium. But this was only a fleeting silence, the calm before the storm.

Howard was jeered and heckled as he defended his ten-point plan, and refused to make or commit the Commonwealth government to making an official apology or providing compensation to the 'stolen generations'.

In a premeditated plan, many of those in the auditorium turned their backs on the Australian prime minister. Howard made a personal apology for past treatment of Aborigines. But the atmosphere was electric, and poisonous, and he was clearly angered, his voice rising and his hand repeatedly thumping the lectern as he continued with a 'hectoring rant'[9] about the *Wik* decision, an attack on Aboriginal leaders, and a robust defence of his ten-point plan. He said that Australians should not engage in national guilt and shaming; 'rather we [Australians] should acknowledge past injustices and focus our energies on addressing the root causes of the current and future disadvantage among our Indigenous people'.[10]

Wilson would never have contemplated turning his back on or heckling the Australian prime minister. However, he recognised the frustration of those attending the conference. He had hoped that the prime minister would make a speech that more fully recognised past injustices and the need to address current concerns of the Aboriginal people. He wanted the prime minister to display a spirit of generosity and reconciliation. Wilson was very disappointed.

However, Wilson was encouraged by the apology made by Kernot, and by Beazley's plea for the Howard government to publicly proclaim profound regret. Kernot said, 'You don't have to wallow in guilt or black armbands to accept that past wrongs were committed against Australia's indigenous people and to acknowledge that the plight of many indigenous people today is a consequence of that history.'[11]

Beazley had grown up in a household where Aboriginal affairs and issues of national importance were regularly discussed. His father, Kim Beazley Snr, a minister in the Whitlam government, was part of a group honoured at the conference for their support of the 1967 referendum that amended sections 127 and 51 (xxvi) of the Australian Constitution to include Aborigines as part of the people of Australia in the national census, and which gave the Commonwealth parliament the power to make laws with respect to 'Aboriginal people'. The junior Beazley said to the conference delegates:

> If the first step to the healing for indigenous Australians is for the Australian Parliament to propose and pass an expression of profound regret for the injustices and dehumanising treatment that have been a part of [their] shared experience of European settlement, then let us so move.[12]

Wilson was heartened by the speeches of Kernot and Beazley. However, he was most impressed with his friend and former colleague Patrick Dodson, who handled the heightened tension of the conference room after Howard's speech with dignity and in a spirit of reconciliation.

While rejecting the ten-point plan, Dodson sought to ease the tension by commenting that the prime minister's personal expression of profound regret was a good start. He stated that it was imperative that the Commonwealth government continue to talk to the Aboriginal community for reconciliation to be progressed further. Talking was part of the process that needed to take place in order for action on reconciliation to then occur.

On the same day, in Canberra, after the tabling in parliament of *Bringing Them Home*, the federal minister for Aboriginal Affairs, Senator John Herron, emphatically ruled out compensation for the 'stolen generations', and refused to commit the government to making an apology. He repeated the prime minister's conference speech, saying, 'We cannot live in the past and we cannot undo what has been done.' Even so, he added that the Commonwealth government would make a full response to the report after careful consideration.

It was already clear that the Commonwealth government would not move from its stated position on the report's two most 'controversial' recommendations: monetary compensation and an apology. It was also clear that the government would continue its attack on the report's finding that the removal policies and practices constituted genocide. The attorney-general rejected the genocide conclusion, and argued that *Bringing Them Home* was a flawed document.

Wilson was not to be deterred by the government attacks and negative responses. With the report now having been tabled, he was free to speak about it. On the first day of the conference he gave a feisty interview on ABC radio. Although the official launch of the report by HREOC would not take place until the next day, Wilson launched a pre-emptive strike, telling ABC radio listeners that he and those involved in the inquiry would continue the 'fight' for justice for the 'stolen generations', irrespective of the Commonwealth's response. He also fervently defended the claim of genocide. He maintained that the removal process came within the definition of genocide in the UN Genocide Convention. He was emotional as he defended the report and inquiry. He reiterated his determination to fight for the recognition of the plight of the 'stolen generations', saying: 'Governments come and go', and '[w]e are on a long haul perhaps but we are heading for reconciliation'.

The next day, 27 May 1997, the second day of the conference, on which he and Mick Dodson publicly launched *Bringing Them Home*, was in a sense the culmination of all that had happened to Wilson in the two years since he had accepted Lavarch's invitation to undertake the inquiry.[13]

He approached the event with much excitement. At long last the time had arrived for members of the public to have the opportunity to read a report that Wilson felt so strongly about. At long last, a chance to directly confront the criticisms of the report. Wilson hoped that, with the launch of the report, the process of healing would commence, and Australia would begin bringing home those who had been forcibly removed from their families and communities.

Earlier in the day, at a press briefing, Dodson had choked up with emotion as he tried to talk about the experience of conducting the hearings. He had been unable to continue for some time, until comforted by HREOC colleagues. On the podium of the convention centre, holding a copy of the report, he was still clearly emotional as he spoke, with long pauses between phrases:

> This story in my hand is the saddest of all stories. Mr Howard, as leader of this nation, you must speak to this nation. We cannot, simply cannot turn away from what this nation did to Aboriginal children.[14]

Wilson followed Dodson at the podium. Draped in his black sweater, colourfully emblazoned with Aboriginal art depictions and the words 'Walking Together', Wilson launched *Bringing Them Home*. He told the audience of nearly 2000:

> I knew very little about the stolen children when I took up this inquiry but as I heard more and more I recognised the suffering has gone so deep and it's still being felt today.[15]

He said that this was no ordinary report. Much of its contents were expressed in the words of Aborigines who had been removed. He asked readers to open their hearts and minds to the report and listen to what the stories said. Wilson said that, while he had spent all his (professional) 'life studying and examining the events of people's lives', the inquiry presented him 'with the greatest discipline of my career':

> I had to learn to listen. Not just with my legally trained mind, nor my Presidential demeanour. But as a human being stripped bare of preconceptions and judgements, and available to be moved and changed.

He said, 'it was a life-changing experience' as he listened to story after story of pain and trauma, often with the storyteller struggling for minutes to utter his or her first words, and straining to hold back the tears. Wilson did not stop, as a judge would have, to ask for corroboration because, 'How could you doubt the authenticity of a story when tears are running down the faces of the storytellers?'

He reiterated the importance of listening: 'Listening is the key to understanding. Understanding is the key to acknowledgement. And acknowledgement is the key to reparation.'

Wilson's appearance at the launch of *Bringing Them Home* was powerful and emotional, not only for him, but also for many in the audience, including former champion tennis player Evonne Cawley. She said that Wilson's performance made her cry, particular when he explained that some government officials had said they were taking children away 'for their own good'. Wilson's 'words evoked her own fears as a Wiradjuri child in the tiny NSW town of Barellan'.[16]

Howard, Beazley and Kernot returned to Canberra after the conference opening session. Beazley suggested that the House of Representatives observe a minute's silence as a mark of respect to Aborigines who had suffered injustice. Howard said it would be churlish and insensitive to oppose the motion. All members of the House of Representatives, except Western Australian Liberal member for Canning, Don Randall, rose from their seats to observe the minute's silence. Randall said it was a Beazley stunt, and that there was a great deal of misinformation being disseminated about Aboriginal child removals. While opposing forcible removals, he said that he knew of many Aboriginal children who had been put into missions in Western Australia at their parents' request.[17]

Beazley did not consider a minute's silence as a stunt. He was deeply moved by the 'stolen generations' issue. Two days later in the House of Representatives, while advocating compensation for those Aborigines who were removed from their parents, Beazley, choked with emotion and tears welling in his eyes, recalled the pain and suffering in the stories he had read in *Bringing Them Home* the night before. He had stayed up till 4 a.m. reading the stories in the report.

The Prime Minister could not be persuaded to change his opposition to compensation. He said the Commonwealth government would not pay compensation because it would open a floodgate of claims. Indeed, his position was not dissimilar to what Wilson held before the inquiry had commenced. Howard also denied Beazley's claim that it was unfair to compensate gun owners for confiscation of their guns and not award compensation to the 'stolen generations'. The former dealt with a contemporary action for current ownership and possession of guns; the latter dealt with the current generation being held responsible for actions of a previous generation.[18] He argued:

> This is asking one generation to accept legal responsibility for the acts of earlier generations that it had no control over and for which acts were within the law of the time.[19]

There were a number of sympathetic profiles and reports on Wilson after the tabling of *Bringing Them Home* in parliament. On 26 May, Catherine Fitzpatrick of the *West Australian* reported:

> Despite attacks on his credibility, Sir Ronald's passion for the inquiry and compassion for indigenous people has inspired respect and admiration. Race discrimination commissioner Zita Antonius [sic] described him [Wilson] as 'a precious national treasure.' Sir Ronald graciously accepted the tributes and standing ovations and refused to respond to detractors who have hurled insults in a bid to undermine the inquiry's findings and recommendations.[20]

Tony Stephens in the *Sydney Morning Herald* wrote:

> What Australians are seeing now in Wilson is something of a third coming. The man who rose to the top of the legal profession as a High Court judge, only to leave early to become president of the Uniting Church in Australia, has carved out another role of public service, which he might see as a public duty, with HREOC and ACFOA [Australian Council for Overseas Aid]. It is likely that by the time he is finished, Wilson, who turned 75 last month, will have made more impact on the nation through his third coming than through the first two. He has become part of the national conscience, joining

> in that role another former High Court judge and man of deep religious conviction, Sir William Deane.[21]

The *Australian*'s columnist Greg Sheridan, a conservative in his specialist field of foreign affairs, stated:

> We shouldn't feel guilty for things we didn't personally do, but if we can feel national pride in, for example, the courage of the Anzacs, so surely we must be able to feel shame at our past treatment of Aborigines.[22]

Along with the sympathetic articles, attacks on Wilson and his role in the inquiry began to mount. On the day *Bringing Them Home* was tabled in the House of Representatives, Christopher Pearson, part-time speech writer for Howard, and editor of the *Adelaide Review*, described Wilson as grandstanding in relation to the report.[23] Pearson wrote a more stinging attack on Wilson a week later, and also took aim at the governor-general:

> The notion of trespass leads to a consideration of the role of Sir Ronald Wilson. Why was this insistently guilty and interested party chosen to preside over the inquiry? Why when his pretence of selflessness is an inadequate mask for the more transparent kinds of egotistical self-assertion, should we have to cringe for him? No doubt he will be spared the realisation of how much his posturings on the question of genocide have affected his reputation, but moderate Aboriginal Leaders should be under no illusions about what a mistake it was to wheel him out. Talking of cringing, Sir William Deane has been another reminder of the frailties to which wilful, vain old men are prone. Not for Holy Billy the vice regal conventions restraining the expression of the tendentious opinion. It almost seems as though it takes a professional politician—like Bill Hayden to understand and respect the constitutional propriety and rules of the game.[24]

Similarly, Piers Akerman, a columnist with the *Daily Telegraph*, criticised Wilson, like others, by bringing up his association with Sister Kate's:

> That the report is flawed is due to the failure of Sir Ronald Wilson, the president of the Human Rights and Equal Opportunities Commission, to maintain the standards usually required by governmental inquiries. Sir Ronald,

> a former board member of Sister Kate's, a Western Australian home which for many years housed young Aborigines separated from their parents, would know full well that there are many Aboriginal children who were separated from their families who *chose* not to talk to this commission.[25]

The debate over *Bringing Them Home* raged across the land among politicians, columnists, in intellectual magazines like *Quadrant*, and at the dinner table. Part of the debate centred on the very use of the term 'stolen generation' or 'stolen generations'. Although the inquiry report did not use the term, many of those supportive of its findings and recommendations did, while many of those contesting the veracity and creditability of the report refused the terminology.

The phrase 'stolen generation' originated with Australian historian Peter Read's 1981 study of the removal of Aboriginal children from their families in New South Wales.[26] But the term created problems and criticism. Did it only mean those actually 'stolen' from their parents' arms, or other circumstances where parents through trickery or undue influence allowed their children to be 'removed'?

Professor Robert Manne, academic and social commentator, nailed the argument when he wrote that it is a term 'that the Aboriginal people have embraced for their collective tragedy'.[27] The semantics and academic arguments were superseded by the everyday reality of common usage.

In addition to the ongoing attacks on Wilson's credibility, the issues that dominated the debate included whether there should be an 'official' apology led by the prime minister in parliament, and whether compensation was justifiable; and especially, whether Wilson was justified in his argument that the removal practices and policies amounted to genocide.

Even his old colleagues from the High Court had their misgivings. Sir William Deane was supportive of the report, but surprised that Wilson, who had always displayed a cautious judicial approach to labelling and language, would have used the term. Deane wrongly thought Dodson had convinced Wilson on this matter.

Sir Harry Gibbs and Sir Daryl Dawson were also surprised by Wilson's advocacy of the genocide label, and with his stewardship of the contents and findings in *Bringing Them Home*. Gibbs said he was 'surprised', but would not elaborate. Dawson, who was very fond of Wilson, and who had a similar judicial philosophy in relation to the federal structures under the Australian

Constitution (as did Gibbs), described *Bringing Them Home* as 'an aberration on the part of Ron'.

Commentator Michael Duffy, writing in the *Australian* stated:[28]

> During the inquiry [Wilson] apologised for his role in the removal of Aboriginal children from their families. This does him credit, but does not explain his report's lack of recommendations for the punishment of those with complicity in genocide. Surely such recommendations would have helped counter any impression that Wilson was the wrong choice for this inquiry.[29]

The inquiry report did not recommend criminal proceedings against any specific person, as the genocide finding related to the overall effect of policies and practices, and did not apply to particular individuals or organisations. Indeed, the inquiry, did not recommend such action for any alleged criminal offences in relation to the removal policies and practices. The inquiry followed the van Boven reparation principles, which focus on civil compensation, symbolic measures and guarantee of nonrepetition of human rights abuses.

Wilson later explained why he felt justified in calling the removal policy 'genocide':

> Genocide is not the attempt to destroy an individual. Genocide is the attempt to destroy a people, a culture. Listen to this, bearing in mind that the history of our laws and practices directed to assimilation testified to an intention to put an end to the Aboriginal race by removing their children in order to bring them up in white society, in many cases all knowledge of their aboriginality was denied to them, they were not allowed to access their family, or their language, or their land, or their culture, or their history.

Bringing Them Home was sympathetically received by most of the media, the academy and many Australians. A Herald–AGB McNair poll taken soon after the report's release suggested that almost two-thirds of Australians believed that parliaments in Australia should acknowledge the nation's responsibility in relation to the past removal policies and practices.[30]

The media analyst company Mervyn Smythe & Associates examined the Australian newspaper media coverage of the 'stolen generations' from just before the 26 May 1997 parliamentary tabling of *Bringing Them Home* until 20 June 1997. It found that the coverage had 'been on the whole extremely favourable…whether one examines the editorials or news/features sections'. It added:

> Despite comments by some [Commonwealth] Government figures, and a few media commentators, the coverage of the report has reflected a situation in which its findings have been seen by most writers/editors as having been proved, as opposed to being still an open question.[31]

For example, Geoff Kitney, in the *Sydney Morning Herald*, stated:

> If ever there was an issue which called out for leadership from the national Government it is the stolen children issue. If ever there was a report which compelled an instant, instinctive, sympathetic, symbolic response from the nation's political leaders this was it. If ever there was a moment in the sorry history of relations between indigenous Australians and European settlers for a genuine, unqualified statement of regret at the unique, government sanctioned, racially-based suffering of Aboriginal people, this was it.
>
> The *Bringing them Home* [sic] report catalogues a great national shame. It reveals, in the harrowing personal testimony of Australians still living, and still suffering the consequences of it, a dark stain on Australian history which ranks with some of the 20th century's most unforgivable systematic violation of human rights.[32]

The media analyst Smythe and Associates also noted: 'Over the course of the coverage there have been a couple of personal attacks by columnists on the authors of the report, particularly Sir Ronald Wilson.' But it added that 'these have been heavily outnumbered by sympathetic profiles in feature articles'.[33]

Author Drusilla Modjeska, speaking in September 1997 at the annual New South Wales Premier's Literary Awards, remarked:

> In this climate, it seems to me that the most important book—if not the best—that has been published this cold and chilly winter has been *Bringing Them Home*, the report of the National Inquiry into the Stolen Generations. If I were a betting man, as my father used to say, I'd bet that this is the book

> that will be remembered by the historians of the future when it comes to writing the narrative of this divided moment in our culture, for the story of those children, and the struggle for the land that surrounds it, is like an open wound through our history.[34]

The popularity of *Bringing Them Home* was noted a month later by Gerard Henderson, director of the Sydney Institute (a conservative think tank), who in the early 1980s had been chief of staff for John Howard when he was treasurer in the Fraser government. Writing sympathetically in the *Sydney Morning Herald*, Henderson noted: 'Today *Bringing Them Home* (AGPS, 1997) is a bestseller which is reviewed in the current issue of *The Times Literary Supplement*.'[35]

Indeed, the foreign media were interested in *Bringing Them Home* and the 'stolen generations' issue. *Dateline*, the American ABC current affairs program, featured the issue in a 1998 broadcast. The British magazine the *Economist* reported Howard's refusal to make a formal apology and Wilson's refusal to back down from the report's genocide claim. It noted that 'Sir Ronald is no stranger to privation. He was orphaned at the age of four and brought up by a brother before leaving school at 14 to earn a living.' The article quoted Wilson: 'I have done a lot of inquiries in my life…But I have never done one like this.'[36]

Wilson expanded on how different this inquiry was in a speech he delivered in the Senate chamber of the Old Parliament House in Canberra on 28 October 1997. Before an overflow audience of Aboriginal and non-Aboriginal people, he said that the numerous other inquiries and royal commissions he had been involved with were wholly intellectual exercises, where he would hear evidence from those compelled to appear before the inquiry, and from the evidence make findings of facts, conclusions and recommendations. He would return home at night time to a good meal and a good night's sleep, untroubled by the events of the day. That was not the case with the 'stolen generations' inquiry. He referred to the evidence given by people, 'very often in the mist of tears' and with great courage. He again referred to the people telling their stories from the heart. He also repeated how the inquiry had been a life-changing event. He said:

> I came to this inquiry a couple years ago as a man over the hill at 73 with about 50 years or more behind me as a hardboiled lawyer mixing it with all

> sorts of antagonists and people in the courts here and in England and yet this inquiry changed me. The reason it changed me is that it penetrated the heart, it got away from my mind which I have had done for the rest of my life in all the briefs I have had.[37]

The tears of the storytellers convinced him that they were reliving the pain, and that it was scandalous for people to say this was ancient history. For Wilson it related to current suffering, 'the reality of today's suffering'. He said that his seven years as HREOC president, where he could advocate for the disadvantaged, had been the greatest privilege of his life, but 'even that can't compared to the privilege of tapping these sources of pain, these wells of human suffering'.

The international media attention on *Bringing Them Home* was noted by *Canberra Times* foreign affairs reporter Ian McPhedran, who wrote:

> Wire service reporters have been run off their feet filing stories on race issues with a particular focus on the stolen children and Pauline Hanson. Those stories have the potential to reach up to two billion people. According to the Canberra correspondent with the Associated Press [a major international agency], Alan Thornhill, the stolen children story was the biggest of the year.[38]

The international coverage was seen by Wilson's longstanding friend Mariele Kuhn in Oxford. On 28 May 1997 she wrote to Wilson, saying how he figured prominently in an article in the British *Independent* on the treatment of Australian Aborigines. She wrote that she was greatly interested in the story and Wilson's part in it. She was proud of him: 'That you are, dear Ron, "one of Australia's most respected former judges" made my heart swell with pride, being an old friend.' She mentioned that the magnitude of the inquiry report and some of the opposition he had received must be keeping him very busy and 'sadly and deeply disturbed'. She said: 'It will take a long time until this dust settles and you and your family can again have some peace of mind.'

Wilson replied to Mariele Kuhn on 9 June 1997:

> We are having a busy time at the moment, defending and advocating for the 'Stolen Children' report. Personally, I am receiving my share of both bouquets and brickbats—but overall I feel very positive about it all. It is important that

> Australia confront its past and do what it can to promote a healing process. The ultimate outcome is vital to the future of the reconciliation process between Aborigines and other Australians.

He added that, because of the recent reconciliation conference in Melbourne, he was hopeful of a grassroots 'people's movement' for the reconciliation process.

The inquiry report generated many letters to the editors of newspapers. Although some were negative, most were supportive of *Bringing Them Home*.[39] Geraldine Walsh, letters editor of the *Sydney Morning Herald*, reported:

> The mail has become much easier to sort. Two piles—one for the broad topic of Aboriginal and race letters, and the other for The Rest (the latter being comparatively few). *Wik* and *Mabo* were knotty subjects. They could be discussed in terms of principle but many found it difficult to come to grips with what the court rulings would mean in practice.
>
> No such difficulty arises with the 'Stolen Children'. Every parent can understand the aching void of having a child snatched from you. Everyone can imagine what it would be like not knowing who your blood family was or where to find it. There were no legal niceties in the letters, just words from the heart. Space prevents us publishing the many individual apologies from those who feel beholden to do so in the absence of a figurehead apologising on behalf of the nation. We have given the gainsayers (they constitute about ⅛), those who have tended to say the separations were a good thing in the long run, a disproportionate representation on the letters page.[40]

15

An Advocate to the End

I cannot rest, because of this sense of trust, to continue to advocate for these people as long as I have breath.

Wilson's tenure as president of HREOC was due to expire on 31 July 1997. A few months previously, the Commonwealth attorney-general, Daryl Williams, had discussed with Wilson his willingness to continue as president until his replacement could be appointed. Wilson had agreed.

The day before the end of his tenure he was working in the Sydney HREOC headquarters when Williams telephoned, and informed him that the government would not be reappointing him.

Apparently, Williams's recommendation was not approved by cabinet.[1] The Commonwealth government was not happy with Wilson's continual highly visible advocacy of *Bringing Them Home*, and his demands for government reparations. In public, Wilson would not verify this story. However, privately he believed this was what had occurred. Even though he did not expect his tenure to be extended, he would have agreed to it. He loved his work at HREOC.

The commission issued a press statement, quoting Wilson:

> I am greatly honoured to have served as President for the last seven and a half years. This was a term appointment. I did not seek reappointment and it is the government's right to decide who should be appointed as my successor. I am proud of the achievements in my term of office and will look back on this period as one of the highlights of my legal and public service career.[2]

Jonathon Hunyor, HREOC's legal officer, was with Wilson when he took the attorney-general's call. Wilson did not admit his disappointment to Hunyor. After hanging up, he told Hunyor that tomorrow was his last day as HREOC president, although he had agreed to stay on for a short period as a hearing commissioner. Then he said, 'Well, let's wrap up what we need to get done.'

What needed to be done included appearing on the evening of his last day at a Melbourne public meeting, where he again discussed *Bringing Them Home* and the need for justice for the 'stolen generations'. He argued that an official (parliamentary) apology from the Commonwealth government was crucial for the healing process. He also said with conviction: 'We are accused by some of guilt, but the word is not mentioned in the report. We are not calling for guilt; we are calling for understanding and acknowledgement.'[3] From the 200 people in attendance, Wilson received a standing ovation.

The next day, 1 August 1997, Wilson held a press conference at the Victorian Equal Opportunity Commission. That night he appeared on ABC TV's *7.30 Report*.

The host of the program, Kerry O'Brien, commenced by saying that Wilson had surprised many people since being appointed HREOC president, almost as if Wilson had undergone a 'Paul on the road to Damascus' conversion. This referred to Wilson's apparent dramatic reversal from conservative states' rights High Court judge to fearless human rights advocate. A smiling Wilson said that was not so, and repeated, as he had many times in the past and would in the future, that while on the High Court he felt constrained by the judicial office and the 'need to behave with proper dignity, decide what he had to decide and speak only when spoken to'.[4] He reiterated that there were times on the High Court where his heart wished to go in one direction but his mind and oath of office took him in another direction. He found this disappointing, and it took a lot out of him. But he never regretted taking this stand and his oath seriously.

Wilson was careful not to criticise the Commonwealth government. In contrast, Wilson was subjected to criticism from members of the federal Liberal and National Party coalition, publicly and in the party room. Peter Nugent, Victorian federal MP, had remarked to several people that in the Liberal party room prime minister Howard spoke in derogatory terms about Wilson.[5] Wilson would not respond to O'Brien's questioning on whether attorney-general Williams had been overruled by other Commonwealth government ministers about allowing him to continue as HREOC president until a replacement could be appointed.

O'Brien asked Wilson if he were concerned that HREOC had been without a sex discrimination commissioner for most of 1997, and that a new president had not been appointed. Wilson said the government had the right to govern, including implementing its ideas on processes and practices. However, he was concerned, because he believed he had worked in a system that was working. However, he said that the government might have reached a different conclusion, and it was its prerogative to manage these HREOC appointments the way it saw as most appropriate. O'Brien asked: did Wilson think that the commission was 'one organisation being singled out for a bit of extra special treatment'? Wilson replied that he was 'not prepared to make that allegation'.

To this juncture, Wilson's demeanour had been calm. O'Brien raised the issue of former Keating Labor minister Gary Johns' opinion piece in the *Australian* expressing concern over HREOC, and suggesting it had developed a culture of arrogance.[6] O'Brien's reference to Johns hit a raw nerve, because Wilson viewed Johns's comments on HREOC as an unfair attack on his commission colleagues. Wilson had always displayed institutional loyalty. He consistently championed the organisations he worked in, and those that worked with him.

It was not only Wilson's respect for other HREOC commissioners and staff that made him upset over Johns's article. He was angered by Johns's criticism, made some eighteen months previously, that Australia spent too much time and money on minorities. Wilson, in a raised voice and with fire in his eyes, said to O'Brien that, because of that article, he was sorry to say that he no longer had respect for Johns. He said the majority could look after themselves or have their interests looked after. With his voice rising higher he said that Johns's criticism 'displayed no sensitivity to the place of [disadvantaged] minorities…'

O'Brien finished the interview by asking Wilson what he saw as the outcome and risks for Australia if the federal government did not agree to compensation and a formal apology, as the inquiry report had recommended? Wilson replied that the risk was, as had been mentioned by the 1991 report of the Royal Commission into Aboriginal Deaths in Custody, 'a continuation of division, injustice and suffering in this country'. That was the stark alternative to seizing this opportunity to make an apology that would go towards the healing process, which went further than addressing material disadvantages. Wilson added that plans were already being implemented to hold a 'Sorry Day' in 1998, which he hoped would amount to a national Sorry Day, with civic events all over Australia, where Aboriginal and non-Aboriginal people could 'look at each other face to face', and 'look in each other's eyes and where the non-Indigenous representatives would say "we are sorry".'

O'Brien finished by saying: 'Sir Ronald Wilson, have a happy retirement, and thank you for speaking to us.'

Retirement in any conventional sense was far from Wilson's mind. He would continue to travel throughout Australia defending the inquiry and report and advocating for recognition and compensation for the 'stolen generations', but he would have to do so as a private citizen.

The controversies and debates unleashed by the release of *Bringing Them Home* continued unabated, especially because of the attachment of the term genocide to the removal policies and practices. To many people, this term is reminiscent of the Nazi Holocaust or mass murders in Rwanda.

Michael Duffy wrote in the *Australian*:

> In demanding that the Prime Minister admit that what happened to Aboriginal children was genocide, his opponents are demanding that they effectively place Robert Menzies and Paul Hasluck in the same circle of hell as Hitler and Himmler. This might be extremely sneaky and clever party politics, but it does nothing to help black and white Australians come together.[7]

The genocide finding even proved worrying for some of the supporters of the report, such as Robert Manne, the editor of the conservative *Quadrant* magazine.[8] In the Stephen Murray-Smith Memorial Lecture, at the Victorian State Library on 27 November 1997,[9] Manne concluded with a discussion of the genocide issue, indicating that there were two ways of looking at it. One was from a legal position, under the UN Genocide Convention.

That is what *Bringing Them Home* did. Manne recited the passage, from the Venezuelan delegate to the UN General Assembly, that summarised the supportive position of including forcible child removals in the Genocide Convention. This passage was included in *Bringing Them Home*, and was quoted by Wilson when launching the report at the Melbourne Reconciliation Conference:

> The forced transfer of children to a group where they would be given an education different from that of their own group, and would have new customs, a new religion and probably a new language, was in practice tantamount to the destruction of their group, whose future depended on that generation of children. Such transfer might be made from a group with a low standard of civilisation…to a highly civilised group…yet if the intent of the transfer were the destruction of the group, a crime of genocide would undoubtedly have been committed.[10]

It should be noted that, while *Bringing Them Home* stated that the removal laws and practices from 1946 (on 11 December 1946, the UN General Assembly adopted a resolution declaring genocide to be a crime under international law) were contrary to the prohibition against genocide, it made no finding of genocide in relation to any specific legislation or state practice. The report made the following general statement:

> …from 1946 laws and practices which, with the purpose of eliminating Indigenous cultures, promoted the removal of Indigenous children for rearing in non-Indigenous institutions and households were in breach of the international prohibition of genocide…[11]

The inquiry was not called on to make a finding of genocide, but then again, it was not asked to make recommendations in relation to the awarding of compensation. It was only requested to examine the justification for compensation. Thus one might wonder why it didn't actually go one step further and specify which legislation and practice amounted to genocide? Considering the likely controversy attached to using the term genocide, arguably it would have been reasonable to expect that, once the report used the label, it would then specify which legislation and state practices amounted to genocide.

While agreeing in general that the removal scheme fitted the genocide summary contained in *Bringing Them Home*, Manne added that the policy of removal was geared to children of mixed descent and not 'full-blood' Aborigines (although some 'full-bloods' were removed). He indicated that this was an important caveat to the legal argument. Manne asserted that, if the 'full-bloods', as a matter of policy, were not being removed in large numbers, it is harder to argue the destruction of the Aboriginal race was attempted through the child removal policy. However, the *Bringing Them Home* report differs on this issue, arguing that children of 'mixed race' are recognised as 'children of the group', and that Aboriginal children were removed because of their Aboriginality, not because of their 'white blood'.[12] Also, there was such a thing as the 'dying pillow' theory, by which the 'full-bloods' were assumed to be dying out through natural causes. Further, it should be noted that there existed legislation proscribing miscegenation or interracial cohabitation, which arguably could be seen to prevent the increase of the 'Aboriginal strain',[13] but this was not part of the removal policy *per se*.

Manne's approach to this genocide issue was to examine it from a historical and conceptual, rather than legal, framework. Under this framework, Manne made a series of points. First, he correctly stated that genocide can be committed without the use of murderous means. Second, in the 1930s, in at least the Northern Territory and Western Australia, there was a policy of eliminating Aboriginal people of mixed descent, as it 'would constitute an unambiguous good'. Third, Manne stated that in other states, while removals occurred, it was not necessarily done for the purpose of eliminating 'the mixed descent population by biological assimilation', and that, especially after World War II, the motive of removal shifted everywhere in Australia 'from biological to sociocultural assimilation'.[14] Fourth, Manne commented that it is important to recognise that officials who were implicated in the biological absorption policies in Western Australia and the Northern Territory did not have a policy of eliminating the 'full-blood' population.

Manne argued:

> If a case is to be made that genocide was committed it can only be made, in my opinion, with regard to a particular policy plan—biological assimilation—at a particular time—the 1930s—and in particular places—the Northern Territory and Western Australia. And even here the case would have to concede, in my opinion, that the policy was more one of intentions

> than effective actions, and that, after 1940, it was, everywhere in Australia, abandoned in both thought and deed.[15]

Manne's discussion exemplifies the complications in the argument on whether the removal policies and practices can be classified as genocide, under the Genocide Convention or by some other criteria or framework. Even so, Manne's discussion only touched the surface of this debate. Genocide arguments are very complicated and, invariably, emotional. Mick Dodson's concerns about using genocide proved to be true. Once he agreed to it, he did not hesitate to publicly advocate its validity. As for Wilson, once Wilkie and Pritchard had convinced him, he had no hesitation in having it included in the report, and after its public release he strongly argued the case for it.

Almost simultaneously with the publication of Manne's 'Stolen Generations' lecture, the conservative think tank, the Melbourne-based Institute of Public Affairs, published a 16,000 word critique of *Bringing Them Home*. The author of *Betraying the Victims: The 'Stolen Generations' Report*[16] was anthropologist Ron Brunton.

Brunton was highly critical of the report and Wilson. He argued, among other things, that *Bringing Them Home* misrepresented many of its sources; made assertions not backed up by evidence; and failed to compare forcible removals with voluntary removals or give consideration to removals justified by legitimate concerns for children's welfare.

Brunton, like others in newspaper columns who criticised the inquiry and its report, mentioned Wilson's link to the Presbyterian Church. Brunton rightly points out that the churches were an important agent in the removal process. This was exactly the point made by Stephen Hall, who had appeared before Wilson when the inquiry was in Perth. Brunton added that, considering the churches' role in the removal process, they only received light criticism in *Bringing Them Home*. This again is true, with the report's chapter on 'Responses of Churches and Other Non-Government Agencies' being only three pages. Mention is made that the experiences of children cared for in church homes and missions varied—some good, some bad—as was generally true of the 'stolen generations'.

It is interesting to note that, in the *Bringing Them Home* chapter devoted to Western Australia, there is a section titled 'Sister Kate's'. This was the only Western Australian mission or children's home to receive such treatment in the report. Speaking in 2003, Wilson said that he was keen to have this section included because of the prominence of the role of Sister Kate's in the removal scheme in Western Australia. He also said that, as he had a role in Sister Kate's, it was important for the integrity of the report to include a section on the home. The section consists of only three paragraphs, which explain that the home was established by Sister Kate Clutterbuck, who had informed A. O. Neville that 'we should of course like to have the poorest and most neglected children, not those who have mothers who love and care for them, but those who are most unwanted in the State'.[17] There could be no more clear statement to support the view Wilson held in the 1960s: that Sister Kate's cared for unwanted or uncared Aboriginal children. One may even argue that this is a self-serving statement.

The report did contain a number of stories that cast the churches in a bad light, including Sister Kate's. Some stories also painted a more positive view of the churches' involvement in the removal schemes.

The report did recommend that the churches make an apology for their role in the removal process, and provide services such as counselling to all those affected by the removals. Three days after the tabling of the inquiry report,[18] and many times subsequently, Wilson said the churches should examine the possibility of assisting the Commonwealth government in funding a compensation tribunal and other reparation measures. At the September 1997 synod of the Western Australian Uniting Church, Wilson advocated for the church to embrace the report. With tears in his eyes, he pleaded for the church to respond positively to the recommendations of the report.

Brunton also made the point that, even though Wilson sat on Sister Kate's management committee while moderator of the Presbyterian Church, he did not hear the protests about the removal process. Brunton commented:

> [Wilson] has been quoted as stating 'I had no knowledge of the wrongness of the practice', a remarkable admission given that he now claims that the practice constituted 'genocide', which is generally seen as the ultimate crime against humanity.[19]

On 16 December 1997, the Howard government released its formal response to *Bringing Them Home*. It was a one-page media release (with some attachments) from minister Herron announcing a 'reparation package'. It addressed only a few of the report's recommendations, mainly in the area of counselling, family reunion services, preservation of records and recording of oral stories. The total package was valued at $63 million.[20] However, this money 'was, in effect, a reinstatement of money cut from ATSIC in the previous budget'.[21]

The Howard government's reparation package pales into insignificance compared with the Canadian situation, which was unfolding almost simultaneously. Canada had its own 'stolen generations', where Indigenous children were sent to residential schools and foster care.[22] The Royal Commission on Aboriginal Peoples (RCAP), established in 1991, commissioned a number of reports and conducted numerous hearings into the residential schools issue. In response to the RCAP, the Canadian federal government on 7 January 1998 released a document: *Gathering Strength: Canada's Aboriginal Action Plan* (Gathering Strength Action Plan).[23] At the same time Jan Stewart, minister of Indian affairs and northern development, stated that the federal government was 'deeply sorry' to those who had suffered physical or sexual abuse at the residential schools.[24]

In addition to the apology, the Canadian federal government, in its Gathering Strength Action Plan, committed C$350 million for a 'Healing Fund' designed to support communities in redressing 'the legacy of physical and sexual abuse at residential schools'.[25]

(More recently, in April 2006, the Canadian federal government announced a C$2 billion deal for former residential school students or 'inmates', which includes individual payments of C$10,000, plus C$3000 for each year spent in a residential school. In addition, individual payments of between C$5000 to C$275,000 are possible for those suffering serious psychological effects from sexual or serious physical abuse. Also, the agreement provides funds for programs of 'healing, truth, reconciliation and commemoration of residential schools and the abuses suffered'. The agreement was part of the settlement of over 7000 lawsuits by former 'inmates' against the Canadian government and a number of churches.[26])

The government's reparation package was far from the end of the matter. Wilson's attackers would not let up. Their anger was also turned on Robert Manne, who until he came out in support of *Bringing Them Home*, had been regarded as one of their own. The editorial board of the *Quadrant* took exception to his stance, which led to Manne's 'resignation' as editor in December 1997.

On 2 May 1998, Wilson wrote to Brunton concerning correspondence between Brunton and race discrimination commissioner Zita Antonios.

Wilson stated that he believed he had answered the substance of Brunton's criticism, which Wilson viewed as based 'on groundless suspicion unsupported by anything like the substantial research that accompanied the preparation of *Bringing Them Home*'. Wilson's letter concluded: 'My sense of stewardship of time convinces me that I have many better things to do than to continue sparring with your unsubstantiated suspicions, suspicions which I dismiss as groundless.'[27]

Brunton's paper was part of an increasing trend of critical articles and publications from early 1998, and continuing into the twenty-first century. Criticism was made of the inquiry's methodology; the report's findings and recommendations; and of Wilson. This criticism can be viewed as part of the larger 'History Wars': namely, a battle of ideas, assertions and conclusions about Aboriginal and non-Aboriginal history in Australia.[28]

Some of the more vociferous and articulate criticism was published in *Quadrant* after Manne's resignation as editor. Throughout 1998, 1999 and 2000, *Quadrant* published many articles criticising the notion of a 'stolen generation' and the findings of *Bringing Them Home*. In fact, it was argued in *Quadrant* that (Commonwealth, state and territory) government policy resulted in a 'rescued generation', not a 'stolen generation'.[29]

A particularly critical article on the inquiry report and Wilson appeared in the 2000 summer edition of the *National Observer* by Melbourne barrister Ian Spry QC.[30] Spry, who had at various times been rumoured as a possible High Court appointee, wrote that, considering Wilson's legal training, it

> would therefore have been expected that he would follow prudently established legal methods, particularly by calling a sufficiently wide range of witnesses to represent fairly every point of view and by enabling witnesses' recollections to be properly tested by cross-examination.[31]

However, Spry commented, 'incredibly, neither of these things (both so clearly essential to the administration of justice, as Wilson himself would have been aware) was done.'[32] Spry wrote that Wilson accepted the Aboriginal stories without them being questioned or challenged by anyone and, more remarkably, this was essential because of the inherent unreliability of childhood memories of many years gone.

Spry asserted that a number of people contacted the inquiry wanting to give evidence that would have shown that the 'stolen generation' claims were fraudulent, but they were turned away by the inquiry.[33] This is a serious allegation. However, Spry fails to support it with evidence, a criticism he made of Wilson. In respect to this allegation, Wilson always maintained that the advertising in newspapers and other sources was a general invitation, and no one was deliberately frozen out of the process. However, not everyone could be heard, including some Aborigines who were removed as children. Wilson welcomed submissions from those involved in the implementation of the removal policy, but their responses were inadequate.

In concluding, Spry's criticism of Wilson was relentless:

> It is evident that the Wilson report now stands finally discredited (although this fact will only reluctantly be acknowledged by those with contrary interests). But in short, how has it come about that a person who has enjoyed fully all of the honours and rewards of public office in this country has so seriously let it down? For his report may be perceived as a betrayal. It has created a false impression in the public mind both within and without Australia that will prove hard to remove. It has seriously affected the credibility of this country, and has diminished severely much of the moral credibility that has been slowly built up.[34]

One can almost discern in Spry's language a disbelief that Wilson could have done what he did when one considers his legal training and judicial record, which displayed no overt sympathetic reception to arguments for Aboriginal justice.

In his 'retirement' interview with Kerry O'Brien on the *7.30 Report*, Wilson had mentioned the proposed 1998 Sorry Day. He had been speaking to a number of Aboriginal people about the concept. Over the following seven months, he consulted numerous people and arranged for a meeting at the HREOC Sydney offices in January 1998.

Thirty people attended the meeting: fifteen Aboriginal and fifteen non-Aboriginal. Wilson led, asking, 'Can we have a Sorry Day on a community basis?' The meeting decided yes, and 26 May 1998, one year after the tabling in the Commonwealth parliament of *Bringing Them Home*, was the date selected. Carol Kendall, a member of the 'stolen generations', became the co-chair of the informal committee. Sir Zelman Cowen, former governor-general, became patron of the National Sorry Day Committee, and John Bond took on the demanding responsibilities associated with being committee secretary.

The National Sorry Day, officially launched in March 1998 at La Perouse in Sydney at a house that was a transit centre for Aboriginal people, including those removed from their families, received extensive media coverage. The sorry day committee developed a statement to explain the concept:

> A day when all Australians can express their sorrow for the whole tragic episode, and celebrate the beginning of a new understanding…Indigenous people will participate in a Day dedicated to the memory of loved ones who never came home, or who are still finding their way home…Sorry Day can help restore the dignity stripped from those affected by removal: and it offers those who carried out the policy—and their successors—a chance to move beyond denial and guilt. It could shape a far more creative partnership between Indigenous and non-Indigenous Australians, with immense benefit to both.[35]

The response from the Australian public was very positive. Aboriginal and non-Aboriginal people from around Australia organised cultural and civic events for the sorry day, and sorry books were provided for people to express their apologies. Nearly one million people wrote condolence messages in the books. On the ABC's 7 p.m. news, over half of the thirty-minute program on the night of 26 May 1998 was devoted to sorry day events.[36]

Having endured a barrage of criticism, much of it personal, since the report had been released, Wilson was encouraged by the positive response on the first sorry day. It convinced him that a 'people's movement' was possible. He now held new hopes for the reconciliation process, although some months after the first national sorry day, Wilson had concerns about the viability of the Council for Aboriginal Reconciliation after the resignation of Patrick Dodson, its chair. Dodson resigned because of his disagreement with prime minister Howard's position on native title and Aboriginal affairs in general. Dodson was replaced by the Queensland activist and former unsuccessful Liberal candidate Evelyn Scott.

Although sorry days in subsequent years attracted hundreds rather than the thousands who took part in the first one, Wilson was always heartened by people's capacity to open their hearts and to say 'sorry', despite the intransigence of the Commonwealth government. Wilson viewed this as an intrinsic good. He considered it all part of the 'Journey of Healing', a campaign launched by many of the 'stolen generations' after the success of the first national sorry day.

The sorry day committee persuaded the prime minister to establish a 'stolen generations' memorial between the High Court and National Library with the following words on it:

> This place honours the people who have suffered under the removal policies and practices. It also honours those Indigenous and non-Indigenous people whose genuine care softened the tragic impact of what are now recognised as cruel and misguided policies.

Howard did make one other gesture. In parliament on 26 August 1999, he made a statement of regret, which was couched in general terms, acknowledging past mistreatment and resulting hurt and trauma of Aborigines, but not specifically the 'stolen generations'.[37]

Gestures were one thing, but the Commonwealth government consistently refused to consider compensation or an apology. Howard would not countenance an apology being made by the Commonwealth parliament. The prime minister's reason for his refusal was legal. He argued that an apology would constitute an admission of legal liability. However, the principle of parliamentary immunity would safeguard against such a consequence from making a parliamentary apology.

In contrast, all Australian state and territory governments have done so.[38] So did many churches, police forces and others. None of these apologies has resulted in adverse consequences, legal or otherwise.

From 1997 to 2000, at numerous places and events, such as Old Parliament House, Canberra (28 October 1997), the Melbourne Press Club (28 August 1997), the National Press Club in Canberra (25 March 1998), the medicolegal meeting in Melbourne (9 May 1998), the Mental Health Conference of Australia and New Zealand in Melbourne (22 September 1999) and the May Macleod Lecture in Sydney on 25 May 2000, Wilson put the case for reparations by Commonwealth, state and territory governments.

At the 1998 National Press Club address in Canberra, his address did not specifically focus on the inquiry, dealing in a more general way with the reconciliation process. Despite questioning from journalists, he refused to be drawn on whether Howard's ten-point plan in response to the *Wik* decision was racist, or to pass judgement on the performance of Aboriginal affairs minister John Herron is the wake of a no-confidence motion in him by the Commonwealth government's Indigenous advisory committee. Wilson did say that, when it came to Aboriginal affairs, he would conclude from the evidence 'that there certainly has not been government for all the people'. This was reported by the newspapers, with the *Canberra Times* byline: 'PM has not "governed for all".'[39]

In the meantime, the *Cubillo–Gunner* case was wending its way through the courts of the Northern Territory.[40] Its origins went back to the 1994 Going Home conference that had so moved Robert Tickner, and been a catalyst for the HREOC inquiry, when QC Ron Merkel had first talked about the possibility of litigation against governments by people who had been removed as children.

In *Cubillo–Gunner*, the plaintiffs were Lorna Cubillo and Peter Gunner. Mrs Cubillo was born in 1938 on a remote pastoral station in the Northern Territory. Her mother had died while she was very young, and her mother's sister cared her for. She claimed that, in or around 1945, patrol officers forcibly took her to a depot at Seven Mile Creek, and she eventually ended up at the Retta Dixon home in Darwin. She stayed there until she was eighteen years of age. Mr Gunner was born in 1948, also on a pastoral station. He claimed he was seven or eight years old when he was removed, and after some time at a transit station, was sent to St Mary's in Alice Springs. He remained there until he was sixteen years of age.

The plaintiffs claimed that their removal and detention constituted wrongful imprisonment and deprivation of liberty. They also alleged that the director of native affairs and the Commonwealth, by virtue of the doctrine of vicarious liability, breached their statutory liability—the duty of care and fiduciary duty to the plaintiffs. The plaintiffs also claimed for breach of 'duty as guardian'. However, even though claims for breach of duty as a guardian were described as a separate cause of action, they replicated the particulars and allegations of breach of statutory duty, breach of fiduciary duty and breach of common law duty of care. The breach of duty as guardian was not developed at trial, or relied upon for any other purpose than being part of the allegations of the other breaches mentioned.

Justice O'Loughlin of the Federal Court of Australia rejected the Commonwealth's strikeout application. He remarked:

> these cases are of such importance—not only to the individual applicants and to the larger Aboriginal community, but also to the nation as a whole—that nothing short of a determination on the merits…is warranted.[41]

Any joy the plaintiffs felt with victory in defending the strikeout application disappeared when Justice O'Loughlin found against the plaintiffs on the merits of the case at trial.[42] The plaintiffs' appeal to the Full Court of the Federal Court was dismissed,[43] and leave to appeal to the High Court of Australia was rejected on the grounds that there was little or no likelihood of success in overturning the lower courts' decisions.[44]

Justice O'Loughlin's August 2000 decision (the trial) held that the Commonwealth was not liable for damages to the two plaintiffs. He accepted that the plaintiffs had suffered pain and suffering, that there had been sexual misconduct and punishment, but not that they had made the case for damages.

Importantly for proponents of *Bringing Them Home*, Justice O'Loughlin did not deny the existence of a 'stolen generation', and recognised that since 1911 there had been a Commonwealth policy of removing part-Aboriginal children from their families and placing them in institutions in Alice Springs and Darwin. However, because of lack of evidence of the practical implementation of that policy by the patrol officers, Justice O'Loughlin was not able to adjudicate on the removals' consensual or forcible nature.[45] Also, Justice O'Loughlin stated that it was not open for the court to judicially review the removal policies.

Even so, he concluded by remarking that the prevailing view of the time (the 1940s and 1950s) was that the best interests of Aboriginal children, particularly 'part-Aboriginal' children, was for them to be assimilated into mainstream non-Aboriginal culture. This required them receiving a Western-style education. However, he added:

> Having made the decision to remove the child, there was a total disregard of the fact that the child was also part Aboriginal, of the fact that the child's mother or family with whom the child was living was or were Aboriginal and the fact that the child had been brought up only aware of Aboriginal culture and unaware of European culture.[46]

O'Loughlin's decision and the subsequent appeal decisions have in many respects effectively closed off the courts as an alternative avenue for the survivors of the removal policies to seek compensation.[47]

One of the most persistent critics of *Bringing Them Home* was Peter Howson, a former federal minister for Aboriginal affairs in the early 1970s. His submissions to the Australian Senate's Legal and Constitutional References Committee Inquiry into the Stolen Generation,[48] which was looking into the Commonwealth government's response to the inquiry's recommendations,[49] were a full frontal assault on *Bringing Them Home* and Wilson. His criticisms were couched in terms of Wilson's failings. In some respects this is understandable. Wilson was the co-chair of the inquiry, and the public front for the report. But the inquiry process and report also involved a team of commissioners and consultants.

Howson's written submission to the Senate committee asserted that Wilson failed to consider evidence that should have been available to him, and that:

> his conclusions were based on fundamental misconceptions about the situation that faced Governments, the churches, the part Aborigine children and their mothers, and about the circumstances of the separation of those children from their mothers.[50]

He was critical that 'Sir Ronald did not check the veracity of stories told to him by Aborigines'; 'did not call evidence from government patrol officers involved in administering Aboriginal welfare'; and 'did [not] call on those missionaries and other church workers who were active in church hostels'. Some of these people were alive, and Howson considered it a failing of Wilson that they were 'incriminated' in the report 'without having any opportunity to defend their conduct'. Howson also wrote that the Senate committee should demand that Wilson make an apology to Sir Paul Hasluck 'for his egregious calumny against one of Australia's most distinguished ministers'.

Wilson made written[51] and oral[52] submissions to the Senate committee defending the inquiry's methodology, findings and recommendations. His written submission reiterated that *Bringing Them Home* acknowledged the difficulty in finding reliable figures of numbers of Aborigines forcibly removed. Nevertheless, based on empirical research, it firmly concluded that 'the number of children forcibly removed lay between one tenth and one third of all [Aboriginal] children'. Wilson rejected the Commonwealth government's claim that no more than 10 per cent of children were removed—whether forcibly or voluntarily. Aboriginal affairs minister Herron had used this

10 per cent figure to counter the argument that there had been a 'stolen generation' of Aboriginal children.

This figure was derived from an Australian Bureau of Statistics household survey, where respondents were asked if they were Aboriginal or part-Aboriginal. If they answered affirmatively, they were questioned if they considered themselves 'stolen'. Of course, this was not a reliable statistical survey, because people's perception of stolen may differ in such a way that may either increase or decrease the numerical conclusion. Also, the survey did not take into consideration Aborigines, forcibly removed, who had died. Even so, the inquiry's estimation, of approximately 150,000 Aborigines being forcibly removed cannot be considered reliable either. Manne argued that it was too high, a more realistic estimation being around 25,000,[53] although it was reported in the *Herald Sun* that now, with the benefit of statistics, there were around '40,000–50,000 children who were taken from their parents…'[54]

Wilson's response to the argument of numbers, and whether one could talk about a generation or generations, was to assert that it was not only the children actually removed who had suffered; one had to consider their parents and other family members. Wilson recalled the 1997 admission of Cedric Wyatt (then head of the Western Australian Aboriginal Affairs Department) at the inquiry hearings in Perth 'that there was probably not one Aboriginal family in Western Australia that did not bear the scars of the removal policies.'[55]

The number of Aboriginal children forcibly removed cannot be severed from the term 'stolen generation' or 'stolen generations'. As previously noted the term's veracity, accuracy and connotations have been vigorously debated, and by 2001 the terms had entered the *Australian Oxford Dictionary*: 'the Aboriginal people who were removed from their families as children and placed in institutions or fostered by white families.'[56]

The terminology debate was reignited by Andrew Bolt of the *Daily Telegraph*, who in a 2001 article reported that prominent Aboriginal leader and chair of ATSIC, Lowitja O'Donoghue, conceded that she was removed, not stolen.[57] Wilson correctly said that *Bringing Them Home* had not utilised the term 'stolen generation' or 'stolen generations', and that the media had initiated using these terms. However, Wilson did refer to the 'stolen' adjective on several occasions in the media. The term created difficulties as to whom could be termed 'stolen', and thus a member of the 'stolen generations', or whether there was even such a thing as the 'stolen generations'. Would a better term have been 'separated' and, consequently, the probability that there would have been more discussion about the effects of separation and subsequent treatment of the children?[58]

In part, this was the position of the editorial of the *Weekend Australian*, under the headline: 'Sad Semantics Betray the Stolen Children'. The editorial considered that the inquiry was dealing with separation, and it could not have been expected to test all the allegations of separation and how they had occurred. The editorial added:

> The important thing is that in hindsight, a reprehensible policy caused untold suffering to many victims, no matter how they were taken or what you choose to call them...The Aborigines who suffered are a removed generation, a lost generation, a still-suffering generation. They and their families had their free will taken away. Their right to decide how they lived was stolen from them.[59]

Wilson's written submission also argued that the Commonwealth government's assertion 'that monetary compensation is inappropriate and improper unless legal liability can be established' was 'a heartless approach'.[60] Wilson returned to this compensation issue in his oral submission. He did not favour very large compensation payments to individuals. Rather, he envisaged a healing commission of, perhaps, three people, two being Aboriginal, who would focus on community-level reparations, not individual compensation. However, Wilson did believe that individual payments, of a few thousand dollars per individual, had a place within the overall reparation measures. They would be little more than a token gesture, in monetary terms, but would, he thought, provide recognition of harm suffered within the context of other measures, for example, such as an apology and endeavours to improve Aboriginal communities. If verification of 'stolen generation' status needed to be established before payment, Wilson said that in most cases this should be achievable through testimony from the person's community and family. Greater compensation for physical and sexual abuses would require an extra inquiry.[61]

Wilson believed that the *Bringing Them Home* recommendation of compensation via extrajudicial means was the best way forward for Australia, reducing the probability of protracted and expensive litigation in the courts. He also viewed the call for an apology as a significant measure in the reconciliation process. Throughout the Senate hearing, he remained a steadfast defender of the inquiry, including all fifty-four recommendations, and the findings, including genocide.

Wilson, again the advocate, appeared before the Senate, as he felt that he had a moral duty to defend the inquiry and its report not only because it had changed his life but, more importantly, because those telling their stories to the inquiry had placed their trust in him and other hearing commissioners.

Wilson always sought to answer attacks on the inquiry and *Bringing Them Home*. He rarely sought to rebut personal attacks against him. His official and public response was clear: they didn't affect him. He was only concerned with such personal attacks to the extent they undermined the report's credibility and acceptance. To a large extent this is factually correct.

Wilson was sufficiently intelligent and aware to appreciate that he was 'fair game' to opponents of the inquiry and report. Even so, Wilson, who always took pride in his professionalism, was emotionally hurt by some of this criticism. Anger, more than hurt, was his general reaction: anger at what he considered a deliberate campaign to discredit him in order to discredit *Bringing Them Home*. But he would not be deterred from defending the inquiry and report.

He did not stop advocating that the reparations the report recommended were practical, achievable and justified. He did not stop defending the report's methodology, especially reliance on the stories told to the inquiry, without corroboration from individual 'native welfare' files previously compiled on the storytellers. Wilson's answer was clear: the inquiry did not have the time or resources to do this, but that necessary and sufficient corroboration was provided by the sheer number of personal stories told to the inquiry (535 orally and around another 1000 in written form) and their similarity. Additional corroboration of an assimilation policy was provided from state and territory government documents as well as testimony and evidence from churches, police officers, academics and researchers.

As to inviting to the inquiry those involved in shaping the assimilation policy and implementing it, such as patrol officers, Wilson said that the inquiry advertised for people to make submissions and appear before the commissioners. An article by former treasury official, Des Moore, published by the Institute for Private Affairs in 1999, incorrectly asserted: 'It will be recalled that Wilson was appointed (by [Prime Minister] Keating) as a Royal Commissioner. As such, he had the power to subpoena witnesses.'[62] Moore was wrong; Wilson was not appointed as a royal commissioner. Moore was not the only report critic to make this mistake. Manne reports that Howson also referred to the inquiry as a royal commission.[63]

Two principal points emerge in relation to Wilson's defence of the inquiry–report's methodology. First, the inquiry could have made a greater effort to have some of those who shaped and implemented the assimilation policy appear before the inquiry. Of course, many of them were dead or elderly and not capable of appearing. This made it even more important to talk to and strongly encourage those who could appear to do so, particularly as the report categorised the removal policies and practices in negative terms as constituting genocide and crimes against humanity. However, as a matter of law, the inquiry could not compel people to appear before them.

The second point concerns corroboration. Manne agreed with Wilson's position. Writing as a critic of Brunton's *Betraying the Victims*, Manne stated:

> Many books on the Stalin terror or the Holocaust rely heavily of testimony of victims. I have never encountered a serious argument suggesting the general unreliability of this kind of evidence. The inquiry into the stolen children heard directly from 535 Aborigines. Is it being suggested that the overall picture that the witnesses painted might represent a kind of collective hallucination?[64]

Wilson steadfastly and relentlessly maintained the faith. As well as all the public advocacy and appearances, he went to see premiers and chief ministers, and many of their senior public servants, to discuss how the recommendations could best be implemented in each state or territory.

Whenever possible, Wilson attended 'Journey of Healing' events, and 'reconciliation' functions, such as the 2000 Sydney Harbour 'walk across the bridges', often wearing his 'Journey of Healing' jumper. These events encouraged him to believe that healing and reconciliation between Aboriginal and non-Aboriginal Australians were possible. He viewed the 'Journey of Healing' as part of a national commitment to confronting the injustices of the past, to telling the truth and to a new sense of self-respect for Australian society.

In May 2000, Wilson was again upset by the Commonwealth government's actions. The Council for Aboriginal Reconciliation had existed for nine years, working towards a document of reconciliation. On 11 May 2000, this document was publicly released. It included an apology for past injustices. Simultaneously, the Commonwealth government released its own declaration of reconciliation document, which continued Howard's opposition to a formal apology.

Wilson agreed with some parts of the council's document, but was disappointed that it did not more specifically associate the request for a formal apology with the 'stolen generations'. Even so, he was more disappointed with the government's simultaneous release of its declaration. The ABC's *7.30 Report* item that evening (11 May 2000) contained comments and footage from several people, including Wilson, who said:

> To release an opposing version, an alternative version, at the very same [moment] as the Council releases its declaration can only promote controversy, and I fear that that is the PM's intention, notwithstanding his professed support for the process.

The life of the Council for Aboriginal Reconciliation closed at the Corroboree event at the Sydney Opera House on 30 and 31 May 2000, where the final Declaration Towards Reconciliation was released.[65] Wilson continued to push the cause of the 'stolen generations', not just to right a grievous wrong, but because he believed that if Australian society had the courage to confront the wrong, its people could build a far better nation. The inquiry had given him a vision of what Australia could be. As he stated in Old Parliament House in Canberra on 28 October 1997:

> We are prepared to look into the face of the Indigenous person opposite and recognise our common humanity, each with a rich heritage of art and culture in a united Australia which respects the land, values our Aboriginal and Torres Strait Islander Heritage, and provides justice and equity for all.[66]

Wilson's activities were not restricted to matters surrounding *Bringing Them Home* and the 'stolen generations'. He was used to being simultaneously involved in many activities. In 1997 he took on the role of president of the Australian Council for Overseas Aid. He remained in the position until 2002. In talking of his four years in that role, he said it allowed him to continue working and advocating for human rights and contributing to developing

'Australia's contribution to the provision of resources in developing countries… [and]…respect for human rights and democratic governance in the developing countries'. In that period he undertook a number of overseas trips, including a trip to the Middle East (Jordan, Israel–Palestine, Lebanon) in October 1998, organised by APHEDA—Australian People for Health, Education and Development Abroad. While there, he spoke to many people on both sides of the Israeli–Palestinian argument. He found the trip fascinating and rewarding, listening to Palestinians in Gaza, who felt like prisoners in their own homes, and Israeli Jews, who were concerned about their security and safety. While he did experience mutual animosity on both sides, he also found significant pockets of great goodwill and moderation of views.

Wilson was also a trustee of the Bringing Them Home Trust. This organisation provided financial assistance to members of the 'stolen generations' to assist them, for example, to return to their country, retrace family, hold family reunions and the like.

In 1999, Wilson became patron of People With Disabilities (WA) Inc (PWD), an organisation constituted to advocate the rights and conditions of people with disabilities. For such an organisation, representing a minority rarely considered or assisted by governments, the media or the public, and operating on a small budget, the support of such an esteemed community figure was beneficial.

Sometimes PWD clients required lawyers. If the client couldn't afford legal representation and the situation was desperate, Kaye Regan, PWD's executive director, would ring Wilson for assistance. Usually, not long after the conversation, a lawyer, often a busy lawyer, would telephone Regan, offering hours of free legal assistance. As they had during the fundraising campaign for the Murdoch University law library, Perth lawyers found it difficult to refuse a request from the former High Court justice.

Wilson's willingness to help PWD and its clients manifested itself in other ways. Whenever needed, he would sign a letter, particularly letters to the editor of the *West Australian*, which significantly increased the chances of publication.

Wilson's modesty and humble demeanour endeared him to many of those who knew him, including Regan. But she could not agree to abide by his request to 'Just call me Ron'. To her, he always remained 'Sir Ronald'. She was constantly in 'friendly' battle with him for refusing to accept taxi vouchers; driving late at night or catching buses to functions; and not allowing her to pick him up or drive him home. After one 'squabble' in an elevator, Wilson said to Regan that he was catching a bus home 'because that was what public transport was for, for the public'.

Regan lost her battle to give him special treatment. Wilson found it slightly amusing. On one occasion he said to Regan, 'I always do as I am told.' She asked him how long he has been doing as he was told? He immediately replied, 'Ever since I met you.'

Regan and the PWD staff adored and revered Wilson, which made him feel uncomfortable. From his perspective, he was merely helping out a section of society that was often neglected by the community's power structures. Later, Regan eulogised Wilson: 'He was so precious and he really was. I don't think there will ever be another person like him because people these days are so materialistic and individual focused.' She added:

> Everyone involved in PWD (WA) felt very privileged to have known him. Anyone who was lucky enough to know him was extremely fortunate as it was a wonderful experience, cherished by all of us at PWD (WA). I feel that I had a very special opportunity. There had been people in the past who on occasions wrote letters to the editor about him calling him a 'bleeding heart' and one of the affluent and privileged. They certainly did not know him as the modest compassionate and community minded person he was. We are very grateful to his family for sharing him with all of us.

Wilson also maintained a very active role in the Uniting Church. Often after Sunday service at his local Applecross St Stephen's Church, he could be found in the kitchen making cups of tea and cleaning dishes. As at home, Wilson enjoyed 'doing the dishes' after a meal.

Wilson's involvement after his term as president of the Uniting Church of Australia was not restricted to his local church. He was asked to mediate in a number of disputes in the church, including at Manguri, the late 1980s incarnation of Sister Kate's Children's Home, operated by Aboriginal people, to provide services to Aboriginal children and families.[67]

At the Eighth Assembly of the Uniting Church of Australia, in Perth in July 1997, issues of homosexuals' ordination for ministry and the blessing of same-sex relationships dominated proceedings. Dorothy McMahon, the high-profile Sydney minister, indicated that unless the church approved the ordination of openly gay people, she would resign, because she was a lesbian.

In stark contrast, the Uniting Aboriginal and Islander Christian Congress strongly opposed homosexuals' ordination. No solution or compromise could be reached.

The assembly resolved to ask three former presidents of the Uniting Church of Australia—Jill Tabart, D'Arcy Wood and Wilson—to consider how the assembly might deal with some outstanding issues relating to sexuality, and report, with recommendations, to the assembly's standing committee. The three consulted widely with congregations, individuals and church elders. However, their report, completed in under a year, failed to make a definitive recommendation on homosexual ministers and same-sex relationships. The report's thrust was 'understanding' and accepting differences and recognising the difference of opinion in this sexuality debate. The former presidents questioned the helpfulness of further intensive consideration of Christian attitudes to homosexuality, particularly concerning vexed issues of homosexual ministers or church leaders and the blessing of same-sex marriages, and concluded:

> Our hope is that we can encourage the Church to recognize we are on a journey of discovery. We each glimpse part of the truth, and on the way we continue to seek the guidance of the Holy Spirit as we search the Scriptures, affirm our differences, learn from each other's insights, and together continue to serve the world for which God's purpose is wholeness of life.[68]

The assembly standing committee accepted the report. Wilson believed that homosexuals should be permitted to be ministers in the church. However, cognisant of the issue's sensitivities, he did not advocate the flaunting of a minister's homosexuality among parishioners. Sensitivities and differences of opinion on this issue within the church were reinforced by the correspondence sent to Wilson by individuals and congregations during and after compiling this report.

To many in the Uniting Church, Wilson was an icon, someone they greatly admired for his deep religious faith and all he had achieved in law and community service. Although some church members did not agree with *Bringing Them Home* and Wilson's persistent calls after the release of the report for the church to become involved in the reparation process, there was little criticism in the report of the church's role in the removal process. However, some church members believed there should have been no criticism at all, because some 'good church members', some alive but many dead, had their reputation unfairly damaged. But *Bringing Them Home* was overwhelming well received within the church. Wilson's reputation was further enhanced, as reflected by Western Australia's synod's nomination of him as an outstanding Western Australian worthy of recognition with a pavement plaque in St Georges Terrace, Perth.

The bronze lettering plaque tradition began in 1979 as part of the 150th anniversary of European colonial settlement in the Swan River district. Each plaque contains a year and a name of a famous Western Australian. The synod suggested 1988, when Wilson was installed the national president of the Uniting Church of Australia. However, Wilson's plaque is dated 1986, at a time when he was still a justice of the High Court. In his modest way, Wilson remarked he was honoured to receive this award, and 'now people could step on him'.

He continued to talk about the 'stolen generations' in church forums. In contrast to his constant and continual refusal to acknowledge that his deep religious conviction had any influence on his role as a prosecutor, Crown advocate, or High Court justice, Wilson openly admitted that he used *Bringing Them Home* as 'a vehicle for recognizing God's moments in the life of the inquiry and the subsequent controversies that have surrounded it'.[69] At the Victorian synod of the Uniting Church in September 2000, Wilson made a passionate speech on this subject. In it he said:

> The first demonstration of God alive and at work in the world in relation to the stolen generations is the age-old battle for truth, the battle between good and evil, between truth and falsehood.[70]

He summarised the criticisms made of *Bringing Them Home*, and stated that the inquiry was not asked to decide whether or not children had been forcibly removed. The Commonwealth government, under prime minister Keating, took that as a given, as reflected in the inquiry's first terms of reference.

He then referred to the 1994 Darwin conference that brought together many Aborigines who, when children, had been removed. Wilson noted the presence at the conference of Aboriginal affairs minister Robert Tickner. Wilson said that Tickner had heard the stories, and that '[t]he mark of God's activity in the world was that those stories cut him to the heart. And he promised a national inquiry.'[71]

With his voice reverberating throughout the hall, and with a passion similar to his 1950s and 1960s prosecuting, Wilson defended the truth of the report. He wanted all Australians to read it with 'an open mind' and 'an open heart':

> *Bringing Them Home* is a truth report. It's the report of a truth commission. And this battleground of truth against falsehood, I believe, is a battleground of the spirit. True, we didn't cross-examine members of the stolen generations with their stories. We couldn't because of the circumstances of the telling.[72]

Some may see this unquestioning belief in the stories as reflective of Wilson having become a zealot for the 'stolen generations'. He noted the courage of the Aborigines telling their stories, and how the inquiry would go into private session to hear them. For example, he said on one occasion:

> We shut the door, turned on the tape and waited for her story. There were no words. It wasn't until tears were coursing down this ebony black face that the words would come.
>
> She had been four years old, her sister six years old. They had been sent from the Territory to Ballarat and fostered out.
>
> She said to me in words that are engraven on my heart, 'But why couldn't they have put us together? They put me in one home and they put my big sister in another home. Now, that home took two children so they could have put me with my big sister. Why didn't they?'
>
> These words were wrenching up memories of 30, 40 years ago, of the tragedy of two little girls separated not only from their communities and extended family, and possibly from their parents, but from each other.
>
> The wonderful thing was, tear-stained face and all, after we'd had an hour together she put a wan smile on her face as she walked out, and said, 'I feel better.'[73]

Wilson did acknowledge that some of the stories may not have been true in every detail. However, there was no suggestion, Wilson maintained, that 'these stories are deliberate untruths'. He strongly disagreed with the Howard's view that the inquiry was dealing with history that was essentially benign. Rather, Wilson said, the effects of separation were a contemporary issue, and he and other commissioners 'felt we were being given a precious trust to tell their stories, until all Australians had heard them'.[74]

He strongly argued for the need to listen and the need to say 'sorry', which he saw as signs of the kingdom of heaven. He believed that the recommendations contained within *Bringing Them Home* were a way to healing and reconciliation, marks of that kingdom: 'They are signposts pointing to the presence of a living God at work in his world.'[75]

Towards the end of his speech Wilson said: 'I cannot rest, because of this sense of trust, to continue to advocate for these people as long as I have breath.'[76]

However, he did not hold much hope that the politicians would provide leadership on the reparations or reconciliation issue. He believed that the commitment for reparations, healing and reconciliation would be through the movement of Holy Spirit, and would come from the Australian people. A people's movement would make governments listen and provide leadership on the unfinished journey of reconciliation.

For Wilson, unity, inclusiveness, justice and equity were marks of the kingdom and presence of God living and working in his world. He concluded the speech with the following words:

> I believe that in the preparation of the report and its publication and its reception by the people of Australia, God has been at work leaving His mark of the kingdom on this land.[77]

Wilson steadfastly refused to concede that his fearless prosecuting style was influenced by a religious conviction that he was on the right side (although he did believe he was on the right side, but not because of a religious conviction), or to believe that a judge should be influenced by their religious faith. However, he saw no problem in making such a connection when it came to the inquiry, and the subsequent advocating of *Bringing Them Home*.

This life-changing experience, this sense of the burden of trust and the signs of the kingdom relentlessly drove him to work hard. It drove him to travel around the state of Western Australia and across the continent to attend meeting after meeting in community halls and churches, to talk to politicians, appear before Senate committees and on television and radio and write to newspapers, at all times pushing the demands for reparations and the truthfulness of *Bringing Them Home*, while enduring personal attacks.

It was tiring work for a man in his late seventies, even an energetic and fit man like Wilson. Leila and the Wilson children, who were proud of Wilson's involvement with the inquiry and *Bringing Them Home*, noticed the toll it was taking on him. However, Wilson continued to push himself. In May 2001, while doing his weekly five-hour voluntary stint at the local Canning Bridge meals on wheels kitchen, he felt dizzy and fell. He had had a minor stroke.

Wilson's doctor instructed him to slow his pace a bit, at least for the short term. But within weeks he was again answering media questions about *Bringing Them Home*, this time from the comfort of his home, where the interviewer, Patrick Carlyon of the *Bulletin* magazine, noticed Wilson's trembling fingers. Again, Wilson defended the inquiry's methodology, his role and the truth of the report.

To the great surprise of Carlyon, Wilson had changed on the use of the term 'genocide'. While he was not retreating, he did believe it sidetracked the debate and acceptance of the report by the Commonwealth government. He acknowledged that the best evidence in regard to the removal policy being genocide was in the 1930s, before the term had gained common usage in international treaty law. Wilson said:

> No one challenges that dreadful consequences followed these [removal] policies. Once you latch onto the term 'genocide' you're arguing about the intent and we should never have used it...
>
> It gave the government an out because the first thing they could do was to reject the report on its finding of 'genocide' and that enabled it [the Howard government] to come out fighting...If there hadn't been that finding then what would they have had to complain about, to criticise?[78]

The front page of the *Bulletin* edition with the article of Carlyon's interview with Wilson contained a photograph of a suited Wilson and the words: 'It was a mistake to use the word genocide.' The words were attributed to 'Sir Ronald Wilson', and were followed with the caption: 'Second thoughts on the Stolen Generation.'

The *Bulletin* article attracted considerable discussion in the media and by some in government. The defenders of Wilson and the report argued that this was not an admission on the incorrectness of using the term 'genocide', but only that its usage was politically unhelpful. Detractors of Wilson and the report latched onto Wilson's admission as further proof of the mistakes in the report, and Wilson's lack of objectivity when heading the inquiry.

One of those detractors, prime minister Howard, was asked in a radio interview with Melbourne Radio 3AW's Neil Mitchell, on 8 June 2001: 'Did you know that Sir Ronald Wilson also in the *Bulletin* this week seemed to be regretting the use of the word genocide in the *Bringing Them Home* report?' Howard, who was confronting criticism at the time from Wilson over the Commonwealth government's treatment of asylum seekers replied:

> Well he may. It was historically untrue and quite provocative to have used that word. And the use of that word has in my opinion dangerously I think compromised that whole debate. I didn't think that report was filled with scholarship and the use of the word genocide was I guess a metaphor for the lack of scholarship in the report.[79]

Wilson did not agree. Rather, he believed that Howard had failed in providing national leadership on the 'healing process' and reconciliation. As far as Wilson was concerned, 'My conscience is clear.'[80]

16

Serious Retirement and the Man

I am content to leave this life. I mean I am ready to die today or tomorrow. My life has had a great sense of privilege that I have had such a good life and comparatively little pain and sorrow in it but I also, perhaps wrongly, have this sense I've done my bit [laughter]. There is a sense of completion coming into my experience.

Just a month after the publication of the *Bulletin* article, and still suffering the effects of his minor stroke, Wilson was on stage at the Adelaide Town Hall. It was the evening of 12 July 2001, the first day of the three-day Adelaide Festival of Ideas.

Wilson was joined on stage by four other speakers: Rick Farley, former executive director of the National Farmers Federation, and member of the Council for Aboriginal Reconciliation;[1] Jackie Huggins of the Bidjara people from central Queensland and Birri-Gubba Juru people from north Queensland, an historian and author, and one of the 'stolen generations'; Mbulelo Mzmane, a South African writer and scholar, and former 'freedom fighter' against the apartheid regime in his country; and Jacob Rumbiak, a West Papuan educationalist and activist, who spent ten years in an Indonesian prison before being cleared of subversion charges.

The topic for the session, which was chaired by renowned media commentator Phillip Adams, was 'RIP: Reconciliation in Paralysis?' The question mark was added at Wilson's request, as he thought it would provide him with more scope to discuss the topic.

In introducing Wilson, Adams remarked about the wreckage of reconciliation, and noted that the term 'stolen generations' had found its way into the *Australian Oxford Dictionary*. He said he had never known of a more ugly moment than in the lead-up to the release of *Bringing Them Home*, when an attempt was made to tarnish the report and attack Wilson.

Wilson commenced speaking in his usual soft manner. Now his voice was affected by his stroke, which also made his hand tremble.

He recalled how the 339th recommendation of the Commission's report mentioned reconciliation, and how within four months of the release of the report in 1991, the governor-general had signed into law the *Council for Aboriginal Reconciliation Act* 1991 (Cwlth). He spoke about the council's first weekend meeting, when Pat Dodson was the inaugural chair and Wilson deputy, when the twenty-five members discussed why they had accepted being on the council and their hopes for it. They formulated a vision of a united Australia, with respect for the land and values of Aboriginal heritage and providing justice and equity for all. They also came up with a goal—that all Australians would acknowledge the reconciliation vision by 2001, the centenary of Australian federation.

Wilson also talked about what he called the 'miracle year'—the year 2000. He referred to 'Corroboree 2000', which included a concert for 2000 people at the Sydney Opera House on 27 May 2000 (the anniversary of the 1967 referendum). It was there that the Council for Aboriginal Reconciliation handed over to the Commonwealth government the document of reconciliation. Among other things, the document included draft legislation that recognised the unique position of Aborigines in Australian society (as the first peoples of Australia) and set out the process of reconciliation, including a series of reconciliation confessions.

The day after the Sydney Opera house event there was the 'Reconciliation Walk' across the Sydney Harbour Bridge, in which approximately 300,000 people participated, including the federal treasurer, Peter Costello, but not prime minister John Howard. Wilson was also there. Similar, but smaller, walks occurred simultaneously in other capital cities. The most spectacular event of that extraordinary year was the Sydney Olympic Games at which,

Wilson said, the Australian public accepted the significance of the Aboriginal involvement in the opening ceremony.

However, Wilson knew more was needed than the attitudinal change that had emerged throughout that 'miracle year' of 2000. There needed to be a commitment to outcomes and a course of action. Unfortunately, he could see no evidence of national leadership. The Commonwealth government would not support the Council for Aboriginal Reconciliation's draft legislation, and it stalled in the Senate after Australian Democrats' Senator Aidan Ridgeway introduced it as a Private Member's Bill. There was a people's movement for reconciliation through local reconciliation groups. There needed to be more of these groups.

Wilson moved on to talk about the 'stolen generations' inquiry and *Bringing Them Home*. He was heartened by Australians' response to the report, which revealed the actual words told by those removed from their families, with two-thirds under the age of five when separated.

He told the audience, as he had told others, of the profound impact of listening to the stories, of how the experience had changed him, and of how he felt he had been given a trust by the storytellers.

Wilson raised the issue of an apology. He said that one of the most telling things of the inquiry was that, after the storytelling, many storytellers asked why they were removed from family, and indicated that they wanted governments to say 'sorry'.

The word 'sorry' raised emotions within Wilson. His quiet voice was replaced by a firmer and louder delivery. He commented that saying 'sorry' was not an admission of guilt, as the Commonwealth government had argued. Rather, an apology was an 'expression of solidarity with the person who had suffered'. He said when one attended a funeral and said sorry to the family of the deceased, one was not admitting responsibility for the death. One was identifying with the sufferer. The audience loudly applauded. Wilson added: 'Sorry is a heart word and directed to healing the suffering. However, to be genuine, an apology must be followed by action.'

Wilson acknowledged what he considered to be some positive Commonwealth government responses. He pointed to the reserving of land on the banks of Lake Burley Griffin for a remembrance of reconciliation, and support for the new independent body called Reconciliation Australia, which replaced the Council for Aboriginal Reconciliation in December 2000. However, Wilson wondered why the Howard government had made the Aboriginal affairs portfolio 'part time'? Why was it joined to the very large and complex immigration portfolio? Were the first peoples of Australia to be viewed on the same level as immigrants to this country?

In response to Howard's call for practical rather than symbolic reconciliation, Wilson said both were needed. It was not a case of one or the other. There was a need for ceremony and practical measures, what Wilson called 'a heart and intellectual response'. Wilson also said that, while not being critical of Aboriginal leaders, he agreed with Hal Wooten, former judge of the Federal Court and RCADIC commissioner, that Aboriginal people had to take more responsibility for the abuse and violence that was occurring in Aboriginal communities.

Returning to the session's title, he said that national leadership had failed the reconciliation process. This brought more applause from the audience. He quickly added that the community would protect the process from rigor mortis. He thought that maybe, rather than 'paralysis' of the reconciliation process, a better word would be 'pause'. This was, Wilson said, because a yearning for justice was part of being human. With his voice rising again, he said that this would eventually lead to national leadership of the process. He concluded: 'The spirit of reconciliation cannot and will not be denied for ever.'

After a lengthy and enthusiastic applause, Adams thanked Wilson, and said that he 'had never heard a better speech in his [Adams'] life in Australian politics.'

Wilson's defiant conclusion was a mark of his dedication to the reconciliation process, and particularly the demands for reparations for the 'stolen generations'. However, his failing health and advancing years—he would be seventy-nine on 23 August 2001—meant he finally had to take retirement seriously.

He did not become a recluse. Rather, he was involved in several organisations, such as the Bringing Them Home Trust and PWD, and occasionally guest lectured at Murdoch's school of law, where he defended his decisions in *Koowarta* and *Mabo (No 1)*. To him they were, as a matter of law, the correct decisions, although he wished he could have decided differently.

On 12 March 2002, he re-entered the public debate over the erroneous and damaging allegations made in the Senate by Senator Bill Heffernan that Justice Michael Kirby of the High Court had used the services of a

Commonwealth car and driver to solicit young male prostitutes. Wilson went on ABC television to express his concerns over the publication of such unsubstantiated claims. Kirby was very grateful. Speaking of Wilson's television appearance, Kirby remarked:

> ...when, in a dark moment, I was attacked in Federal Parliament he went on the television that night. He did so when most official voices (and virtually all judicial voices) were silent. He did so to express his sense of grave disquiet about the way in which the matter had been raised without any notice, contrary to the rules of the Parliament and contrary to conventions going back hundreds of years. So he is a person of sterling integrity.

Initially, Wilson did not find it easy to take retirement seriously. He had been 'formally retired' since he resigned from the High Court in 1989. He considered his busy 1990s the most significant part of his life:

> Prior to my formal retirement my whole life was governed by a conventional legal career and the appointment to the Human Rights Commission enabled me to become an advocate for the dignity of every member of the human race. And I have also been able to advocate for the betterment of people in third world conditions through my four years as President of the Australian Council for Overseas Aid.

With his resignation from the Australian Council for Overseas Aid in 2001, Wilson thought it was at last time to really 'retire'. Although he liked the idea of declining further civic and community duties and activities, and being able to 'just go for walks along the river in the morning and read and doze in the afternoons', he wondered if he was 'lacking responsibility' if he did not 'continue to look for ways in which to make a contribution to society'.

His body was deteriorating. In early 2003 he abandoned his voluntary meals on wheels work, 'because I got tired of standing on my feet for five hours straight.' He also politely refused most invitations to attend conferences or public meetings.

Enjoying his retirement meant staying in bed to around 8 a.m., listening to ABC radio over breakfast, then walking around the Swan River for about an hour. No more jogging; instead, a brisk walk. The river had a 'stilling peaceful effect'; it was a major source of relaxation. He often spontaneously prayed on these daily walks 'because I am stimulated by the beauty and the river and it lifts one's spirit and you tend to meditate a bit while walking'.

Then back home, sitting outside in the sun to read the newspapers and a few magazines from various organisations he had been or was still associated with. After lunch he would be ready to check his emails and read some more before dinner. After washing the dishes, he would sit down with Leila to watch ABC TV's 7 p.m. news, followed by the *7.30 Report*. Wilson wouldn't watch much television after that. He enjoyed the occasional documentary, and always tried to tune into the ABC's *Four Corners*. Usually he was in bed by 9.30 p.m. Occasionally he would take a book or magazine to bed, but most nights he was content to just lie there until he dozed off to sleep.

Of course, he enjoyed having family over for dinner. Most weeks, he and Leila would visit their youngest daughter Robyn, who lived in a nearby suburb, to enjoy a meal with her, her husband Jeffery, and their four boys. After dinner they would play bridge, with Wilson displaying a keen competitive streak, perhaps not unlike a prosecutor.

In addition to Robyn's four children, there were Helen's two daughters, Ian's son and Bruce's two daughters from his first marriage. Bruce divorced Kerry in 2000 and remarried in 2003 to Robyn Dale, who instantly brought four children to the family, and therefore another four grandchildren for Leila and Wilson. In 2005, Geoff became engaged to Ahlia Harris, who had two children from a previous marriage.[2] Leila and Wilson loved spending time with all the grandchildren and engaging in friendly argument on a number of issues. Four of the grandchildren, Allyson, Lynette, Michael and Emily, followed in the footsteps of their famous 'papa' by studying law.[3]

Wilson felt he was very privileged to have five children, to see them mature into adults with a sense of justice and community service. Some of the children participated in religious and church services in their adulthood, but apart from Robyn, the children's religious convictions are not as strong as that of their parents.[4] Speaking of his children in 1994, Wilson said: 'We've been blessed with family, and by and large, although they've given us our concerns and anxieties (and still do), they've been an enormous blessing.'[5] Wilson and Leila wanted their children to be happy, but also to contribute to society.

The importance Wilson and Leila placed on 'good deeds' was well known to many of those who came in contact with them. Sir Daryl Dawson recalled a time when his wife Lady Lou Dawson said to Wilson and Leila that Robyn was a beautiful girl with beautiful eyes. Wilson replied: 'Well that is not important. We don't go on about those things. It is what you do and what you are that is important. Not that you are beautiful.'

The children had gone into different fields of work. Bruce is a professor of sociology at the Royal Melbourne Institute of Technology. Helen, because of failing health, retired from teaching. Geoff has had a varied career in the public service (including a time as welfare officer in Kalgoorlie) and private sector, and is currently working at one of his father's former workplaces, the Western Australian Supreme Court, as a communications and technology officer. Robyn, a former nurse, became a full-time homemaker, and more recently, a youth counsellor with her local Baptist Church. Ian, having completed a PhD on political violence in Indonesia, is a research fellow at the Asia Research Centre, Murdoch University.

Wilson's marriage to Leila was happy, built on mutual respect and support. But while Leila considers Wilson to have been a dedicated husband and father, she always lived with the warning he had given her when he proposed marriage: she and family came third in priority. First was his faith and second was his public duty. Leila believes that their life together followed those priorities. Even so, it didn't detract from Wilson's dedication to being a good husband and father.

In a 1994 interview, when talking about why he had a happy marriage, he said he was blessed to have five children and a wife who was a homemaker who carried extra burdens in his absence from home, and with whom he shared common interests. At his swearing-in ceremony to the High Court in 1979, Wilson acknowledged the unwavering support Leila had provided to him and the family and without that support he could not 'have done what I have done.'[6]

In fact, Leila had been the rock on which the family had survived and grown. While Wilson was a devoted father when home, the difficulty for Leila was that he was away so often. This did create some tension between husband and wife, particularly as she had to deal with the sicknesses and injuries when Wilson was away. Any tension that did arise between the two never developed into an argument. Wilson just refused to argue with Leila. This frustrated and annoyed her. Sometimes she wanted to have a good oldfashioned domestic argument to clear the air. Wilson point blank refused to do so. While it made her angrier, it never lingered. In later years, she commented:

> That was just the way he was. Maybe it was different in his workplace, where he would argue his point, but with me he would not argue. Ron seemed to be able to always stay under control.

Leila has an independent spirit, and pursued several charitable and voluntary activities, including being on the board of Ngala Mothercraft Centre and state president of Australian Churchwoman. Because Ian came into the household more than a decade after Geoff was born, Leila had a long duration (thirty years) serving in the Scotch College canteen and clothes shop. She enjoyed it, especially because it kept her in contact with younger mothers.

In his 1994 interview for the Battye Library Oral History Project, Wilson cited another reason for his successful marriage, referring to a Ceylonese man named Gerald Cooray, whom he had met at a church conference in 1950 and become close friends with:

> [W]e often discuss things about life in general, and one discussion I can remember we discussed our attitude to marriage from our respective cultures' point of view. He said to me, 'The difference between your culture and mine is that in our culture we love the girl we marry,' and that had behind it the whole system of arranged marriages. 'We love the girl we marry whereas in your culture you marry the girl you love,' and it's that degree of acceptance that typified his culture, which I think I've imported into my own lifestyle and acceptance of marriage. It doesn't mean that I love Leila any the less but it does mean that I accept that fact that I'm married, and for me, however fed up I might get at home sometimes, there's no question of pulling the plug because I'm married.[7]

Leila did not read the transcript of the 1994 interview until after Wilson died. Around that time, while clearing Wilson's study, she found Wilson's 1944 correspondence with Mariele Kuhn while he was serving in the RAF in England. Wilson wrote about his reserved nature: 'Maybe I have to really fall in love with someone before I shall be able to gain complete freedom in all my relationships.'[8] Leila wondered if Wilson ever did fully open himself up to her, and about the implications attached to that.

After reading the 1994 interview and other material about her husband, Leila remarked:

> The more and more I read about my husband the less I think I knew him. In many respects he was a secretive man, keeping many of his thoughts to himself. He seemed to live life in compartments. Once one task was completed, he closed the door on that and moved on to the next challenge and so on.

She loved him and had a happy marriage. There were difficult times, and the frequency of Wilson's absence from home placed additional demands on her, particularly with raising the children. Leila viewed Wilson as a devoted husband and father who looked to the good things in people.

Wilson had a reserved nature. Indeed, he remarked: 'On reflection, I would agree that I am not a particularly gregarious person. Very often, when in a group I am quite content to listen to the conversation without contributing to it.'

He did not form close friendships easily. Most of his friends came from the church scene:

> I have close friends through the church. We did things together, mostly associated with affairs of the church particularly when I was in Nedlands, and I left there in '89. So it was in that earlier period. But now there would not be any close friends that I would enjoy their company just for the sake of being with them and chatting and sharing confidences and things of that kind. From time to time I have regretted a sense of loneliness I think by reason of that fact.

Mostly, Wilson would focus on the job at hand. With that went a sense of detachment from things going on around him that were superfluous to the current task. He did not inquire into these 'superfluous' things; he was not that curious. For example, in the early 1960s, he did not become involved in the churches' opposition to the death penalty. He just did his job of prosecuting and remained detached from the end result. He remained detached from student politics at university and, even though he was a senior law officer for the Crown, oversaw the management committee at Sister Kate's Children's Home and was a member of a number of Aboriginal 'support groups', he had no idea that there was such a thing as a state government policy of child removals from families until the 'stolen generations' inquiry.

Although reserved and detached, he was an engaging individual, well liked, and indeed adored by many who worked with him. At social gatherings, while he did not crave the spotlight, people gravitated towards him. He had, as remarked by Lady Lou Dawson, 'star quality, charisma'.

Wilson had the ability to bring people together and to negotiate consensus among people with differing views. However, he had firm views of his own, and sometimes used his status to ensure they prevailed. He also was mindful to allow an airing of other views. He was caring of others. He displayed genuine interest in the lives of those who worked with and for him.

Wilson was keenly interested and committed to helping those less fortunate. This is why he relished his job as HREOC president, and why he was involved in community and advocacy groups. He strove to do the best job possible to help people facing discrimination or needing help. He saw it as part of his civic duty, reflecting his sense of justice for his fellow human being. To him it was the epitome of being a Christian: not to be concerned about oneself but to do good community deeds. This belief and commitment drove Wilson to give himself to many causes and organisations, and personally to live a simple life 'so others may simply live'. He never thought, as a former High Court justice or a knight of the realm, that he should be treated differently to others. That is why he didn't like being referred to as 'Sir', and why he kept saying to people, 'Just call me Ron.'

Although Wilson tackled every task zealously, and often passionately, the zeal and passion ended with the job. All that changed when he became involved with the 'stolen generations' inquiry. He had described himself as being 'fairly controlled' emotionally, but:

> I have probably learnt to show a bit more emotion through the national inquiry…and I am not averse to giving them [members of the stolen generations] a hug when the opportunity arises and that kind of thing, but subject to that, most of my emotions would certainly have been reserved within the family.

It is true that after his 1991 appointment to HREOC, Wilson became more and more outspoken on human rights and justice issues, but it was not until being involved in the 'stolen generations' inquiry that Wilson, as he said, underwent a 'life-changing experience'. Wilson opened his heart to the members of the 'stolen generations', who trusted him with their stories, and he was determined to share these stories with other Australians and to advocate for reparations, regardless of the effect it may have on the reputation of the commission or himself.

It was a religious experience. Wilson, the man who had constantly denied that his deep religious faith affected him as a Crown lawyer or High Court justice, believed that his championing of *Bringing Them Home* and the calls for reparations for the 'stolen generations' were driven by his deep religious commitment. He said that the report and its reception by the Australian public were signs of the work of God.

What are Wilson's impacts on the legal history of Australia, and on Australian society? In Western Australia he made changes to criminal prosecution that had reverberations into the twenty-first century. He brought a new level of professionalism and confidence to the Western Australian Crown Law Department. His professional career had many firsts, including being the first High Court justice from Western Australia, where he decided important constitutional and other cases and wrote 'well-crafted' judgements. He was often in the minority, particularly in matters of the division of Commonwealth–state legislative powers.

However, Wilson's mark on the law and society was much greater than just orthodox 'measurable' legal achievements. Justice Michael Kirby said:

> I think his [Wilson's] great contribution is that he showed how a highly orthodox, conservative lawyer can grow up. How he can grow out of the cocoon, can expand his mind in harmony with his heart and with the sense of spirituality in which he was raised.

Kirby went on to indicate how many lawyers who were pillars of their church and prayed to God were 'distinctly unkind to disadvantaged people' and 'blind to injustices to minorities...Most people of that ilk never grow up. They never see the injustices. To the end of their life they don't see contradictions.'

Wilson was a significant person in his church, and his contributions to the relatively new Uniting Church were of major importance. Through his role as president of the Uniting Church of Australia he played an integral part in seeking a greater role for the laity in the church, for the status of Aborigines in the church and for the church's position in relation to reconciliation and matters of human rights and justice.

Kirby opined that Wilson did 'grow up,' although '[i]t was too late to affect his decisions in the High Court'. He became a champion of the disadvantaged, and it was the capacity to change that Kirby most admired. He thinks this was unusual for a lawyer of his generation, background and training. Kirby deplored the fact that this 'blossoming' following Wilson's High Court days led to some 'disparaging comments', which he believed were unjustified and not 'far short of contempt'. For Kirby, 'Sir Ronald's life is a marvellous and unusual story.' He added:

> Indeed, it is a life that Ingmar Bergman would have made a wonderful film out of. It would have been a film after the manner of *Wild Strawberries* (1957). It would be a man who had all the honours of the world, but looked into his soul, and found the need for something more. I believe that the desire to do this was planted by his early life and by his spiritualism and Christianity…

It is the 'stolen generations' inquiry for which Wilson will be best remembered, more so for those members of the community not intimately connected to the legal profession or system. The inquiry report, *Bringing Them Home*, was a catalyst for a major political and community debate in Australia, and the report retains a presence in the nation's consciousness. The report was, and remains, an important document in the continuing debate over justice, reconciliation and public policy in relation to the first peoples of the continent.

The report has particular relevance to the contemporary focus on abuse of children in Aboriginal communities. Some critics of the report have argued that it has stymied official government or parliamentary action in removing Aboriginal children from dangerous home environments. Others would say the report is a timely reminder that whatever solution is proposed, even if removal from family and communities is the only option, at least in the short term, governments must be mindful of the need to place these children in environs where they can still retain their Aboriginality while they are protected from further abuse.

Wilson celebrated his eightieth birthday on the 23 August 2002. He was in high spirits as he enjoyed a small gathering of 'Murdoch friends' for afternoon tea in the office of the Vice-Chancellor of Murdoch University, Professor John Yovich; and particularly enjoyed the later celebrations with his family.

The ageing process was catching up with him. Over the next couple of years he suffered from a series of minor strokes. After each stroke, his memory became a little less acute and the tremor in his hands a bit more pronounced. Theo Mackay, of the Anglican Social Responsibilities Commission and a colleague of Wilson's on the Bringing Them Home Trust, remarked that he couldn't help but notice that once Wilson had his first couple of strokes 'his processes started to slow down and occasionally he just didn't keep up in meetings, and the other side effect of his strokes was his handwriting became very jittery'.[9]

In July 2004, after another stroke, he was hospitalised for a week while a series of tests was performed. It was discovered that two parathyroid glands were not functioning properly. He returned to hospital for a few days in December 2004 for an operation on those glands.

Not long after, Wilson returned to his daily walks, but he moved slower. He continued to reject most invitations to events. He still attended some, including the main oration of Law Week in May, the Ronald Wilson lecture, which had been established in 1990 in his honour.[10] Since his eightieth birthday, Leila noticed a marked deterioration in Wilson's keenness to be involved in community events or engage in dialogue with people outside the family. Not that he became a recluse, as he still was involved in some, church, community and university events, but the energetic Wilson was replaced by a man who, in Leila's words, 'was preparing to die'.

On 6 July 2005, Wilson was enjoying lunch with Leila and grandson Peter Christie. Peter asked Wilson a question. He did not respond. He seemed to go blank, with Leila describing it as 'being lost for fifteen minutes'. On the morning of 8 July, Wilson found it difficult to get out of bed. He could not stand up. Leila took him to St John of God Hospital in Murdoch. He was diagnosed as having had a trans ischemic attack (TIA), both at lunch time on the 6 July and on the morning of 8 July. A TIA is a warning that a stroke may be coming. The medical staff told Wilson and Leila that it may be a good idea for him to remain in hospital for the weekend. Wilson didn't want that. He decided to go home.

On the morning of 15 July, Wilson and Leila visited Wilson's doctor. The doctor measured Wilson's blood pressure—a low reading. Leila had another appointment to attend to. Wilson decided to catch a taxi back home. Leila telephoned home at noon. There was no answer. She was not unduly worried. She thought Wilson was probably having a nap. Leila tried again at 12.30 p.m. Again no answer. Now she was worried.

She returned home to find Wilson in the kitchen, the place in the home he considered himself to be in charge of after meals. He was standing, but bent over at the sink with a cup of tea nearby. He had been dead since late morning.

Death held no fear for the man born nearly eight-three years earlier in the port town of Geraldton. In 2003 he had remarked:

> I am content to leave this life. I mean I am ready to die today or tomorrow. My life has had a great sense of privilege that I have had such a good life and comparatively little pain and sorrow in it but I also, perhaps wrongly, have this sense I've done my bit [laughter]. There is a sense of completion coming into my experience.

Epilogue

I would like to think when I die there would have been more people to have cause to regret my passing or to thank God for my living than not…What is driving this feeling? Just the liking to be useful, or to have people thankful to me for whatever I have done or any way in which I have helped them.

Wilson died on 15 July 2005. Two days later, the Sunday evening news programs reported his death. Political and religious leaders paid tribute to him. The next day, the *West Australian* contained an article about his life under the headline 'Human Rights Fighter Dies' and the sub-headline 'Ronald Wilson was an outspoken and tireless supporter of the Stolen Generation.'[1] This article was accompanied by a photograph of Wilson in his 'Walking Together' sweater, standing between two female artists from the Kaltjiti community in South Australia. The national newspaper, the *Australian*, included a brief article under the headline 'Sir Ronald Remembered As a Man for All People',[2] and a feature article headlined 'Seeking Justice for All', which reflected on his passion and faith and championing of the underprivileged.[3] In an editorial, the *Australian* said that Wilson was a courageous and compassionate man who enlisted in the RAAF in World War II and served the community in many ways. The editorial said: 'Sir Ronald was a fine and distinguished Australian who will be sorely missed.' But it also said: 'By bringing a UN-sanctioned definition of "genocide" to bear on the stolen generations, Sir Ronald abandoned common sense, polarised the debate and alienated ordinary Australians.'[4]

That week's death notices in the *West Australian* contained numerous tributes to Wilson. They came from family members, politicians of all political persuasions, lawyers, academics, community organisations, the church, and from members of the general public who had met him personally or been touched by Wilson's championing of the disadvantaged and the 'stolen generations'. Recurring words used in the notices were 'a man of faith and conviction', 'justice', 'humility', 'passion' and 'integrity, honesty and courage'. His support for justice for Aboriginal people and for the 'stolen generations' were remembered.[5]

The premier of Western Australia, Dr Geoff Gallop, told the ABC News:

> Sir Ronald Wilson has made a very significant contribution to our way of life, the way we understand ourselves, he had a particular passion for Indigenous Australians and he backed [this] up with a great deal of courage...When it came to the stolen generation report Ronald Wilson looked beyond the statistics and went to the human reality of what had happened.

Gallop telephoned Leila and offered a state funeral. Leila declined the premier's offer. She indicated that it is not what Wilson would have wanted: 'He didn't like a fuss being made of him when alive and I know the same would be the case in death.' Also, Leila and the family wanted to control the funeral process, and they feared that if it became an official state funeral, they might have had to comply with certain protocols that may have clashed with their wishes.

A cremation ceremony was held on the morning of the 22 July 2005 at the main Perth metropolitan cemetery, Karrakatta. The chapel was crowded. Distinguished figures, such as the premier and the Chief Justice of the Western Australian Supreme Court, David Malcolm, sat with members of the public, including Aboriginal people and people in wheelchairs. John Button, the man Wilson had prosecuted in 1963 for the murder of his girlfriend, was there. Forty years later, the court held that Button's conviction was unsafe. Over time, Button's dislike of Wilson had given way to enormous respect for a 'fellow Christian' and for his advocacy of human rights. Button believed that Wilson's human rights advocacy was in part driven by guilt over his prosecuting days:

> I believe Wilson would have had some guilt at having been the person that successfully prosecuted some innocent people like me and Darryl Beamish and this drove him to do good deeds such as his human rights work.

Wilson did not have such guilt. He always believed and maintained he acted appropriately in all his prosecuting trials.

Button was 'genuinely saddened' by Wilson's death. He said, 'I knew I would regret it if I didn't attend the funeral. I wanted to pay my respects to a deeply Christian man who had after his prosecuting days, in his later life, done much good.'

Leading the casket into the Karrakatta chapel was Wilson's granddaughter Allyson. Six other grandchildren acted as pallbearers: Michael, Tim, Laura, Emily, Peter and Caleb. Some of the other grandchildren followed: Michaela, Alice, Daniel, Jack and Jalada. Three grandchildren were not there: Lynette was overseas, and Eythan and Ayesha were considered too young to be at the Karrakatta service.[6]

The service was led by Reverend Geoff Blyth, a former moderator of the Western Australian synod of the Uniting Church, whose service reinforced the unassuming nature of Wilson. Blyth acted as Wilson's chaplain during Wilson's reign as moderator of the Uniting Church in Western Australia.[7] On Leila's invitation, Wilson's former law student and Crown Law Department colleague, Justice Michael Murray, spoke of Wilson's impressive legal career, his doggedness and determination as an advocate and his encouragement of his work colleagues, particular the junior lawyers.[8]

The president of the Uniting Church of Australia, the Reverend Dr Dean Drayton, in a passionate eulogy spoke of Wilson's distinguished service to the church. He also referred to *Bringing Them Home*, how Wilson had endured unjustified personal attacks and how the Commonwealth government had 'turned its back on the report'. Drayton also said that he believed that history would record Wilson's fight for justice and for the 'stolen generations'.

Wilson's two youngest sons, Geoff and Ian, spoke of their father. Two of the grandchildren, Peter and Emily, had already read verses from the Bible and Allyson had read the poem 'Separation'.

Geoff talked about his father's modesty. Although each sibling held different views about their father, they all agreed he loved them. Geoff said:

> His legacy to us is manifold. My brothers and sisters and I all have a keen sense of social justice, and all have clear ideas of right and wrong. We do not always agree, but that too is dad's legacy, as he and Mum always taught us to think for ourselves, and blessed us with the ability to do so. We also find it hard to judge, because ironically perhaps, Dad never judged a person. He accepted everyone as they were, and attempted to understand him or her, and to empathise and to relate.

Ian said that he was lucky to be able to enter the Wilson family. He talked about the love his parents had for all their children. Ian said that his dad sought to understand his rebellion as a teenager, and that he was never judgemental. He concluded by describing his father as 'an amazing man', who was 'too amazing to be summed up in any eulogy'. Ian said that the family would miss their dad, 'but his character, personality, conviction and love for his family will continue to inspire us, humble us, and fill us with warmth and love throughout our lives'.

Aboriginal music was played, before Reverend Sealin Garlett, chairperson of the Uniting Aboriginal and Islander Christian Congress, concluded the eulogies and tributes. He thanked Wilson for 'showing respect' for Aboriginal culture and the injustices his people had suffered, and for seeking to rectify the wrongs of the past. Garlett thanked 'God for allowing a humble, gentle man to walk with us on our journey'.

The family placed flowers on the coffin. Wilson was cremated. Leila was happy with the service. She thought it was 'what he would have wanted'.

Another service was held in the afternoon at St Stephen's Uniting Church in Applecross, Wilson's local church. The family had planned for the morning service to be a celebration of his legal and public service. The afternoon service was to be more personal, with a greater involvement of the grandchildren.

Blyth again led the worship. He described how the unassuming, gracious man was well loved and looked up to with respect by people in the church and by many of the younger members of the congregation. He also noted that, although Wilson was a gentle man, he also was a man of strong principles and strength of character.

Wilson's son in-law Jeffery read a passage from Romans.

He was followed by Jill Tabart, the president of the Uniting Church of Australia (1994–97), who came from Tasmania for the service. She mentioned how Wilson had been encouraging to her, and spoke of his commitment to fighting injustices, particularly in relation to Aboriginal people.

Wilson's eldest son then took to the lectern. Bruce mentioned that because of his father's professional and church commitments he was often away from home. He wanted more of his father, and Wilson's absence from home made things difficult for his mother. However, when his father was home he was dedicated to the children. Bruce described his father as 'an ordinary man, made remarkable by his faith, and by his openness to learning', and that one of Wilson's major legacies he 'has left many people is his capacity for embracing difference, indeed, being excited by "otherness"'.

Bruce touched on his father's modesty, and how he never found it easy to talk about himself. The 'stolen generations' inquiry experience created a new awareness in his father. Listening to the stories told by Aboriginal people led to his father recognising 'the value of not having to stick to a schedule, nor to run the agenda, and that he learned things about himself, and about how to just "be" with people'. Bruce added that the grandchildren benefited most from this new awareness.

Following Bruce, Michael Christie spoke on behalf of the seventeen grandchildren. Michael, with all the other grandchildren, apart from Lynette behind him, said what they really appreciated was their grandfather's 'ability and willingness to spend time and participate doing the things kids like to do', such as kicking the football around, teaching them marching songs or telling them stories. Michael said:

> Papa's wonderful smile and laughter were a definite highlight and will be the picture in my memory of him for the rest of my life; it had a way of filling me with joy. And then there were his hugs that were something special from a man that couldn't contain his love and affection.

Michael mentioned how Wilson loved to play the devil's advocate to encourage a debate with the grandchildren. But he was not judgemental. He was prepared to listen and respected what they said. He added:

> We as his grandchildren did not see him as a man in terms of his career achievements or titles or position in society although they were known and respected. Rather we saw him as the man he was behind closed doors, the Papa we knew up close and personal. What we saw

> when we looked at Papa was absolute unconditional love, to look at the man was to look at love. The way he treated us and the way he acted personified love. His selflessness and tireless acts of sacrifice perhaps more greatly demonstrated this. I think he was the greatest dishwasher in the world, or at least the most experienced, not to mention a fine gravy stirrer.

Michael mentioned how his grandparents were always there when the grandchildren needed them. He remarked on his famous grandfather's humility. He concluded the eulogy by saying how much Papa loved his grandchildren, and how they all in returned loved and respected him. Michael said:

> He was our hero, our innocence, our rock and we are all much better people from knowing him. We were truly blessed to be his grandchildren and forever grateful for all the happy times and legacy he has placed in our hearts. It's been an absolute privilege to have him journey with us in our lives and we will miss him so much for the rest of our lives. We love you Papa; words cannot truly express how great you are.

In death as in life Wilson remained a figure of controversy. A day after he was cremated, the *Weekend Australian* published an article by columnist Christopher Pearson,[9] who had written many negative comments on Wilson and *Bringing Them Home*. Much of the article dealt with Wilson's tenure as a prosecutor, a part of Wilson's career that had attracted criticism. Pearson said that, while much had been said about Wilson's 'mildness, modesty and unassuming ways', he also had 'a persistent monomaniacal streak'. He referred to Wilson being called 'the Avenging Angel,' and he quoted Estelle Blackburn, author of *Broken Lives*,[10] the 1990s book that reignited the debate on John Button's innocence or guilt, who described Wilson as a 'very ambitious and over-zealous prosecutor at the time'.

Pearson wrote that Wilson's 'righteous indignation' was kept in check during his High Court days, but dominated his period as HREOC president. Pearson reported that Wilson had once said that during this period he had 'never felt better', and this had 'something to do with getting angry'. Pearson commented:

> It was an artless admission; the sort of thing you would expect only from someone with quite limited self-understanding. Plainly the burdens of judicial office and the presidency of the Assembly of the Uniting Church had taken their toll. What was keeping him going was afflatus and his regular fix of Old Testamental prophetic wrath. What routinely overwhelmed his judgment, in the HREOC years and afterwards, was seeing indigenous issues through a prism of rage.

Pearson then moved to the *Beamish* case, in which Wilson had been the prosecutor. Pearson referred to an article by Peter Ryan, former editor of Melbourne University Press, in the 2005 May edition of *Quadrant*.[11] Ryan's article dealt with the 1966 pamphlet of Professor Peter Brett[12] on the Darryl Beamish conviction for the murder of Jillian Brewer and the quashing of that conviction by the Western Australian Court of Criminal Appeal on 1 April 2005.

Pearson surmised that 'since Brett's book came out in 1966, Wilson was in a state of denial about irreparable wrong done to poor Beamish'. This is a surprising statement, considering that Pearson commenced his article by saying that there were two versions of the convention of speaking about the dead: one being to say only good about them (*de mortuis nil nisis bonum*) and the other being 'nothing but the truth' (*nil nisi verum*). Pearson's article does not attempt to follow the former, but his surmising or 'guess' on what Wilson felt about the *Beamish* case does not comply with the latter maxim either. Pearson never interviewed Wilson over his 'feelings' about the *Beamish* case.

And there was more: '[Wilson's] sermons and denunciations of whited sepulchres in the meantime were probably all the more passionate because, in his lucider moments, he knew that he was one himself.' However, Pearson provided no evidence or quote from Wilson to support his own 'sermonising' on Wilson's thoughts of the 'Beamish affair'.

Pearson repeated his previous criticisms of *Bringing Them Home* and Wilson, including the methodology, writing that the report 'was as ill-considered and counterproductive accusation as I can remember anyone in public life making during the past 30 years'. He added:

> The frisson this self-described 'voice of the voiceless' so obviously derived from reiterating the charge was sickening to watch. The report itself is a disgrace. Wilson abandoned the habits of a lifetime of careful weighing and

> testing of evidence in favour of the most shameless partisan kind of advocacy research. His use of sources was extremely loose and he repeatedly refused to hear evidence that ran counter to his prejudices, including testimony from people who believed that separation policies had worked to their advantage. Not surprisingly, the test cases based on the report's findings have collapsed under the weight of their implausibility when tried in court.

In conclusion, Pearson commented that probably the worst outcome or consequences of *Bringing Them Home* is that it

> has had the effect of dissuading many social workers and government departments from intervening in cases where removing abused part-Aboriginal children from dysfunctional communities was necessary, sometimes leaving them in mortal peril.

There is an argument to be made that the 'stolen generations' debate has resulted in a hesitancy on the part of child welfare authorities to act when the safety of an Aboriginal child is in question. This is an issue of contemporary relevance in light of the increased media focus during 2005 and 2006 on reported abuse and neglect of Aboriginal children, particularly in remote Aboriginal communities.[13]

The 15 May 2006 ABC TV *Lateline* program interviewed Alice Springs Crown prosecutor Nanette Rogers, who detailed incidences of terrible child abuse in Aboriginal communities. This reignited the debate about remote Aboriginal communities and Aboriginal child welfare.

A week after Pearson's column, Wilson Tuckey, the outspoken Western Australian Liberal member of the House of the Representatives, who had the nickname 'Ironbar' as a result of being convicted of assaulting an Aboriginal man with a length of steel cable in 1967 while a publican in Carnarvon, said that a 'posthumous apology' was 'owed' to public servants and churches. Tuckey said the removals were done because of genuine concerns for the children, and 'they have been "blackguarded" by the late Ronald Wilson and the "kangaroo court" of his inquiry into the so-called "stolen generations".'[14]

If he were alive, Wilson probably would not have been surprised by this criticism. Soon after the release of *Bringing Them Home*, Tuckey said the inquiry report lacked balance. His parliamentary colleague, Chris Gallus, a former opposition spokesperson for Aboriginal affairs, was reported to have asked Tuckey to display 'more sympathy in his response to the stolen children report'.[15] Speaking in 2003, Wilson said of Tuckey: 'I don't find him to really be constructive.'

While Wilson's stewardship of the 'stolen generations' inquiry continued to be criticised after his death, the plaudits also continued. On 22 March 2006, the Western Australian government announced the Sir Ronald Wilson Leadership Award, to be presented to a Western Australian 'for furthering social justice and advancing equality'. In announcing the award, citizenship and multicultural minister Margaret Quirk described Sir Ronald as 'one of Western Australia's most distinguished servants'. She added: 'His commitment to advancing the cause of indigenous people made him arguably without peer in this area.'[16]

At the annual Sir Ronald Wilson Lecture on 11 May 2006, Federal Court judge Robert Nicholson delivered a eulogy honouring Wilson's life and achievements.[17] Indeed, it was Nicholson who had suggested to the Francis Burt Law Education Centre that it sponsor a lecture focusing on 'community justice and law' and name it after Wilson. Not only was this because Wilson had been Western Australia's first High Court justice, but also, as Nicholson said at the eulogy, 'In reality there was very much more to be recognised…'

Nicholson acknowledged that Wilson 'was first and foremost a deeply committed Christian', which 'permeated his entire outlook and activities', and '[i]f there is one single element which explains and knits together his views, involvements and achievements it was his Christian view of what should be justice in the world'.[18]

Nicholson touched on Wilson's role as a crown prosecutor, and the 'contradiction' between the forceful prosecutor and the champion of human rights. He said:

> Those who knew him in this role described him as relentless in properly and professionally advancing the case of his client, the State of Western Australia. Some have found it difficult to reconcile the Ron of human rights fame with the Ron of prosecutorial fame. The answer is possibly that whatever Ron did, he did to the maximum of his capacity, sparing nothing in application and preparation. His nickname of the 'Avenging Angel' is evocative of both the goodness of the man as well as his total devotion to duty, whatever that duty might be. When the task was to secure a conviction and penalty, he went

> all out for that result. When the task was to defend human rights, the same man went all out for that result.

It is true that Wilson always undertook whatever role he had seriously and gave it all his attention. However, such an attitude opened him up to criticism, and created some perceived or actual tensions in his various roles and tasks during a long period of professional, community and religious service and commitment.

Nicholson's eulogy noted Wilson's love of advocacy, and how he was prepared to go 'to the heart of the issues' he was advocating, 'no matter how controversial or difficult they were'. None probably proved more controversial or difficult than the 'stolen generations' inquiry. Nicholson remarked that the inquiry 'brought to the fore all his personal talents, all his experience throughout his professional life and his beliefs as an individual', and how the 'report still challenges our nation'.

Nicholson concluded the eulogy by acknowledging Wilson's humility, talents, the respect he engendered and the significance of his life:

> We all know that Ron Wilson was a great Australian, a great Western Australian, a great member of the legal profession. He was one of us. He led us from humility and with talent. His memory is secure in our history and in the hearts of those who worked with him or observed him in his professional endeavours. It is fitting that this Lecture should continue its community purpose after his life but in accordance with the vast reach of his ideals. Vale Ron.

Such a eulogy should have satisfied Wilson's desire that more people than not regretted his departure from this life and that he had been useful to people.

In December 2006, Leila, her five children and some of the grandchildren gathered at the base of Bluff Knoll, which climbs to 1073 metres above sea level, and is part of the sweeping mountain landscape that makes up the Stirling Ranges, just north of the south-west coastal town of Albany. Bluff Knoll, called Bular Mial (many eyes) or Bula Mial (his eyes) by the local Aboriginal Nyoongar population, was Wilson's favourite location in Western Australia. He enjoyed hiking in the Stirling Ranges and the Porongurups, and had climbed to Bluff Knoll's summit. He loved the high he got from hiking, the beauty of the mountain peaks and spectacular cloud formations. As when walking on the banks of the Swan River near his home in Applecross, Wilson sometimes prayed as he admired nature's beauty and wonders.

There is no elaborate headstone at Karrakatta Cemetery to commemorate the legal and community service of the first High Court justice from Western Australia and human rights advocate. Wilson did not crave such honours. Rather, he had sought to lead a 'simple life' and help others as best he could. Wilson had lived what he called 'a fortunate life'.

Leila knew Wilson would consider himself fortunate to have his ashes sprinkled into the air at Bluff Knoll. And they were.

NOTES

1
The Boy from Geraldton

The main sources for this chapter are: interviews by the author with Wilson, Jim Wilson and Joan Tonkin; interviews with Wilson by Jane Fleming, Robert Meadows and Geraldine Byrne and Stuart Reid; and J. Margo, 'Darling Dynasty Keeps Its Mouth Shut and Pen Dry', *Sydney Morning Herald (Good Morning Weekend)*, 1 January 1983, p. 23.

1 Mahatma Gandhi first coined the axiom. Refer to L. Spearman, Sir Ronald Wilson and the High Court, unpublished supervised legal research paper, School of Law, Murdoch University, 2004, p. 12.

2 J. Margo, 'Darling Dynasty Keeps Its Mouth Shut and Pen Dry', *Sydney Morning Herald (Good Morning Weekend)*, 1 January 1983, p. 23. The account presented here in relation to the Darlings is largely taken from this article, and verified as far as memory and knowledge would allow, by Wilson and his brother Jim.

3 Gordon Darling retired from the board of BHP in 1986, and embarked on a life of philanthropic activism in the arts and the building of relationships with Asia. He served as the first chair of the National Gallery of Australia (1982–86).

4 J. Fleming, Interview with Wilson, Perth, December 1993.

5 S. Reid, Transcript of interview with Wilson, Battye Library, Perth, 30 November 1994, p. 208.

6 Based on interviews the author conducted with some of Wilson's High Court colleagues: Sir Anthony Mason, Sir Gerard Brennan, Sir Harry Gibbs, Sir William Deane and Sir Daryl Dawson. Dawson and Deane confirmed that Wilson had an inferiority complex when it came to his education, a complex they believed was not justified, as Wilson could hold his own with his colleagues.

7 C. M. H. Clark, *A History of Australia VI: The Old Dead Tree and the Young Tree Green 1916–1935*, Melbourne University Press, Melbourne, 1987, p. 322.

8 ibid., p. 326.

9 Fleming, Interview with Wilson, December 1993.

10 Reid, Transcript of interview with Wilson, 27 September 1994, p. 8.

11 ibid., p. 9.

12 Fleming, Interview with Wilson, December 1993.

13 R. Meadows and G. Byrne, Transcript of interview with Sir Ronald Wilson, Battye Library, Perth, November 1993, p. 1. An abbreviated version of this interview is published in *Brief*. Refer to 'From Basement to Bench: An Interview with Sir Ronald Wilson AC KBE', *Brief*, 1994, 21 (1), p. 11. Republished in 2005 as 'From Basement to Bench: An Interview with Sir Ronald Wilson, first published in *Brief* in February 1994', *Brief*, 2005, 32 (7), p. 6.

14 Reid, Transcript of interview with Wilson, 27 September 1994, p. 20.

15 For a detailed history of the Supreme Court of Western Australia, refer to G. Bolton and G. Byrne, *May It Please Your Honour: A History of the Supreme Court of Western Australia from 1861–2005*, Supreme Court of Western Australia, Perth, 2005.

16 J. Molony, *The Penguin Bicentennial History of Australia*, Penguin, Melbourne, 1987, p. 281.

17 Meadows and Byrne, Transcript of interview with Wilson, November 1993, p. 2.

18 ibid., p. 12.

19 Reid, Transcript of interview with Wilson, 27 September 1994, pp. 27–8.

2
Duty Calls

The main sources for this chapter are: interviews by the author with Wilson; interviews with Wilson by Stuart Reid, Robert Meadows and Geraldine Byrne; and correspondence between Wilson and M. Kuhn.

1 R. Meadows and G. Byrne, Transcript of interview with Wilson, Battye Library, Perth, November 1993, p. 3.

2 B. Galligan, 'World War II', in T. Blackshield, M. Coper and G. Williams (eds), *The Oxford Companion to the High Court of Australia*, Oxford University Press, South Melbourne, 2001, pp. 730–1.

3 Meadows and Byrne, Transcript of interview with Wilson, November 1993, p. 3.

4 Refer to J. M. Bennet, *Sir Archibald Burt: First Chief Justice of Western Australia, 1861–1879*, Federation Press, Leichhardt, 2002.

5 Meadows and Byrne, Transcript of interview with Wilson, November 1993, p. 5.

6 ibid., pp. 4–5.

7 R. Wilson, letter to Mariele Kuhn, 11 July 1944, Wilson's personal files.

8 R. Wilson, letter to Mariele Kuhn, 28 July 1944, Wilson's personal files.

9 S. Reid, Transcript of interview with Wilson, Battye Library, Perth, 27 September 1994, pp. 14–15.

10 ibid., 29 September 1994, p. 33.

11 R. Wilson, letter to Mariele Kuhn, 5 December 1945, Wilson's personal files.

3
A Lawyer or Padre?

The main sources for this chapter are: interviews by the author with Wilson, Leila Wilson, John Toohey, Ron Cannon and Peter Travers; interviews with Wilson by Margaret Robertson, Stuart Reid, Robert Meadows and Geraldine Byrne; F. Alexander, *Campus at Crawley*, F. W. Cheshire for University of Western Australia Press, Melbourne, 1963; and M. Dixon, *Looking Back: A Short History of the UWA Law School 1927-1992*, University of Western Australia Library, Crawley, 1992.

1 M. Robertson, Edited transcript of interview with Sir Ronald Wilson, Western Australian Bar Association Oral History Project, Perth, 19 December 2000, p. 2.

2 Australian Student Christian Movement, *The ASCM 1947*, Brown Prior Anderson, Melbourne, 1947, p. 1.

3 Wilson was extremely delighted with McCaughey's vice-regal appointment. He thought it fitting for a man of 'impeccable manners and integrity'.

4 It is not unusual for contemporary Australian law schools to have an annual first year intake of over 200 students.

5 Reid, Transcript of interview with Wilson, 29 September 1994, p. 36.

6 B. Hawke, *The Hawke Memoirs*, William Heinemann Australia, Melbourne, 1994, p. 12.

7 ibid., p. 21.

4
The Prosecutor

The main sources for this chapter are: interviews by the author with Wilson, Leila Wilson, Leopold Woods, Bart Kakulas, Paul Nichols, Owen Leitch, Peter Panegyres, Chief Justice David Malcolm, Judge Michael Murray, His Excellency Judge Kevin Parker, and Judge Hal Jackson; interviews with Wilson by Margaret Robertson, Stuart Reid, Robert Meadows and G. Byrne; interview with Leopold Woods by Stuart Reid; R. D. Wilson, Jury selection and service in Philadelphia: A description, comparison and evaluation, unpublished LLM dissertation, University of Pennsylvania Law School, 1957; N. Mattingley, The abolition of capital punishment in Western Australia, 1960–1984, unpublished honours thesis, History Program, Murdoch University, 1990; and M. Keefe, Wilson's legacy: Button, Beamish, Cooke 40 years on, unpublished supervised legal research paper, School of Law, Murdoch University, 2004.

1 G. Bolton and G. Byrne, *May It Please Your Honour: A History of the Supreme Court of Western Australia from 1861–2005*, Supreme Court of Western Australia, Perth, 2005, p. 200.

2 S. Reid, Transcript of interview with Sir Ronald Wilson, Battye Library, Perth, 29 September 1994, p. 56.

3 ibid., 14 October 1994, p. 79.

4 R. Meadows and G. Byrne, Transcript of interview with Wilson, Battye Library, Perth, November 1993, p. 8.

5 R. D. Wilson, Jury selection and service in Philadelphia: A description, comparison and evaluation, unpublished LLM dissertation, University of Pennsylvania Law School, 1957.

6 M. Lang, 'System Flawed: Expert', *West Australian*, 23 January 1995, p. 4.

7 However, note that in the Stuart Reid interview of 1994 Wilson commented that the jury system is a safeguard to the system: 'It's very protective of the trial process—that's when you have a verdict of a jury—and I don't think there's a lot in the procedures that could be improved.' Refer to Reid, Transcript of interview with Sir Ronald Wilson, 14 October 1994, p. 88.

8 Wilson, Jury selection and service in Philadelphia, p. 144.

9 S. Reid, Transcript of interview with Leopold Woods, Battye Library, Perth, 25 January 1996, p. 93.

10 ibid.

11 ibid., p. 94.

12 M. Keefe interview with Woods, in M. Keefe, Wilson's legacy: Button, Beamish, Cooke 40 years on, unpublished supervised legal research paper, School of Law, Murdoch University, 2004, pp. 9–10

13 Reid, Transcript of interview with Sir Ronald Wilson, 14 October 1994, p. 86.

14 N. Mattingley, The abolition of capital punishment in Western Australia, 1960–1984, unpublished honours thesis, History program, Murdoch University, 1990.

15 Bolton and Byrne, *May It Please Your Honour*, p. 216.

16 In both Western Australia and South Australia the last executions took place in 1964. The last execution in New South Wales was in 1940; Victoria, 1967; Queensland, 1913; Tasmania, 1946; and Northern Territory, 1952. There has never been an execution in the Australian Capital Territory. Refer to I. Potas and J. Walker, 'Capital Punishment', *Australian Institute of Criminology Trends and Issues in Crime and Criminal Justice*, Australian Institute of Criminology, Canberra, February 1987.

17 N. Mattingley, The abolition of capital punishment in Western Australia, 1960–1984, p. 33.

18 It would appear that the Catholic Church was not prominent in this campaign. In more recent times the Catholic Church has become a more visible opponent of capital punishment.

19 Reid, Transcript of interview with Leopold Woods, 30 January 1996, p. 108.

20 P. Conole, *Protect and Serve: A History of Policing in Western Australia*, Western Australian Police Service, Perth, 2002, pp. 294–5.

21 ibid., p. 295.

22 R. Wilson, 'Truth and Justice', *Australian Journal of Forensic Sciences*, 1983, 16, pp. 2, 13.

23 *Button v The Queen* [2002] WASCA 35 (25 February 2002); *Mickelberg v The Queen* [2004] WASCA 145 (2 July 2004); *Beamish v The Queen* [2005] WASCA 62 (1 April 2005); *Mallard v The Queen* [2005] HCA 68 (15 November 2005).

5
The Prosecutor's Trilogy

The main sources for this chapter and the next are: interviews with Wilson by the author, Margaret Robertson, Stuart Reid, and Robert Meadows and Geraldine Byrne; interviews by the author with Leopold Woods, Bart Kakulas, Owen Leitch (short contact by phone) and Chief Justice David Malcolm; P. Brett, *The Beamish Case*, Melbourne University Press, Melbourne, 1966; T. Winton, *Cloudstreet*, Viking, Camberwell, 1991; E. Blackburn, *Broken Lives*, Stellar Publishing, Claremont, 1998; R. Drewe, *The Shark Net*, Penguin, Camberwell, 2000; M. Keefe, Wilson's legacy: Button, Beamish, Cooke 40 years on, unpublished supervised legal research paper, School of Law, Murdoch University, 2004; and the various transcripts and case reports in relation to the trials and appeals in the matters of *Cooke*, *Button* and *Beamish*.

1 T. Winton, *Cloudstreet*, Viking, Camberwell, 1991, p. 365.

2 R. Drewe, *The Shark Net*, Penguin, Camberwell, 2000, p. 182.

3 N. Hasluck, *Offcuts from a Legal Literary Life*, University of Western Australia Press, Nedlands, 1993, p. 129.

4 *Beamish v The Queen* [2005] WASCA 62 (1 April 2005), para 36.

5 ibid., para 41.

6 G. Bolton and G. Byrne, *May It Please Your Honour: A History of the Supreme Court of Western Australia from 1861–2005*, Supreme Court of Western Australia, Perth, 2005, p. 179.

7 *Beamish* trial transcript, p.176, cited in P. Brett, *The Beamish Case*, Melbourne University Press, Melbourne, 1966, p. 40.

8 *Beamish* trial transcript, pp. 173–4, cited in ibid.

9 P. Brett, *The Beamish Case*, Melbourne University Press, Melbourne, 1966, p. 41.

10 *Beamish v Queen* [2005] WASCA 62 (1 April 2005), para 48.

11 ibid., para 48, quoting from *Beamish* trial transcript, p. 402.

12 Bolton and Byrne, *May It Please Your Honour*, p. 216.

13 *Beamish v The Queen* [1962] WAR 85.

14 Winton, *Cloudstreet*, p. 365.

15 Drewe, *The Shark Net*, p. 235.

16 Anonymous, 'More than 300 at QC's Funeral', *Daily News*, 14 January 1969, p. 3.

17 Bolton and Byrne, *May It Please Your Honour*, p. 216, citing *West Australian*, 13 January 1969, p. 2.

18 ibid., p. 206.

19 Button cross-examined by Wilson, *Button* trial transcript, *The Queen v John Button* SCWA, 1 May 1963, pp. 289–90.

20 Questioning of Charles Button formed part of a *voir dire* in order to test whether allegations of lying by John Button could be put to the jury.

21 *Button* trial transcript, *The Queen v John Button* SCWA, 1 May 1963, p. 316.

22 ibid., p. 728.

23 ibid., 4 May 1963, p. 733.

24 ibid., p. 783.

25 ibid., 6 May 1963, p. 786.

26 ibid., p. 786–7.

27 Drewe, *The Shark Net*, p. 279.

28 Quoted by Robert Drewe in memoirs of his early life in Perth, where he had met Cooke, who at one staged worked for Drewe's father: ibid., p. 228.

29 E. Blackburn, *Broken Lives*, Stellar Publishing, Claremont, 1998, pp. 89–90.

30 Anonymous, 'Cooke Convicted, Gets Death Sentence', *West Australian*, 28 November 1963, pp. 1, 20 and 24.

31 Bolton and Byrne, *May It Please Your Honour*, p. 195.

32 Drewe, *The Shark Net*, pp. 318–19.

33 *Cooke* trial transcript, *The Queen v Cooke* SCWA, 27 November 1963, p. 199.

34 ibid., p. 205.

35 ibid., p. 207.

36 ibid., p. 256.

6
The Prosecutor's Trilogy Concludes

1 G. Bolton and G. Byrne, *May It Please Your Honour: A History of the Supreme Court of Western Australia from 1861–2005*, Supreme Court of Western Australia, Perth, 2005, p. 243. Wilson and Burt appeared against each other in numerous significant criminal, civil and constitutional cases, including *Tonkin v Brand* [1962] WAR 2, which concerned certain prescribed government electoral duties. This case was argued before Wilson had taken silk.

2 P. Brett, *The Beamish Case*, University of Melbourne Press, Melbourne, 1966, p. 16.

3 Professor Brett assisted Professor Zelman Cowen, then Dean of Melbourne University's Faculty of Law, in preparing an opinion requested by the Law Society of Western Australia, and in commenting on Beamish's notice of appeal to the Privy Council. As such, Payne argues that Brett's 'pamphlet is far from being the "dispassionate and objective discussion" which it is held out to be'; D. Payne, 'Book Reviews: *The Beamish Case*', *University of Western Australia Law Review*, 1965–66, 7, pp. 576, 583.

4 ibid., p. 603.

5 *Beamish v The Queen (No 2)*, unreported, CCA of SCWA, no 20 of 1964, 22 May 1964, p. 9.

6 Beamish's second appeal transcript, *Beamish v The Queen (No 2)* CCA of SCWA, 19 March 1964, p. 245. Although in Wilson's cross-examination of Cooke, Cooke

did say that he wasn't sure of the actual sequence of events as to when Brewer spoke.

7 ibid., 20 March 1964, pp. 333–4.

8 ibid., p. 334.

9 ibid., pp. 323–4.

10 ibid., pp. 359–60.

11 ibid., pp. 379–80.

12 ibid., p. 389.

13 ibid., p. 375.

14 ibid., p. 395.

15 Button's appeal transcript, *John Button v The Queen* CCA of SCWA, 8 April 1964, p. 222.

16 ibid., pp. 227–8.

17 ibid., p. 261.

18 ibid., pp. 256–7.

19 *Beamish v The Queen (No 2)*, unreported, CCA of SCWA, Library no 20 of 1964, 22 May 1964; and *Button v The Queen*, unreported, CCA of SCWA, 22 May 1964.

20 *Beamish v The Queen (No 2)*, unreported, CCA of SCWA, Library no 20 of 1964, 22 May 1964, per Wolff CJ, p. 47.

21 ibid., pp. 63–4.

22 ibid., pp. 69–70.

23 ibid., p. 1.

24 ibid., p. 71.

25 *Button v The Queen*, unreported, CCA of SCWA, 22 May 1964, p. 7.

26 ibid., p. 12.

27 ibid., p. 29.

28 ibid., p. 30.

29 ibid., per Jackson J, p. 4.

30 ibid., p. 5.

31 Refer to Hansard, *WA Parliamentary Debates*, vol. 168, 14 October 1964, pp. 1555–63.

32 ibid., p. 1753.

33 P. Brett, *The Beamish Case*, p. 53.

34 R. Wilson, Letter to Attorney-General of Western Australia, October 1966, Crown Law Department Archives.

35 D. Payne, 'Book Reviews: *The Beamish Case*', p. 599.

36 Reverend Jenkins's statement, 12 November 1964, cited in *Beamish v The Queen* [2005] WASCA 62 (1 April 2005), para 380.

37 Anonymous, 'Jurists Seek New Look at Beamish Affair', *West Australian*, 11 August 1969, p. 2.

38 E. Blackburn, *Broken Lives*, Stellar Publishing, Claremont, 1998.

39 R. Wilson, letter to Wendy Page, 13 September 1998, Wilson's personal files.

40 In Blackburn's book, *Broken Lives*, it is mentioned that Button and Wilson met in 1988 (p. 382). However, from correspondence between Button and Beamish, the year in fact was 1989.

41 J. Button, letter to Wilson, 27 November 1989, Wilson's personal files.

42 J. Button, letter to Wilson, 19 April 1990, Wilson's personal files.

43 B. Christian, 'Mother, 96, Clings to See Her Son's Name Cleared', *Subiaco Post*, 10 June 2000, pp. 1, 22.

44 B. Christian, 'Beamish: Action after 40 Years', *Subiaco Post*, 10 June 2000, pp. 1, 22, 71. Note that although it is one article, on p. 22 it is called 'Beamish Gets the Green Light after 40 Years' and on p. 71 it becomes 'Green Light for Beamish'.

45 K. Welham, 'Don't Pity This Killer', *Sunday Times*, 3 September 2000, p. 25.

46 B. Christian, 'Beamish Appeal Backed by Facts', *Sunday Times*, 10 September 2000, p. 15.

47 R. Gibson, 'Trial by Media Proves Showcase for the Law', *West Australian*, 29 May 2001, p. 5.

48 *Button* trial transcript, *The Queen v Button* (2002) CCA of SCWA, 29 April 1963, p. 22.

49 *Button v The Queen* [2002] WASCA 35 (25 February 2002), para 314.

50 R. Gibson, J. Butler and T. Robb, 'FREE AT LAST: Justice for Button after 39 Years' (emphasis in original), *West Australian*, 26 February 2002, p. 1.

51 *Beamish v The Queen* [2005] WASCA 62 (1 April 2005), para 411.

52 ibid., para 398.

53 ibid., para 409.

54 ibid., para 410.

55 ibid., para 412.

56 ibid., para 422.

57 ibid., para 422.

58 K. Shine, 'Cleared of Murder after 44 Years', *Australian*, 2 April 2005, pp. 1–2.

59 R. Guilliat, 'Silent Witness', *Sydney Morning Herald (Good Weekend)*, 11 June 2005, pp. 21, 26.

60 As described by Steytler, Wheeler and McClure JJ in *Beamish v Queen* [2005] WASCA 62 (1 April 2005), para 48.

61 R. Guilliat, 'Silent Witness', p. 26. Also refer to K. Shine, 'Finally Cleared of Murder after 44 Years', *Australian*, 2 April 2005, pp. 1–2.

62 M. Keefe, interview with Tom Percy, in M. Keefe, Wilson's legacy: Button, Beamish, Cooke 40 years on, unpublished supervised legal research paper, School of Law, Murdoch University, 2004, p. 24.

63 ibid.

64 ibid., p. 27.

65 ibid., p. 28.

66 *Beamish v The Queen* [2005] WASCA 62 (1 April 2005), paras 319–20.

67 *Mallard v The Queen* (2002) 28 WAR 1, paras 19–20, cited in *Beamish v The Queen* [2005] WASCA 62 (1 April 2005), para 320.

68 Organised by the Australian Academy of Forensic Sciences and the World Psychiatric Association at the University of NSW; paper later published as R. Wilson, 'Truth and Justice', *Australian Journal of Forensic Sciences*, 1983, 16, p. 2.

69 ibid., p. 7.

70 ibid.

71 ibid.

7
Crown Advocate, Church Moderator and Family Man

The main sources for this chapter are: interviews by the author with Wilson, Leila Wilson, Bruce Wilson, Helen Ladhams (née Wilson), Geoff Wilson, Robyn Christie (née Wilson), Peter Panegyres, Chief Justice David Malcolm, Justice Michael Murray, His Excellency Judge Kevin Parker, Fred Chaney, Beryl Grant, Des Cousins; interviews with Wilson by Margaret Robertson, Stuart Reid, Robert Meadows and Geraldine Byrne; interview with Lady Wilson, Geoff Wilson, Ahlia Harris, Jeffery Christie and Robyn Christie by L. Batterham; and various law reports and Crown solicitor's court file notes.

1 Advice given to Michael Murray by Wilson: Author, interview with Justice Michael Murray, Perth, 22 November 2004.

2 *R v Commonwealth Conciliation and Arbitration Commission; Ex parte Association of Professional Engineers' Association, Australia* (1959) 107 CLR 208, concerning issues of government undertaking and an industrial undertaking within the context of 'industrial dispute' in the arbitration power (section 51 (xxxv)) of the Australian Constitution. New South Wales and the intervening states (including Western Australia) attempted to argue that engineers in state departments and instrumentalities were immune from this Commonwealth legislative power because their work conditions could never be deemed 'industrial'. Such an argument was a circuitous way of seeking to reintroduce the discredited doctrine of implied immunities (which prohibited Commonwealth legislative power being expressed over state departments and instrumentalities). Refer further to L. Zines, *The High Court and the Constitution*, 2nd edn, Butterworth, Sydney, 1987, pp. 7–15.

3 *The Federated State School Teachers' Association of Australia v Victoria* (1928) 41 CLR 569. The case was concerned with whether 'state teachers' constituted an industry, and whether disputes between the state and the teachers it employed could be deemed 'industrial dispute' under section 51 (xxxv) of the Constitution. The High Court held that it could not.

4 S. Reid, Transcript of interview with Wilson, Battye Library, Perth, 20 October 1994, p. 112.

5 B. d'Alpuget, *Robert. J. Hawke: A Biography*, Schwartz, East Melbourne, 1982, p. 77.

6 B. Hawke, *The Hawke Memoirs*, William Heinemann Australia, Port Melbourne, 1994, pp. 39–40.

7 Reid, Transcript of interview with Wilson, 20 October 1994, p. 112.

8 M. Roberts, Edited transcript of interview with Wilson, Western Australian Bar Association Oral History Project, Perth, 19 December 2000, p. 7.

9 The independent bar in Western Australia was formed by Francis Burt, Terry Walsh, John Wickham and Gresley Clarkson. All QCs, they held their inaugural meeting on 30 September 1963.

10 R. Meadows and G. Byrne, Transcript of interview with Wilson, Battye Library, Perth, November 1993, p. 15.

11 Robertson, Edited transcript of interview with Wilson, p. 5.

12 He had also broken his leg in grade 2 of primary school.

13 Meadows and Byrne, Transcript of interview with Wilson, November 1993, p. 33.

14 R. Wilson, Technical Training Year, Nedlands Presbyterian Church, 1966, Wilson's personal files.

15 Anonymous, 'Take a New Look, Says Church Head', *West Australian*, 5 May 1965, p. 26.

16 For a history of Sister Kate's, refer to J. Leeming, Nearly White: Assimilation policies in practice in Western Australia at Sister Kate's Children's Home from 1933 to 1964, unpublished honour's thesis, UWA, 1986; Uniting Church Synod of Western Australia, Submission to the National Inquiry into the Separation of Aboriginal and Torres Straight Islander Children from Their Families, Uniting Church Synod of Western Australia, Perth, 12 September 1996; and V. Whittington, *Sister Kate: A Life Dedicated to Children in Need of Care*, University of Western Australia Press, Crawley, 1999.

17 Q. Beresford, *Rob Riley: An Aboriginal Leader's Quest for Justice*, Aboriginal Studies Press, Canberra, 2006, p. 46.

18 ibid., pp. 46–7.

19 S. Hawke, *Polly Farmer: A Biography*, Fremantle Arts Centre Press, Fremantle, 1994, p. 16.

20 Beresford, *Rob Riley*, p. 44.

21 For example, refer to ALSWA, *Telling Our Story*, ALSWA, Perth, 1995, p. 84.

22 ABC TV, *7.30 Report*, 1 May 1997.

23 For a history of the separation policies in Western Australia, refer to A. Haebich, *For Their Own Good: Aborigines and Government in the South West of Western Australia 1900–1940*, University of Western Australia Press, Nedlands, 1988; Q. Beresford and P. Omaji, *Our State of Mind: Racial Planning and the Stolen Generations*, Fremantle Arts Centre Press, Fremantle, 1998; A. Haebich, *Broken Circles: Fragmenting Indigenous Families 1800–2000*, Fremantle Arts Centre Press, Fremantle, 2000; A. Buti, *Separated*, Sydney Institute of Criminology, Sydney, 2004.

24 Other relevant amending statues, include the *Aborigines Act Amendment Act* 1911 (WA); *Aborigines Act Amendment Act* 1936 (WA); *Native Administration Amendment Act* 1941 (WA); *Native Welfare Act* 1954 (WA); and *Native Welfare Act Amendment Act* 1960 (WA).

25 ABC TV, *7.30 Report*, 1 May 1997.

26 *Freightlines and Construction Holdings Ltd v New South Wales* (1967) 116 CLR 1.

27 ibid., 3.

28 *Freightlines and Construction Holdings Ltd v New South Wales* [1968] AC 625.

29 Reid, Transcript of interview with Wilson, 20 October 1994, p. 114.

30 ibid.

31 ibid.

32 P. D. Durack and R. D. Wilson, 'Do We Need a New Constitution for the Commonwealth?', *Australian Law Journal*, 1967, 41, p. 231.

33 ibid., p. 232.

34 ibid., pp. 237–8.

35 ibid., p. 241.

36 ibid., p. 242.

37 ibid.

38 Reid, Transcript of interview with Wilson, 20 October 1994, p. 125.

39 Hansard, *WA Parliamentary Debates*, 182, 24 April 1969, pp. 3436–7.

40 ibid., p. 3436.

41 ibid.

42 ibid., 30 April 1969, p. 3557.

43 ibid.

44 ibid., p. 3558.

45 ibid.

46 L. Batterham, Interview with Lady Leila Wilson, Geoff Wilson, Ahlia Harris, Jeffery Christie and Robyn Christie.

47 ibid.

8
The Solicitor-General

The main sources for this chapter are: interviews by the author with Wilson, Leila Wilson, Bruce Wilson, Helen Wilson, Geoff Wilson, Robyn Wilson, Peter Panegyres, Sir Daryl Dawson, William Deane, Jim Thomson, Judge Mary Ann Yeats, Justice Christine Wheeler, Judge Hal Jackson, Sir Charles Court, Ian Medcalf, Chief Justice David Malcolm, Judge Michael Murray, His Excellency Judge Kevin Parker, Beryl Grant, Des Cousins, Reverend David Robinson; interviews with Wilson by Margaret Robertson, Stuart Reid, Robert Meadows and Geraldine Byrne; various Crown Solicitors' court file notes; law reports and newspaper articles.

1 M. Robertson, Edited transcript of interview with Wilson, Western Australian Bar Association Oral History Project, Perth, 19 December 2000, p. 12.

2 G. Bolton and G. Byrne, *May It Please Your Honour: A History of the Supreme Court of Western Australia from 1861–2005*, Supreme Court of Western Australia, Perth, 2005, pp. 227–8.

3 ibid., p. 228.

4 G. Whitlam, *The Whitlam Government 1972–1975*, Viking, Melbourne, 1985, p. 3.

5 R. Wilson and I. Burkitt (on behalf of NEAF), letter to Chaney, May 1972, Wilson's personal files.

6 See further, J. Edelman and N. Gray, 'Toohey, John Leslie', in T. Blackshield, M. Coper and G. Williams (eds), *The Oxford Companion to the High Court of Australia*, Oxford University Press, South Melbourne, 2001, pp. 673–5.

7 *Gough v Gough* (1956) 95 CLR 369.

8 A. Barblett, Justice, Transcript of speech, Opening Ceremony of the Family Court of Western Australia, Special Sitting, 1 June 1976, p. 10, Wilson's personal files.

9 For example, refer to *Hematite Petroleum v Victoria* (1983) 151 CLR 599; *Fencott v Muller* (1983) 152 CLR 570; *Commonwealth v Tasmania (Tasmanian Dams Case)* (1983) 158 CLR 1.

10 *Western Australia v Hamersley Iron Proprietary Limited* (1969) 120 CLR 75.

11 ibid., 84.

12 *MacRobertson Miller Airline Service v Commissioner of State Taxation (Western Australia)* (1975) 133 CLR 125.

13 S. Reid, Transcript of interview with Wilson, Battye Library, Perth, 20 October 1994, p. 120.

14 *Oteri v The Queen* [1976] 1 WLR 1272.

15 ibid., 1276.

16 *Munro v Lombardo* [1964] WAR 63.

17 *New South Wales v Commonwealth* (1975) 135 CLR 337.

18 Reid, Transcript of interview with Wilson, 20 October 1994, p. 118.

19 R. Smith, 'The Assembly', in W. W. Emilsen and S. Emilsen (eds), *The Uniting Church in Australia: The First 25 Years*, Circa, Armadale, Victoria, 2003, pp. 7, 10.

20 The long title was: 'An ACT to Make Provision for the Inauguration of the Uniting Church in Australia in Accordance with the Basis of Union and to Constitute the Uniting Church in Australia Property Trust (WA) and for Other and Incidental Purposes.'

21 If $50,000 were 'handed over', it did not come from the personal resources of Wilson, as Leila was abreast of the couple's financial and bank details. She never observed such a transaction.

22 T. Woods, 'Today Is U-Day', *West Australian*, 22 June 1977, p. 7.

23 M. Owen, 'Western Australia: Renewal and Change', in W.W. Emilsen and S. Emilsen (eds), *The Uniting Church in Australia*, pp. 224, 228.

24 P. D. Durack and R. D. Wilson, 'Do We Need a New Constitution for the Commonwealth?', *Australian Law Journal*, 1967, 41, p. 231.

25 Refer to Anonymous, 'Current Topics: Appointment of a Western Australian High Court Justice of the High Court', *Australian Law Journal*, 1979, 53, pp. 471–2.

26 Anonymous, 'Labor Says Wilson Is a "Court Man"', *West Australian*, 23 May 1979, p. 4.

27 Cited in Anonymous, 'Current Topics: Appointment of a Western Australian High Court Justice of the High Court', p. 471.

28 ibid., pp. 471–2.

29 Anonymous, 'Labor Says Wilson Is a "Court Man"', *West Australian*, 23 May 1979, p. 4.

9
The High Court

The main sources for this chapter are: interviews by the author with Wilson, Leila Wilson, Bruce Wilson, Helen Ladhams (née Wilson), Geoff Wilson, Robyn Christie (née Wilson), Sir Harry Gibbs, Sir Anthony Mason, Sir Gerard Brennan, Sir William Deane, Sir Daryl Dawson, Jeremy Allanson, Kenneth Martin QC, Peter van Hattem, Melanie Sloss SC and Richard Price; interviews with Wilson by Margaret Robertson, Criena Fitzgerald, Stuart Reid, Robert Meadows and Geraldine Byrne; M. Coper, *The Franklin Dam Case*, Butterworth, North Ryde, 1983; and various law reports.

1 The same Durack who co-authored the 1967 *Australian Law Journal* article with Wilson.

2 F. Brennan, 'The Law and Politics of Human Rights in an Isolated Country without a Bill of Rights', *Brief*, 2003, 30 (5), p. 9.

3 ibid.

4 ibid.

5 Was also minister of external affairs.

6 Was also minister for customs and excise.

7 M. Leiboff and M. Thomas, *Legal Theories in Principle*, Thomson Law Book Co, Pyrmont, 2004, p. 139.

8 *Australia Acts* 1986 refers to the enactment of legislation of the same name in the Australian and UK parliaments to close the remaining avenues of appeals from state courts to the Privy Council.

9 Refer to the *Privy Council (Limitation of Appeals) Act* 1968 (Cwlth) and *Privy Council (Appeals from the High Court) Act* 1975 (Cwlth).

10 J. Hocking, *Lionel Murphy: A Political Biography*, Cambridge University Press, Melbourne, 1997, p. 264.

11 Refer to J. Priest, *Sir Harry Gibbs: Without Fear or Favour*, Scribblers Publishing, Mudgeeraba, 1995, pp. 79–80.

12 *MacPherson v R* (1981) 147 CLR 512.

13 ibid., 519.

14 ibid., 524.

15 For example, refer to *Van Der Meer v R* (1988) 82 ALR 10.

16 *Barton v R* (1980) 147 CLR 75.

17 *Zecevic v DPP (Victoria)* (1987) 162 CLR 645.

18 ibid., 652.

19 ibid.

20 P. Durack, 'Wilson, Ronald Darling', in T. Blackshield, M. Coper and G. Williams (eds), *The Oxford Companion to the High Court of Australia*, Oxford University Press, South Melbourne, 2001, pp. 714, 716.

21 ibid.

22 R. Meadows and G. Byrne, Transcript of interview with Wilson, Battye Library, Perth, November 1993, pp. 20–1.

23 While written submission arguments were introduced during the tenure of the Mason Court (1987–95), they did not become standard practice until the Brennan Court (1995–98). Refer to S. Gageler, 'Counsel, role of', in Blackshield, Coper and Williams (eds), *The Oxford Companion to the High Court of Australia*, pp. 167–8.

24 Although Deane did join Wilson in eight cases.

25 See R. Heath, 'Buildings', in Blackshield, Coper and Williams (eds), *The Oxford Companion to the High Court of Australia*, 2001, pp. 71–3.

26 G. Barwick, *A Radical Tory*, Federation Press, Annadale, 1995, p. 232.

27 (Edited text), 'Confidence, Humour in Installation Speech', *Murdoch News*, 3 March 1980, p. 3.

28 ibid.

29 J. Hocking, *Lionel Murphy: A Political Biography*, p. 248.

30 G. Barwick, *A Radical Tory*, Federation Press, Annadale, 1995, p. 219.

31 For example, Professor George Winterton considers that 'Barwick was a highly competent, though not great judge. Ironically, the very qualities which contributed to his success at the Bar—self-assurance, combativeness and ability to identify the nub of an issue—detracted from his performance as a judge, making him appear insufficiently impartial and his judgments on occasion too simplistic or dogmatic.' See G. Winterton, 'Barwick, Garfield Edward John', in Blackshield, Coper and Williams (eds), *The Oxford Companion to the High Court of Australia*, pp. 56, 58.

32 During Wilson's time on the High Court he had eight associates: Jeremy Allanson, Kenneth Martin, David Craig, Peter van Hattem, Melanie Sloss, Cameron Sweeney, Jennifer Wall and Richard Price.

33 L. O'Connor, letter to author, 8 December 2004.

34 Australia signed the convention on 13 October 1966.

35 *Koowarta v Bjelke-Petersen* (1982) 153 CLR 168. This issue of whether the race power, post 1967, can only be used for the benefit of Aborigines has been judicially considered by the High Court since Wilson's tenure on that court, in the *Kartinyeri v Commonwealth (Hindmarsh Island Bridge case)* (1988) 195 CLR 337. In that case, out of the four justices who considered the issue, Justice Michael Kirby was alone in holding that the race power cannot be used to enact 'detrimental and adversely discriminatory special laws by reference to a people's race'. It should be noted that Justices William Gummow and Kenneth Hayne assumed that the Commonwealth parliament and the Australian electorate in 1967 intended that legislation would only be passed for the benefit of Aboriginal peoples, but the constitutional text of the race power (section 51 (xxvi)) does not prevent detrimental laws towards Aborigines. Justice Mary Gaudron did not see the race power as being limited to only beneficial laws, although she did find if difficult to identify a circumstance where laws detrimental to a racial minority would be valid, and she said that 'prima facie, at least (the (race) power) presently only authorises laws which operate to the benefit of Aboriginal Australians.'

36 However, note that the case did not decide whether the Act conformed with the UN *Convention for the Elimination of All Forms of Racial Discrimination*.

37 *Koowarta v Queensland* (1982) 153 CLR 168, 198.

38 ibid., 244.

39 ibid., 248.

40 ibid., 251.

41 ibid.

42 ibid., 250.

43 D. Rose, 'Comment on the External Affairs Power', *Federal Law Review*, 1984, 14, pp. 216, 217.

44 *Koowarta v Queensland* (1982) 153 CLR 168, 247–52.

45 ibid., 249.

46 C. Fitzgerald, Transcript of interview with Wilson, Battye Library, Perth, 23 March 2000, pp. 1–3, 9, 20, 22. Also refer to L. Spearman, Sir Ronald Wilson and the High Court, unpublished supervised legal research paper, School of Law; Murdoch University, 2004, pp. 24–5.

47 In more recent times, some may argue that it is the Commonwealth government, through the Commonwealth parliament, that breaches international treaties, and the states are seeking to preserve them.

48 *Koowarta v Queensland* (1982) 153 CLR 168, 252–3.

49 In the March 1983 federal election, the ALP lost seats in Tasmania. In part, it is believed that this was the result of many Tasmanians disapproving of 'Canberra' interfering into 'its affairs'.

50 *Commonwealth v Tasmania (Tasmanian Dam Case)* (1983) 158 CLR 1.

51 The regulations were held by a majority of the court—Gibbs, Wilson, Deane and Dawson—to be invalid. It should be noted that *World Heritage Properties Conservation Act* 1983 (Cwlth) relied on four sources of Commonwealth power: the external affairs power (Section 51 (xxix)) (this was also the head relied on for the regulations); the corporations power (Section 51 (xx)); the race power (Section 51 (xxvi)); and an implied power said to be inherent in having a national government and Commonwealth parliament. Professor Tony Blackshield writes that the focus of the case 'has been mainly on the majority view of the external affairs power, though some of the majority observations on the corporations power were potentially much more far-reaching.' See T. Blackshield, 'Tasmanian Dam Case (1983)', in Blackshield, Coper and Williams (eds), *The Oxford Companion to the High Court of Australia*, pp. 658, 659.

52 However, the majority judges did state that the external affairs power in relation to international agreements was not limited to complying with international obligations. Murphy and Deane spoke of recommendations of international bodies, and Mason of implementation of 'benefits; emanating from international treaties'. Refer further to L. Zines, *The High Court and the Constitution*, 2nd edn, Butterworth, Sydney, 1987, p. 250.

53 Note that Mason thought the subject matter was not of international concern, as did the minority Justices: Gibbs, Wilson and Dawson.

54 *Tasmanian Dam Case* (1983) 158 CLR 1, 197.

55 J. Quick and R. Garran, *The Annotated Constitution of the Australian Commonwealth*, Australian Book Co, London, 1901, p. 631.

56 S. E. K. Hume, 'The External Affairs Power: The State of the Debate', in Samuel Griffith Society, *Proceedings of the Sixth Conference of the Samuel Griffith Society*,

Townhouse Hotel, Carlton, 17–19 November 1995, <http://www.samuelgriffith.org.au/papers/html/volume6/v6chap2.htm>, 30 October 2006.

57 P. Durack, 'The External Affairs Power: What Is to Be Done?', Samuel Griffith Society, *Proceedings of the Sixth Conference of the Samuel Griffith Society*, Townhouse Hotel, Carlton 17–19 November 1995, <http://www.samuelgriffith.org.au/papers/html/volume6/v6chap2.htm>, 30 October 2006.

58 *Tasmanian Dam Case* (1983) 158 CLR 1, 197 (case references omitted). Wilson referred to *Engineers Case* (*Amalgamated Society of Engineers v Adelaide Steamship Co. Ltd* (1920) 28 CLR 129), where the High Court held against a doctrine of state reserve powers, in which the Commonwealth cannot encroach on powers reserved by the Constitution for the state or on the state.

59 *Tasmanian Dam Case* (1983) 158 CLR 1, 204.

60 Meadows and Byrne, Transcript of interview with Wilson, November 1993, pp. 17–18.

61 ibid., p. 18.

10
Mabo and More

The main sources for this chapter are: interviews by the author with Wilson, Leila Wilson, Bruce Wilson, Helen Wilson, Geoff Wilson, Robyn Wilson, Sir Harry Gibbs, Sir Anthony Mason, Sir Gerard Brennan, Sir William Deane, Sir Daryl Dawson, Jeremy Allanson, Kenneth Martin QC, Peter van Hattem, Melanie Sloss and Richard Price; interviews with Wilson by Margaret Robertson, Criena Fitzgerald, Stuart Reid, Robert Meadows and Geraldine Byrne; B. A. Keon-Cohen, 'The Mabo Litigation: A Personal and Procedural Account', *Melbourne University Law Journal*, 2000, 24, p. 35; J. Hocking, *Lionel Murphy: A Political Biography, Cambridge University Press*, Melbourne, 1997; J. Priest, *Sir Harry Gibbs: Without Fear or Favour*, Scribblers Publishing, Mudgeeraba, 1995; T. Blackshield, M. Coper and G. Williams (eds), *The Oxford Companion to the High Court of Australia*, Oxford University Press, Melbourne, 2001; P. H. Russell, *Recognizing Aboriginal Title: The Mabo Case and Indigenous Resistance to English-Settler Colonialism*, University of Toronto Press, Toronto, 2005; and various law reports.

1 L. Bartlett, 'Interview with Wilson', 720 ABC Perth Radio, *Morning Program*, 30 May 2000.

2 Anonymous, 'Sir Ronald Is Assembly Choice', *Western Impact*, June 1985. p. 1.

3 ibid.

4 ibid.

5 ibid.

6 *The Church of New Faith v The Commissioner of Pay-Roll (Victoria)* (1983) 154 CLR 120.

7 *The Church of New Faith v The Commissioner of Pay-Roll* (1983) 1 VR 97, 108–9.

8 *The Church of New Faith v The Commissioner of Pay-Roll* (1983) 154 CLR 120, 124.

9 ibid., 164–77.

10 An earlier case that had a 'religious' element to it was the so-called DOGS (Defence of Government Schools) case (*A-G (Vic) ex rel Black v Commonwealth* (1981) 146 CLR 559), although this case did not have to determine what a religion was as such. In this decision, Wilson, writing a separate opinion, agreed with the majority (Murphy dissenting) in upholding the Commonwealth power to provide funding for religious-denomination schools.

11 Published as R. Wilson, 'Life and Law: The Impact of Human Rights on Experimenting with Life', *Australian Journal of Forensic Sciences*, 1985, 17, p. 61.

12 ibid., p. 82.

13 Here Wilson was quoting from R. McCormick, 'To Save or Let Die', *Journal of the American Medical Association*, 1979, 229, p. 174, cited in ibid., p. 82.

14 T. Blackshield, 'Murphy Affair', in T. Blackshield, M. Coper and G. Williams (eds), *The Oxford Companion to the High Court of Australia*, Oxford University Press, Melbourne, 2001, p. 486.

15 ibid.

16 The politician in question is Bob Ellicott, attorney-general in the Fraser government, who had been part of the prosecution team in the Sankey case (*Sankey v Whitlam* [1977] 1 NSWLR 333, *Sankey v Whitlam* (1978) 142 CLR 1), which involved the private prosecution of former prime minister Gough Whitlam and three of his cabinet ministers, including Murphy, in relation to charges of illegality over alleged contravention of the 1927 Financial Agreement. Murphy's name was removed from the record for the High Court case. The charges were dismissed. There had been speculation that the real target of the prosecution was Murphy, as a conviction would have provided reasons for his removal from the High Court pursuant to section 72 of the Constitution. Refer to T. Blackshield, G. Frickle and A. Simpson, 'Litigants, Notable, 1945–2001', in Blackshield, Coper and Williams (eds), *The Oxford Companion to the High Court of Australia*, pp. 440, 441; and J. Hocking, *Lionel Murphy: A Political Biography*, Cambridge University Press, Melbourne, 1997, pp. 259, 285–6.

17 M. Wilkinson, 'Big Shots Bugged', *National Times*, 25 November–1 December 1983, p. 5.

18 Hocking, *Lionel Murphy: A Political Biography*, pp. 287–8.

19 ibid., p. 289.

20 This would involve a joint sitting of the House of Representatives and the Senate.

21 J. Priest, *Sir Harry Gibbs: Without Fear or Favour*, Scribblers Publishing, Mudgeeraba, 1995, p. 101.

22 *R v Hoar* (1981) 148 CLR 32.

23 Blackshield, 'Murphy Affair', in Blackshield, Coper and Williams (eds), *The Oxford Companion to the High Court of Australia*, p. 487.

24 *R v Murphy* (1985) 158 CLR 596.

25 Cited in Priest, *Sir Harry Gibbs*, p. 104.

26 ibid.

27 *R v Murphy* (1985) 4 NSWLR 42.

28 Blackshield, 'Murphy Affair', in Blackshield, Coper and Williams (eds), *The Oxford Companion to the High Court of Australia*, p. 489.

29 Priest, *Sir Harry Gibbs*, p. 108.

30 ibid.

31 R. Meadows and G. Byrne, Transcript of interview with Wilson, Battye Library, Perth, November 1993, p. 26.

32 Cited in Priest, *Sir Harry Gibbs*, p. 110.

33 Meadows and Byrne, Transcript of interview with Wilson, November 1993, p. 26.

34 On that day the Commonwealth government gave the award also to Mason, Brennan, Dawson, Deane and Toohey.

35 Anonymous, 'Sir Ronald Is Assembly Choice', *Western Impact*, June 1985, p. 1.

36 Recalled by Reverend Drayton, while speaking at Wilson's funeral service on 22 July 2005.

37 Murdoch Senate, Minutes, 17 October 1988; Anonymous, 'Murdoch Senate Approves Amalgamation Terms', *On Campus*, 18 October 1988, pp. 1–3.

38 Anonymous, 'Amalgamation: Decision to Preserve Murdoch's Contribution to WA', *On Campus*, 15 June 1989, pp. 1–2.

39 *Mabo v Queensland (No 1)* (1988) 166 CLR 186.

40 P. H. Russell, *Recognizing Aboriginal Title: The Mabo Case and Indigenous Resistance to English-Settler Colonialism*, University of Toronto Press, Toronto, 2005, p. 191.

41 ibid., p. 194.

42 ibid., p. 191.

43 ibid., p. 193.

44 *Mabo v Queensland (No 1)* (1988) 166 CLR 186. There of course was another *Mabo* case, which recognised the existence of a common law native title in Australia; see *Mabo v Queensland (No 2)* (1992) 175 CLR 1.

45 *Mabo v Queensland* (1986) 64 ALR 1.The matter also had come before Justice Deane on 28 October 1982 in relation to a strikeout application by the state of Queensland, but the matter was never pursued before him, and the state withdrew its strikeout application. It had also come before Justice Toohey in April 1987. Also there was a trial before Justice Moynihan of the Queensland Supreme Court in October–November 1986. For a chronology of the *Mabo* litigation, see B. A. Keon-Cohen, 'The *Mabo* Litigation: A Personal and Procedural Account', *Melbourne University Law Review*, 2000, 24, p. 893, appendices.

46 He was ably assisted by barrister Barbara Hocking and solicitor Greg McIntyre, who both spoke at the 1981 Townsville Conference, and who provided the initial intellectual impetus to propose an action along the lines of the *Mabo* litigation.

47 *Mabo v Queensland (No 1)* (1988) 166 CLR 186, 218.

48 Russell, *Recognizing Aboriginal Title*, p. 210.

49 *Mabo v Queensland (No 1)* (1988) 166 CLR 186, 216, 229.

50 ibid., 204.

51 *Mabo v Queensland (No 1)* (1988) 166 CLR 186, 206.

52 For a succinct discussion on the various judgements as they relate to denial of equality, refer to R. Bartlett, *Native Title in Australia*, Butterworth, Sydney, 2000, pp. 18–21.

53 R. Wilson, 'Reconciliation', Address to the National Press Club, Canberra, 25 March 1998 (CD filming of the address).

54 C. Fitzgerald, Transcript of interview with Wilson, Battye Library, Perth, March 2000, p. 10.

55 *Walton Stores v Maher* (1988) 164 CLR 387.

56 The *Walton Stores* judgement was delivered on 19 February 1988 (heard on 7–8 May 1987), and the *Mabo (No 1)* hearings occurred on 15–17 March 1988.

57 This area of law relates to the doctrine of estoppel.

58 M. Lang, 'Premier WA Judge Resigns', *West Australian*, 2 February 1989, p. 53.

59 ibid.

60 L. Haultain, 'Interview with Wilson', ABC Radio National, *The Law Report*, 5 August 1997.

61 *Mabo v Queensland (No 2)* (1992) 175 CLR 1.

62 Also in a lecture he gave students in 2004, he did say that he stood by his decisions in *Koowarta* and *Mabo (No 1)*, but did not elaborate. The author was in attendance at all three lectures.

63 Meadows and Byrne, Transcript of interview with Wilson, November 1993, p. 25.

64 *Philip Morris Inc v Adam Brown P. Brown Male Fashions P/L* (1982) 148 CLR 457.

65 ibid., 548.

11
The President

The main sources for this chapter and the next are: interviews by the author with Wilson, Leila Wilson, Bruce Wilson, Helen Wilson, Geoff Wilson, Robyn Wilson, Gregor Henderson, Desmond Cousins, Susan Roberts; interviews with Wilson by Margaret Robertson, Stuart Reid, Robert Meadows and Geraldine Byrne; interview with Gregor Henderson by William Emilsen; interview with Rob and Sue Osborn by Linley Batterham; and Wilson's speeches and writings.

1 R. Wilson, President's report, 1991, Wilson's personal files.

2 A. Dutney, 'The World Calling: The Uniting Church Begins a Second Decade', *St Mark's Review*, 1988, Spring, p. 15.

3 *Journey*, 1988, May, pp. 12, 14; cited in ibid., p. 21.

4 W. Emilsen, Transcript of interview with Gregor Henderson, Uniting Church Archives, United Theological College, North Parramatta, 30 September 2004, p. 6.

5 ibid.

6 Thus the centenary was actually in 1988, but the Koreans were celebrating it a year later in 1989.

7 J. Fleming, Interview with Ronald Wilson, Perth, December 1993.

8 Emilsen, Transcript of interview with Gregor Henderson, 30 September 2004, p. 4.

9 R. Wilson, President's report, 1991, Wilson's personal files.

10 R. Wilson, President's report (draft), 1991, Wilson's personal files.

11 J. Fleming, Interview with Ronald Wilson, Perth, December 1993.

12 ibid.

13 Wilson, President's report, 1991.

14 The account as described here was detailed in R. Wilson, Pilgrimage to Mapoon, Uniting Church Archives, United Theological College, North Parramatta, August 1990.

15 T. Koch and I. Gerard, 'Paradise Refound, and Grog's Been Banished', *Weekend Australian*, 24–25 July 2006, p. 8.

16 Anonymous, 'UCA Apologises to Aborigines', *Western Impact*, March 1991, p 12.

17 ibid.

18 ibid.

19 ibid.

20 Emilsen, Transcript of interview with Gregor Henderson, 30 September 2004, p. 8. Wilson became a member of the Applecross parish when he moved to that suburb from Nedlands in 1991.

21 Women did take an active role in many aspects of church affairs, but Wilson was mindful of the need to encourage and enhance this.

22 Emilsen, Transcript of interview with Gregor Henderson, 30 September 2004, pp. 5–6.

23 ibid., p. 10.

24 R. Wilson, President's report, 1991, Wilson's personal files.

25 S. Reid, Transcript of interview with Sir Ronald Wilson, Battye Library, Perth, 29 November 1994, p. 172.

26 Subsequently it became the School of Economics, Commerce and Law.

27 In 2004, Simmonds was appointed a justice of Supreme Court of Western Australia.

28 L. Batterham, Interview with Rob and Sue Osborn, Perth, 20 October 2005.

29 Discrimination on the grounds of race (*Racial Discrimination Act* 1975 (Cwlth)), sex (*Sex Discrimination Act* 1984 (Cwlth)) or disability (*Disability Discrimination Act* 1992 (Cwlth)). HREOC also deals with issues of *Privacy Act* 1988 (Cwlth).

30 J. Beaumont, 'Sir Ronald Wilson: A Remarkable Man', *ITA*, 1990, July, p. 25.

31 ibid.

32 C. Connolly and P. Vout, 'A New Era for the Human Rights Commission?', *Polemic*, 1990, 1, p. 20.

33 ibid.

34 Australia did eventually sign the protocol on September 1991, and it came into force in Australia on Christmas Day 1991.

35 Connolly and Vout, 'A New Era for the Human Rights Commission?', p. 21.

36 ibid.

37 ibid. *Tasmanian Dams* refers to the previously discussed *Commonwealth v Tasmania* (1983) 158 CLR 1, where Wilson was in minority (see chapter 9); and Richardson to *Richardson v Forestry Commission* (1988) 164 CLR 261.

12
Royal Commission, Reconciliation and Rights

The main sources for this chapter are: interviews by the author with Wilson, Leila Wilson, Bruce Wilson, Helen Wilson, Geoff Wilson, Robyn Wilson, Gregor Henderson, Desmond Cousins, Susan Roberts, Jonathon Hunyor, Diana Temby; interviews with Wilson by Margaret Robertson, Stuart Reid, Robert Meadows and Geraldine Byrne; interview of Rob and Sue Osborn by Linley Batterham; various HREOC decisions; Wilson's speeches; and the two reports and commentary on the Royal Commission into the Commercial Activities of Government and Other Matters; and TV interviews.

1 Editorial, 'Inquiry Needs Outside Chief', *West Australian*, 28 November 1990, p. 10.

2 A. Burns and M. Lang, 'Senior WA Legal Figures', *West Australian*, 6 December 1990, pp. 8–9.

3 ibid.

4 In 2004, Le Miere was appointed a justice of the Western Australia Supreme Court.

5 R. Hay, F. Crago and M. Tannock, 'Royal Commission in Retrospect: A Different Perspective', *Brief*, October 1992, p. 18.

6 M. Lang, 'Tougher Task Still Ahead', *West Australian*, 1 July 1992, p. 9.

7 ibid.

8 G. A. Kennedy (chairman), *Report of the Royal Commission into the Commercial Activities of Government and Other Matters*, Part 1, Western Australia State Government, Perth, 20 October, 1992.

9 For discussion on the report and its findings against politicians and public servants, refer to A. Peachment, 'WA Inc: Failure of the System or Crime of the Employee', in M. Brogan and H. Phillips (eds), *Past As Prologue: The Royal Commission into Commercial Activities of Government and Other Matters: Proceedings from a conference on the Part II Report of the Royal Commission and the Reform of Government in Western Australia*, Perth International Hotel, Edith Cowan University, 4 November 1994, pp. 80–1.

10 ibid.

11 ibid. For a discussion and examination of WA Inc and other 'commissions of inquiry' over the period of 1991–2004 in Western Australia, refer to A. Peachment (ed.), *The Years of Scandal*, University of Western Australia Press, Crawley, 2006.

12 G. A. Kennedy (chairman), *Report of the Royal Commission into the Commercial Activities of Government and Other Matters*, Part 2, Western Australia State Government, Perth, 12 November 1992.

13 This report finding is discussed by M. L. Barker, 'Past As Prologue: A Second Anniversary Reflection on the Work of the Royal Commission into WA Inc', in M. Brogan and H. Phillips (eds), *Past As Prologue*, pp. 10, 13.

14 ibid. As reported by Baker, Cowan made this allegation on 6WF ABC Radio, *Morning Program*, 14 October 1994.

15 B. Nicholson, 'Report Claim "Ridiculous"', *West Australian*, 15 October 1994, p. 4.

16 S. Reid, Transcript of interview with Wilson, Battye Library, Perth, 29 November 1994, p. 177.

17 ibid, p. 176.

18 R. Wilson, People in Glasshouses: Human Rights and Australia, Western Australian Press Club, Perth, 8 July 1991, Wilson's personal files.

19 R. Wilson, Mitchell Oration 1991: Human Dignity for All: A Pie in the Sky?, South Australian Equal Opportunity Commission, Adelaide, 20 September 1991, pp. 11–12.

20 Published in 1992 as R. Wilson, 'The Domestic Impact of International Human Rights Law', *Australian Journal of Forensic Sciences*, 1992, 24, p. 57.

21 *McInnis v The Queen* (1979) 143 CLR 575.

22 *Kioa v West* (1985) 159 CLR 550.

23 R. Wilson, 'The Domestic Impact of International Human Rights Law', p. 63.

24 ibid.

25 ibid.

26 ibid., refer to Editor's note, p. 57.

27 Hansard, *House of Representatives*, 10, 30 May 1991, p. 4498.

28 ibid., p. 4824.

29 ibid.

30 The following made up the initial members of the Reconciliation Council: (chair) Patrick Dodson; (deputy chair) Wilson; (Aboriginal members) Archie Barton, Sol Bellear, Essieina Coffey, Mary Graham, Pastor Bill Hollingsworth, Rose Murray, Professor Lowitja O'Donoghue, Wenten Rubuntja, Esme Saunders, Alma Stackhouse, Galarrwuy Yunupingu; (Torres Strait Islander members) Bill Lowah, Pastor Alan Mosby; (representing the wider community) Robert Champion de Crespigny, Ted Egan, Rick Farley, Jennie George, Senator Cheryl Kernot, Ray Martin, Peter Nugent MP, Professor Margaret Reynolds, Hon. Helen Sham-Ho MLC, Ian Spicer.

31 S. Bevis, 'Lift Aborigines' Status: Keating', *West Australian*, 22 February 1992, p. 3.

32 ibid.

33 ibid.

34 *Mabo v Queensland (No 2)* (1992) 175 CLR 1.

35 Hansard, *House of Representatives*, 8, 4 June 1992, p. 3586.

36 P. Russell, *Recognizing Aboriginal Title: The Mabo Case and Indigenous Resistance to English-Settler Colonialism*, University of Toronto Press, Toronto, 2005, pp. 283–6.

37 ibid., p. 287.

38 J. Walker and L. Taylor, 'Promises Have Hollow Ring', *Weekend Australian*, 6–7 August 1994, p. 11.

39 R. Tickner, *Taking a Stand: Land Rights to Reconciliation*, Allen & Unwin, Crows Nest, 2001, p. 123.

40 L. Tickner, 'Plan for Mabo Poll "Not Racist"', *West Australian*, 13 July 1993, p. 8.

41 M. Irving, 'Aborigines Bid to Expand *Mabo*', *Australian*, 8 November 1993, p. 2.

42 ibid.

43 ibid.

44 M. Lang, 'Lawyers Divided on Plan's Classes', *Australian*, 6 November 1993, p. 8.

45 ibid.

46 *Mabo v Queensland (No 1)* (1988) 166 CLR 186.

47 G. Meertens, 'Hard to Go Back on *Mabo*: Ex-judge', *West Australian*, 17 July 1993, p. 14.

48 Under section 109, the Commonwealth legislation has supremacy over state legislation, and thus the state legislation is invalid to the extent of the inconsistency.

49 *Western Australia v Commonwealth (Native Title Act Case)*; *Teddy Biljabu v Western Australia* (1995)183 CLR 373.

50 G. Armstrong, 'Rights Pact Fear over *Mabo* Law', *West Australian*, 4 December 1993, p. 8.

51 Russell, *Recognizing Aboriginal Title*, p. 300.

52 Refer to R. Wilson, 'Why Human Rights Matter for Everyone', *Murdoch University Electronic Journal of Law*, 1996, 3, <http://www.murdoch.edu.au/elaw/issues/v3n3/wilson.html> 30 October 2006.

53 ibid.

54 For example, *Ardeshirian v Robe River Iron Associates*, 18 May 1990, unreported, HREOC, Sir Ronald Wilson; *Murray v Forward*, 17 September 1993, unreported, HREOC, Sir Ronald Wilson; *Mead v Southern Districts Football League*, 15 November 1991, unreported, HREOC, Sir Ronald Wilson; and *Tamanivalu v Western Australian Rugby Union Inc*, 17 August 1994, unreported, HREOC, Sir Ronald Wilson.

55 For example, *Tully v Ceridale Pty Ltd*, 19 June 1990, unreported, HREOC, Sir Ronald Wilson; and *Proudfoot v ACT Board of Health*, 17 March 1992, unreported, HREOC, Sir Ronald Wilson.

56 For example, *X v McHugh*, 8 July 1994, unreported, HREOC, Sir Ronald Wilson; and *Scott v Telstra Corporation Ltd*, 6 September 1995, unreported, HREOC, Sir Ronald Wilson.

57 Under an agreement between the Western Australian Equal Opportunity Commission and HREOC, the state institution, as an agent of HREOC, often processed complaints, at least at the initial stages, that came under the purview of the Commonwealth body, such as complaints under the RDA.

58 *Mead v Southern Districts Football League*, 15 November 1991, unreported, HREOC, Sir Ronald Wilson, para 9.

59 H. McGlade, 'Reviewing Racism: HREOC and the *Racial Discrimination Act* 1975 (Cwlth)', Indigenous Law Bulletin, 1997, 4, pp. 12–14.

60 L. McNamara, 'Long Stories, Big Pictures: Racial Slurs, Legal Solutions and Playing the Game', *Australian Feminist Law Journal*, 1998, 10, pp. 85, 96.

61 ibid., p. 97.

62 *Tamanivalu v Western Australian Rugby Union Inc*, 17 August 1994, unreported, HREOC, Sir Ronald Wilson.

63 McNamara, 'Long Stories, Big Pictures: Racial Slurs, Legal Solutions and Playing the Game', p. 102 (original footnotes omitted).

64 Wilson's concern with HREOC being embroiled in political controversy was also on display when in 1996 he expressed to this author his concern that the commission may be blamed for any industrial dispute between the Western Australian Prison Officers' Union and the state government resulting from the commission holding that the policy of the justice department in segregating HIV prisoners was contrary to the *Disability Discrimination Act* 1992 (Cwlth). However, no such industrial dispute eventuated.

65 The following account of the Jevons affair and the quotes cited come from Muirhead, J. H., In the Matter of a Petition to His Excellency the Governor of Western Australia As Visitor of Murdoch University, F. R. Jevons and Murdoch University, *Report of his Excellency's Assessor The Hon J. H. Murihead AC QC*, 30 May 1996.

66 ibid., pp. 15–16.

67 ibid., p. 16.

68 ibid., p. 19.

69 ibid., p. 29.

70 ibid., pp. 35–6.

71 Believed to be Learned Hand; refer to R. Wilson, Degree Ceremony, Perth Concert Hall, 22 March 1995, Wilson's personal files.

72 The source to Judge Learned Hand was written in Wilson's personal speech notes; however, no detailed citation was present. The author has been unable to independently verify the attribution of quote to Judge Hand.

13
Bringing Them Home

The main sources for this chapter and the following two are: interviews by the author with Wilson, Leila Wilson, Jonathon Hunyor, Meredith Wilkie, Diana Temby, Mick Dodson, Fred Chaney, Sir William Deane, Sir Daryl Dawson, Sir Harry Gibbs, Susan Roberts; short contacts with John Bond, Stephen Hall and Kaye Regan; interviews by Linley Batterham with John Bond and Theo Mackay; HREOC, *Bringing Them Home*, Australian Government Publishing Service, Canberra, 1997; and various newspaper and other print articles, TV footage and radio transcripts, Wilson speeches and letters held in his personal files, and 'stolen generations' cases.

1 The Commonwealth laws included as legislation passed by Commonwealth parliament governed Aboriginal affairs in the Northern Territory.

2 N. D'Souza, 'The Stolen Generation: From Removal to Reconciliation', *University of New South Wales Law Journal*, 1988, 21, pp. 204–5.

3 P. Keating, 'Speech by the Honourable Prime Minister, P J Keating MP, Launch of the International Year for the World's Indigenous People: Redfern 10 December 1992', *Aboriginal Law Bulletin*, 1993, 3, p. 4.

4 ibid.

5 *Williams v Minister, Aboriginal Land Rights Act 1983* (1994) 35 NSWLR 497.

6 An earlier version of Merkel's conference paper can be found as R. Merkel, 'Government Culpability for the Forced Removal of Aboriginal Children from Their Families', *Australian Law Bulletin*, 1990, 2 (47), p. 4.

7 P. Carlyon, 'White Lies', *Bulletin*, 12 June 2001, p. 27.

8 C. Sidoti, 'Between Two Worlds: Australia's Stolen Children', *Current Affairs Bulletin*, December 1997/January 1998, p. 4.

9 ABC TV, *7.30 Report*, 1 May 1997.

10 The complete list of members: Annette Peardon, Brian Butler, Yami Lester, Irene Stainton, Floyd Chermside, Barbara Cummings, Grant Dradge, Carol Kendall, Lola McNaughton, Isabel Coe, Peter Rotimah, Nigel d'Souza, Maureen Abbott, Margaret Ah Kee, Bill Lowah, Matilda House and Jim Wright.

11 ALSWA, *Telling Our Story*, ALSWA, Perth, 1996. This report was submitted to the inquiry by the ALSWA. The organisation also produced another more substantial report for the inquiry: ALSWA, *After the Removal*, ALSWA, Perth, 1997.

12 His life story is told in great detail in the biography by Q. Beresford, *Rob Riley: An Aboriginal Leader's Quest for Justice*, Aboriginal Studies Press, Canberra, 2006.

13 R. Wilson, The National Inquiry into the Removal of Aboriginal Children: Healing the Nation, State Aboriginal Health Conference, Perth, 21 November 1995, Wilson's personal files.

14 Regional Aboriginal Co-Commissioners: Annette Peardon, Marjorie Thorpe, Dr Maryanne Bin Salik, Sadie Canning, Olive Knight, Kathy Mills, Anne Louis, Laurel Williams, Jackie Huggins, Josephine Ptero-David and Professor Marcia Langton. Also Queensland anti-discrimination commissioner John Briton was involved in some of the hearings.

15 R. Wilson, Occasional Address, Graduation Ceremony, University of Technology Sydney, 2 October 1998, Wilson's personal files.

16 Wilson also relayed this story in the video produced by HREOC called *Bringing Them Home*.

17 Evie's story is reproduced in HREOC, *Bringing Them Home*, Australian Government Publishing Service, Canberra, 1997, pp. 147–9.

18 Although for some the telling of the story was far from therapeutic, as it brought up painful memories. The inquiry did provide some counselling support for storytellers but, because of financial restraints, it was inadequate.

19 R. Wilson, Justice for the Stolen Generation, Gold Coast Intercontinental Hotel, 22–24 November 1999, Wilson's personal files.

20 C. Wyatt, Secretary, Department of Aboriginal Affairs, Oral submission, Western Australian Government, Perth, 14 May 1996.

21 For further details of the Louis Johnson story refer to S. Mickler, *The Myth of Privilege*, Fremantle Arts Centre Press, Fremantle, 1998; and A. Haebich, *Broken Circles: Fragmenting Indigenous Families 1800–2000*, Fremantle Arts Centre Press, Fremantle, 2000, pp. 17–64.

22 S. Hall, *No Better Than Anyone Else*, Anglican Church Social Justice Committee, Perth, 1996.

23 J. Bond, 'National Sorry Day – Australia', in European Centre for Conflict Prevention (ed.), *People Building Peace 2: Successful Stories of Civil Society*, Riener Boulder, London, 2005, pp. 647–8.

24 'Josie's Story', in ALSWA, *Telling Our Story*, pp. 84–6. 'Josie' is a pseudonym. *Telling Our Story* was submitted to the inquiry, along with another document produced by the legal service: ALSWA, *After The Removal*, ALSWA, 1995. 'Josie' also gave oral evidence to the inquiry as part of the ALSWA submission.

25 HREOC, *Toomelah Report: Report on the Problems and Needs of Aborigines Living on the NSW–Queensland Border*, Australian Government Publishing Service, Sydney, 1988.

26 HREOC, *Our Homeless Children: National Inquiry into Homeless Children*, Australian Government Publishing Service, Sydney, 1989.

27 For example, refer to R. Wilson, Keynote address, Boat People Symposium, Centre for Research in Culture and Communication, Murdoch University, 15 October 1996, <http://wwwmcc.murdoch.edu.au/ReadingRoom/boat/Wilson.html>, 30 October 2006; and. R. Wilson, 'Why Human Rights Matter for Everyone', *Murdoch University Electronic Journal of Law*, 1996, 3 <http://www.murdoch.edu.au/elaw/issues/v3n3/wilson.html>, 30 October 2006.

28 Article II of the Genocide Convention defines genocide as: 'any of the following acts committed with the intent to destroy, in whole or in part, any national, ethnical, racial or religious group, as such: (a) killing members of the group; (b) causing serious bodily or mental harm to members of the group; (c) deliberately afflicting on the group conditions of life calculated to bring about its physical destruction in whole or in part; (d) imposing measures intended to prevent births within the group; and (e) forcibly transferring children of the group to another group.' Australia ratified the Genocide Convention on 8 July 1949.

29 A. O. Neville, in Commonwealth of Australia, *Aboriginal Welfare: Initial Conference of Commonwealth and State Aboriginal Authorities*, Australian Government Publishing Service, Canberra, 1937, p. 3. Also refer to A. O. Neville, *Australia's Coloured Minority*, Currawong Publishers, Sydney, 1947.

30 Neville in Commonwealth of Australia, *Aboriginal Welfare: Initial Conference of Commonwealth and State Aboriginal Authorities*, p. 3.

31 Neville, *Australia's Coloured Minority*, pp. 177–8.

32 Correspondence from a native welfare file found in ALSWA, *After the Removal*, p. 27. For privacy reasons, the names are pseudonymous.

33 T. Austin, *Never Trust a Government Man*, Northern Territory University Press, Darwin, 1997.

34 As early as 1901, the Commonwealth's first attorney-general, Alfred Deakin, had alluded in parliament to the 'dying race theory': 'We have power to deal with people of any race within our borders, except the aboriginal inhabitants of the continent, who remain under the custody of the States. There is that single exception of a dying race, and if they be a dying race, let us hope that in their last hours they will be able to recognize not simply the justice, but the generosity of the treatment

which the white race, who are dispossessing them and entering into their heritage, are according them.' *Post and Telegraphy HR*, vol. 4, 1901, p. 4851.

35 T. Austin, *I Can Picture the Old Home So Clearly: The Commonwealth and 'Half-caste' Youth in the Northern Territory 1911–1939*, Aboriginal Studies Press, Canberra, 1993, pp. 17–19; Q. Beresford and P. Omaji, *Our State of Mind: Racial Planning and the Stolen Generations*, Fremantle Arts Centre Press, Fremantle, 1998, p. 33.

36 Austin, *I Can Picture the Old Home So Clearly*, p. 196.

37 P. Brock, *Outback Ghettoes: Aborigines, Institutionalisation and Survival*, Cambridge University Press, Cambridge, 1993, p. 133.

38 H. Moseley (Commissioner), *Report of the Royal Commissioner Appointed to Investigate, Report, and Advise Upon Matters in Relation to the Condition and Treatment of Aborigines*, Government Printer, Perth, 1935.

39 Recommendation 10. Refer to HREOC, *Bringing Them Home*, pp. 295, 653.

40 *Industrial and Reformatory Schools and the Training Act* 1864 (Qld); *Neglected and Criminal Children's Act* 1864 (Vic); *Destitute Persons Relief Act* 1866 (SA); *Better Care of Destitute Children Act* 1866 (NSW); *Public Charities Act* 1866 (NSW); *Industrial Schools Act* 1967 (Tas); and *Industrial Schools Act* 1874 (WA).

41 For example, the *Aborigines Protection Act* 1869 (Vic) and the *Aborigines Protection Act* 1886 (WA).

42 A table of all relevant legislation in all jurisdictions is provided in HREOC, *Bringing Them Home*, pp. 600–48.

43 Tasmania did not pass any Aboriginal-specific legislation for child removals because the state did not acknowledge that there was any of the Aboriginal population left there, although the Tasmanian legislature enacted the *Cape Barren Island Reserve Act* 1912 (Tas), which provided for the removal of Aboriginal families from mainland Tasmania to Cape Barren Island off the north coast.

44 Between 1863 and 1911, the Northern Territory was annexed to South Australia, and after that the Commonwealth parliament was responsible for Aboriginal affairs there. Until the 1967 referendum, which gave the federal parliament power to enact laws for Aborigines, the Commonwealth constitutional power to enact laws for Aborigines in the territories was done pursuant to Section 122 of the Australian Constitution (the Territories Power).

45 Until the *Aborigines Welfare Act* 1954 (Cwlth), Aborigines in the Australian Capital Territory were covered by the various Aboriginal-specific statutes enacted by the legislature of New South Wales.

46 For further examination of the guardianship power, and the duties it entails, refer to A. Buti, *Separated: Aboriginal Childhood Separations and Guardianship Law*, Sydney Institute of Criminology Series, Sydney, 2004.

47 Refer to HREOC, *Bringing Them Home*, p. 222.

48 UN Human Rights Commission, Revised Set of Basic Principles and Guidelines on the Right to Reparation for Victims of Gross Violations of Human Rights and Humanitarian Law, prepared by Mr Theo van Boven pursuant to Sub-commission decision 1995/117, UN doc. E/CN.4/Sub.2/1996/17, 24 May 1996. The van Boven principles have been revised by the Bassiouni principles. Refer to UN Human Rights Commission, The Right to Restitution, Compensation and

Rehabilitation for Victims of Gross Violations of Human Rights and Fundamental Freedoms: Final Report of the Special Rapporteur, M Cherif Bassiouni, submitted in accordance with the Commission resolution 1999/33, E/CN.4/2000/62, 19 January 2000.

49 Commonwealth Government, (submissions to) National Inquiry into Separation of Aboriginal and Torres Strait Islander Children from Their Families, 1996, pp. 26–32.

50 S. Pritchard, 'The Stolen Generations and Reparations', *University of New South Wales Law Journal Forum*, 1997, 21, pp. 259, 264. Also refer to R. Graycar, 'Compensation for the Stolen Children: Political Judgments and Community Values', *University of New South Wales Law Journal*, 1997, 21, p. 253.

51 Refer to HREOC, *Bringing Them Home*, pp. 287, 652.

52 B. Boxill, 'Morality of Reparations', *Social Theory and Practice*, 1972, 2, p. 118. Also refer to J. Braithwaite, 'Setting Standards for Restorative Justice', *British Journal of Criminology*, 2002, 42, p. 563.

53 Editorial, 'Canada's Act of Atonement', *Sydney Morning Herald*, 9 January 1998, p. 12.

54 HREOC, *Bringing Them Home*, p. 3.

14
In the Eye of the Storm

1 R. Wilson, Speech, Community Meeting, Old Parliament House, Canberra, 28 October 1997; transcript of tape, courtesy of John Bond.

2 *Wik Peoples v Queensland* (1996) 187 CLR 75.

3 S. Hawke, *Polly Farmer: A Biography*, Fremantle Arts Centre Press, Fremantle, 1994.

4 J. Woodford, 'No Action on Stolen Children', *Sydney Morning Herald*, 20 May 1997, p. 1.

5 M. Kingston, 'Report That Won't Stay under the Carpet', *Sydney Morning Herald*, 20 May 1997, p. 6.

6 T. Wright, 'For Pete's Sake, It's Time to Right the Wrongs', *Sydney Morning Herald*, 21 May 1997, p. 15.

7 J. MacDonald, 'Payout for "Genocide" Rejected', *West Australian*, 22 May 1997, p. 34.

8 M. Kingston, 'Children's Fate Demands Justice', *Sydney Morning Herald*, 22 May 1997, p. 15. Two days later, in the same newspaper, journalist Mike Seccombe wrote an article espousing the attributes of Wilson while at the same time being less than complimentary towards attorney-general Williams. Refer to M. Seccombe, 'Kookaburra' column, *Sydney Morning Herald*, 24 May 1997, p. 30.

9 Anonymous, 'A Sorry Response', *Herald Sun*, 1 June 1997, p. 44.

10 J. Howard, Opening Speech, Australian Reconciliation Conference, Melbourne Convention Centre, 26 May 1997. <http://www.austlii.edu.au/au/special/rsjproject/rsjlibrary/car/arc/speeches/opening/howard.htm> 30 October 2006.

11 C. Kernot, Opening speech, Australian Reconciliation Conference, Melbourne Convention Centre, 26 May 1997, <http://www.austlii.edu.au/au/special/rsjproject/rsjlibrary/car/arc/speeches/opening/kernot.htm>, 30 October 2006.

12 K. Beazley, Opening Speech, Australian Reconciliation Conference, Melbourne Convention Centre, 26 May 1997, <http://www.austlii.edu.au/au/special/rsjproject/rsjlibrary/car/arc/speeches/opening/beazley.htm>, 30 October 2006.

13 Jackie Huggins, Indigenous co-commissioner to the inquiry, and Coral Edwards, a healer, also spoke at the launch.

14 The launch, including excerpts of Dodson's speech, was broadcast on ABC TV, *7.30 Report*, 27 May 1997.

15 R. Wilson, *Bringing Them Home* launch speech, Australian Reconciliation Conference, Melbourne Convention Centre, 27 May 1997, Wilson's personal files.

16 K. Sweetman, 'Tennis Star's Secret Terror', *Herald Sun*, 28 May 1997, p. 3.

17 R. Markey, 'MP Sits Out House Motion of Sorrow', *West Australian*, 27 May 1997, p. 4.

18 The Commonwealth government's gun buyback scheme was instigated in response to the 1996 Port Arthur massacre, where a single gunman went on a rampage killing more than thirty people in the historic Port Arthur settlement in Tasmania.

19 R. Markey, 'PM Rejects Tearful Beazley Payout Bid', *West Australian*, 29 May 1997, p. 6.

20 C. Fitzpatrick, 'Passion Runs Deep in New Man', *West Australian*, 30 May 1997, p. 4.

21 T. Stephens, 'The Turbulent Knight', *Sydney Morning Herald*, 4 September 1997, p. 13.

22 G. Sheridan, 'A Rueful Goodbye to the Acceptable Face of Conservatism', *Australian*, 21 November 1997, p. 13.

23 C. Pearson, 'Black Overkill Tests Beazley's Leadership', *Australian Financial Review*, 26 May 1997, p. 19.

24 ibid.

25 P. Akerman, 'The Other Side of the Stolen Children', *Daily Telegraph*, 5 June 1997, p. 11.

26 P. Read, *The Stolen Generations: The Removal of Aboriginal Children in New South Wales 1883 to 1969*, NSW Ministry of Aboriginal Affairs, Sydney, 1981.

27 R. Manne, *Left Right Left: Political Essays 1977–2005*, Black Inc, Melbourne, 2005, pp. 217–18. Manne's essay on the 'stolen generations' is titled: 'In Denial and the Stolen Generations' (pp. 217–305), which originally appeared as R. Manne, 'In Denial and the Stolen Generations', *Australian Quarterly*, 2001, 1.

28 Different from the former Labor minister in the Hawke ministry.

29 M. Duffy, 'Crime Demands Punishment', *Australian*, 28 February 1998, p. 24.

30 H. Brown, 'When the Quality of Mercy Is Stretched to the Limit', *Courier-Mail*, 31 May 1997, p. 23.

31 Mervyn Smythe & Associates, *An Analysis of the Media Coverage of* Bringing Them Home, Vol 1, June 1998, p. viii.

32 G. Kitney, 'Howard Heightens the Hurt', *Sydney Morning Herald*, 30 May 1997, p. 21.

33 Mervyn Smythe & Associates, *An Analysis of the Media Coverage of* Bringing Them Home, Vol 1, June 1998, p. vi.

34 D. Modjeska, 'A Bitter Wind beyond the Treeline', *Sydney Morning Herald*, 18 September 1997, p. 19.

35 G. Henderson, 'Never Too Late to Atone', *Sydney Morning Herald*, 14 October 1997, p. 19.

36 Anonymous, 'Lost Childhood', *Economist*, 14 June 1997, 343, p. 44.

37 R. Wilson, Speech, Community Meeting, Old Parliament House, Canberra, 28 October 1997, transcript of tape, courtesy of John Bond.

38 I. McPhedran, 'PM Not in the Foreign Media Race', *Canberra Times*, 3 June 1997, p. 2.

39 The report also generated personal mail for Wilson, overwhelmingly complimentary, but there were also a small number of unflattering comments on the report and Wilson.

40 G. Walsh, 'Postscript', *Sydney Morning Herald*, 2 June 1997, p. 16.

15
An Advocate to the End

1 K. Middleton and B. Foley, 'AG Declines New Term for Human Rights Head', *Age*, 1 August 1997, p. 12.

2 HREOC, Sir Ron Wilson: Statement from the Human Rights Commission, 31 July 1997.

3 K. Middleton and B. Foley, 'AG Declines New Term for Human Rights Head', *Age*, 1 August 1997.

4 Wilson made numerous speeches and participated in fundraising events while a justice of the High Court, but these speeches and activities did not create controversy, unlike the inquiry report and his advocacy of it.

5 L. Batterham, Interview with John Bond, 26 October 2005.

6 G. Johns, 'Who's Watching the Watchdog?', *Australian*, 31 July 1997, p. 11.

7 M. Duffy, 'How to Bypass the Reconciliation Roadblock', *Australian*, 14 July 1997, p. 11.

8 As a matter of full disclosure, this author, as a human rights solicitor at the ALSWA, had argued on behalf of his 'stolen generation' clients, in both written (*Telling Our Story* and *After the Removal*) and oral submissions before the inquiry, that the removal policies and practices could have been labelled genocidal.

9 R. Manne, 'The Stolen Generations', *Quadrant*, 1998, 42 (1–2), p. 53. During Manne's tenure as editor, a number of articles by philosopher Raimond Gaita supported the association of genocide with the policy of removing Aboriginal children from their families. Refer to R. Gaita, 'Genocide and Pedantry', *Quadrant*, 1997, 41 (7–8), p. 41; and R. Gaita, 'Genocide: The Holocaust and the Aborigines', *Quadrant*, 1997, 41 (11), p. 17.

10 UN Document A/AC6/SR83 (1948) 195, cited in HREOC, *Bringing Them Home*, Australian Government Publishing Service, Canberra, 1977, p. 271.

11 ibid., p. 278.

12 ibid., p. 272.

13 For example, refer to the *Northern Territory Aboriginals Act* 1911 (SA), section 22; and *Aboriginals Protection and the Restriction of the Sale of Opium Acts Amendment Act* 1897 (Qld), section 9.

14 Indeed, as Manne rightly indicated, sociocultural assimilation does not come within genocide—at least pursuant to the Genocide Convention, which excludes cultural genocide. It should be noted that the report talks about 'eliminating Indigenous cultures', and does not mention the destruction of the 'national, ethnical, racial or religious group', as required under the Genocide Convention. Refer to HREOC, *Bringing Them Home*, p. 278.

15 Manne, 'The Stolen Generations', *Quadrant*, 1998, 42 (1–2), pp. 53, 63.

16 Brunton, R., 'Betraying the Victims: The "Stolen Generations" Report', *IPA Backgrounder*, 10, 1998.

17 HREOC, *Bringing Them Home*, p. 110. This quote is taken from P. Jacobs, *Mister Neville*, Fremantle Arts Centre Press, Fremantle, 1990, p. 218.

18 J. MacDonald, 'Wilson Pushes for Payments Fund', *West Australian*, 30 May 1997, p. 4.

19 Brunton, *Betraying the Victims: The 'Stolen Generations' Report.*

20 J. Herron, 'Bringing Them Home: Commonwealth Initiatives', media release, Canberra, 16 December 1997.

21 D. Celermajer, 'A Sorry Nation?', *Arena*, 1998, 36, pp. 35, 37.

22 Refer to A. Armitage, *Comparing the Policy of Aboriginal Assimilation: Australia, Canada and New Zealand*, University of British Columbia Press, Vancouver, 1995; J. Miller, *Shingwauk's Vision: A History of Native Residential Schools*, University of Toronto Press, Toronto, 1997; and J. Milloy, *A National Crime: The Canadian Government and the Residential School System 1879 to 1986*, University of Manitoba Press, Winnipeg, 1999.

23 Government of Canada news release, 'Canada's Aboriginal Action Plan Focused on Communities, Founded on Reconciliation and Renewal', Ottawa, 24 September 2006 (to coincide with the minister's address), commented: 'At the heart of this Action Plan is a commitment to address the needs of communities by building a real partnership with Aboriginal people, including the development of mechanisms to recognise sustainable and accountable Aboriginal governments and institutions. An essential aspect will be to work closely together with Aboriginal people to define the partnership and shape a common vision of the relationship between us… Canada's Aboriginal Action Plan has four objectives: renewing the partnerships; strengthening Aboriginal governance; developing a new fiscal relationship; [and] supporting strong communities, people and economies.'

24 ibid.

25 Also at the request of the federal government, the Law Commission of Canada (LCC) prepared a 'report addressing processes for dealing with institutional child physical and sexual abuse, including past institutional abuse in Residential Schools'. Refer to LCC, *Restoring Dignity: Responding to Child Abuse in Canadian Institutions*, LCC, Ottawa, 2000.

26 Indian Residential Schools Settlement: Official Court Website, <http://www.residentialschoolssettlement.ca>, 1 November 2006.

27 R. Wilson, Letter to R. Brunton, 2 May 1998, Wilson's personal files.

28 The major focus of the so-called history wars relates to the early colonisation of Australia. Some historians have argued that, in contradiction to the version of history that has Australia as having been peacefully settled, the land being *terra*

nullius, there was widespread violence towards Aborigines, with many thousands killed. Refer, for example, to H. Reynolds, *The Other Side of the Frontier*, rev. edn, Penguin Books, Ringwood Victoria, 1990; and L. Ryan, *The Aboriginal Tasmanians*, 2nd edn, Allen & Unwin, St Leonards, 1996. A debate has subsequently arisen between these scholars and, notably, historian and journalist Keith Windschuttle, who argues that the number of killings is overstated and without empirical foundation. Refer to K. Windschuttle, *The Fabrication of Aboriginal History*, McLeay Press, Sydney, 2002. For comment on the 'problem' of history, truth and law, refer to I. McCalman and A. McGrath (eds), *Proof and Truth: The Humanist As Expert*, Australian Academy of the Humanities, Canberra, 2003.

29 For example, refer to P. Howson, 'Rescued from the Rabbit Burrow', *Quadrant*, 1999, 43 (6), p. 10; and R. Marsh, '"Lost", "Stolen" or "Rescued"', *Quadrant*, 1999, 43 (6), p. 15.

30 I. Spry, 'The Discrediting of the Wilson Report: False "Stolen Generation" Claims', *National Observer*, Summer 2000, p. 55.

31 ibid., p. 56.

32 ibid.

33 ibid., pp. 57–8.

34 ibid., p. 61.

35 J. Bond, 'National Sorry Day—Australia', in European Centre for Conflict Prevention (ed.), *People Building Peace 2: Successful Stories of Civil Society*, Riener Boulder, London, 2005, pp. 647, 649.

36 ibid.

37 J. Howard, Transcript of the prime minister, the Hon. John Howard MP, Motion of Reconciliation, 26 August 1999. <http://www.pm.gov.au/media/Speech/1999/reconciliation2608.cfm>, 1 November 2006.

38 South Australia: 28 May 1997; Western Australia: 28 May 1997; Queensland: 3 June 1997; ACT: 17 June 1997; New South Wales: 18 June 1997; Tasmania: 13 August 1997; Victoria: 17 September 1997; and Northern Territory: 24 October 2001. In late 2006, the Tasmanian government announced a compensation scheme with a total cap of $5 million. Under section 5 of the *Stolen Generations of Aboriginal Children Act* 2000 (Tas), ex gratia individual payments of up to $5000 per individual and $20,000 per family have been made available to members of the stolen generation. Refer to R. Grace, 'Tassie to Compensate Stolen Generations', *Australian*, 26 September 2006, <http://www.theaustralian.news.com.au/story/0,20867,20600691-2702,00.html>, 1 November 2006.

39 A. Contractor, 'PM Has Not "Governed for All", Says Author', *Canberra Times*, 26 March 1998, p. 2.

40 *Cubillo v Commonwealth* (2000) 103 FCR 1 (*Cubillo* trial). Also refer to *Cubillo v Commonwealth* (1999) 89 FCR 528 (*Cubillo Strikeout Application*) and *Cubillo v Commonwealth* (2001) 112 FCR 455 (*Cubillo* appeal).

41 *Cubillo Strikeout Application* (1999) 89 FCR 528, 599.

42 *Cubillo* trial (2000) 103 FCR 1.

43 *Cubillo* appeal (2001) 112 FCR 455.

44 *Cubillo v Commonwealth* (HCA D10 and 11/2001 3 May 2002). The reasoning of O'Loughlin J, reaffirmed on appeal, brings into reality the multiple legal and evidential obstacles involved in pursuing litigation to redress the alleged wrongs of past Aboriginal child separations or removals. Refer further to J. Clarke, '*Cubillo v Commonwealth*', *Melbourne University Law Review*, 2001, 25, p. 218; and R. van Krieken, 'Is Assimilation Justiciable? Lorna Cubillo and Peter Gunner v Commonwealth', *Sydney Law Review*, 2001, 23, p. 239.

45 Also refer to supplementary submission by M. Flynn, Senate Legal and Constitutional References Committee, for the committee's inquiry into the Stolen Generation, vol 9, 2000, pp. 2798–9. The *Cubillo–Gunner* decision was preceded by the 1997 decision in *Kruger v Commonwealth* (1997) 190 CLR 1, where the plaintiffs were again unsuccessful. This was an ill-conceived challenge based on constitutional law. Once again the decision in this case did not deny the existence of a policy of removing Aboriginal children from their families.

46 *Cubillo* trial (2000) 103 FCR 1, 482.

47 Of course, one needs to be somewhat circumspect in saying 'never' in relation to litigation. It may be possible that, at some stage, based on the particular facts of a case, a 'stolen generation' plaintiff will succeed in court. However, as time goes on this becomes less and less likely, as evidentiary and time limitation difficulties become more insurmountable. It should be noted, though, that compensation has been awarded to a 'stolen generation' claimant in New South Wales via the administrative process of the Criminal Injuries Compensation Tribunal. Refer to Valerie Linow, New South Wales Victims of Crime Compensation, Notice of Determination, February 2002. Linow received $35,000. Further, some members of the Stolen Generations (how many is unclear) have been awarded approximately $4000 each under the Victorian Criminal Injuries Compensation scheme for sexual assaults while in the care of the state of Victoria. Refer to A. Cornwall, *Restoring Identity: Final Report*, Public Interest Advocacy Centre, Sydney, 2002, p. 47.

48 Submission by Peter Howson, Senate Legal and Constitutional References Committee for the Committee's Inquiry into the Stolen Generation, vol 5, 2000, pp. 1728–35; and supplementary submission by Peter Howson, Senate Legal and Constitutional References Committee for the Committee's Inquiry into the Stolen Generation, vol 9, 2000, pp. 2804–9.

49 The Senate committee's report made ten recommendations, including a Commonwealth parliamentary apology and the establishment of a 'reparations tribunal'. Refer to Senate and Constitutional References Committee, *Healing: A Legacy of Generations*, Parliament of the Commonwealth of Australia, Canberra, 2000.

50 Submission by Peter Howson, Senate Legal and Constitutional References Committee, for the Committee's Inquiry into the Stolen Generation, vol. 5, p. 1728, p. 1729. He also provided oral testimony: refer to Hansard, L&C pp. 722–33, 18 August 2000.

51 Submission by Sir Ronald Wilson, Senate Legal and Constitutional References Committee for the Committee's Inquiry into the Stolen Generation, Vol. 5, 2000, pp. 1583–7.

52 Hansard, *L&C*, pp. 735–65, 4 September 2000.

53 R. Manne, 'In Denial: The Stolen Generation and the Right', in R. Manne, *Left Right Left: Political Essays 1977–2005*, Black Inc, Melbourne, 2005, pp. 217, 239.

54 K. O'Sullivan, 'Kay O'Sullivan Says It Is Time to Apologise to Aborigines', *Herald Sun*, 26 May 1997, p. 18.

55 Hansard, *L&C*, p. 740, 4 September 2000.

56 B. Moore, *The Australian Pocket Oxford Dictionary*, 5th edn, Oxford University Press, South Melbourne, 2001, pp. 1087–8.

57 A. Bolt, 'Stolen Generation Myth Sells Us All Short', *Daily Telegraph*, 24 February 2001, p. 19. Also refer to S. Rintoul, 'Going Home', *Australian Magazine*, 21–22 April 2001, pp. 12–17.

58 Refer to A. Buti, *Separated*, Sydney Institute of Criminology Series, Sydney. 2004, pp. 5–6.

59 Editorial, 'Sad Semantics Betray the Stolen Children', *Weekend Australian*, 24–25 February 2001, p. 18. The debate on the veracity of the term continues. At the 2006 Age Melbourne Writers' Festival, Manne and Bolt vigorously debated the issue: Storey Hall, Royal Melbourne Institute of Technology, 3 September 2006.

60 Submission by Sir Ronald Wilson, Senate Legal and Constitutional References Committee for the Committee's Inquiry into the Stolen Generation, p. 1586.

61 Hansard, *L&C*, p. 749, 4 September 2000.

62 D. Moore, 'Sir Ronald Wilson Should Apologise', *Institute for Private Affairs*, September 1999 <http://www.ipe.net.au/nltr8.html>, 23 September 2006.

63 R. Manne, 'In Denial: The Stolen Generation and the Right', p. 263.

64 R. Manne, 'Rumble Turns into a Raw Deal', *Sydney Morning Herald*, 2 March 1998, p. 15.

65 For a brief analysis of the Council for Aboriginal Reconciliation, refer to A. Gunstone, The Formal Australian Reconciliation Process: 1991–2000, National Reconciliation Planning Workshop, Old Parliament House, Canberra, 30–31 May 2005.

66 R. Wilson, Speech, Community Meeting, Old Parliament House, Canberra, 28 October 1997, transcript of tape, courtesy of John Bond.

67 For a brief history of Manguri, refer to J. Maey, 'The Manguri Story', *Western Impact*, November 1999, p. 7.

68 J. Tabart, D. Wood and R. Wilson, *Three Former Presidents Report to Assembly Standing Committee: Issues of Sexuality*, Uniting Church of Australia, 1998, p. 6.

69 R. Wilson, 'Bringing Them Home: Signs of the Kingdom', *Crosslight*, October 2000, p. 8.

70 ibid.

71 ibid.

72 ibid.

73 ibid.

74 ibid.

75 ibid., p. 9.

76 ibid.

77 ibid.

78 P. Carlyon, 'White Lies', *Bulletin*, 12 June 2001, pp. 27.

79 N. Mitchell, interview with John Howard', Radio 3AW, *Morning Show*, 8 June 2001.

80 Carlyon, 'White Lies', *Bulletin*, 12 June 2001, p. 30.

16
Serious Retirement and the Man

The main sources for this chapter are: interviews by the author with Wilson, Leila Wilson, Bruce Wilson, Helen Wilson, Geoff Wilson, Robyn Wilson, Ian Wilson, Sir Daryl Dawson, and Justice Michael Kirby; interview with Wilson by Stuart Reid; interview with Theo Mackay by Linley Batterham; State Library of South Australia, *Adelaide Festival of Ideas 2001* (CD), State Library of South Australia and Radio Adelaide 101.5 FM, 12 July 2001.

1 Farley died in early 2006.

2 Geoff and Ahlia married in April 2006.

3 Allyson and Lynette Ladhams are the daughters of Helen; Michael is the son of Robyn; and Emily is Bruce's daughter.

4 Robyn is a regular attendee at her local Baptist church.

5 S. Reid, Transcript of interview with Wilson, Battye Library, Perth, 29 September 1994, p. 58.

6 As quoted in F. Brennan, 'The Law and Politics of Human Rights in an Isolated Country without a Bill of Rights', *Brief*, 2003, 30 (5), p. 9.

7 Reid, Transcript of interview with Wilson, 29 September 1994, p. 59.

8 R. Wilson, letter to Mariele Kuhn, 5 December 1945, Wilson's personal files.

9 L. Batterham, Interview with Mackay, Perth, 8 November 2005.

10 Refer to Anonymous, 'The Sir Ronald Wilson Lecture', *Brief*, 2005, 32 (7), p. 20, for a list of the speakers and topics for the annual lectures.

Epilogue

The main sources for this epilogue are interviews with Leila Wilson and John Button; funeral speeches and eulogies from Bruce Wilson, Geoff Wilson, Ian Wilson, Michael Christie, Reverend Dr Dean Drayton, Reverend Sealin Gartlett, Dr Jill Tabart and Justice Robert Nicholson; C. Pearson, 'Conscience Has the Final Say', *Weekend Australian*, 23–24 July 2005, p. 20; and various newspaper articles and death notices in relation to the death of Wilson.

1 G. Parker, 'Human Rights Fighter Dies', *West Australian*, 18 July 2005, p. 9.

2 K. Brown and P. Taylor, 'Sir Ronald Remembered As a Man for All People', *Australian*, 18 July 2005, p. 2.

3 K. Brown, 'Seeking Justice for All', *Australian*, 18 July 2005, p. 10.

4 Editorial, 'A Brave Campaigner for the Less Fortunate', *Australian*, 18 July 2005, p. 8.

5 For example, refer to Deaths, *West Australian*, 20 July 2005, p. 66; Deaths, *West Australian*, 21 July 2005, p. 50; and Deaths, *West Australian*, 22 July 2005, p. 54.

6 Alice and Emily O'Neil Wilson (the children of Bruce Wilson and his first wife, Kerry O'Neil); Allyson and Lynette Ladhams (the children of Helen and Ian Ladhams); Tim and Laura Dale (the children of Robyn Dale (Bruce's current wife) from a previous marriage); Michaela and Jack Hayes (the children of Robyn Dale from a previous marriage); Michael, Peter, Caleb and Daniel Christie (the children of Robyn and Jeffery Christie); and Jalada Wilson (the son of Ian and his ex-wife Nur Khamidah ('Ida')); and Eythan and Ayesha Harris (the children of Ahlia Harris from a previous marriage). Ian has no children with his current partner, Hartini Hassan ('Tini') who attended both services at Karrakatta and St Stephen's Uniting Church.

7 As a lay member of the church, Wilson could not give out communion. Blyth did this on behalf of Wilson.

8 Justice M. Murray, Tribute, A Service of Celebration for the Life of Sir Ronald Wilson AC, Karrakatta Cremation Chapel, 22 July 2005.

9 C. Pearson, 'Conscience Has the Final Say', *Weekend Australian*, 23–24 July 2005, p. 20.

10 E. Blackburn, *Broken Lives*, Stellar Publishing, Claremont, 1998.

11 P. Ryan, 'Ripe Justice', *Quadrant*, 2005, 49 (5), p. 95.

12 P. Brett, *The Beamish Case*, Melbourne University Press, Melbourne, 1966.

13 A. Wilson, 'Ending a Tradition of Abuse', *Australian* (*Weekend Inquirer*), 20 May 2006, p. 17.

14 Anonymous, 'Tuckey Dismisses "Stolen Generation"', *West Australian*, 22 May 2006, p. 5.

15 R. Markey, 'Howard Told to Be More Sympathetic', *West Australian*, 4 June 1997, p. 30.

16 K. Franzen, 'Social Justice Award Honours Sir Ronald Wilson', *West Australian*, 25 March 2006, p. 42.

17 Justice R Nicholson, Eulogy, Sir Ronald Wilson Lecture 2006, Perth, 11 May 2006.

18 Although Wilson had denied that his Christian faith 'dictated' his legal career.

BIBLIOGRAPHY

Books and monographs

Alexander, F., *Campus at Crawley*, F. W. Cheshire for University of Western Australia Press, Melbourne, 1963.

Armitage, A., *Comparing the Policy of Aboriginal Assimilation: Australia, Canada and New Zealand*, University of British Columbia Press, Vancouver, 1995.

Austin, T., *I Can Picture the Old Home So Clearly: The Commonwealth and 'Half-caste' Youth in the Northern Territory 1911–1939*, Aboriginal Studies Press, Canberra, 1993.

——, *Never Trust a Government Man*, Northern Territory University Press, Darwin, 1997.

Bartlett, R., *Native Title in Australia*, Butterworth, Sydney, 2000.

Barwick, G., *A Radical Tory*, Federation Press, Annandale, 1995.

Bennet, J. M., *Sir Archibald Burt: First Chief Justice of Western Australia, 1861–1879*, Federation Press, Leichhardt, 2002.

Beresford, Q., *Rob Riley: An Aboriginal Leader's Quest for Justice*, Aboriginal Studies Press, Canberra, 2006.

Beresford, Q. and Omaji, P., *Our State of Mind: Racial Planning and the Stolen Generations*, Fremantle Arts Centre Press, Fremantle, 1998.

Blackburn, E., *Broken Lives*, Stellar Publishing, Claremont, 1998.

Blackshield, T., 'Murphy Affair', in T. Blackshield, M. Coper, and G. Williams (eds), *The Oxford Companion to the High Court of Australia*, Oxford University Press, Melbourne, 2001, pp. 486–8.

——, 'Tasmanian Dam Case (1983)' in T. Blackshield, M. Coper, and G. Williams (eds), *The Oxford Companion to the High Court of Australia*, Oxford University Press, Melbourne, 2001, pp. 658–9.

Blackshield, T., Frickle, G. and Simpson, A., 'Litigants, Notable, 1945–2001', in T. Blackshield, M. Coper, and G. Williams (eds), *The Oxford Companion to the High Court of Australia*, Oxford University Press, Melbourne, 2001, pp. 440–4.

Bolton, G. and Byrne, G., *May It Please Your Honour: A History of the Supreme Court of Western Australia from 1861–2005*, Supreme Court of Western Australia, Perth, 2005.

Bond, J., 'National Sorry Day—Australia', in European Centre for Conflict Prevention (ed.), *People Building Peace 2: Successful Stories of Civil Society*, Riener Boulder, London, 2005. pp. 647–53.

Buti, A., *Separated: Aboriginal Childhood Separations and Guardianship Law*, Sydney Institute of Criminology, Sydney, 2004.

Brett, P., *The Beamish Case*, Melbourne University Press, Melbourne, 1966.

Brock, P., *Outback Ghettoes: Aborigines, Institutionalisation and Survival*, Cambridge University Press, Cambridge, 1993.

Brunton, R., 'Betraying the Victims: The "Stolen Generations" Report', *IPA Backgrounder*, 10, 1998.

Clark, C. M. H., *A History of Australia VI: The Old Dead Tree and the Young Tree Green 1916–1935*, Melbourne University Press, Melbourne, 1987.

Commonwealth of Australia, *Aboriginal Welfare: Initial Conference of Commonwealth and State Aboriginal Authorities*, Australian Government Publishing Service, Canberra, 1937.

Conole, P., *Protect and Serve: A History of Policing in Western Australia*, Western Australian Police Service, Perth, 2002.

Coper, M., *The Franklin Dam Case*, Butterworth, North Ryde, 1983.

Corwall, A., *Restoring Identity: Final Report*, Public Interest Advocacy Centre, Sydney, 2002.

d'Alpuget, B., *Robert. J. Hawke: A Biography*, Schwartz, East Melbourne, 1982.

Dixon, M., *Looking Back: A Short History of the UWA Law School 1927–1992*, University of Western Australia Library, Crawley, 1992.

Drewe, R., *The Shark Net*, Penguin, Camberwell, 2000.

Durack, P., 'Wilson, Ronald Darling', in T. Blackshield, M. Coper, and G. Williams (eds), *The Oxford Companion to the High Court of Australia*, Oxford University Press, South Melbourne, 2001, pp. 714–16.

Edelman, J. and Gray, N., 'Toohey, John Leslie', in T. Blackshield, M. Coper, G, Williams (eds), *The Oxford Companion to the High Court of Australia*, Oxford University Press, South Melbourne, 2001, pp. 673–5.

Gageler, S., 'Counsel, Role of', in T. Blackshield, M. Coper, and G. Williams (eds), *The Oxford Companion to the High Court of Australia*, Oxford University Press, South Melbourne, 2001, pp. 167–8.

Galligan, B., 'World War II', in T. Blackshield, M. Coper, and G. Williams (eds), *The Oxford Companion to the High Court of Australia*, Oxford University Press, South Melbourne, 2001, pp. 730–2.

Haebich, A., *Broken Circles: Fragmenting Indigenous Families 1800–2000*, Fremantle Arts Centre Press, Fremantle, 2000.

——, *For Their Own Good: Aborigines and Government in the South West of Western Australia 1900–1940*, University of Western Australia Press, Nedlands, 1988.

Hall, S., *No Better Than Anyone Else*, Anglican Social Responsibilities Commission, Perth, 1996.

Hawke, B., *The Hawke Memoirs*, William Heinemann Australia, Melbourne, 1994.

Hawke, S., *Polly Farmer: A Biography*, Fremantle Arts Centre Press, Fremantle, 1994.

Heath, R., 'Buildings', in T. Blackshield, M. Coper, and G. Williams (eds), *The Oxford Companion to the High Court of Australia*, Oxford University Press, South Melbourne, 2001, pp. 71–3.

Hocking, J., *Lionel Murphy: A Political Biography*, Cambridge University Press, Melbourne, 1997.

Jacobs, P., *Mister Neville*, Fremantle Arts Centre Press, Fremantle, 1990.

Leiboff, M. and Thomas, M., *Legal Theories in Principle*, Thomson Law Book Co., Pyrmont, 2004.

Manne, R., 'In Denial: The Stolen Generation and the Right', *Australian Quarterly Essay*, 2001, 1.

——, 'In Denial: The Stolen Generations and the Right', in R. Manne, *Left Right Left: Political Essays 1977–2005*, Black Inc, Melbourne, 2005, pp. 217–305.

McCalman, I. and McGrath, A. (eds), *Proof and Truth: The Humanist As Expert*, Australian Academy of the Humanities, Canberra, 2003.

Mickler, S., *The Myth of Privilege*, Fremantle Arts Centre Press, Fremantle, 1998.

Miller, J., *Shingwauk's Vision: A History of Native Residential Schools*, University of Toronto Press, Toronto, 1997.

Milloy, J., *A National Crime: The Canadian Government and the Residential School System 1879 to 1986*, University of Manitoba Press, Winnipeg, 1999.

Minow, M., *Between Vengeance and Forgiveness*, Beacon Press, Boston, 1998.

Molony, J., *The Penguin Bicentennial History of Australia*, Penguin, Melbourne, 1987.

Moore, B., *The Australian Pocket Oxford Dictionary*, 5th edn, Oxford University Press, South Melbourne, 2001.

Neville, A. O., *Australia's Coloured Minority*, Currawong Publishers, Sydney, 1947.

Owen, M., 'Western Australia: Renewal and Change' in W. W. Emilsen and S. Emilsen, (eds), *The Uniting Church in Australia: The First 25 Years*, Circa, Armadale, Victoria, 2003, pp. 224–55.

Peachment, A. (ed.), *The Years of Scandal*, University of Western Australia Press, Crawley, 2006.

Potas, I. and Walker, J., *'Capital Punishment': Australian Institute of Criminology Trends & Issues in Crime and Criminal Justice*, Australian Institute of Criminology, Canberra, February 1987.

Priest, J., *Sir Harry Gibbs: Without Fear or Favour*, Scribblers Publishing, Mudgeeraba, 1995.

Quick, J. and Garran, R., *The Annotated Constitution of the Australian Commonwealth*, Australian Book Co., London, 1901.

Read, P., *The Stolen Generations: The Removal of Aboriginal Children in New South Wales 1883 to 1969*, NSW Ministry of Aboriginal Affairs, Sydney, 1981.

Reynolds, H., *The Other Side of the Frontier*, rev. edn, Penguin Books, Ringwood, 1990.

Russell, P. H., *Recognizing Aboriginal Title: The Mabo Case and Indigenous Resistance to English-Settler Colonialism*, University of Toronto Press, Toronto, 2005.

Ryan, L., *The Aboriginal Tasmanians*, 2nd edn, Allen & Unwin, St Leonards, 1996.

Smith, R., 'The Assembly', in W. W. Emilsen and S. Emilsen (eds), *The Uniting Church in Australia: The First 25 Years*, Circa, Armadale, Victoria, 2003, pp. 7–33.

Tickner, R., *Taking a Stand: Land Rights to Reconciliation*, Allen & Unwin, Crows Nest, 2001.

Whitlam, G., *The Whitlam Government 1972–1975*, Viking, Melbourne, 1985.

Windschuttle, K., *The Fabrication of Aboriginal History*, McLeay Press, Sydney, 2002.

Winterton, G., 'Barwick, Garfield Edward John', in T. Blackshield, M. Coper and G. Williams (eds), *The Oxford Companion to the High Court of Australia*, Oxford University Press, South Melbourne, 2001, pp. 56–8.

Whittington, V., *Sister Kate: A Life Dedicated to Children in Need of Care*, University of Western Australia Press, Crawley, 1999.

Winton, T., *Cloudstreet*, Viking, Camberwell, 1991.

Zines, L., *The High Court and the Constitution*, 2nd edn, Butterworth, Sydney, 1987.

Journal articles

Anonymous, 'Confidence, Humour in Installation Speech', *Murdoch News*, 1980, 7, p. 3.

——, 'Current Topics: Appointment of a Western Australian High Court Justice of the High Court', *Australian Law Journal*, 1979, 53, p. 471.

——, 'From Basement to Bench: An Interview with Sir Ronald Wilson AC KBE', *Brief*, 1994, 21 (1), p. 11.

——, 'From Basement to Bench: An Interview with Sir Ronald Wilson, First Published in *Brief* in February 1994', *Brief*, 2005, 32, 7, p. 6.

——, 'Lost Childhood', *Economist*, 14 June 1997, 343, p. 44.

——, 'Sir Ronald Is Assembly Choice', *Western Impact*, June 1985, p. 1.

——, 'The Sir Ronald Wilson Lecture', *Brief*, 2005, 32 (7), p. 20.

Beaumont, J., 'Sir Ronald Wilson: A Remarkable Man', *ITA*, July 1990, p. 25.

Boxill, B., 'Morality of Reparations', *Social Theory and Practice*, 1972, 2, p. 118.

Braithwaite, J., 'Setting Standards for Restorative Justice', *British Journal of Criminology*, 2002, 42, p. 563.

Brennan, F., 'The Law and Politics of Human Rights in an Isolated Country without a Bill of Rights', *Brief*, 2003, 30 (5), p. 9.

Carlyon, P., 'White Lies', *Bulletin*, 12 June 2001, p. 27.

Celermajer, D., 'A Sorry Nation?', *Arena*, 1998, 36, p. 35.

Clarke, J., 'Cubillo v Commonwealth', *Melbourne University Law Review*, 2001, 25, p. 218.

Connolly, C. and Vout, P., 'A New Era for the Human Rights Commission?', *Polemic*, 1990, 1, p. 20.

d'Souza, N., 'The Stolen Generation: From Removal to Reconciliation', *University of New South Wales Law Journal*, 1998, 21, p. 204.

Durack, P. D. and Wilson, R. D., 'Do We Need a New Constitution for the Commonwealth?', *Australian Law Journal*, 1967, 41, p. 231.

Dutney, A., 'The World Calling: The Uniting Church Begins a Second Decade', *St Mark's Review*, Spring 1988, p. 15.

Gaita, R., 'Genocide and Pedantry', *Quadrant*, 1997, 41 (7–8), p. 41.

——, 'Genocide: The Holocaust and the Aborigines', *Quadrant*, 1997, 41 (11), p. 17.

Graycar, R., 'Compensation for the Stolen Children: Political Judgments and Community Values', *University of New South Wales Law Journal*, 1998, 21, p. 253.

Hay, R., Crago, F. and Tannock, M., 'Royal Commission in Retrospect: A Different Perspective', *Brief*, October 1992, p. 18.

Howson, P., 'Rescued from the Rabbit Burrow', *Quadrant*, 1999, 43 (36), p. 10.

Keating, P., 'Speech by the Honourable Prime Minister, P J Keating MP: Launch of the International Year for the World's Indigenous People: Redfern 10 December 1992', *Aboriginal Law Bulletin*, 1993, 3, p. 4.

Keon-Cohen, B. A., 'The *Mabo* Litigation: A Personal and Procedural Account', *Melbourne University Law Review*, 2000, 24, p. 893.

McCormick, R., 'To Save or Let Die', *Journal of the American Medical Association*, 1979, 229, p. 174.

McGlade, H., 'Reviewing Racism: HREOC and the *Racial Discrimination Act* 1975 (Cwlth)', *Indigenous Law Bulletin*, 1997, 4, p. 12.

McNamara, L., 'Long Stories, Big Pictures: Racial Slurs, Legal Solutions and Playing the Game', *Australian Feminist Law Journal*, 1998, 10, p. 85.

Manne, R., 'The Stolen Generations', *Quadrant*, 1998, 42 (1–2), p. 53.

Marsh, R., '"Lost", "Stolen" or "Rescued"', *Quadrant*, 1999, 43 (6), p. 15.

Merkel, R., 'Government Culpability for the Forced Removal of Aboriginal Children from their Families', *Australian Law Bulletin*, 1990, 2 (7), p. 4.

Payne, D, 'Book Reviews: *The Beamish Case*', *University of Western Australia Law Journal*, 1965–66, 7, p. 576.

Pritchard, S., 'The Stolen Generations and Reparations', *University of New South Wales Law Journal*, 1998, 21, p. 259.

Rose, D., 'Comment on the External Affairs Power', *Federal Law Review*, 1984, 14, p. 216.

Ryan, P., 'Ripe Justice', *Quadrant*, 2005, 49 (5), p. 95.

Sidoti, C., 'Between Two Worlds: Australia's Stolen Children', *Current Affairs Bulletin*, December 1997–January 1998, p. 4.

Spry, I., 'The Discrediting of the Wilson Report: False "Stolen Generation" Claims', *National Observer*, Summer 2000, p. 55.

van Krieken, R., 'Is Assimilation Justiciable? Lorna Cubillo & Peter Gunner v Commonwealth', *Sydney Law Review*, 2001, 23, p. 239.

Wilson's writings and speeches

Tabart, J., Wood, D. and Wilson, R., Three Former Presidents Report to Assembly Standing Committee: Issues of Sexuality, Uniting Church of Australia, 1998.

Wilson, R., *Bringing Them Home* Launch Speech, Australian Reconciliation Conference, Melbourne Convention Centre, 27 May 1997, Wilson's personal files.

——, 'Bringing Them Home: Signs of the Kingdom', *Crosslight*, October 2000, p. 8.

——, Degree Ceremony, Perth Concert Hall, 22 March 1995, Wilson's personal files.

——, 'The Domestic Impact of International Human Rights Law', *Australian Journal of Forensic Sciences*, 1992, 24, p. 57.

——, 'Life and Law: The Impact of Human Rights on Experimenting with Life', *Australian Journal of Forensic Sciences*, 1985, 17, p. 61.

——, Justice for the Stolen Generation, Gold Coast Intercontinental Hotel, 22–24 November 1999, Wilson's personal files.

——, Jury Selection and Service in Philadelphia: A Description, Comparison and Evaluation, unpublished LLM dissertation, University of Pennsylvania Law School, 1957.

——, Keynote Address: Boat People Symposium, Centre for Research in Culture and Communication, Murdoch University, 15 October 1996, <http://wwwmcc.murdoch.edu.au/ReadingRoom/boat/Wilson.html>, 30 October 2006.

——, Mitchell Oration 1991: Human Dignity For All: A Pie in the Sky?, South Australian Equal Opportunity Commission, Adelaide, 20 September 1991.

——, The National Inquiry into the Removal of Aboriginal Children: Healing the Nation, State Aboriginal Health Conference, Perth, 21 November 1995, Wilson's personal files.

——, Occasional Address: Graduation Ceremony, University of Technology Sydney, 2 October 1998, Wilson's personal files.

——, People in Glasshouses: Human Rights and Australia, Western Australian Press Club, Perth, 8 July 1991, Wilson's personal files.

——, Pilgrimage to Mapoon, Uniting Church Archives, United Theological College, North Parramatta, August 1990.

——, President's Report, 1991, Wilson's personal files.

——, President's Report (Draft), 1991, Wilson's personal files.

——, Reconciliation: Address to the National Press Club, Canberra, 25 March 1998, CD filming of the address.

——, Speech, Community Meeting, Old Parliament House, Canberra, 28 October 1997, transcript of tape, courtesy of John Bond.

——, Submission by Sir Ronald Wilson, Senate Legal and Constitutional References Committee for the Committee's Inquiry into the Stolen Generation, vol. 5, 2000, pp. 1583–7.

——, Technical Training Year, Nedlands' Presbyterian Church, 1966, Wilson's personal files.

——, 'Truth and Justice', *Australian Journal of Forensic Sciences*, 1983, 16, p. 2.

——, Why Human Rights Matter for Everyone, *Murdoch University Electronic Journal of Law*, 1996, 3 <http://www.murdoch.edu.au/elaw/issues/v3n3/wilson.html>, 30 October 2006.

Newspaper articles and stories

Akerman, P., 'The Other Side of the Stolen Children', *Daily Telegraph*, 5 June 1997, p. 11.

Anonymous, 'Amalgamation: Decision to Preserve Murdoch's Contribution to WA', *On Campus*, 15 June 1989, pp. 1–2.

——, 'Cooke Convicted, Gets Death Sentence', *West Australian*, 28 November 1963, pp. 1, 20, 24.

——, 'Jurists Seek New Look at Beamish Affair', *West Australian*, 11 August 1969, p. 2.

——, 'Labor Says Wilson Is a "Court Man"', *West Australian*, 23 May 1979, p. 4.

——, 'More than 300 at QC's Funeral', *Daily News*, 14 January 1969, p. 3.

——, 'Murdoch Senate Approves Amalgamation Terms', *On Campus*, 18 October 1988, pp. 1–3.

——, 'Sir Ronald Is Assembly Choice', *Western Impact*, June 1985, p. 1.

——, 'A Sorry Response', *Herald Sun*, 1 June 1997, p. 44.

——, 'Take a New Look, Says Church Head', *West Australian*, 5 May 1965, p. 26.

——, 'Tuckey Dismisses "Stolen Generation"', *West Australian*, 22 May 2006, p. 5.

——, 'UCA Apologises to Aborigines', *Western Impact*, March 1991, p 12.

Armstrong, G., 'Rights Pact Fear over Mabo Law', *West Australian*, 4 December 1993, p. 8.

Bevis, S., 'Lift Aborigines' Status: Keating', *West Australian*, 22 February 1992, p. 3.

Bolt, G., 'Stolen Generation Myth Sells Us All Short', *Daily Telegraph*, 24 February 2001, p. 19.

Burns, A. and Lang, M., 'Senior WA Legal Figures', *West Australian*, 6 December 1990, pp. 8–9.

Brown, H., 'When the Quality of Mercy Is Stretched to the Limit', *Courier-Mail*, 31 May 1997, p. 23.

Brown, K., 'Seeking Justice for All', *Australian*, 18 July 2005, p. 10.

Brown, K. and Taylor, P., 'Sir Ronald Remembered As a Man for All People', *Australian*, 18 July 2005, p. 2.

Christian, B., 'Beamish: Action after 40 years', *Subiaco Post*, 10 June 2000, pp. 1, 22, 71.

——, 'Beamish Appeal Backed by Facts', *Sunday Times*, 10 September 2000, p. 15.

——, 'Mother, 96, Clings to See Her Son's Name Cleared', *Subiaco Post*, 10 June 2000, pp. 1, 22.

Contractor, A., 'PM Has Not "Governed for All", Says Author', *Canberra Times*, 26 March 1998, p. 2.

'Deaths', *West Australian*, 20 July 2005, p. 66.

'Deaths', *West Australian*, 21 July 2005, p. 50.

'Deaths', *West Australian*, 22 July 2005, p. 54.

Duffy, M., 'Crime Demands Punishment', *Australian*, 28 February 1998, p. 24.

——, 'How to Bypass the Reconciliation Roadblock', *Australian*, 14 July 1997, p. 11.

Editorial, 'A Brave Campaigner for the Less Fortunate', *Australian*, 18 July 2005, p. 8.

——, 'Canada's Act of Atonement', *Sydney Morning Herald*, 9 January 1998, p. 12.

——, 'Inquiry Needs Outside Chief', *West Australian*, 28 November 1990, p. 10.

——, 'Sad Semantics Betray the Stolen Children', *Weekend Australian*, 24–25 February 2001, p. 18.

(Edited text), 'Confidence, Humour in Installation Speech', *Murdoch News*, 3 March 1980, p. 3.

Fitzpatrick, C., 'Passion Runs Deep in New Man', *West Australian*, 30 May 1997, p. 4.

Franzen, K., 'Social Justice Award Honours Sir Ronald Wilson', *West Australian*, 25 March 2006, p. 42.

Gibson, R., 'Trial by Media Proves Showcase for the Law', *West Australian*, 29 May 2001, p. 5.

Gibson, R., Butler, J. and Robb, T., 'FREE AT LAST: Justice for Button after 39 Years', *West Australian*, 26 February 2002, p. 1.

Guilliat, R., 'Silent Witness', *Sydney Morning Herald (Good Weekend)*, 11 June 2005, pp. 21–6.

Henderson, G., 'Never Too Late to Atone', *Sydney Morning Herald*, 14 October 1997, p. 19.

Irving, M., 'Aborigines Bid to Expand *Mabo*', *Australian*, 8 November 1993, p. 2.

Johns, G., 'Who's Watching the Watchdog?', *Australian*, 31 July 1997, p. 11.

Kingston, M., 'Children's Fate Demands Justice', *Sydney Morning Herald*, 22 May 1997, p. 15.

——, 'Report That Won't Stay under the Carpet', *Sydney Morning Herald*, 20 May 1997, p. 6.

Kitney, G., 'Howard Heightens the Hurt', *Sydney Morning Herald*, 30 May 1997, p. 21.

Koch, T. and Gerard, I., 'Paradise Refound, and Grog's Been Banished', *Weekend Australian*, 24–25 July 2006, p. 8.

Lang, M., 'Lawyers Divided on Plan's Classes', *Australian*, 6 November 1993, p. 8.

——, 'Premier WA Judge Resigns', *West Australian*, 2 February 1989, p. 53.

——, 'System Flawed: Expert', *West Australian*, 23 January 1995, p. 4.

——, 'Tougher Task Still Ahead', *West Australian*, 1 July 1992, p. 9.

MacDonald, J., 'Payout for "Genocide" Rejected', *West Australian*, 22 May 1997, p. 34.

——, 'Wilson Pushes for Payments Fund', *West Australian*, 30 May 1997, p. 4.

McPhedran, I., 'PM Not in the Foreign Media Race', *Canberra Times*, 3 June 1997, p. 2.

Maey, J., 'The Manguri Story', *Western Impact*, November 1999, p. 7.

Manne, R., 'Rumble Turns into a Raw Deal', *Sydney Morning Herald*, 2 March 1998, p. 15.

Margo, J., 'The Darling Dynasty Keeps Its Mouth Shut and Pen Dry', *Sydney Morning Herald (Good Morning Weekend)*, 1 January 1983, p. 23.

Markey, R., 'Howard Told to Be More Sympathetic', *West Australian*, 4 June 1997, p. 30.

——, 'PM Rejects Tearful Beazley Payout Bid', *West Australian*, 29 May 1997, p. 6.

——, 'MP Sits Out House Motion of Sorrow', *West Australian*, 27 May 1997, p. 4.

Meertens, G., 'Hard to Go Back on *Mabo*: Ex-judge', *West Australian*, 17 July 1993, p. 14.

Middleton, K. and Foley, B., 'AG Declines New Term for Human Rights Head', *Age*, 1 August 1997, p. 12.

Modjeska, D., 'A Bitter Wind beyond the Treeline', *Sydney Morning Herald*, 18 September 1997, p. 19.

Nicholson, B., 'Report Claim "Ridiculous"', *West Australian*, 15 October 1994, p. 4.

O'Sullivan, K., 'Kay O'Sullivan Says It Is Time to Apologise to Aborigines', *Herald Sun*, 26 May 1997, p. 18.

Parker, G., 'Human Rights Fighter Dies', *West Australian*, 18 July 2005, p. 9.

Pearson, C., 'Black Overkill Tests Beazley's Leadership', *Australian Financial Review*, 26 May 1997, p. 19.

——, 'Conscience Has the Final Say', *Weekend Australian*, 23–24 July 2005, p. 20.

Rintoul, S., 'Going Home', *Weekend Australian*, 21–22 April 2001, pp. 12–17.

Seccombe, M., 'Kookaburra', *Sydney Morning Herald*, 24 May 1997, p. 30.

Sheridan, G., 'A Rueful Goodbye to the Acceptable Face of Conservatism', *Australian*, 21 November 1997, p. 13.

Shine, K., 'Cleared of Murder after 44 Years', *Australian*, 2 April 2005, pp. 1–2.

Sweetman, K., 'Tennis Star's Secret Terror', *Herald Sun*, 28 May 1997, p. 3.

Stephens, T., 'The Turbulent Knight', *Sydney Morning Herald*, 4 September 1997, p. 13.

Tickner, L., 'Plan for *Mabo* Poll "Not Racist"', *West Australian*, 13 July 1993, p. 8.

Walker, J. and Taylor, L., 'Promises Have Hollow Ring', *Weekend Australian*, 6–7 August 1994, p. 11.

Walsh, G., 'Postscript', *Sydney Morning Herald*, 2 June 1997, p. 16.

Welham, K., 'Don't Pity This Killer', *Sunday Times*, 3 September 2000, p. 25.

Wilkinson, M., 'Big Shots Bugged', *National Times*, 25 November–1 December 1983, p. 5.

Wilson, A., 'Ending a Tradition of Abuse', *Australian (Weekend Inquirer)*, 20 May 2006, p. 17.

Woodford, J., 'No Action on Stolen Children', *Sydney Morning Herald*, 20 May 1997, p. 1.

Woods, T., 'Today Is U-Day', *West Australian*, 22 June 1977, p. 7.

Wright, T., 'For Pete's Sake, It's Time to Right the Wrongs', *Sydney Morning Herald*, 21 May 1997, p. 15.

Interviews

Interviews by the author with Wilson (transcripts held on file with author)

Buti, A., Interview with Sir Ronald Wilson, Perth, 15 April, 6 May, 13 May, 3 June, 24 June, 30 June, 8 July, 2003.

Other interviews by the author (transcripts held on file with author)

Buti, A., Interview with Jeremy Allanson, Perth, 7 December 2004.

——, Interview with Professor Geoffrey Bolton, Perth, 21 April 2005.

——, Interview with Sir Gerard Brennan, Sydney, 12 November 2003.

——, Interview with Ron Cannon, Perth, 16 March 2005.

——, Interview with Fred Chaney, Perth, 23 August 2005.

——, Interview with Sir Charles Court, Mandurah, 18 October 2004.

——, Interview with Robyn Christie, Perth, 3 February 2004.

——, Interview with Laurence Claus, Perth, 17 December 2004.

——, Interview with Des Cousins, Perth, 13 April 2005.

——, Interview with Mick Dodson, Canberra, 14 February 2004.

——, Interview with Sir Daryl Dawson, Melbourne, 15 February 2004.

——, Interview with Sir William Deane, Canberra, 13 February 2004.

——, Interview with Robert Ellicott QC, Sydney, 24 April 2004.

——, Interview with Sir Harry Gibbs, Sydney, 11 February 2004.

——, Interview with Beryl Grant, Sydney, 15 September 2004.
——, Interview with Reverend Gregor Henderson, Canberra, 13 March 2004.
——, Interview with Jonathon Hunyor, Sydney, 11 February 2004.
——, Interview with Judge Hal Jackson, Perth, 25 November 2004.
——, Interview with Justice Michael Kirby, Sydney, 23 April 2004.
——, Interview with Bart Kakulas, Perth, 13 December 2004.
——, Interview with Helen Ladhams, Perth, 30 July 2004.
——, Interview with Ian Ladhams, Perth, 30 July 2004.
——, Interview with Chief Justice David Malcolm, Perth, 29 November 2004.
——, Interview with Kenneth Martin QC, Perth, 7 December 2004.
——, Interview with Sir Anthony Mason, Sydney, 11 November 2003.
——, Interview with Ian Medcalf, Perth, 30 October 2004.
——, Interview with Judge Michael Murray, Perth, 22 November 2004.
——, Interview with Paul Nicholls, Perth, 21 December 2004.
——, Interview with Kerry O'Neil, Melbourne, 15 February 2004.
——, Interview with Peter Panegyres, Perth, 19 January 2005.
——, Interview with His Excellency Judge Kevin Parker, The Hague, 27 January 2005.
——, Interview with Richard Price, Perth, 7 December 2004.
——, Interview with Susan Roberts, Sydney, 12 February 2004.
——, Interview with Reverend David Robinson, Perth, 7 September 2004.
——, Interview with Lucy Robinson, Perth, 7 September 2004.
——, Interview with Justice Ralph Simmonds, Perth, 29 November 2004.
——, Interview with Melanie Sloss SC, Melbourne, 13 November 2003.
——, Interview with Diana Temby, Sydney, 29 September 2004.
——, Interview with Jim Thomson, Perth, 13 December 2004.
——, Interview with Joan Tonkin, Perth, 18 September 2004.
——, Interview with John Toohey, Perth, 21 January 2005.
——, Interview with Peter Travers, Perth, 20 October 2004.
——, Interview with Peter Van Hattem, Perth, 7 December 2004.
——, Interview with Justice Christine Wheeler, Perth, 13 December 2004.
——, Interview with Meredith Wilkie, Sydney, 11 February 2004.
——, Interview with Bruce Wilson, Melbourne, 16 February 2004.
——, Interview with Geoff Wilson, Perth, 30 October 2004.
——, Interview with Hazel Wilson, Perth, 21 September 2004.
——, Interview with Ian Wilson, Perth, 22 March 2005.
——, Interview with Jim Wilson, Perth, 21 September 2004.
——, Interview with Lady Leila Wilson, Perth, 3 February 2004.
——, Interview with Leopold Woods, Perth, 20 November 2004.
——, Interview with Judge Mary Ann Yeats, Perth, 20 December 2004.

Other interviews with Wilson (transcripts held by Battye Library)

Fitzgerald, C., Interview with Sir Ronald Wilson, Perth, 23 March 2000.

Meadows, R. and Byrne, G., Interview with Sir Ronald Wilson, Perth, November 1993.

Reid, S., Interview with Sir Ronald Wilson, Perth, 27 September, 29 September, 14 October, 20 October, 29 November, 30 November, 1994.

Other interviews with Wilson (transcripts held on file with author)

Fleming, J., Interview with Sir Ronald Wilson, Perth, original transcript held by Fleming, December 1993.

Robertson, M., Interview with Sir Ronald Wilson, Western Australian Bar Association Oral History Project, Perth, original transcript held by Robertson, 19 December 2000.

Other interviews (transcripts held on file with author)

Batterham, L., Interview with Rob and Sue Osborn, Murdoch University, original transcript held by Batterham, 20 October 2005.

——, Interview with Lady Leila Wilson, Geoff Wilson, Ahlia Harris, Jeffery Christie and Robyn Christie, Perth, original transcript held by Batterham, 22 October 2005.

——, Interview with John Bond, Perth–Canberra (via telephone; original transcript held by Batterham), 26 October 2005.

Emilsen, W., Interview with Gregor Henderson, Sydney, original transcript held at Uniting Church Archives, United Theological College, North Parramatta, 30 September 2004.

Other interview (transcript held with Battye Library)

Reid, S., Transcript of interview with Leopold Woods, Perth, 25 January 1996.

Author's short contacts

Richard Bartlett (via email)

John Bond (in person)

John Button (by telephone)

Robert Castiglione (by telephone)

Russell Elsegood (via email)

Stephen Hall (via email and telephone)

Dr Peter Johnston (in person)

Owen Leitch (by telephone)

Kath Mallott (by telephone)

Lee O'Conner (in writing)

Michael Owen (by telephone and email)

Bob Pearce (by telephone)

Kay Regan (via email)

Thesis and unpublished research papers

Breen, M., The History of the District and Family Court during Sir Ronald Wilson's time As Solicitor-General of Western Australia: 1969 to 1979, unpublished supervised legal research paper, School of Law, Murdoch University, 2004.

Cohen, R., Sir Ronald Wilson and the Human Rights and Equal Opportunity Commission: A Critical Analysis, unpublished supervised legal research paper, School of Law, Murdoch University, 2005.

Keefe, M., Wilson's Legacy: Button, Beamish, Cooke 40 Years On, unpublished supervised legal research paper, School of Law, Murdoch University, 2004.

Leeming, J., Nearly White: Assimilation Policies in Practice in Western Australia at Sister Kate's Children's Home from 1933 to 1964, unpublished honours thesis, University of Western Australia, 1986.

Loh, T., Sir Ronald Wilson: Analysis of his most important High Court Decisions, unpublished supervised legal research paper, School of Law, Murdoch University, 2004.

Mattingley, N., The Abolition of Capital Punishment in Western Australia, 1960–1984, unpublished honours thesis, History Program, Murdoch University, 1990.

Pinkerton, R., Cooke, Beamish and Button: A Critical Analysis: The Role of the Media and Sir Ronald Wilson in These Cases, unpublished supervised legal research paper, School of Law, Murdoch University, 2004.

Rogers, D., How the Decisions of Wilson J in *Mabo* and *Koowarta* Have Influenced Aboriginal Society and the Law, unpublished supervised legal research paper, School of Law, Murdoch University, 2004.

Spearman, L., Sir Ronald Wilson and the High Court, unpublished supervised legal research paper, School of Law, Murdoch University, 2004.

Reports and submissions

Aboriginal Legal Service of Western Australia, *After the Removal*, Aboriginal Legal Service of Western Australia , Perth, 1997.

——, *Telling Our Story*, Aboriginal Legal Service of Western Australia, Perth, 1996.

Commonwealth of Australia, *Aboriginal Welfare: Initial Conference of Commonwealth and State Aboriginal Authorities*, Australian Government Publishing Service, Canberra, 1937.

Commonwealth Government, *(Submissions to) National Inquiry into Separation of Aboriginal and Torres Strait Islander Children from Their Families*, Australian Government Publishing Service, Canberra, 1996.

Flynn, M., Supplementary Submission by M. Flynn, Senate Legal and Constitutional References Committee for the Committee's Inquiry into the Stolen Generation, vol. 9, 2000, pp. 2798–9.

Howson, R., Submission by the Honourable Peter Howson, Senate Legal and Constitutional References Committee for the Committee's Inquiry into the Stolen Generation, vol. 5, 2000, pp. 1728–35.

——, Supplementary Submission by the Honourable Peter Howson, Senate Legal and Constitutional References Committee for the Committee's Inquiry into the Stolen Generation, vol. 9, 2000, pp. 2804–9.

Human Rights and Equal Opportunity Commission, *Bringing Them Home*, Australian Government Publishing Service, Canberra, 1997.

——, *Our Homeless Children: National Inquiry into Homeless Children*, Australian Government Publishing Service, Sydney, 1989.

——, *Toomelah Report: Report on the Problems and Needs of Aborigines Living on the NSW–Queensland Border*, Australian Government Publishing Service, Sydney, 1988.

Kennedy, G. A. (Chairman), *Report of the Royal Commission into the Commercial Activities of Government and Other Matters*, Part I, Western Australia State Government, Perth, 20 October, 1992.

——, (Chairman), *Report of the Royal Commission into the Commercial Activities of Government and Other Matters*, Part II, Western Australia State Government, Perth, 12 November 1992.

Law Commission of Canada, *Restoring Dignity: Responding to Child Abuse in Canadian Institutions*, Law Commission of Canada, Ottawa, 2000.

Mervyn Smythe & Associates, *An Analysis of the Media Coverage of* Bringing Them Home, vols 1 and 2, June 1998.

Moseley, H. (Commissioner), *Report of the Royal Commissioner Appointed to Investigate, Report, and Advise upon Matters in Relation to the Condition and Treatment of Aborigines*, Government Printer, Perth, 1935.

Muirhead, J. H., In the Matter of a Petition to His Excellency the Governor of Western Australia as Visitor of Murdoch University, F. R. Jevons and Murdoch University, *Report of his Excellency's Assessor The Hon J. H. Muirhead AC QC*, 30 May 1996.

Senate and Constitutional References Committee, *Healing: A Legacy of Generations*, The Parliament of the Commonwealth of Australia, Canberra, 2000.

Tabart, J., Wood, D. and Wilson, R., *Three Former Presidents Report to Assembly Standing Committee, Issues of Sexuality*, Uniting Church of Australia, 1998.

Uniting Church–Synod of Western Australia, *Submission to the National Inquiry into the Separation of Aboriginal and Torres Straight Islander Children from Their Families*, Uniting Church–Synod of Western Australia, Perth, 12 September 1996.

Wyatt, C. Secretary, Department of Aboriginal Affairs, oral submission, Western Australian Government, Perth, 14 May 1996.

Hansard: parliamentary debates and committee hearings

Post and Telegraphy, HR vol. 4, 1901, p. 4851.

Hansard, Western Australian Parliamentary Debates, vol. 168, 14 October 1964, pp. 1555–63, 1753.

——, *Western Australian Parliamentary Debates*, vol. 182, 24 April 1969, pp. 3436–7.

——, *Western Australian Parliamentary Debates*, vol. 182, 30 April 1969, pp. 3557–8.

——, *House of Representatives*, no 10, 30 May 1991, pp. 4498, 4824.

——, *House of Representatives*, no 8, 4 June 1992, p. 3586.

——, *L&C* (Senate Legal and Constitutional Standing Committee), 18 August 2000, pp. 722–33.

——, *L&C*, 4 September 2000, pp. 735–65.

Internet sources

Beazley, K., Opening Speech, Australian Reconciliation Conference, Melbourne Convention Centre, 26 May 1997, <http://www.austlii.edu.au/au/special/rsjproject/rsjlibrary/car/arc/speeches/opening/beazley.htm>, 30 October 2006.

Denholm, M., 'First Payout Deal for Stolen Generation', *Australian*, 18 October 2006, <http://www.theaustralian.news.com.au/story/0,20867,20600691-2702,00.html>, 1 November 2006.

Durack, P., 'The External Affairs Power: What Is to Be Done?', *The Samuel Griffith Society: Proceedings of the Sixth Conference of The Samuel Griffith Society*, Townhouse Hotel, Carlton 17–19 November 1995, <http://www.samuelgriffith.org.au/papers/html/volume6/v6chap2.htm>, 30 October 2006.

Grace, G., 'Tassie to Compensate Stolen Generations', *Australian*, 26 September 2006, <http://www.theaustralian.news.com.au/story/0,20867.20479825-1702,00.html>, 1 November 2006.

Howard, J., Opening Speech, Australian Reconciliation Conference, Melbourne Convention Centre, 26 May 1997, <http://www.austlii.edu.au/au/special/rsjproject/rsjlibrary/car/arc/speeches/opening/howard.htm>, 30 October 2006.

——, Transcript of the Prime Minister, The Hon. John Howard MP Motion of Reconciliation, 26 August, 1999, <http://www.pm.gov.au/media/Speech/1999/reconciliation2608.cfm>, 1 November 2006.

Hume, S. E. K., 'The External Affairs Power: The State of the Debate', *The Samuel Griffith Society: Proceedings of the Sixth Conference of The Samuel Griffith Society*, Townhouse Hotel, Carlton 17–19 November 1995, <http://www.samuelgriffith.org.au/papers/html/volume6/v6chap2.htm>, 30 October 2006.

Indian Residential Schools Settlement: Official Court Website <http://www.residentialschoolsettlement.ca>, 1 November 2006.

Kernot, C., Opening Speech, Australian Reconciliation Conference, Melbourne Convention Centre, 26 May 1997, <http://www.austlii.edu.au/au/special/rsjproject/rsjlibrary/car/arc/speeches/opening/kernot.htm>, 30 October 2006.

D. Moore, 'Sir Ronald Wilson Should Apologise', *Institute for Private Affairs*, September 1999, <http://www.ipe.net.au/nltr8.html>, 1 November 2006.

Television and radio

Bartlett, L., Interview with Wilson, 720 ABC Perth Radio, *Morning Program*, 30 May 2000.

Haultain, L., Interview with Sir Ronald Wilson, ABC Radio National, *Law Report*, 5 August 1997.

Mitchell, N., Interview with the Prime Minister, the Hon. John Howard MP', Radio 3AW, *Morning Show*, 8 June 2001.

O'Brien, K., Interview with Wilson, ABC TV, *7.30 Report*, 1 August 1997.

Stein, G., 'Interview with Sir Ronald Wilson', ABC Radio, *World Today*, 13 December 1996.

ABC TV, *7.30 Report*, 31 March 1993.

ABC TV, *7.30 Report*, 4 December 1993.

ABC TV, *7.30 Report*, 1 May 1997.

ABC TV, *7.30 Report*, 20 May 1997.

ABC TV, *7.30 Report*, 27 May 1997.

ABC TV, *7.30 Report*, 11 May 2000.

ABC TV, *Lateline*, 15 May 2006.

Legislation cited

Aborigines Act 1905 (WA).

Aborigines Act Amendment Act 1911 (WA).

Aborigines Act Amendment Act 1936 (WA).

Aboriginal Heritage Act 1972 (WA).

Aboriginal Land Rights (Northern Territory) Act 1976 (Cwlth).

Aborigines Protection Act 1869 (Vic).

Aborigines Protection Act 1886 (WA).

Aboriginal Protection and Restriction of the Sale of Opium Act 1897 (Qld).

Aborigines Welfare Act 1954 (Cwlth).

Australia Act 1988 (UK, Cwlth and all Australian States).

Better Care of Destitute Children Act 1866 (NSW).

British Nationality Act 1948 (UK).

Cape Barren Island Reserve Act 1912 (Tas).

Colonial Laws Validity Act 1865 (UK).

Criminal Code 1913 (WA).

Destitute Persons Relief Act 1866 (SA).

Disability Discrimination Act 1992 (Cwlth).

District Court Act 1969 (WA).

Family Court Act 1977 (WA).

Family Law Act 1975 (Cwlth).

High Court of Australia Act 1979 (Cwlth).

Human Rights and Equal Opportunity Commission Act 1986 (Cwlth).

Industrial and Reformatory Schools and the Training Act 1864 (Qld).

Industrial Schools Act 1874 (WA).

Industrial Schools Act 1967 (Tas).

Judiciary Act 1903 (Cwlth).

Land Act 1962 (Qld).

Law Reform Commission Act 1973 (Cwlth).

Land (Titles and Traditional Usage) Act 1993 (WA).

Legal Practitioners Act 1893 (WA).

Marine Act 1948 (WA).

Matrimonial Causes Act 1959 (Cwlth).

Merchant Shipping Act 1894 (Imp).

National Parks and Wildlife Conservation Act 1975 (Cwlth).

Native Administration Amendment Act 1941 (WA).

Native Title Act 1993 (Cwlth).

Native Welfare Act 1954 (WA).

Native Welfare Act 1963 (WA).

Native Welfare Act Amendment Act 1960 (WA).

Neglected and Criminal Children's Act 1864 (Vic).

Northern Territory Aboriginals Act 1911 (SA).

Petroleum and Mineral Authority Act 1973 (Cwlth).

Privacy Act 1988 (Cwlth).

Privy Council (Appeals from the High Court) Act 1975 (Cwlth).

Privy Council (Limitation of Appeals) Act 1968 (Cwlth).

Public Charities Act 1866 (NSW).

Public Service Act 1904 (WA).

Queensland Coast Islands Declaratory Act 1985 (Qld).

Racial Discrimination Act 1975 (Cwlth).

Royal Commission Act 1968 (WA).

Royal Commissions Amendment Act 1990 (WA).

Road Maintenance (Contribution) Act 1958–1965 (NSW).

Seas and Submerged Lands Act 1973 (Cwlth).

Sentencing Act 1995 (WA).

Sex Discrimination Act 1984 (Cwlth).

Solicitor-General Act 1969 (WA).

Statute of Westminster 1931 (Imp).

Stolen Generations of Aboriginal Children Act 2006 (Tas).

Theft Act 1968 (Imp).

Trade Practices Act 1974 (Cwlth).

Uniting Church in Australia Act 1976 (WA).

World Heritage Properties Conservation Act 1983 (Cwlth).

World Heritage (Western Tasmania Wilderness) Regulations 1983 (Cwlth).

Cases cited

A-G (Vic) ex rel Black v Commonwealth (1981) 146 CLR 559.

Amalgamated Society of Engineers v Adelaide Steamship Co. Ltd (1920) 28 CLR 129 (*Engineers Case*).

Barton v R (1980) 147 CLR 75.

Beamish v The Queen [1962] WAR 85.

Beamish v The Queen (No 2), unreported, CCA of SCWA, no 20 of 1964, 22 May 1964, 9.

Beamish v The Queen [2005] WASCA 62, 1 April 2005.

Button v The Queen, unreported, CCA of SCWA, 22 May 1964.

Button v The Queen [2002] WASCA 35, 25 February 2002.

The Church of New Faith v The Commissioner of Pay-Roll [1983] 1 VR 97.

The Church of New Faith v The Commissioner of Pay-Roll (Victoria) (1983) 154 CLR 120.

The Federated State School Teachers' Association of Australia v Victoria (1928) 41 CLR 569.

Commonwealth v Tasmania (Tasmanian Dams Case) (1983) 158 CLR 1.

Cubillo v Commonwealth (1999) 89 FCR 528.

Cubillo v Commonwealth (2000) 174 ALR 97.

Cubillo v Commonwealth (2001) 112 FCR 455.

Cubillo v Commonwealth, HCA D10 and 11/2001 3 May 2002.

Fencott v Muller (1983) 152 CLR 570.

Freightlines and Construction Holdings Ltd v New South Wales (1967) 116 CLR 1.

Freightlines and Construction Holdings Ltd v New South Wales [1968] AC 625.

Gough v Gough (1956) 95 CLR 369.

Hematite Petroleum v Victoria (1983) 151 CLR 599.

Kartinyeri v Commonwealth (Hindmarsh Island Bridge Case) (1988) 195 CLR 337.

Kioa v West (1985) 159 CLR 550.

Koowarta v Bjelke-Petersen (1982) 153 CLR 168.

Kruger v Commonwealth (1997) 190 CLR 1.

Mabo v Queensland (1986) 64 ALR 1.

Mabo v Queensland (No 1) (1988) 166 CLR 186.

Mabo v Queensland (No 2) (1992) 175 CLR 1.

Mallard v The Queen (2002) 28 WAR 1.

Mallard v The Queen [2005] HCA 68 (15 November 2005).

MacPherson v R (1981) 147 CLR 512.

MacRobertson Miller Airline Service v Commissioner of State Taxation (Western Australia) (1975) 133 CLR 125.

McInnis v The Queen (1979) 143 CLR 575.

Mickelberg v The Queen [2004] WASCA 145, 2 July 2004.

Munro v Lombardo [1964] WAR 63.

New South Wales v Commonwealth (Seas and Submerged Lands Case) (1975) 135 CLR 337.

Oteri v The Queen [1976] 1 WLR 1272.

Philip Morris Inc v Adam Brown P. Brown Male Fashions P/L (1982) 148 CLR 457.

R v Commonwealth Conciliation and Arbitration Commission; Ex parte Association of Professional Engineers' Association, Australia (1959) 107 CLR 208.

R v Hoar (1981) 148 CLR 32.

R v Murphy [1985] 4 NSWLR 42.

R v Murphy (1985) 158 CLR 596.

Richardson v Forestry Commission (1988) 164 CLR 261.

Sankey v Whitlam [1977] 1 NSWLR 333.

Sankey v Whitlam (1978) 142 CLR 1.

Tonkin v Brand [1962] WAR 1.

Van Der Meer (1988) 82 ALR 10.

Walton Stores v Maher (1988) 164 CLR 387.

Western Australia v Commonwealth (Native Title Act Case); Teddy Biljabu v Western Australia (1995)183 CLR 373.

Western Australia v Hamersley Iron Proprietary Limited (1969) 120 CLR 75.

Williams v Minister, Aboriginal Land Rights Act 1983 [1994] 35 NSWLR 497.

Wik Peoples v Queensland (1996) 187 CLR 75.

Zecevic v DPP (Victoria) (1987) 162 CLR 645.

Human Rights and Equal Opportunity Commission decisions

Ardeshirian v Robe River Iron Associates, 18 May 1990, unreported, HREOC, Sir Ronald Wilson.

Mead v Southern Districts Football League, 15 November 1991, unreported, HREOC, Sir Ronald Wilson.

Murray v Forward, 17 September 1993, unreported, HREOC, Sir Ronald Wilson.

Proudfoot v ACT Board of Health, 17 March 1992, unreported, HREOC, Sir Ronald Wilson.

Scott v Telstra Corporation Ltd, 6 September 1995, unreported, HREOC, Sir Ronald Wilson.

Tamanivalu v Western Australian Rugby Union Inc, 17 August 1994, unreported, HREOC, Sir Ronald Wilson.

Tully v Ceridale Pty Ltd, 19 June 1990, unreported, HREOC, Sir Ronald Wilson.

X v McHugh, 8 July 1994, unreported, HREOC, Sir Ronald Wilson.

Court transcripts

Beamish's Second Appeal Transcript, *Beamish v The Queen (No 2)*, CCA of SCWA, 17–20 March 1964.

Button's Trial Transcript, *The Queen v Button*, SCWA, 29–30 April, 1–4, 6 May 1963.

Button's Appeal Transcript, *Button v The Queen*, CCA of SCWA, 1964, 8 April 1964.

Cooke's Trial Transcript, *The Queen v Cook*, SCWA, 25–27 November 1963.

International conventions, covenants and other documents

United Nations, *Convention on the Elimination of all Forms of Racial Discrimination*

United Nations, *Convention on the Prevention and Punishment of Genocide* (Genocide Convention)

United Nations, *Convention for the Protection of the World Cultural and Natural Heritage*

United Nations, *Convention on the Rights of the Child*

United Nations, *Declaration on the Rights of Indigenous People*

United Nations, *International Covenant of Civil and Political Rights*

United Nations, *First Optional Protocol of the International Covenant of Civil and Political Rights*

Human Rights Commission, *Revised set of basic principles and guidelines on the right to reparation for victims of gross violations of human rights and humanitarian law prepared by Mr Theo van Boven pursuant to Sub-Commission decision 1995/117*, UN Doc. E/CN.4/Sub.2/1996/17, 24 May 1996.

Human Rights Commission, *The Right to Restitution, Compensation and Rehabilitation for Victims of Gross Violations of Human Rights and Fundamental Freedoms: Final Report of the Special Rapporteur, M Cherif Bassiouni, Submitted in Accordance with the Commission Resolution 1999/33*, E/CN.4/2000/62. 19 January 2000.

Others

Australian Student Christian Movement, *The ASCM 1947*, Brown, Prior, Anderson, Melbourne, 1947.

Barblett, A., Transcript of Speech: Opening Ceremony of the Family Court of Western Australia, Special Sitting, 1 June 1976, Wilson personal files.

Barker, M. L., 'Past As Prologue: A Second Anniversary Reflection on the Work of the Royal Commission into WA Inc', in M. Brogan and H. Phillips (eds), *Past As Prologue: The Royal Commission into Commercial Activities of Government and Other Matters: Proceedings from a Conference on the Part II Report of the Royal Commission and the Reform of Government in Western Australia*, Edith Cowan University, Perth International Hotel, 4 November 1994, p. 10.

Button, J., Letter to Wilson, 27 November 1989, Wilson's personal files.

——, Letter to Wilson, 19 April 1990, Wilson's personal files.

Christie, M., Remembering Papa: A Service of Celebration for the life of Sir Ronald Wilson AC , St Stephens Uniting Church, Applecross, 22 July 2005.

Drayton, D., Tribute: A Service of Celebration for the Life of Sir Ronald Wilson AC, Karrakatta Cremation Chapel, 22 July 2005.

Government of Canada, Federal government news release, 'Canada's Aboriginal Action Plan Focused on Communities, Founded on Reconciliation and Renewal', Canadian Government, Ottawa, 24 September 2006.

Garlett, S., Music and Reflection: A Service of Celebration for the Life of Sir Ronald Wilson AC, Karrakatta Cremation Chapel, 22 July 2005.

Gunstone, A., The Formal Australian Reconciliation Process: 1991–2000, National Reconciliation Planning Workshop, Old Parliament House, Canberra, 30–31 May 2005.

Human Rights and Equal Opportunity Commission, *Bringing Them Home* (video), 1997.

——, *Sir Ron Wilson: Statement from the Human Rights Commission*, 31 July 1997.

Kuhn, M., Letter to Wilson, 28 May 1997, Wilson's personal files.

Linow, V., New South Wales Victims of Crime Compensation, Notice of Determination, February 2002.

Murdoch Senate, Minutes, 17 October 1988.

Murray, M., Tribute: A Service of Celebration for the Life of Sir Ronald Wilson AC, Karrakatta Cremation Chapel, 22 July 2005.

Nicholson, R., Eulogy: Sir Ronald Wilson Lecture 2006, Perth, 11 May 2006.

O'Conner, L., Letter to author, 8 December 2004.

Peachment, A., 'WA Inc: Failure of the System or Crime of the Employee', in M. Brogan and H. Phillips (eds), *Past As Prologue: The Royal Commission into Commercial Activities of Government and Other Matters: Proceedings from a Conference on the Part II Report of the Royal Commission and the Reform of Government in Western Australia*, Perth International Hotel, Edith Cowan University, 4 November 1994, p. 80.

State Library of South Australia, *Adelaide Festival of Ideas 2001* (CD), State Library of South Australia, and Radio Adelaide 101.5 FM, 12 July 2001.

Tabart, J., Tribute: A Service of Celebration for the life of Sir Ronald Wilson AC, St Stephen's Uniting Church, 22 July 2006.

Wilson, B., 'Remembering Dad, Celebrating his Life', A Service of Celebration for the life of Sir Ronald Wilson AC, St Stephen's Uniting Church, Applecross, 22 July 2005.

Wilson, R., Letter to Attorney-General, Western Australia, October 1966, Crown Law Department Archives.

——, Letter to Mariele Kuhn, 11 July 1944, Wilson's personal files.

——, Letter to Mariele Kuhn, 28 July 1944, Wilson's personal files.

——, Letter to Mariele Kuhn, 5 December 1945, Wilson's personal files.

——, Letter to Mariele Kuhn, 9 June 1997, Wilson's personal files.

——, Letter to R. Brunton, 2 May 1998, Wilson's personal files.

——, Letter to Wendy Page, 13 September 1998, Wilson's personal files.

R. Wilson and I. Burkitt (on behalf of NEAF), Letter to Chaney, May 1972, Wilson's personal files.

INDEX